THE FALL OF ROBESPIERRE

THE FALL OF ROBESPIERRE

24 HOURS IN REVOLUTIONARY PARIS

COLIN JONES

OXFORD

UNIVERSITY PRESS

OXFORD
UNIVERSITY PRESS

Great Clarendon Street, Oxford, OX2 6DP,
United Kingdom

Oxford University Press is a department of the University of Oxford.
It furthers the University's objective of excellence in research, scholarship,
and education by publishing worldwide. Oxford is a registered trade mark of
Oxford University Press in the UK and in certain other countries

Published in the United States of America by Oxford University Press
198 Madison Avenue, New York, NY 10016, United States of America

British Library Cataloguing in Publication Data
Data available

Library of Congress Control Number: 2021935694

ISBN 978-0-19-871595-5

Printed and bound in Great Britain by
Clays Ltd, Elcograf S.p.A.

Links to third party websites are provided by Oxford in good faith and
for information only. Oxford disclaims any responsibility for the materials
contained in any third party website referenced in this work.

For Jo

*It wasn't about principles;
it was about killing*

Marc-Antoine Baudot,
on the overthrow of Robespierre

Acknowledgements

This is a book about Paris and in writing it, I have derived continuous inspiration from the work of two very great and very different historians of the city and its people in the eighteenth century, namely, Daniel Roche and the late Richard Cobb, to whom I would like here to pay homage. I have also taken infinite pleasure from the fact that while researching and writing, I have had Louis-Sébastien Mercier's *Tableau de Paris* and *Le Nouveau Paris* at my elbow and Hilary Mantel's *A Place of Greater Safety* in the back of my mind.

I originally chose to tell the story of 9 Thermidor in the 'Mercier way' described in the Introduction—up close, in detail, and with an eye to time, space, and sequence—out of a sense of curiosity and fun. As historians, we always write under the constraints imposed by our evidence, but I felt it would be interesting to add a further level of complexity and challenge. I found myself attracted less to the work of other historians than to experimental authors I like such as George Perec, whose 1969 novel, *La Disparition* is written without recourse to the letter 'e', and Raymond Queneau, whose 1947 *Exercices de style* recounts a mundane incident on a Parisian bus from 99 different angles and in 99 different styles. The two men belonged to the Oulipo tradition of 'writing under constraint'. What I learned from my own, lesser challenge in constraint—writing hourly chapters and compressing the narrative within a single day—was that it provokes and stimulates the imagination in unexpectedly rewarding and pertinent ways. In my case, it directed my thinking afresh to issues of place, time, timing and story-telling that proved to lie at the heart of the argument of this book. The result, I hope, is not just an exercise in style but an enhanced pathway towards understanding a key historical event.

The idea for the book followed on from conversations with my wonderful agent, the late Felicity Bryan, whose death came towards the end of the writing stage. I was privileged to have benefited from her unmatchable vitality, energy, and invigorating enthusiasm for nearly 30 years. I thank Catherine Clarke of the Felicity Bryan Agency for her help in the completion stages. At OUP, Luciana O'Flaherty and her team have guided me calmly through everything.

In the years spent researching and writing the book, I have learnt so much from the many friends who have patiently listened to me talking about it in conferences, seminars, over coffee or drinks, and around dinner tables, and have offered interest, critical insights, and moral support. I can't name them all: but I hope they know who they are and that they realize the depth of my gratitude. Among the many, I would like to thank the following for particular assistance with the project in some material or intellectual way: Stephen Clay, Laurent Cuvelier, Vincent Denis, Robert Darnton, Ariane Fichtl, Mette Harder, Martyn Lyons (a long time ago!), Jonathan Sachs, Steve Sawyer, Pierre Serna, Anne Simonin, and Charles Walton. I am also exceptionally lucky to have had as readers of an earlier draft of my manuscript David Bell, Alex Fairfax-Cholmeley, David Jordan, Simon Macdonald, and Michael Sonenscher. I could not have been in better hands. *Salut et fraternité* for their time, their kindness, and their friendship. Simon has also been a source of endless encouragement and the communicator of a large number of archival finds. I should stress that all errors remaining are strictly my own achievement. I also thank Natalie Smith for research and bibliographical assistance and Miles Irving who drew the maps. Dominique Lussier was an excellent indexer.

I was supremely fortunate to have been awarded a Major Research Fellowship from the Leverhulme Trust, which I acknowledge with enormous gratitude. The Trust's generosity in funding what it esteems as valuable and cutting-edge research makes it a jewel in the British research landscape. I was able to work on the project in a number of locations, where I delivered papers on the topic. These include University of Richmond, Virginia where I held the Freeman Professorship (2013); the National Humanities Center, North Carolina (2014) where I was Carl and Lily Pforzheimer Fellow; and the University of Chicago, where I have been Visiting Professor since 2018. Thanks are due to the University's Modern France Workshop for interest and encouragement. I oversaw the production process while Fellow at the Institut d'études avancées in Paris for 2020–21— a pleasure that even COVID-19 failed to spoil (though it tried hard). I wish also as ever to thank my colleagues in the School of History, Queen Mary University of London, especially Julian Jackson, Miri Rubin, and Quentin Skinner, for the gift of their friendship and support.

I can't list all the venues where I have delivered papers and talks, but would mention the honour bestowed in being asked to give plenary lectures which helped me crystallize my ideas. These include the Oxford University Faculty of History lecture, 2011; the University of Richmond Douglas Southall Freeman lecture, 2013; the Social History Society plenary lecture, 2014; and the Voltaire Foundation Besterman lecture, 2015.

The book has been developed over the years and some outputs overlap with the finished manuscript, notably 'The Overthrow of Maximilien Robespierre and the "Indifference" of the People', *American Historical Review*, 119 (2014), pp. 688–713; '9 Thermidor, Cinderella of French Revolutionary *Journées*', *French Historical Studies*, 38 (2015), pp. 9–31; 'Robespierre's Fall', *History Today*, 65 (August 2015), pp. 39–44; 'Robespierre, the Duke of York and Pisistratus during the French Revolutionary Terror', *Historical Journal*, 61 (2018), pp. 643–72 (with Simon Macdonald); and 'La vie parisienne des Conventionnels en 1793', in P. Bastien & S. Macdonald, eds., *Paris et ses peuples*. Presses de l'Université de Quebec à Montréal (2019), pp. 75–88.

Finally, I think of the time spent with this book in my head in the company of my wife, Josephine McDonagh, to whom, with love, it is dedicated.

Table of Contents

Prefatory Note and Abbreviations   xvii

List of Figures and Maps   xix

Introduction: The Fall of Robespierre Up Close   1

Prelude: Around Midnight   11
*Rousseville's lodgings, Rue Saint-Honoré (Tuileries)—Vernet's
wanderings: from the Place du Trône-Renversé (Montreuil/Quinze-Vingts)
to the Rue de Birague (Arsenal)—La Force Prison (Droits-de-l'Homme)—
Legracieux's lodgings, Rue Denfert (Chalier)—Home of Guittard de
Floriban, Rue des Canettes (Mutius-Scévole)*

PART I: ELEMENTS OF CONSPIRACY
(Midnight to 5.00 a.m.)

00.00/Midnight   27
Robespierre's lodgings, 366 Rue Saint-Honoré (Piques)

01.00/1.00 a.m.   43
CPS Committee Room, Tuileries palace (Tuileries)

02.00/2.00 a.m.   56
*CPS offices, Tuileries palace—CPS Committee Room, Tuileries
palace—Tallien's quest: the streets of Paris*

03.00/3.00 a.m.   69
*Across the city—Conciergerie prison, Palais de Justice, Ile de la Cité
(Révolutionnaire)—Bénédictins-Anglais prison, Rue Saint-Jacques
(Observatoire)*

04.00/4.00 a.m.   84
Various locations, CPS offices, Tuileries palace

PART II: SETTINGS FOR A DRAMA
(5.00 a.m. to Midday)

05.00/5.00 a.m.   103
Streets leading to Les Halles (Marchés)

06.00/6.00 a.m.   114
Robespierre's lodgings, 366 Rue Saint-Honoré

07.00/7.00 a.m.   126
*Municipal offices, Maison Commune (Maison-Commune)—Place du Panthéon
(Panthéon)—Jacques-Louis Ménétra's section (Bon-Conseil)*

08.00/8.00 a.m.   140
École de Mars, Plaine des Sablons, Neuilly—The streets of the city

09.00/9.00 a.m.   150
*Offices of the municipal Police Administration, Mairie, Ile de la Cité
(Révolutionnaire)—Giot's itinerary: Rue de Hautefeuille (Marat), Panthéon
(Panthéon), Temple prison (Temple)*

10.00/10.00 a.m.   164
*Revolutionary Tribunal, Palais de Justice, Ile de la Cité (Révolutionnaire)—
Thibaudeau's route: from Rue Hautefeuille (Marat) to the Tuileries palace—
Robespierre's lodgings, 366 Rue Saint-Honoré*

11.00/11.00 a.m.   176
*Tuileries palace and gardens—Vestibule to the Convention hall and
Tuileries palace environs—Convention hall, Tuileries palace—CPS
Committee Room, Tuileries palace*

PART III: A PARLIAMENTARY COUP
(Midday to 5.00 p.m.)

12.00/12.00 Midday   191
Convention hall, Tuileries palace

13.00/1.00 p.m.   200
*Convention hall, Tuileries palace—Tuileries gardens—Public galleries,
Convention hall, Tuileries palace—Across the city*

14.00/2.00 p.m.   215
*Salle de l'Égalité, Maison Commune—Revolutionary Tribunal,
Palais de Justice, Ile de la Cité—Maison Penthièvre, Place des Piques
(Piques)—Convention hall, Tuileries palace—Police Administration offices,
Ile de la Cité, and sectional meetings—Across the city*

15.00/3.00 p.m.   233
*National Guard Head quarters, Rue du Martroy (Maison-Commune)—
Convention hall, Tuileries palace—Courtyard, Palais de Justice, Ile de
la Cité—Convention hall, Tuileries palace—Hanriot's ride: the eastern
sections—Across the city: sectional committee meetings*

16.00/4.00 p.m.   251
Convention hall, Tuileries palace—Vergne's home, Ile Saint-Louis
(Fraternité)—La Force prison—Conciergerie courtyard, Palais de Justice,
Ile de la Cité—CPS Committee Room, Tuileries palace—Place de la
Maison Commune (or Place de Grève) (Arcis)—Mairie and Police
Administration HQ, Ile de la Cité—Hanriot's raid: from the Maison
Commune to the Tuileries palace—CGS offices, Hôtel de Brionne (Tuileries)

PART IV: A PARISIAN *JOURNÉE*
(5.00 p.m. to Midnight)

17.00/5.00 p.m.   269
Théâtre de la République, Palais-Royal environs (Montagne)—The
streets of the city—Police Administration HQ, Mairie, Ile de la Cité—Place
de la Maison Commune—CGS and CPS offices, Tuileries palace
complex—Place de la Maison Commune—Maison Commune
Council Chamber—CGS offices, Hôtel de Brionne—Vergne's home,
Ile Saint-Louis

18.00/6.00 p.m.   282
Council chamber, Maison Commune—Fouquier-Tinville's lodgings,
Palais de Justice, Ile de la Cité—Place du Carrousel (Tuileries)—Place
du Trône-Renversé—Council Chamber, Maison Commune—Mairie
and Police Administration HQ, Ile de la Cité—Talaru prison
(Montagne) and the prison network—Rue Saint-Guillaume
(Fontaine-de-Grenelle)

19.00/7.00 p.m.   298
Place de la Maison Commune—Convention hall, Tuileries palace—Maison
Commune—Jacobin Club (Montagne)—Luxembourg prison
(Mutius-Scévole)—Coffinhal's raid: Rue Saint-Honoré (Tuileries)—Police
Administration HQ, Mairie, Ile de la Cité—Across the city

20.00/8.00 p.m.   314
Police Administration HQ, Ile de la Cité—Fouquier-Tinville's
office, Palais de Justice, Ile de la Cité—Maison Commune—Convention
hall, Tuileries palace—Place du Carrousel—Convention hall, Tuileries
palace—Place du Carrousel—Convention hall, Tuileries palace—CPS
Committee Room, Tuileries palace—Convention hall, Tuileries palace

21.00/9.00 p.m.   335
Convention hall, Tuileries palace—Tuileries palace environs—Place
de la Maison Commune—Council chamber, Maison Commune—Across
the city—Convention hall, Tuileries palace—Maison Commune—Quai
de Gesvres (Arcis)

22.00/10.00 p.m.   351
*Police Administration HQ, Mairie, Ile de la Cité—Maison
Commune—Across the city—Convention hall, Tuileries palace—Jacobin
Club—Convention hall, Tuileries palace—Maison Commune—
Guillaume-Tell section and across the city—Paris prisons*

23.00/11.00 p.m.   373
*Salle de l'Égalité, Maison Commune—Café des Subsistances, Palais
de Justice, Ile de la Cité—Across the city—Convention hall, Tuileries
palace—Lombards section and across the city—Révolutionnaire
section—Place Saint-Sulpice (Mutius-Scévole) and across the city—Place
de la Maison Commune and Place du Carrousel—Maison Commune*

PART V: MIDNIGHT, AROUND MIDNIGHT, AFTER MIDNIGHT

Midnight   397
Salle de l'Égalité, Maison Commune

Around Midnight   403
*Private lodgings, Quai de l'École (Muséum)—Convention hall,
Tuileries palace—Place de la Maison Commune—Mairie, Ile de
la Cité—Temple prison—Maison Commune—Gravilliers section—Across
the city—École de Mars encampment, Plaine des Sablons—Guyot's
wandering: from the Maison Commune to the Sans-Culottes section—
Bourdon's expedition: from the Gravilliers section to the Place de la
Maison Commune*

After Midnight   419

Afterword: 9 Thermidor From Afar   432
*Against the people—Conspiring against Robespierre: a myth?—
Robespierre conspirator?—The Commune and the people—Public
opinion redivivus—The people's choice: institutions over personalities*

Notes   457
List of Characters   525
Note on Sources   533
Bibliography and Printed Sources   537
Index   555

Prefatory Note and Abbreviations

The day on which Robespierre fell—27 July 1794—is widely known as 9 Thermidor Year II in the Revolutionary Calendar. Generally, however, I have used the familiar Gregorian dating system, except where particular events or laws are usually referred to in Revolutionary Calendar terms (e.g. the Law of 14 Frimaire). All dates in the new Calendar were in Year II (1793–4) unless otherwise stated.

All day and night timings shown are either derived directly from sources or else are estimates based on the copious existing documentation. All dialogue is drawn directly from sources: none is invented, and there is a minimum of adaptation.

In the notes, I have located places within Paris with reference to the 48 sections instituted in 1790. See Map 2 and legend, pp. 00–0. In the endnotes I have identified the present-day arrondissement. To avoid confusion, I have used hyphens for multi-word sections: thus 'Maison-Commune' is the section of that name, but 'Maison Commune' refers to the city hall.

Many of the main streets and public buildings were officially renamed during the Terror. Saints' names were often omitted: e.g. the Rue Saint-Honoré was sometimes called the Rue Honoré, the Faubourg Saint-Antoine the Faubourg Antoine. However many of these official renamings were not widely used by Parisians and did not pass into the language. Consequently, I have adopted the new Revolutionary names only where they became widely used: thus the old (and present-day) Place de l'Hôtel-de-Ville was generally referred to as the Place de la Maison Commune; whereas the Place du Carrousel outside the Tuileries palace was rarely referred to by its new official name of Place de la Réunion. I have tried always to opt for the sensible and least confusing name.

The following abbreviations are used throughout:

Cn.   Citizen
CPS   Committee of Public Safety (*Comité de salut public*)
CGS   Committee of General Security (*Comité de sûreté générale*)
HQ   Headquarters
NG   National Guard (*Garde nationale*)

List of Figures and Maps

Introduction

Map 1. Central Paris in 1794   8

Map 2. The 48 Paris sections   10

Prelude

Figure 1. Rousseville, Report to the Committee of Public Safety, around midnight, 8–9 Thermidor (F7 4781)   12

Part I

Figure 2. Committee of Public Safety order summoning Lecointre, notary, 1.00 a.m.?, 9 Thermidor (AFII 47 pl. 363, pi. 31)   64

Figure 3. Princesse de Monaco to Public Prosecutor Fouquier-Tinville, 8–9 Thermidor (W 431)   73

Part II

Map 3. The Maison Commune neighbourhood   127

Figure 4. Petition of the Saint-Marcel citizen-washerwomen to National Commander François Hanriot, no date (AFII 47 pl. 368, pi. 37)   161

Map 4. The Tuileries complex   175

Part III

Figure 5. François-Auguste de Parseval-Grandmaison, 'Portrait de Robespierre . . . à la séance du 9 thermidor'   207

Figure 6. Paris National Guard Commander François Hanriot, order book, 9 Thermidor (AFII 47 pl. 368, pi. 38)   236

Figure 7. Committee of Public Safety to Legion Chiefs, around 3.30 p.m. (AFII 47 pl. 363, pi. 2)   245

Part IV

Figure 8. Committee of Public Safety, Arrest Warrant for Paris Mayor Fleuriot-Lescot, after 10.00 p.m. (AFII 47 pl. 363, pi. 10)   359

Figure 9. Joseph, Acting Commander, Faubourg-Montmartre National Guard battalion, to Acting Commanding Officer, Place du Carrousel, 12 midnight (AFII 47, pl. 364, pi. 10)   391

Part V

Figure 10. Jean-Louis Prieur, Léonard Bourdon at the Maison Commune, 9–10 Thermidor   421

Figure 11. Vincenot, Commander, Arsenal National Guard battalion, to Acting Commanding Officer, Place du Carrousel, 9–10 Thermidor (AFII 47 pl. 367, pi. 3)   428

Figure 12. Goubert, Commander, Marchés National Guard Battalion, to Acting Commanding Officer, Place du Carrousel, 12.30 a.m., 9–10 Thermidor (AFII 47 pl. 367, pi. 53)   429

Figure 13. Contou, Commander, Fontaine-de-la-Grenelle National Guard battalion, to Acting Commanding Officer, Place du Carrousel, 9–10 Thermidor (AFII 47 pl. 365, pi. 2)   430

Afterword

Figure 14. 'Triomphe des Parisiens' saluting 'the generous and intrepid athletes of liberty' (British Library, French Revolution Pamphlets)   453

Introduction: The Fall of Robespierre Up Close

From up close, things are different from when one judges them from afar...
Revolutionary crises are composed of infinitely small things and these form
the essential base of all events. In general, there is much about them that will
astonish the observer. Nearly all have been not only unanticipated; they fall
within the category of things that no wise man can believe possible.

T he French Revolution, stated Louis-Sébastien Mercier, author, journalist, politician, and matchless commentator on his native Paris in the
late eighteenth century, was 'all about optics'. Only by getting 'up close' and
drilling down into 'infinitely small' details of the revolutionary process could
one gain a satisfactory understanding of the often improbable and invariably
unpredictable course of great Revolutionary events.

Time seemed to speed up in 1789. Mercier's fellow statesman, Boissy
d'Anglas, expressed wonder that, from the vantage-point of 1795, it seemed
that French men and women had lived six centuries in the space of six years.
Parisians had become keenly aware of time. They lacked bells tolling the
hours (following the nationalization of ecclesiastical property and the closure
of most churches), but their pockets now contained watches alongside
wallets, handkerchiefs, and snuff-boxes. They politely apologized for not
giving an exact time if they had forgotten their timepiece.

Parisians were never more time-alert than on the days of popular action
within Paris (the so-called *journées*) when time seemed to accelerate particularly frenetically. *Journées* punctuated political life throughout the decade
from 14 July 1789, conventionally held to be the start of the Revolution, to
18 Brumaire/9 November 1799, when the advent of Napoleon is generally
seen as marking its end. They seemed to follow their own rules and
procedures at a headlong pace that could push out of shape and utterly

transform the overall course of events in ways that, as Mercier put it, 'no wise man [would] believe possible'. In order to understand the logic and mechanics of any particular Parisian *journée* and follow the twists and turns of its course, Mercier's advice was thus to take a microscope and get up close to the action. On a Revolutionary *journée,* he wondered, when every moment seemed to count and be big with consequence, how

> can one write such a history if one loses track of the sequential narrative (*enchaînement*) of each day? For such and such an event was produced so unanticipatedly that it seems less to have occurred than to have been created out of nothing . . .

It seemed that each participant was part of an invisible, intricately linked chain leading hectically who knew where.

The subject of this book is one of those days of action that so fascinated Mercier: 27 July 1794, or 9 Thermidor Year II in the nomenclature of the French Revolutionary Calendar introduced in 1793. He did not supply a full account of it, as at that moment he was a political prisoner, in gaol in the former monastery of the Bénédictins-Anglais, up on the Rue Saint-Jacques on the Left Bank, fearing for his life. Yet this did not deter him from following, reflecting on, and feeling part of the action in all its complexity. The day saw the fall from power of Maximilien Robespierre, one of the Revolution's most charismatic and outstanding politicians, and it signalled the beginning of the end for the type of government through terror in which he had played a key part over the previous year. It is a day whose outcome historians invariably view as a kind of parliamentary *coup d'état* performed by Robespierre's opponents within the political elite. I hope to show that its outcome was determined not just by politicians' machinations, but also as a result of a huge process of collective action by the people of Paris who since 1789 had cut an increasingly significant figure in national politics.

In order to understand how the people of Paris achieved its role as one of the significant actors in the drama of the day, we need to understand in outline the city's role within the Revolution's history back to the first revolutionary *journée.* On 14 July 1789, Parisians famously stormed the Bastille, the notorious state prison and arms dump on the eastern edge of the city. They did so in order to protect themselves against an attempt by King Louis XVI and his ministers to erase the gains the Revolution had made thus far. By their actions that day, Parisians forced the king to confirm the creation of a single unitary 'national assembly', and to allow the establishment of a constitutional monarchy grounded in principles to be laid out in the historic Declaration of the Rights of Man and the Citizen, promulgated on 26 August 1789.

The constitutional monarchy ultimately failed. By the time of another key day of Parisian popular action on 10 August 1792, Louis XVI's huge popularity in 1789 had almost entirely dissipated and a ruler earlier hailed as the 'restorer of French liberties' was being compared to despotic tyrants of Antiquity. The advent of war against continental Europe in April 1792 played an important part in this turnabout: the king's failure to rally to the flag even at a moment of utmost national emergency destroyed his political legitimacy. The Parisian revolt of 10 August obliged the king to step down. He was subsequently tried by a new assembly, the National Convention, elected by universal male suffrage, before being executed in January 1793.

The Convention underlined the epochal importance of the king's over-throw by declaring retrospectively in October 1793 that the day on which they had voted a Republic, 21 September 1792, marked the dawn of an era that would be celebrated in a new way of marking time. (Its post-dated inauguration meant that by the time the new calendar got going, Year II of the era of equality was already under way.) The new calendar, drawing on the decimal system that French scientists regarded as naturally grounded in human reason, divided the year not into weeks but into ten-day *décades*. Many of the new decadal days of rest were given over to celebrations and commemorations of various kinds. There were still twelve months, but because the calendar was calculated from 21 September 1792, each started on or around the third week of the old calendar months. A new nomencla-ture was introduced, replacing the former mishmash of Roman gods and emperors and Christian saints with a system of names evoking states of nature and the rural economy. The new months reflected the climate (at least in the temperate zones of the northern hemisphere). Thermidor was the hot month (from the Greek, *thermon*, for summer heat); it was preceded by Messidor (June–July), the harvest month (*messis*, harvest in Latin, May–June); by Prairial, the meadow months (*prairie*, meadow in French, April–May), and by Floréal, the month of flowers (*flos*, flower in Latin, March–April). Similarly, each former saint's day was blessed with a name grounded in nature. The date 9 Thermidor for example became the Day of the Mulberry.

The 10 August *journée* that triggered this change in the recording of time had confirmed the people of Paris as a political actor in their own right in the new Republic. Social groups that had been outside or on the fringes of public life hitherto were now hailed as key elements within a 'popular movement' that expressed itself not simply through armed intervention on *journées* but also through political and ideological engagement within expanded parameters of democratic space, now inclusive of newspapers and pamphlets, public meetings and demonstrations, political associations and clubs, as well as the local committees and assemblies within the 48 sections into which since 1790 Paris had been divided. The leading edge of the popular movement was the group known from 1791–2 onwards as 'sans-culottes', a term which signified that they were 'without breeches'— that is to say, that they preferred the trousers of the working man over the breeches that were the normal mark of gentility prior to 1789. In Year II, the sans-culottes came to supply the loudest voices and the most dynamic actors within the popular movement, and they powerfully impacted public opinion.

Within this inclusive democratic space, the Paris popular movement aspired to represent the people of France as a whole. This claim was put to the test in the summer and autumn of 1793, however, when most of the rest of the country mounted vigorous protests at what they regarded as unwarranted interference by Parisians in the political process. By two further *journées*—on 31 May and 2 June 1793—the Parisian popular movement joined forces with radical deputies in the Convention known as Montagnards to expel from the assembly more than a score of moderate deputies, or 'Girondins'. Parisians justified this assault on nationally elected delegates by highlighting the desperate state of the nascent Republic's military position, and they accused the Girondins of obstructing a war of national defence. Even as the armies of the allied powers advanced across French frontiers, provincial protests against the *journées* swelled dangerously into civil war conditions, with the 'Federalist Revolt' affecting numerous areas across France, particularly in and around the major cities of Lyon, Marseille, and Toulon. The security situation was further aggravated by unrest in western France in and around the Vendée department in that took on the complexion of a royalist rebellion.

The Convention overcame all these threats to its existence—military disintegration, Federalist Revolt, and peasant insurrection in western France—by dint of introducing a state of emergency which involved the suspension of normal constitutional arrangements, including most of the individual freedoms enshrined within the Rights of Man declaration. In particular, the deputies created a Committee of Public Safety, composed of twelve deputies, that it set at the heart of what was viewed as a 'Revolutionary Government'. (In this context, 'Revolutionary' signified that the state was not operating formally within a constitution: the radical constitution agreed in 1793 was never to be implemented.) The Committee was endowed with semi-dictatorial, emergency powers in order to conduct the fight against external and internal threats. This notably took the form of terror, the intimidation and disciplining of internal dissidents by the exertion through multiple channels of state violence.

The Committee's formidable iron fist was intermittently encased with a velvet glove. In particular, the government favoured socially and economically progressive policies that would attach not just Parisian sans-culottes but the popular classes across the nation to the cause of the Republic. This was the central plank of a strategic alliance struck in the summer of 1793 between the Montagnard deputies in the Convention and the sans-culottes of the Parisian popular movement. The alliance was brokered by Maximilien Robespierre, who in July 1793 became a key member of the Committee of Public Safety. More than any other political figure, Robespierre grasped that the legitimation of the Revolutionary Government's rule through terror would best be achieved by a matching commitment to social reforms that mobilized the nation in general, and Parisians in particular.

Robespierre's ideological validation played a major part in the government's seizure of the political and military initiative in the course of 1793–4 in ways that ended civil warfare and gave French armies the edge over their European foes. One might therefore have expected Robespierre to take much personal credit from the great watershed victory in the battle of Fleurus on 26 June 1794, which relieved the French northern frontier and opened up the Low Countries to the advance of the republican armies. In fact, for reasons we will explore in the course of the book, this was not at all the case. The relationship between different forces and figures within the Revolutionary Government had altered in telling ways. Robespierre was at daggers drawn with his colleagues within the Revolutionary Government, had partially withdrawn from public life, and seemed to be stirring up dissent within Paris against the very government of which he was a member. His behaviour tested the patience of his colleagues in government to the extreme, and ultimately it snapped. On 9 Thermidor, they launched a frontal attack on Robespierre in the Convention, and placed him under arrest.

To understand 9 Thermidor, we will need to comprehend Robespierre's position and motivations as well as those of the men within the Convention who passed from being his allies to his antagonists. But we also must penetrate into the minds and preoccupations of the people of Paris. For ultimately, it was the action of Parisians that, after many of the sudden ups-and-downs that for Mercier were characteristic of such *journées*, determined the outcome of the day.

Although the issues of 9 Thermidor were of national scale in their importance, they were settled by Parisians *intra muros*. Mercier once quipped that 'Paris is so big that one could stage a battle at one end of it without the other end knowing anything about it'. This was emphatically not the case on 9 Thermidor, however: there was popular involvement and mobilization in every one of the city's 48 sections. Furthermore, because the day occurred so unexpectedly and passed so swiftly, there was no chance for the environs (let alone the whole of France) to become involved. Most of France woke up on 10 Thermidor to find that Robespierre had fallen. It was the most Parisian of Revolutionary *journées*.

Seeing how Parisians—sans-culottes certainly, but many others too—came together to act collectively on 9 Thermidor involves not just digging down to the level of 'infinitely small' details but also locating those details within the city, both spatially and temporally—situating the action on the map and by the clock, so to speak. The outcome of the *journée* depended on decisions made in the course of these 24 hours by hosts of individuals caught up at all levels of the drama and at key moments in the flux of the day. We can grasp the flow of the day best by tracking news and information, and also rumour, gossip, emotions, orders and decrees, men and women, horses, guns, pikes, and cannon, as they travelled within and around the city over these 24 hours. From the most elevated through to the most humble city-dweller and across Paris from the historic heart to its furthermost periphery, Parisians sought to read the runes and to comprehend the minutiae of the day so as to determine their best course of action. How should they act? And for whom? To mobilize or not to mobilize? To rally to Robespierre and the Commune (the municipal government)? Or to support the National Convention? The day's outcome depended on a million micro-decisions made by Parisians across the expanse of the city and through the 24 hours of the day.

Writing the kind of microscopic, multi-layered, and multi-perspectival history of Paris and Parisians that this book attempts is only possible because archival documentation for the day is quite exceptionally rich, allowing us to access literally hundreds and hundreds of micro-narratives that cover fragments of the day from a multitude of angles. For fuller discussions, see Note on Sources, pp. 533–6; and Jones (2014): 'The Overthrow', pp. 696–7. There is a copy of the Barras instruction in W 500, d. 3. It would be difficult to think of another day in the whole of the eighteenth century on which sources are so copious and dense. A few days after the event, Barras, the deputy whom the government charged with the security of the city, initiated a punctiliously thorough review of everything that had happened within each of the 48 sections on 8, 9 and 10 Thermidor. 'Gather together all details', he instructed sectional authorities:

> A fact that seems minor may illuminate a suspicion or lead to the discovery of a useful truth. Inform me of all orders that you gave and all that you received; but above all, be precise on the dates and the hours; you will appreciate their importance.

This call engendered nearly 200 micro-accounts of at least part of the day from vantage points all over the city. Many of these were broken down for key periods of the day into quarter-hourly chunks. Besides this capital source deriving from the Barras enquiry, the Convention also set up an official commission to make a report on the day, which was presented in the Convention exactly a year later. In addition, newspaper reports and later political memoirs invariably contain accounts of the day. And finally, literally hundreds of individual police dossiers over the next year or so also provide similar micro-accounts of episodes and moments of the day.

This mosaic of thousands of fragments of experience distilled and of minutiae remembered composed a drama that seemed larger than real life. When 'events become at once terrible and singular' in this way, they produce, Mercier noted, a situation in which even 'dramatic fiction would be far from matching historical facts'. The 9 Thermidor proved a day when fact proved if not stranger than fiction certainly as gripping and surprising. Changing our customary focus as historians so as to get 'up close' to Parisians, their city, and their actions in the drama of 9 Thermidor allows us to view in a new and unexpected light not only Robespierre, the Revolution, the uses of terror, and the people of Paris but also the way in which we write the history of an epochal event.

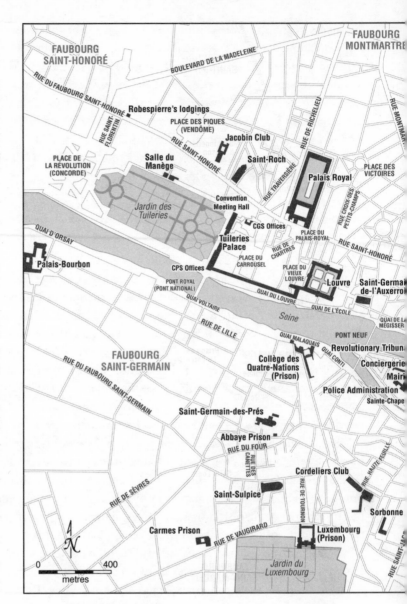

Map 1. Central Paris in 1794

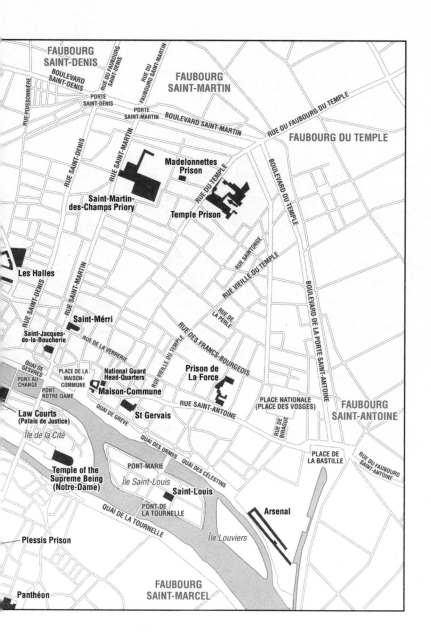

FAUBOURG
SAINT-DENIS

FAUBOURG
SAINT-MARTIN

BOULEVARD
SAINT-DENIS

RUE POISSONNIÈRE

RUE DU FAUBOURG SAINT-DENIS

RUE DU FAUBOURG SAINT-MARTIN

PORTE
SAINT-DENIS

PORTE
SAINT-MARTIN

BOULEVARD SAINT-MARTIN

RUE DU FAUBOURG DU TEMPLE

FAUBOURG DU TEMPLE

RUE SAINT-DENIS

RUE SAINT-MARTIN

BOULEVARD DU TEMPLE

Madelonnettes
Prison

RUE DU TEMPLE

Saint-Martin-
des-Champs Priory

Temple Prison

RUE SANTONGE

RUE VIEILLE DU TEMPLE

Les Halles

RUE SAINT-DENIS

RUE SAINT-MARTIN

RUE DE
LA PERLE

Saint-Mérri

RUE DES FRANCS-BOURGEOIS

Saint-Jacques-
de-la-Boucherie

RUE DE LA VERRERIE

RUE VIEILLE DU TEMPLE

QUAI DE
GESVRES

PLACE DE LA
MAISON-
COMMUNE

National Guard
Head-Quarters

Prison de
La Force

BOULEVARD DE LA PORTE SAINT-ANTOINE

PONT AU
CHANGE

PONT
NOTRE-DAME

Maison-Commune

PLACE NATIONALE
(PLACE DES VOSGES)

FAUBOURG
SAINT-ANTOINE

RUE SAINT-ANTOINE

Law Courts
(Palais de Justice)

QUAI DE GRÈVE

St Gervais

RUE DE
BIRAGUE

Île de la Cité

QUAI DES ORMES

PLACE DE
LA BASTILLE

RUE DU FAUBOURG
SAINT-ANTOINE

QUAI DES CÉLESTINS

PONT-MARIE

Temple of the
Supreme Being
(Notre-Dame)

Île Saint-Louis

Saint-Louis

QUAI DE LA TOURNELLE

PONT DE
LA TOURNELLE

Arsenal

Plessis Prison

Île Louviers

Panthéon

FAUBOURG
SAINT-MARCEL

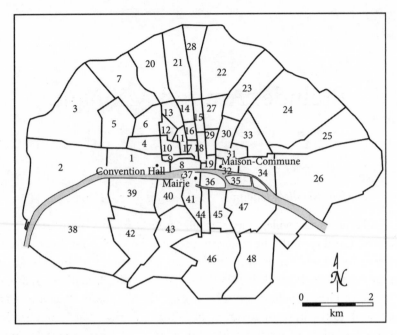

SECTIONS

1 Tuileries	1	27 Gravilliers	27
2 Champs-Elysées	2	28 Faubourg-du-Nord	28
3 République	3	29 Réunion	29
4 Montagne	4	30 Homme-Armé	30
5 Piques	5	31 Droits-de-l'Homme	31
6 Le Peletier	6	32 Maison Commune	32
7 Mont-Blanc	7	33 Indivisibilité	33
8 Muséum	8	34 Arsenal	34
9 Gardes-Françaises	9	35 Fraternité	35
10 Halle-au-Blé	10	36 Cité	36
11 Contrat-Social	11	37 Révolutionnaire	37
12 Guillaume-Tell	12	38 Invalides	38
13 Brutus	13	39 Fontaine-de-Grenelle	39
14 Bonne Nouvelle	14	40 Unité	40
15 Amis-de-la-Patrie	15	41 Marat	41
16 Bon-Conseil	16	42 Bonnet-Rouge	42
17 Marchés	17	43 Mutius-Scévole	43
18 Lombards	18	44 Chalier	44
19 Arcis	19	45 Panthéon-Français	45
20 Faubourg-Montmartre	20	46 Observatoire	46
21 Faubourg-Poissonnière	21	47 Sans-Culottes	47
22 Bondy	22	48 Finistère	48
23 Temple	23		
24 Popincourt	24		
25 Montreuil	25		
26 Quinze-Vingts	26		

Map 2. The 48 Paris sections

Prelude: Around Midnight

Rousseville's lodgings, Rue Saint-Honoré (Tuileries)

Pierre-Henri Rousseville rents a room above an inn on the Rue Saint-Honoré. Until recently the street featured on the crowd-lined itinerary for tumbrils (or carts) bearing convicted counter-revolutionaries to the guillotine at the nearby Place de la Révolution. People still gather here in droves. It is one of Paris's liveliest and most urbane thoroughfares. It is also only a short walk to the heart of government in the Tuileries palace complex. It is an excellent place of residence for politicians as also for government spies. Rousseville follows the latter vocation: he is an official 'government observer', who reports to the CPS, the Committee of Public Safety.

Tonight, Rousseville is putting the final touches to a confidential report for his masters. His report, headed 'Liberty, Equality, Fraternity, Probity or Death', is addressed 'CR'. This designates the 'Citizen Representatives', the elected deputies, 'representatives of the people' who compose the CPS. But Rousseville is pretty sure that his report will pass before the eyes of another 'CR', namely, Citizen Robespierre. Maximilien Robespierre, the most prominent member of that committee, is Rousseville's main point of contact with the CPS. His lodgings at 366 Rue Saint-Honoré are only a short distance from Rousseville's.

Like many spies, Rousseville has a chequered past. A priest prior to 1789, he flirted with the royalist cause as a secret agent in the early years of the Revolution, before undergoing radicalization. Elected parish priest at Belleville on the north-east edge of Paris, he attended the famous Jacobin Club, France's premier political association, and became linked to the far left groupings who waged war on Christianity. He published a 'dechristianizing' pamphlet urging the marriage of priests, before practising what he preached and taking wedding vows. He went on to have spells as government commissary on the eastern front in Alsace, and as police agent for the

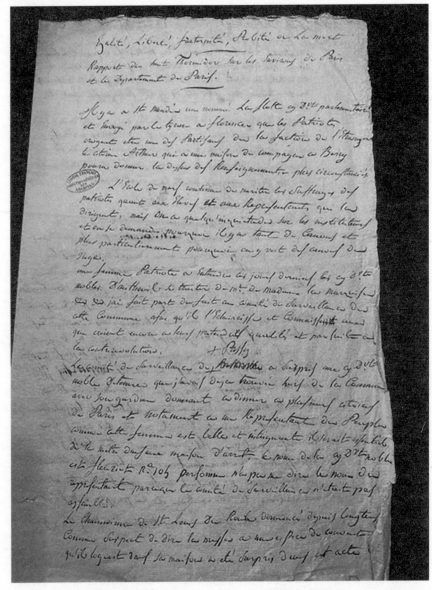

Figure 1. Rousseville, Report to the Committee of Public Safety, around midnight, 8–9 Thermidor (F7 4781)

ministry of the Interior and for the Paris departmental authorities before, in early 1794, he secured employment with the CPS.

Since its creation by Convention decree in April 1793, the CPS has been struggling to stave off military disaster and domestic implosion. It is authorized to conduct the war effort in which France has been engaged since April 1792 by all available means, including powerful authoritarian attacks on anyone who opposes the government line—through terror, that is. War had helped trigger the overthrow of the monarchy and the creation of a Republic in late 1792. But it was also threatening to bring that Republic crashing to the ground. In its work, the Committee cooperates closely with the CGS (Committee of General Security), which controls security and police matters. These two 'Committees of Government', as they are called, each composed of 12 deputies, form the core of the 'Revolutionary Government' ruling France. Making common cause, the 24 men have achieved great success, crushing waves of internal rebellion and expelling invading foreign armies. In the battle of Fleurus a month before, on 26 June 1794, French forces inflicted a major defeat on their Austrian foes, opening up the Low Countries to French advance.

Despite their record of joint success, there are ideological and personal issues causing friction between the two Committees of Government. These are getting worse, and have started to threaten government stability. One deep line of fracture is over policing. Robespierre, Rousseville's handler on the CPS, is highly critical of CGS agents. The CGS believes that in order to catch a thief, one sometimes has to set a thief. It employs individuals who do not seem as squeakily virtuous and patriotically clean as Robespierre would wish. The CGS's spy chief, Jean-Baptiste Dossonville, is a case in point. The bar that he ran in 1791–2 in the Bonne-Nouvelle section on the north-west boulevards became a rallying-ground for royalists. Then he got involved in the counterfeiting of assignats, the Revolution's fragile new paper currency. Was he up to his ears in counter-revolutionary crime and corruption? Or playing a cunning double-game? The CGS thinks the latter, and has entrusted him with sweeping powers over local institutions. Robespierre is less sure. And indeed, arriving in the CPS in-tray tomorrow will be a lengthy report from the Amis-de-la-Patrie sectional authorities, dated today, 26 July, with over a dozen witnesses denouncing Dossonville for a grim catalogue of corrupt and nefarious acts.

It is men like Dossonville who have made Robespierre fear that the whole CGS police force might be an elaborate front for the Republic's enemies. For nearly a year now, he has been convinced that foreign powers coordinated by British Prime Minister William Pitt, have hatched a 'Foreign Plot' threatening the Republic from within by suborning corrupt representatives in government. Robespierre's worries led him in April 1794 to create a parallel security agency, the Police Bureau—or 'Bureau of Administrative Surveillance and General Police', to give its full name. The Bureau is under the CPS aegis and run by himself and his closest political allies, Louis-Antoine Saint-Just and Georges Couthon. The duplication of policing duties with the CGS is souring relations and engendering mutual suspicion.

Robespierre distrusts the CGS and the Dossonvilles of the world, but he trusts Rousseville. For reasons unknown to others and maybe even to Rousseville, Robespierre is convinced that Rousseville is a true patriot. It is Robespierre who signed the CPS decrees appointing him to the Police Bureau and advancing his career, providing him with a decent salary, and allowing him to requisition horses for his travels from government stables on the Rue Saint-Honoré. When Robespierre wants an arrest made, Rousseville is a favoured agent. Conversely, Robespierre orders arrests on Rousseville's say-so. The ex-priest and ex-*enragé* has become one of the highest and most notorious officials in the CPS Police Bureau. He struts around bars and coffee-houses in a striking red waistcoat listening out for what is being said. Sometimes royalists spot him entering, and send up a quiet warning whistle.

For some time now, Rousseville has been touring Paris's rural environs, reporting on counter-revolutionary wrongdoings. Since April, Ancien Régime nobles are no longer allowed to reside within Paris. But droves of aristocratic refugees—Rousseville estimates 2,000 or more—have formed nests of sedition in Versailles, Neuilly, Passy, Auteuil, and other communes outside city walls. The Bois de Boulogne and the Bois de Vincennes are infested with clandestine meetings of aristocrats. In some places, aristocrats call each other by their abolished titles; priests who have abjured the Revolution hold mass; and private homes are full of the kind of religious bric-à-brac (engravings, crucifixes, prayer-books) that most Parisians now keep out of sight. There is a danger too of these counter-revolutionaries infecting the patriotism of the École de Mars, the military academy recently established on the Plaine des Sablons, on the Paris side of the village of Neuilly.

This evening, however, Rousseville sets aside his worries about an aristocratic ring encircling Paris. His report focuses on the state of opinion in Paris itself—'the Revolution's premier boulevard', as he calls it—at a critical moment in the Republic's short life. He is aware of Robespierre's anxieties about the workings of a Foreign Plot. That conspiracy now embraces, Robespierre has warned, the use of assassination as a legitimate weapon.

He and fellow CPS member, Jean-Marie Collot d'Herbois, were targeted in assassination attempts in late May: a deranged individual called Henri Lad-miral fired shots at Collot, while a teenage girl called Cécile Renault, with two penknives in her pocket, was arrested at Robespierre's lodgings talking of 'seeing what a tyrant looked like'. Robespierre is certain that the British government orchestrated these attacks. He and CPS colleague Bertrand Barère responded to them by jointly sponsoring a law prohibiting French troops from taking British prisoners of war. Death on the battlefield is now all the British have the right to expect from republican troops. Pitt and his ilk, Robespierre believes, are also using bribery and corruption to subvert the Revolution from within. He is sure that that corruption has reached the heart of the bureaucracy, the Convention and the Revolutionary Govern-ment, and, not least, the CGS police forces.

Rousseville reassures his master that these seditious efforts have failed to win much support within the city of Paris itself: 'the people', he writes, 'is full of confidence in the Convention'. Yet he must know that it is not just would-be murderess Cécile Renault who is concerned with 'tyranny'. It seems to be spreading within the political elite. Rousseville is aware that there has been a series of odd but worrying incidents just recently, involv-ing mysterious groups of armed men, notably at the Paris Arsenal and outside the poor-house and prison of Bicêtre, to the south of the city. Counter-revolutionary comments are routinely reported in bread queues and late-night bars. The city seems full of outsiders from the provinces up to no good. Neighbourhood parties—or 'fraternal banquets', as they are called—to celebrate the victories of French armies at the front, have been insidiously taken over by aristocrats seeking to mislead faithful street militants. A few days ago, it was reported that chalk signs had been mysteriously placed on the doors of lodgings of certain deputies in the Rue Traversière, close to the Convention hall. Was this making them marked men?

Vigorous action, Rousseville concludes, is immediately required. It is an excellent starting point that the people of Paris is 'full of confidence' in the Convention. But now is the time for all patriots to rally to the cause. They must, he concludes, 'surround loyal deputies with their trust, their care and their force'. 'The Committees of Government, the Convention and the people must be united in a solid mass of 25 million individuals, all sworn for the cause of freedom'. Firm action to crush conspirators and to ensure unity will allow Robespierre's dream of a purer, more virtuous Revolution to prevail.

Vernet's wanderings: from the Place du Trône-Renversé (Montreuil/Quinze-Vingts) to the Rue de Birague (Arsenal)

Alexandre Vernet is on his way home to the Rue Troussevache in the Lombards section, on the Right Bank near the market of Les Halles. The weather during the day has been fine, and in the afternoon, Vernet walked out to the Place du Trône-Renversé ('Overturned Throne') on the eastern edge of the city. Since 14 June, all guillotinings of individuals sentenced by the Revolutionary Tribunal for counter-revolutionary offences have taken place here. Vernet witnessed today's executions.

Paris-born, Vernet is by trade a breeches-maker, a *culottier*. The Revolution has not been kind to breeches-makers. Since events took a radical turn, breeches have changed from being a mundane mark of polite gentility to a cause of suspicion. The model patriot on the streets of Paris is now the man who disdains gentility and goes 'without breeches' or 'sans-culotte'. That term was first used contemptuously by the aristocratic Right to designate Parisians who yearned for a political role in the Revolution but did not have a decent suit of clothes to stand up in. But street radicals now glory in the name, and they dress accordingly, sporting the long trousers of the working man rather than 'aristocratic' knee-breeches. They also wear a red bonnet, a sign of new-found freedom, decked with the red-white-and-blue cockade that is a badge of patriotism, and the short jacket known as the *carmagnole*. Even some deputies in the Convention adopt the style, though emphatically not Maximilien Robespierre, who remains loyal to an impeccably correct form of dress: tidy culottes, silk stockings, powdered hair. This is of little comfort to a man like Vernet, apprenticed for a career making breeches. He has been reduced to eking out a meagre living buying and selling second-hand clothes at Les Halles.

We cannot be sure of Alexandre Vernet's political opinions. But we do know that men of his social type are quintessential sans-culottes. For these number a great many individuals from the artisanal trades specializing in luxury goods and services left high and dry after 1789 by loss of clients. The emigration of most aristocrats and their families and a move away from ostentatious consumption means that workers in the fashion trades (notably textiles and furnishings but also jewellery, fancy goods, domestic service, hairdressing, and so on) go hungry. An empty stomach can be a first step on the road to political radicalism.

The Parisian popular movement is composed of working people across the whole city, master and journeymen artisans, shopkeepers and shop assistants and petty clerks in the main. But many of the most ardent sans-culottes in the city are to be found in the populous eastern and south-eastern faubourgs of Saint-Antoine and Saint-Marcel. Located in the former, the Place du Trône-Renversé attracts sans-culotte crowds. In that respect it is more suitable for public executions than the Place de la Révolution on the far western side of the city, which from mid-1793 until recently was the location for the guillotine. That site attracted criticism. The passage of the tumbrils bearing prisoners from the Conciergerie prison on the Ile de la Cité along the Rue Saint-Honoré to that vast public square opening out onto the meadows of the Champs-Elysées had become one of the great rituals of the city. But traders and shopkeepers complained that the tumbrils were bad for business. Doctors highlighted the deleterious effect of viewing the procession and guillotinings on the health of children and pregnant mothers. Bales of straw failed to stem the blood that ran in swollen rivulets off the scaffold, staining the ground and giving off a nauseous stench. As a consequence, on 14 June 1794, the government shifted the instrument of decapitation southeast, to the peripheral Place du Trône-Renversé, which looks out on barren scrubland and open countryside beyond city gates.

Why do crowds of Parisians troop out in numbers to the Place to witness capital punishments? The spectacle is less dramatic than often said. Crowds at a guillotining are so big that most individuals present see very little. And they must not blink, for the blade is as fast as lightning. This is very unlike the horrific mutilating tortures of Ancien Régime justice, where death came as a release after hours of excruciating physical torture. In fact a guillotining is less grand guignol spectacle than a kind of austere morality play. The assumption is that once the Revolutionary Tribunal has done its work in identifying counter-revolutionaries, the act of punishment is a routine, transparent, and devastatingly swift demonstration of the sovereignty of the people.

Recently, however, popular anxieties about the guillotinings have begun to surface, as judicial terror intensifies. Concern focuses partly on numbers, partly on victims and partly on process. In the year that the guillotine was on the Place de la Révolution, it disposed of around a thousand condemned individuals; in the space of just six weeks in its present location, it has accounted for many more. Tumbrils used to carry a dozen or so individuals to their fate; now it is 40, 50, or more. And it is not just aristocrats who are led to their fates, but also people from humble backgrounds. Today, for example, alongside a good sprinkling of the aristocratic *haut gratin*, there was a grocer, an inn-keeper, an actress, and a chamber-maid. Is this what the reign of equality amounts to? One wonders how many Parisians have a friend or relation among the victims. The tumbrils promiscuously mix social classes, and include the Revolution's adherents as well as its opponents: many victims shout 'Long Live the Republic!' from the scaffold, sparking doubts about what exactly is going on. Spy Rousseville has reported hearing women in the street saying, 'this is the year for patriots to go to the guillotine', and stories are circulating about malpractice within the Revolutionary Tribunal and dark doings in the city's prisons. Recently, the appearance on a tumbril of a particularly young-looking teenager brought a rough growl from the crowd, 'No children'. The execution of 16 Compiègne Carmelite nuns on 17 July produced a troubled atmosphere of something akin to awe: in contravention of the law against religious dress being worn in public, they were in their habit, prayed together at the foot of the scaffold and marched courageously up to the guillotine one at a time chanting the *Veni Creator* through to the final swish of the blade.

Does Alexandre Vernet share these concerns about the use of the guillotine? Or has his attendance sprung from a simple quest for afternoon entertainment? It is not clear. In any case, the execution crew are a quietly efficient bunch and the guillotine got through its daily batch some time after 7.00 p.m. Vernet set out for home via the Faubourg Saint-Antoine, where he met up with workmates and had a glass or two, or maybe more. With the bars starting to close from around 11.00 p.m., Vernet knew he risked being picked up by night patrols, along with street-walkers and vagrants. Tiredness may have been setting in as he walked, and as the night was clear and dry, Vernet settled down on a quiet spot for a doze in the Marais, nearly a kilometre from his home. He selected his spot injudiciously. It was just behind the National Guard (NG) guardhouse on the Rue de Birague, by the Place des Vosges in the Arsenal section. He is about to be rudely awakened and hurled protesting into the cells.

La Force Prison (Droits-de-l'Homme)

'The Police Administrator has just left. He came to announce that tomorrow I will go before the Revolutionary Tribunal, which means the scaffold. This isn't at all like the dream I had last night. In it Robespierre no longer existed and the prisons were open. But thanks to your obvious cowardice, there soon will be no one left in France capable of making my dream come true.'

Theresa Cabarrus wrote this scathing letter the previous day to her lover, deputy Jean-Lambert Tallien. Her referral to the Revolutionary Tribunal has not in fact occurred today, but the threat of the scaffold remains real enough. Is her note a dismissive farewell? Or a challenge to action?

The Cabarrus-Tallien love affair has been intense, and is closely linked to the precipitous course of the Revolution. Tallien was a petty clerk in Paris before 1789. Radical journalism, engagement in political clubs and involvement in street action gave him enough of a profile to be elected to the Convention. At 27 years old, he was the second youngest deputy in the assembly. Full of restless energy, he was sent out in 1793 to south-western France as a deputy on mission in the provinces, that is, a roving commissioner with sweeping powers to enforce government policies. In October, he entered Bordeaux, with the task of punishing the city for its involvement in the Federalist Revolt against the Convention that summer. And in Bordeaux, he met Theresa Cabarrus.

Widely acknowledged to be one of the most beautiful women of her generation, Cabarrus has already stimulated more than her fair share of sexual intrigue and gossip. She comes from an aristocratic family in southwest France that has served Spanish as well as French kings. Now 20 years old, she was married at 15 to a feckless Parisian magistrate, became a mother at 16, and was divorced at 19. She was presented at court in Versailles in 1789 and this and her links with emigrated nobles led her to seek anonymity away from Paris. No sooner did she encounter Tallien than she was pleading the cause of local dignitaries threatened by the stern justice that Tallien had been sent to mete out. Within weeks, François Héron, another government spy with an exotic background (in his case as a privateer) reported to Paris that the two were having sex and protecting aristocrats from revolutionary justice. Neither is recommended behaviour for a deputy on mission.

In February 1794, Tallien was recalled, leaving Cabarrus dangerously unprotected in Bordeaux, where the presence of the precocious teenager, Marc-Antoine Jullien, a roving CPS spy who is Robespierre's personal protégé, made her life uncomfortable. So she fled in her lover's wake, seeking refuge at Fontenay-aux-Roses, some 5 miles from the capital, in a property owned by her former husband's family. Rousseville was on the prowl in the area, however, and on 31 May he reported that Citizenness Cabarrus had been visited for several nights by the deputy Tallien at Fontenay, but that she was now believed to be in Paris.

And in Paris she indeed was; and by then in prison, a situation for which Robespierre was largely responsible. Another of his favoured agents, hot-headed Servais-Beaudoin Boulanger, who is an officer in the Paris NG high command, was tracking her moves as she ventured back and forth between Fontenay-aux-Roses and Paris, with Tallien often in tow. In Paris, she lodged in a house in the Champs-Elysées section, owned by Robespierre's landlord no less, cabinet-maker Maurice Duplay. Was this a trap? At all events, Robespierre was certain enough of Cabarrus's movements to sign her arrest warrant on 22 May and give it to Boulanger to enforce. Boulanger followed her out to Versailles, where he arrested her and had her transferred to the La Force prison in Paris, located in the Marais just off the Rue Saint-Antoine. The gaoler signed her into the admissions register converting her beauty into the physiognomic calibrations of police bureaucracy: 'four feet eleven tall, dark hair and eyebrows, normal forehead, dark eyes, average nose, small mouth, round chin . . .'. A strip search followed before she was led away into solitary confinement, where she has remained for three weeks, losing weight and becoming ill. A story has it that, on learning of her travails here, Robespierre permitted her the use of a mirror, but only, he stipulated, once a day.

In this dark and hostile site, Cabarrus has won favours from her gaolers by drawing likenesses of them, for she trained as an artist as a young girl. With writing implements that she has managed to secure in return, she corresponds imploringly with her lover, as the spectre of the Revolutionary Tribunal floats ever closer.

Tallien is not in gaol, but his life and liberty hang by a thread. He is a marked man—marked by Robespierre. It is not just sleeping with the aristocracy and his corrupt and unprincipled behaviour in Bordeaux that Robespierre holds against him. He is suspicious of Tallien's former links to the deputy Georges Danton (whom Robespierre helped dispatch to the scaffold in April 1794 for corruption and counter-revolutionary intent). Even before that, Robespierre held against Tallien his alleged involvement in the 1792 'September Massacres' (2–4 September 1792). These were provoked by a city-wide panic at the deteriorating military situation. News of the fall of Verdun in late August 1792, the last defensive fortress protecting Paris from the invading German army, led to popular mobilization for the front on one hand and on the other a crude determination to eradicate counter-revolutionary prisoners within the city. Rumours of an aristocratic 'prison plot' served as justification, triggering groups of Parisian radicals touring the city's gaols killing to right and left.

Robespierre publicly defended and justified the massacres as an expression of popular will, even claiming (with heartless inaccuracy) that only one actual patriot had been killed. But he was privately revolted by these shocking incidents, and blocked Tallien's election for Paris in the election to the Convention later that month, forcing him to secure nomination from the Seine-et-Oise department.

Robespierre's longstanding dislike for Tallien crystallized into hatred in June 1794, when Robespierre and his closest political allies, Saint-Just and Couthon, forced a nervous Convention to agree to the so-called Law of 22 Prairial (10 June 1794), facilitating and speeding up convictions by the Revolutionary Tribunal for counter-revolutionary offences. Like many colleagues, Tallien feared that this might be used against deputies and he challenged Robespierre in the Convention over the law, only to be crushed in debate. 'Tallien is one of those individuals', Robespierre high-handedly informed the deputies, 'who ceaselessly speaks of the guillotine as something of concern to him, so as to slander and worry the Convention'.

Robespierre is frighteningly formidable in such circumstances. Deputy Bourdon de l'Oise, who also protested against the 22 Prairial Law, was humiliated so woundingly by Robespierre that he was ill in bed for a month. His condition was not helped by rumours soon going around Paris that he and Tallien had been assassinated. Tallien is made of sterner stuff and, following the clash in the Convention, wrote Robespierre a letter in which he professed the firmest patriotism. Far from being the libertine voluptuary he is reputed, he claimed, he lives a quiet, frugal family life at his mother's house on the Rue de la Perle in the Marais. Robespierre's response was to use his authority within the Paris Jacobin Club to have Tallien's membership rescinded within 48 hours. Robespierre is in no mood to build bridges.

Claude Guérin, yet another CPS police spy reporting to Robespierre's Police Bureau, has organized a watch on Tallien's moves around the town. His reports reach Robespierre. Tallien realizes he is being followed, Guérin notes. He anxiously looks around him to left and right. He wanders the streets aimlessly, visiting restaurants and *bouquinistes*, strolling in the Tuileries gardens, chatting to fellow deputies before popping into the Convention to listen to debates. A visit to his lover's prison is out of the question: it would spell death for both. But Tallien has smuggled a reply to Cabarrus: 'Be as prudent as I'll be brave and above all stay calm.' Is he fobbing off an ex-lover? Or is he planning something? A couple of days ago he confidently told an acquaintance that 'by the end of the week the tyrant will be brought low'.

Legracieux's lodgings, Rue Denfert (Chalier)

Stanislas Legracieux is in his Left Bank lodgings, writing a letter to fellow Jacobins in his home town of Saint-Paul-Trois-Châteaux in the former Dauphiné province in south-eastern France. Saint-Paul is also the birthplace of Legracieux's friend, Claude-François Payan, a strong supporter of Robespierre, who has become, as National Agent, a leading official within the Paris Commune—that is, the municipality—second in importance only to the Mayor, Jean-Baptiste Fleuriot-Lescot. It is most likely Payan's influence that has secured Legracieux a nicely remunerated place in the central bureaucracy which he has journeyed to the capital to take up.

Legracieux is beside himself with excitement. Today, he witnessed truly dramatic events within the walls of the National Convention. Robespierre openly exposed and denounced the Foreign Plot that has been threatening to divide the nation and engulf the Revolution. He promised (Legracieux is paraphrasing) to rip aside the veil hiding corrupt traitors who conceal the face of tyranny beneath the smile of hope. He stood rock-like against his enemies in the Convention, Virtue personified, facing down the conjoined forces of crime and corruption.

Legracieux is scandalized that, despite the depths of iniquity that Robespierre revealed to his fellow deputies, the assembly refused to publish his speech and to send it out to the provinces. The people is thus being denied the right to know the virtues of the pure and the wickedness of the treacherous. To Legracieux's indignation, Robespierre's enemies went further still: they dared to treat this guardian of freedom as a dictator! Robespierre had to rely on his own strength of character to endure this reception in the Convention.

The day was, however, to have a silver lining. For that evening, Legracieux recounts, Robespierre attended the 'sanctuary of patriotism' that is the famous Paris Jacobin Club. The Club gets its name from its meeting place, the monastery of the Jacobins, a former Dominican house on the northern side of the Rue Saint-Honoré, only a few hundred yards from Robespierre's lodgings. From its foundation in autumn 1789 as the Society of Friends of the Constitution, it has consistently attracted the most radical deputies from the national assembly, but membership is also open to private individuals committed to the patriotic cause. Debates and decisions here have a record of powerfully impacting the national assembly. So it bodes well for Robespierre that his numerous friends and admirers in the Club warmly embraced his wish to punish traitors, wherever they are to be found. With reckless enthusiasm the order of the day, hats were flung repeatedly in the air in his support.

And so tomorrow, Legracieux tells his provincial friends, 27 July 1794, the subject of debate in the Jacobins will be the present conspiracy. War to the death against tyrants will ensue. And subsequent days will witness the triumph of the Republic of liberty and equality, hatred for tyrants, and the just vengeance of the people against those who betray it. Unity will prevail, under Robespierre's sage guidance. The wicked must vanish from the face of the earth . . .

Home of Guittard de Floriban, Rue des Canettes (Mutius-Scévole)

Midnight is approaching, ending the day of 26 July 1794. The sun set at 7.36 p.m. A new moon was visible from 4.51 in the afternoon—or was it? For the sky was cloudy. The weather has not been outstanding for this time of year, with rain on most days. Tomorrow, 27 July, the sun is due to rise at 4.22 a.m.

Célestin Guittard de Floriban, 69-year-old widower, bourgeois, and rentier, keeps a diary. Its mundane inscriptions are spasmodically spiced by a collection of marginal stars and asterisks which denote sexual relations with his long-term dining companion, one Madame (or rather, now, Citizenness) Sellier. For some months now, Floriban has developed a dual daily pastime: in his diary he records the temperature and he then itemizes the list of the day's guillotined. On 23 July, his diary shows, the temperature rose to 22 degrees, and 55 individuals were guillotined. On 24 July: 23 degrees, 36 guillotinings. The 25 and 26 July were both fine days: the temperature remained at 23 degrees, as first 38 victims, then a further 52 were executed.

Floriban's Left Bank home on the corner of the Rue des Canettes adjoins the Place Saint-Sulpice. The street is crowded and airless, which probably explains why up at the Observatory on the southern edge of the city at an elevation 30 metres higher, scientists will record at midday on 27 July a maximum temperature of only 18 degrees—whereas Floriban will register 23. The day of the 27th will remain cloudy and warm. Floriban will note a light shower in the morning; the Observatoire records it at 9.15 a.m. Apart from that, 27 July will see no rain.

Floriban records time in his diary with the old Gregorian Calendar, studiously ignoring the official Revolutionary version. He may not even be aware that on the upcoming *décadi*, 10 Thermidor – 28 July—there are plans afoot to celebrate two teenage heroes, Joseph Bara and Agricol-Joseph Viala, who have given their lives for the fatherland in war. Robespierre has been making a fuss about them, and at his suggestion their bodies will be placed with great pomp in the Panthéon, the old Sainte-Geneviève church, now a republican shrine for national heroes.

Plans change. In fact, 24 hours or so from now, at the end of 28 July, after duly noting his meteorological data, the prosaic diarist will break into dramatic capitals to announce:

> – GREAT CONSPIRACY. Today would have been one of the greatest events that France has ever known if conspiracy had had its way.

The date 27 July 1794 (9 Thermidor Year II) will indeed prove to be a day of conspiracy and counter-conspiracy, of conspiracy alleged, conspiracy discovered, conspiracy foiled. The fate of the Revolution, the state of Paris, and the destiny of France will be in the balance. And at the heart of the action in these 24 hours in the month of Thermidor will be Maximilien Robespierre. In weeks to come, Floriban will remain poised over his diary. But by the end of the fateful day of 9 Thermidor, Robespierre's spy Rousseville, his panegyrist Stanislas Legracieux and indeed the hangover-bound *sans-culotte* Alexandre Vernet will all be facing imprisonment. Tallien will have taken vigorous action in defence of his lover, Theresa Cabarrus. And as for Robespierre himself? Twenty-four hours from now, Robespierre will be on the run from the law, and fearing for his life . . .

PART

I

Elements of Conspiracy (Midnight to 5.00 a.m.)

Paris is sleeping. Since the storming of the Bastille in July 1789, the city has been living one the most turbulent and passionate episodes in its history. The young French Republic is in the throes of a life and death struggle against the combined armed forces of Ancien Régime Europe, while it also endeavours to master nationwide dissension and civil conflict. Though democratically elected, the National Convention has placed normal democratic procedures in abeyance, and embraced the use of terror as a means of overcoming opposition.

War and terror have transformed the city, endowing its inhabitants with a new kind of political energy. The largest city in continental Europe, Paris once revelled in its reputation as the hedonistic home of European politeness, enlightened thinking, and leisured consumption. Now, Parisians view themselves as the knowing vanguard of world-historical democratic transformation.

Politics since 1789 has been a chronicle of recurrent crises and abrupt shifts in direction, and a new crisis is brewing. It all centres on one of the leading figures in the Revolution, Maximilien Robespierre. Robespierre has a huge reputation as a patriot and a democrat. The most eloquent and incorruptible of champions of the people, he is currently a key member of a government that seems to be carrying all before it. Yet at this moment, while most Parisians are slumbering in their beds, Robespierre is considering his position. He realizes his enemies are depicting him as a dictator, a tyrant-in-the-making. At this very moment, he fears that they are conspiring against him, as though their lives depended on it. As indeed they are. And indeed they do.

00.00/Midnight

Robespierre's lodgings, 366 Rue Saint-Honoré (Piques)

- I expect nothing from the Montagne; they want to do away with me as a tyrant; but the bulk of the Convention will hear me.

Robespierre is speaking to his landlord, master cabinet-maker Maurice Duplay, in his lodgings at 366 Rue Saint-Honoré. Recently, he has been going to bed early. Tonight that has not possible.

The long, emotional speech that Robespierre gave in the Convention earlier in the day was the first time he has spoken there since mid-June. He may have enraptured spectating provincial Jacobin Stanislas Legracieux, but he also provoked furious and personalized opposition among many deputies, not least his habitual long-term political allies, the radical deputies of what is called the Montagne, or 'Mountain'. (In the Manège, the Convention's meeting hall through to May 1793, the group gained the name by colonizing the uppermost benches of the steeply raked seating.) This evening, Robespierre has repeated his Convention speech in the altogether more sympathetic forum of the Jacobin Club. The Club is the Republic's premier political association, a debating chamber that forms policies that deputies carry into the legislature. Its galleries are open to the general public, and members of the public may join for a fairly substantial subscription. The Club also serves as the hub of a vast network of affiliate and supporting clubs and associations throughout the length and breadth of the country, containing probably in excess of 150,000 members. Club meetings rarely last much past ten o'clock, but tonight has been an exception. Although his speech encountered lively opposition, in the end his demands for political purges to crush the plots that threaten the Republic have been enthusiastically acclaimed, as Legracieux excitedly noted, in stormy debates which delayed his return home.

By his oratory, Robespierre has raised the political stakes to a new level—but he feels vindicated. He has been talking about the Foreign Plot and other conspiracies for so long now as though in a void. Today the Convention has given him positive evidence to prove his point: there is an evident plot against him that is being led by his old Montagnard allies in the Convention, who are claiming that he aspires to dictatorship. They think a tyrant is waiting in the wings.

The theoretical strength of the Convention is 749 deputies. Roughly one-third of them count as Montagnards. The remainder is balanced between the Centre, often disparaged as 'the Plain' or 'the Marsh' (or *Marais*) and the ever-diminishing ranks of the Right. Despite their minority status, the energetic and determined Montagnard group has been able largely to impose its collective will about government policy on the direction of the Revolution for a year or more now. The men of the Plain have lacked coordination—as well as the courage and the vision—to put their numerical advantage to the test. The hundred or so replacement deputies who have taken the seats of the deputies who have been purged or else who have resigned or died in post, are probably among the most reticent. But Robespierre now seems to be thinking—as he is faced with blatant conspiracy on the Montagnard benches—that this is the moment for him to mobilize just such moderate individuals, who form 'the bulk of the Convention' (as he notes) as a force to save the Republic, and indeed himself.

Does Robespierre for an instant reflect, one wonders, as he leaves Duplay to make his way to his bedchamber with the clock showing after midnight, that today marks a year to the day since, on 27 July 1793, he was elected onto the CPS? He respects anniversaries: he tends not to miss 14 July commemorations. Maybe he also recalls that 6 May 1789, when the Third Estate began its resistance to Louis XVI at the outbreak of the Revolution, was his own birthday? Yet now his mind needs to focus on the immediate future rather than on what must seem a long-distant past. Fortunately, his small, spartan rented room offers few distractions from thinking. For over a month now, he has been doing little else. Studiously avoiding the Convention and the CPS, he has kept himself to himself here at his lodgings, save only for walking his dog, a mastiff called Brount, at the edge of the city, and for evening visits to the Jacobin Club, which is conveniently close to the Duplay residence. Duplay is a Jacobin, and landlord and tenant often attend the Club together.

Robespierre was an obscure provincial lawyer in Arras when in 1789 he was elected by the Artois province to the Estates General. In the new National Constituent Assembly, and then in the Jacobin Club, he carved out an enduring reputation as the unswerving defender of the popular classes and the cause of popular sovereignty. Right-wing enemies contemptuously dubbed him the 'populomaniac deputy' and 'the people's Don Quixote', but he never flinched from launching tirades against prominent figures in the new regime who were in his estimation deceiving the people: Mirabeau, for example, the eminent yet corrupt leader in the Constituent Assembly; Lafayette, commander of the Paris NG; Dumouriez, the Girondins' favourite 'patriot' general, who turned traitor and ran off to the Austrians; and the meddlingly troublesome duke of Orleans, Louis XVI's cousin. 'The Incorruptible', as he became known, stood above the often compromised political morals of the new political elite. He claimed, and still claims, not only to represent the people but in some proud sense even to embody it: '*je suis peuple*'. This identification is grounded in a vague but adamantine belief in the perennial goodness of the people, always at risk from the corrupt hands of the great and the powerful.

Robespierre's dual commitment to the popular cause and the Jacobin Club has not wavered, even in the dark days following King Louis XVI's attempt to flee Paris in the so-called 'Flight to Varennes' in June 1791. The king had never really understood let alone sympathized with the cause of Revolution. Dragged out of Versailles in October 1789, he and his family were placed in the Tuileries palace in central Paris. Free in theory, they instantly felt they were prisoners. Louis's decision to try to escape from the city split the political class, causing a massive rift within the Jacobins. Even before the humiliated king had been brought back to the capital from Varennes, where he and his family were intercepted, support for republicanism burgeoned among the Jacobin Club membership—but not among those who were deputies. All of the latter, except for Robespierre and a handful of others, abandoned the club, creating a new (if short-lived) Feuillant Club.

In the Assembly, the Feuillants adopted the policy of supporting the errant monarch as a means of forcing him to legitimize a new constitution. In this delicate situation, the Paris NG under Lafayette's command brutally crushed a popular demonstration calling for the removal of the king, that

was held on the Champ de Mars on the south-west corner of the city on
17 July 1791. It was followed by a campaign of harassment of popular radicals
and republicans across the city. Hitherto, Robespierre had lodged in the Rue
Saintonge on the eastern reaches of the Marais. But he felt vulnerable there
in the tense post-Champ de Mars atmosphere and Duplay came to his aid,
offering him lodgings that provided greater protection: 366 Rue Saint-
Honoré houses Duplay's carpentry business as well as his home and the
street gate opens onto a courtyard where his tough-armed carpenter appren-
tices and journeymen ply their master's trade.

With the advent of the Legislative Assembly in September 1791 marking
the end of his tenure as a deputy, Robespierre chose not to return to Arras
but to remain in Paris and further develop his role as defender of popular
sovereignty, partly through journalism and partly through a continued role
at the Jacobin Club. In this period he soldered lasting and powerful links
with the emerging sans-culotte movement of street radicals, notably in the
days leading up to the *journée* of 10 August 1792 that overthrew the king.
After joining the insurrectionary Paris Commune created at the moment of
transition to a Republic, he played an active role in radicalizing the capital
and electing its deputies (himself included) to the new assembly, the
Convention.

By this time, war with Europe had begun to redefine what the Revolution was all about. Robespierre had initially distanced himself from calls for
war that started to be made in the national assembly in late 1791 and early
1792 by a loose grouping of deputies known as Girondins or Brissotins (some
of them hailed from the Gironde department around Bordeaux, while the
journalist deputy Jacques-Pierre Brissot, formerly Robespierre's friend and
ally, was their most high-profile leader). Yet although Robespierre naturally
embraced the patriot cause once war against the Austrians was declared in
April 1792, Girondin antagonism towards him and his fellow Montagnards
grew steadily, as the scale of the international conflict widened to involve
most of the other European powers, including Britain. Girondins were
fiercely critical of the way that the Montagnards favoured a populist and
authoritarian approach to the conduct of the war. In particular, they loudly
attacked Parisian sans-culottes, especially after the bloody episode of the
1792 September Massacres. With sans-culotte pressure building up against
them, one of the Girondin group, deputy Maximin Isnard, while presiding
at the Convention on 28 May 1793, warned a deputation from the Paris
Commune that were they to launch an attack on the nation's

representatives, 'Paris would be destroyed, and people will scan the banks of the Seine for traces of the city'. Robespierre in contrast defended the Parisian people against such Girondin provocations and worked with them to have Brissot and his colleagues expelled from the Convention.

The mutual hatred between the two sides climaxed in the two *journées* of 31 May and 2 June 1793. On those days, the Montagnards coordinated with the Parisian sans-culotte movement to force the Convention to arrest and expel the Girondin leadership—initially 22 (and ultimately 29) deputies plus two ministers. Instrumental in the operation was François Hanriot, a humble sans-culotte thrust by the crisis into the role of de facto Paris NG commander. In an inspired, if sinister stroke, Hanriot amassed some 80,000 guardsmen around the Convention hall and threatened the deputies with being overrun unless they took action against the Girondins.

The ensuing parliamentary purge sparked huge tracts of provincial France into armed anti-Parisian resistance in the Federalist Revolt of mid-1793. On top of this, the Convention's armies suffered a rash of military defeats at this time on the frontiers: foreign troops spilled over every border from the Pyrenees to the Rhine; the loyalty of the generals could not be counted on; a peasant royalist uprising triggered civil war in the Vendée department in western France; famine threatened; and central government was paralysed by faction-fighting. When Robespierre joined the CPS on 27 July 1793, the Republic's fortunes were at their nadir.

What a difference a year makes! In twelve months, the Republic has made an astonishing recovery. This point was underlined in the Convention only two days previously, on 25 July 1794 (7 Thermidor), by Robespierre's CPS colleague Bertrand Barère. He highlighted just how far France has come since those dark mid-1793 days. Gradually over the late summer of 1793, with the Girondins out of the way (22 of them would be guillotined in October), the Montagnards re-staffed and re-energized the two Committees of Government—the CPS and the CGS—to make them capable of effective action on all fronts. Military action brought the Vendée under control. The Federalist Revolt was snuffed out, and the principal cities which had supported it (Lyon, Marseille, Toulon) recaptured from the rebels and brutally punished. Lyon in particular was singled out for special treatment. The city lost even its identity. It was henceforth 'Ville-Affranchie' ('Freed City') and its ramparts and many private residences were razed, while a military commission meted out brutal repression. In addition, every frontier was cleared of foreign troops. Indeed, following the battle of Fleurus in late June 1794,

French troops are taking the battle to their foes and pushing into the Low Countries. On other fronts there is marked improvement too. Although there are still food shortages, the spectre of famine has been lifted, with special measures keeping Paris provisioned. The judicial system, organized around the Revolutionary Tribunal in Paris, is ridding France of traitors, while police forces are foiling plots, notably within the city's prison system.

Although Barère concluded his peroration by celebrating the growing spirit of calm throughout the country, he did spot a cloud on a largely sun-drenched horizon: namely, people from the poorer classes had been heard around the Convention hall calling for 'a new 31 May', a further sans-culotte-led purge of the assembly. Although deputies now fully accept the outcome of the anti-Girondin *journées* of 31 May and 2 June 1793, no one wants a repeat performance. Barère's speech stressed that such action now would not only be dangerous for the Revolutionary cause; it would also be redundant since, although there remains some way to go before the Repub-lic is fully triumphant, in essence the government could not be working better. Threats from Paris are completely out of kilter with reality and would take France down the road to counter-revolution.

Robespierre was not present in the assembly for Barère's speech. And his sense of present 'reality' is very different from that glowingly elaborated by his CPS colleague. The champion of the popular cause absolutely rejects the latter's implicitly blaming the people of Paris for threatening the Republic. It is not the people who pose the problem, but their representatives in the national assembly. For Robespierre, talk of a replay of the 31 May *journée* is a distraction from recognizing that a foreign-financed conspiracy has pene-trated to the heart of the political system over recent months. Foreign powers are secretly suborning revolutionaries, planting propaganda in the press, and stimulating in-fighting within the political elite. Many of the most egregiously corrupt politicians involved in this Foreign Plot have been executed, following trials before the Revolutionary Tribunal in March and April 1794: first, the radical Hébertist grouping around the municipal politician Jacques-René Hébert, then a more moderate set of deputies around Georges Danton and Camille Desmoulins, who wanted to slow down the pace of terror. Unfortunately, Robespierre believes, the canker of corruption has not been completely eradicated. For some months, he has pestered CPS colleagues to wake up to the reality of this conspiracy and to call for the removal of foreign-financed plotters. By turning a deaf ear to his pleas, they have themselves become part of the problem. Fail to face facts about the enemy, and one becomes the enemy oneself.

Robespierre's deep pessimism about the government of which he forms part is grounded in a conviction that it has broken the contract it made with the people in 1793. Corruption within the government has not only polluted that relationship, he believes, it has also had a massively deleterious effect on the people themselves. The highly unitary notion of the people that he cherished in the early part of the Revolution has started crumbling under the experience of government. He now feels there is not one but two peoples: one is formed by 'the mass of the people, pure, simple, thirsty for justice, friends of freedom'. It is this 'virtuous people who spilt its blood to found the Republic'. The other, in contrast, is 'an impure breed', a 'concoction of ambitious intriguers, a chattering, charlatanesque, artificial people who mislead public opinion' and who constitute the source of all the nation's ills. A corrupt government gives sustenance to the 'impure breed' rather than the 'virtuous people'.

It was with a sense of purifying government that Robespierre agreed to enter the CPS on 27 July 1793. It was an elevation, he claims, that he did not actively seek. Certainly, being placed on a powerful body that was running the country under crisis conditions was something entirely new to him. He had been the conscience of the Revolution and the gadfly targeting corrupt politicians. His career was built on being an outsider looking in; now at a stroke he had insider status thrust upon him. This transition from poacher to gamekeeper did not come easily, for Robespierre generally ascribes to the classical republican view that the danger of corruption always lurks near the heart of government. He had hardly been a CPS member for three weeks before he was reporting his shock to the Convention at criminal behaviour within the committee. His complaints about the bad faith of his colleagues died away in subsequent months, but they have re-emerged with a vengeance in recent weeks.

Robespierre's impracticality is notorious. Danton's jibe that Robespierre couldn't boil an egg to save his life was harsh. But he certainly brought to his place within the CPS next to no managerial or practical skills. Almost alone among prominent politicians in the Convention, he had never even sat on an assembly committee, nor developed the skills of political fixing, of quests for compromise, and of creating consensus that go with managing a committee or serving as rapporteur. He has never really run anything in his life. Trained and then practising freelance as a provincial lawyer prior to 1789, his expert knowledge is highly limited. His acquaintance with the culture of international relations is nugatory. He expresses (and indeed rather glories in) a total ignorance of military affairs, save for a predilection for 'patriotic' rather than aristocratic generals. And he is little more than a dunce in matters financial ('Money frightens Robespierre', Danton once said). Indeed, he is one of a handful of colleagues who are too disorganized even to manage to collect their pay-cheque as deputy in person.

Although when he entered the CPS, Robespierre had a neophyte's enthusiasm for reforming committee processes, he soon tired of being the new managerial broom, and came to specialize in what he does best: talk. His legislative record is thin. It is his speeches and character rather than his concrete achievements or the range of his practical competencies that have brought him to the CPS. It seems true what Jean-Paul Marat once said of him:

> – the only ambition he has is to speak at the rostrum . . . He has so little about him of a party leader that he flees any group that seems tumultuous and pales at the sight of a drawn sabre.

What he offered from the outset (his CPS colleague Jacques-Nicolas Billaud-Varenne believes) were 'the most austere virtues, the most complete dedication and the very purest of principles'. His colleagues have allowed him to showcase these virtues, for everyone's benefit, in a powerful and charismatic eloquence that has crowned the Revolutionary Government with a powerful aura of legitimacy, and heightened levels of popularity and republican assent to their common purpose. This has been changing recently, but in the course of the last year he has provided Revolutionary Government with exemplary service by being able to combine an ability to win popular support for government policy with a toughness that keeps a potentially unruly Convention docile and uncomplaining.

One has only to glance at Robespierre's speeches in the national assembly or Jacobin Club from the earliest days of the Revolution to grasp his powerfully distinctive voice and inspiring vision of a new, regenerated world of political virtue. In the Constituent Assembly between 1789 and 1791, he fearlessly championed the people, fought for individual rather than a property franchise, argued a powerful case for freedom of expression, championed religious toleration, demanded humane judicial reforms, including the abolition of the death penalty, and joined the anti-colonialist cause (which has culminated in the abolition of slavery in February 1794).

He made major contributions to debates on the 1793 Constitution, the world's most democratic charter (though currently on hold). Before the Revolution, Robespierre also spoke up for the right of women to form part of intellectual debates and public life. If he has recently gone quiet on that cause, it is mainly because deputies mostly believe that women belong in the realm of private life. Women, however, sense that he is a sympathetic spirit and he enjoys much female popularity, leading his enemies to sneer at his 'idolaters' in the public galleries.

At his best, he can weave a spell over listeners of both sexes that allows them to glimpse a better, fairer world. When Robespierre is fully on song, his rhetoric has mesmerizing, quasi-magical powers, that no other politician can match. Some aspects of this uplifting vision, grounded in individual rights, have had to be put on hold because of the war emergency. Even so, and despite still being mocked by some fellow deputies as a utopian vision-ary, he has retained a sense of the Revolution as offering the opportunity for regenerated humanity to accede to a noble destination, which he conceives of as that republic of virtue that has formed the basis of his great set-piece speeches over the last year. Billaud-Varenne's better grasp of detail made him, rather than Robespierre, the CPS drafter and rapporteur of the Law of 14 Frimaire (4 December 1793), the piece of legislation setting out the mechanisms of the Revolutionary Government. Similarly, Barère's compe-tence in international relations makes him the optimal presenter of news from the front, and it is he rather than Robespierre who introduces major reform of poor relief. Yet it is Robespierre who has assumed the task of presenting a coherent and passionate moral rationale for Revolutionary Government, both inspiring and justifying government activities. This encompasses the use of terror. Terror is nothing new: it has been an embodiment of sovereignty across the ages, especially at moments of state crisis. The Revolutionary Government, Robespierre argues, has put this on a new and morally defensible basis, due to the fact that sovereignty in the new Republic is embodied in the people not in the person of the ruler. Given this grounding, the government now freely deploys terror in the exercise of what he calls a 'despotism of liberty against tyranny'. This brings virtue and terror into conjunction in a way that is new in the history of humanity:

> – Virtue without which terror is destructive; terror, without which virtue is impotent. Terror is only prompt, severe and inflexible justice; it is thus an emanation of virtue.

Robespierre's deep emotional engagement in his speeches adds to their impact. His heart is always on his sleeve. He is painfully sincere in all his words and actions, offering an exemplary model of high-minded action in the style of his great idol, Jean-Jacques Rousseau, the arch-apostle of moral transparency. The high spot of the whole Revolution for Robespierre was probably when, on 8 June 1794 (20 Prairial), he officiated over the Festival of the Supreme Being, which followed on from legislation which he had designed and steered through the assembly, establishing a Deist form of worship which sought to consign atheism to the past. The enthusiastic response that he perceived the festival eliciting from the people of Paris played to his passionate conviction that the Revolution marked a new epoch in history. He does not see returning now to the democratic 1793 Constitution as a government priority: indeed he views those who call for it in present circumstances as the dangerous heirs of the Hébertist radicals who had been crushed in the spring. Rather, he urges the government to work with the existing national assembly towards human regeneration through social institutions like public festivals, his Supreme Being project, educational reforms, and social welfare schemes. Combined with terror, these will direct the people onwards in the pathways of virtue.

There are no shades of grey in Maximilien Robespierre's oratory, nor indeed in his worldview. His speeches depict a black-and-white world in which the pure, the morally upright, and the patriotic heroically combat all manner of corrupt men and women in the noble task of humanity's self-fashioning in virtue. This arch-simplification of the political landscape, fortified by the inevitable polarization of politics at time of war, combines with an unwavering, self-sacrificial, Rousseau-esque commitment to the cause. The kind of melodramatic, sentimental narrative arc which structures his speeches, and which often evokes his own death in the cause of freedom, is not new: he was using it even before the Revolution got under way, and he has drawn on it throughout his Revolutionary career. Nor is it Robespierre's alone. But it is undoubtedly his signature trope, which has the power to instil an added frisson in his listeners.

Robespierre's ability to thrill and to inspire his audience through the power of his words is all the more striking in that he is not at all a natural orator. He admits to suffering stage fright, at least up to the moment when he opens his mouth. His voice, inflected by an unfashionable provincial accent, is thin and often sounds slightly strained. It carries poorly in the cavernous assembly hall. His physical posture at the rostrum is constrained and awkward and he lacks expansive, Danton-esque gestures. He also has a habit, which some find infuriating (though it also prompts close attention) of speaking slowly and making dramatic pauses, while maybe adjusting the green-lens spectacles he often wears. His speeches can be very long—and for the unconverted seem even longer.

Perhaps Robespierre's Achilles heel as a speaker, however, is his sensitivity to ridicule and humour. He is famously thin-skinned and stands so firmly on his dignity as almost to invite mischievous deflation. Under the Constituent Assembly, his aristocratic opponents provoked Robespierre by writing and pronouncing his name as Roberts-pierre, alleging a (completely fictitious) family connection to the infamous Robert Damiens, Louis XV's would-be assassin in 1757. Then again, a matter of weeks earlier, CGS member Marc-Guillaume-Alexis Vadier tweaked Robespierre's tail over the affair of an obscure visionary prophetess called Catherine Théot who, Vadier claimed, called herself the 'Mother of God' and regarded Robespierre as the Messiah, a thought that sparked waves of poorly suppressed giggles at his expense in an assembly which had been pretty sombre of late. Robespierre has personally prohibited the Théot case going to the Revolutionary Tribunal in a way that people suppose means either he has something to hide or simply does not want to expose himself to further ridicule.

Despite these weak spots, Robespierre has achieved rhetorical mastery over his audience in a variety of ways. He is particularly adept at handling parliamentary procedure, and knows how to command attention through interventions in debate and the use of points of order. If one of his own points of order is rejected, he may retort with verbal violence, invoking the loftiest principles and his own emotional disarray at being challenged so stridently, that the speaker has to give way. On one famous occasion he only managed to seize the rostrum by shouting 'Let me speak or else kill me'. On the other hand, once at the rostrum he is also a past-master at overriding objections and points of order from the floor: when the pro-Girondin deputy Carra at one stage in August 1793 tried to put a point of order as Robespierre tore into him, Robespierre cut him dead with: 'it is not seemly for conspirators to interrupt freedom's defender'. Robespierre can also on occasion affect a silent, basilisk-like, Medusan stare that can stop grown men in their tracks and induce devastating despair. Finally, he falls back on invoking the assent of his supporters in the public galleries or else associating them with his putative victimhood as a means of silencing and intimidating opponents.

If Robespierre's mood is unsettled tonight, and his feelings intense
and brooding, it is because today—or rather, yesterday, 26 July or 8
Thermidor—this repertoire of techniques of rhetorical domination has
been found wanting. The long, two-hour speech he delivered in the
Convention was the first he has delivered there since 12 June. It ended by
inspiring loud and articulate hostility that he has simply not experienced as a
CPS member.

Robespierre presented his remarks as coming from a simple deputy, a
mere citizen rather than a member of the government, from which, he
freely admits, he has absented himself for the last six weeks. Shorn of
responsibility to government, he felt freer, he claimed, to speak truth to
power, to unveil plots and to denounce conspiracies. By 'unburdening his
heart', he hoped that the 'useful truths' he offered might harmonize
discord in the Convention and guide the thinking of the people. He
represented himself as an ardent outsider, a passionate oppositional force,
who equates his own identity and destiny with that of the people's
revolution he has always championed. Public freedom is being violated,
and his innocent name is being calumniated and outraged. His enemies are
the Revolution's enemies: attacks on him are attacks on the Revolution
and on the people. His opponents supply the British press with stories of
his tyrannical intentions, they exaggerate his passing involvement in
policing, and they diffuse lies about his alleged plans to send scores of
fellow deputies to the Revolutionary Tribunal and the guillotine. The
conspirators are erecting 'a system of terror': frightened deputies no longer
sleep soundly in their beds at night. They laughably claim he wishes to be a
dictator. He is no dictator—'If I were', he grimly noted, his enemies
'would be grovelling at my feet'.

At the start of his speech, Robespierre announced that in the interests of
encouraging harmony, he was not about to make accusations. Yet as his
speech developed, it became clear that he does in fact have specific targets in
view, namely, the groups of immoral, often atheistical and sometimes
ruthless men, who, he believes, with foreign aid have been conspiring
against him and against the Republic for some months now. Former nobles,
émigrés and crooks—he must be thinking of Dossonville—have insinuated
themselves within the CGS bureaucracy. The financial administration is
another target. The CPS has kept out of financial affairs, but recent legislation adversely affecting small savers suggests that the Convention's Finance
Committee, headed by fellow deputies Cambon, Mallarmé, and Ramel, has

fallen into corrupt and aristocratic hands, while their treasury chief, Lhermina, is a hypocritical counter-revolutionary.

Dramatically, Robespierre did not spare the Committees of Government
from his verbal assaults. Not only is the CGS bureaucracy riddled with
counter-revolutionaries, according to Robespierre, but the whole committee has gone along with Vadier's use of the Catherine Théot affair to
undermine and ridicule him. The CPS is little better, and although Robespierre generally eschews naming names, his veiled references are pointed.
The armies may be winning battles at the front, but war policy—in the
hands of his CPS colleague Lazare Carnot—threatens to unleash tyranny. It
is worrying that Paris is being left defenceless by Carnot's decision to transfer
sectional artillery units from Paris to the front. Robespierre has another
colleague, Barère, in his sights when he berates the 'academic lightness'
which he displays on announcing military successes in a way that risks
playing into 'military despotism'. Robespierre had bitter, if anonymized,
words too for his colleagues Billaud-Varenne and Jean-Marie Collot
d'Herbois, who hypocritically claim his friendship even as they plot against
him and whisper that he is a new Catiline, the Roman aspirant to dictatorship, or else Pisistratus, the Athenian tyrant.

The counter-revolutionary acts that these members of government are
committing have caused dysfunctionality in the conduct of policies agreed
by the Convention. They have not only deferred the advent of the republic
of virtue but they are also threatening to unravel all that the Revolution has
achieved. The CPS and the CGS are not doing their job. The forces of order
need to clamp down to prevent hardened counter-revolutionaries from
openly conspiring in the capital. The Revolutionary Tribunal should be
defended and the institution strengthened to allow it to do its work effectively. The law prohibiting the taking of British prisoners of war has not been
executed rigorously enough; it must be properly enforced.

As ever, Robespierre's 8 Thermidor speech was full of rhetorical flights
aimed to display his passionate commitment to the Revolutionary cause. He
sought to elicit pity, admiration, and emulation. He is, he declares, no
dictator but rather 'freedom's slave, the living martyr of the Republic, the
victim even more than the enemy of crime'. He peppered his talk with
anecdotes that showed him suffering the slings and arrows of his outrageous
opponents: insults he endured from fellow deputies when presiding over the
glorious festival of the Supreme Being; calumnies spread about him by the
Duke of York, commander of the British armed forces on the continent;

ridicule directed at him (by Vadier); treachery (from Cambon); rivalry (of Carnot); and so on. He ended his peroration with a flourish, asserting that he had always combatted crime, and could no longer form part of a government that governed criminally. The game-keeper has clearly returned to poaching.

Robespierre's speech purported not to accuse; yet it did little else. It was an outright rejection of the paean of praise for the government that Barère had enunciated the previous day. Remarkably, a word indicating conspiracy (conspirator, conspiracy, plot, faction, etc) cropped up almost every single minute of his two-hour speech. Despite claiming to be preaching harmony, his speech performed discord and exudes menace. Notwithstanding the signature evocations of his own death, Robespierre's speech made him sound to deputies less like a man who is ready to die than a man who wants to kill.

While mentioning almost no one except Finance Committee stalwarts by name, he made a precise list of demands: traitors in the Convention and even at the heart of government need to be rooted out; the CPS and the CGS must be purged; the CGS's bureaucracy has also to be subordinated to the renovated CPS, and its officials weeded out for traitors; and the Finance Committee and its officials require much the same treatment.

Robespierre has been such a key figure in the Revolutionary Government and has given the lead in so many initiatives involving and legitimating terror, that his speech, punctuated with occasional outbreaks of applause, was heard with rapt yet increasingly appalled attention. He was seemingly showing the assembly that his and the people's enemies now come from the Montagnards, his former allies. His appeal is thus (as he indicated to landlord Duplay that night) to the centrist deputies of the Plain. Good, upright men—*hommes de bien*—he stresses, must grasp that his intentions towards them are now pure, and that he and they have a common enemy in men of blood, perverted men, corrupt men.

The unexpected length and the explosive contents of the speech left the Convention in a quandary. The deputies' baffled uncertainty over how to react was evident in the first two interventions that ensued, from Montagnards who were deep-dyed enemies of Robespierre. First, Laurent Lecointre sprang to his feet to propose immediate publication of the text: the printing and circulation of speeches as pamphlets was an honour reserved for only the most significant discourses. Yet the gesture can only have sprung from Lecointre's fear for his own skin, since for months he has been openly expressing his hatred of the Incorruptible. Next, Bourdon de l'Oise, one of Robespierre's perennial whipping boys, offered a craftier and braver response by calling for the text to be passed first for comment to the CPS and CGS. As Robespierre immediately grasped, this was tantamount to sending the text to men he had just accused of being traitors.

Robespierre's ally Couthon rushed to his aid, demanding that the speech should not merely be published, but also sent to every commune in the land. The debate seemed to be drifting, when it was startlingly transformed by the Montpellier businessman, Joseph Cambon, chair of the Finance Committee that Robespierre had singled out for attack. He hurled himself to the rostrum to launch a blistering attack. In a furious (but also doubtless frightened) rant, Cambon passionately defended the work of his committee, vaunted his own patriotism as quite as deeply felt as Robespierre's, and concluded:

> – It's time to tell the whole truth: a single individual is paralysing the will of the Convention, and that man has just spoken; it is Robespierre!

Cambon's fury and the surprisingly high level of applause it elicited knocked Robespierre off his stride, and he riposted weakly, admitting he knew nothing about finance and confessing he was basing his critique on hearsay, triggering a contemptuous riposte from Cambon. It has been a long time since Robespierre received this kind of treatment in public. The enthusiastic response that Cambon elicited from across the deputies' benches is a worrying sign for him.

As if to emphasize the new anti-Robespierre mood, Billaud-Varenne now pitched in again: had Robespierre bothered to attend the CPS for the last six weeks he would not have made so many false statements. He proposed that Robespierre's speech should indeed go the Committees of Government for consideration. Deputies impetuously shouted their support.

Although the most obvious targets of Robespierre's speech were clear enough, the studied vagueness about the scale of the purges that he was proposing had been triggering nervous anxiety. Étienne-Jean Panis, a deputy who had once been close to Robespierre, now daringly opened up a new line of attack. He simply wanted to know: did Robespierre's list for purging include his own name? He had recently been told when walking out of the Jacobin Club that it did. Was this true? And was Robespierre's notorious *bête noire*, deputy Joseph Fouché, also on the list? Robespierre was by now completely on the back foot. Challenged again to name names, with deputies almost baiting him, he desisted point-blank, and ignored the question of whether he did in fact have a proscription list.

A whole line of Montagnard deputies, including another of Robespierre's arch-enemies, Louis-Stanislas Fréron, rose to condemn the idea of Robespierre's speech having wide circulation. As CGS member André Amar noted, sending it out for instant diffusion would deprive those accused in Robespierre's speech of a legitimate right to reply. Finally it was agreed that the speech should indeed be published, but only circulated for now to members of the Convention.

As the session was closing, one of the Convention's scribes asked Robespierre for the manuscript of his speech. It has been his practice to revise his speeches before they are published. His notes for the session were a mess, so he weakly indicated that he would forward the text at a later date.

The moderate deputy Jean-Baptiste Mailhe has fallen foul of Robespierre so often in the past that he counters despair about his destiny by fetishistically trying to sit next to Robespierre in the Convention hall on every occasion. Now, Mailhe saw a humiliated and chastened Robespierre return to his seat muttering to himself, 'I am lost!' The Montagnards had deserted him, he had lost the floor in the Convention, and the term 'dictator' was being bandied about. Would the Jacobin Club later that evening at least prove welcoming? Would they defend him against the grave charge of conspiring to become a dictator?

01.00/1.00 a.m.

CPS Committee Room, Tuileries palace (Tuileries)

Robespierre's ears must be burning. Angry raised voices coming from the CPS meeting room in the Tuileries palace have been audible in the outer offices for nearly an hour now and show no sign of stopping. There is a fracas at the heart of the Revolutionary Government, and, despite his absence, it is all about him, his character and his intentions.

It is not unknown for the committee which has run the country over the last year to be engaged in furious dispute, even at this late hour. Members do have their disagreements and disputes, increasingly so in fact. A quarrel in May which pitted Robespierre against military expert Lazare Carnot was so noisy that it caused crowds to assemble outside in the Tuileries garden, obliging clerks to shut the windows so as to prevent passers-by from hearing earfuls of confidential government business.

The most vociferous participants in tonight's quarrel are Robespierre's CPS colleagues, Collot d'Herbois and Billaud-Varenne, who have just returned from the Jacobin Club, and are laying into Robespierre's ally, Saint-Just. Robespierre has been speaking in the Club: not just speaking, in fact, but launching a personalized frontal assault on Revolutionary Government (of which he forms part) and the two men in particular. Despite his six-week absence from the CPS and assembly, Robespierre has remained a frequent attender at the Jacobin Club. Since 12 June, the day of his last speech in the Convention, he has spoken at more Jacobin Club meetings than he has not, and since 9 July he has intervened in nine out of the Club's ten meetings. The increased frequency of his Jacobin attendance has been marked by an ostentatious ramping up of attacks on the government. But tonight has put things on a different level. Collot and Billaud are infuriated. They are also very frightened.

The two men are directing their uncontrolled fury at their colleague Saint-Just, whom they believe is part of a plot against them led by Robespierre, and probably supported by Couthon. Their indignation is all the more righteous, moreover, in that the men believe that their opponents have broken the terms of an informal understanding hammered out only days earlier, on 22–3 July (or 4–5 Thermidor) that sought to end the toxic atmosphere that has been developing within the Committees of Government. Collot and Billaud fear that they have been taken for fools.

Even though Robespierre and Couthon had been aggressively critical of government in recent weeks at the Jacobin Club, there were enough vestiges of goodwill and common purpose remaining to explore a viable resolution of conflict. Accordingly, it was agreed that joint CPS/CGS meetings should be held in order to work towards conciliation. Robespierre was absent the first day, 22 July, though Saint-Just eloquently pleaded his cause. That meeting was positive enough for Saint-Just to believe that his colleagues' wish for conciliation was sincere, and he used his influence over Robespierre to encourage him to attend a further joint meeting of the two committees the following day.

The 23 July meeting began tensely as colleagues eyed each other in silence. Robespierre had returned after a six-week absence to what must have seemed to him the lair of his enemies. While he covered any nervousness he may have felt with icy looks of disdainful hauteur, his ally Saint-Just sought to transcend his own and everybody's embarrassment, breaking the silence to launch an elevated paean of praise for Robespierre as 'a martyr of liberty'. This stimulated Robespierre into a long speech in which he bitterly complained about the way that many seated around the green table were attacking him in speeches and actions. Matters looked as though they were getting out of hand, and names of potential victims of a purge may have been mooted. Carnot was forthright in opposition, however, and showed no sign of willingness to compromise. Billaud and Collot combined together, however, in a charm offensive to win Robespierre over. 'We are your friends,' wheedled Billaud. 'We have come so far together . . .' The emollient words coaxed Robespierre into entering into dialogue. Although it was not spelled out, the implication was that there would be a cessation of personal attacks on each other. CPS and CGS members assumed that the moratorium would be accompanied by Robespierre's backing down from the idea of a purge of the Convention.

There was agreement too on changes to the procedures of revolutionary justice that Saint-Just had been demanding for some time. On 26 February and 3 March, he had got the Convention to decree the so-called 'Laws of Ventôse', which among other things envisaged the establishment of four Popular Commissions in Paris that would serve to filter political suspects, freeing some, deporting others, and sending only the most egregious cases to the Revolutionary Tribunal. Only two of these commissions have ever really functioned, under the label Commission du Muséum, which is based in the section of that name. Now, as a major concession to Saint-Just and Robespierre, four such commissions are to be instituted. It was also agreed that there will be four additional itinerant tribunals to cope with suspects in the departments. The idea is to lessen pressure on the Paris Revolutionary Tribunal while maintaining judicial terror here and throughout the country. The measures will also have the effect of reducing the prison population of Paris that has reached problematic levels.

Another token of goodwill over an issue that has been festering for some time was an agreement that a number of Paris sections should send their NG artillerymen to serve at the front. This has long been a routine arrangement, of whose military rationale Carnot approves, but Saint-Just, Robespierre, and their allies in the Club have recently made a political issue of it. Although their anxiety seems largely unsubstantiated, they are claiming that this would leave the capital dangerously undefended. Artillerymen are among the most patriotic of sans-culottes, so their absence could de-radicalize the capital's armed forces. In the event, sparked by the ambient spirit of compromise, Saint-Just agreed to Carnot's proposal to expedite the gunners of four sections into regular military service behind the front line.

Finally, it was agreed that Barère would make a speech to the Convention about the external situation, which he delivered on 7 Thermidor, while Saint-Just would be deputed to draw up a report for the Convention so as to present a united CPS/CGS front that scotched rumours about divisions within the Revolutionary Government. This is a major concession, though there is still some way to go before total unanimity is reached, since Billaud and Collot strongly urged Saint-Just to make no mention of religious affairs. Robespierre's Cult of the Supreme Being remains a bone of contention.

In the interim, a decree on the establishment of Popular Commissions has duly been passed, and sectional artillerymen have been despatched to the army. Yet Robespierre and Couthon have shown absolutely no wish to abide by the spirit of détente. On the evening of 24 July (6 Thermidor) both men attended the Jacobin Club where Couthon launched a bitter tirade against the CGS and a further call for a purge of those deputies, 'whose hands are laden with wealth and with the stench of the blood of the innocent victims that they have immolated'. Although the Committees of Government contained men of virtue, Couthon proclaimed, the CGS in particular is surrounded by scoundrels making corrupt and arbitrary decisions. Even in the Convention, even in the Jacobin Club, he added (worryingly for those present), agents of the Foreign Plot were to be found. He was not, he underlined again, attacking the Convention as a whole, only a handful of 'impure individuals who seek to corrupt public morality and to build a throne for crime on the tomb of morals and virtue'. 'Good men,' he concluded, 'must now rally and separate themselves from these five or six turbulent creatures.' Robespierre put in his pennyworth too, proclaiming that 'the moment has come to strike down the last heads of the hydra; the factious must not hope for pardon'. All this was fighting talk: it blew the negotiated truce out of the water.

Couthon further aggravated matters by going back on the issue of the NG gunners being evacuated from Paris. He blamed Louis-Antoine Pille, Carnot's appointee as chief of the army commission (effectively army minister) for this decision. Pille's deputy, Jacobin and Robespierre ally, Prosper Sijas, has been conducting a personal vendetta against him, so that the continuation of the feud is manifestly a proxy attack on Carnot. It breaks the terms of the CPS/CGS truce, and ignores Saint-Just's acquiescence in artillery deployments.

René-François Dumas, President of the Revolutionary Tribunal, another fervent supporter of Robespierre in the Club, then waded in with a further cause of contention, namely, the curious case of Jean-François Magendie. Magendie had been petitioning the Convention for some time, claiming that outstanding sums owed to him by the wealthy former court banker, Magon de La Balue, guillotined a week earlier, should be paid out of his estate. Magendie was handing out copies of his petition to left and right at the door of the Jacobin Club on 6 Thermidor. What caught the eye in the pamphlet was not its substance but rather the suggestion, made in passing, that using the phrase 'for God's sake' ('sacré nom de Dieu') should be viewed as a counter-revolutionary, capital offence. This was doubtless a sycophantic proposal on Magendie's part, meant to curry favour with Robespierre. Yet it was so ludicrously ill-judged that when it came to Robespierre's ears he will have realized straight away the fun at his expense that his enemies would make of the idea. He was still bruised by the ridicule that had come his way over the Catherine Théot case, and it seemed easy to assume that the whole Magendie business was a ruse to make him look ridiculous.

After attacking Magendie, Robespierre went on to endorse Couthon's calls for a purge of deputies. The clearly puzzled deputy for the Ile-de-France (Mauritius), Benoît Gouly, stepped forward to ask for greater clarity:

> – At each of our meetings for three weeks now, Robespierre and Couthon have been stating that they have great truths to reveal to the people. I ask that in a special meeting tomorrow they explain about the plots that are being hatched against the fatherland.

It seems a fair, even helpful question. Is this not the time for clarity, for naming names? Who are the guilty men? And are there only five or six of them as Couthon has said? But Couthon and Robespierre did not receive it that way. Both glared furiously at Gouly, before Robespierre took to the rostrum to launch an attack on the proposal. Clearly timing was a sensitive issue.

The Jacobin Club agreed that a delegation should go to the Convention next day to present a petition outlining their grievances over the gunners, Pille's actions in the military bureaucracy, and the Magendie case. This they did, on 7 Thermidor, when they also highlighted anxiety about the workings of a Foreign Plot (one of Robespierre's favoured themes). In the same session, Barère was making his agreed state-of-the-nation speech and, ironically enough, it contained a carefully crafted olive branch for Robespierre. Flourishing a very obvious nod towards the compromise he believed had been struck on 23 July (but which seemed under attack in this very session), Barère evoked the threats of a new 31 May-style purge of the assembly recently uttered in the environs of the Tuileries palace, before going on:

> – Yesterday . . . a representative of the people, notorious for his patriotism, that he has merited by five years of work and by the imperturbable principles of independence and freedom, heatedly refuted these counter-revolutionary words.

The compliment must by then have sounded hollow, not least because Robespierre was absent from the Convention for Barère's speech and the

Jacobin petition, even though the Jacobin delegation seemed to be ventrilo-quizing their hero.

Far from desisting from attacks, Robespierre has thus ratcheted them up. Billaud and Collot must be wondering whether Robespierre, Saint-Just, and Couthon were ever sincere in the truce negotiations. Or were they just playing for time and getting themselves ready to strike? Maybe Robespierre really is aiming to be dictator . . .

Tonight's quarrel involving Collot, Billaud, and Saint-Just is taking place in the main CPS Committee Room, situated at the heart of the apartment in the old Tuileries palace in which Queen Marie-Antoinette was lodged between 1789 and 1792. The room retains some of its erstwhile splendour: a huge chandelier, Gobelins tapestries, rich carpets, and an ornate oval table covered with green baize, around which members sit. The room lies within an intricate complex of corridors and rooms that has invaded most of the southern half of the palace, down to and including, on the river end of the palace, the old Pavillon de Flore, now renamed Pavillon de l'Égalité. When it moved into these premises in May 1793, the CPS shared the space with a number of other Convention committees, but these have been driven elsewhere, allowing CPS staff to expand from less than 50 in mid-1793 to more than 500. The CGS offices are in the Hôtel de Brionne, a former aristocratic mansion that is linked to the northern edge of the Tuileries by a covered walkway. Tonight a group of its members have come to make joint session with their CPS colleagues.

The statutory membership of the CPS is twelve, though it currently stands at eleven. In theory, the Convention renews its membership on a monthly basis, but in fact the team has been unchanged since September of last year, with the sole exception of the aristocratic Hérault de Séchelles who was ejected for financial and political misdemeanours in December 1793 (and subsequently executed). The Committee is dedicated to working in a truly collective manner, and key business is transacted as a group. Although Robespierre and Barère report mostly to the Convention on CPS policy and decision-making, there is no *ex officio* chair. Full minutes are not taken, and all members have taken an implicit vow of silence about committee business. What happens around the green table, stays around the green table. 'God forbid,' exclaimed Robespierre in November 1793, for once echoing his colleagues, 'that I should ever reveal anything about what happens in the Committee.'

Some CPS members come in as early as 7.00 a.m., but formal plenary meetings take place from 10.00 a.m. until around midday when a number remove to the Convention Hall as the assembly's main business starts up. At the end of the Convention's session, CPS members dine, invariably separately from each other, but then many regroup from around 8.00 p.m. or later. Those who are assiduous members of the Jacobin Club may come on from there at around 10.00 p.m. Business sometimes continues till 2.00 or 3.00 a.m. Tonight it is clearly going to be longer. Between the set meeting times (and sometimes within them) members of the team work on the different tasks which they have assumed in separate bureaux.

The nature of CPS business means that physical presence at the green table is rather patchy. André-Jean Bon Saint-André, for example—a sea-captain, then a Protestant pastor under the Ancien Régime—has embraced the navy brief, and spends most of his time in key ports around France. Pierre-Louis Prieur (called 'Prieur de la Marne' after the department that elected him) is another long-term absentee, as he is almost permanently stationed with armed forces at the front. Military affairs overall have become the responsibility of military engineer Lazare Carnot, who is a pretty constant presence in CPS offices, though he spends parts of the day closeted away with his administrators. The Burgundian engineer and savant, Claude-Antoine Prieur 'de la Côte d'Or', also specializes in military affairs, notably armaments and war manufacture. He is more often surrounded by his administrative team and their files than by his colleagues around the green table. This is true too of the zealous Norman lawyer Robert Lindet, who has a demanding area of responsibility—infrastructure, economic policy, and the enforcement of the price freeze policy known as the Maximum—that requires him to be in constant consultation with his officials.

Robespierre's young ally, Saint-Just, vaunts his military expertise, which has been sharpened by effective spells as a deputy on mission with the armies on the northern front. But since his return from the front on 29 June he has been most engaged with the work of the CPS Police Bureau established in April. He, Robespierre, and the Auvergnat lawyer Georges Couthon are the only three CPS members to participate in the Bureau's management. Couthon managed a spell in the provinces in the summer of 1793, helping to crush the Federalist Revolt in Lyon; but his mobility is increasingly inhibited by paralysis of the lower limbs. He powers himself around in a wheelchair, and is invariably carried to his seat in the Convention and Jacobin Club by ushers and colleagues. Nowadays, he does not attend the evening meetings of the Committee, and spends a good amount of time in floating health baths on the river Seine.

The three pillars of the CPS, the most regular in their attendance as well as among the most assiduous at paperwork, are Barère, Billaud-Varennes, and Collot d'Herbois. The Gascon lawyer and man of letters Bertrand Barère is the key point of liaison with the Convention on policy issues. Corresponding with deputies on mission—a massive responsibility, as there are often scores of the deputies away in the departments enforcing Revolutionary legislation—is the task of Billaud-Varenne, another ex-lawyer, and Collot d'Herbois, who enjoyed a colourful pre-1789 career as a dramatist and itinerant theatre director. The two were the last to be added to the 'Twelve Who Rule' in early September 1793. Then, their notorious radicalism was considered to be a means of placating the sans-culotte movement. Radical they remain, but each is now every inch a CPS man.

The eleven men on the CPS are very different characters, but they have much in common. All are in the prime of life: Saint-Just is by far the youngest at 26, Jean Bon Saint-André and Collot at 44 the oldest. All hail from solid bourgeois and/or professional backgrounds. Most started the Revolution as monarchists, but all had become firm republicans by 1792. Although some were initially close to the Girondins, by early 1793 all had passed into Montagnard ranks and most are members of the Jacobin Club— only Carnot, Prieur de la Côte d'Or, and Lindet are not members. Despite policy differences that have developed between them, all are firm supporters of the CPS's role at the heart of Revolutionary Government. None blenches at policies of terror. All support the Revolutionary Tribunal.

The pressure of work is relentless. The core members are used to 16- or 18-hour days. Some of them have beds brought in so they can snatch some sleep rather than go home (even though carriages are kept ready for them in the courtyard). Maybe 800 to 900 CPS letters, decrees, and orders are transmitted each day, and multiple signatures are required for them to be valid. Members sign on trust, and can be caught out. Carnot tells the story that he unknowingly appended his signature to the arrest warrant of his favourite restaurateur, that he alleges Robespierre slipped by him out of spite. As this suggests, personality has become the medium through which policy issues are refracted across the board. This is true for the conduct of war, procedures of judicial terror, religion, public morality, and the thorny issue of policing.

Robespierre's suspicions about CGS officials are notorious, but CPS members for their part suspect that Robespierre, Saint-Just, and Couthon's jealously guarded stewardship of the Police Bureau allows them to keep tabs on their political enemies and build up a private power base. The enlargement of the CPS remit to include policing has poisoned relations with the CGS. Robespierre enjoys the ardent friendship of two CGS members, the great painter Jacques-Louis David and young Philippe Le Bas, who has married the daughter of Robespierre's landlord Maurice Duplay. The other CGS members feel spied on by these men, and nurture grudges against Robespierre for his treatment of them in the past. He regards CGS stalwarts Amar and Vadier with unconcealed contempt.

Disputes between and within the committees have started to overlap in complex patterns in regard to policy, procedures, and personalities. CGS members have been feeling generally frozen out of policy making by the CPS, or rather by Robespierre and his allies within it. Many were particularly infuriated by the radical changes to Revolutionary justice procedures introduced by the Law of 22 Prairial in June, which was presented to them (as in fact to the majority in the CPS) as a fait accompli by Robespierre and Couthon, who went on to bully it through the assembly. Broadly speaking, the law is all about getting more people convicted in a fraction of the time and on the basis of much less hard evidence. But it was the way that Robespierre and Couthon broke with collective responsibility and pushed the bill through themselves which galled their colleagues. Robespierre's other recent focus—the Cult of the Supreme Being—has similarly infuriated many CPS as well as CGS members. The Deist form of worship profoundly irritates CGS members who have a Protestant background (Philippe Ruhl, Moise Bayle, and Jean-Henri Voulland) and also those who are outright atheists (notably Vadier, Amar, and Jean-Antoine Louis du Bas-Rhin). All the Cult's critics are anxious about the role that Robespierre may be ascribing himself within it.

Tonight's joint session of the CPS and CGS has been set up to consider the situation following Robespierre's speech in the Convention. Pending the arrival of Collot and Billaud, they are getting on with their business. Since around 8.00, Saint-Just has been seated at a side-table preparing the speech that he plans to deliver in the Convention later today (as agreed in the 22–3 July sessions).

As Collot and Billaud entered the CPS committee-room in a state of high dudgeon, Saint-Just looked up from the table and asked airily, 'What's new at the Jacobins?' The young man's studied insouciance provoked an explosion of rage from both men. For at the Jacobin Club they have been on the receiving end of the rowdy acclaim for Robespierre that had so elated provincial Jacobin Legracieux. It seems unthinkable to Collot that Robespierre's acolyte does not know what Robespierre is up to, which appears to be: plotting their execution.

> – You're asking what's new? And you really don't know? Are you not in the graces of the principal author of all political squabbles, who now wants to lead us all to civil war? You're a coward and a traitor. You deceive us with your hypocritical airs. You're just a bag of clichés. What I have witnessed tonight leaves me in no doubt: you are scoundrels, the three of you, and you are all determined to lead the fatherland to ruin. But liberty will survive your horrible plotting! In our midst, you are preparing plots against the committees of government. And you have calumnies against us in your pockets.

CGS member Élie Lacoste has been serving over the last week as elected Jacobin President and has witnessed at first hand the nasty storm that Robespierre and Couthon are whipping up there. He now joins Collot, attacking Saint-Just and his two allies as 'a triumvirate of rogues' while the usually equable Barère also rises angrily to the occasion:

> – You insolent pygmies. A cripple, a child and a scoundrel! You couldn't even run a farmyard.

Completely taken aback by this violent verbal assault, Saint-Just goes pale and stutters unconvincingly, emptying his pockets and shuffling his papers towards Collot to protest his innocence.

Billaud and Collot go on to recount what they have just had to suffer at the Jacobin Club. Both men had not attended the Club for quite a time, but they still maintain considerable credit in Jacobin circles. They had a solid wedge of support in the Club this evening, including fellow Montagnard deputies Javogues, Dubarran, and Bentabole, though it was soon clear that they were outnumbered by Robespierre's supporters.

At the start of the meeting, both Collot and Billaud tried to catch the eye of the Jacobin President, the magistrate, Nicolas-Joseph Vivier (Élie Lacoste's stand-in). Yet on the basis of reaction within the assembly, he accorded priority at the rostrum to Robespierre, who cut straight to the chase:

- By the agitation of this assembly, it is easy to see that it is not unaware of what happened this morning in the Convention. And it is easy to see that the factious are frightened of being unveiled in the presence of the people. And I thank them for showing themselves so clearly, for this has allowed me to see who are my enemies and the enemies of the fatherland.

Collot and Billaud then had to sit through a repetition of Robespierre's long conspiracy-drenched speech in the Convention. This was received with enthusiasm, but also with critical voices from Collot and Billaud's supporters. 'We don't want dominators at the Jacobins!' Javogues yelled at Robespierre at one moment.

Keeping their indignation under wraps, the two men waited patiently for Robespierre to end, so that they could riposte, as they had done so effectively that morning in the Convention. But Robespierre had a melodramatic last gesture with which to confound them:

- The speech that you have heard is my last will and testament. I have seen today that the league of evil-doers is too strong for me to hope to escape. It is without regrets that I succumb. I leave you my memory. It will be dear to you; you will defend it.

As the room noisily expressed its emotion, Robespierre continued:

- And if I succumb, well, my friends, you will see me drink hemlock in calm.
- If you drink hemlock, I will drink it with you!

The latter cry is from the painter Jacques-Louis David, who has rushed through the hall to offer Robespierre a fraternal accolade (from which ultra-sensitive Robespierre instinctively shrank).

With Collot still being denied permission to speak, Revolutionary Tribunal President, Dumas, who had been vocal in the Club two days earlier, inserted himself into the debate. The fact of conspiracy was self-evident, he stated. Then, looking towards Collot and Billaud:

- It is strange that men who for several months have kept silent now ask to speak, doubtless to oppose the stream of thunderous truths that Robespierre has just issued. It is easy to recognise them as the heirs of Danton and Hébert; they shall also be, I prophesy, the heirs of their fates as well.

As the audience enthusiastically took in the enormity of this threat from a man who presides over the Revolutionary Tribunal, Collot finally got the Jacobin President's nod to speak, only to be met with disapproving jeers.

'I too was under the assassin's knife!' he proclaimed in self-justification, recalling Ladmiral's attempt on his life several months earlier, only for mocking laughter to be heard. Collot drew on his actor's training to make himself heard above the hubbub: yes indeed, he said, he has his suspicions about Robespierre. If the latter had deigned to come to the CPS over the last six weeks, his speech would not contain so many errors. Infuriated at the taunts of Robespierre's supporters, Billaud also sought to re-enter the debate but the din was so loud that his voice was drowned out and the audience saw only his angry gesticulations.

At this critical moment, with cries of 'To the guillotine with them!' starting to be heard, the crippled Couthon was carried to the rostrum to speak. The room quietened to catch his words.

> - Citizens, I am convinced of the truth of the facts that Robespierre has enunciated. We are witnessing the deepest of all conspiracies thus far. It is certainly the case that there are pure men in the committees of government; but it is no less certain that there are scoundrels too. I too want a discussion (*beckoning at Collot and Billaud*): not of Robespierre's speech but of the conspiracy. We shall see the conspirators appear at this rostrum. We shall examine them. We will catch them out. We shall note their vacillating replies. They will grow pale in the presence of the people. They shall be convicted. And they shall perish.

The respectful silence in which Couthon was initially heard transformed into a wild yell of collective approval.

Couthon's speech placed Collot and Billaud in an impossible position. They knew that if they spoke, it would be as conspirators in a show trial. The crowded hall has been agitated into a frightening state of lynch-mob frenzy. The two men's supporters in the hall had been overwhelmed, and they made for the door to further shouts of 'To the guillotine!' Some heard Dumas mocking them menacingly as they left: 'You won't be talking so much in two days' time!' To those present, he jeered, 'We'll cut their cackle!' . . .

Collot draws to a close his account of the humiliating ordeal he and Billaud have faced in tonight's Jacobin Club meeting. His CPS and CGS colleagues are aghast. He turns his glowering fury again on Saint-Just:

> - You are preparing a report, but knowing you, you are doubtless preparing our arrest warrant. You can take our lives, have us killed, but do you think the people will be merely spectators of your crimes? No usurpation goes unpunished, when the rights of the people are at stake.

Saint-Just blandly confesses that he has already sent the first 18 pages of his report to his secretary to be written up for tomorrow. He seems to be prevaricating, which infuriates Collot even more, and the men bicker and yell incoherently. Saint-Just claims that Collot has been plotting with radical deputy Joseph Fouché against Robespierre and himself for months. And yes, there may be some deputies named to be purged tomorrow. But he makes a major concession with the aim of calming Collot down, namely, that before he gives his speech tomorrow he will present it to this committee for its approval. And Fouché can come along to see the men make their peace.

Saint-Just's concession takes some heat out of the discussion. Voices are lowered, and overt anger starts to drain away. Collot's adrenaline levels normalize. After being initially wrong-footed by Collot's explosive anger, Saint-Just is getting his equanimity back. He is in soothing vein. If Robespierre rejected the agreement made on 22–3 July, this does not mean that he himself has. He can see their point of view. He wants to be part of the team. Their lives are not at risk. There is no coming storm.

Despite Saint-Just's protestations of sincerity and collegiality, several members of the committee remain unconvinced about him. After some sotto voce exchanges among themselves, most present agree to wait for Saint-Just to evacuate the premises. Some colleagues, however, are already leaving the simmering atmosphere to catch up with sleep before what could be a momentous day ahead. CGS member Jean-Henri Voulland has made it to his lodgings on the Rue Croix-des-Petits-Champs, a quarter of a mile or so from the Tuileries. Earlier in the day, he wrote a letter to a group of fellow patriots in his home town of Uzès in the department of the Gard. They had heard about dissensions in the Committees of Government, and were worried, like Voulland, that any impression of division within the committees would be exploited by the Republic's enemies at home and abroad. But, still influenced by the conciliatory meetings of 22–3 July, Voulland assured them that all such rumours are baseless. The citizens of Uzès should sleep calmly in their beds knowing that the committees are united.

Yet after yesterday and today's events, Voulland is wondering whether that message is still correct. He is well aware of all that Robespierre has done for the Revolution. But petty issues of wounded *amour propre* seem to have embittered him, and today he has really thrown down the gauntlet. Voulland hopes he is still recuperable for the Revolutionary cause. Yet in hoping Robespierre will return to the fold, is Voulland merely whistling in the dark?

02.00/2.00 a.m.

CPS offices, Tuileries palace

D eputy Laurent Lecointre is writing an urgent message to the CPS in the vestibule outside its offices. He wants to deliver a warning. But given the gravity of the political situation, the Committee has given orders to the skeleton staff on night duty to refuse entry to all comers. If the Committees won't see him, perhaps they will read his letter.

Lecointre is alert to the possibility that a move is about to take place within Paris that will involve Paris NG commander François Hanriot mobilizing the city against the Convention. Hanriot is a firm supporter of Robespierre. Given what happened in the Convention earlier in the day, Lecointre is worried something is already afoot. The last time that Robespierre called as emphatically for a purge of the Convention was in spring 1793. That led on to the *journées* of 31 May and 2 June, when Hanriot played a key role in forcing the Convention to expel the Girondin deputies. Barère might have complimented Robespierre in the Convention of 25 July for not openly calling for a new popular *journée*, but Lecointre is far more suspicious about his intentions. He believes that Robespierre is indeed intending to whip up a 31 May-style *journée*.

At around 9.00 p.m. last evening, Lecointre conveyed his anxiety to CGS member Louis-Stanislas Lavicomterie and the deputy Dubois-Crancé whom he chanced upon in the street. Lavicomterie promised to convey his message to the CPS and CGS, which he knew were in joint session. Then at 10.00 p.m., Lecointre got a tip-off that his own brother had received orders to report for NG duty in his section early next morning for a special mission. Lecointre does not know what this might amount to, but he is worried. Worried enough in fact to come to seek an audience with the CPS at around 1.30 a.m., only to find the two committees in secret session. Collot is still venting his spleen against Saint-Just, and wants no interruptions.

Lecointre is desperately concerned that the CPS is incommunicado. Were Robespierre to give the nod, Hanriot, working in collaboration with the mayor of Paris, Fleuriot-Lescot, and the Commune's National Agent, Payan (both men notorious supporters of Robespierre), would pose a huge threat. On his way to and from the CPS offices, Lecointre has encountered two other deputies, Stanislas Fréron and Joseph Cambon, who are similarly trying to wake the CPS up to the dangers that they face. They must be able to overhear Collot ranting behind closed doors, but they too are refused access to the committee.

For all these men, the potential danger to the Republic is also a mortal threat to themselves. After the thwarting of Robespierre yesterday, they all fear his revenge. Like Carnot and Lindet, Cambon is the kind of political moderate with technical proficiency, who over the last year has been drawn to support Montagnard positions by a patriotic desire to carry the war to the enemy. A wealthy Protestant businessman before the Revolution in his native Montpellier, he has a high profile in the assembly. He served briefly on the CPS in 1793, and then was elected chair of the Convention's Finance Committee. Finance is outside the remit of the CPS, which means that Cambon is effectively finance minister, and has won plaudits for getting to grips with France's huge national debt, which had sparked the Revolution in the first place. Although he and his family in Montpellier have profited from purchasing 'national lands' (that is, the confiscated property of the church and of émigrés), Cambon is generally seen as being above corruption, and enjoys high esteem in moderate as well as Montagnard circles. He has, however, been growing increasingly impatient with the way that Robespierre's absence is affecting firm CPS policy and personalizing issues. This means that Robespierre's attack on him in the Convention—he and his collaborators on the CPS Ramel and Mallarmé were almost the only names Robespierre mentioned—was the last straw. Yet by standing up to Robespierre in the Convention, Cambon has, he realizes, burnt his boats. Every evening, he is in the habit of sending the day's newspaper to his family in Montpellier. This evening, on the evening papers which contain the parliamentary report he writes: 'Tomorrow either Robespierre or I will be dead.'

The stakes are equally high for Stanislas Fréron, who also joined in yesterday's chorus of disapproval towards Robespierre in the Convention debate. The son of a famous author, Fréron *fils* also made his living in the late

Ancien Régime and early years of the Revolution by his pen. His radical journalism in the early 1790s matched the violence of 'Friend of the People', Jean-Paul Marat, and helped ensure his election to the Convention as a deputy for Paris. He is one of the slew of deputies sent out on mission in mid to late 1793 and early 1794 to crush the hydra of federalism, royalism, and counter-revolution. He was despatched along with the Provençal deputy, Paul Barras, to the department of the Var on the Italian border, where the Federalist Revolt had morphed into outright treachery, with rebels handing the French fleet at anchor in Toulon harbour over to Britain's Royal Navy. Fréron and Barras besieged the city and then captured it (with the notable help of a young Corsican artillery captain who is an enthusiast for Robespierre and who is called, improbably, Napoleone Buonaparte), and then proceeded to pacify the area.

Yet by the time Barras and Fréron returned to Paris in May 1794 they were not trailing clouds of glory but rather radiating growing suspicion that their repression had been inhumane and that they had used their powers to enrich themselves at the expense of the battle zone. In order to try to clear the air, the two men visited Robespierre in his home. Only with difficulty getting past landlord Duplay's wife and daughters who act as Robespierre's guardians, they found him at his toilette. Emerging from having his hair powdered, he totally ignored the two men, continuing his grooming by brushing his teeth in their presence and spitting out water at their feet, before sitting impassive and disdainful to hear their statement, and then allowing them to usher themselves out.

Robespierre has no first-hand experience of what is involved in the work of deputies on mission. They have been vital in bringing back into the fold provinces that have taken up arms against the Convention in the Federalist Revolt and in enforcing obedience to Revolutionary Government. The Montagnard faction has thrown themselves particularly energetically into these missions, and even the crippled Couthon managed a spell in Lyon. But Robespierre is (along with Barère in fact) a rarity on the CPS in never having been on mission. His knowledge of violent opposition to the Revolution outside Paris is entirely at one remove, based on contacts and correspondence with a select number of informants.

Among Robespierre's most trusted sources is his younger brother Augustin, whom he helped get elected to the Convention. Augustin served as deputy on mission in the south-east. He too was present at the capture of Toulon, and is thus well placed to relay gossip about Barras and Fréron. But

there are others. Robespierre's teenage protégé, Marc-Antoine Jullien, provides similar intelligence for the CPS on the action of deputies on mission in
the west and south-west. Jullien was critical of the extreme violence shown
by deputy Jean-Baptiste Carrier in putting down the pro-royalist peasant
revolt in the Vendée. He then moved on to Bordeaux from where he
conveyed a stream of tales about the misdoings of deputy on mission Tallien,
not least with his mistress, Theresa Cabarrus. A number of ambitious radicals
from Lyon, now based in Paris, also supply Robespierre with stories about
the highly sanguinary repression of Federalist Lyon in late 1793 and 1794
after Couthon's return to Paris. In this case, the guilty men are alleged to be
his CPS colleague Collot d'Herbois and the Loire-Inférieure deputy, Joseph
Fouché.

Fouché preys on Robespierre's mind. Although Robespierre has known
him since his Arras days—at one stage, the man was said to be wooing
Maximilien's sister Charlotte—he cordially detests him. The ex-Oratorian
teacher turned radical atheist represents for Robespierre the *nec plus ultra* of a
certain kind of dangerous, immoral, and politically reckless deputy on
mission. Fouché combines four elements, each of which attracts Robespierre's enmity. First, there is his excessive use of violence in putting
down the Federalist revolt and its aftermath. There was substantial demoli-
tion within the city and allegedly 1900 executions in Lyon down to the first
months of 1794. As the guillotine was accounted too slow to deal with the
numbers involved, many victims were shot in groups in the so-called
mitraillades (essentially firing squads of cannon using grapeshot, or *mitraille*).
This excessive level of vengeful violence, Robespierre believes, recruits for
the counter-revolutionary cause.

Second, Fouché is alleged to be venal and corrupt, and is suspected of
having lined his pockets in his travels at the expense of the Republic. He is a
prime suspect for being drawn by greed into the Foreign Plot. Third, Fouché
is also one of the most brazen atheists in the Convention, who in his period
of service in the Nièvre and surrounding departments in late 1793 made
active dechristianization (attacks on priests, pillage of churches, religious
iconoclasm, and so on) a central plank of his strategy. His activities in this
area were linked to militant atheists in the Paris Commune who have since
been executed. This anti-clerical posture makes him an implicit critic of
Robespierre's Cult of the Supreme Being. Robespierre thinks that the new
form of worship will be welcomed by all Christians and will help to dissolve
popular religious antagonism towards the Revolution. Fouché and others,

who have experienced at first hand extreme violence meted out in the name of religion by peasants in the Midi and the west, know by bitter experience that this is hopelessly out of touch with the strength of religious feeling in the provinces. But Robespierre won't be told.

The fourth and final of Fouché's sins in Robespierre's eyes is that he stands up to him. Recalled from his mission in late March, he showed no remorse for his actions in the Nièvre or in Lyon, even when Robespierre castigated him in person back in Paris. The fact that he was elected President of the Jacobin Club in early June (in Robespierre's absence) shows a decent level of support for him there. But Robespierre got his revenge by having him expelled from the Club a few weeks later. Sniping between the two men has continued. Fouché realizes that the group of radical sans-culottes from Lyon who have grievances against Collot and himself have Robespierre's ear and are poisoning him against them both. His name must already be inscribed, Fouché thinks, on the list that he and others believe Robespierre maintains of those who are to be expelled in a coming purge. Despite an honoured place on what he views as Robespierre's 'tablets of death', he seems to have access to intelligence about what goes on around the CPS green table, probably through Collot d'Herbois, his former ally at Lyon, and CGS member Vadier, another radical atheist. A few days previously, in private correspondence, Fouché confidently predicted the imminent overthrow of Robespierre, once divisions within the committees of government have widened.

No one knows if Robespierre does indeed have a list of enemies for purging. If he does, though, Fouché must be at the head of it. It must also include Fréron and the whole cohort of Montagnard deputies, whose profile on mission resembles that of Fouché and Fréron. Certainly Fréron must be in that number. And Barras and Tallien too, no doubt. How many other similar cases are there? The excesses of the ferocious Joseph Lebon in Arras and Cambrai seem to have evaded Robespierre's condemnation, partly because of the man's friendship with the Robespierre brothers. But there is no shortage of potentially guilty men. Carrier, the scourge of Nantes and the Vendée, is one. Others include radical dechristianizers like Claude Javogues, Collot's supporter in the Jacobin bear-pit tonight, for his turbulent mission in the Lyonnais and Forez; André Dumont for his activities in the Somme and Pas-de-Calais; Didier Thirion, held to have committed atrocities in the Sarthe; and Rovère, who is alleged to have organized roving bands that went around the Bouches-du-Rhône plundering national lands and the property of those who had engaged in the Federalist Revolt. And then there is Léonard Bourdon, whom many hold responsible for excessive repression meted out during time in Orléans and Burgundy. Robespierre detests them all.

One effect of Robespierre making such swingeing attacks in the Convention yesterday, but without pronouncing the names of those he had in mind for a purge, is that anyone at whom he has looked askance in the recent past is fingering their collar apprehensively. This is one way government by terror works: even those who have been meting out terror can feel frightened out of their wits. So it is not just the wild men on the Left who are nervous about their future. Men from the Right and Centre also feel targeted. Dubois-Crancé is a case in point. A soldier of some distinction before 1789, his alleged sin was, while on mission in Lyon in the summer of 1793, to have failed to stop royalist troops from escaping the city. On 25 July, recalled from a mission in Brittany, Dubois went straight into the Convention and presented an eloquent self-defence. Robespierre had been misled, he stated baldly. Given the mood that Robespierre is in, this was probably not a good line. For Robespierre has long nurtured hostility towards him. The previous month he had Dubois expelled from the Jacobins.

Laurent Lecointre, currently scribbling away in the CPS vestibule, is another in Robespierre's bad books. Since the autumn of 1793, this deep-dyed opponent of Robespierre has gone further than any other deputy in offering him brazen defiance. So far, he has lived to tell the tale, and indeed seems fortified by his encounters. He made his name as a patriotic and precociously republican NG commander in the aristocratic vipers' nest of Versailles, his home city. After Robespierre, Couthon, and Saint-Just drove through the Law of 22 Prairial, Lecointre had to be talked by CGS members Amar and Moise Bayle out of doing something rash that he and all the Convention would regret. He did not overthrow one tyrant, he maintains, to see another take his place. He also had done his very best to wreck Robespierre's enjoyment of the Festival of the Supreme Being a day or two earlier. Robespierre's preeminent place in the festivities and procession, by dint of the event happening in the fortnight that he served as President of the Convention, was widely criticized. Montagnard Marc-Antoine Baudot was among a group of deputies who in the festive procession followed Robespierre at 20 paces distance, yelling out cat-calls and insults in his hearing. He witnessed Lecointre going up to Robespierre and yelling in his face: 'I despise you as much as I hate you' and calling him a dictator 20 times or more. Robespierre bitterly alluded to that encounter in his speech yesterday.

Since mid-July, Lecointre has again been chafing at the bit. A day or so ago, he spoke to Robert Lindet and the CGS's Vadier about taking action of some sort. The advice he received was the same: wait and see. This is not altogether surprising since at that moment the 22–3 July truce was still shakily in place. For some months now, Lecointre has commandeered a little group that he says is ready to undertake an assault on Robespierre, probably in the Convention (assuming, that is, that the latter can be persuaded to stop sulking in his tent *chez* the Duplays). Many of this number are among the threatened deputy on mission group, notably Tallien, Fréron, Barras, Rovère, and Thirion, plus the maverick ex-CGS member Guffroy.

This group overlaps with that of disgruntled ex-supporters of Danton, who have never forgiven Robespierre for overthrowing their hero in the spring. They form a Dantonist network that includes two deputies for the Aube department which Danton had also represented, namely, Edme-Bonaventure Courtois, Danton's ex-schoolmate, and Garnier de l'Aube, plus individuals such as Jean-François-Bertrand Delmas and Louis Legendre, on both of whom Robespierre keeps files containing spy reports on their activities. Although this putative faction undoubtedly grumbles more than it conspires, some of the wider Dantonist grouping, notably Panis, did spring into action in the attack on Robespierre after his speech at the Convention yesterday.

Dantonist Bourdon de l'Oise, who has been almost as openly anti-Robespierre as Lecointre, is on the fringes of this group too, though he has his own plans. When dictating his will to a notary, he made a vow to kill Robespierre in the Convention. He clearly intends to make a performance of it, as he plans to dress in the blood-spattered clothes he wore when storming the Bastille and the beplumed hat marked with bullet-holes that he had donned going into battle against the Vendéen rebels, and he intends to use his blood-smeared sabre for the deed itself.

How serious is such plotting? Lecointre's conspiracy is an open secret in the Convention and Robespierre was told of its existence more than a month ago. One wonders whether, despite their posturing, Lecointre or Bourdon are really up to the task. Lecointre's craven behaviour in the Convention yesterday suggests he is not the dedicated tyrannicide he imagines himself to be. Indeed, one wonders exactly what he will do after writing his note of warning to the CPS in their outer offices, and accepting that they will not give him an interview. Will he continue plotting? Or will he go home to bed and pull the sheets over his head?

2.30 a.m.

CPS Committee Room, Tuileries palace

The atmosphere is still eerily tense around the green table. Saint-Just continues to pore over his report for later today, while the other members of the Committee get on with routine business. It is the practice for the CPS clerks to bring a big batch of paperwork to the committee room around 2.00 a.m. for signatures. Normal committee life has to go on regardless. There is a war to win.

The Committee has, however, received Lecointre's scribbled letter about his brother and has sent out a messenger summoning him. Lecointre's concerns about Hanriot's conduct have led them to issue a further order to summon one of Paris's two gendarmerie commanders, Jean Hémart, to test his loyalty for the coming day if the going gets rough. This is a good choice, not least since there is no love lost between Hémart and NG commander Hanriot. Indeed Hémart has only just emerged from a short spell cooling his heels in gaol for accounting errors seized on by Hanriot. Still seeking to ingratiate himself with his colleagues, Saint-Just signs this order when it is presented to him. The high emotion evident an hour or so ago is receding, allowing the combined committees to become more proactive. Plans are starting to be made.

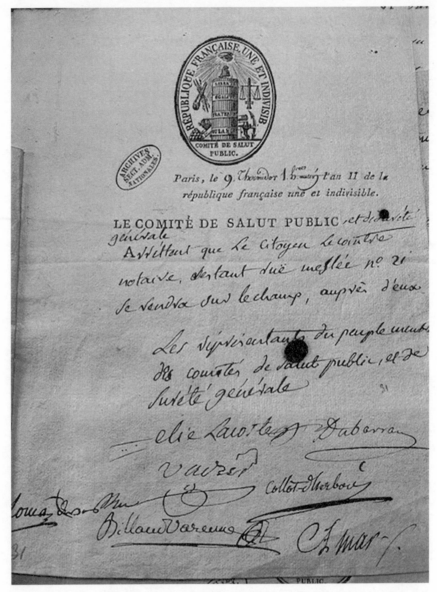

Figure 2. Committee of Public Safety order summoning Lecointre, notary, 1.00 a.m.?, 9 Thermidor (AFII 47 pl. 363, pi. 31)

2.00 a.m.–3.00 a.m.

Tallien's quest: the streets of Paris

A lot of impromptu political networking is taking place across the city. The frightening imprecision of Robespierre's threats yesterday has had an impact across the political spectrum. There is a great deal of potential for stimulating support for some sort of attempt to restrain Robespierre from the course of action on which he seems determined. Yet if there is much dry tinder, is there a match? Tallien seems to be that match. For Tallien, it is the life of his lover Theresa Cabarrus as well as his own that is on the line.

Tallien is a cool customer and earlier in the evening was seen at the theatre. But for some little time now, under cover of darkness, he has been combing the streets of Paris, visiting the homes of potential allies. His task is made easier by the fact that deputies' lodgings are very concentrated. Most in fact are in the environs of the Tuileries palace and the Palais-Royal and along the Rue Saint-Honoré.

Busy on his rounds, Tallien is extending his contacts out from the group of core Montagnards to include members of the Plain, the middling, and even Right-wing deputies who thus far have resisted being drawn into the Girondin or Montagnard camps. He has grasped that Robespierre sees such men as his allies tomorrow against his former Montagnard colleagues. Tallien wants to get to them first.

Tallien has made a beeline for three of the most senior and respected such deputies, namely, the Ardéchois Boissy d'Anglas, the Provençal canon lawyer Durand-Maillane, and the Breton ex-parlementaire Palasne-Champeaux. All of them boast an engagement in national politics dating back to 1789 and all cherish their political independence. So much bad blood has developed over the course of the last two years that it seems counter-intuitive that such individuals could ever be on the same political side as someone like Tallien. The men have always felt closer to Robespierre than to Tallien-style demagogues. After the purge of the Girondins in June 1793, some 73 deputies wrote a strong letter of protest. The Revolutionary Government gaoled them forthwith and the '73' are still in prison. Yet Robespierre has adamantly rejected calls from the Left for the men to go before the Revolutionary Tribunal (and thence no doubt to the guillotine). Many of the imprisoned deputies feel that their life depends to some extent on Robespierre's ability to keep the Parisian popular movement under control, and they write to him expressing their gratitude, feigned or otherwise. Robespierre plays up to this: his is the finger in the dyke, holding back the floods of anarchy and popular violence. It is thus understandable that Boissy d'Anglas and his friends fear that with Robespierre gone, the balance of power would shift strongly to the left, putting not just the '73' but also themselves at risk. Boissy d'Anglas only avoided imprisonment with the '73' by a whisker, and feels highly exposed. In a rather rambling section of his speech yesterday, Robespierre appeared to have been distancing himself from any responsibility towards the '73'. This may be because he is aware that CGS members Amar and Jagot have recently visited many of the men in gaol and promised to improve their conditions.

Switching horses and abandoning Robespierre might thus seem a perilous option for deputies like Boissy d'Anglas, as Tallien is well aware. At least there are no warm feelings involved: any support men from the Plain and the Right offer Robespierre is strictly instrumental and unsentimental. He has served to shield them from what they have perceived is worse. This means they can be quite dispassionate about changing tack—if they are sure Robespierre's role is changing. And this won't be the first time they have weighed their options. For several weeks now, Fouché has also been visiting deputies, saying, 'You are on the list! Me too!' He and others brandish purported lists of deputies set to be delivered over to the Revolutionary Tribunal that they claim to have inveigled out of sources close to Robespierre. These (quite possibly totally fabricated) lists show not just the five or six Couthon has mentioned but up to 50 names. Fouché may even be out on the streets now, his arguments strengthened by Robespierre's conduct yesterday.

Robespierre, Tallien tells his interlocutors, is becoming more and more dangerous and unpredictable. Most deputies probably do not know the extent to which he has opted out of CPS business but they will certainly have remarked his long absence from the Convention. This troubles

deputies for he does not seem to be sick: the newspapers show he is a
consistent attender and speaker at the Jacobin Club—more so than ever in
fact. There, moreover, he and Couthon are following the puzzling strategy
of attacking the Revolutionary Government of which they form part.
Robespierre seems to be losing the credentials and the credibility to pose
as saviour of the Right and Centre. His free-wheeling aggression has been
amplified and given added resonance by his speech on 8 Thermidor which
combined self-indulgence with precision targeting. There will be a purge,
quite probably a replay of 31 May 1793. Members of the Committees of
Government and unnamed deputies will be removed. Executions will
increase over and above the present high rate, and the moment will soon
come round when it is the turn of Durand-Maillane and his ilk. If the last
obstacle preventing a further purge of the Convention falls tomorrow, can
they really think themselves safe?

Tallien's case is strengthened by the fact that Robespierre seems to have
moderates as well as radicals in his sights. In normal times, the men of the
Centre and Right would probably cheer to the rafters Robespierre's purging
radical deputies on mission such as Fouché, Fréron, and indeed Tallien
himself. Yet why on earth is Robespierre picking on the widely respected
Joseph Cambon? Maybe some of Cambon's acts in righting the financial ship
of state have caused problems for the holders of *rentes*, as Robespierre
suggested. But Robespierre's reaction, when Cambon challenged him with
ferocious passion to explain himself, was telling. He gave the impression of
not understanding on what grounds apart from personal grievance he had
threatened the lives of Cambon and his allies in the Finance Committee, all
respected men with good records of patriotic state service.

Then again, what exactly lies behind Robespierre adding Dubois-Crancé
to the total? He seems to have made up his mind against him on the basis of
evidence he is not willing to share (and which probably derives from tittle-
tattle supplied by his Lyonnais informants). In 1793, Dubois-Crancé recommended changes to promotion procedures that allowed swift advancement
for talented soldiers and introduced the so-called *amalgame*, by which volunteers and soldiers of the line were combined into regiments together. These
were crucial reforms that created the armed forces that have won the day at
Fleurus. Why then target a moderate patriot with this kind of record of
achievement? Revealingly, when he came to the assembly to defend himself
on 25 July, Dubois challenged any deputy present to contradict his claims.
No one stepped forward. Is his name on the list a personal whim of

Robespierre's? And is he merely one among many moderates now doomed to the scaffold?

As morning approaches, Tallien gets a sense that going repeatedly over these arguments is beginning to work. He is wearing down the resistance of his interlocutors. He may be on the brink of making allies that will astonish sleeping Robespierre.

03.00/3.00 a.m.

Across the city

P aris as a whole is in bed experiencing the restful rhythms of the night.
A few plotters and counter-plotters are still abroad at this hour, keeping
company with the more enterprising burglars, prostitutes, and night-
walking denizens of the dark hours. If extraordinary events may be in
gestation, the realm of the ordinary and the everyday persists.

On the Left Bank, in a house on the Rue de Conti, in the Fontaine-de-
Grenelle section, Marie-Antoinette Laurent, a native of Guise in the
department of the Ardennes, has just died. Also at 3 o'clock, over in the
Homme-Armé section in the Marais, Marie-Thérèse Hua, the wife of
the clerk Ambroise Guérin, is giving birth to a boy, whom they name
Jules Messidor.

Jules Messidor's arrival in this world and Marie-Antoinette's departure
from it are reminders that, whatever the outcome of the political events in
train, 27 July 1794, 9 Thermidor Year II, Mulberry Day, will be a normal
day of births and deaths like any other. Paris contains something over half a
million inhabitants. This year, there will be roughly 24,000 births and nearly
30,000 deaths, and around 9,000 marriages. Bearing seasonal fluctuations in
mind, this means that today we might expect on average some 65 individuals
to be born, and around 80 to die. (In fact, the Revolutionary Tribunal in its
present mood is boosting the latter number.)

Dying and being born are not what they used to be. In the new Republic,
they have been secularized. Families may seek religious endorsement for life
events if they wish, but this is an option rather than a legal necessity. Priests
are no longer required to officiate, bless, and make a formal record, as they
have since the sixteenth century. On 20 September 1792, the registration of
births, marriages, and deaths passed under the authority of the state, and is

now administered by municipalities. Sunday observance has disappeared too, replaced by 'decadal' holidays every ten days. Besides the fêtes that adorn many of these days, there is a whole programme of larger events, like the splendid Bara and Viala festival planned for the following day, 10 Thermidor. In contrast, the Paris municipality is light, if inventive, on ceremonial around births, marriages, and deaths. New rules agreed by the Commune require that 'lugubrious' black coffin drapes, for example, be replaced by a tricolour palette: white for the young, red for those of virile age and blue for the old with inscriptions, 'He grew (or "was living", or "had lived") for the fatherland.' Coffins are to be carried at shoulder height by four men wearing a tricolour sash and belt and a special tunic reaching down to their knees.

The ceremonial for the 25 marriages due to take place today is similarly spare. Currently sleeping soundly, one hopes, before their big day are Jean-Baptiste-Guillaume Viard, who manufactures weights and measures, and Marguerite Moutard. They will be called on at the Maison Commune by municipal official, Pierre-Louis Paris, to state their intentions, at which point the latter is empowered by law to declare baldly and without religious frills that 'in the name of the law, the couple is joined in marriage'.

Matters are equally cut-and-dried as regards divorce, a practice which, flying in the face of church lore, the Republic instituted in September 1792. The new practice has been welcomed in the city, particularly by women, and reaches well down the social order. Later today, on the Rue Saint-Jacques, one of Paris's prime printing neighbourhoods, Françoise-Nicole Soisy, under guidance from a justice of the peace, will begin legal process against her printer husband, Charles-Adrien Hénault (who has already abandoned the marital home and his 9-year-old daughter).

Even the most rudimentary ceremony will, however, be denied those due to be executed today at the Place du Trône-Renversé, after trial and conviction by the Revolutionary Tribunal. Once the guillotine has done its work, the public executioner and his aides place bodies and severed heads in huge baskets. They sit on their lids to close them up, and then cram them in carts, painted red and lined with lead to prevent leakages of bodily fluids. The carts head south over open ploughland to reach the cemetery of the old Picpus convent. This newly nationalized property has served as graveyard for the executed since the guillotine moved to the south-east of the city on 14 June. Nearly 1,300 individuals have already been buried there, and the site has reached its third grave-pit.

The execution crew divest corpses of clothes in the monastery's former chapel. They are allowed some bounty from the bodies, but most of their quotidian effects are sent to Parisian hospitals for cleaning and further use. The naked cadavers and heads are thrown in and covered with wooden planks and with quicklime, huge barrels of which have been carted here recently to deal with steeply rising demand and environmental hygiene. For, as was the case with the Place de la Révolution, the Picpus death-pits have begun to exude a rotting stench.

3.00 a.m.

Conciergerie prison, Palais de Justice, Ile de la Cité (Révolutionnaire)

Those readying themselves for their final journey today include 27-year-old Marie-Thérèse-Françoise de Choiseul, princesse de Monaco, who is now in a cell in the Conciergerie prison attached to the law courts (the Palais de Justice) on the Ile de la Cité. The princesse's husband has enlisted with the royalist rebels in the Vendée insurrection, so there is a case for her to answer. No opportunity, however, has been provided for her to defend herself. Sentenced to death yesterday by the Tribunal, the princesse secured a stay of execution by pleading pregnancy, alleging intercourse with an unnamed man three months earlier. If a convicted woman is found to be pregnant, she must give birth before the sentence is carried out. But first she must be tested by the Tribunal's medical panel, comprising a physician, a pharmacist, and a midwife. They are ever alert to the claim that this privilege is being abused by women seeking to live longer. Physician Thiéry is a Robespierre appointee, and he and his colleagues are tough over such claims. It is generally held that pregnancy can only be medically ascertained after four to five months, but this does not deter the panel from declaring the princesse not pregnant after three. The Tribunal has as little time for medical certainties as for legal niceties.

Last evening in her cell in the Conciergerie, the princesse wrote a letter (marked 'very urgent') to Antoine-Quentin Fouquier-Tinville, the Tribunal's public prosecutor:

Citizen,
   I wish to advise you that I am not pregnant. I wanted to tell you. I did not soil my mouth with this lie out of fear of death, or to avoid it, but to give myself one more day, so

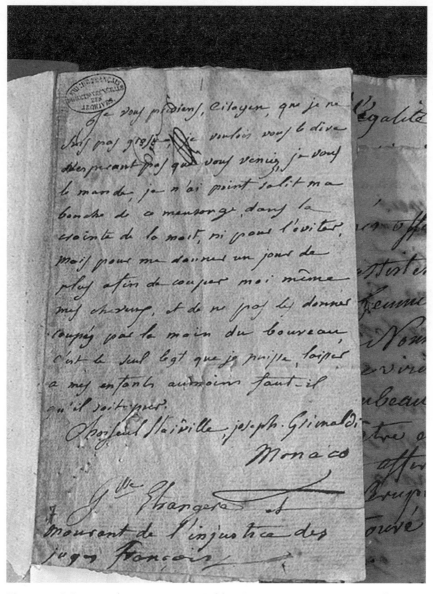

Figure 3. Princesse de Monaco to Public Prosecutor Fouquier-Tinville, 8–9 Thermidor (W 431)

that I can cut my hair myself, and not have it done by the executioner. It is the only legacy that I can leave to my children; at least it must be pure.

Choiseul-Stainville-Joseph-Grimaldi-Monaco, foreign princess, dying from the injustice of French judges.

She has broken a window in her cell and used the glass to cut her plaited hair. She stores this now alongside letters she has written to her children and their governess. To her children she writes:

I have postponed my death by one day not out of fear but because I wanted to cut off these sad remains of myself that you might have them . . . I have spent one more day in this agony, but I do not complain . . .

She asks that they bring out this personal memento three or four times a year in loving memory of their mother.

Such mementoes designed to give meaning to a death shorn of its usual ceremonial accompaniment are frequent among victims of the Revolutionary Tribunal. Some bequeath a lock of hair, others a favoured jewel, a handkerchief, or a last portrait. Jean-Antoine Roucher, who was guillotined two days previously alongside fellow poet André Chénier, sent his family and friends a final sketch of himself by a fellow inmate along with a poem:

> *Dear and sweet ones, be not amazed*
> *If sadness makes my face seem fraught;*
> *As skilful hand my image made*
> *The scaffold called, of you I thought.*

Today, the stoical princesse de Monaco faces Roucher's fate.

3.00 a.m.

Bénédictins-Anglais prison, Rue Saint-Jacques (Observatoire)

Louis-Sébastien Mercier is soundly asleep within the Bénédictins-Anglais prison. Conditions in this, Mercier's third gaol, are infinitely better than the first two. Rounded up in the autumn of 1793 as one of the '73' deputies gaoled as supporters of the expelled Girondins, he spent his first night with others of the '73' at the La Force prison, lying cramped on filthy, vermin-infested straw in an overcrowded cell with his head virtually in a slop-bucket. A move followed, just days ago, to the Madelonnettes, a former convent cleared of its nuns in 1793 and organized as an overflow prison for political prisoners (who currently include the Marquis de Sade). Yet the repressive regime, insatiable vermin and insanitary filth here was so insufferable that the 73 petitioned the CGS for better treatment. After a visit from CGS members Amar and Voulland, the group has now been shifted elsewhere, with Mercier and around 40 others being conveyed here, in open carriages so that they could be targets for public scorn.

This former house of the English Benedictine order is located at the southern, countrified end of the Rue Saint-Jacques, the healthiest part of Paris in Mercier's view. It has been stripped of most of its rococo furnishings: the organ from the chapel will be played up at the Panthéon tomorrow at the Bara and Viala ceremonies. But it is clean, airy, and not overtly repressive. It is also tantalizingly close to Mercier's home, a third-floor apartment just off the same thoroughfare, facing the courtyard of the church of Saint-Étienne-des-Grés. Here, just after midnight on Sunday, 6 October 1793, an armed delegation of sectional sans-culottes under CGS orders roughly seized him from the arms of his wife Louise Machard. She was still nursing a one-year-old baby and was five months pregnant with another.

Mercier boasts that in the worst of circumstances, his pillow is always soft, and on this night he is sleeping the soundest of sleeps, the sleep of the just. Like the princesse de Monaco, he too fears death tomorrow, though not by guillotine. He has observed that the paving stones covering the drainage pipes in the prison courtyard have been ominously lifted. The official story is that this is a routine exercise in sewage control. But Mercier is overcome by the paralysing fear that the black hole is destined to be the tomb of the inmates, victims of collective assassination by a bloodthirsty Parisian mob in a replay of the infamous 1792 September Massacres, when armed mobs wiped out half the city's prison population. Paris is haunted by popular violence.

Mercier certainly finds it difficult to shake off his own vivid, nightmarish remembrance of those murderous days, which for him mixed banality, farce, and transcendental evil in equal measure:

> – It was the day after the September Massacres, and I was walking slowly down the Rue Saint-Jacques, motionless in astonishment and horror and amazed to see the skies, the elements, the city and its human population all struck dumb. Two carts full of corpses were already passing me; a driver calmly and in full daylight was taking them, half buried in their black and bloodied clothes, to the far-off quarries of Montrouge . . . A third cart comes along. A foot sticks up in the air from out of the pile of corpses. I am dumbfounded in veneration. Though the eye of the executioner could not perceive it, this foot shone with immortality. I will recognise that foot on the Last Day of Judgement, when the thunderous Eternal Being will pass judgement on kings—and on *Septembriseurs*, the perpetrators of the massacres.

Revolutionary politics has not proved to be Mercier's forte. On the back of some celebrity as an author and dramatist before 1789, he launched himself into political journalism, co-editing the *Annales patriotiques et littéraires* newspaper, and then entering national politics by way of election to the Convention by the Seine-et-Oise department in September 1792. He rallied to the Girondin rather than to the Montagnard cause, but even Madame Roland, the Girondin muse, accounted him 'a zero in the Convention', his somewhat squawky Punch-and-Judy voice failing to command attention or respect. Although he and Robespierre had both been witnesses at the wedding of Camille Desmoulins in December 1790, there is now no love lost between them and indeed since then Robespierre has played a major part in speeding to the guillotine both bride and groom plus the other witnesses at the ceremony, the Girondins Brissot, Pétion, and the comte de Sillery. Mercier's most notorious intervention in debates was a maladroit clash with Robespierre about the proposed new constitution in June 1793, which resulted in him being brutally slapped down. Within hours of the fiasco, he would be organizing the petition of the '73', which got him where he is today.

Yet Mercier doesn't see Robespierre's apparent protection of the '73' as a mark of humanity: for him, the '73' are Robespierre's hostages, whose fate he deliberately holds in the balance so as to prevent Right-wing deputies within the Convention from getting out of line. Nor is he fooled by the crocodile tears and the professions of respect shown to their 'dear colleagues' by the CGS's Amar and Voulland, on their visit to the Madelonnettes. He knows just how vulnerable he and his fellow prisoners will be, if new waves of *Septembriseurs* come calling.

It is richly ironic that Mercier should now mortally fear the people of Paris, for he had sung their praises and indeed their political acumen with no little enthusiasm in his sprawling, 12-volumed *Tableau de Paris* that catapulted him to fame prior to 1789. It offered a loving description of his native city and its inhabitants as if from the level of the street. Mercier commends the people of Paris for making the Revolution in the first place. But it is they, he now believes, the 'mistaken multitude', as he calls them, who have wrecked the revolution they created. The September Massacres revealed a level of cruelty that he never suspected in a population that seemed the most civilized in Europe. The Montagnards should be ashamed for taking as political partners sans-culotte radicals who claim to speak for the people. The consequence is that the country has now to endure 'government by fools'.

There are currently around one hundred prisons in Paris, half of which are sectional gaol-houses like the one in the Marais where Alexandre Vernet is currently cooling his heels. At the other extreme are huge institutions which have a history going back well into the Ancien Régime: the medieval Conciergerie gaol, for example, where the princesse de Monaco sleeps, and the seventeenth-century poor-houses of Bicêtre, three miles south of the city, and La Salpêtrière in the Faubourg Saint-Marcel in the south-east. Others are newcomers, like the Madelonnettes and the Bénédictins-Anglais or the former abbey of Port-Royal, now renamed Port-Libre, or else former colleges of the university. Others are ex-aristocratic homes. The most magnificent of these is the Luxembourg palace on the Left Bank, the former residence of the comte de Provence, Louis XVI's brother. There is a gamut of smaller establishments too, such as the Talaru prison on the Rue de Richelieu (whose inmates have included the proprietor-marquis of the same name).

Some of the institutions within this honeycomb carceral world claim to offer a degree of insulation against the scaffold. The prison at the Pension Belhomme, formerly a clinic for the insane run by an entrepreneurial cabinet-maker, Jacques Belhomme, is the most notorious case in point. It and similar semi-private retreats serve as sanctioned bolt-holes for those who have secured favour from some element within national or local power systems and who can pay handsomely for seclusion. Until just recently, only two of the 160 largely aristocratic inmate population in the Couvent des Oiseaux on the rue de Sèvres, in the south-west of the city, have been referred to the Revolutionary Tribunal in the previous six months.

Yet despite these chinks in the carceral world, fear is omnipresent throughout the prison network. The memory of the 1792 September Massacres is still raw and fresh in many prisons, and their stone floors and walls are still literally stained by the blood of their victims. The La Force prison was the scene of infamous atrocities, including the hacking to death and mutilation of Queen Marie-Antoinette's former favourite, the princesse de Lamballe. Her assassins, it was said, went on to mutilate her genitals and drape them over her face, then waved her ghastly severed head on the end of a pike outside the window where the queen was imprisoned. Crude brutality of a similar order was also meted out in the Left Bank prisons of the Carmes and the Abbaye (formerly attached to the abbey of St-Germain-des-Prés), as well as at the Conciergerie, and in Bicêtre and the women's prison of La Salpêtrière. In all, around 1200 individuals were killed. Priests who had refused the new constitution were the most conspicuous target of the murder gangs, but many common-law criminals and simple suspects (and, at La Salpêtrière, prostitutes) were also victims. Most of these individuals were butchered in cold blood, some also having to endure the pathetic travesty of a trial by so-called 'popular commissions'. Most estimates of deaths in the massacres are far higher than reality, and the blood-lust exhibited is invariably viewed as having been the work of the whole Parisian population (even though probably only a few hundred wild men were involved).

When in early 1793, the thirst for popular violence seemed to be swelling again, the government sought to pre-empt it by establishing judicial processes that dealt exemplarily with counter-revolutionary offences. This was the thinking behind the creation of the Revolutionary Tribunal on 10 March 1793: 'Let us exercise terror,' Danton urged the Convention, 'so as to pre-empt the people from doing so.' Mercier's imprisoned colleague, Denis Blanqui, feels that this judicial framework has become just a legitimate form of prison massacre, '"Septembrization" through legal forms'. Prisoners feel hated—and vulnerable. They realize that the hungry popular classes envy the regularity and alleged quality of the meals they get served. With the numbers of the guillotined rising, there are even whispers that the meat being served up in prisons is human flesh.

It was popular fears about counter-revolutionary plotting within the prisons that ignited the September Massacres, and in a worrying recent development, many of the individuals brought before the Revolutionary Tribunal are said to be participants in 'prison plots'. This development began in mid-June following accusations against prisoners out at Bicêtre to the south of Paris: the guillotining of some 76 Bicêtre prisoners was followed by show trials involving gaols within the city. Executions accounting for 315 prisoners from the Luxembourg took place in four waves in early to mid-July, and there were further batches of 49 from the Carmes on 23 July, and then 165 executions from Saint-Lazare in three batches from 24 to 26 July. There is no end in sight: even today, Benoist, former gaoler at the Luxembourg and now himself a prisoner at the Carmes, is writing to the CGS promising new lists of prison plotters.

Mercier is no wiser than anyone else in determining who exactly is orchestrating this new dance of death, as capital sentences increase exponentially. It is not solely Robespierre's work of course, for the executions have continued unabated during his self-exile from government over the last six weeks. But he has played a key role in it in two major ways. First, by the brutal simplification of judicial procedure introduced by the notorious Law of 22 Prairial which he and Couthon drove through the CPS and the Convention. Second, in early June, he personally approved a memo allowing Martial Herman, minister-level appointee at the Commission for Civil Administration, Prisons, and Tribunals, to seek out counter-revolutionaries in the prisons and refer them direct to the Revolutionary Tribunal. The move began with a discussion in the CPS which deplored the high proportion of the lower classes being guillotined while aristocrats seemed to be protected in the city gaols. Herman came up with plans aimed 'to purge the prisons at a stroke and to clear the soil of freedom from these dregs and rejects of humanity'.

Embracing the mission of reducing prison numbers personally licensed by Robespierre, Herman established a network of *moutons*, as they are called, or prison informers, spies, and denouncers, to discover (invent might be a more accurate term) conspiracies. He draws on legislation introduced by Saint-Just in the spring—the Law of 23 Ventôse (13 March)—which was confirmed by the 22 Prairial law, which makes any attempt or wish to escape justice a counter-revolutionary offence worthy of outlaw status. In theory an outlaw does not even have to be referred to the Revolutionary Tribunal: like enemies of the people held to have borne arms against the Republic (notably in the Vendée and other civil war zones), they could be taken out and shot. In fact, cases of overt prison resistance are still referred to the Tribunal, though once there they are given short shrift.

Robespierre and Herman are said to have known each other since well before the Revolution, when both were practising law in their native Arras. The story has it that it was Robespierre who summoned him from his judicial and political duties in the Pas-de-Calais in 1793 to sit as President of the Revolutionary Tribunal. Herman certainly proved the loyal CPS servant in his new role, excelling in his astute management of the Dantonist trial, for which he was promoted to his present position, which effectively combines the tasks of the Interior and Justice ministries. Writing to Robespierre over the appointment of a judge, Herman gave him the nod of approval by saying that the candidate in question seemed to be 'one of us'. This sense of being on Robespierre's austerely spartan, virtue-promoting wavelength is an important part of the chilly dedication to Robespierre that Herman brings to his job. In private, he criticizes Robespierre's enemies on the CPS for making a fuss about destroying domestic enemies and holds out the wish that these 'could be all exterminated on one day so that we could all enjoy the happiness that the Republic promises us'.

The advent of the prison plots has been roughly contemporary with a sharp deterioration in general conditions within the prisons. Partly this is due to simple overcrowding. In January, the prison population was 5,000; in July it is just shy of 8,000. In late spring, the CPS decided that all counter-revolutionary suspects throughout France had to be despatched to Paris for trial. Even though this is far from universally observed, provincial influxes have swelled the prisons to what seems like breaking point. Carts of prisoners brought in from outside often face a wearying trek around the city, in an effort to find a gaoler who can take them in. The mushrooming of prison numbers has also led the Government to reduce spiralling maintenance costs by introducing a new austerity.

In 1793, many prisons allowed well-off inmates a surprising degree of latitude. Gaolers largely connived in allowing the purchase of better living conditions in the form of bedding, furnishings, and food. They also were often relatively free and easy about prison visiting, the writing and receiving of letters and the provision of books and newspapers. Mercier, for example, was able to maintain a steady correspondence with his wife, Louise Machard, sometimes openly, sometimes through covert means (placing letters at the bottom of a basket of fruit, for example). His wife in turn procured for him the little necessities of his life: a magnifying glass, candles, paper, clean linen, handkerchiefs, a toothpick, material for a curtain, plus plentiful food. Mercier made an early decision: 'I won't complain; I will live.' His complaints are still surprisingly few. There are flea and mice infestations to cope with, but boredom is the main problem, even if there is the occasional wave of despair ('Be braver than me,' he entreats his wife. 'I kiss you. I am crying.'). But his idea of living seems more like living to eat. His wife is instructed to keep the 'good cheer' coming: salad, cabbage, carrots, asparagus, artichokes, grapes, chocolate, sugar lumps, mackerel, sausages, grilled songbirds, rice, pork and mutton, a bottle of wine a day . . .

Recently, however, it has been becoming more difficult for Mercier's wife to answer his requests. For from May 1794, the CPS and the Paris Commune, alleging the need to clamp down on the hatching of prison plots, escapes, and suicide attempts and also to institute a more egalitarian ethos, have enforced a much stricter regime. Mercier's wife is suddenly accused of smuggling in letters containing 'enigmatic and ambiguous wording'. And it is not only the Mercier couple who are under increased suspicion. Following a systematic roll-call in mid-May throughout the prison network, all inmates were obliged to hand over sharp and cutting objects (knives, razors, pins, needles, compasses, corkscrews, and even nappy pins and toothpicks) as well as jewels, cash, paper money reserves, and other precious possessions. In the Port-Libre prison, prisoners have had musical instruments confiscated, as well as pets: nearly 200 dogs were ejected from this prison alone, while one female inmate there witnessed her cat being grilled and eaten by the warders. The police commissioner, militant sansculotte, and Cologne-born cobbler Wichterich (whose Germanic accent prisoners love to mock) reported for duty at the Luxembourg the day following the confiscations sporting a pink and black satin suit and silver buckles on his shoes that all assumed were his spoils from the exercise. Although visits from a barber are sometimes allowed, some prisons have seen male prisoners sprouting unkempt beards and letting their fingernails grow. A new mealtime regime has been instituted too, based on a common table and often comprising a lunch of verminous salted meat with cabbage or potatoes, plus some bread at night. This replaces brought-in meals eaten in the cell. Inmates eat with their hands as knives are forbidden.

Many prisoners try to maintain habits of leisure and sociability, but these too suffer. Candles are now often forbidden, confining inmates to their cells from earlier in the evenings. Their personal effects are rifled through by warders accompanied by huge mastiffs straining at the leash. Censorship is stricter on books. A particular loss is easy access to newspapers—'our sole point of contact with humanity', regrets one inmate—which prisoners liked to follow closely to see what is happening in the Convention and at the Revolutionary Tribunal. Henceforth they depend on the wild rumours that spread around the prison system as a result of prisoner transfers and they listen out for the headlines in the cries of the newspaper hawkers in streets outside (though vendors sometimes add malicious gloating over the rising number of guillotinings, and throw in a neck-chop gesture too). Greater surveillance is demanded as regards messages and signs to individuals outside the prison. In some gaols, prisoners are threatened with potshots if they so much as look out of windows.

Prison warders are getting tougher: the Revolutionary Government seems to be more on their backs than before to deliver greater stringency and observance of regulations. Formerly only too open to bribes, they are now more prudent. Guyard, the new gaoler at the Luxembourg is a client of Couthon from his days in Lyon and is rumoured to have led prison massacres there. Another newly promoted warder, Haly at Port-Libre, displayed wild animals from Africa in fairs and markets prior to 1789, and he has taken to his task in much the same spirit: he shows female aristocrats in their cells to his inebriated dinner guests as though they were zoological specimens. Brutality is more in evidence. The duchesse de Duras was informed by her gaoler that every aristocrat is going to be guillotined. Another gaoler makes it clear to inmates that they are merely 'guillotine fodder'. Some seek sexual favours from women inmates to keep them off the death lists.

Realizing the endorsement that the Revolutionary Government has given spies within the prison, however, warders are keen to treat *moutons* better.

Some of them get to live a life of petty splendour. Ferrières-Sauveboeuf, the main *mouton* at La Force, who is alleged to have put the Revolutionary Tribunal on to the princesse de Monaco, is a former count, who travelled in the Levant and performed diplomatic services for the crown prior to 1789, but who then made a reputation as a radical in both the Jacobin and Cordeliers clubs. Realizing that he will be in prison some little time, he has decorated his cell in an oriental manner, including watercolours of the Bosphorus, keeps caged nightingales, has his meals served separately to him, and is to be found in the evening puffing on a hookah.

The presence of such men is deeply unsettling for inmates. All feel that they are being watched and try hard not to betray their feelings. Knowing that imprudent reactions to the news can give them away, aristocratic prisoners try to avoid reactions betraying schadenfreude when they hear reports of republican defeats, but find it difficult to prevent stifled smiles, nervous twitches, and involuntary foot-tapping, even though they know they are being carefully watched. The nerve-jangling moment when prison gates open to allow in an empty tumbril, and the reading of a list of names to be taken away to the Conciergerie prison to await trial before the Revolutionary Tribunal, is another test of resilience. The speed with which the named are now disposed of—trial within 24 hours, execution within 36 hours is becoming the new norm—is horrifying. Moreover, even prisons that have seen relatively few executions are now being hit. The Couvent des Oiseaux had more than a dozen of the *haut gratin* of the inmate population suddenly carted off two days ago. They are scheduled for the guillotine today. It is much the same at the Talaru prison: the eponymous marquis was removed, quite possibly due to a confusion over names on 23 July and executed forthwith. The Tribunal will now convict almost anyone who shows up in the dock who is of ecclesiastical status or who bears an aristocratic name.

04.00/4.00 a.m.

Various locations, CPS offices, Tuileries palace

I t is the dark before dawn, and Saint-Just is working by candlelight on the report that he plans to deliver to the Convention later today. For several hours now, he has maintained a cooperative stance towards the other committee members in the room, even though they have made their distrust of him crystal clear. He has tried to calm them down. No, there is no plan for a 31 May-style revolt tomorrow. No one is under the knife. No, the lives of members of the CPS and CGS are not threatened. There is absolutely no need, as colleagues have mooted, for the committees to arrest alleged ringleaders, Mayor Fleuriot-Lescot, National Agent Payan, and NG Commander, François Hanriot. Indeed to do so would be an act of usurpation, depriving the people of Paris of their magistrates and their elected general.

In order to appease the members of the committee, Saint-Just has agreed that before he presents his speech to the Convention tomorrow morning, he will run it by colleagues in a meeting at 11.00 a.m. Yet despite this veneer of cooperative civility, which is seemingly in the spirit of the fractured 22–3 July truce, the events of the night have transformed his feelings about the content of his report. Tonight's farrago and the conjugated anger of Collot and Billaud are making him see things rather differently. The report must reflect that.

One of the most positive things to emerge from the joint CPS/CGS conciliatory truce meetings was the understanding that Saint-Just would present today's report to the Convention as a move towards healing rifts and facilitating more harmonious relations within the committees. Robespierre seems to have done his best to scupper things since then, but Saint-Just plans to override this, and to use the occasion not only to re-solder together the elements of the government team so as to make the CPS better fit for purpose but also to present a road-map indicating the way forward for the Revolution as a whole. Unlike his friend and idol, he is not obsessed with conspiracies nor with the CGS and its nefarious agents. He can think more positively and constructively.

Victory at Fleurus has offered the Convention an opportunity for advancing beyond war mobilization and progressing towards the creation of the sort of society that the Revolution has always been about. The year 1789 had shown that the idea of happiness as the goal of social organization was imaginable. It was a new idea in Europe, in the world. At the CPS's request, Saint-Just has for some time been contemplating the type of social institutions needed to found the new Republic. He is now in a position that, with just a little more time, he will be able to present to the Convention a far-ranging programme of reform. Today's speech should be the first instalment in a larger schedule of political harmonization and social transformation. Like Robespierre, he believes that in the construction of a new social order, innovative republican institutions can be created that will usher citizens towards cherished values of fraternity grounded in interpersonal trust and friendship. Fighting for the fatherland—for *la patrie*—he believes is not about fighting for French soil. *La patrie* forms a 'community of affections' between patriots, an emotional community that makes the defence of *patrie* possible.

Far-ranging laws on education and welfare will prepare pathways towards a self-consciously Spartan ideal society from which excessive wealth will be banished allowing egalitarian fraternity to flourish. Republican society will come to embody true social justice, which is his (and Robespierre's) watchword. Probably without even noticing it, he has recently been signing himself as 'Saint-Juste'. The supplementary 'e' is an unconscious downpayment on his preoccupation with the ideal of a more equal and fairer society.

Saint-Just is hoping that 9 Thermidor will mark a major moment in his career. In 1790, before the two had met, he wrote Robespierre a fan-mail letter beginning, 'You, who hold together the tottering country against the torrent of despotic intrigue, you whom I know only like God, through his miracles', and ending with assurance that 'you are a great man; you are not merely the deputy of a province, but of humanity and the Republic'. When he entered the Convention in 1792, he was at 25 years old its youngest member, and had no real career behind him except some random, often unsavoury episodes, a few intellectually adventurous writings, plus a little dabbling in local politics. He situated himself firmly under his hero

Robespierre's wing and from day one has spent all his political life with a reputation as Robespierre's servile acolyte.

Saint-Just made his mark in the Convention in 1792 by a maiden speech on the king's trial, in which he fully supported Robespierre's unbending attitude towards Louis XVI. He heightened his profile by taut, fresh-minted aphorisms: 'no one reigns innocently'; 'this man must either rule or die'; and 'the revolution begins where the tyrant ends'. His trenchant opinions significantly shaped the outcome of debates, even influencing Robespierre's own position. Yet it is still the case that if deputies say the name Saint-Just, they think Robespierre. The two seem linked by inseparable bonds of personal and ideological affinity. Since his election to the CPS in July 1793, Saint-Just has always shown eagerness to do his master's bidding, attacking the Girondins and their supporters, acting as a hired gun shooting down the Dantonist faction, expatiating on the Foreign Plot, running the Police Bureau, and so on. This has not made him popular. Like Robespierre, he does not suffer fools gladly, and his arrogance irritates many deputies, even on his own side. As with his mentor, he attracts cheap shots. Camille Desmoulins said of him that he walked around with his shoulders bearing his head as if it were the holy sacrament. People say that he wears a dandyishly high cravat line to hide ghastly neck scars from some unspecified but horrible skin disease. Yet he has his 'idolaters', some of them cranks. The former female radical Théroigne de Méricourt—now, poor woman, closely confined in a state of severe mental disturbance—seems to be expecting him to live up to his name and do her justice.

Despite a spotless record of personal fidelity, however, Saint-Just must now be wondering: is this to be the moment to emerge as his own man from under Robespierre's shadow? He is of course grateful to his older colleague for offering him his friendship and for embodying an ideal model of republican living and an inspiring vision of the future. But even Saint-Just finds Robespierre increasingly difficult to deal with. In his speech at the Convention yesterday, the older man drove a coach and horses through the truce that Saint-Just had carefully brokered only a few days before. It is true that Robespierre has some justification for distrusting those whom he regards as his opponents in the CPS and CGS. Saint-Just must have squirmed when during the negotiations he heard Billaud's wheedling comments towards Robespierre. 'We are your friends; we have come so far together'—this, from a man who behind Robespierre's back has been talking of him as a tyrant, a proto-Pisistratus. Even so, Robespierre's scattershot assault has made Saint-Just's job all the harder.

By claiming that the only way for the Revolution to advance is for extensive purges of the Committees of Government and the Convention, Robespierre has put himself out on a limb. Saint-Just does not want to join him there. Robespierre used words related to conspiracy literally a hundred times in his speech yesterday; Saint-Just will not use the words 'conspiracy' nor 'conspirator' and will deploy only a handful of related terms. Whatever Robespierre thinks, conspiracy is not the Republic's big problem now.

Even putting personal ambition and indeed modesty to one side, Saint-Just feels he may be the only deputy who can break the current political deadlock and take the Revolution triumphantly forward. All the same, the behaviour of Collot and Billaud in the CPS this evening has shown Saint-Just that neither of them can be offered unconditional support. Collot's vehement personal insults have deeply upset him, and he plans to inflect his speech in ways that show his anger. Like Robespierre, Collot has broken the truce terms by engaging in personal attacks, so Saint-Just can feel justifiably unfettered. In addition, he deplores the willingness that Collot and Billaud displayed this evening to whip up fear in both the CGS and the CPS in a way that threatened to effect a kind of *coup d'état* against Paris's municipal government. The two men also seem critical of the Revolutionary Tribunal. Saint-Just worries where all of this might lead. Although he has promised Billaud and Collot that he will talk the language of conciliation in the assembly, he cannot simply overlook all that has happened in the last few hours.

In spite of what he has to tell the Convention about the extent of Billaud and Collot's misdeeds, he believes that the biggest problem about the CPS in recent months is not the Committee's divisions (which foreign powers are counting on), but rather its dispersal. Institutional dysfunctionality lies at the heart of the problems of government rather than evil groups of conspiring individuals. For some time, he will argue, the size and coherence of the CPS has been affected by a cumulation of factors, notably, long absences on departmental missions (Jean Bon Saint-André, Prieur de la Marne, Collot, himself), illness (Couthon), and the tendency of the 'technicians' in the committee (Lindet, Carnot, Prieur de la Côte d'Or) to focus on their area of expertise rather than on decision-making in common. Plus, there has been the effective freezing out of Robespierre. The consequence is that a handful of individuals have too much power in their hands.

If Collot and Billaud are the names that come easiest to Saint-Just in this regard, he may well also have in mind Barère. And he will certainly be thinking Carnot. No love is lost between Saint-Just and Carnot. Carnot was elected to the CPS because of his considerable military experience and he lords it over army issues. Saint-Just in contrast entered the CPS with no real military knowledge, but studied military matters closely over the course of 1793. Serving as deputy on mission with the Army of the Rhine along with his bosom friend and colleague Philippe Le Bas in autumn 1793, he brought energy and personal bravery to the post. Then in the spring of 1794, again with Le Bas, he played an even more prominent role with the Army of the North and indeed takes much credit for the French victory in the battle of Fleurus.

Colleagues on the CPS have got used to the sound of Carnot and Saint-Just bickering angrily over military matters, ranging from choice of generals (Carnot favours military experience, Saint-Just patriotic sentiment) through to tactics and strategy (Saint-Just tends to be more aggressive). Carnot has committed to a grand strategy of territorial expansion, based on extending French frontiers notably in maritime Flanders along the English Channel, so as to prepare for an assault on the Netherlands. There are colleagues who heartily approve such an idea: Barère is well aware how military victories bolster patriotic support for the Revolutionary Government. Then again, the thought of extending the tax base and offering opportunities for plunder that will allow war to pay for itself appeals to Cambon's finance committee. Saint-Just in contrast is altogether more sanguine about an expansionist policy and on the northern front favours a defensive approach focused on securing the frontier. Like Robespierre, he fears that military adventurism will allow a charismatic leader to emerge and sweep away the reforms the Revolution has effected. To forestall any move towards military despotism, Saint-Just fervently focuses on new social institutions, not conquests. The costs of these can be met by progressive taxation and through policies of social redistribution as well as through terror against those unwilling to join the 'community of affections'. This community is predicated on a community of the hated who are to be eradicated by the use of terror. Saint-Just's sincere attachment to his ideas cannot be doubted, but neither can his potential ruthlessness in carrying them out. 'He would give his own head to found the Republic,' one deputy has quipped, 'and 100,000 other heads as well.'

Robespierre, whose understanding of military matters is poor and who originally opposed France going to war on the grounds, famously, that 'no one likes an armed missionary', tends to follow the prompts of his young ally on military matters. Where Saint-Just bends his ear as regards the northern front, moreover, his brother Augustin plays a similar role on the south-eastern frontier, where he has been serving as deputy on mission. Influenced by the young artillery commander Buonaparte, Augustin favours a powerful thrust into Piedmont that would even threaten Vienna, while Carnot opposes such moves for fear of exposing French supply lines to British coastal incursions. Augustin's return to Paris from the front in mid-July to appeal to the CPS failed to move Carnot, adding supplementary fuel to the fires of Robespierre's ill-feeling.

The conflict between Carnot and Saint-Just has been simmering for months. In April, a dispute over firearms and personnel flared into a full-scale slanging match between the two men. Saint-Just reacted angrily to some of Carnot's proposals, threatening him with the guillotine, whereupon Carnot lost control and with icy disdain accused him and Robespierre of being 'ridiculous dictators'.

Rumour acts to amplify and possibly distort the picture. It is whispered that Saint-Just has indeed argued that Robespierre should be given special powers which could be viewed as dictatorial. Deputies occasionally witness angry exchanges in meetings, and even get the impression that CPS members are treating Robespierre with contempt. Because of the conventions about collective confidentiality over the CPS's goings-on, however, there is uncertainty about how serious and frequent these arguments are, and the extent to which they are hampering the work of government. It is known that there was a big row over the way that Couthon and Robespierre drove through the Law of 22 Prairial on the Revolutionary Tribunal without proper referral to the committee. Robespierre was alleged to have been crying tears of rage at the end of it. After a further, very major fall-out in mid-June, with military matters again the trigger for further hostilities between Saint-Just and Carnot, Robespierre started absenting himself completely from CPS meetings.

Today, Saint-Just realizes that he has a golden opportunity to gain the political high-ground against Carnot now that the terms of the 22–3 July truce have been lifted. For it is generally acknowledged that, by insisting that 18,000 men be removed from the Army of the North to strengthen French forces across a broader front, Carnot spoiled the Army of the North's chances of following up its victory at Fleurus with an even greater knockout blow against the Austrians. This mis-step has put Carnot on the back foot, which is where Saint-Just likes him.

Saint-Just realizes that Carnot is equally distrustful of Robespierre. During a military posting in Arras prior to the Revolution, Carnot had become acquainted with Robespierre when the latter was an aspiring young lawyer. But any friendship has long gone sour. Robespierre's social views are far too extreme for the sedately moderate Carnot, who has also grown to dislike Robespierre's apparent inability to serve the Revolutionary Government as dutifully as he should. He also detests the way that Robespierre, Couthon, and Saint-Just run their Police Bureau as a private fiefdom, only bringing matters to the rest of the CPS when they need to garner signatures. Then there is the recurrent squabble around the issue of the additional powers that Saint-Just has seemed to wish to accord Robespierre. What exactly Saint-Just intends is unclear: he is probably evoking a practice of the Roman Republic, whereby the emergency powers of dictator could be temporarily be given to an individual in time of crisis. But this limited and specific usage is being distended through use and is employed almost interchangeably with 'despot' and 'tyrant'.

Unlike Robespierre, Carnot is not a figure to take grievances noisily into the public sphere. He hates the Jacobin Club and speaks sparingly in the Convention. However, he has taken the precaution of creating a new newspaper aimed at soldiers at the front. The first issue of the *Soirée du Camp* was printed on 19 July. It contains nothing of political note or relevance. But it forms Carnot's precautionary mouthpiece in case Saint-Just and Robespierre's 'dictatorial' aspirations are extended and they start to call for military backing.

If Saint-Just really had ideas about making Robespierre a dictator, he seems to have renounced them, or maybe put them on hold for this speech. His main priority as regards Robespierre will be to bring him back onside as a working member of government. He realizes that he will have to make clear his unimpaired personal belief that Robespierre's conduct has always been irreproachable and that he has never heard him being anything but measured in his views about members of the Convention. (It may prove difficult for this part of his speech to sound altogether convincing.) Robespierre has been expressing his pain. But the root of the problem lies in the excessive power which two or three CPS members enjoy. Saint-Just wants to reorganize the

CPS so that it truly is a collective form of government. He will suggest that all CPS orders should have at least six signatories.

Saint-Just is aware that his criticism of Carnot, Collot, and Billaud may seem like a denunciation, as to some extent it is. He wants to bring Collot and Billaud's behaviour out into the open, and to oblige them to explain themselves. Hopefully if they see the error of their ways and return to their tasks refreshed and repentant, Robespierre may be brought back onside: 9 Thermidor doesn't have to be the prelude to a bloody purge of Robespierre's list of 'conspirators'. A way forward is possible in which the CPS will work more effectively and in the intended collective spirit. Dysfunctions within Revolutionary Government can be remedied without the need for a major blood-letting. Further *jours de gloire*—further days of glory—remain ahead, with a revivified CPS still at the helm.

4.00 a.m.

The same, somewhat removed

What are others still working in the CPS offices at this time thinking? Attendance has thinned out. CGS member Voulland has made his way home, and those remaining have been temporizing, waiting for Saint-Just to make his departure. Despite his protestations, they do not trust him. His ties to Robespierre run too deep, and his insolence towards members of the committees in the past is still deeply etched in their memory.

Carnot, Barère, and the still gently fuming Collot d'Herbois and Billaud-Varenne comprise the core of the group remaining. They have accepted Saint-Just's presence, but are clearly thinking and planning beneath the surface. Billaud must realize that Saint-Just thinks him a hypocrite for posing in the negotiations on 23 July as a fraternal ally of Robespierre. But in fact the two men, with Collot, have indeed been fellow travellers on the paths of republicanism and democracy since the early 1790s. Billaud's conception of first the Revolution and now the Revolutionary Government is extremely close to Robespierre's. The men stood shoulder to shoulder over the fate of the king, the expulsion of the Girondins and (with some tensions) the culling of the Dantonist and Hébertist factions in spring 1794. Billaud formulated the Law of 14 Frimaire on Revolutionary Government (4 December 1793) which set out the framework for the dominance of the CPS and the CGS over the war effort, the running of the economy and the deployment of terror, and Robespierre has always been fully signed up to the Law's provisions. Billaud is as committed to egalitarianism as Saint-Just and Robespierre and indeed he too has been formulating 'social institutions' for a virtuous and fraternal Republic.

The tensions between Billaud and Robespierre seem to owe most to the vanity of small differences. For if their social and political views are very similar, their personalities are sharply contrasted. Robespierre's disdainful, holier-than-thou imperiousness in public arenas jars with Billaud's more morose and introverted temperament. For some time now, Billaud has been taciturn and distant when Robespierre and Saint-Just are in the same room. Saint-Just accuses him of ponderous silences and endless muttering of the phrase, 'we are on the edge of a volcano'. (It is unclear who or what he thinks will erupt, but the phrase has been given topicality by the eruption of Mount Vesuvius, reported in the press just a few days earlier.)

Collot is Billaud's CPS twin. Both men entered the CPS in September 1793. They discharge their duties as regards correspondence with deputies on mission, a huge task, with commendable efficiency. Their signatures are side by side on more CPS decrees than any of their colleagues. Collot is well aware that Robespierre holds his repression of the Federalist Revolt in Lyon against him, as he worked alongside Robespierre's bugbear Fouché. He must also realize that his theatrical background and actorly ways grate against Robespierre's obsession with authenticity. Conversely, Collot may sardonically reflect on the extent to which Robespierre's famed incorruptibility and martyrish leanings have themselves become a bit of a performance. There is only a limited number of times that Robespierre can melodramatically offer to lay down his life for the cause without thoughts of 'crying wolf' crossing deputies' minds. Had yesterday's death-threat been the first time that Robespierre had made such an offer, it might have had more credibility. Saint-Just appreciates Robespierre's utter sincerity and rectitude, which form the basis for his fame and the admiration that he attracts; but his colleagues sniff rank hypocrisy. For all his wearying talk of the hideousness of faction, moreover, Robespierre acts as if he were a faction leader, marking down his enemies and nurturing his supporters. Like Billaud, Collot thinks that for Robespierre there are no conspirators except for men he doesn't like.

Collot is certainly not the only deputy to resent the self-aggrandizing and Manichean flavour of Robespierre's rhetoric. All talk and no action doesn't quite express it, but a lot more talk than action certainly does. Even before his conspicuous absences from the CPS and the Convention, Robespierre was not one for late-night sessions. He provided the soundtrack, so to speak, of many of the Convention's greatest and most humane legislative achievements: the abolition of slavery, legislation on social protection, welfare for soldiers' and their families, a freeze on food prices, the *levée en masse*, laws on cultural heritage, the restructuring of poor relief. But his actual input into drafting legislation has been minimal. He may be a man of vision, but he is no action man. Moreover, those few decrees in which Robespierre has played a leading role, notably the Cult of the Supreme Being, the 22 Prairial law and the establishment of the Police Bureau, have proved highly divisive. He likes to take collective credit for CPS achievements, it is noted, but retains the right to criticize and even denounce his colleagues. He is notably unwilling to join in praise for military victories, which makes colleagues suspect that he is waiting for defeats so that he can attack his colleagues full-on.

Following the purge of the Dantonist faction in the Convention in the spring, other CPS and CGS members have set their face against further acts of exclusion. They have watched with disbelief and intense irritation as Robespierre has rejected this view and taken his purge campaign and his anti-conspiracy tirades into the Jacobin Club rather than trying to sort out matters following the accepted protocols of collective CPS responsibility. Much of all this may be unfair to Robespierre. But Robespierre's actions have been such that fairness no longer really comes into it.

Robespierre's behaviour has also pushed Bertrand Barère onto the Billaud-Collot wavelength. Barère's influence and political longevity—no deputy has served longer on the CPS—owe much to his constitutional flexibility, his capacity for going with the political flow, and his skills in doing deals and making compromises. There is nowhere that Barère feels more comfortable than on the fence. Heaven knows, on the CPS he has more than adequately and loyally stuck by Robespierre when the latter needed support: he sang his praises after the Ladmiral assassination attempt; he co-sponsored the law forbidding the taking of English prisoners of war; and he covered for him in the Convention over the 22 Prairial law. He has openly acknowledged all that government owes the man. In return, Robespierre has been free with snide remarks. So despite this record of unremitting bending over backwards to accommodate his difficult colleague, the worm in Barère has finally turned. Robespierre's demand for heads seems insatiable and his wilful and exasperating snubbing of the 22–3 July negotiations, plus his rabble-rousing speech yesterday evening in the Jacobins, seems impossible to bear. Barère now views Robespierre as having crossed the line from being a difficult colleague to being an impossible one.

What to do about Robespierre? A point of no return seems to have been reached for the men sitting around the green table. In past months, they have consistently rejected approaches from conspirators like Lecointre and Bourdon de l'Oise. Besides the fear he evokes in his colleagues, a sense of collective solidarity has been in play here, as well as the hope, once covertly expressed by Lindet, that Robespierre was 'digging his own grave' anyway. But Robespierre's speech yesterday has produced a new, sinister sense of imminence. They are coming speedily to the collective conclusion that, one way or another, their colleague is a liability rather than an asset. He needs to be stopped. But how?

The only way to remove Robespierre from his perch is to eject him from the Convention. This can be done in one of three ways, none of them easy. The first is by popular direct action, that is, by organizing a mass movement in Paris on the lines of the 31 May *journée*, so as to force the Convention's hand. This seems to be what Robespierre is already favouring against his enemies, and his opponents' sense of Robespierre's popularity in the city deters them from risking such an approach against him. It is Robespierre who parades around as if he had public opinion behind him. He is the crowd-stirring celebrity, not they.

The second strategy for silencing Robespierre might seem a very obvious one, but it is in fact extremely risky. The Convention has the right to rotate the membership of the Committees of Government, so in theory the CPS could seek to persuade the deputies to take this step. If they tried to do this, however, they would instantly create a rift at the heart of government which would reduce its efficiency and could work out to their own disadvantage. They might well lose, such is Robespierre's ability to frighten deputies.

The third strategy would be to do what the CPS did in the spring of 1794 to expel Danton. Danton was a figure whose Revolutionary credentials were huge—possibly even greater then than Robespierre's now—but the Committees of Government viewed his campaign for a relaxation of the Terror as a threat. They expeditiously ordered his and his alleged supporters (including Robespierre's old school-mate Camille Desmoulins) to be arrested at night. When this was announced to the Convention next day as a fait accompli, Danton's friend Louis Legendre stood up to argue that a deputy should have the right to defend himself before the Convention. He was faced down by Robespierre in a way that left him quivering in his shoes. Robespierre and Saint-Just then collaborated in drawing up a charge-sheet against Danton which combined the plausible with the frighteningly, almost laughably mendacious. Prevented from speaking in his own defence in the Convention, Danton was further silenced when he started making his opinions loudly known during his trial before the Revolutionary Tribunal. The

CPS took speedy action to change legal procedures so as to stop him speaking.

Can the CPS do to Robespierre what it did to Danton? And if so, how exactly should it go about it? The auguries do not look good, certainly for the moment. The decree ordering the arrest of Danton, Desmoulins, and their followers was signed off by all members of the CPS and the CGS, and this unanimity was essential in getting the Convention onside on the following day. But currently the Government Committees are disunited: CGS members Le Bas and David are unabashed Robespierre supporters, as are Couthon and Saint-Just on the CPS. The Convention's receptivity to such a move would thus be far from clear. The alleged assassination plots being hatched by Lecointre and Bourdon de l'Oise are extreme and unrepresentative of the overall view of the assembly, at least as things stand. Furthermore, the committee is not even sure that it could find someone physically to arrest Robespierre. The CPS has no troops of its own to act as an executive force, any more than the Convention for that matter, save for a small ceremonial guard that reports to Hanriot, and ultimately to the Commune. This lack of control still rankles among many deputies when they think back to how Hanriot's NG contingents bullied them into defenceless submission on 31 May and 2 June last year.

In spite of the genuine threat that Robespierre now poses, it would thus seem dangerously premature to launch a head-on attack on him at this moment. A 31 May-style coup is simply out of the question, while it is still too early to be able to count on the Convention. Indeed, going public with their plans would be perilous in terms of national security, as well as their own necks. Precipitate action could backfire against them and produce the opposite effect, putting Robespierre fully in control, with deadly consequences for his colleagues. Their main strategy, at least for the moment, is therefore to play a waiting game, and to see what Saint-Just comes up with in his speech in the Convention.

They do, however, take a few infant steps, out of Saint-Just's hearing, that will prepare them if it comes to a confrontation in the near future. First, they decide to minimize the chances of Robespierre organizing an operation to purge the Convention, by neutralizing NG Commander Hanriot. He will be dismissed and replaced with a rotating system of command among the six Legion Chiefs. They have already sounded out the mounted gendarmerie commander, Hémart, to verify that he can be relied on to take charge tomorrow if needed. In addition, they have prudently called up

Robespierre's potential allies, Mayor Fleuriot-Lescot and National Agent
Payan, to come and sit twiddling their thumbs in their vestibule awaiting an
invitation to speak to the committee—which never comes. It is a way to
keep them out of mischief.

In addition, they now decide to work on a proclamation for tomorrow
that will legitimate their NG proposal and alert deputies and indeed the
general public to the current state of political uncertainty. An exhortatory
proclamation to the people of Paris is the kind of thing that Barère can be
counted on to do well. He is supremely gifted at being vague. And as it is
completely unclear how things will work out later today, it is best to give no
hostages to fortune. Barère will find a way of stressing the need to rally
around the Committees of Government, come hell or high water.

With Barère taking a quill in hand, the men around the green table realize
that they are on a knife-edge. In the coming stand-off with Robespierre,
they will need more support from the Convention and the people of Paris
than they can currently count on. And they don't want to have to blink first.
They should at least have a clearer idea of how things stand once Saint-Just
has come back to report to them the contents of his big speech.

Approaching 5.00 a.m.
The same, somewhat removed

S aint-Just's speeches are always carefully crafted and full of aphoristic turns of phrase and impeccably honed coinings. He still has some fine-tuning to do. This may be the moment for him to slip away. Before he leaves, he reiterates his promise to be back at 11.00 in the morning to show his colleagues his report before he delivers it. There is talk of Fouché being there to reply to accusations. The Convention's formal agenda starts at midday, so this will allow time for consideration and amendment.

Is Saint-Just sincere in that promise? Or is he already thinking that he can make more impact by going over their heads and appealing direct to the Convention? To do so would be to break the aura of collective responsibility and the code of silence that has always prevailed over CPS business. But the stakes may just be too high for any other course of action to be appropriate. And after all, it was the Convention that elected him to the CPS in the first place, and his prime responsibility must be to the representatives of the nation, not to a clique of committee colleagues. He will make it clear from the start that he is speaking in a personal capacity, from the heart and above faction. Although he will make positive statements about the Jacobins and their proclaimed grievances, his target audience (echoing Robespierre's speech yesterday) will be the middling deputies of the Plain, the *gens de bien*. Hopefully this will help pull Robespierre back onside.

As he leaves his remaining colleagues, and sweeps past Fleuriot-Lescot and Payan waiting impatiently in the CPS vestibule, Saint-Just must be feeling that if he can play his difficult hand well later today, he will have averted a major political crisis, avoided likely bloodshed, protected his greatest friend against attacks (and also offered the great man a lifeline), and also set the government, and indeed the Republic, on a firm course towards a better future. The Convention will be called on to examine Billaud and Collot's behaviour in the light of his critique; to re-impose the truce he helped to broker a few days ago; to proceed to reorganize the CPS so that it works properly as a collective body; and to agree to give him just a few more days to perfect his second report on social institutions. If all goes as Saint-Just hopes, 9 Thermidor Year II, Mulberry Day, could be a day of glory which posterity will never forget.

PART
II

Settings for a Drama
(5.00 a.m. to Midday)

The sun is rising. The small circle of individuals caught up in the feverish yet inconclusive rounds of plotting in the last few hours are snatching some rest. Despite the endless evocation of conspiracy, there is remarkably little conspiring actually now taking place. Robespierre is not girding his loins. He has not lifted a finger overnight to coordinate with his main sympathizers and supporters.

It is much the same with Robespierre's opponents in the Committees of Government. They realize that a crisis is imminent, and that they may have to try to remove Robespierre from government before he does the same to them. But they are painfully aware that the current balance of forces within the city strongly favours him, not them. Believing it unlikely that he will make his move today, they have chosen to put conspiring on hold and to wait and see what Robespierre's ally Saint-Just has to say in the Convention later today. It is not completely out of the question that he might offer an olive branch in the spirit of the 22–3 July truce negotiations.

After Robespierre's behaviour yesterday, there is no shortage of deputies worried about his intentions. But the nervy wait-and-see attitude prevalent among the Committees of Government is also shared by long-disgruntled members of the Convention such as Lecointre, Bourdon de l'Oise, and Fouché. These men have been conspiring for months but seem better at producing hot air than hard action. Tallien at least seems more committed to action, though it remains to be seen whether the deal that he thinks he brokered late last evening with deputies from the Plain and the Right will hold under pressure in the light of a new day.

The city's inhabitants, moreover, are blissfully ignorant about the crisis brewing within the political elite. They are under the impression that they are waking to a 9 Thermidor that really is just another normal day in the history of Revolutionary Paris.

05.00/5.00 a.m.

Streets leading to Les Halles (Marchés)

T he sun rose at 4.22 a.m. this morning and it is already getting light at Les Halles, Paris's central market. For a couple of hours now, carts bearing produce to sustain the city's everyday life have been trundling through the gloom to this place 'where Morpheus never sprinkles his poppy-dust', as Mercier once put it. Despite extensive recent development of the built environment in the centre of the city, one only has to walk a mile or two outwards from the square in front of Notre-Dame cathedral, which marks the centre of Paris, to find vegetable plots, fruit-trees, and market gardens which supply Les Halles. They spill out profusely both sides of the so-called Farmers-General wall, built in the 1780s to mark the city limits. Wheat fields come up to Grenelle and Montrouge in the south, and in the north to Belleville and Montmartre. The latter boast vineyards as well as more than a dozen windmills. Clamart is famed for its peas, Argenteuil for its asparagus, Montmorency for its cherries, Montreuil for its strawberries.

The drivers of food-carts observe a strict embargo on noise: the city police have always striven to give Parisians a sound night's sleep. Produce arrives at Les Halles along set itineraries: the Rue d'Enfer in the south, and the Rues Saint-Martin and Saint-Denis in the north, with Rue Poissonnière the route for bringing fresh fish from northern ports. All are broad streets with street lighting, though the story is that the horses know the way by heart, allowing the drivers to slumber, whip in hand. Advancing under the same sound constraints are the carts which have left the great city hospital, the Hôtel-Dieu on the Ile de la Cité, bearing corpses along the Rue Saint-Jacques for interment at the burial grounds out at Clamart at the south-east edge of the city. Noise cannot be totally removed from the passage of these vehicles.

Horses' hooves, squeaky axles and an uneven roadway ensure that. Louis-Sébastien Mercier claims that such furtive dawn cart-parades disturb many sleeping couples in houses along the route, who set about vigorously contributing to the city's demographic vitality.

Teams of municipal street-cleaners are also quietly at work. About this time too domestic servants go out and sweep the street. Street cleaning operations convey the contents of city latrines and gutters, plus mountains of horse manure out to the environs for conversion into fertilizer. Adding to the detritus are legions of domestic animals—getting on for a million cats, countless dogs, legions of poultry, rabbits, and cage-birds. All of these may provide dietary variation in tough times: the city's keenest pet-owners are the poor.

It is at this early hour too that a ghostly army of manual and semi-skilled workers seeking employment is walking from the outer sections towards the centre, where most economic activity takes place. Many day-labourers are heading for one of the main labour-markets of the city. The biggest of these is the old Place de Grève, now Place de la Maison Commune, situated in front of the former Hôtel de Ville housing the main municipal offices. There are also more specialized labour-markets too: porters and the like aim for the quais at the centre and east, while the Pont-au-Change attracts locksmiths.

The main thoroughfares along which this semi-silent army moves are densely dotted with coffee-houses, bars, and taverns. Many walkers stop for a *café au lait*. This has been the staple breakfast of the Parisian labouring classes for some decades now, though market porters at Les Halles still prefer a shot of cheap red wine or eau-de-vie. There is generally not much more than rudimentary sociability at this early hour. Being on one of the recruitment sites bright and early is advisable. Drink-fuelled unruliness will wait for a homeward-bound stop-off at the end of the day.

Bars and coffee-houses are largely male preserves at this hour. Women, in contrast, have a much stronger presence in another site of early morning sociability and exchange: the queue. Lining up outside food shops is not supposed to start happening till 6.00 a.m., but the regulation is widely breached: early birds may catch the worm. Police spies are an invariable, silent presence here, testing the temperature of public opinion at this early hour before moving on to pursue their *métier* elsewhere—in cafés, bars, marketplaces, public squares, gardens, and other sites where crowds gather. They are, however, particularly attentive to queues, as are any passing

National Guard patrols: for crowd anger about food can generate *murmures* in a queue that might trigger an *attroupement* (a gathering), or even a *rassemblement* (an unruly crowd) and lead on to a rebellion or an *émeute*, (a riot). The lexicon of popular discontent is finely calibrated.

'Queue' is a freshly coined word. It used to signify simply a tail or a pigtail; now it describes these solemn lines of glum, quietly muttering and complaining consumers. Right-wing newspapers mischievously claim that the word derives from 'gueux', meaning 'beggar' or 'good-for-nothing'. Such a derivation, patriotic journalists indignantly proclaim, is an insult to the dignity of the needy in a republican state whose constitution stipulates support for its poorer members. The 1793 Constitution inserted the right to subsistence among the fundamental Rights of Man for the first time (the 1789 Declaration had been more liberal than socially radical in its approach). Even though the 1793 Constitution is in abeyance in this period of Revolutionary Government, the Declaration of Rights that prefaces it is taken at face value. Ensuring that no one goes hungry is a serious political desideratum.

The constitutional commitment to the right to subsistence is grounded in an implicit contract made over the summer and autumn of 1793 between the Parisian sans-culotte movement and the Montagnard grouping within the Convention. The upshot is that in return for popular support, markets will be regulated in the interests of urban consumers. Prior to this, Montagnards in the Convention were as committed to the principles of free trade as any economic liberal. As late as February 1793, for example, even Robespierre was still loftily claiming 'the people should rise not to collect sugar but to fell tyrants', and denigrating popular concern with 'measly merchandise'. His antagonism towards calls for market regulation at that time was also fuelled by deep hostility towards street radicals, notably the so-called *enragés* headed by the radical priest, Jacques Roux, who advocated price-controls alongside more far-reaching schemes for social levelling. The pressing need to find ways of attaching the popular masses to the Revolutionary cause, however, especially with war under way, made Robespierre and his Montagnard peers change their tune. They adopted the *enragé* programme (while gaoling most of their leaders), that includes regulating markets towards favouring small consumers.

The symbol of the pact between government and people emergent during the previous year is the Price Maximum, the nationwide system of price-setting initially established in May 1793, and amended and extended on a number of occasions since. The Maximum purports to moralize and revolutionize trade by fixing prices and profits in a transparent and even-handed way. It sets a price for all commodities adjudged to be of prime necessity, based on a supplement of 33 per cent over 1790 prices, with further supplementation for transport costs and an allowance for wholesaler and retailer profit. It aims to deliver on promises to the urban consumer by reducing social inequalities and generating trade that follows the precepts of a moral economy in which fair is prioritized over free.

In the summer of 1793, under strong sans-culotte pressure for effective action against the aristocracy of wealth as well as that of birth, strict methods for the enforcement of the Maximum were established. First, a law of 26 July 1793 pushed through by Collot d'Herbois designated the death penalty for hoarding and created special 'hoarding commissioners' (commissaires aux accaparements) in each of Paris's 48 sections to lead the attack on wealthy merchants who sought to profit from artificially high prices. Second, in early September, a special, 7,000-strong 'people's militia' (armée révolutionnaire) was set up, composed in the main of radical sans-culottes, including many of the city's artillery companies. Its units scoured the countryside in the environs of the capital forcing farmers to bring their produce to market and, under the banner of terror, either requisitioned their produce or forced them to sell at low prices.

The CPS member who has been accorded special responsibility for making the Maximum work as well as presiding over economic policy generally is Robert Lindet, a tirelessly dutiful and effective operator. Judging that extreme circumstances justify special measures, he has undertaken massive policies of requisitioning. One element of this is the practice of confiscating hoarded goods found in an individual's possession. Cn. Ducy, a wholesale merchant living in Rue de la Tour in the Temple section, for example, had his stocks impounded several weeks ago and just yesterday his sacks of flour were sent to Les Halles to be sold off at the Maximum price, while other dry goods (rice, vermicelli, lentils, beans, and so on) were despatched to the Hôtel-Dieu to feed the sick poor. But it is not only commodities that are subject to requisition. Property formerly belonging to the church (nationalized in 1790) and to émigrés is diverted to government use.

The CPS enjoys the authority to requisition labour as well as property. This is justified by the great law of 26 August 1793 instituting a levée en masse, effectively a conscription of national labour for the war effort. This extends beyond army recruitment to conscription of labour for war-related industries. Under the monarchy, Parisian manufacturing catered for well-heeled consumers within the city and was dominated by fashion, luxury goods, construction, and the food trades, plus a huge service sector. From 1793, government set about transferring personnel and skills from these sectors into arms manufacture. 'Ancien Régime Paris sold ridiculous fashions, innumerable knick-knacks, dazzling ribbons and furnishings,' proclaimed Barère. Now, in contrast, 'Republican Paris will become France's arsenal.' 'Let locksmiths cease to make locks,' Billaud-Varenne proclaimed, in much the same spirit. 'The locks of liberty are bayonets and muskets.'

The CPS established a central institution, the 'Paris Manufactory', to preside over this unheard of transformation. Extensive property and numerous workers have been requisitioned for the task, under the general supervision of CPS arms supremo, Prieur de la Côte d'Or, who has also mobilized elite scientists and engineers to help with standardized production, quality control, and greater efficiency. Hundreds of forges and foundries have been set up on public squares. Workshops are also established across the city, with much finishing work being done on boats moored off the Ile de la Cité. Saltpetre refineries in the abbey of Saint-Germain-des-Prés, in the Luxembourg gardens and out at the gunpowder factory at Grenelle, just beyond the Champ de Mars, are supplied with saltpetre scraped off the walls of cellars by enthusiastic teams of militants within the 48 Paris sections. French gunpowder production is six times higher than it was in 1790. In the first flush of enthusiasm, the government gave itself the task of producing a thousand rifles a day. They are only managing a daily 500, but even so, when cannon production and work on boots and uniforms are added in, this still makes Paris the foremost centre for military manufacture in Europe.

The government's industrial policy for Paris is all about production, meaning other considerations often get short shrift. Heavy industry makes streets and neighbourhoods dirtier, noisier, smellier, and more polluted than ever before. The deterioration in the urban environment is particularly marked in the upmarket Faubourg Saint-Germain. The elegant former homes of émigré nobles are a godsend for a government looking for factory space.

The Revolutionary Government prides itself on incarnating popular sovereignty, which makes the welfare of the Parisian population a key concern. In many ways what it has achieved in the city through a kind of command economy in highly unpropitious political and material circumstances is remarkable. Huge armies are being supported on all fronts, yet

employment levels in Paris are high and there is bread in the shops. 'We'd
have to be real buggers,' a police spy has heard a woman declaring in the
popular Courtille neighbourhood in the east of the city, 'if we didn't love
our [sic] Convention.'

   The comment reflects generally high levels of support across the city for
the egalitarian goals of the Revolutionary Government. CPS spy Rousseville's comment that the people of Paris retain confidence in the Convention
remains broadly true. There is an implicit, latent acceptance that material
sacrifices are acceptable if they are linked to winning the war against Europe.
This is partly an acknowledgement that French armies are fighting to save
Revolutionary social and political gains—the abolition of feudalism, personal
and economic freedoms, democratic practices, representative government,
and all the rest. But it also expresses an awareness of the number of Parisians
in those armies. Paris generated more volunteers than any other city in
1792–3, and then supplied huge numbers more in 1793–4 in the *levée en
masse*. A great many Parisian families have at least one family member under
arms, some more. Those who frequent the public galleries of the Convention know that the loudest cheers of the day always greet the announcement
of military victories. These are normally made by Barère, who loves gilding
the lily in stirring speeches that he calls his *carmagnoles*. If Robespierre's
speech yesterday was the event that electrified those sitting on the deputies'
benches, the public galleries erupted more rapturously at what happened
next: the presentation of enemy standards captured at the siege of Nieuport
in Belgium. Robespierre may even have left the chamber by the time this
happened: Barère's comment at the start of his celebratory *carmagnole*,
'Cursed be the moment when the successes of our armies are heard coldly
in this place' seems rather pointedly aimed at his colleague. Robespierre may
be unimpressed, yet popular thirst for military victories is unquenchable.

   The blood sacrifice that Parisian men risk at the front justifies belt-
tightening at home. All the same, belt-tightening, it is firmly believed should
be a universal requirement. It is a problem, then, when the very government
which instituted the Maximum starts to distance itself from implicit principles of social equality. Since the elimination of the Left-wing Hébertist
movement in the spring of 1794, the Revolutionary Government has tended
to follow Bertrand Barère's axiom that the aim of policy should be to
encourage trade and not to kill it. Significant revisions of the Maximum
have been introduced to allow greater freedom and to include the retail and
transport sectors. These changes are inflationary, and favour agrarian

producers rather than urban consumers, Maximum notwithstanding. The Law on Hoarders remains on the statute-book, and continues to have a deterrent effect at local level: anyone engaged in economic practices that militants in the sections judge as unfair risks having their names added to local lists of political suspects, and can end up in gaol. Yet the post of hoarding commissioner has gone, and economic offenders constitute a tiny group in the docks of the Revolutionary Tribunal. In addition, the Paris *armée révolutionnaire* was abolished in March 1794: it was held to have disrupted as much as lubricated trade, since its activities often degenerated into pilfering and pillaging hapless peasant farmers. Government now seeks to coax farmers back onto the Parisian marketplace.

The fear that in trying to balance social justice with economic vitality, the government is tilting in favour of the latter is confirmed by an accompanying shift of direction in government economic policy as regards wage regulation. Growing laxness in regard to farmers and merchants is accompanied by growing severity as regards workers. Government and private employers, in the interests of production, have been keeping a watchful eye on wage costs. In theory the Maximum imposes a ceiling on wages just as it does for prices; it is supposed to be 50 per cent above 1790 levels. In fact, a wage Maximum has simply not been implemented by the Paris Commune. This means that all wages in the city, not only in war manufacture, have drifted upwards, not least due to manpower shortages caused by mass war mobilization. Workers have still felt the pinch, however, and pushed for yet higher wages by petitions, strikes, go-slows, and so on. In February and March, port workers and other trades took collective action. Print workers in the state print shops adjacent to the Tuileries palace have also been involved, as have tobacco workers who occupy the former Hôtel de Longueville just across the Place du Carrousel from the Tuileries. After a lull, problems with other groups of workers arose, notably among workers in arms manufacturing.

One would think that sans-culotte pressure would be supportive of such moves. But there is less common ground over employment policy than one might think: the composition and ideology of sans-culotte elites tend to favour small-property owners over wage-earners. At the Commune, moreover, National Agent Claude-François Payan is unflinchingly tough on worker agitation. He imprisons strikers on public order charges, refers them to the Revolutionary Tribunal, and works closely with the CPS's Police Bureau. He views the industrial war effort as a patriotic campaign, so that any sort of resistance from below may be considered as an infraction of military discipline and patriotic altruism. For Payan, strikes are counter-revolutionary; strikers are enemies of the people.

In addition, the government's monetary policy aggravates matters for consumers and workers alike. The Revolution's main answer to the financial crisis which caused its outbreak in 1789 was the establishment of a paper currency, the assignat, secured against the nationalized lands of the church. But the government has endlessly struggled against its depreciation. Aware that the excessive issues around the currency have fuelled inflation, the government has committed to a policy of withdrawing them from circulation, celebrated in spectacular public burnings—an assignat bonfire of 20 million in notes has in fact been announced in the newspapers for today at 10.00 a.m. in the former Capucines convent. On the other hand, the assignat presses are never idle. Indeed the severity that the Commune showed insubordinate print workers this spring was partly motivated by the fact that many work on printing the assignats which are driving the economy.

The government worked hard in late 1793 and early 1794 to prop up the assignat so as to inspire economic confidence. Yet the value of the currency against metal has not ceased to decline, with the liberalization of economic policies from the spring of 1794 accelerating the downward slide. Wages are paid in paper (assignats) while those who have coin get discounts. Currency issues thus further fuel popular discontent.

In the bread-queues, complaints about a lack of revolutionary egalitarianism take on special force on an empty stomach. 'It is worth noting,' a spy reported one voice from the crowd saying,

> that if everyone shared the same dearth, then it really would be proven that there is a lack of commodities; but the people are saying that there are individuals stuffed with everything while those who really made the revolution, the poor patriots, are lacking life's necessities.

Ordinary Parisians have to content themselves with salted herring and vegetables, the complaints go, while the rich scoff salmon and pike, and *restaurateurs de luxe* serve up guinea-fowl, pâtés, hams, and turkeys. While the poor wait patiently in line, the wealthy access the black market for private suppliers or else frequent restaurants where for high prices and payment in coin you can eat for a week at one sitting. The fanciest establishments are in the vicinity of the Tuileries palace where the Convention meets, particularly in and around the Palais-Royal (now Maison-Égalité). Here, financiers and aristocratic hangers-on are to be found cheek-by-jowl, people are scandalized to discover, with deputies from the Convention. There still seems to be one rule for the rich and another for the poor.

Government policy, moreover, appears to be driven by the erroneous assumption that the poor live by bread alone. Certainly there are large numbers of Parisians who have to get by on bread, with a few vegetables and some scraps of cheese thrown in, and it is socially just to focus policy around the staple foodstuff of the majority of the French people. But over the course of the eighteenth century, the tastes of ordinary Parisians have changed, in line with a transformation of consumer behaviour affecting housing, furnishings, clothes, and fashion. People don't want to be fobbed off with staples. Once-exotic colonial produce such as sugar, coffee, and chocolate have come to be adjudged as mainstays. Symptomatically, Robespierre's first act on entering the CPS in July 1793 was to urge placing coffee on the Maximum on the grounds that it had become a popular necessity rather than an aristocratic luxury. The Royal Navy's blockade of French ports, however, has caused many of these products to become rarer and more expensive. Regret turns to anger when people see the elite paying huge off-Maximum prices out of reach of poorer households. Most food riots in Paris since 1789 have in fact focused on commodities other than bread (such as soap and sugar, in grocery riots in February 1793). Popular resentment of unequal distribution also affects attitudes towards prisoners in the city gaols. Aristocrats behind bars seem to be living scandalously better than the patriotic sans-culottes who put them there. This can't be right.

Issues relating to food consumption suggest that the equality preached by the Revolutionary Government is out of reach. The moral economy of the bread queue and the workplace seems to be at odds with a government that is strengthening its centralized clamp on workers and consumers while relaxing rules on trade and enterprise that benefit independent farmers, merchants, and manufacturers.

Anger drives protest. 'We are dying of hunger,' a police spy noted one worker complaining, 'while they mock us with pretty speeches.' This is an exaggeration, for there is no shortage of bread; but meat, dairy produce, oil, and tallow for candles are currently in short supply. Though overt royalism is rare, grumbling about the economy is often spiced with nostalgia for better days. The occasional counter-revolutionary voice is heard—'Fucking Republic, it's made us short of everything.' Radicals claim that the best way to bring back abundance to the city would be to place a guillotine on every street corner. In March, a CPS poster in an arms manufactory was defaced, with an anonymous hand writing 'stupid brutes', 'deceivers of the people', and 'thieves' and 'murderers' under the names of Prieur de la Côte d'Or and Robert Lindet, and 'cannibal' under the name of Robespierre. The Revolutionary Government and the Commune continue to vie with each other in expressing outrage against such deeds, that they ascribe to 'intriguers', 'aristocrats', and the like. But the culprits have still not been found.

There is a distinct danger of the Revolutionary Government losing touch with the people of Paris who, after all, put it in power in the first place. Two recent events underline this possibility. The first centres on the great French victory at Fleurus on 26 June. An undignified spat flared up over how this republican triumph should be celebrated. News of the victory generated a spontaneous movement of festivity throughout Paris. In the evenings, people across the city left their homes and set up impromptu street parties, lasting till almost midnight, with all participants bringing their share of food and wine and candles. These 'fraternal banquets', as they came to be called, played into a strain of patriotic militarism which predates 1789, but which has been intensified by the current conflict with Ancien Régime Europe.

At first the authorities welcomed these novel and rather touching festive expressions of popular patriotism. One newspaper caught the mood nicely when it described them as 'a first draft of the image of happiness that the Republic will represent when it has vanquished all its foes'. Yet national and municipal authorities were not slow to enforce a sharp about-turn. National Agent Payan at the Commune led the charge, waxing indignant at the banquets as evidence of an aristocratic plot to undermine Revolutionary Government by encouraging sans-culottes to think kindly of the very people they should be eradicating. Believing that the war will soon be over, scolds Payan, is a counter-revolutionary plot: 'You will only enjoy the sweetness of peace once you have hurled all these would-be friends of peace into their graves.' Robespierre has possibly been influenced by CPS spy Rousseville's opinion that the feasts 'involve great consumption and favour immorality and libertinage'. Robespierre concludes that the fraternal banquets are a case of the 'impure breed' tricking the 'virtuous people'. He and Barère have strongly backed up Payan in the Convention and the Jacobin Club.

The second episode which suggests growing divergence between government and people is the decision to enforce a Wage Maximum in Paris for the first time. Elsewhere in France, the imposition of the Maximum has related to both prices and wages, but in Paris the Commune managed to defer implementation of the wage restrictions of the legislation. It is the Commune which now leads the change. It accepted the need for the measure on 5 July, in the context of continuing worker insubordination throughout the city and CPS worries about production costs in war manufacture. A new schedule of wages was drawn up, and published just a few days previously, on 23 July (5 Thermidor). The Commune has made every effort get it out to the sections with great despatch. It has produced an immediate shock, for the new wage limits are set against a theoretical increase in line with prices, and this means often massive wage reductions. Carpenters will have their daily wages more than halved while those of the highest-paid blacksmiths in arms factories will be cut by nearly two-thirds. (Workers are happily not aware but while their wages are thus targeted, the salary of National Agent Payan and also of CPS office workers is about to be considerably augmented.)

There has been a swelling of discontent, even angry disbelief, among the working population about this measure. On 24 July, the carpenter François La Flèche, who runs a business in the Faubourg-Montmartre section, informed his 40 workers that henceforth he would have to pay them according to the schedule of the new Wage Maximum, that is, at half the current rate. This morning he is planning to go to the meeting of his sectional authorities to tell them his workers' response. He states:

> - If foodstuffs sell at the price of the Maximum, they will work, but for as long
> as food sells above the Maximum price, they won't.

And indeed the men have now gone on strike. This moreover could be the tip of an iceberg. For the Commune is receiving messages that a major demonstration against the Wage Maximum is planned to take place today, 9 Thermidor.

It is clear that the 1793 Montagnard/sans-culotte alliance hammered out in mid-1793 is currently under strain. Fleurus has put on the agenda the issue of how long the emergency regime of Revolutionary Government has to continue. There is a lot of anger about the Wage Maximum, it is true, but it is the Commune rather than the Committees of Government or the Convention that is getting most flak over it, as indeed over the fraternal banquets ban too. And it is national rather than municipal government that attracts popular plaudits for battlefield success.

06.00/6.00 a.m.

Robespierre's lodgings, 366 Rue Saint-Honoré

Robespierre is an early riser. Furnishings are sparse in his small rented upstairs room in the home of Maurice Duplay, and the ambiance austere: a table, four chairs, some well-stocked bookshelves, and many piles of paper. A bed covered by a blue counterpane with white flowers contrived from one of Mme Duplay's old dresses provides a rare homely touch. During the day Robespierre has the run of the house. The Duplays have kitted out a little side room on the ground floor which he uses as an office, and he is always welcome in the family quarters. His practice since Arras days has been to wake early and work until around 8.00 a.m. when he begins to attend to his toilette and get dressed for the day. In this sense, 27 July 1794—Robespierre tends to think instinctively in terms of the old calendar—is a day like any other, with its regular routines.

Robespierre is fortunate to be starting Mulberry Day, 9 Thermidor Year II, in a location he finds congenial, the home of someone he sees as a kindred spirit. When Robespierre comes home to the household of Maurice Duplay, he leaves much of his political public persona at the door. At 366 Rue Saint-Honoré, he finds a material, perceptible, and relatable everyday example of the hard-working, patriotic 'virtuous people' that he eulogizes in his speeches. Although Duplay prides himself on being a proud sans-culotte, he is no horny-handed son of toil. Born in a village in the Auvergne mountains, his move to Paris in his youth has allowed him to make his fortune. He sank profits from his carpentry business into property, increasing his wealth. Now, he gains political and social credit and status from housing the eminent Robespierre. It is surely on Robespierre's say-so that since late 1793 he has been a juryman on the Revolutionary Tribunal. Duplay's politics bring him work too. Jacobins are customarily suspicious of entrepreneurs, but Duplay's commitment to the republican cause makes him the kind that Revolutionary Government can do business with. He secures commissions to provide for Revolutionary festivals that now punctuate the calendar. Timber for these constructions is probably lying in the courtyard that Robespierre's bedroom looks down on.

Maurice Duplay takes excellent care of his tenant. He and his wife, both in their fifties, preside over a comfortable and contented household. Three of their five children live with them: Eléonore and Victoire and their teenage brother Jacques-Maurice, the benjamin of the family. Daughter Sophie's husband, the Auvergnat lawyer Antoine Auzat, is currently serving as army transport commissioner on the northern front, and at this moment the couple is stationed near the northern front. Sister Elisabeth is married to the dashing, blue-eyed young Philippe Le Bas, the friend and supporter of Robespierre also from his home department, the Pas-de-Calais, which he represents in the Convention. The couple's home on the Rue de l'Arcade, situated not far from the neighbourhood, is owned by Duplay senior. Elisabeth must frequent her parents' home a great deal, for since their marriage in August 1793, despite being elected to the CGS in October, Le Bas has spent nearly all of his time away from Paris serving as deputy on mission to the armies (though he did manage to be back for the birth of the couple's son on 16 June). In his most recent mission, Le Bas served alongside Saint-Just, who is also part of the Duplay circle. Besides his strong political affiliation with Robespierre, Saint-Just has also courted Le Bas's sister Henriette.

Also lodging at 366 for a year now is Maurice Duplay's nephew, Simon. Known as 'Jambe-de-Bois' ('Pegleg'), Simon lost a leg fighting the Prussians in the first of the infant Republic's most glorious triumphs, the battle of Valmy of 20 September 1792. Hailed by Goethe, who was present on the German side, as marking 'a new era in the history of the world', this battle had pushed back allied troops enough to allow the new National Convention to establish itself. It was the most significant French victory in the war against Europe before Fleurus. Following the young man's return to Paris, the unworldly Robespierre used him for secretarial tasks, including collecting his monthly salary as a deputy in the Convention, before procuring him employment in the CPS offices, in the Police Bureau, where he seems to find the work congenial. Simon's wooden leg shows that the Duplays have made the kind of sacrifice for the fatherland that is not at all uncommon in

Paris. It is a further symbol of their patriotic commitment and sans-culotte credentials.

The Duplays coddle Robespierre in a cosy family life that, frankly, seems more bourgeois than sans-culotte and is certainly far removed from the current acrimony of national politics. It is one of many paradoxes about him that although he places great store on the authenticity, sincerity, and transparency of the self he presents to the world, he seems an altogether less chilly and remote figure in the Duplay household. He is more human here, more likeable. He revels in being at the bosom of the family, revealing a facet of his personality that most of his peers scarcely imagine. The Duplays provide the kind of harmonious domestic milieu that Robespierre never enjoyed as a boy. His mother died when he was five years old, and his father abandoned his young family soon after, leaving him, his brother Augustin and his sister Charlotte to various relatives for their upbringing. At 366 Rue Saint-Honoré, Maximilien's benign disposition wins him the Duplay family nickname 'Bon-Ami' or 'Good-Friend'. He kindly defends the youngsters against the scolding of their mother. In the evenings, he reads them all poetry and extracts from the French classics—Voltaire, Rousseau, Racine, Corneille. The Duplays indulge his whims, moreover, keeping his linen spotless, serving him the *café au lait* and oranges that are austere Maximilien's little luxuries, and ensuring fresh supplies of butter and milk despite problems of supply caused by the Maximum. They are pleased to welcome select political friends and allies to dine at the family table and to share its leisure moments. The Duplay daughters stroll with him in the Champs-Élysées accompanied by his dog, Brount, and he occasionally picnics with them in the Jardin Marbeuf to the west of the city and in surrounding villages. He is so nice, so normal, so ordinary.

Although the Duplay provide him with a surrogate family, Maximilien is a thoughtful elder brother to Augustin whom he contrived to get elected to the Convention for Paris in September 1792. Aged 31, Augustin has always found it difficult to escape the shadow of his brother. Maximilien's scholarship to the Collège Louis-le-Grand in Paris was especially extended so as to accommodate Augustin, who followed in his brother's footsteps, going on to train as a lawyer in the city, before returning to Arras, as his brother had done. Here, Augustin energetically engaged in Maximilien's campaign for election to the Estates General, and himself continued along a political pathway, co-founding the Arras branch of the Jacobin Club and serving in local office, where he worked with Philippe Le Bas. His brother's decision to pluck him from his Arras niche and make a Parisian deputy of someone who had only visited the capital a few times confirms a pattern of dependency which it has proved difficult for Augustin to shake off. He faithfully follows Maximilien's political line on the issues of the day, but fellow deputies have quickly realized the extent to which his talents are inferior. He has a reputation not as a statesman but rather as a loudmouthed hothead with a proclivity for womanizing. 'All lungs, no brain' was Camille Desmoulins' unkind summation.

Moving out of shared residence with Maximilien at 366 Rue Saint-Honoré into lodgings of his own on the nearby Rue Saint-Florentin perhaps marked a move towards becoming his own man. Even more important in this respect has been his service as deputy on mission in the provinces, a role his desk-bound brother has never taken. Since returning fully to Paris from late June, Augustin has networked in the Convention and the Jacobin Club to promote his reputation, though not altogether successfully. He nurtures plans for a military offensive against Piedmont, which he developed at the front with Buonaparte, and which ultimately targets Vienna. But the CPS (from which his brother is absenting himself) has not taken his plans seriously.

Augustin's mind is perhaps currently taken up with an unhappy phase in his relationship with his sister. Charlotte Robespierre is three years younger than Maximilien and a year older than Augustin. She retains the habit into adulthood of calling her younger brother by the nickname of 'Bon-Bon' ('Sweetie'), partly by fond reference to his second name ('Bon'), partly as a nod towards his good nature as a child. In 1792, her brother suggested she come to Paris from their native Arras and she too moved into the Duplay household. It was not very long, however, before she and Madame Duplay fell out over who looked after Maximilien better. Feeling that their landlady had too strong an influence over her brother, she moved with both brothers to another apartment on the nearby Rue Saint-Florentin. Madame Duplay fought back, visiting Maximilien when he had fallen ill and then exerting emotional blackmail over him to return to the Duplay home. Maximilien guiltily conceded to his return with the wistful words, 'They love me so.'

Charlotte has now gone on to fall out spectacularly with Augustin. The tiff started when she was accompanying him on his mission in the south-east in late 1793. It worsened when on his second mission he took along his current mistress, a Madame Saudraye. The quarrel reached a point, following his return to Paris in June 1794, whereby Augustin left the Rue

Saint-Florentin lodgings he shared with Charlotte to move in with a fellow deputy near to Les Halles. Maximilien managed to pack their sister off to Arras, but she was back in Paris in no time, and since then has taken lodgings with a female friend. Her brothers have turned their back on her. 'She has not a drop of blood in her that is like ours,' Augustin wrote to his brother a few weeks ago.

It seems, moreover, that there are now two women between poor, misunderstood Charlotte and her beloved Maximilien. Hostile witnesses claim that Madame Duplay's motherly concern springs from a wish for him to marry their eldest daughter, the somewhat severe Eléonore. It is whispered that the two are affianced already or even that he has taken her for his mistress. Others are less sure. In his cell awaiting trial, Danton claimed Robespierre was a virgin who had no balls. In fact, Robespierre's sexual identity is a closed book, although his enemies resent how curiously attract-ive he is to women. From the public galleries of the Convention and the Jacobin Club, a strong female following dotes on his every word and applauds his every peroration. Robespierre pays—or affects to pay—no attention to such 'idolaters'. They are the price of fame. Robespierre has become a celebrity.

Robespierre has enjoyed celebrity status for some time. It is not just that his principled politics and obdurate defence of what he regards as the people's cause has won him fame, admiration, and even reverence among a wide array of Parisians. Nor is it just a question of him being recognized in the street, which he is (at least in the political bubble around the Tuileries complex). It is that people whom he has never met feel they are on intimate and affectionate terms with him. He is famous—and loved for being famous. This is how celebrity works. Augustin tells his brother with grim amazement how while on mission in south-east France he met 'thousands of intriguers who bombastically repeat your name, and claim to be on intimate terms with you'. Maximilien receives fan letters by the sackload. Entrepreneurial artists sell engravings and table-top busts of the great man and lockets with his image. Homages to his virtues are humbly and profusely offered. Since the Renault and Ladmiral assassination attempts, the Convention hall has endlessly resonated, and indeed still resonates, with letters from pro-vincial patriots praising his bravery. Ardent revolutionaries change their name to Robespierre—like the Montmartre sans-culotte, Charles-François Le Gentil, who now passes as Robespierre Le Gentil. Babies are named Maximilien or even Maximilienne. Robespierre is asked to serve as a godfather. Women offer their hand in marriage. People call their pets after him too (or at least prison gaolers do so: guard-dog 'Robespierres' ensure no counter-revolutionary escapes their jaws).

The Duplays more than indulge the celebrity of 'Good-Friend' Maximilien, with Eléonore leading the cult. Robespierre's bedroom may be spartan in its furnishings but in his little office on the ground floor and in the family salons are drawings, engravings, and multi-coloured busts and mementoes fabricated by the Robespierre bric-à-brac industry. The Duplays also seek to protect him from the excesses of the cult, and the other dangers of celebrity. For Robespierre receives death threats as well as fan mail.

> - Tiger covered with the purest blood of France, executioner of your country [says one]. This hand that presses yours with horror will pierce your inhuman heart...Every day I am with you; I see you each day; at any moment, my uplifted arm can seek out your breast!

With this kind of threat circling around Robespierre, the Duplay womenfolk form themselves into a protective barrier against the outside world. Would-be assassins may come to call. So the women patrol the Duplay courtyard, screening visitors, and turning many away. It is they who intercepted Cécile Renault when she appeared with her concealed penknives on 23 May. The women smelled a rat at once and called on men nearby to take her to the CGS offices. There are other, more recent suspicious incidents.

Is Robespierre really as much at risk as the fiercely protective Duplay women seem to suggest? Is he exaggerating threats to his person? Following meetings with him in late 1793, the actress and political radical Claire Lacombe (currently in gaol as a political suspect) opined that he was a coward with 'fear written in his face'. Since that encounter, moreover, Robespierre has become genuinely convinced that Prime Minister William Pitt and the British government are committed to using assassination of French republican leaders as a war strategy and that he is number one on their death list. 'Robespierre dreams conspirators,' Public Prosecutor Fouquier-Tinville tells a friend. His nightmares follow him into his daily life. He largely masters the tension and stress. His constitution has not broken down as it did earlier in the year. But his fears make him happy to acquiesce in the defensive barrier against the outside world that the solicitous Duplays provide.

Furthermore, for some little time now work acquaintances of Duplay and enthusiasts for Robespierre at the Jacobin Club have been forming another line of defence around him, accompanying him in the street, armed with wooden clubs. The three men who offered main force to conduct Cécile Renault to the CGS on the day of the assassination attempt were not idle bystanders but three prominent members of this protection group: Jean-Baptiste Didier, Charles-Louis Châtelet (or Duchâtelet), and Servais-Beaudoin Boulanger. Didier is a journeyman locksmith from Choisy, outside Paris and a family friend of Duplay's wife, who comes from the same village. When Didier came to live in Paris in 1794 it was said he lived in Robespierre's lodgings, though he then moved to the converted buildings of the former Conception monastery at 355 Rue Saint-Honoré, just around the corner from the Duplays. Châtelet, like Didier and Duplay a juryman on the Revolutionary Tribunal, was a moderately successful landscape painter before the Revolution and had worked on Marie-Antoinette's famous 'hamlet' in Versailles. Boulanger was originally an apprentice jeweller in the Saint-Eustache area, but became a high-ranking figure in the post-1789 army. Through sans-culotte links and service in the National Guard of his section, Halle-au-Blé, he secured promotion to a key role within the *armée révolutionnaire*. For reasons which are unclear, Robespierre offered him patronage and protection, and in the spring of 1794 he was attached with the rank of general as an aide-de-camp to Paris NG commander, Hanriot. This allows him to serve as a key Robespierre henchman.

Other members of the bodyguard group have all done sterling service within the Paris popular movement, many in Robespierre's own Piques section. They include Francois-Pierre Garnier Delaunay, a career lawyer and vocal Jacobin who has become judge within the Revolutionary Tribunal; Léopold Renaudin, a lute-maker by trade; and goldsmith Pierre-François Girard. The most prominent of them all is the printer Charles-Léopold Nicolas, whose protection of Robespierre goes back to Constituent Assembly times. A fervent Jacobin, Nicolas has used his political links to build a tidy fortune. He secured the commission to publish the Club's in-house newspaper, *Journal de la Montagne*, as well as the acts of the Revolutionary Tribunal (on which he is a juryman) and other commissions totalling well over 100,000 livres. It is his company in fact that printed the official Wage Maximum of 5 Thermidor which has so enraged Parisian workers. This is a reminder that the loyal group of Parisians who form Robespierre's milieu, and who are the closest to 'the people' that he idolizes, contains more bosses than workers.

Such men profit from Robespierre's long shadow, and can derive economic benefit from it (as Duplay and Nicolas well know) and political leverage too. Others probably like the vicarious celebrity it affords them. But there is altruism in the motives too. Girard, for example, freely admits that he does not get much gratification from the role: Robespierre treats many of the group arrogantly, as if they were not there. The only occasion on which Robespierre has addressed a word to him was to ask him the time. No matter: Girard views such protection as a patriotic duty necessitated by the current wave of counter-revolutionary assassination attempts.

It is very difficult to assess how substantial the threats to Robespierre really are. One suspects that what the Duplays and their milieu are partly at least responding to is their lodger's self-sacrificial rhetoric and his perennial talk of his coming death. The clash with his sister Charlotte suggests some degree of emotional overheating on all sides. Ambient stress within the household has reached Philippe Le Bas too. His new wife was recently horrified to meet a group of deputies including Bourdon on the Champ de Mars who threatened to kill 'Good Friend' Robespierre with their own hands. A few days ago, when she was out walking in the Jardin Marbeuf, her husband suddenly turned to her and blurted out:

> – If it wasn't a crime I would blow your brains out and kill myself too. At least we would die together. But no! we have our poor child . . .

Although one wonders whether Robespierre is even aware of it, the strain of living around his person at this tense political moment is having a depressive effect on the Duplay milieu.

For the moment, however, Robespierre is safe and sound in his little nook. Some of the bodyguard group will arrive later in the morning, after he has breakfasted, to walk with him to the Convention hall on this important day. He now sets to work before the family has risen and before Duplay's workers have entered the courtyard to start their daily routine. No one has ever imagined Robespierre idly daydreaming or twiddling his thumbs. If he is up, he is at work and today he has a speech at the Convention to prepare.

Robespierre's routines must help him to manage pressure. Despite the martyrish rhetoric yesterday, one doesn't make two two-hour speeches in a day if one is dropping with angst, fatigue, or moral exhaustion. He must be aware that he will need to be nimble on his feet, for yesterday's speech will have put his Montagnard opponents on the alert. Saint-Just's set-piece report is scheduled first on the agenda, but Robespierre will follow on. He is not exactly sure what Saint-Just will say, for the younger man has been completing his speech at the CPS offices. But the two see eye-to-eye, so he expects him to follow the lead he gave yesterday at the Convention. Both men will be looking for support from the centre-ground within the Convention as they seek to isolate the corrupt men in power.

This is not a bad moment to catch up with the newspapers as a way of gauging Parisian opinion. Yesterday evening's papers will have something to say about his speech. The *Messager du soir* reads:

> - Robespierre spoke early and unveiled the conspiracy which he has discussed in the recent meetings of the Jacobins. His speech is so important that it is impossible, in the small amount of space that we have, to provide even a rough idea of it or the discussion that followed.

This is disappointingly laconic. At least, Robespierre can reflect, they are not distorting his words as journalists have been doing recently, and he knows that his Jacobin Club triumph last night came too late to be included in the morning papers. In a day or two, though, newspapers will be ensuring that his speech, whose publication the Convention rejected, will be reaching a national audience. He accepts the time lag: he is not looking for immediate results or a quick fix. He is thinking beyond the window offered by the current day. Popular action takes time to mobilize, in which print and talk each have a role to play.

Reading newspapers has been one of the ways that Robespierre has kept in the political loop while he has been absenting himself from the CPS and the Convention. He has also been religiously attending the Jacobin Club and finds time to riffle through government papers brought to his home. Saint-Just comes regularly with files from the CPS offices. It seems that the business that has most preoccupied him at 366 Rue Saint-Honoré over the last six weeks are the affairs of the CPS Police Bureau. Simon Duplay, 'Duplay Jambe-de-Bois', is now an official on this body, and this also allows Robespierre to stay involved.

The CPS Police Bureau was established in late April by the law of 27 Germinal driven through the Convention by Saint-Just. It is placed under the CPS as a whole, but in the three months of its existence, it has been managed either individually or collectively by a CPS sub group consisting of Robespierre, Saint-Just, and Couthon. Robespierre monopolized its management through till early June while Saint-Just was away on mission at the northern front, and he and Couthon continue to play a part after Saint-Just's return.

The Bureau is set up in a way that resembles the semi-detached arrangements that Carnot provides in the CPS for the armed forces, and Lindet for food supply. As in those cases, other members of the CPS are routinely brought in for signatures, invariably without discussion or consultation. Unlike those other areas of special responsibility, however, the Police Bureau has powers that overlap seriously with the work of the CGS, which has general responsibility for national policing and security. Originally tasked with surveillance only over erring state functionaries, the Bureau now deals with police issues of all kinds. It grows too. Currently office staff, working under Augustin Lejeune, who prides himself on his friendship with Saint-Just, number around 50.

Most CGS members resent the Bureau as a rival, and share their bad feelings with like-minded CPS members. Robespierre's tendency to keep his cards close to his chest exacerbates the problem. Whereas Saint-Just does not rule out working with the CGS, Robespierre systematically refuses to refer business their way. Indeed, he seems to be angling for greater autonomy, nurturing links with other more compliant bodies. One such is the so-called Commission du Muséum, a Popular Commission of the sort that he and Saint-Just advocated bolstering in the 22–3 July truce negotiations. Another is the powerful Commission of Civil Administration, Prisons, and Tribunals, established after the abolition of the ministries in April. The chief of that commission is Martial Herman, fervent admirer of Robespierre. Another Robespierre follower, National Agent Payan at the Commune, also coordinates closely with the Police Bureau on security matters. The Bureau seems to have the monopoly of the services of police spies like Rousseville and Guérin, authorized by the CPS as a whole, but reporting, as far as it is known, principally to Robespierre and Saint-Just. Robespierre recently placed a gendarme at the entrance to the Bureau's offices, which are situated on the second floor of the Tuileries palace, directly above the main CPS offices. The simple message, even to his government colleagues: keep out.

Despite internal differences, the CPS has always respected its ethos of collective responsibility. Yet the Police Bureau plays fast and loose with this approach and Robespierre observes his own rules, engendering suspicion, misunderstandings, and conflicts. His critics fear he is establishing the Bureau as a parallel policing body and a private fiefdom, even a launch pad for personal power. Robespierre closes down sectional committees in Paris where he suspects peculation (and where criticisms of himself are voiced), only for the CGS to overturn his decisions. The institutional inefficiency of government is being compromised by internecine hostility. In his speech in the Convention yesterday, Robespierre went out of his way to minimize his role in the Police Bureau. Yet by signally under-representing the scale of his involvement, he has increased rather than diminished suspicions. The most striking product of these tensions has been the affair of the wild prophetess and Robespierre-worshipper, Catherine Théot. Rather than ride out the potential ridicule that would come his way if her trial went ahead, Robespierre acted unilaterally, instructing Public Prosecutor Fouquier-Tinville to drop the case. Affronted by this slapdown, CGS member Vadier, who had brought the affair forward in the first place, is using the episode as an anti-Robespierre propaganda weapon in the committees and across the Convention.

It is ironic that Robespierre's involvement in the work of the Police Bureau raises suspicions about his ambitions. For although the remit of the Bureau is wide, there are precious few cases that rise above a mind-numbing level of pettiness. Robespierre's enemies may fantasize about him creating a well-oiled and hyper-efficient bureaucratic machine, but the fact is that the vast majority of cases that he sees are utterly humdrum: an official filling his pockets, a drunk bad-mouthing the CPS, an elected officer overstepping his authority, small-scale denunciations, the whingeing culture of the bread queue, and so on. He despatches most with marginalia which rarely get beyond the laconic: 'Arrest', 'Require more information', and the like. The Police Bureau, as it has been working under Robespierre's partial management, is far from the launch pad for the seizure of power that some deputies may fear.

Robespierre's experience of micromanaging the moral and political minutiae which forms the basis of the Bureau's business gives him the sense of being close to the realities of the Revolution on the ground. It must stimulate him to reflect on how much there remains to do to bring the French people up to the appropriate political and moral level for this epochal Revolution. The 'virtuous people' is still under pressure from the 'impure breed' he so detests. Proper civic education will be essential, as will the kind of new social institutions that Saint-Just is currently mapping out.

The moment certainly does not seem right for any relaxation of terror. The people are not yet ready. Robespierre's speeches yesterday made it clear enough: the Revolutionary Government must remain in place; the Revolutionary Tribunal must be given every support; laws against enemies of the Republic on the battlefield and anywhere else need to be properly enforced.

Rights are for tomorrow; terror is for today. The 'virtuous people' need to be protected from their enemies by continuing institutions of terror, and by Robespierre's continuing vigilance on the people's behalf. This encompasses a burning wish to extirpate enemies of the people wherever they may be found, even among his erstwhile colleagues.

The Convention session yesterday showed Robespierre that his colleagues are happy to pin his back against the wall. But a good night's sleep has restored his spirits. He is not letting stress weaken him. And he can take consolation from the fact that he has been in similar situations before, and lived not only to tell the tale but also see his policies and the Republic triumph. In the past, reactionary aristocrats and then enraged Girondin supporters threatened him with physical violence. In October and November 1792, the Girondin Louvet de Couvray launched a vicious and well-supported attack on him as an 'object of idolatry' and 'dictator', charges not so very different from what he now faces in the Convention. Robespierre had seen off Louvet and all the others in style. Why should he not do the same to his conspiring enemies on Mulberry Day? His best defence has always been his belief in the people—and their belief in him. The response he got in the Jacobin Club last night has confirmed for him that this lifeline is still very much intact. With the people on his side, what has he to fear?

07.00/7.00 a.m.

Municipal offices, Maison Commune
(Maison-Commune)

As one of the clerks who serves the committees of the Paris municipality, Blaise Lafosse has a busy day ahead of him. He is already at his desk in the Maison Commune, the old Renaissance city hall or Hôtel de Ville, located on the Right Bank towards the east of the city. He has to complete the minutes of the Municipal Council which met three days before, on 24 July, and then put the final touches to preparations for today's meeting that is due to start at 1.30 p.m. The Municipal Council is 48 strong and takes executive action on municipal matters. Today's agenda includes items as diverse as the disposal of street rubbish, the removal of faecal matter collecting around the Ile des Cygnes to the west of the city, watering the boulevards so as to keep dust under control during the summer months, a new uniform for the fire services, nursing personnel within and the supply of eggs to the Hôtel-Dieu, Paris's great hospital, some financial and émigré issues, and so unglamorously on. Councillor Jean-Baptiste Avril will also be delivering an awaited report on the city's cemeteries. And they will have to look at the Bara and Viala festival to be held on 10 Thermidor, as plans are behind schedule. Though utterly mundane, this is the kind of routine business that allows the municipality to keep a city as huge and complex as Paris running. The extra time an early start provides will hopefully stand Lafosse in good stead.

He has come in early from his lodgings a mile or so away to the north of Les Halles in the Rue du Jour in Contrat-Social, one of the 48 sections into which the city is divided. These are the key units which ensure the city's administration, and they also form the base level of democratic involvement.

Since 1792, all adult males across the city enjoy the right to vote in national, municipal, and sectional elections. In Contrat-Social, the section's general assembly in which voting and other major sectional business takes place meets in the Saint-Eustache church, now a national property.

The sectional framework was set up in a rather haphazard way in 1790, and sections vary greatly in size and population as well as social composition and political complexion. The western sections of the city tend to house a more socially respectable population, though aristocratic emigration has thinned out elites in areas such as the Faubourg Saint-Germain. The outer ring of sections is normally larger and less densely populated. The average

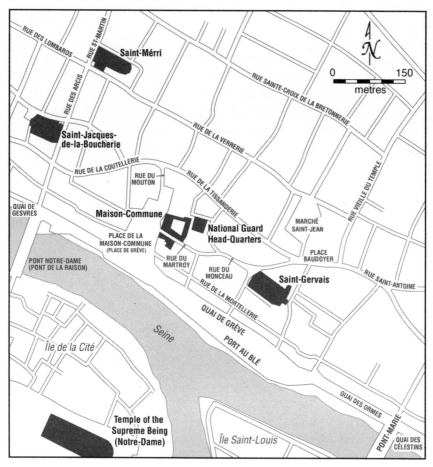

Map 3. The Maison Commune neighbourhood

population size of a section is around 15,000, though there is considerable divergence around the mean: Révolutionnaire on the Ile de la Cité and Fraternité on the Ile Saint Louis are among the smallest with around 5,000 inhabitants. More populous sections included Gravilliers on the Right Bank, and Panthéon and Unité on the Left, with more than 20,000 each. Originally the section names referenced local landmarks and though some of these remain in place (Invalides, Temple, Tuileries), other have been renamed 'patriotically'. Some names commemorated revolutionary heroes and martyrs modern (Marat, Lepeletier, Chalier) and ancient (Guillaume-Tell, Mutius-Scévole, Brutus), while others evoked revolutionary values (Fraternité, Unité, Indivisibilité, Réunion), constitutional and political points of reference (Droits-de-l'Homme, Contrat-Social, Montagne, Amis-de-la-Patrie), and sans-culotte associations (Homme-Armé, Piques, Bonnet-Rouge, Sans-Culottes).

If the Convention forms the national representation, the Paris Commune performs the same function for the capital city. The municipal 'parliament' is the General Council to which each of the 48 sections elects three members. In theory 144 members strong, the Council meets twice every ten days on the fifth and tenth of each *décade*, and offers a forum for speech-making and policy decisions. Its composition offers few points of resemblance to the well-heeled municipal assemblies of the Ancien Régime. Indeed, the old privileged orders are remarkable by their virtual absence from its current membership. Only a handful of councillors have a smidgeon of noble blood, and such has been the recent strength of anti-clericalism across the city, there are very few churchmen either.

The only priest, or rather ex-priest, on the General Council at present is Jean-Pierre Bernard, who has renounced his vocation, married, and accumulated an impressive roster of paid roles: as well as an ecclesiastical pension and the emoluments he receives as caretaker of his former church, he serves as a head of administration in the Mairie and has just received a plum position in the saltpetre bureaucracy. Such cumulation of posts is formally forbidden, but not uncommon.

While bearing in mind the tendency in these egalitarian, sans-culotte days to deflate one's social standing, the General Council is largely populated by individuals from middling and even relatively humble social positions. Roughly one-third is made up of artisans and employees, and a further third are merchants and businessmen. They are established figures in the main, of middling age: less than 10 per cent are under 30, and two-thirds are in their forties and fifties. The doyen of the group is the 68-year-old architect Pierre-Jean Renard, while the youngest member is the wood-worker Jean-Baptiste Aubert, both from the Poissonnière section.

Writers and professionals (lawyers, doctors, etc) are disproportionately represented and are often vocal in the forum of the General Council. Pierre-Louis Paris, for example, self-proclaimed man of letters, is due to officiate at a wedding later today. There are a dozen painters. The great Jacques-Louis David, who organizes the big republican festivals, as well as being a deputy and member of the CGS, must be an inspiration to his fellow artists. Painter Laurent Cietty has secured contracts for decorations associated with the great republican festivals, and indeed is preparing the upcoming Bara and Viala festivities. Others, such as Jean-Léonard Faro, and Claude Bigaud, have simply thrown themselves into Revolutionary politics full-time. For them, as for the good number of councillors whose prior occupation was in the now languishing luxury trades (hairdressing, perfumery, fashion, and so forth), municipal office provides a more reliable income stream.

The Council includes a handful of wealthy individuals. These include Jean-Jacques Arthur and René Grenard, business partners in one of Paris's finest wallpaper production companies prior to 1789. From its base on the Rue Louis-le-Grand overlooking the fashionable western boulevards, the Arthur and Grenard firm had supplied wallpapers to the Royal Household. In sans-culotte circles, the hyper-enthusiastic Arthur probably doesn't men-tion his former client, nor one assumes does he draw attention to his purchase of national lands (that is, property confiscated from nobles and the church in the Revolution) out at Bercy which he has equipped like a minor country seat. At the other end of the spectrum, there are very few out-and-out workers. Jean-Guillaume Barelle from the Faubourg-du-Nord, paid 20 sous a day as a building worker, is something of an exception. The ninth day of the *décade* is workers' payday, moreover, so he may prefer a more relaxing recreation to transacting municipal business.

The Commune's governing body and its other committees meet in the Maison Commune, the former Hôtel de Ville. The building's florid Ren-aissance façade looks out on the Place de la Maison Commune, which many still persist in calling by its traditional name, the Place de Grève. 'Grève' means shoreline, and the southern edge of the square runs away to the edge of the Seine, where numerous docks are located specializing in receiving and stocking raw materials brought up along the Seine river-network from deep in the French interior. Before 1789, Paris's ceremonial head based here was the *Prévôt des marchands* (the Merchants' Provost). The Prévôt presided over bodies of worthies who performed many, but not all municipal tasks, as he shared power with the *Lieutenant général de police*, a royal nominee with ministerial-level authority and an exceptionally wide remit of responsibilities. The two sets of Ancien Régime bodies were ousted in 1789, and Paris's municipality now has responsibility for the whole range of activities formerly split between them. Quiet at this early hour, Lafosse's workplace will soon become its normal bustling hive of activity, swarming with clerks, couriers, ushers, messenger-boys, porters, committees, and officials.

The Commune boasts not just an exceptionally wide remit but also a proud record of radical political action from the Revolution's very first days. It originated in the summer of 1789 as the city defended itself against a move by Louis XVI to bring the forces of Revolution to heel. The 407 Parisian electors to the Third Estate of the Estates General oversaw the city's defence and the storming of the Bastille, mutating in the process into a new, independent municipality headed by a mayor. It was at this moment that the national tricolour was created as the iconic symbol of the Revolution, combining the red and blue ceremonial colours of the city of Paris with the white of the Bourbon monarchy. The tricolour has survived the end of the monarchy, and currently bedecks every flagpole in the city and is the main element in the cockade sported on his red bonnet by every republican patriot, Cn. Lafosse included.

The overthrow of the king on 10 August 1792 was set in motion by radical members of a self-appointed Insurrectionary Commune ringing the tocsin from the Maison Commune's bell-tower. A new Revolutionary tradition thereby evolved, further exemplified in the *journées* of 31 May and 2 June 1793: when the Commune rings this warning-bell, Parisians rise up in arms to defend the sovereign rights of the people and to save *la patrie*. The Maison Commune's tocsin is supplemented by many churches throughout the city, though a large number of church-bells have been melted down for cannon in the war effort, transforming the urban soundscape. (Since they have gone silent, Mercier ruefully notes, they have never made more noise.) The ancient bells of Notre-Dame cathedral, now the 'Temple of the Supreme Being', are the most prestigious of those that remain. A supplementary warning operation that the country is in danger is the firing of the alarm cannon (*canon d'alarme*) set up on the Ile de la Cité at the middle of the Pont Neuf where the famous equestrian statue of Henri IV once stood. It was fired on 31 May 1793, a *journée* currently on many minds.

The Commune's iconic vanguard role within the Revolution is grounded in Parisians' active political engagement and democratic commitment. From 1789, the mayor and municipal officials were democratically elected, at first under a property franchise and since the overthrow of the monarchy under the principle of universal manhood suffrage. The principle of election extends from the top to the bottom of municipal governance—at least in theory.

One of the three elected councillors from each section is chosen to serve on the Municipal Council, meeting today. Sixteen of these 48 are designated as administrative officials and these compose the Municipal Bureau, which manages six major municipal services or departments: subsistence and food supply; finance and taxes; public works; public institutions; national lands; and police. The scale of these services is such that many are housed outside the Maison Commune: public buildings and national lands services are located in buildings adjacent to the city hall and around the Marais, while police, finance, subsistence, and food supply are housed at the Mairie (the mayor's offices over on the Ile de la Cité). The Maison Commune is the flagship heading a flotilla of municipal services scattered around the east of the city.

The members of the Municipal Bureau work collectively with regular officials to ensure the execution of municipal decrees and policies framed by either the Municipal Council or the General Council. The meetings of both the latter bodies are chaired by the Mayor, in the presence of the National Agent. While the Mayor serves as the high-level outward-facing representative of the city, the National Agent is effectively the chief executive officer of the Commune, with powers of surveillance and managerial oversight over the whole of its business and the entirety of its administrative staff.

The democratic principles grounding the Commune's activities have been attenuated within the last year. Under the Law of 14 Frimaire (4 December 1793), which enshrined the centralization of executive power on the CPS, elections became less frequent. Two-thirds of existing councillors were appointed by the CPS following resignations and deaths and also as a result of purges of political opponents and backsliders. Mayor Jean-Baptiste Fleuriot-Lescot was also put in place by the CPS in spring 1794 without election. Around the same time, the CPS appointed Claude-François Payan to the post of National Agent. The current incumbents of these two key posts wield considerable power as a result of being placed under the CPS, but they enjoy less freedom of action and independence than their predecessors.

Mayor Fleuriot-Lescot owes his prominent position to the Revolution. Born in Brussels to French parents in 1751, he trained as a sculptor and in 1789 was working in a modest position in an architect's practice. He climbed the ladder of political advancement with great speed, and was elected to the Commune by the Muséum section in 1792. Although without legal training, he was then appointed as deputy to public prosecutor Fouquier-Tinville in the Revolutionary Tribunal in early 1794 and subsequently, when the ministries were replaced by executive commissions in April 1794, he was awarded the Public Works portfolio. He had not been in post for a month before appointment to the Paris mayorship followed. His debt to the CPS, and especially Robespierre, who gave the appointment his blessing, is a guarantee of his fidelity. It is said that he would send his own father to the guillotine if it would advance him in Robespierre's favour.

Fleuriot's opportunistic placidity contrasts with the cold and controlled, yet restless energy of National Agent Claude-François Payan. Payan is a provincial. In the early part of the Revolution, he and his older brother Joseph-François threw themselves into local politics in their home department of the Drôme. Up in Paris on political errands, Claude-François caught the eye of Robespierre, who secured him a position at first within the CPS bureaucracy and then as juryman in the Revolutionary Tribunal. In the spring, he presided over the General Assembly in Robespierre's section, Piques. His assiduity and commitment to the cause have led to rapid promotion to the post of National Agent while he is only 27. At roughly the same time, his elder brother was appointed to a position in the national Education Commission.

There is a kind of political purity about the National Agent's commitment to the Revolution that must appeal to Robespierre (and make Lafosse feel he has a tough task-master). 'People are always saying to the judges, take care, spare the innocent,' he informed a political ally back in the Midi.

– But I say, in the name of the Fatherland, tremble for fear of saving one guilty person . . . individual humanity and moderation parading as justice is a crime.

The chilly certainty of purpose that informed his spell in the Revolutionary Tribunal has rubbed off on his general outlook.

Payan is one of Robespierre's 'adulators', but like Herman in the Civil Administration commission (and possibly Dumas, President of the Revolutionary Tribunal), he is also something of an intellectual who shares Robespierre's spartan but inspiring vision and speaks the same fierce language of patriotic virtue versus vice. Sometimes these men seem more like Robespierre than Robespierre himself. They take his black-and-white rhetoric as a prompt for action. Payan's categorical refusal to envisage the popular fraternal banquets movement as anything more than a dastardly aristocratic manoeuvre, for example, shows his dogged consistency of purpose. So does his uncompromising stance on labour relations. The vision which these men share is one of patriots combatting nefarious hordes of counter-revolutionaries, aristocrats, and conspirators. Justice for the patriots can only be achieved by making huge and bloody inroads into the ranks of enemies of the people.

A month ago, when the Catherine Théot affair was breaking, bringing Robespierre a good deal of criticism, Payan wrote him a long letter urging action that was so audaciously severe that he counselled Robespierre to burn it as soon as he had read it. Robespierre should, he urged, use the Théot imbroglio as a launch pad for reasserting authority within Paris. He should attack head-on not only Vadier and his cronies in the CGS, along with their bureaucracy for that matter, but also the raft of moderates and troublemakers within the Convention, such as Bourdon de l'Oise, who are generating calumnies of all sorts. In addition, he should not only crack down on journalists; he should simply take over the press so that public opinion will no longer be misled. This is the way to bring the people of Paris back onside. It is also the way to put the idea of dictatorship in Robespierre's head.

Has Robespierre replied? Is he mulling over this course of action? The letter must at very least confirm for him that the Commune is in loyal hands. In fact, Robespierre has already contributed very directly to making the Commune one of his strongholds. The CPS drive since the turn of 1794 to reduce the Commune's autonomy has the uniform support of members of the CPS, including Collot d'Herbois and Billaud-Varennes, who are often seen as champions of sans-culotte influence. Yet it is Robespierre who has directed operations vis-à-vis the Commune, overseeing the dismissal of key elected officials and closing down the neighbourhood political clubs which have always formed a key part of sans-culotte political sociability. He has also had the lion's share of responsibility for new appointments at the Commune, starting with Payan, the most effective operator and indeed the most formidable character in the core group.

The team of officials recently put in place has in fact been largely fished from a pool of names of proven patriots that Robespierre composed at some time in the spring of 1794. This has served as a handy vade mecum for a great many appointments. For the Commune, Robespierre recommended Lubin and Moenne to be Payan's deputies. The 28-year-old painter Jean-Jacques Lubin has served as Vice-President of the General Council under Pache's mayoralty, but subsequently come close to being compromised for his friendship with Pache and Hébert and rash statements such as his wish that half the members of the Convention be guillotined. He restored his credit by having a fellow citizen in his section, the Champs-Élysées, gaoled as a suspect for daring to say that 'Robespierre was marching towards a dictatorship through anarchy and oppression'. Yet Lubin's brother, still tainted by links with ex-Mayor Pache, is due to be referred to the Revolutionary Tribunal today, which must be preying on Jean-Jacques' mind. Jacques Moenne, the second of Payan's deputies, is another Robespierre 'patriot', a Lyonnais book-keeper who became an assiduous Paris Jacobin and is associated with sans-culottes from his native city who are close to Robespierre. His promotion vacated the post of deputy chair of the General Council, which has fallen to the 27-year-old Jean-Philippe-Victor Charlemagne, a schoolmaster and another ardent pro-Robespierre patriot.

Many individuals on Robespierre's list display more pro-Robespierre sentiments than relevant expertise or even technical competence. About Cn. Bourbon, chosen in April to be deputy clerk to the Commune, for example, little is known by anyone save for the fact that on taking his oath he decided, in an anti-monarchical flourish, to change his name to Fleury.

Blaise Lafosse has arrived at his office too early for this morning's gossip. He is doubtless ignorant of the turbulence of the meeting yesterday evening at the Jacobin Club. Both Fleuriot and Payan are Jacobins and may have been present there last night, though Payan will have arrived late after a visit to the theatre. Nor will Lafosse yet know about Fleuriot and Payan being summoned to the CPS offices in the middle of the night. Lafosse has much to do, but also much to catch up on. But at this moment, his focus is on just another day and just another committee.

7.00 a.m.

Place du Panthéon (Panthéon)

C arpenter Maurice Duplay's workers may well be arriving early today to complete the construction of audience seating around the entrance to the Panthéon, the name now given to the former church of Sainte-Geneviève, which towers over the Latin Quarter. Arrangements are behind schedule, and today's task is to get things finished for tomorrow's festivities that will honour the boy martyrs Joseph Agricol Viala and little drummer-boy Joseph Bara, who died heroically fighting the Republic's enemies.

It was Robespierre who in recent months took up the martyrdom of these two teenagers, and suggested placing their remains in the Panthéon (designated since 1791 as a shrine for national heroes). Robespierre's acolyte, pageant-master Jacques-Louis David, has been commissioned to choreograph the day. He has planned a huge multi-media spectacular, requiring participation by the people of Paris, with a procession between the Tuileries gardens outside the Convention hall over to the Left Bank, involving mass bands, singers, and dancers. There is a good deal of anticipation of the event. His own great painting, 'The death of the young Bara', is still far from ready, but theatres are already staging Bara and Viala-related performances, poetry is extolling their virtues, written accounts of the day are being circulated in today's newspapers, and engravings of the festivities (still yet to take place) may be purchased on the Pont-au-Change.

David laid out his plans for festivities several weeks ago, but management of the event has since gone badly awry. There has been quibbling about the time the festivities are to commence and about responsibilities for different parts of the day. The CPS realized that the Commune has fallen behind on planning, and pushed the Mayor into writing to all sections on 25 July, ordering them to convene a general assembly to allow the deputations to meet and rehearse their parts. The distinguished composer François-Joseph Gossec, who has written a patriotic hymn to be sung on the day, personally supervised rehearsals in the Brutus section yesterday. Sections are also being treated to musicians and choir boys and girls from the national institute of music to help with rehearsals. But on the evening of 8 Thermidor, Mayor Fleuriot-Lescot was still complaining that not all sections had received proper instruction. It remains unclear how far preparations have got.

A key ceremonial part in festivities will be played by the President of the Convention, a post to which deputies vote fortnightly. At the moment, the President is Collot d'Herbois, who currently has more pressing things on his mind. Robespierre too appears to have lost all interest in the business. Despite his leading role as sponsor of the festival, he made no mention of the fête in his speeches yesterday. Adding to problems, pageant-master David has been sick. Not too sick to have planned to take his own children to the festival. Nor too sick to have flamboyantly supported Robespierre on the previous evening at the Jacobin Club. But sick enough on getting home from the Club that night to take a medicinal emetic that will force him to stay in his bed on both 27 and 28 July. One wonders: is this a diplomatic illness? Does David already regret his promise at the Jacobin Club last night to drink hemlock with Robespierre?

7.00 a.m.

Jacques-Louis Ménétra's section (Bon-Conseil)

U nder a system of pork rationing introduced several months ago, some
300 pigs are led down to the weighing station at the hospital at La
Salpêtrière in the south-east of the city to be registered, numbered with red
dye, and then divided up and distributed to pork-butchers across the city.
Each of the 48 sections has a delivery every two days. The most populous
sections get most: the Gravilliers section on the Right Bank and the Panthéon section on the Left, each of which contains a population of between
20,000 and 25,000, get eleven pigs, and the least populous five per delivery.
There has been some consternation in recent days about how this rationing
system is working at ground level and in a number of sections officials are
coming in early today to sort things out. No one wants an unruly queue.

Sectional officials and committees play a crucial part in the mundane
workings as well as the democratic processes of the city. Elections for the
municipality are probably less valued by local people than those conducted
in sectional general assemblies for the committees dealing with intra-
sectional business. Each section elects a Civil Committee, established in
the immediate aftermath of the summer crisis of 1789. Their form and
membership have changed in a number of ways since then, but they remain
a key part of neighbourhood life, enjoying responsibilities for law and order,
public health and welfare, and with ensuring citizens go safely about their
business. The twelve committee members tend to be solid citizens who
command local respect. Each committee's president (a rotating office)
presides over the twice-decadal general assembly of the section and has the
right to convoke extraordinary assembly meetings in times of crisis. The post
has been salaried since May 1794. The daily allowance of 3 livres will not

enrich anyone at current prices but may offset losses caused by the Revolution.

Currently presiding at (or chairing) the Civil Committee of the Bon-Conseil section, which is adjacent to Contrat-Social, north of Les Halles is 50-year-old glazier, Jacques-Louis Ménétra. Prior to 1789, he specialized in the manufacture of lanterns and street lamps. He is still full of tales about a rollicking youth spent tramping France in his *tour de France* apprenticeship learning new glazing techniques interspersed with bedding honest house-wives, undefended girls, and frustrated nuns. To hear him, his life then was a chronicle of night-time escapades and fights with the city watch, spiced with rollicking bouts of drunkenness and good cheer. He has a nice turn in anecdotes: he played tennis with a Prince of the Blood, and chess with *philosophe* Jean-Jacques Rousseau, hobnobbed with public executioner San-son and then had the little Dauphin watching his antics while he mended broken windows out at Versailles, and so on.

Ménétra has put such rumbustiousness behind him to become a solid citizen. A pillar of his section's National Guard force, he is the elected deputy to the sectional justice of the peace as well as President of the Civil Commission. A matter of days earlier, he just failed to get himself elected to the Commune's General Council, losing out to his friend Antoine Jemptel. He consoles himself by playing a role in the sectional Beneficence Com-mittee which dispenses poor relief to his needy neighbours.

Though unsalaried and usually appointed locally rather than elected, the members of the sectional Beneficence Committees are among the hardest working of local officials. They provide a more flexible system for aiding the poor than the well-meaning but formulaic (and invariably underfunded) schemes of central government. A municipal endowment which they sup-plement with charitable income allows them to provide assistance for the sick poor but also for the old and infirm, pregnant women and nursing mothers and the families of the temporarily unemployed, as well as the families of 'defenders of the fatherland' (that is, soldiers). They continue Ancien Régime traditions of charity, but in a now expansive, secularized form that seeks to be responsive to all citizens in need (not simply dutiful Catholics). They play a role in giving the poorer classes a sense of civil entitlement associated with the egalitarian mission of the Republic. Méné-tra's whole life has revolved principally around Number One. But he has been moved in his mature years to appreciate what the Revolution has achieved: a Republic that strives to take care of its citizens.

As Civil Committee member, Ménétra is, in theory, well situated to ensure citizen rights are respected, and to defend the people against their enemies. In practice, there is now a rival for this role in the form of the section's Revolutionary Committee. A decree of the Convention on 21 March 1793 established what was then called a 'surveillance committee' within each commune throughout France, and within Paris in each section. Their initial surveillance role was focused on foreigners and outsiders, but their powers were much extended during the political crisis of the summer of 1793. In particular, Revolutionary Committees draw up lists of political suspects in accordance with the Law of Suspects on 17 September 1793, and can arrest and imprison at will. They dispense *cartes de sûreté* (in essence identity cards) as well as 'certificates of civism' (*certificats de civisme*) for those needing patriotic validation. Many committees use their powers with quiet authority in a way that maintains the peace and keeps counter-revolutionary manoeuvres at bay. But they can also serve individual interests. There is outright corruption going on in some sections. The Revolutionary Committee in the Bonnet-Rouge section, over on the Left Bank, is running a veritable racket, covertly requiring kickbacks from potential suspects. More frequently, key figures on the committees use their authority to build up or maintain a following through patronage.

Such practices were a staple of neighbourhood life under the Ancien Régime. But they now have a deadly tinge. For the Revolutionary Committees' powers of arrest, imprisonment and identification of suspects can blaze a pathway to the guillotine. This has been increasingly the case in the last year, particularly as deadly conflicts within the political classes, not least those involving the Dantonists and Hébertists, have produced a ripple effect of distrust at local level. Jacques-Louis Ménétra has felt the mood changing towards fear and suspicion. He has a sense that anyone now with even one foot in public life is being watched, and that past conduct is being measured by a yardstick of republican virtue. In these circumstances, Ménétra glumly realizes, withdrawing from public life has become more dangerous than staying in. He is careful not to refuse any posts that come his way.

With the strong pressures towards centralization and conformity coming from the CPS (and in a diluted way from the Commune), local sectional life is less vibrant than it was. Yet moves towards government centralization risk sapping the vitality out of the sans-culotte movement. It makes one wonder: is the whole popular movement that has been so crucial in pushing the Revolution forward in decline?

08.00/8.00 a.m.

École de Mars, Plaine des Sablons, Neuilly

A few weeks ago, 17-year-old Hyacinthe Langlois was sent by his department in Normandy to join France's new military academy, the École de Mars. It is located on the edge of the Bois de Boulogne to the west of the city, on the so-called Plaine des Sablons close to the village of Neuilly. Education is a key element in the Revolutionary Government's mission to transform the hearts and minds of French men and women. Robespierre has long advocated imaginative reforms (though recently the subject has slipped down his list of priorities). It was his CPS colleague, Bertrand Barère, who in early June steered a plan for the École through the Convention. Every department was invited to select half a dozen of its most patriotic youths for training in the new École in the three branches of the military arts (infantry, cavalry, and artillery) so that they can become future republican heroes on the field of battle.

Some 80 pupils will come from the city of Paris and it will not be hard to find recruits. Arms, cannon, uniforms are everywhere; cavalrymen cavalcade on the boulevards; drill parades take over public gardens; beautiful women hang off every brocaded military arm; tricolour flags flutter in all public places; even children join in the fun, making grenadier hats out of paper, using sticks as weapons and marching up and down to improvised drumming.

The École will be less fun. Composed, Barère insisted, of nothing but 'tents, arms and canons', the École is a spartan encampment—or rather Sparta revisited by Enlightenment notions of classical Antiquity. The École's commander, Louis-Florentin Bertèche, is a character who could have been lifted from ancient annals. Made famous for receiving 42 Prussian sabre wounds about his person as he saved his general's life in the battle of Jemappes in 1792, his dark, mutilated face and hands must frighten the boys as much as they would instil fear in the enemy. (Though he is unaware of the fact, he is on borrowed time, as unrelated denunciations of him have reached the CPS, which is taking steps to dismiss him.)

On arrival, recruits have their hair unceremoniously cropped. Tears have sprung to many teenage eyes as the pigtails and tresses which they believed to be authentically republican are cursorily removed. Jacques-Louis David has been invited to design a new style of uniform for them: Roman tunics and cuirasses with Scottish kilts and a Prussian shako (plus a short stabbing sword on the ancient Roman model) in an improbably colourful *opéra-comique* mélange.

At this moment, there are around 3,500 boys in the encampment organized into Caesarean 'centuries' and 'thousands' rather than regiments and companies. High wooden palisades keep the world out, forcing villagers from Neuilly to make a detour around the camp perimeter in order to reach Paris, and they occasionally lob rocks and stones over the wall in protest. Neuilly is becoming a refuge for aristocrats and there are fears of a brothel opening up in the village to service the École. On the reports of CPS spy Rousseville, more than a hundred villagers were taken into custody as political suspects. The École's instructors—veterans devoted, it is said, to Hébertist views and the bottle (not necessarily in that order)—encourage fears of hostile forces who will break into the camp and slaughter them all. The boys are anxious about this implausible claim. They experience a greater risk to life from within the camp: poor-quality rations and deficient water supplies have started to cause deaths from dysentery. Discipline is fiercely enforced, so it is little surprise that some boys begin to wonder what they have let themselves in for: they miss their families, and 'nostalgia' (the doctors' term for pathological, sanity-threatening melancholic homesickness) causes some to mope and go into decline.

The boys have been up since dawn today. Reveille at 5.00 a.m.—deafening cannon shot, drums, and trumpets—discourages slouching. There are theory lessons later in the day, but much of the morning is spent in drills and exercises within the camp. Langlois is particularly pleased to have been chosen to be among the delegation of boys who will have a place of honour, marching behind the deputies of the Convention in the city tomorrow, on the decadal rest-day of 10 Thermidor for the processional festivities associated with the pantheonization of their role models, the young martyrs Bara and Viala. Their effigies are displayed prominently alongside a massive statue of liberty in the huge hall in which they have their classes.

Despite his pride and enthusiasm at being selected in this way, Langlois shares the homesickness afflicting many of his peers. On one occasion, he was found weeping by a delegation being shown round by the Montagnard Jean-Pascal Peyssard, one of the deputies chosen by the Convention to run the École. Among the group was a thin, pale man, elegantly dressed and coiffed, whose eyes blinked as he addressed the lad through his spectacles, to ask what was the matter. When told the cause of the distress was an ill-fitting uniform, the man instructed Peyssard to procure him a new one. Langlois must be grateful for this act of kindness. It came from Maximilien Robespierre.

Does Robespierre see the École, as some in Paris have started to whisper, as a kind of praetorian guard for himself? It is surely relevant that one of Robespierre's favourites, Philippe Le Bas, son-in-law of his landlord Maurice Duplay, has been appointed alongside Peyssard to command the camp. And Robespierre's doctor, fellow Jacobin and juror on the Revolutionary Tribunal, Joseph Souberbielle, is in charge of medical services. But if Robespierre does have such designs, he is conducting them with implausibly secret efficiency. Indeed, the worry in the Jacobin Club, expressed in debates on 24 July, is that it is Carnot who is plotting to use the École against the city of Paris, and presumably against Robespierre. Rumours about the large number of siege cannon being brought to the École ostensibly for artillery lessons for the boys have set alarm bells ringing.

None of these wild suppositions, we can be sure, has reached Hyacinthe Langlois and his friends. One wonders whether Le Bas and Peyssard give them much credence either. At any rate, the boys are eagerly looking forward to their proud parade on 10 Thermidor to celebrate Bara and Viala. If they consult their Revolutionary Calendar, they will see that the Day of the Mulberry is followed by the gloriously unmartial-sounding Day of the Watering Can.

8.00 a.m.

The streets of the city

Wile the boys out at the École de Mars are currently agitated by the prospect of the Bara and Viala festival on Watering-Can Day, those of their Parisian peers who work as newspaper vendors are fanning out across the city. Workers based in the city's print shops, mostly located on the Left Bank in the Marat section and around the Palais-Royal on the Right Bank, have been busy overnight producing this morning's newspapers, and they now are on their sleepy way home, passing a wave of shop assistants, clerks, functionaries, professional men, and the like streaming into the heart of the city to their places of work. The paperboys are carrying their wares to the addresses of subscribers or else hawking their stock on the street. They yell this morning's headlines as they go, so as not to be drowned out by the familiar shouts of other street traders alerting households to their arrival: the milkmaid's '*À la crème!*', the water-carrier's '*À l'eau! À l'eau!*', the broom-maker's, '*Balais, Balais!*', the market gardener's '*Ma belle salade!*'. The silence of the early hours has long gone.

News-boys, who number in their hundreds, jostle for custom: there are 51 newspapers currently being produced in the capital. Although some are specialist journals and not all publish daily, there is a great deal of variety and volume on offer on today's streets: this is proof that the freedom of the press, one of the most cherished of the liberties accorded by the Declaration of the Rights of Man, is not as extinct as some critics of Revolutionary Government claim.

The freedom of speech proclaimed in 1789 has brought French citizens a larger, richer, and more varied textual, visual, and aural diet than ever before. In 1789, Paris boasted only one daily paper that carried political reportage. As soon as the Revolutionary crisis hit, numbers shot up: there were 184 new titles in 1789, 305 in 1790. The number of print-shops increased three- or four-fold. The boom in new titles and a huge growth in readers have massively extended the parameters of democratic debate. For since 1789, the main news that newspapers carry is politics.

Print also acts as a relay to other forms of political communication. Speeches and sermons are published as pamphlets or else reworked as posters that litter walls and monuments. Songs exist in printed form too. The Revolution inaugurated a vibrant singing culture. Just over a hundred new songs were published in 1789; the figure for 1793 was 590 and numbers for 1794 look like they will surpass that. Theatre has felt the dynamic winds of change too: the pre-1789 system of tight state regulation ended, and the number of theatres in the city expanded strikingly, to nearly 40 in total. This also means more plays than ever before have published form, allowing authors to reach a big audience outside the places of performance.

Since 1789, print interacts productively with other sociable activity: political clubs, reading rooms, NG posts and guardrooms, popular societies and sectional assemblies, as well as taverns and coffee-houses, family settings, street corners, parks, public gardens, and the like. These offer a hugely expanded number of venues where the printed word, often read aloud, is absorbed and subjected to keen debate. Print gets everywhere and lubricates the processes of participatory citizenship inside and outside the home. Paris provides a disproportionate share of national newspaper production, while literacy rates are at their highest, and theatre audiences and newspaper subscribers at their most numerous here too. Significantly, many journalists who made their names in Paris in the early years of the Revolution have turned their celebrity to political advantage and been elected to the Convention, sometimes by departments far from the capital.

Freedom of the press has taken some hard knocks since 1789, and so have journalists. Royalist and aristocratic journals were closed down in the aftermath of the overthrow of Louis XVI in August 1792. Pro-Girondin titles were next to go, over the spring and summer of 1793, and these were followed by those associated with the victims of the factional trials of March and April 1794. Journalists who have seen the scaffold in the last year or so include not just royalists but also Girondin luminaries like Brissot, Gorsas, Fauchet, and Carra; left-wing critics of Revolutionary Government such as Jacques-René Hébert; and Dantonist moderates including Camille Desmoulins. Others either died in gaol (Jacques Roux) or are still languishing there (Mercier).

The guillotine and the prison cell act as a strong brake on free political expression. Since the spring, newspaper editors have been particularly careful to stick close to the government line. Editorial comment and opinion pieces are increasingly squeezed out by simple factual reporting: the staples of most newspapers are news of victories at the front, the proceedings of the Convention and the Jacobin Club, and lists of those executed by the Revolutionary Tribunal, plus the roster of this evening performances at the theatre. For key items, editors often delay reporting until they have checked text in the *Bulletin des lois*, or else papers that observe a strict Jacobin line. The politically marginal *Correspondance politique de Paris et des départements*, for example, alert to the sensitivity of the Law of 7 Prairial (26 May 1793) which, on Barère and Robespierre's prompting, prohibited the taking of British prisoners of war, explained to its readers that it would provide a verbatim rendition of the law without further commentary, on the grounds that 'its smallest details are interesting and so the least reporting error would be dangerous'. Such editorial caution is understandable.

A particularly sensitive danger zone surrounds Robespierre, whose extreme touchiness over misreporting is notorious. In the early years of the Revolution, there was no more ardent proponent of free speech and a free press. He promoted an elevated view of the role of newspapers, along with schools, popular societies, civic festivals, and military service, in enlightening public opinion and leading the people towards virtue. In the interim between the Constituent Assembly and the Convention, he even tried his hand at journalism himself, editing *Le Défenseur de la Constitution*.

As time has gone on, however, Robespierre's views have gone into reverse. Open counter-revolution and external and internal war, he now feels, place too much pressure on such free institutions; the survival of the state comes first. 'Freedom of the press,' he was reported as musing in the Convention following the expulsion of the Girondins in mid-1793, 'is only for times of tranquillity.' Indeed he inscribes in his private notebook, 'We must proscribe writers, as the most dangerous enemies of the people.'

It was the Girondin attacks on him that confirmed Robespierre in the view that it is often the alleged champions of the Revolution who are its worst and most pernicious enemies, deliberately spreading calumny, stimulating error, obfuscating the truth, and misleading the people. By January 1794 Robespierre was proposing the public burning of all copies of his schoolmate Camille Desmoulins' dissenting news-sheet, the *Vieux Cordelier*. Desmoulins' coruscating repartee at Robespierre's expense—'*brûler n'est pas répondre*' ('Burning isn't an answer')—contributed to Robespierre's role in despatching him to the guillotine a few months later.

Desmoulins' chastisement has not caused Robespierre to moderate his hatred for journalists. Any thought that the execution of the Dantonist and Hébertist factions in the spring would make politics more transparent and authentic has proved sadly incorrect. The problem persists. 'How can it be permitted,' the pro-Jacobin *Journal des Hommes libres* has asked, that even though terror is the order of the day,

> – . . . large amounts of false news circulate from the centre of Paris . . . and carry uncertainty into the minds of patriots and serenity into the souls of aristocrats?

'False news' was very much Robespierre's complaint too. In a debate about a month ago he lambasted the bad faith of journalists working for the semi-official newspaper of record, the *Moniteur*, for blatant misreporting. In a recent speech, he pointed out, he had noted the claim made in English newspapers that he was accompanied by an armed guard when walking around Paris. He rebutted the accusation, casting his arms around to declare sarcastically 'As you can see, it is a most constant fact.' Yet he consequently objected bitterly that the speech had been completely misreported: the *Moniteur* had unaccountably missed the maximum irony that his words implied, giving readers the impression that he did in fact have a bodyguard. (This is a particularly touchy subject for Robespierre, given the fact that he is indeed often accompanied around the streets by a group of armed men.) The *Moniteur* defended itself by pointing out that its account was taken word-for-word from the *Journal de la Montagne*, the Jacobins' own in-house newspaper. But this clearly did not satisfy Robespierre. His fear remains that the Republic's advantage on the battlefield is being sabotaged by journalistic false-friends and covert enemies within the print media. Journalists are becoming the enemy.

> Whosoever has ideas about the Revolution and its enemies must grasp their tactic. They have several, but one of the simplest and most powerful is to mislead public opinion about principles and about men.

'False news' is being generated in London and diffused by the British government's journalist agents in Paris who spread corruption. It forms a key part of the Foreign Plot.

If Robespierre and his supporters are increasingly hostile to the workings of the freedom of the press under existing conditions, they also are manifesting similar scepticism about theatrical freedoms. From 1793, ardent Jacobins promoted the idea that the stage should be a forum for political pedagogy leading the people along the pathways of republicanism and virtue. A decree of the Convention on 2 August 1793 instructed all theatres to play every ten days state-endorsed plays championing civic virtue. It also threatened with closure any theatre vaunting anti-republican values. Theatre proprietors are put under pressure to stage CPS-endorsed pieces as well as other patriotic plays, whose stock features include republican homilies, depictions of heroic political *journées* and military victories, references to iconic figures such as Brutus and republican martyrs Marat and Lepeletier, with robust attacks on kings, nobles, non-juring ecclesiastics who have refused the loyalty oath to the Republic, and other stock villains. There is much audience participation in singing republican anthems before, after, and often during performances.

As well as this exhortatory pressure on Parisian theatres, the government also utilizes negative measures. As Joseph Payan put it in a co-authored report on behalf of the Education Committee within the last few weeks:

> Newspapers are like theatres; they have moral impact. For this reason they must be placed under some kind of control... [The shape of that control] relates to the very principles of freedom, and can therefore only be answered within the context of the principles of the Revolutionary Government and the supreme law of the safety of the people.

Thus bad dramatists should be subject to fierce repression as potential enemies of the people, in league with foreign powers. Joseph evidently sees eye-to-eye with his brother, Robespierre's confidant, Claude-François, the Commune's National Agent, for at this very time the latter has been urging Robespierre to take over the press and to repress bad journalists alongside the bad dramatists attacked by his brother.

Political orthodoxy is, however, proving to be even more difficult to enforce on the stage than on the page. The law of 2 August 1793 has been largely flouted. Currently, only half the new plays produced can be classified as 'patriotic'. Much of the other half is just traditional fare. Proving to be the most popular play of the Revolutionary decade in fact is Anseaume's *Les deux chasseurs et la laitière* ('Two Huntsmen and a Milkmaid'), a light musical piece composed in 1763, featuring two actors, an actress and a pantomime bear. The Ambigu-Comique theatre on the Boulevard du Temple staged it in the course of the present month, proving that even at this high-water moment of republican enthusiasm, Parisians often prefer entertainment to propaganda, and laughter to sternly austere republican exemplars. More than 50 plays have been produced since 1792 whose title contains the name Harlequin, as opposed to a mere two for Brutus. In republican theatre, Harlequin ranks over Brutus. And so does a pantomime bear.

Aware of the problem, the government sacked its two theatre censors for incompetence in March 1794. But their successors, Faro and Le Lièvre from the Commune's Police Administration, face the same problems. For it is not just a case of bad authors and bad actors, as Payan would have it, but also 'bad' audiences, who express their views in ways that challenge the censor. Parisians have long had a notorious propensity to find in scripts hidden political meanings which reflect the popular mood of the times. On visiting the city in 1779, the Scottish traveller John Moore had noted how

> by the emphatic applause they bestow on particular passages of the pieces represented at the theatre, they convey to the monarch the sentiments of the nation respecting the measures of his government.

This practice continued from Day One of the Revolution and is still in place. Indeed the case is sometimes made that the right to heckle is enshrined within the Declaration of the Rights of Man as a form of free speech.

Three *causes célèbres* during the period of Revolutionary Government have highlighted government sensitivity to what it views as inappropriate audience reactions to evocations of terror. The first concerned Marie-Joseph Chénier's *Caius Gracchus*, first performed in 1792. Later, in 1793, because of inappropriate audience reaction to the phrase, 'laws, not blood' it was dealt with severely. Chénier's *Timoléon* suffered a similar fate in autumn 1793. Here the trigger for government outrage was spotted in rehearsals, namely, the words, 'we need laws and morals, not victims'. It was also noted that one of the villains of the piece was taken to bear a deplorable resemblance to Robespierre. The play was withdrawn and Chénier was allegedly forced to burn the offending manuscript of his play in the offices of the CGS. Perhaps the most notorious case concerned the performances in August 1793 of the former deputy, François de Neufchâteau's stage version of Samuel Richardson's novel of sensibility, *Pamela*. The CPS had forced the theatre in question, the old Comédie-Française no less, to change the play's aristocratic protagonists into commoners, but even then there was a problem: the phrase, 'Ah! Only persecutors are to be condemned/ And the best of all are the tolerant', received thunderous applause. Furious at this 'uncivic' reaction, the CPS closed down the show and gaoled the playwright and the actors, whom it held responsible for the audience's reaction. Robespierre was particularly offended by the *Pamela* case, comparing the actresses involved to Marie-Antoinette and urging that they be treated just as severely (presumably by the guillotine). They are currently in prison awaiting referral to the Revolutionary Tribunal. But the shows go on—and so does the laughter and the pointed applause.

For Robespierre, the noise of laughter in Parisian theatres must be like a reproach to government. Sometimes that laughter simply expresses a frivolity of purpose out of touch with these austere republican times. But the further danger is that laughter is a sign of opposition and critique: not merely, then, a stinging admission of the failings of republican pedagogy to transform the immaturity of the people, but also a worrying sign of the penetration of the capital by enemies of the people and Foreign Plotters, desirous of corrupting the public.

Robespierre's critique of newspapers and theatres is often echoed by his colleagues in Revolutionary Government. Couthon, Collot, Barère, and Amar have all spoken forthrightly on the issue. Yet there is no doubt that, out of all those at the heart of government, it is Robespierre who is most preoccupied with the issue. The former champion of the free press is now its bitterest foe, and he communicates his anxieties to key followers such as Payan. His views about the prevalence of 'false news' are linked to his convictions about the seriousness of the Foreign Plot. Even before he gave up coming to CPS meetings, his colleagues noted, he had been dwelling obsessively on this question. His contributions all focus on 'arrests, newspapers and the Revolutionary Tribunal', his colleagues complain. His behaviour has made them increasingly irritated at his seeming unwillingness to put his shoulder to the wheel in the hugely demanding work of government. Yet, conversely, the failure of Robespierre's consistent efforts across the spring and early summer to convince his colleagues only strengthens his own convictions about the tentacle-like reach of France's enemies. Where the fate of the whole revolution is in the balance, unwillingness to take seriously the Foreign Plot and its machinations is coming to be, in Robespierre's eyes, a counter-revolutionary offence that could only be countenanced by an enemy of the people.

09.00/9.00 a.m.

Offices of the municipal Police Administration, Mairie, Ile de la Cité (Révolutionnaire)

—'Virtue is the order of the day!'

The command which Claude-François Payan, the Commune's National Agent and ardent Robespierre supporter, issued yesterday gave the city's police forces today's marching orders in unequivocal terms. The command is not an early stirring of Robespierre's political moves towards a republic of virtue. Much more banally, it is a call for the better policing of prostitution.

The Commune's idea of cleaning up the city overlooks the material filth of the streets so as to target what it regards as moral pollution. The triumph of virtue leads through the persecution of vice, in sex work as in more elevated political spheres. Since the overthrow of the king, the Commune has been determined to reverse the laisser-faire attitude towards sex evident in the early part of the Revolution. Payan is following Chaumette, his predecessor in post, in advocating an attack on public prostitution in all its forms from street-walking to pimping and brothel-keeping, and embracing issues of public health and venereal infection.

Government, both municipal and national, has little patience with women playing a role in public life. The promises of freedom of expression and the expansion of the public sphere after 1789 brought more women into public life than ever before. But since 1792–3, the movement has been waning. Attacks on prostitution and sexual irregularity form only the thin end of a much larger wedge of intolerance about women's presence in any form of public life. Women's most high-profile political association, the

Society of Revolutionary Republican Women, was banned in late 1793 and many of the most politically active women have suffered cruelly. Militants from the Society like Claire Lacombe and Pauline Léon are in gaol, while Olympe de Gouges, author of the path-breaking *Declaration of the Rights of Women* (1791), ended up on the scaffold, as did the Girondin *salonnière* Madame Roland. Théroigne de Méricourt has gone mad over it all, and is stalking Saint-Just by post. Influenced by the hyper-masculine military culture now in evidence, political figures stress a Rousseauist complementarity of gender roles which consigns women to the home. Even (and for some, especially) the women who frequent the public galleries of the Convention and the Jacobin Club may find themselves roundly assailed.

It is proving easier to drive women out of public life than off the streets, however, and Payan must realize that his conception of virtue as the order of the day has a long way to go before it is effective. Unsurprisingly, police cells this morning are not bursting with newly harassed sex workers. Achieving his goal is also not made easier by the heterogeneity of the city's police forces and their reporting structures. At local level, the National Agent can work on public order issues through the police commissary in each section, an updated version of the pre-Revolutionary *commissaires du Châtelet*, and in theory an elected office. These officials work alongside the sectional Civil and Revolutionary Committees and they are also under the orders of a number of other authorities, including the CGS and CPS. In addition, the city NG has a policing function, notably in night patrols across the city, in which literally thousands participate. The Guard reports to its Commander, Hanriot, who takes his orders from the Commune. There is also an elected justice of the peace in each section, who is an *ex officio* member of the sectional Civil Committee.

This morning's business for the city's police commissaries is characteristically humdrum. At 7.00 a.m., for example, the Droits-de-l'Homme commissary discovered that milkmaid Marguerite Thouin had brought into the city from Vincennes in her mule's saddle-bags not just standard, permissible amounts of milk, eggs, and butter, but also quality joints of meat destined for private clients on the Tuileries section. The police point out that this represents an infraction of the laws of the Maximum. Her protestations of innocence do not convince. At 8.00 a.m., there is another Maximum issue: illegal loading of goods on the Ile Saint-Louis.

Other morning business for police commissaries is equally mundane. In Gardes-Françaises, kitchen-maid Antoinette Roque has petitioned for her

30-month baby to be taken into the foundling hospital: she can't cope with single parenthood. There is a sad case over at the Invalides: a young lad swimming in the Seine has strayed out of his depth and drowned. In Bonne-Nouvelle, there has been a problem with a locked door that needed main force to open it to allow saltpetre collection. A rotting, disarticulated pig carcase is the problem needing solving over in the north-west sections of the city. The locals are stealing pieces for food, under the impression that as the meat is not yet sprouting maggots it must be safe to eat.

Despite the appearances of calm, however, the city authorities have been alerted to the strong possibility of worker demonstrations later today against the Wage Maximum which the Commune promulgated on 23 July (5 Thermidor). Hanriot put the NG on alert over the issue on 25 July. There is the additional worry that the protesters may come out tomorrow and ruin the festivities in honour of Bara and Viala. Although Hanriot originally rather pooh-poohed Mayor Fleuriot-Lescot's worries on this point, stating grandly that reason and good behaviour are needed in public festivities rather than armed men, Fleuriot is this morning insisting on a stronger NG presence.

The question of worker demonstrations has developed into an issue into which the Commune's own Police Administration will be drawn. The offices of this administrative service are located at the Mairie, the mayor's offices on the Ile de la Cité in the former residence of the senior magistrate (*Premier Président*) of the old Parlement of Paris. It is encrusted within a tangle of ancient narrow streets which join it to the Quai des Orfèvres. In 1792, the number of municipal councillors appointed to staff the police administration was four, but the sheer volume of the work that comes their way has led to an increase in numbers. Currently, they are 20 strong. Their key roles are the policing of suspects (in conjunction with the sectional Revolutionary Committees) and supervision of the prisons, domains that are closely linked. Individuals adjudged to be suspects may be imprisoned in one of the city's hundred gaols, which are currently creaking at the joints under the weight of prisoner numbers. Three-quarters of the 8,000 inmates are Parisians. The Law of Suspects of 17 September 1793 defined a political suspect extremely broadly, and the Commune's gloss outlined in October 1793 was wider still: 'Individuals who, without doing anything against freedom, have also done nothing for it'. To a large extent, the identity of a political suspect is in the eye of the beholder. And that can be perilous if the beholder is a member of one of the sectional Revolutionary Committees tasked with political surveillance.

The expansion of the number of Police Administrators has been accompanied by a high turnover in personnel. This is due to a mixture of political rivalries and proven charges of corruption. There was a major clear-out in the spring, partly as a consequence of an anti-Hébertist purge and partly due to the growth of CPS powers at the expense of the autonomy of the Commune. Only one of the 20 men currently in post was appointed before 1794, namely, Etienne Michel of the Réunion section, and even he has suffered a brief spell in prison. Nearly all of the newcomers have been appointed by the CPS, and they conform to the general pattern in containing a good admixture of individuals with links to or sympathies for Robespierre. They represent a decent enough cross-section of Parisian sansculotterie. A good number have backgrounds in the luxury trades (including three jewellers, two painters, two watchmakers, two tailors, a cabinet-maker, an engraver, and an artisan in mirror-making), while Michel is a manufacturer of rouge employing half a dozen or more workers. The literacy level of several is low. The Cologne-born cobbler Martin Wichterich (whose confiscation of prisoners' shoe-buckles so impressed his charges) is among the humblest and least articulate. 'Have patience,' he told a group of prisoners on one occasion with Delphic certainty and in very bad French. 'Justice is just, truth is true, and this lastingness cannot indefinitely last.'

The Police Administrators have been anticipating a busy day, what with Payan's new war on vice and the threat of a major Wage Maximum demonstration. But there is no sign of anything yet that is beyond the banal. The main business during the night shift has been the arrest of a couple of political suspects. At 3.00 a.m., duty administrators Faro and Teurlot sent out a squad to pick up a locksmith and his wife on the Rue des Lavandières in Muséum. The woman was found to have a coin with the face of the late tyrant (aka Louis XVI) on one side as well as some suspicious-looking keys: people have been guillotined for less. At 4.00 a.m. the same officers sent out an emissary with another arrest warrant, on an undisclosed charge. The sleeping hours are good moments to make discreet arrests.

Routine business this morning includes the overnight theft of a major cache of jewellery from a shop near Saint-Roch comprising watches, diamond bracelets, gold chains, necklaces, and so on, plus 30 to 40 *bonnets rouges*. (The thief must be a patriot.) Suspects have to be interrogated, but it is not a bad idea to let them stew in their own juice before starting to question them. There are imprisonments and prison transfers to sort out, and prison inspections to get under way. Alexandre Vernet, whom the Arsenal NG found sleeping outside their guardroom on the Rue de Birague early this morning, is discovered not only to be drunk and disorderly but also to have been missing his guard-duty back in his home section, Lombards. He is going to be sent to La Force prison, making 9 Thermidor a day for him to remember.

Administrator Teurlot made an early visit to the Abbaye prison to inspect the state of the drains. This measure of urban hygiene, evident in other prisons, has been interpreted by many inmates as a prelude to another round of September Massacre-style attacks. The sewers will become the prisoners' tomb: the rumour mill is in full flow. In the Bénédictins-Anglais, Mercier is shivering in his shoes. Yet nothing yet seems to indicate that the rumours have a foundation.

9.45 a.m.

Giot's itinerary: Rue de Hautefeuille (Marat), Panthéon (Panthéon), Temple prison (Temple)

Christophe-Philippe Giot boasts a very fine moustache. It is the sort that old soldiers wear, as is appropriate for a veteran who joined the army in 1759 to fight in the Seven Years War. Expansive, spreading across the face to join up with bushy side-whiskers and leaving only the chin bare, the moustache also approximates to the style favoured by ardent sans-culottes. Suspicions have recently been raised that aristocrats have been using such moustaches to hide their political views. But Giot is the genuine article. For his valorous actions on 14 July 1789 he was officially recognized as a 'Vainqueur de la Bastille', and since then he has been active in all the great Parisian *journées*. On 5–6 October 1789, 10 August 1792, 31 May 1793, and 2 June 1793, he was there; he helped ensure success. His reward has been promotion through his section (Marat) to the rank of Adjutant to the First National Guard Legion.

The National Guard is one of the most important institutions to have emerged from the Revolution in 1789. Since the early days of the Revolution, much political discussion has tended to focus on the Paris NG commander, a post initially held by Lafayette, and currently filled by François Hanriot. Below this is a body suffused with democratic and patriotic spirit. Its history has reflected the development of the Revolution itself, while it also has contributed to that history in significant ways. Originating as the bourgeois militia which in the summer crisis of 1789 both protected the city against the royalist threat and ensured the maintenance of law and order, it radicalized in tempo with the Revolution. During the summer of 1792 as the overthrow of the monarchy loomed and with the survival of the Revolution seemingly in the balance, calls for universal male suffrage were accompanied by the opening of the NG ranks to all adult males (and not only to those who reached the requirements of a property franchise). The *journées* of 31 May and 2 June 1793 are often saluted as an achievement of the people of Paris; but they were more accurately a triumph for the NG, whose intimidatory encirclement of the Convention forced the deputies to agree to the expulsion of the Girondin deputies. The right to insurrection enshrined within the 1793 Constitution burnishes the idea that it has become one of the inalienable Rights of Man. All citizens now bear arms as well as rights.

Since late 1792, the National Guard draws very heavily on the 150,000–160,000 adult males that a city of 600,000 can boast. Adolescents are exempt from service, as also are those aged over 60. Thus 70-year-old Floriban, the bourgeois rentier over in the Mutius-Scévole section obsessed with meteorology and guillotinings, regularly pays for a replacement when his time comes around. Then there are the state functionaries and members of sectional committees who also have exemption from service, plus the men fighting at the front. With these subtractions one reaches a level for the force of 116,000 men—four out of every five Parisian males, then. These are organized in nearly 1,000 companies, each of around 120 men.

The Guard's structure mirrors the administrative organization of the city into sections. Companies are grouped into 48 sectional battalions. (The number of companies in a battalion thus depends on the section's size.) A hierarchical structure to make the force more manageable groups sections into six Legions, each commanded by a Legion Chief, and each containing eight sections. The First Legion of which Giot is Adjutant, for example, covers the Faubourg Saint-Marcel (Observatoire, Sans-Culottes, Chalier, Finistère) sections, continuing along the Left Bank down to the Pont-Neuf (Chalier, Marat), and the island sections of Fraternité (Saint-Louis) and Cité (containing Notre-Dame).

In addition to this, there is one artillery company of up to 120 men in each section, with two cannon. The gunners have a separate reporting structure. They are headed by an Artillery Adjutant Major, currently Cn. Fontaine. The men cultivate a sense of themselves as a militant sans-culotte elite. Part of this derives from earlier involvement in the Paris *armée révolutionnaire*, notably in its role in conquering the rebel city of Lyon in the Federalist Revolt. One of Fontaine's aides, the training officer, Instructor (*Instituteur*) Cosme Pionnier from the Gravilliers section, is said to have been involved in the *mitraillades* against Lyonnais rebels.

Sectional battalion commanders rank with the presidents of the Civil and Revolutionary Committees as figures of sectional importance. Indeed, turn-out is usually higher for NG posts than for elections to civilian bodies. The erosion of the principle of election to sectional posts under the Revolution-ary Government affects the NG posts less too. Giot's section is highly politicized, which suggests he has garnered much respect. He lives on the Rue Hautefeuille, and at 8.00 a.m. this morning, left wife and children at home and walked up to the First Legion HQ, which is located close to the Panthéon. There he checked over the daily reports received from each of the sections under his Legion's command, signing that all was in order. A shower of rain shortly after 9.00 may have obliged him to delay his leaving, but now as the hour approaches 10, he is on his way to the NG Head quarters for the whole city, which is located to the rear of the Maison Commune on the Right Bank. Here, on the hour, he is scheduled to receive his orders for the day.

Giot's commander, First Legion chief Fauconnier, is already present at HQ, consulting with the other Legion chiefs. When he emerges, he informs Giot that he has assigned him three tasks for the day. First, that morning, he must organize a lottery within the Legion to select some 300 guardsmen to be present on the Place du Panthéon the following day to ensure good order for the Bara and Viala ceremonies. (So Hanriot has finally accepted Fleuriot-Lescot's concern over the issue.) Second, he will drill and rehearse the youth contingents of sectional NG companies in preparation for that festival. His parade-ground will be the open space outside the old Notre-Dame cathedral (now the Temple of the Supreme Being). Third, Fauconnier instructs Giot to do a tour of duty today at the Temple prison; he will have to fit in his parade-ground drilling around that. Giot sets out for the Temple, which is located in the north-east edge of the Marais.

The sinister gothic pile that is the Temple prison served as the headquar-ters of the Templar Order in the Middle Ages, before being adapted for more secular purposes. In 1789, it was part aristocratic housing complex, part manufacturing zone (whose artisans were exempt from guild restrictions) and part debtors' prison. It has secured a place in Revolutionary mythology, however, by being designated as the prison where Louis XVI was kept, along with his family, following his deposal in 1792. Since then, courtesy of the guillotine, the Bourbon family has progressively diminished: Louis XVI was executed in January 1793, Queen Marie-Antoinette in October 1793, and then Louis's sister, the saintly Madame Elisabeth, in May 1794. Only remaining now are the young pretender to the throne, nine-year-old Louis-Charles, and his elder sister, 15-year-old Marie-Thérèse.

The two children endure a life of melancholy solitude within prison walls. Left largely to her own devices, the princess rises from her bed around noon, while the former dauphin has been subject to a regime of political re-education which one imagines must seriously pain and confuse a child who has known more than his share of suffering. In July 1793, several months after his father's execution, he was removed from his mother and sister and placed under the care of Antoine Simon, a sans-culotte cobbler from the Marat section. Simon was under instruction from the Commune to give the child a life that would make him lose his sense of rank and entitlement. Yet he and his wife are in their fifties and have no children of their own, nor seemingly any idea what a normal upbringing is, let alone a republican one. He may in fact owe his appointment to the fact that he has worked as a herniotomist, for Louis-Charles does in fact require a herniary truss. The fact that the boy was bamboozled into testifying to the Revolutionary Tribunal in October 1793 that his mother had forced an incestuous relationship on him shows a child who has altogether lost his bearings. This episode seems to have pushed him towards mutism, which adds to his isolation. Things are not made easier by the ending of the arrangement with Simon, who in early 1794 decided to focus more on his responsibilities for the Marat section on the Commune's General Council. Since then Louis-Charles has been living with only his rough-edged guards as companions.

The Commune and the Convention seem to have given up the aim of making a little sans-culotte out of the boy-pretender. But they are aware of his and his sister's value as bargaining chips in any future diplomatic arrangements. They also realize that he would be a massively powerful symbol of counter-revolution were he to escape. One of the watchwords of the Vendée rebels in western France is 'Vive Louis XVII!'. The arrangements for guarding him are therefore punctiliously thorough. The prison regime is overseen by prison director, the ex-engraver François Le Lièvre. His brother, Jacques-Mathurin, also a former engraver, now serves on the Commune's General Council for the Lombards section. Both men retain a radical edge that dates back to 1793 when they advocated attacks on merchants without revolutionary credentials, and taught women how to pillage grocer shops. (Perhaps this is a tall story.)

Each day three members of the Commune's General Council who also are members of the Police Administration put in a shift supervising the prisoner. The arrangement is not popular. Louis-Pierre Tessier, for example, a dry-goods merchant representing the Invalides section, spent all of 25 July on sectional business and on the following day attended to issues at the Gros-Caillou military hospital within his section. But he was told at 7.00 a.m. on 26 July that he would also be obliged to do a tour of duty that night at the Temple. Leaving work that evening, he dropped in at his home to pick up his nightcap and a copy of the day's *Moniteur,* and to bid his family farewell, before trekking across the city to arrive at the Temple some time after 9.00 p.m. He is still there as midday approaches, when Giot will call to check over the establishment. One of the other two Police Administrators on the shift is Joseph Soulié, a poor tailor from the Gardes-Françaises section who, it is claimed, is illiterate and has only been placed on the Commune and the Police Administration a couple of months earlier at National Agent Payan's insistence.

The first things the Administrators do in taking up their position is to view the ex-dauphin and his sister, to ensure they are both present and correct. They also inspect the NG troupe, containing more than 200 men, who have been sent to protect the prison overnight. The Temple is one of the few neuralgic points in the city—the others are the Convention, the Maison Commune, the Treasury and the Arsenal—which require a daily NG force on rota duty. These additional duties tend to be drawn for by lot, on top of the regular service that guardsmen perform.

It is the Paris NG Commander, François Hanriot who has responsibility for these key areas of urban and national security. Along with Paris Mayor Fleuriot-Lescot (to whom he reports) and National Agent Payan he is one of the three most important figures in the city's life. Unlike them he can boast of election rather than CPS nomination. In a bitterly fought contest in July 1793, he prevailed over the choice of most political moderates, Nicolas Raffet from the Montagne section.

Despite these democratic credentials, Hanriot divides Parisian opinion. His lightning ascent since 1793 seems to confirm him as a man of the people, and he has a niftily demotic turn of phrase when it is needed. Son of a peasant father and domestic servant mother from Nanterre on the edge of Paris, he served as a petty customs official at the city barriers until 1789, when he played a role, it is said, in the popular attack on customs posts, and was briefly imprisoned for his efforts. Settling subsequently in the south-east corner of the city in the Sans-Culottes section within the Faubourg Saint-Marcel, one of the poorest yet most populous parts of the city, he built up a reputation and power base as a radical, and was elected commander of his section's NG battalion. He was hand-picked by the organizers of the *journées* of 31 May and 2 June 1793 to command the National Guard of the whole city, before subsequently winning the electoral contest for the post.

To his credit, Hanriot has played a key role in maintaining order over the last turbulent year. He is a well-known face on Paris streets, visiting sections, checking up on guard-rooms (he is particularly vigilant over erasing wall-graffiti that shame modesty), and the rest. His cheery daily bulletins, which are carried in many newspapers, are angled to go down well with the more radical parts of the working population. 'In a free country,' he instructs his men, 'law and order must be maintained not by pikes and bayonets but by reason and philosophy.' Appeals to a sans-culotte better nature can, however, achieve a jarring and at times almost comic level of sententiousness, on the lines of 'Brothers in arms, let us always be sublime and watchful!' or 'We republicans want only a cabin as our home and only good morals, virtues and love of the fatherland as our wealth.' Then there are some unreconstructedly Rousseauist views about women: they really should not make a fuss in queues and would be better advised staying at home, 'preparing soup and darning socks'.

Hanriot has enemies as well as admirers. Political moderates marvel at how he managed to steer clear of indictment with the radical Hébertists in March 1793, with whom he has always cultivated strong links. (The support of Robespierre may well have been a factor in this.) His elevation to the rank of divisional general caused mirth: this squat, dumpy, snub-nosed figure was not a proper soldier and had never fought a single campaign. But he loves colourful braided uniforms, and the fast horses that he gallops around the outer boulevards with little attention to pedestrian life and limb, and he flaunts his rank in the company of raffish aides-de-camp. Presumably it is for them and their mistresses that he has rented a box at the Opéra Comique costing 2,000 livres a year (at a time when the wage of a manual worker is a few livres a day).

Hanriot likes to throw his weight around. His NG command is linked to the rank of 31st Divisional commander, which also gives him command over all armed forces in the city including the gendarmerie, a mixture of mounted and foot troops, some 2,000 strong and scattered around the city. Hanriot regards the chief of the 29th Gendarmerie battalion, Jean Hémart, as disloyal,

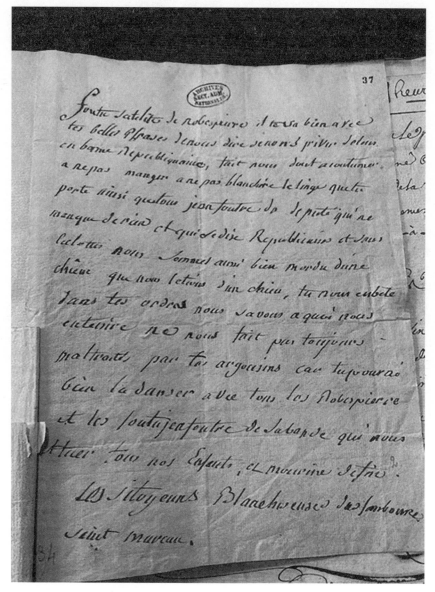

Figure 4. Petition of the Saint-Marcel citizen-washerwomen to National Commander François Hanriot, no date (AFII 47 pl. 368, pi. 37)

and used an accounting oversight as pretext for having him briefly incarcerated. Hémart only emerged on 21 July. Has this taught Hémart a lesson? Or is his blood still boiling? We may see later today, as Hémart was summoned last night by the CPS to ensure his support for them during the coming day, as they plotted to remove Hanriot from his command.

It seems that Hanriot's position may be going to his head. He has got wind of a denunciation of his behaviour to the CPS by one of the sections (he is trying to discover which one). On 21 July, an old acquaintance wrote to give him a friendly but firm warning about where his conduct might be leading:

> – Public opinion is starting to judge you harshly. People don't like your aides-de-camp with their epaulettes. Their insolence and your way of talking to people and presenting yourself when you go out together is displeasing even to those in the CPS who seem to protect you. Your time is coming to an end and you should save your skin if you can.

The 'citizen washer-women' of his native Faubourg are rather more direct:

> – You fucking Robespierre henchman. You've got a cheek telling us to be good republicans and to get used to doing without food or linen—that you and those fucking deputies wear, you who want for nothing and call yourselves republicans and sans-culottes. You pester us with your orders and you can go and be hanged along with all the Robespierres and his fucking band who are having our children killed and die from famine . . .

Yet if Hanriot's popularity may be on the wane, there is still continued respect for the institution he heads. Generally speaking, Parisians are proud to belong to a force with such an illustrious set of achievements in its short life. There is grumbling about tours of duty, which come around normally at the rate of one or two days a month, with additional demands, as for the Bara and Viala festival. 'Everyone does his guard-duty,' Mercier noted, 'the silly and the wise, the deaf and the attentive.' It is true that each battalion has a small number of full-time replacements. Yet even so, the Paris NG remains one of the most democratic institutions of the Republic.

The vitality and democratic spirit within the Paris NG contrast with the current state of many of the other municipal and sectional institutions. Over recent months, the CPS in particular has squeezed a lot of the energy and autonomy out of the sans-culotte movement. The government thoroughly approved the support that came from the sections in the transition to Revolutionary Government in 1793; but they do not want the sections behaving, as Collot d'Herbois put it, like 'a little republic in each section'.

Political clubs are moribund, or under the surveillance of the Jacobin Club. Sectional committees have been politically filtered by purges and many wallow in factionalism. General assemblies have been much weakened: they are only allowed to meet twice a week; there are fewer elections within them as the practice of CPS selection has become current; and they often seem to be run by small groups of local militants, some of whom sport personal agendas beneath their red caps and ideological statements, and keep a watchful eye over people speaking out of turn. The Commune has been effectively neutered as an independent force and brought firmly under the control of the Committees of Government.

The sans-culotte core of the popular movement is clearly suffering from the controlling actions of Revolutionary Government. Yet this has signally failed to quash public opinion within the city. The backchat recorded by police spies in queues, bars, and public places shows that. Then again, despite being under the censors' cosh, the press and the theatre both display defiant sparks of vitality. It is a matter of real import, then, that conversation and debate in NG guardrooms, in adjoining bars, and at parade-grounds is still pretty free. Solidarity is stimulated by the fact that companies are usually assembled topographically, so they reproduce neighbourhood friendships and solidarities. The Law on Suspects works against overt criticism of government. But paid government spies don't have access to NG guardrooms. Neither do sectional militants and government bureaucrats who claim exemption from guard service. To a considerable degree, the National Guard has retained its role as a site of discussion and debate within a city increasingly feeling the disciplinary and controlling pressure of central government.

10.00/10.00 a.m.

Revolutionary Tribunal, Palais de Justice,
Ile de la Cité (Révolutionnaire)

Antoine-Quentin Fouquier-Tinville, public prosecutor attached to the Revolutionary Tribunal, has been looking forward to 9 Thermidor. Not because of anything about the official business he has to transact on the day, but simply for the date. In the new Revolutionary Calendar, the 9th of the month (like the 19th and 29th) precedes a decadal holiday. It means that this evening there will be no business to prepare for tomorrow. The Committees of Government will be preoccupied with the Bara and Viala festivities. Tomorrow Fouquier will be free. Later today, he can start to relax. He intends to relax. Three days earlier, while celebrating the promotion of a colleague, Fouquier met Cn. Vergne, who lives on the Ile Saint-Louis, which now forms the Fraternité section. Vergne invited him to dine at his home today, along with several neighbours who include Fouquier's colleagues, Tribunal Vice-President Pierre-André Coffinhal and juror (and clog-maker) Charles-Huant Desboisseaux.

Coffinhal and Fouquier have paid the price for their notoriety across Paris: when out late one night a month or so ago in the Palais Royal they endured a disgraceful assault by a NG patrol who pretended not to recognize them. One trooper grabbed Fouquier by the throat in the guardhouse and shook him hard, while fellow guardsmen laughed at his discomfort. Dining in a private residence *chez* Vergne is thus probably safer all round. The rendezvous is set for mid-afternoon, by which time Fouquier can feel sure he will have responsibly discharged his duties by sending to the guillotine a few tumbrils-ful of those individuals shivering in the dock at this moment, as with clocks chiming he prepares to enter the main courtroom of the Palais de Justice on the Ile de la Cité.

If Fouquier is anticipating some leisure time after today's business, Tribunal President René-François Dumas's mind is focused elsewhere. Last night at the Jacobin Club, he led the cheering for Robespierre, targeting bitter barbs and menaces at Robespierre's enemies, Billaud-Varenne and Collot d'Herbois as the two men stumbled, humiliated and angry, out of the Club. He is hoping that this morning in the Convention, Robespierre will lead an attack against these and other enemies of the people. A purge of the Committees of Government and the Convention will bring a host of new victims to the Tribunal, where Dumas will be eager to do his bit.

There is an additional reason for Dumas's hopes that Robespierre will act decisively today: the magistrate is worried that his own life may be under threat. His brutal and sadistic manner in trying and sentencing has given him like Fouquier a dark celebrity in Paris. He cannot count on being safe on the street from those who want to do him harm or exact revenge for sentences passed on friends or family members. He has two loaded pistols on his desk in the Tribunal. At his home on the Rue de Seine (Unité), he has a peephole that allows him to scrutinize visitors for evil intent.

In addition, Dumas has heard that a few days previously, political enemies from his native Jura department have testified against him to the CGS. Dumas, their story runs, connived in his brother's emigration. The brothers were steeped in corruption prior to the Revolution. And Dumas has accepted bribes from defendants at the Tribunal in return for their freedom. Dumas is fighting back in the Jacobin Club against his enemies, who have inveigled themselves into the CGS bureaucracy. But he is at serious risk of being unmasked as a counter-revolutionary suspect. He is not at all sure whether his relationship with Robespierre gives him political immunity. Things are delicately poised and time is closing in. Swift action taken by Robespierre against Dumas's enemies in the CGS will be a personal blessing.

For his part, Fouquier will have been cheered by the stories about Dumas going the rounds, for there is no love lost between the two men. They are physically very different. Dumas 'the Red', ruddy-faced and flame-haired, contrasts strongly with Fouquier, who has dark hair, pale skin, and darting eyes. Fouquier had to fight Dumas off from displacing him as prosecutor a few months ago, and he hates the way his rival flagrantly cosies up to Robespierre, who seems only too receptive to his invidious whispering.

Yet Dumas and Fouquier have more in common than they would like to admit. Both are imperious, irascible characters, habituated to getting their own way, and unwilling to brook inefficiency or foot-dragging from their officials. Fouquier boasts that he has sent one of his clerks to the guillotine, if only *pour encourager les autres*. Dumas shouts down everyone in his court and treats his fellow judges with disdain.

Ironically, Dumas's offices in the Palais de Justice face on to the apartment of Fouquier and his family. Most nights, as Dumas makes for his home after working late, Fouquier beds down on a mattress in his office rather than return to his apartment and his wife and children and risk bumping into Dumas. He dines frequently at the Café des Subsistances, the refreshment stand or *buvette* within the court complex, where he can meet and converse with Tribunal colleagues, and pour out his troubles to the bar-staff. He rises early to breakfast here too. He was already champing at the bit by the time President Dumas was ready to stride into the courtroom to begin the day's procedures.

There are two sessions of the Tribunal, which run concurrently, both starting at 10.00 a.m. Fouquier has composed the indictment for both. His and Dumas's deputies are readying themselves to begin proceedings in the Salle de l'Égalité, located in the former criminal court of the Paris Parlement. Dumas and Fouquier will be in the Salle de la Liberté, which is located in the old Grand'Chambre, the ceremonial home of the former Parlement. It is now unrecognizably different, its ancient trappings and regalia replaced by wall posters of the 1793 Declaration of the Rights of Man and plaster busts of Martyrs of Liberty Marat, Lepeletier, and Brutus.

Dumas enters, followed by three subaltern judges, Cns. Maire, Deliège, and Félix. The men wear a tricolour cockade and sash over dark legal robes, while their headgear is crowned by huge black plumes. Maire and Deliège have a good amount of experience, but Félix is new to the job: though appointed by the Law of 22 Prairial, he only got back to Paris three days ago after meting out republican justice to the Vendée rebels in Angers, where he is said to have ordered the executions of thousands. He should feel more than at home in his new billet.

The judges dominate the courtroom from a raised dais at one end of the room. In the pit just beneath them sits Fouquier in solitary splendour, facing onto benches where the court clerks are seated. Before the Law of 22 Prairial, these rows were also occupied by 'unofficial defenders', private individuals who had volunteered to take on the role of defence ascribed by the law. These posts have now been abolished as part of the provisions of legislation carefully designed to facilitate convictions. To the right of the judges the defendants, just brought up from the filthy Conciergerie cells, sit docilely on benches which have been extensively increased and banked in order to cope with the growing numbers of the accused in each session. Across from them are benches where a jury of nine sits, drawn from a pool of 60 jurymen, nominated by the CPS. Whereas the Tribunal's judges have legal training as well as experience in presiding over subaltern courts, jurymen just have to be good patriotic citizens. Today, they include two carpenters and two shoemakers. All have patriotic backgrounds in local politics.

Although Fouquier is bound by law to oversee the trial selection of jurymen by drawing lots, in the case of high-profile and politicized trials he personally selects 'solid' jurors, who can be counted on to convict, whatever transpires. A good number of these men are associated with Robespierre: Maurice Duplay is his landlord, for example, while jurymen Nicolas, Didier, and Renaudin and judge Garnier-Delaunay count among his bodyguard. They have a reputation for shouting down and threatening with denunciation as aristocrats any juror who might incline to see a guilty defendant's point of view. Today no such precautions have been necessary and maybe lots have indeed been drawn, for the jurors are a random and unremarkable crowd. It must be anticipated that the session will be open and shut.

At the back of the courtroom, enclosed behind a rail at chest height, the public stands, watching judicial drama about to unfold. There is, it must be said, much less enthusiasm in the room than was once the case. Crowds used to build up excitedly through the day, with a huge number present for the sentencing. It was better than the theatre. But these days the accused are not even present at the later stages of their own trial, draining the day of much of its drama. Any remaining tension relates less to the actual court proceedings, than to the certainty that nearly all defendants will be mounting the scaffold steps to the guillotine. For some months now, the Tribunal has been 'a tribunal of blood', a machine designed to produce capital convictions.

The Law of 22 Prairial (10 June 1794), hastened through an irritated and fearful Convention by Robespierre and Couthon, has accelerated Tribunal procedure, overriding what the Law's sponsors saw as the pettifogging formalism of the court's actions thus far, and bringing the Tribunal more closely under CPS control. 'The time required to punish an enemy of the people,' Couthon stated, 'should be no longer than the time needed to recognize one.' The regulations that have most radically changed the atmosphere in the courtroom are the denial of the right of the accused to a public defender; the removal of the requirement to call witnesses and to have oral testimony in circumstances where guilt is demonstrated by the moral conviction of the jury (rather than material evidence); and the stipulation that the Tribunal has only two sentences to dispense: freedom or death.

The 22 Prairial Law has made it quicker and easier to identify and convict 'enemies of the people', but the increase in the numbers coming before the Tribunal has other causes too. The legislation is part of a wider move to centralize revolutionary justice in the capital: since April, all counter-revolutionary offences throughout France are supposed to be tried in Paris. Wagon trains from across the country now bring up hordes of offenders, worsening already serious overcrowding in the capital's prisons. In addition, Popular Commissions, set up in the spring, though still not fully operative, are assigned the task of filtering imprisoned suspects, and sending only those who seem obviously guilty to the Tribunal. Finally, since early June, the Commission of Civil Administration, Tribunals, and Prisons is permitted to refer suspects directly to the Tribunal. This has been done at the request of Robespierre's friend and admirer, the Commission chief, Martial Herman, and with Robespierre's explicit authorization.

Since Robespierre waved through the measures giving new powers to Herman, the supply of prisoners being referred to the Tribunal has mushroomed. Herman and his equally zealous second-in-command, Emmanuel-Joseph Lanne, consciously operate under the provisions of the Law of 23 Ventôse introduced by Saint-Just, which stipulated a death-sentence for prisoners fleeing or attempting to flee justice. Organizing an escape plot (or even thinking about it) seems to count. Heaven knows there are many individuals ill-disposed towards the Revolutionary Government to be found in Parisian gaols. There are real escape plots too, and only last night two inmates succeeded in breaking out of the Luxembourg prison. But Herman and Lanne use existing legislation against anyone who seems even to wish to be free, thus engendering plot denunciation from within the prison network on an industrial scale, as evidenced in the exponentially rising number of executions.

In the courtroom, the day's business begins with President Dumas reading out the list of the accused to ensure that all are present. One name on the list is not responded to. Dumas moves swiftly on to instruct the jury who, with right hand raised, take a solemn oath to do their duty. This done, he asks each of the accused their names, ages, professions, and their financial situation before and after 1789. Prosecutor Fouquier then stands to read out the indictment. He has received information about the accused from a range of sources: the CGS, Herman, the Popular Commissions and judicial and police bodies from throughout France. Fouquier is a stickler for legal process and takes pride in his compositions. However, he has been complaining bitterly at the lack of useful documentation coming through, especially from the Popular Commissions. Bureaucratic slip-ups are not at all uncommon. Characteristically, the man thought to be missing from the defendants today was in fact tried and executed several weeks earlier. The volume of defendants has swollen faster than Fouquier and his clerks can keep up with, and key documents often get lost in paper trails. Individual defendants are only given sight of their indictment the evening before in the prison, or even on the morning of their trial. This aggrieves Fouquier's sense of professionalism: he has to write indictments with little idea about the crimes alleged. Mountains of letters and petitions lie unanswered on his desk. But the big problem in his role as Public Prosecutor is a chronic lack of adequate documentation for the task in hand.

Fouquier's indictments against the 47 alleged enemies of the people today run through the standard legal phrasing for counter-revolutionary crimes in all its sprawling woolliness. They have conspired against the Republic by signing liberticidal decrees to favour Federalism, participating in plots organized by the king against the people's welfare, obstructing food supply, maintaining correspondence and intelligence with foreign and domestic enemies, emigrating, making counter-revolutionary remarks, and so, in this vein, on. Some 40 to 45 minutes later in the Salle de la Liberté, with the indictment out of the way, Fouquier sits down so as to allow President Dumas to lead with questions, first to five witnesses testifying on a handful of the individuals in the dock, and then to the accused. Dumas does not suffer fools gladly. In fact he does not suffer anyone gladly, and today he has additional, personal reasons for not beating around the bush. His questioning of the accused is always perfunctory and intimidating. Those who dare answer back are shouted down with a fury at which even Fouquier sometimes winces.

Trials in the Revolutionary Tribunal these days have little to do with establishing the truth. They have a ritualistic rather than a forensic air about them. The jurors have the right to ask defendants questions, but rarely do, as they tend to assume that the prisoners simply would not be here unless their guilt had already been established by subaltern authorities and tribunals. An aristocratic pedigree or a prior career in the church are additional grounds for presumption of guilt. Jurors have few qualms about the current practice of the *fournée* ('batch', as in a batch of bread ready for oven-baking), grouping together into a single bloc defendants from disparate backgrounds and with very varied offences against their names. A number of jurors seem distracted during the trials too, manifesting scant interest in the business in hand. Artists Jean-Louis Prieur and Claude-Louis Châtelet, for example, idly sketch the accused across the court from them. Even so, the jurors view themselves as the very heart and soul of the whole judicial edifice: the fact that they are, juror François Trinchard states, 'good sans-culottes, men of purity, men of nature' is the best imaginable guarantee of the legitimacy of revolutionary justice. Patriotism trumps legal forms when it comes to adjudicating counter-revolutionary crimes.

After some basic back and forth, Dumas's task is to resume the questions on which the jury must come to a decision. Once this is done, the jurors will retire to consider their verdict. Before 22 Prairial, trials were sufficiently complex that a meal-break was taken at 3.00 p.m. and the court resumed at 6.00 p.m. That has not happened for quite some time. Despite the growth in the number of defendants, the *fournées* tend to be tried with much swifter despatch than earlier trials. The fact that Fouquier has already conferred with the public executioners to bring six tumbrils to the Conciergerie courtyard by early afternoon shows a degree of certainty about the outcome. Very soon after, Fouquier hopes to be off to his anticipated dinner, while Dumas will be free to join in events which are about to unfold in the National Convention, where, with his fingers crossed, his eyes (and his hopes) will be fixed on Robespierre.

10.00 a.m.

Thibaudeau's route: from Rue Hautefeuille (Marat) to the Tuileries palace

A couple of hours after his neighbour, First NG Legion Adjutant Christophe-Philippe Giot, has left for his day's work, Antoine Thibaudeau, deputy for the Vienne department, emerges from his rented rooms, which are also on the Rue Hautefeuille in the Marat section. He is on his way to today's session in the Convention hall, in the Palais-National, formerly the Tuileries palace, on the other side of the Seine. It is a 25- to 30-minute walk.

Thibaudeau left the Convention hall in the early evening yesterday after hearing Robespierre's long tirade, feeling depressed and anxious about the political situation in which the Revolution finds itself. The night has been long and hard. He ruminates what today will bring. Although he habitually sits on the Montagnard benches and contributes to the Convention's Education Committee, he has always cherished his independence, and feels an outsider to the faction-fighting taking place among his fellow deputies. He is probably ignorant of the Jacobin Club's turbulent session the previous evening.

Thibaudeau has a number of possible routes to the assembly-hall which take him through the historic heart of the city. In terms of direction, the easiest would be to cross the river by way of the Ile de la Cité—across the Pont Saint-Michel on to the Ile, and on to the Right Bank by way of the law courts, the site of the Revolutionary Tribunal and the Conciergerie prison. Hordes of the families and friends of plaintiffs at the Tribunal will already be milling dolefully and emotionally about here. This is a grim place, a place to avoid. Across the river here, moreover, virtual slum neighbourhoods run along the Right Bank. Mercier counselled holding one's breath as essential for anyone traversing the area. So Thibaudeau is more likely to choose to direct his steps westwards through the Latin Quarter towards the Pont-Neuf. Though the old Henry IV statue has gone, the bridge is famous for the pyramids of oranges that vendors picturesquely construct here and also for shoe-cleaners who are adjudged the best in Paris at removing the city's famously noxious mud. The deputy might also push a little further west and cross the river by the Pont National (formerly the Pont Royal), built in the late seventeenth century, and linking the Faubourgs of Saint-Honoré on the north and Saint-Germain to the south. This is an altogether easier, more leisurely, less busy and less noisome route—it may be better for reflection on what the day will bring.

Like most rank-and-file Conventionnels, one imagines, Thibaudeau is hoping that today will alleviate rather than aggravate the situation after yesterday's turbulent session. Being outside factional struggles makes him perhaps more optimistic about a solution to the political deadlock than those at the heart of government. Surely the members of the committees now at loggerheads are closely enough aligned by common interests, ideological commonalities, and personal solidarities to find a way to work this crisis through in some way? Surely they can see that national interest requires a united patriotic front that transcends personalia?

If today really is going to be a question of a number of deputies being ejected from the Convention, as Robespierre seemed to be proposing yesterday, Thibaudeau wonders, then who will prevail? There is little love lost between Thibaudeau and Robespierre. Indeed, Robespierre disgusts him, and not just because of his overweening conduct in the Convention. Thibaudeau cannot forgive Robespierre's refusal to support his family back in Poitiers when over the last year they were attacked by over-zealous deputies on mission. He does recognize that Robespierre is currently the biggest political figure in the assembly, and would be difficult to replace. But yesterday Robespierre was vigorously attacked, weakly defended and visibly shaken. His position looks very fragile, even though he seems to have big ideas in mind. What does Robespierre really want? Thibaudeau wonders. Where is he going? Where will he stop?

10.45 a.m.

Robespierre's lodgings, 366 Rue Saint-Honoré

Locksmith Jean-Baptiste Didier is joining Robespierre and the Duplays in the family breakfast-room at 366 Rue Saint-Honoré, prior to Robespierre's departure for the Convention. Didier is a familiar face here. Before his move to the old premises of the Conception monastery, virtually next door, he is said to have lived here, and even to have shared Robespierre's room. He has become a member of Robespierre's loose bodyguard group. It must have been through Robespierre's good graces that Didier was appointed a juryman in the Revolutionary Tribunal, and there he has tried to live up to Robespierre's ideals. He is one of the 'solid' jurymen who likes to ensure that enemies of the people do not escape the blade of justice.

Robespierre's support has given Didier professional advancement impressive patriotic credentials. But his admiration for Robespierre is not based on material interest alone. As with many who think of themselves as sans-culottes, Robespierre's speeches and his conduct throughout the Revolution have opened up new horizons and strengthened Didier's political commitment. He feels that when Robespierre speaks resonantly and movingly of social justice and popular sovereignty, he is addressing him and his peers, and stimulating their engagement. He exudes a deep sense of loyalty and gratitude towards Robespierre for opening his mind in ways that have changed his whole outlook on life, and those feelings are further fortified by his personal acquaintance with the 'Good Friend' in the welcoming Duplay household.

This morning, Didier has already been to the Revolutionary Tribunal, probably to see if he is needed on today's juries. He is excused service, but a shower of rain at around 9.15 a.m. makes him delay his departure from the Ile de la Cité until between 10.00 and 10.30, when he sets out for the

Duplays. He knows the routines of Robespierre and the Duplay family. While they complete their breakfast, he drinks a cup of coffee.

After rising early to work in his room, Robespierre normally dresses and has his hair powdered before presenting himself for the day and descending to the Duplay quarters. Madame Duplay and daughter Eléonore indulge Robespierre's fondness for coffee and his taste for oranges. That may be all he consumes at this time of day, for he is notoriously abstemious. He then readies himself for the Convention, getting his papers together and maybe taking a last peep at the notes for the speech he intends to make following Saint-Just's oration with which the day's formal business will begin. His brother Augustin, whose lodgings are only a few minutes away, drops in: he will accompany his brother to the Convention, offering moral support and fraternal advice as Maximilien readies himself for the debates.

Didier will be aware that Robespierre's friend Saint-Just is planning to make a major speech today, but one wonders whether he knows much more than that. Robespierre plans to shift his primary political allegiance away from the Montagnards with whom he has hitherto been associated. This is a massive and risky move. Yet he seems keen to make it appear that this is just one day like any other. In a way today is better than yesterday. Yesterday's events have given the situation clarity. The conspirators have come out into the open. He can see the scale of the problem facing him. He is thus doubtless quite sincere when, as he and Didier leave the house, he seeks to placate the alarm that the Duplays have been expressing about his fate, reassuring his landlord once again:

– Don't be alarmed. The majority of the Convention is pure; I have nothing to fear.

This is not Dutch courage on his part. In yesterday's dramas the Montagnards showed themselves in their true colours, and Robespierre believes that this will also have been remarked by the deputies of the Plain to whom he now looks for support. He endured a bad moment in the Convention following his speech. But the ovation he received at the Jacobin Club provided comfort and new inspiration. He realizes he is in a strong position: his friend Hanriot commands the Parisian NG; his allies Fleuriot and Payan run the Commune; he enjoys much support within the Paris sections. And today his close ally Saint-Just will be opening the debate and setting the political tempo in a way that will work well with Robespierre's plans. His position is better supported than when he faced the Girondin threat in late

1792 and 1793. He prevailed then, he will prevail now. His cause—rooting out the enemies of the people at the heart of government—is of the best.

Most important of all, his triumph at the Jacobins last night suggests he has lost none of his popularity. The people is on his side. It is still receptive to his words. For Robespierre, that is crucial. His action today must be geared—as it was in the 31 May/2 June 1793 crisis—around the action of the Parisian people in forcing through change. He will be the prophet of the people, pointing out the path that needs to be followed. It is unlikely that resolution will be achieved today: the people need to be carefully readied for their intervention. There is still some way to go. Given all of this, why indeed, he asks himself, should Duplay be alarmed today? There is nothing to fear.

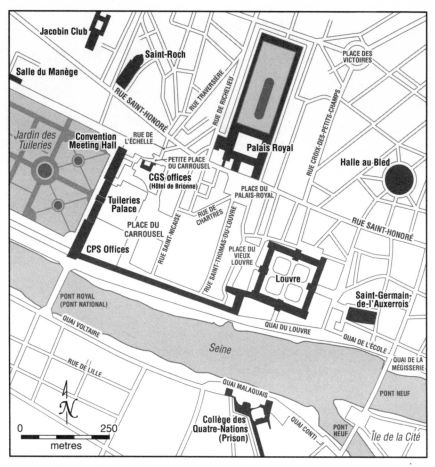

Map 4. The Tuileries complex

11.00/11.00 a.m.

Tuileries palace and gardens

S till no doubt ruminating about what the day will bring, deputy Thibaudeau is approaching the precincts of the old Tuileries palace where
the Convention meets. The Tuileries is the palace that the absolutist kings
never really loved. From the seventeenth century, Versailles enjoyed the
royal affections, and within Paris kings favoured the Louvre. The declaration
of the Republic offered the building a new start, as the Convention decided
to move here from the old riding school (the Manège, a few hundred yards
to the west) in which assemblies had met since October 1789. Following
some restoration work, the Convention duly relocated there in May 1793.

At the approach to the Tuileries on the eastern side is a large open square,
the Place du Carrousel, now renamed Place de la Réunion, which is
surrounded by dense and run-down housing, plus a number of nationalized
aristocratic mansions. Prior to the fighting that occurred here on 10 August
1792 as Louis XVI was being overthrown, there were three separate courtyards along this eastern side of the palace. The walls were largely destroyed
in the day's fighting, and the courtyards are now separated from each other
simply by railings and ruins. But Thibaudeau may well be approaching the
palace from the west, through the gardens. One wonders in fact whether he
encounters the Robespierre brothers, accompanied by the faithful Didier,
also on their way to the assembly by this garden route.

Laid out in the mid-seventeenth century by André Le Nôtre, Louis XIV's
gardening impresario, the Tuileries gardens have seen better days. The
punctiliously geometrical designs of Le Nôtre's formal design have suffered
from the passage of huge crowds, whether engaged in anti-monarchical
rioting in 1792 or else in the less belligerent thronging of the gardens for state

ceremonies such as the inauguration of the Cult of the Supreme Being in June 1794. Le Nôtre may well be turning in his grave, all the more because in line with sans-culotte wishes to nurture the raw materials of prime necessity in preference to merely decorative flora, his signature parterres have been denuded of flowers and planted with potatoes. (This a rather canny choice of plant in fact, for no self-respecting sans-culotte would ever steal from it in order to eat. The Parisian popular diet revolves around bread, not scrumping potatoes.)

Despite a republican makeover, the Palais-National itself, with poly-chrome marble pillars, huge chandeliers, and the like, has not lost all traces of erstwhile royal sumptuousness. But it is now wholly occupied by a government hard at work. Most of the suites of rooms house government committees and their staff. The offices of the CPS in the old Pavillon Flore (Pavillon de l'Égalité) are where last night's rowdy arguments around the green table took place. Draped over the top of the dominating central block of the palace, formerly the Pavillon de l'Horloge, now the Pavillon de l'Unité, is a huge red bonnet with a streamer more than 30 feet long hanging from it. The Unité Pavillon contains the entrance for deputies—or rather entrances, for one enters via a spacious corridor which links the courtyard on the east and the gardens on the west. Access is guarded by a company of gendarmes and by National Guardsmen from the Paris sections, serving in rota. The changing of the guard is at noon, and at present men from the Panthéon are preparing to be relieved by a company from Bonne-Nouvelle.

Entering the corridor from the west, Thibaudeau will turn left into the section of the palace leading to the north. Making his way up a richly decorated ornamental staircase towards the Convention hall, he will enter via one of two ante-rooms into a large vestibule, known as the Salle de la Liberté, so named because of the ten-foot high statue of Liberty placed in its middle. It is a place of everyday sociability for the deputies, as is evidenced by the numerous small traders who have set up business hereabout. There are *buvettes*, coffee-sellers, tobacconists, book and newspaper vendors, and a stall selling tricolour cockades and other revolutionary bric-à-brac. There are also lurking pickpockets about. Deputies and members of the public need to hold onto their wallets and their watches. Today there will be pilfering as usual.

Surprisingly few of the deputies now starting to crowd into the palace live further away from the Tuileries than Thibaudeau. Some lived in Paris before 1792 and stay in their residences across the town, but most are to be found in a limited number of neighbourhoods. A very large majority of the 749 deputies spend most of their lives and have lodgings within two of Paris's 48 sections, Tuileries and Montagne, in a zone covering the Palais Royal, the Tuileries, and the Jacobin Club, and then extending westwards along the Rue Saint-Honoré. Around half of the deputies have addresses in these two sections, about 100 of them on the Rue Saint-Honoré (a fact that eased Tallien's task the previous evening of priming centrist deputies for today's events). This political bubble had one of the largest concentrations of hotels under the Ancien Régime, but the availability of hotel rooms is not the only factor in this crowding, as more than three-quarters of the deputies are in private lodgings. Quick and easy access to the Convention hall in the Tuileries counts for a lot in deputies' accommodation decisions. So does proximity to the shops, coffee-houses, bars, and restaurants of the neighbourhood. Most deputies are in Paris without their families, so that the infrastructure of a bachelor's life is strongly present. The area includes, despite the austere frowns of the more spartan Jacobins, a number of hot zones for gambling and prostitution too, not least the Palais-Royal. It is also a buzzing information hub, with coaches and couriers pouring in from across the country delivering messages to the government bureaucracy. News, gossip, and ingoing and outgoing intelligence are aplenty here and there are newspapers at every corner. It is easy to stay abreast.

Many deputies share lodgings with their friends and political allies or else deputies from the same department. But there is no straightforward pattern. Many deputies live cheek-by-jowl and share at least a staircase with avowed enemies. The political bubble generates repressed tensions and awkward situations, but can also produce unexpected sociability and fellow feeling.

Beyond this crowded hub, there is an outer penumbra of sections around the Tuileries—Piques (Robespierre's section), Lepeletier, and Guillaume-Tell to the north-west, Muséum, Gardes-Francaises, Halles-au-Blé, and Lombards to the east—that also house many deputies. There is also a large-ish contingent on the Left Bank especially in the sections of the former Faubourg Saint-Germain (Fontaine-de-Grenelle, Unité, and Marat). This was the neighbourhood in which before 1789 many of the old nobility had their *hôtels particuliers*, or private mansions, but there are few still around now. Some residences have been turned into government offices and some into prisons. The large-scale removal of the aristocracy has left space that deputies, who are rather well paid, can take advantage of. The weaver Jean-Baptiste Armonville, probably the sole member of the Convention to hail from a genuinely working-class background, is lodged at the Hôtel de Taranne, which prior to 1789 specialized in hospitality for grands seigneurs and foreign princes. There are surprisingly few deputies located in the outer sections or, even more strikingly, to the east of the Rue Saint-Denis. It is said that many deputies at present are sleeping away from their lodgings, for fear of midnight arrest. Even so, the deputy who has regular dealings with the people of the faubourgs is a very rare bird. Although the Convention sounds with endless invocations of the people, the deputies know very little about the lives of the majority of Parisians close up.

11.30 a.m.

Vestibule to the Convention hall and Tuileries palace environs

Although the Convention session starts each day at around 10.00 a.m., the proper order of the day does not get under way until noon. Before that, the minutes from the previous day's meeting are recited and agreed; there may be some special announcements; and then there is a period when messages from across France are read to the assembly. Some of these will be applauded, many will receive honourable mentions, a good number will find their way into the minutes. None gives rise to debate. Quoracy is 200 out of a possible 749 deputies, a figure that is sometimes less easy to achieve than one would imagine. More than 60 deputies, virtually all of them Montagnards, are currently away working as deputies on mission all over the country. Others are ill, feigning illness or simply keeping a deliberately low profile. At the moment, meetings are averaging around 400.

The initial moments of the Convention's day can be dull, and one wonders whether anyone is either counting deputy numbers or listening to patriotic letters. They will have perceived that the public galleries are filling up early. Duplay is there. Maybe he preceded Robespierre so as to procure a seat. Members of the public are checked at the door for social respectability and political orthodoxy: an entrance pass, tricolour cockade on display, no beggars, no drunkards, and so on. As the public files into the galleries, ushers cleanse the chamber with vinegar (it can get quite smelly in there).

Deputies in the Salle de la Liberté, in larger numbers than usual at this time, are eagerly seeking and exchanging news before formal business begins. Like Thibaudeau, most are in a state of perplexity about what is going on. Talk focuses on what happened the previous evening, following the meeting of the Convention, when Robespierre went to the Jacobin Club. There, people recount, he not only re-read his speech in the Convention but also made additional disparaging remarks about his fellow deputies and colleagues. He said he could not hope to escape the clutches of the large number of evil men wanting him dead. He will succumb without regret, and calmly swallow hemlock if evil prevails. (Painter-politician Jacques-Louis David, who yesterday said he would do the same, has in fact this morning swallowed an emetic and is lying abed in his apartment in the Cour Carrée of the Louvre palace. It is being said that Barère has warned him off today's events.)

Deputies in the know are passing on the story that in the Jacobin Club yesterday evening, Couthon proposed the expulsion from the Club of all deputies who voted against printing and diffusing Robespierre's speech. Is this true? If so, it is a very large group. Was Couthon threatening all of them or only the ringleaders? He had his colleagues, Collot and Billaud, driven out of the Club as though they were traitors. Someone says that a new 31 May *journée* was proposed. Rumours have started to circulate too about the furious quarrel that ensued last night in the CPS offices, pitching Collot and Billaud against Saint-Just. And has Cambon arrived yet, to see whether today will bring the death of Robespierre or himself?

Many deputies, like Thibaudeau, have seen the storm clouds gathering but remain in the dark about the exact form the fight will take or its outcome. If he were a betting man, Thibaudeau might be tempted to put money on Robespierre ejecting his rivals now, as he did with the Dantonists in the spring. He will be interested too in seeing how slippery Barère deals with today: he wagers he will have a different speech in each pocket, depending on how things go.

Neither Thibaudeau nor the vast majority of the assembly realizes that Tallien and his contacts from the previous evening have been covertly coordinating their plans, giving each other Dutch courage. Now they are anxiously trying to nurture the bonds of their new solidarity. Anti-Robespierre veteran Bourdon de l'Oise shakes right-wing stalwart Durand-Maillane warmly by the hand, with the words, 'Ah! The fine fellows of the right!' Durand then strikes up a conversation with radical Montagnard Rovère, a likely name on Robespierre's list (assuming he has one). Tallien joins the conversation. The deputies he saw last night seem well enough disposed, but Tallien must be wondering how reliable the pact

with deputies of the Plain and the Right that they have desperately con-
tracted in the early hours is going to prove when things get rough. These
deputies are not renowned for courage or resilience.

The socializing deputies are aware that in the Convention hall, routine
business is still in progress. It is a difficult chamber for a presiding chair to
manage. It is some 20 metres high and its acoustics are bad: even bellows-
lunged Danton complained. Things are made worse by the way the hall has
been organized. The space, more than 40 metres long by about 15 metres
wide, has been configured with the seating laid out in a way that makes it
extremely broad and rather thin. Ten long and slightly raked lines of green-
cushioned benches, stretching almost the full length of the room, are situated
on the left as Thibaudeau enters from the Salle de la Liberté. Deputies thus
have the gardens to their backs. A wide corridor halfway down the room
divides the files of benches into two. This leads out to an external corridor
downstairs from which there are several other points of access into the hall.
These are the locations through which the public enters either to access the
public galleries or else the space where the bar of the house is placed.

Delegations of non-deputies are easily and conveniently received at the
bar of the house. Two days ago, for example, the Paris Jacobin Club
delegation was present here to make its formal representations to the
deputies. The bar faces on to the central wooden, stage-like structure across
the hall, atop of which sits the assembly's acting President, who chairs
business from a silk-embroidered chair designed by David. He is flanked
on each side by raised tables at which sit the secretaries of the Convention,
who take the minutes. The presidents are elected by and from deputies for a
fortnight at a time, while the complement of six secretaries, also serving
deputies, are rotated by half every fortnight. Guarding this structure and
scattered through the hall are uniformed ushers wearing plumed hats. The
wooden structure with the President's chair also contains the speaker's
rostrum, to which deputies accede by one of two sets of steps. To the rear
of the President's seat is a small room. Members of the ruling committees
sometimes assemble here so that they can hear proceedings without being
seen. Above the President's seat are draped colourful enemy flags seized on
the field of battle, that have recently started to be displayed here. They
include the five standards seized at the end of the siege of Nieuport in
Belgium ten days earlier on 16 July, whose arrival yesterday provoked such
wild applause, following the bitter disputes that Robespierre's long speech
had instigated.

The hall has been constructed to hold up to 800 deputies, which gives it at present an air of barn-like semi-desertion. The public galleries on the second floor are even more capacious, taking up to 1,400 spectators and these now appear to be full. The public looks down on the assembly from benches in five wide galleries, separated one from the other by Greek columns. There is a further public gallery at each end of the hall, with blue cushions. At the level of these galleries are statues of figures that the deputies have decreed should also preside over their activities. All are republican heroes: on the garden side, are the Greeks (Demosthenes, Lycurgus, Solon, and Plato), while on the courtyard side, there are the Romans (Camillus, Valerius Publicola, Cincinnatus, and Brutus).

The Brutus in this Roman galaxy is Lucius Junius Brutus, who overthrew the monarchy and established the Roman Republic (sixth century BCE). His repute in France has been endorsed by David's famous 1789 painting, 'The lictors bring to Brutus the bodies of his sons'. In the interests of the public good, Brutus had overridden personal feeling and family ties and ordered the execution of his sons for their crimes. How will the bonds of family stand up to today's events?

Yet there is another Brutus statue in the hall too, which represents a rather different form of devotion to the *res publica*. The first Brutus's even more celebrated descendant, Marcus Junius Brutus, is also present in effigy. His statue stands behind the President's chair alongside the two more recent Martyrs of Liberty, the former deputies Marat and Lepeletier, both assassin-ated by counter-revolutionaries the previous year. Marcus Junius Brutus led the plot to assassinate Julius Caesar in 44 BCE, when the latter seemed to be aiming for dictatorial powers over the Roman Senate. This may seem as apposite a figure for the day of 9 Thermidor as it was for the Ides of March . . .

And indeed at least one deputy, now chatting artlessly, is carefully ready-ing himself to enter the Convention hall with an assassin's dagger concealed on his person, seemingly determined to play the role of Marcus Junius Brutus to Robespierre's Julius Caesar: Jean-Lambert Tallien.

11.45 a.m.

Convention hall, Tuileries palace

The deputies are filing into the Convention hall in greater numbers now as the moment for the opening of the official business at noon approaches. The routine items dealt with since 11.00 a.m. have been characteristically varied. More than 20 missives have been read out. Besides anecdotes and homilies concerning local acts of patriotism, there is praise abounding for the Convention's laws—on the Supreme Being, on begging, on poor relief, on the refusal to take British or Hanoverian troops prisoner on the field of battle, and for military victories. Most missives are from popular societies based in towns and villages from across France, and are dated from about a month before. The tone of the letters is uniformly patriotic, super-laudatory, and hyper-enthused. They include the tail-end of a huge wave of more than 200 letters over the past month or so expressing anguish at the assassination attempts made on Robespierre and Collot d'Herbois on 22 May and sending good wishes to both. What a difference two months makes!

A regular feature of these sessions is the commendation of acts of patriotic generosity. Today, three examples have stood out. The commune of Pré-chac in the Gironde is sending 75 pounds of bandages and a great deal of old linen to military hospitals at the front. The popular society at Sucy-en-Brie (now renamed Sucy-Lepeletier) is forwarding to the state treasury metals they have stripped from the local temples of fanaticism (aka churches) along with much saltpetre scraped off cellar walls. And then the Bois d'Oingy society in the department of the Rhône has subscribed to equip a local lad as a cavalryman for the front. They duly provide details of the patriotic dowry, and a detailed description of the volunteer (34 years old, five feet two in height, brown hair and eyes, snub nose, round and tanned face, etc) and his horse (four years old, four feet five and a half inches in height, white star on forehead, brown coat, three white hooves, etc). As is often the case, these three communications come from locations each with a population of a thousand or fewer. All this may be dull. Yet it shows Parisians that the Convention enjoys a renown and prestige well beyond the bounds of the city, and serves as a reminder how far the patriotic élan of 1793–4 and support for the Convention has reached down within French society. It is grass-roots democracy in routine action. There will be little else that is routine taking place in the hall today.

From his place on the deputy benches, Thibaudeau senses a certain nervousness in the hall, a sense of imminence and expectation. Deputies' faces express a range of emotions. Actorly Collot d'Herbois has taken his place in the President's chair. Barère is there, serene and affable as ever. Saint-Just and Robespierre, who have entered together, move close to the rostrum and seem to show little reaction from yesterday's events. This a moment when all those deputies whose insides must be churning need to remain stoically calm.

The agenda states that Saint-Just will be the first to speak. It has been agreed that he will present a report on the government and the state of public opinion, following the arrangements accepted during the intra-governmental negotiations on 22–3 July. The idea then was that he would today expatiate firmly on the spirit of unity within the Committees of Government. Deputies will indeed be keen to see how he addresses that issue after all that has happened in the last few days, indeed in the last few hours. And as deputies are waiting for President Collot to call the meeting to order and summon Saint-Just to make his report, the latter scribbles a note and hands it to an usher, who leaves the chamber.

11.59 a.m.

CPS Committee Room, Tuileries palace

As the Convention has been going through the preliminaries to the formal order of the day, the joint meeting of the CPS and the CGS is already under way in the CPS offices at the other end of the building. Convened for 10 a.m., it is attended by most members currently in Paris, though not by Collot d'Herbois, who is currently chairing the Convention, nor by Robespierre nor Saint-Just, who are already in the assembly. The meeting's main business is to consider Saint-Just's report on the Republic, as was agreed in the session last night. The idea also seems around that they will discuss with Fouché the charges against him. Fouché has made himself available, but not Saint-Just, who promised to be there by 11.00 a.m.

When Couthon wheeled himself into the committee-room, the discussion was focusing on whether or not to arrest Hanriot. Couthon did not attend last night's CPS meetings, so this must be news to him. Disregarding the conversation, he launched straight away into an attack against the deputy Dubois-Crancé, who had defended himself ably in the Convention on 25 July against attacks from Robespierre. Couthon presented a sheaf of papers which he claimed to be irrefutable proofs of the deputy's guilt, presumably over his conduct at the siege of Lyon in 1793. Attacking Dubois-Crancé in this way also allows Couthon to include in his condemnation Fouché too, another Lyon veteran.

Couthon threatens the other committee members that he will not take no for an answer on this affair. But Carnot, as a trained military engineer, a man who knows a thing or two about siegecraft, stops him in his tracks and a slanging match quickly flares up:

Couthon: 'I always knew you were the most evil of men!'
Carnot: 'And you the most treacherous.'

Couthon's intervention has drawn discussion away from the Hanriot question, prolonged the meeting more than anticipated, and exacerbated division in the ranks of the committees. It has also diverted committee
members' minds from the question: where exactly is Saint-Just? Couthon
is still mid-tirade when a messenger brings in a note for him that he reads,
then rips up and throws away. But CGS member Philippe Ruhl has managed
to read its contents. The letter is the note that Saint-Just has just despatched
from the Convention hall. It says: 'Injustice has closed my heart; I am going
to open it completely before the Convention.'

Saint-Just faithfully promised last night that he would show his report to
the committees before delivering it before the Convention. He has gone
back on his word. Ruhl immediately smells a rat. Couthon, he fears, has
deliberately staged this diversionary tactic to keep the committees of
government away from discussing the Hanriot issue or taking stock of
Saint-Just's absence or attending the Convention at this crucial hour.
So Robespierre and his fellow conspirators have shown their hand. Because
of Couthon's cunning ruse, the agenda in the Convention is starting with a
signal act of collegial treachery. Ruhl reacts swiftly:

– Come, friends. Let us go and unmask traitors or present our heads to the
Convention.

Leaving Couthon in his wheelchair trailing behind, the group rushes out
down the corridors towards the Convention hall. They can be there in just a
couple of minutes. The curtain is going up on an historic drama.

PART

III

A Parliamentary Coup (Midday to 5.00 p.m.)

Parisians are now bustling cheerfully through their day. But the political elite is entering uncharted terrain and on the cusp of a crisis whose shape and dimensions it is still struggling to discern. The main actors are hurriedly taking up positions for the imminent drama which will be staged within the precincts of the National Convention hall. Things are moving very fast. Deputies do not realize that Saint-Just opened his speech without consulting his colleagues in government. This has transformed the whole situation.

Despite a night of nervy plotting and counter-plotting, this will be a drama whose script is still being written. No one has a master plan, only a variety of hopes, wishes, considerations and notional projects that conflict on essentials. Spontaneity and improvisation seem now to be the order of the day.

Among Robespierre's enemies, however, one man at least is more than prepared to force the pace of the day. Unbeknownst both to Robespierre's friends and enemies, Jean-Lambert Tallien has grasped that his own and his mistress's fate depends on the gamble he is about to take.

12.00/12.00 Midday

Convention hall, Tuileries palace

—This has got to end!

The deputies assembled in the Convention hall to listen to Saint-Just's speech on the harmonious workings of government crane their necks round to see Jean-Lambert Tallien sweeping into the hall from the Salle de la Liberté, shouting at the top of his voice as he poses a furious point of order against Saint-Just.

It was the CPS/CGS reconciliation meeting of 22–3 July (4–5 Thermidor) that decided that Saint-Just would present a speech to the Convention today. The idea was that he would stress the spirit of unity reigning among the Committees of Government. Since then, much water has passed under that particular bridge. Saint-Just has chosen to break his promise to run his speech past his CPS colleagues in advance of his intervention. It would be pointless, he has concluded: they would refuse him the right to speak. He has already sent Couthon a message about his intentions, indicating how his encounter with Billaud and Collot last night has 'afflicted his heart' and made him ill-disposed towards them. His controlled anger, evident in his air of awkwardness and the slightly wild look in his eyes, will be reflected in the content of his speech. He intends to defend Robespierre, with whom he entered the Convention hall, and will make no bones about how badly his CPS colleagues have treated them both. He will be true to his values by presenting his speech not as a compromise text from within the government but as a personal act of good faith, supporting Revolutionary institutions and spoken from the heart, in the name of the *patrie*. Saint-Just believes in the community of affections between patriots. The hearts of those fellow deputies that are pure and patriotic will certainly go out to him. For those who are not pure and patriotic he has other ideas.

He begins his speech:

- I belong to no faction; I combat all factions. They will only die out through the action of institutions that produce sureties, that set the bounds of authority and that force human pride to bow the knee under the yoke of public freedom. The course of things has brought it about that this tribunal for speeches could become the Tarpeian rock for whosoever should come to inform you that members of the government have strayed from the paths of wisdom . . .

But before deputies have the chance to puzzle through what Saint-Just is driving at, Tallien has come storming into the Convention hall, loudly stopping him in his tracks. He had been in conversation outside with the staunch Montagnard deputy Goupilleau de Montaigu, when he saw the session beginning. 'This is the moment to attack Robespierre and his accomplices,' he told Goupilleau:

- Come into the hall and witness the triumph of the friends of liberty. By this evening, Robespierre will be no more.

There is universal surprise in the hall at Tallien's loud, impetuous gesture. From his position in the Chair, Collot who, like his CPS and CGS colleagues, is not privy to Tallien's intentions, is as astonished as anyone. He follows assembly protocols in allowing Tallien to speak on his point of order: Saint-Just is supposed to be speaking about the unity of government, but in fact, Tallien declares, he is demonstrating and exacerbating its divisions:

- The speaker started by stating he belonged to no faction. I say the same. I belong only to myself—and to liberty. And it is for liberty that I am going to make the truth be heard . . . Division is everywhere. Yesterday, a member of the government set himself aside from it and pronounced a speech in his own name. Today another member of government does the same. They have come here to assail the fatherland, to aggravate its troubles, to hurl it into the abyss. I demand that the veil be completely torn asunder . . .

Tallien has used a point of order not only to silence Saint-Just but also to implicate Robespierre in his attack. The audacity of this open assault takes everyone aback. For Thibaudeau, it seems like an electric shock has been roughly administered to those assembled. This is accentuated when these opening remarks spark off three orchestrated rounds of cheering from a clutch of deputies whom Tallien has clearly primed for the occasion. The investment of his time with Durand-Maillane and his ilk late last night is making its first return. Others present have been well aware of the existence of tensions at the heart of government, but the secrecy about what goes on around the CPS green table means that they do not have a clear picture. They are astounded at what is suddenly happening.

Saint-Just has planned to strike out independently from Robespierre today. But most deputies have been anticipating His Master's Voice, a view confirmed by Saint-Just's opening words. They have always viewed him as Robespierre's faithful and ruthless henchman. Seeing Saint-Just and Robespierre enter the hall together, and with Robespierre obviously champing at the bit to follow his ally to the rostrum, they have been expecting a coordinated intervention from the two men. Saint-Just's opening, high-flown reference to being putatively hurled like a political outcast from the Tarpeian rock as under the Roman Republic seems to endorse this, for this kind of homage to his own putative death is very much a Robespierre touch. Even if they detest Tallien (and many do), a great many deputies rather enjoy him taking Saint-Just down a peg or two.

It is at this moment, with Collot doing his best to maintain some semblance of order, that members of the disrupted joint meeting of the CPS and CGS, led by Ruhl, rush in to the assembly hall. They are in a state of fluster and high dudgeon over what they adjudge to be Couthon's artful and pernicious attempts to keep them out of the assembly at this vital moment, and what appears to be Saint-Just's conspiratorial deceit. Their flighty indignation transmits itself to Collot in the President's chair. He knows that Saint-Just promised to report his speech in advance to CPS colleagues. He must have assumed at the start of business that he had done so. But a wave of chaotic shouting now throws the assembly into complete disorder. It looks like a carefully laid plot by these three men is being sprung. It seems that the three had hoped to give the Convention a double-barrelled attack from Robespierre and Saint-Just, while Couthon was cunningly keeping the three men's major opponents out of the assembly. Cunning or coincidence? There are more than enough deputies willing to believe the worst of the three men, and that their endless talk of conspiracies has been a cover for their own plotting.

Like Billaud, Collot has a very low opinion of Tallien as a low, louche, and treacherous character. Yet in the circumstances he is more than happy to give him the floor. And in the tumult that has been following the opening salvoes, with Thibaudeau's 'electric shock' still running erratically round the room, Tallien will have observed that Robespierre's supporters seem to be rather few on the ground. He continues:

- I have just been demanding that the veil be torn asunder. I am delighted to have just seen this done and that the plotters have been unmasked and that soon they will be destroyed and liberty will triumph.

Tallien claims to have been silent in the past out of fear of the tyrant and his proscription list. The session at the Jacobins last evening has, however, made him fear for the country as this new Cromwell rallied his army. He is here with a dagger—his mother had glimpsed him hiding it under his coat this morning as he set out for the assembly. He brandishes it aloft:

- I armed myself with a dagger to pierce his breast if the Convention did not have the courage to decree his arrest.

Tallien is echoing Julius Caesar's assassin, Marcus Junius Brutus, whose bust looks down on him in the hall. But it is more theatrical gesture than threat. He makes no physical attack on Robespierre and seems to be respecting republican legality and parliamentary protocol.

Tallien channels Brutus, but he is also defending his mistress, gaoled Theresa Cabarrus. His professed devotion to the public good may be genuine enough, but it is also infused by personal animosity fuelled by Robespierre's overt antagonism to him and his lover. The rumour may be even running that Cabarrus supplied the dagger he is currently brandishing—an implausibly sentimental scenario (and logistically difficult).

Saint-Just has been struck dumb by what is happening before his eyes. He had thought today would be a day of personal glory when he removed himself permanently from under Robespierre's shadow. Instead it all seems to be about Robespierre. Robespierre himself is now evidently furious and is straining angrily to make a point of order. But the level of applause for Tallien is building, as initial collective astonishment gives way to approval and admiration. Loud expressions of support are making themselves heard around the hall, building on the orchestrated clapping of Tallien's supporters. The Convention is discovering just how much it hates Robespierre.

Tallien now widens the attack. Robespierre, he states, is at the heart of a vast conspiracy against the public good and is planning another *journée* which will lead to the condemnation of all his enemies. To pre-empt the worst, Tallien demands that the National Guard commander François Hanriot be placed under arrest. Then the Convention can turn its attention to the Law of 22 Prairial and its sole author, Robespierre. Action also needs to be taken against Revolutionary Tribunal President, Dumas. The excited applause is going to Tallien's head. In his elation that his huge gamble is paying off, he is losing his drift.

Collot approves Tallien's motion to arrest Hanriot, which is in line with CPS discussions yesterday night. He can accept the attack on Dumas, for he knows that the CGS already have him in their sights for counter-revolutionary activities. But he is worried that Tallien may now go onto the offensive against the Revolutionary Tribunal itself. Everyone remembers his antagonism to the Law of 22 Prairial. For CPS members, attacking the Revolutionary Tribunal is off limits, and indeed Collot fears that if Tallien continues on this track, he may soon go beyond attacking revolutionary justice to oppose the CPS which has been managing it. He needs to neutralize him before he goes too far, and so he invites his newly arrived colleague Billaud-Varenne to intervene.

By the Convention's rules of procedure, a speaker opposed to the previous speech should be allowed to take the rostrum. With Saint-Just looking too dumb founded to continue, a furious Robespierre is calling out that he should be accorded the right to reply. Collot is not going to allow that to happen.

As Billaud makes his way to the rostrum, one deputy hears Barère urge him *sotto voce* to focus his attacks on Robespierre rather than Couthon or Saint-Just. Robespierre is (after Hanriot) the principal target: isolating him should make him even more vulnerable. Tallien has already shown the dangers in widening the list of the accused. Barère may also be thinking that with Robespierre out of the way, Couthon and even Saint-Just may be retrievable. It is prudent to stay focused on Robespierre. He is the only 'tyrant' currently under consideration.

Infuriated by what he assumes is Couthon and Saint-Just's concerted trickery this morning, Billaud comes out swinging wildly. He has barely begun when he suddenly claims to see in the public galleries one of the individuals who made threats against him last night in the Jacobins, and he insists that he be ejected and imprisoned.

After the man is hustled out, Billaud continues. He pours out his heart to the deputies about the attacks on him and the threats against the Convention that were uttered at the Jacobin Club and then in the CPS committee room the previous evening. This is a significant move on his part, for it breaks the wall of silence of CPS members in the Convention about what goes on around the CPS green table. Billaud is astonished, he states, to see Saint-Just at the tribune after he specifically promised last night to submit his speech to both committees and to withdraw it if they disapproved. If that was not bad enough, Couthon's diversionary actions this morning have exposed a nefarious plot. Billaud and the other CPS members have escaped Couthon and Saint-Just's wiles. But the Convention is under threat from the three men.

Does Saint-Just have no supporters and Robespierre no defenders in the house? The deputy Philippe Le Bas steps forward and demands the right to speak for St-Just, which indeed, according to the Convention's procedural rules, he should have. Le Bas, Saint-Just's close friend and son-in-law of Robespierre's landlord Duplay, is a member of the CGS but missed last night's proceedings. In the present context, however, the deputies will have none of him, and with cries of '*Vive la République!*', he is slapped down and threatened with the Abbaye prison for his pains. Things have turned very nasty very quickly.

Billaud has now hit his stride, and is intensifying the assault on Robespierre. The Convention is in mortal danger. The National Guard is armed against it and Hanriot its commander has been denounced as a traitor. Billaud attacks not just Hanriot but also his general staff. Robespierre has defended them against his CPS colleagues, yet all are politically suspect. Furthermore, when asked to nominate colleagues to go on mission in the provinces, Robespierre claimed he could not think of 20 deputies worthy of the role. He has also had good patriotic sans-culottes in the Paris sections arrested under his own authority. After having everything his own way for six months, he distanced himself from his colleagues when they put up resistance to the 22 Prairial Law. Yesterday night in the Jacobin Club, he launched attacks on Billaud and Collot that were taken further by Revolutionary Tribunal President Dumas.

Billaud's undisciplined, scattershot speech demonstrating the dangers deputies now face from Robespierre draws gasps of indignation interspersed with applause. A cry, 'May tyrants perish!', is heard. Yet Billaud, who had not anticipated making this speech, has started to lose his thread. He rushes hectically along, blurting out new charges, and washing the dirty linen of the CPS in public: Robespierre protected a secretary of the CPS who had stolen 14,000 livres: he long defended Hébert; he angrily assailed Billaud when he first started to attack Danton; he has a personal espionage system working against the deputies...

Billaud's references to the spring purge of the Hébertist and Dantonist factions makes Robespierre react angrily, but his rush towards the rostrum to reply is greeted by yells from across the whole assembly of 'Down with the tyrant!' His path is blocked on both points of access to the rostrum by the Convention's ushers and also by today's secretaries. These include Jean-Étienne Bar and André Dumont, with help provided by Louis Legendre and Jacques Brival. Dumont is one of the group of deputies that Robespierre has in his sights over the radical anti-clerical policies he pursued when on mission in the northern departments. He has also been trying (without success) to get Robespierre to support the case of his brother who has been unjustly imprisoned. He is only too delighted to block Robespierre's way.

Billaud rounds off his speech by giving voice to what has become the mood of the assembly:

- No deputy would wish to exist under a tyrant!

The assembly loudly roars its approval. Prompted by Tallien's references to Julius Caesar and Oliver Cromwell, deputies recognize that in the person of Robespierre they are indeed dealing with a tyrant.

The Montagnard deputy Charles Duval, still rubbing his eyes at the spectacle taking place before him, finds himself thinking: the spell is broken. That magic by which Robespierre, through sheer power of personality, eloquence, and fear, has kept the Convention docile and respectful seems to be vanishing before the eyes of the deputies. From the Montagnard benches, ex-soldier Jean-François Delmas (and one wonders if he is aware that Robespierre's files contain vicious attacks on him) along with lawyer and fellow Montagnard, Jean-Pierre Couturier, step forward to push the debate onwards by urging the arrest of Hanriot, and the extension of the warrant to include his general staff. With the debate continuing, the Convention reels off a decree ordering the arrest of Hanriot and Boulanger and other aides-de-camp, to which list the name of Revolutionary Tribunal President Dumas is added.

Bertrand Barère is now summoned to speak. He receives raucous cheers as secretaries Dumont and Bar push aside the infuriated Robespierre on the steps up to the rostrum to allow him to pass. Thibaudeau's wager that Barère has two speeches for today's eventualities in his pocket rather short-changes him, for he can take most things in his stride. But the directness of Tallien's assault on Robespierre and the fervent response it is eliciting have taken things in a new direction. Barère likes to manage and regulate, not to allow spontaneity to take the assembly who knows where. In line with the tenor of last night's discussions in the CPS, he has also drafted a proclamation about present dangers which will be decreed and published so as to win over the public.

Barère is well used to balancing on political tightropes. He is categorical that the continued existence of the CPS is vital to the survival of the Republic. But he makes no bones about it: division in the government is helping the Republic's enemies. The British and the Austrians must be rubbing their hands in glee at the attacks being made against the Revolutionary Government in the last few days—and indeed in this very session. Unity has been crucial in the CPS's crushing the Republic's enemies and keeping freedom alive. This is now under threat.

> - The Committees of Government are the shield, the refuge, and the sanctuary of centralized government... their existence makes it impossible for royalty to recover, for aristocracy to return to life, for crime to dominate, for the Republic not to triumph.

Yet while singing the CPS's praises, Barère is also hedging his bets. He is alert to the danger that the Tallien-led attack on Robespierre could spill over into a generalized assault on the powers of the CPS. His fulsome praise for the committee aims to firewall it against possible attacks.

Significantly too, Barère makes no direct reference to Robespierre. Only two days previously, on 25 July, Barère was generous in his praise of Robespierre for seeming to oppose the moves to purge the assembly under popular pressure. Yet even if the last 48 hours—indeed the last 48 minutes— have changed all that, Barère is still cautious about the dangers of tackling Robespierre head-on. Although he probably does believe his own taunt that Robespierre could not organize a farmyard (let alone an insurrection), he realizes that Robespierre's allies do not lack organizational skills or experience. So while speaking vaguely of internal divisions, he focuses deputies' minds less on Robespierre than on the threat posed by Paris's NG. It is not enough, he states, simply to order the arrest of commander Hanriot and his general staff. The practice of having a sole commander of the Paris NG must be suppressed in the interests of democracy. So, seemingly, there will be no direct replacement for Hanriot. The Convention scramble together a decree abolishing the post of NG commander and setting in place the more democratic practice whereby the six Legion Chiefs perform the role on a weekly rota basis. But then in the confusion the deputies seem to go back on this, by decreeing that the gendarmerie commander Jean Hémart, whose loyalty the CPS sounded out in the middle of the previous night, should be appointed interim NG commander.

The decree against Hanriot and his ADCs also goes on to state that the mayor of Paris and the Commune's National Agent must at this moment do their duty. The safety of the representatives of the people in the Convention is on their heads, and they must deal with any turbulence that aristocratic parties whip up in Paris. Hémart will be commanded to deliver this message in person at the NG headquarters which are adjacent to the Maison Commune.

Barère goes on to propose that his proclamation be issued and disseminated across the 48 sections of Paris and also be sent out at once to all communes across the country, and to all the armies. He has made a few minor changes on the hoof to the drafted text, which now reads:

> Citizens! Despite the Republic's striking victories, a new danger threatens the Republic, all the more worrying for having ensnared some elements of public opinion . . . Personal passions have usurped the place of the public good . . . the Revolutionary Government is under attack . . . aristocracy seems to triumph and the royalists are ready to re-emerge . . . Citizens, do you wish to lose in a single day six years of revolution, of sacrifices and of courage? Do you wish to go back beneath the yoke that you broke?

The people should be clear, Barère enjoins: the threats to the people's gains from the Revolution are coming from the military (he is thinking of Hanriot's NG) and it is crucial that the whole people join together to support the committees and thwart royalist and aristocratic designs.

A remarkable omission from the text is any direct reference at all to Robespierre. Robespierre's aura may have been irrevocably damaged, but Barère has preferred to float in the realm of the vague, an element in which he excels. Perhaps those used to reading the runes will see an oblique reference to him in the evocation of the role of 'personal passions' in potential usurpation. The fear that Robespierre has inspired is not easily dissipated. That—one imagines—is the power of tyrants.

13.00/1.00 p.m.

Convention hall, Tuileries palace

'Tyrant.'

The word has been uttered, the accusation is out in the open. Robespierre is a tyrant. A term used about Louis XVI is now being deployed to describe a regicide deputy. Ironically too, it was Robespierre who, along with Saint-Just, most cogently outlined the term's definition and parameters during the king's trial. 'No king can reign innocently,' Saint-Just had proclaimed, which implied that the very institution of monarchy was an illegitimate and intolerable power-grab by an individual trampling over the rights of fellow citizens. Robespierre, abandoning his erstwhile opposition to all forms of capital punishment, argued powerfully that the French Republic was obliged to end the life of the usurper of the collective freedom of the French people: 'The king must die, so that the Republic may live.'

As was the case with their predecessors in 1789, the deputies do their political thinking in a way that refracts through the writings of thinkers such as Montesquieu, Rousseau, and Mably. The Enlightenment idealization of Greek city states and the Roman republican era encompassed a sense of foreboding about the fragility of the republican condition and its vulnerability to tyrannical usurpation. But ancient history also provided the notion of dictatorship embodied in the epic example of Cincinnatus, the fifth-century Roman patrician summoned from his estates to assume sole power during a state emergency crisis, only to return to his plough once the crisis had been resolved. In the often chaotic military circumstances in 1792–3, with the survival of the Republic looking highly precarious, the Convention went down this road, placing power not in a single individual but in a collectivity: the Committees of Government. Saint-Just's decree of

10 October 1793, that government should be 'revolutionary until the peace', accepted restrictions on individual rights and constitutional normality in the name of the Republic's survival until war ended. The Law of 14 Frimaire codified this state of affairs, enshrining the concentration of executive and legislative power in the two Committees of Government, the CPS and the CGS. Importantly, however, the law stipulated that 'the Convention is the sole centre of impulsion of government', and that the assembly has the right to change the composition of the Committees of Government at will. Even though the assembly has not chosen to rotate committee membership since September 1793, this arrangement maintains the notion that the extension to the Committees of Government's powers, that in most other circumstances would be called dictatorial, is a temporary measure. The CPS has sought further to justify their sweeping powers by appealing to the legislature's roots in popular sovereignty. 'The people exercises dictatorship over itself,' Barère once put it, through the Convention. Robespierre has gone further, adumbrating a 'despotism of virtue' that Revolutionary Government incarnates on the Convention's behalf and in the people's interests.

In the sense that devotion to the *res publica* overrides any thought of personal ambition or interest, every member of the Committees of Government is committed to the self-effacing and patriotic virtues involved in somehow 'being Cincinnatus' (whose statue adorns the Convention hall). The Cincinnatus example was almost certainly in the mind of Saint-Just a couple of months earlier when at a CPS meeting he advocated promoting Robespierre to a vaguely specified elevated role within the Committees. He may also have been influenced by the thinking of the radical journalist Jean-Paul Marat, the 'Friend of the People', who in the early years of the Revolution tirelessly called for the institution of a dictator to see the French state through hard times. In the Convention, he had specified that he intended the term in the sense of 'a guide, a chief, and not a master'.

Carnot's response to Saint-Just's proposal was to call him and Robespierre 'ridiculous dictators'. The angry riposte highlighted a growing tendency in political discourse to conflate the notions of dictator and tyrant. The aspirants to dictatorial power most frequently cited are those that Tallien has evoked as tyrants in today's debate, namely, Julius Caesar, who succeeded in this task, establishing the imperial system, and, more recently, Oliver Cromwell, who had overthrown the English king and then parliament to establish sole power. Catiline, famously attacked by Cicero for conspiring to overthrow the Republic, is another who attracts the labels 'dictator' and 'tyrant'.

And although Tallien's speech has not touched on it, there is a further context for tyranny of which many deputies will be aware. It relates to the figure of the sixth-century BC Athenian tyrant Pisistratus. As every reader of Plutarch in the Convention (thus every deputy) will know, Pisistratus seized power as a result of a ruse. He entered the forum displaying self-inflicted body wounds which he alleged had been rained on him by his political opponents, and when the Athenians allowed him to form a small bodyguard for his defence, he used the group to stage a coup and impose his personal rule. Saint-Just's undelivered speech today waxes indignant about how Billaud-Varenne had sought to inveigle himself into Robespierre's good graces, even though he had recently been calling him Pisistratus behind his back.

For some time now, in the corridors of power, Billaud has indeed been making this sly comparison. The conspicuously martyrish, self-sacrificial rhetoric that Robespierre so often deploys bears metaphorical resemblance to wound-display. When Marat was killed in his bath, Robespierre manifested something akin to assassination-envy, while in the follow-up to the baulked attempt on his own life by Cécile Renault, he postured as though parading wounds he did not have. The comparison also evokes a charge of patriotic pretence that has often in the past been levelled against Robespierre: despite his passionate commitment to transparency and authenticity and his invocations of his own victimhood, Robespierre has often been charged with dissimulation, hypocrisy, and play-acting (as well as for having a club-bearing personal bodyguard). As well as being Catiline, Caesar, and Cromwell, therefore, Robespierre is also Pisistratus.

Robespierre is a 'tyrant' and dictator in a further way that in some respects echoes Antiquity: that is, he builds up his popularity, mimicking the way the tyrants of Antiquity played the *hoi polloi* or plebeians. Robespierre's opponents have long been scandalized at how flagrantly he plays to the public galleries. At the height of the polemics between Montagnards and Girondins in late 1792, he was assailed by Louvet for wanting to be a dictator, and exercising 'a despotism of opinion'. The association has never entirely gone away, though when a speaker dared use the phrase against him in the Jacobin Club in February 1794, Robespierre had his membership rescinded in a flash.

Despite the classical resonance for this kind of popular support, Robespierre is held to control opinion in ways unknown in Antiquity. Indeed, the means at his disposal for influencing opinion are of a completely different order from anything available in the Ancient World. Robespierre may berate journalists for diffusing 'false news' but in fact he is a past master at playing to his own advantage on all the registers of publicity made available by the development of print culture across the eighteenth century and the emergence of public opinion as a force to be reckoned with and appealed to.

Print accords Robespierre's self-promotion vast reach through his speeches, as he and his colleagues well know. He is highly attentive to having the full and corrected text of his speeches in print. He polices publication with a copy-editor's zeal and hauls over the coals those editors who don't reach his standards. He attacks 'false news' spread by immoral journalists. And, while putting his own spin on all he says, he closes down critical voices. One reason why he will have felt cheered by the rhapsodic reception he received in the Jacobin Club yesterday evening was that he knew that repeating his Convention speech verbatim there will ensure it national coverage, thus bringing it before the eyes of the people. For the text will get out to the Club's many provincial affiliates in brochure form as well as in newspaper reportage and thereby be read by huge numbers of militants across the land. The Jacobin press machine will thus compensate for the Convention's refusal to circulate the speech outside the assembly.

The exceptional popularity that Robespierre is held to enjoy was a major factor in persuading the joint meeting of the Committees of Government yesterday night to defer precipitate action against him. The material forces he has at his disposal through Hanriot's NG and Payan and Fleuriot-Lescot's Commune are already very considerable. Robespierre's 'exclusive celebrity' (as Billaud puts it) among the people of Paris and 'frightening popularity' (Collot's phrase) is just too great. Today, however, almost accidentally, the Convention seems to have stumbled into the most effective way of preventing his celebrity being deployed. It is stopping him from speaking.

- So I will never be allowed to speak?!

Robespierre's sudden interjection brings the Convention's attention back to his person. Barère has been reading out the proclamation he drafted last night aimed at rallying the people to offer resistance to armed attacks on the Convention. He has adroitly taken the spotlight away from Robespierre and towards the threat posed by Hanriot. The latter's dismissal has been decreed and a new NG command structure introduced. Yet if Barère hoped to pass lightly over the threat posed by Robespierre, it is Robespierre in person who thrusts himself back into the limelight by his demands to speak.

How is Robespierre's mind processing what is happening around him and how should he best respond? He is manifestly astonished by what is taking place. His half-threat yesterday about his powers—were he dictator, he expostulated, people would be grovelling at his feet—is coming back to haunt him. No one is grovelling at his feet. In fact, he is being brutally silenced, his legitimate appeals to be heard unheard. Twisting the knife, an unnamed deputy shouts out to him:

- You didn't want us to hear Danton.

There is a definite whiff of Dantonist revenge in what is going on. The arrest of Danton and his alleged allies and followers in the spring had been made under cover of darkness, and when the CPS simply announced the arrests in the assembly the following day, there was uproar, with Danton's friend, the Parisian butcher Louis Legendre demanding that Danton and his ally Desmoulins be permitted to speak in their defence. It was Robespierre who faced down this threat, reducing Legendre to a quivering wreck by his cold, unbending insistence that the affair was now in the hands of the Revolutionary Tribunal. Legendre has already been in the thick of the action today, exercising his role as secretary to bar Robespierre access to the rostrum, and he now cries out:

- If my eyes were pistols, I would send you down to hell.

At this critical juncture, another of Robespierre's arch-enemies within the Committees of Government is given access to the rostrum. It is Vadier. Robespierre and he have a long and bitter history of mutual suspicion and altercation. Vadier now adds colourful detail to the charges already made: Robespierre was responsible for the Law of 22 Prairial; he was personally responsible for imprisoning the patriotic militants of the Indivisibilité section; he has a personalized spy system targeting his enemies.

Deputies are agog at being provided with so much information about what has been going on around the CPS's green table—all the more as Vadier ramps up his contribution by focusing on the Catherine Théot case which had already set the two men at loggerheads in June. Mixing humour, sarcasm, and contempt to the pent-up anger of his attacks on 'the tyrant' (as he is applauded for calling Robespierre), he stresses that it was Robespierre alone who forced Fouquier-Tinville at the Revolutionary Tribunal to drop the case, on the grounds that the would-be prophetess had a letter to Robespierre hidden under her mattress that stated that his mission was predicted by Ezekiel. (This somewhat arcane reference was probably equating Robespierre's sponsorship of the Cult of the Supreme Being with Ezekiel prophesying a new Jerusalem).

Vadier is reprising his greatest hit. The Théot case allows the deputies welcome relief from the atmosphere of high tension. Laughs come raining down. He continues:

> -...I have since received another letter from an individual called Chénon, a notary in Geneva and head of a sect of Illuminés. He proposes to Robespierre a supernatural constitution.

The sardonic reference to Robespierre's favoured Cult of the Supreme Being triggers laughter, and Vadier continues:

> To hear Robespierre speak, one would think he was the only defender of freedom; he is despairing, he is going to leave everything behind; he is of a rare modesty (Laughter) and his perpetual refrain is 'I am oppressed; I am not allowed to speak'...He says, 'So-and-so is conspiring against me and I am the friend par excellence of the Republic; therefore he is conspiring against the Republic!' This is a novel form of logic...

The strident mockery stimulates Robespierre, perennially thin-skinned where his personal dignity is concerned, into another furious effort to be heard. But again he is shouted down:

> - We don't listen to conspirators!

Vadier has put Robespierre back at the heart of the debate, but even so there is a risk that his knockabout humour will cause the deputies to lose focus. Realizing what is happening, Tallien returns to the rostrum to urge the assembly to get back to the point. Robespierre exclaims:

> - I would know how to do that.

The comment comes out as a dark threat and is greeted by murmurs.

> Robespierre: My enemies are abusing the National Convention!
> Across the assembly: Down with Robespierre!

Resisting Robespierre's heckling, and aware of the fragility of the evidence for Robespierre's 'tyranny', Tallien makes the case that the events of the previous day by themselves are sufficient to convict Robespierre of conspiracy. Robespierre's speech at first in the Convention and then in the Jacobin Club was linked to his behind-the-scenes efforts to subvert the unity of the committees and to increase his own powers through his role in the sinister Police Bureau.

As Tallien is concluding his peroration, Robespierre stands forward.

- I demand to be executed.

André Dumont, who has done a sterling job preventing Robespierre from ascending the stairs to the rostrum, ripostes:

- You deserve it a thousand times over...
- Robespierre: Set me free from this criminal spectacle.

Collot in the chair struggles to keep order in the resultant tumult, with cries of 'Arrest him!' ringing in all ears.

Robespierre begins pouring out insults against the Montagnards on their benches. But then he takes a new tack. The suddenness of the attacks unleashed on him has made him quite forget the strategy with which he entered the Convention this morning, namely, an appeal to moderate deputies in the assembly. His remark to Duplay before he set off from his lodgings shows that it was from that quarter that he anticipates support at this time of need. His speeches yesterday prepared the ground for this move, with talk of *hommes de bien* (men of probity). Turning his back to the Montagnards so he can address the rest of the assembly, he speaks:

- It is to you, men of purity, men of virtue, not to the brigands, that I address my words.

His appeal is met with stony silence and averted gazes. The men of the Centre and the Right, marshalled by Tallien's late-night interlocutors, refuse to come to his aid. They have been too thoroughly primed. They sit on their hands. Only Durand-Maillane steps forward to declare in sepulchral tones:

- Villain! The virtue that you invoke commands humanity to send you to the scaffold!

This thunderous fulmination, in combination with the studied passivity of moderate deputies, is an over powering blow for Robespierre. In exasperation, surely now mingled with fear as well as defiance, he turns once again to the Collot in the chair:

- On what grounds, President, are you supporting the assassins?
- Tallien: You heard him. He treats us as assassins!

Secretary Dumont joins in again:

- We don't want to kill you; it's you that wants to kill public opinion.

In long sessions, it is customary for the President to retire for a while, with another deputy stepping up to take the chair. At this moment, Jacques-Alexis Thuriot is taking over the President's chair from Collot. Robespierre is almost losing his voice. To his frenetic vociferations, Thuriot remarks 'You will have to wait your turn' – a comment which triggers shouts of 'No! No!' from the assembly. Robespierre is not going to be allowed a turn. What started out as the concerted plan of a small anti-Robespierre clique has become the seemingly unanimous wish of all the deputies. Robespierre paces wildly around the space in front of the rostrum before slumping on a bench.

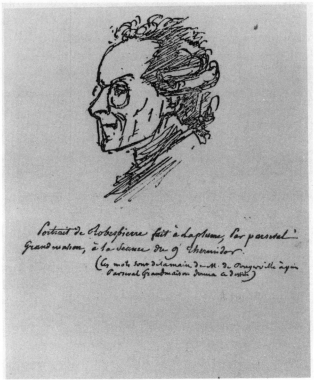

Figure 5. François-Auguste de Parseval-Grandmaison, 'Portrait de Robespierre ... à la séance du 9 thermidor'

The Dantonist deputy Garnier de l'Aube mocks him:

– The blood of Danton is choking you!

Robespierre: Ah! So it is Danton you are avenging! Cowards, why then did
    you not defend him?

Thuriot rings the presidential bell to call a halt to this kind of diversion, and
Robespierre's desperate attempts to speak are frustrated by further presidential bell-ringing. Maybe some of the deputies remember the story told about
Danton's trial in the Revolutionary Tribunal, when the presiding judge—it
was Martial Herman, in fact, Robespierre's ally from Arras days—rang his
bell with equal determination to drown out Danton's thunderous plaints.
'Danton, don't you hear my bell?' Herman demanded, to which Danton
riposted. 'The voice of a man fighting for his life ought to overcome the
ringing of a bell.' Robespierre is certainly fighting for his life, but his lungs do
not allow his voice to carry in the same way as his old foe.

Robespierre is being reduced to impotent silence. Yet presidential bell-
ringing still leaves open the key question under consideration, the question
of the day in fact: what is to be done with Robespierre the tyrant?

1.30 p.m.

Tuileries gardens

Robespierre's bodyguard, the locksmith Jean-Baptiste Didier, is getting very agitated indeed. After he had walked the Robespierre brothers to the Convention hall, he stayed around for a little while in the vestibule. He could see into the chamber and observed Tallien intervening. But the stuffiness of the room has got to him and, not realizing the gravity of what is taking place in the Convention hall, he left the palace to take the air in the Tuileries gardens.

After a little while, he noted that passers-by were being attracted by the noisy fracas of the Convention session. Yet they, and Didier, are refused access, for the ushers who regulate admission to the galleries have activated a ban on entry and egress from the hall while the drama plays out.

Panic suddenly grips Didier as he grasps what is going on: his hero is under attack. And he is being denied popular reinforcements. This is shaping up as a parliamentary coup aimed against Robespierre—but also against the cause of the people that he embodies. The people of Paris are being shut out from this assault on their sovereignty. Didier is beside himself with anxiety and perplexity. What can he do to support Robespierre?

1.45 p.m.

Public galleries, Convention hall, Tuileries palace

Jean-Baptiste Van Heck, is having serious misgivings about what he is
seeing and hearing. Van Heck is known as one of the most energetically
patriotic members of the Cité section on the Ile de la Cité. He has been
highly active in sans-culotte politics, winning his spurs as a patriot long
before the *journées* of 31 May and 2 June 1793, in which he played a leading
role. He currently serves as elected commander of the Cité NG battalion.

For some weeks now Van Heck has noted what seems to him to be
storm-clouds forming over the patriots who made the Revolution. What he
has seen today with his own eyes looks like a group of moderates bringing
down the most celebrated patriot of all, for whom he has deep respect. He
finds Thuriot's endless bell-ringing utterly unfair. Surely Robespierre has a
right to reply? If Van Heck is a regular in the public galleries—the *habitués*
are numerous—he will also get the sense that the Convention's zealous
assault on Robespierre is breaking its own procedural rules. Calling a fellow
deputy a tyrant is out of the ordinary within the assembly. The rules forbid
personalia in speeches. This is one reason (there are others) why Robespierre
has tended not to name the individuals he attacks. Deputies are launching
vicious personal attacks without being called to order and are being encouraged to out-do each other in personal vituperation. Then again the rules
have it that speakers on the two sides of a debate are heard alternately. No
opposition to the assault on Robespierre is evident. It is all one-way traffic.
The rowdy allies of Tallien, the persistent presidential bell-ringing of Collot
and Thuriot in the assembly chair, and the nifty footwork of today's
secretaries Dumont, Legendre, and Bar around the speaker's rostrum, have
combined to silence Robespierre, save for a series of angrily frustrated

expostulations which have done nothing to advance his cause. It is doubtful that anyone in the hall has ever seen him looking quite so angry, frightened, and desperate as he is now. Given the apparent unanimity which is emanating from the deputies' benches, moreover, he is beginning to look guilty as charged. If it were down to a show of hands, Robespierre would clearly be declared a tyrant. But Van Heck is undecided where exactly tyranny lies in all this.

Van Heck has qualms, then, but he does not voice his anxieties. Indeed, one of the most striking things about the Convention session in progress is the absence of the expression of support for Robespierre in the public galleries. Robespierre is well known for having devoted supporters. Yet they have found themselves out-manoeuvred by Robespierre's enemies. It is possible that Robespierre's absence from the Convention for the last six weeks has reduced his following, with his adulators focusing instead on the Jacobin Club where he is a perennial presence. Even so, this silence is deafening. The puncturing of Robespierre's aura in this single session has been remarkably rapid and surprisingly wholesale. It has opened up the chink of a possibility in the minds of his CPS colleagues that despite their worries about Robespierre's extreme popularity, his stock as the people's champion has been overrated. Robespierre may even be in free-fall.

1.45 p.m.

Across the city

To remain in the heights of celebrity one perhaps needs to nourish the flame more than Robespierre has recently been doing. Despite playing to the public galleries, he has often seemed uncomfortable with the trappings of celebrity, shrinking from his own spotlight and giving every appearance of being unwilling to burnish his reputation in ways he finds demeaning. His wilful self-removal from the public eye has not helped. It is as if his absence from the Convention has made the hearts of his followers grow forgetful. Even some who are highly sympathetic to Robespierre wonder what he is playing at. Lanne, his political ally at the Commission of Civil Administration, Prisons, and Tribunals, feels that Robespierre is wrong not to provide the CPS with the facts behind the allegations he is making. He and his superior, Herman, also agreed that it is ill-considered of Robespierre to be absenting himself from CPS meetings.

While Robespierre has been focusing on his own purity of purpose, opponents have been finding space within the wider public sphere to encourage doubts about his character and suspicion of his intentions. Journalists and newspaper editors do not enjoy the freedom of manoeuvre to state baldly the kind of opinions that one hears (and police spies note) in queues, bars, and public spaces. But they have become particularly expert at using subtle, deniable ways of critiquing Robespierre (or 'Roberspierre', as some, infuriatingly for him, persist in calling him).

A range of tricks are in play, some of them cunningly typographical. On the last page of a recent issue of the *Trois décades* newspaper, an erratum announced, 'instead of "Robespierre and Vadier will be referred to the Revolutionary Tribunal", please read "the calumniators of Robespierre and

Vadier will be referred to the Revolutionary Tribunal."' Then again, on 3 Thermidor, the editor of the *Abréviateur universel* apologized for a typo that had crept into the report of one of Robespierre's speeches in which he had been assailing his arch-enemy Fouché: instead of using the verb *taire*, the text had *faire*. So, the editor told his readers, Robespierre's speech should read 'It was we who *silenced* false denunciations', and *not*, they emphasized 'It was we who *made* false denunciations'. And in today's issue being hawked on the streets at this very moment, the journal makes a similar faux-apology regarding their report of the speech by the pro-Robespierre delegation of the Jacobin Club in the Convention on 25 July. The speech implied that their aim was 'to bloody (*'ensanglanter'*) the pages of history'. The text, it seems, should have read 'to represent' (*'représenter'*).

Besides these faux-errata, recent newspaper items in the *Feuille de la République* reveal further coded political attacks aimed at cultivating a spirit of resistance to Robespierre in the wider public. The paper followed a Dantonist line prior to Danton's proscription. Its overt political criticism was non-existent thereafter, yet it kept its Dantonist allegiance intact for those who understood its strategy of typographical resistance to the government. On 23 July, the newspaper carried a review of a new and much applauded one-act comedy by the playwright Antoine-Jean Dumaniant which had just played at the Théatre de la Cité-Variétés, entitled 'Hypocrite en révolution'. It is, the paper explained, about

> one of those crafty men who by their robust oratory under the cloak of patriotism influence uneducated citizens and popular assemblies, and for a while seduce worthy sans-culottes who imprudently give their support to such false patriots. We might note such individuals so that each of us can point out the deceitful knaves who usurp a false popularity in the sections that they wish to use so as to overthrow the Republic.

It does not require much work of the imagination to see in this a pen-portrait of the Incorruptible.

Then again, the *Moniteur*, the *Feuille de la République*, and other news-sheets recently advertised the appearance in French translation of a seventeenth-century English tract allegedly by William Allen, *A Political Treatise*, that had been written by 'an enemy of the tyranny of Cromwell'. This was in fact Edward Sexby's notorious *Killing No Murder*, originally published in 1657 and reissued by Allen in 1685. This open call to tyranni-cide was now clearly targeted at Robespierre rather than Oliver Cromwell.

There is, it seems, a new tyrant in their midst, for those who can decipher hidden messages.

One probably needed a good classical education and a detective's eye to pick up some of the references in the press to Robespierre and the trappings of tyranny. Classical educations are, however, far from rare in the political and social elite. Parisian theatre audiences have long shown a hyper-responsiveness to classical and historical allusion, an ear for current affairs, and a taste for word-play that is widely savoured and not solely among the elite. Parisians' weapons of the weak had been sharpened in similar struggles against absolutist monarchy before 1789. How far has this covert talk of tyranny penetrated the wider Parisian public opinion, and sapped Robespierre's credibility and popularity—and prepared Parisians for today's events?

14.00/2.00 p.m.
Salle de l'Égalité, Maison Commune

T he session of the Municipal Council for which clerk Blaise Lafosse was busying himself at 7.00 a.m. this morning has been under way within the Maison Commune for around half an hour. Lafosse is taking minutes.

Like the Revolutionary Tribunal, the Maison Commune has its own Salle de l'Égalité. In its case, this is the meeting room formerly known as the Zodiac Room, on account of the wooden Renaissance carvings of the heavenly signs. The Commune has been more forgiving towards the astrological symbols than to decorative vestiges of royalty and aristocracy. In late 1793 and early 1794, it commissioned one of its own, councillor Daujon, a sculptor, to scour the building to erase or chisel off all offending coats of arms, crowns, and fleurs-de-lys that were legion in this erstwhile, pre-1789 centre of monarchical loyalism. All portraits of full-robed magistrates have similarly been removed. Tricolour flags and effigies of martyrs of liberty have replaced them.

Of the 48 councillors who are members of the Municipal Council, only 22 are present, but this is a quorum so business may begin. In the chair, Mayor Fleuriot is still smarting from having been called out by the CPS during the night along with National Agent Payan—and all to no purpose at all: they were not even afforded an audience. The two men are anxious about the worker demonstrations against the Wage Maximum that are threatening for today, and they share concerns that these may spill over onto tomorrow, when the Bara and Viala pantheonization is planned.

Neither Fleuriot nor Payan has yet heard the news of what is going on this morning in the Convention. So they dutifully focus their minds on the first items on their agenda. Is it waste disposal or the new uniforms for the fire service, one wonders, that is currently being discussed? Or that anticipated paper from councillor Avril about cemetery reform?

2.00 p.m.

Revolutionary Tribunal, Palais de Justice, Ile de la Cité

The trials taking place in the Revolutionary Tribunal are well advanced. In its own Salle de l'Égalité, notable incidents have occurred. Three days previously, a certain Madame Maillé was due to be executed along with her 17-year-old son—the latter for hurling rotten fish at a gaoler. When the guards called the mother's name, her homonym, a Madame Mayet, stepped forward in error. The court soon realized a mistake had been made, but convicted the substitute all the same, along with the young man, packing both off to the guillotine. Today it is the turn of Madame Maillé to be tried. But on entering the court-room this morning she glimpsed the benches on which her son had been found guilty and she was suddenly seized with hysterical convulsions. She had to be carried out and ministered to in an adjoining room. By the time she started to recover it was clear that she cannot be tried today. Her case will now take place tomorrow.

Meanwhile in the Salle de la Liberté, there have been some raised eyebrows about the mental and physical state of 69-year-old ex-financier Puy de Vérine, blind and deaf, brought into the docks having soiled himself and in an evident state of mental incapacity and distress. But trials do not stop for such trifles, and while proceedings continue, President Dumas finds time to sign an order instructing that the princesse de Monaco will be added to the list of the defendants going to the guillotine this afternoon.

Suddenly, however, an even more striking incident occurs: a group of men announcing themselves to be agents of the CPS enter the courtroom, surround the dais, and declare, in pursuance of a government Convention decree just rendered, that President Dumas is hereby placed under arrest. He is hurried out of the building. The rather flabbergasted subaltern judge Maire assumes the presiding role as the trial continues.

As he is led away, Dumas is heard muttering, 'I am lost!'.

What do those present make of this extraordinary event? News of the attack on Robespierre and his colleagues has not yet penetrated the law courts. Fouquier and others must assume that Dumas is being taken into custody for other reasons. They may have wind of the investigations that the CGS have been making for several days now over his conduct as judge and also his alleged *émigré* links. Now, it seems, the CGS has got its man.

2.00 p.m.

Maison Penthièvre, Place des Piques (Piques)

Despite the Convention banning movement into and out of their public galleries so as to allow the dramatic events unfolding in the Convention hall to proceed undisturbed, the story of the attack on Robespierre is leaking into the city. Within the Tuileries complex, petitioners to the CPS and other government committees have picked up the scent. Another vector for transmission is the team of agents and gendarmes that the CPS sends out to do its business. Collot d'Herbois has already sent messengers to the Revolutionary Committee of the Tuileries section to remain at their posts *en permanence*, and instructed them to place seals on the property of Robespierre and Couthon.

The Maison Penthièvre, a former *hôtel particulier* in the Place Vendôme, half a mile to the north-west of the Tuileries, houses the government's Commission for Administration, Prisons, and Tribunals. Once the Convention's decrees have been duly authenticated by its clerks, they are routinely forwarded to the print works in the offices here, where the Commission's chief, Martial Herman, is responsible for signing off on decrees for printing and distribution.

Herman is in a state of shock. In the last few minutes, the utterly routine signing-off procedure has suddenly become far from routine. For he has seen the text of the decrees ordering the arrest of Hanriot and his general staff as well as of Dumas, followed by Barère's proclamation. The messenger-boy must also have passed on the news about how Robespierre is under attack. Two days earlier, Herman had confided in his colleague Lanne that a well-regarded patriot had told him confidentially that in a few days Robespierre was going to make 'a decisive speech for liberty' that would hopefully extend his power. What has gone wrong?

Herman now fears for Robespierre—and for himself. For he counts himself a friend, and his career owes everything to his patronage. Indeed, he can almost account himself Robespierre's loyal lieutenant for matters penal, for he plays a key role in detecting prison plots and thus supplying the Revolutionary Tribunal with 'guillotine fodder.' President Dumas takes them on from there. If Robespierre had been plotting any sort of action today, as his enemies in the Convention are now charging, he surely would have kept Herman in the picture, as well as his other key lieutenants such as Payan and Fleuriot at the Commune and indeed Dumas? Herman instantly regrets his letter to Robespierre in which he spoke of a potential judge as being 'worthy of being one of us'. The phrase which played so neatly into Robespierre's black-and-white estimations of humanity will not look good on Herman's charge-sheet if his closeness to Robespierre is held against him.

2.00 p.m.

Convention hall, Tuileries palace

It is difficult to see a way back for Robespierre. The deputies seem to be massing for the kill, while the public galleries seem firmly on the Convention's side. From their places on the benches, deputies have watched Robespierre's face transform over the last hours from pale and tense to completely and angrily despondent. He has tried pleading, entreaties, and outright threats to be heard, but to no avail. He now seems to be determined to alienate everyone except his very closest friends and supporters. He has just been calling his colleagues murderers to their face. Tallien is right: the question of what to do with Robespierre has to be instantly addressed.

The focus thus far has been on neutralizing the threat of Hanriot's NG and of getting a proclamation out to the people of Paris. There is a lot of incidental talk of arresting Robespierre and there is much cheering at the suggestion. But to bell the cat, a motion and a formal vote are required. At last, possibly stimulated by Robespierre's insults, the obscure Aveyron deputy Louchet steps forward and states:

- I demand an arrest warrant against Robespierre!

Initially, support for Louchet's call for a *mise en arrestation* is slow to emerge, with nervous clapping limited to isolated places across the hall, but gradually it grows and becomes unanimous. So the Convention seems to be finally grasping the nettle, and taking into cognizance what it is in the process of doing. Or is it? For another little-known deputy, Lozeau from the Charente-Inférieure goes one step further than Louchet, and calls for a *mise en accusation*, a warrant of impeachment.

Lozeau is probably moved by the fact that in law Louchet's idea of an arrest warrant (*mise en arrestation*) does not necessarily involve imprisonment. In 1793, a number of Girondin deputies were permitted to remain in their homes while under arrest, and subsequently fled. But differentiating between the two warrants is rather academic as regards Robespierre: no one can imagine him being allowed to serve out his period of arrest *chez* the Duplays. He will go into prison with a round-the-clock guard on him. Ironically, however, the deputies are rather contradicting themselves over this point of law. For in the debates over the Law of 22 Prairial, Bourdon de l'Oise, Tallien, and others had sought guarantees from Robespierre that the severe legislation would not be used to generate *mises en accusation* against deputies. Robespierre rode over them roughshod in debate. His intransigence then gives an added sheen of legitimacy to today's attacks on him, and some gleeful schadenfreude.

Most deputies probably have little thought for legalistic formalism at the moment: they just want Robespierre to be removed altogether from political life. They accept that this implies the road to the guillotine via the Revolutionary Tribunal. Yet if they remember the Danton trial for its ruthless efficiency, many minds will also wander back to the trial of Marat which the Girondins set up in April 1793. Despite compelling evidence against him, Marat was acquitted and left the Tribunal on the shoulders of his supporters. Could Robespierre do the same? Could his popularity maybe sway the verdict in his favour? CPS members will be aware that following the 22 Prairial reforms the bench of judges and the pool of jurors have been packed with Robespierre nominees from his patronage list, including men who form part of his informal escort group. Can the Tribunal be counted on to convict? For those deputies who are holding back on a disorderly rush to judgement, there is the thought that a delay permitted by a simple arrest warrant would benefit the prosecution, since it would allow more evidence to be amassed against Robespierre. For the truth of the matter is that despite today's huffing and puffing, the evidence against Robespierre for 'conspiracy' presented today is thin, highly circumstantial and subject to contrary interpretation.

With the deputies mulling over the best way forward on this issue, Robespierre's brother Augustin, seeing the way things are going and the seeming inutility of any form of resistance, bravely steps forward:

- I am as guilty as my brother. I share his virtues, I wish to share his fate.
I demand an arrest warrant against me too.

Robespierre is palpably moved by his brother's loyalty. His efforts to get a hearing are still unavailing but he vehemently assails his fellow deputies.

Eager to cut him short, the Montagnard Charles Duval asks:

- President, can one man be master of the Convention?
An unknown deputy rejoins: He has been for too long!
Fréron (joining the debate for the first time): Ah! How difficult it is to strike down a tyrant!

Fréron has a point: despite all the shouting and the clear consensus that has emerged about Robespierre's status as a tyrant, the deputies still seem surprisingly timid about disposing of him. Debate over the kind of warrant to be used is distracting. After some further desultory exchanges, Thuriot from the chair finally ends the procrastinatory hair-splitting over the warrant and puts to the assembly the motion for an arrest warrant. It is carried unanimously.

At this moment, Philippe Le Bas also steps forward. His friends, wanting him to retreat from supporting Robespierre (and perhaps mindful too of Le Bas's six-week old baby son), have surreptitiously been tugging at his coat-tails to force him to sit, so firmly in fact that his jacket has torn. But Le Bas is determined:

- I do not wish to share the opprobrium of this decree. I also wish to be arrested.

The desirability of extending the arrest warrants to others in Robespierre's ambit is suddenly taken up. CGS member Élie Lacoste wades in, claiming to have heard Augustin Robespierre state at the Jacobins, 'they say the Committees are not corrupt; but if their agents are, then they must be too!' Augustin must surely share his brother's fate.

Fréron now steps in to declare:

- Citizen colleagues: from this day onwards liberty and the *patrie* will emerge from their ruins!
Robespierre, attempting to heckle: Yes, the brigands are triumphing!

Fréron is encouraged by the strong rumble of disapproval following Robespierre's interjection to pick up the baton. Possibly prompted by Tallien, he now seeks to widen the charges to involve not just Augustin Robespierre and Le Bas but also Couthon and Saint-Just. The three men, Fréron asserts, planned

> – ... to form a triumvirate reminiscent of the bloody proscriptions of Sulla; it was to be erected on the ruins of the Republic ... Couthon is a tiger dripping with the blood of the Convention. As his royal pastime, he dared speak in the Jacobin Club of five or six heads from the Convention. But that was only the start. He wanted to make of our corpses steps by which to ascend the throne.

Fréron is introducing a new, mildly sinister but also slightly ridiculous edge to the debate. The classical allusions seem a little forced, the reference to royalty even more so. Couthon grasps an opportunity. Pointedly indicating his paralysed legs, he exclaims with maximum irony:

> – I was aiming to climb the throne ... !

Such a fierce appeal to sympathy may strike a chord with many deputies, since despite his latter-day closeness to Robespierre, Couthon has friends on the deputy benches. But Élie Lacoste acts swiftly to bring the threads of the debate together in a way that moves things forward and keeps the deputies focused. As a fellow member of the Revolutionary Government, he has seen Robespierre at close quarters. He has also, on a period as deputy on mission attached to the Army of the North in mid-1794, fallen foul of Saint-Just. And more recently as President of the Jacobins, he has witnessed the machinations of Robespierre and Couthon at first hand. Where Tallien has offered passion, Billaud anger, Vadier ridicule, and Fréron improbable colour, Lacoste's approach is clinical. His view is that the triumvirate of Robespierre, Couthon, and Saint-Just have for several months been thwarting the efforts of government, disturbing public tranquillity, and seeking to undermine liberty. There seems also to be collusion with foreign powers that risks splitting the government apart (though he is vague on this point).

The interventions by Fréron and Lacoste have given the debate fresh impetus. They have also brought in a new word: triumvirate. The implicit classical reference is to the three-man imperial rule of Julius Caesar, Pompey, and Crassus at the end of the Roman Republic. At Fréron's suggestion, the Convention formally votes the arrest of the two Robespierres, Couthon, Saint-Just, and Le Bas.

2.00 p.m.

Police Administration offices, Ile de la Cité, and sectional meetings

The Police Administration never sleeps; but it does observe meal-breaks. Catching up with the paperwork on overnight business, and pre-emptive surveillance of key sections to check on worker demonstrations over the Wage Maximum, have triggered healthy appetites. All functionaries in the Mairie take their meal-break between 2.00 and 4.00 p.m. They have left just before news about the goings-on in the Convention that morning infiltrates the building.

Sectional committees which have been meeting this morning transacting routine business are also breaking up in order to eat. Gangs of saltpetre collectors have been at work, and sectional welfare committees have been attending to cases of need. Revolutionary Committees have been dealing with standard policing issues. The committee in the Unité section on the Left Bank has been meeting since 10.00 a.m. in the premises of the ancient Saint-Germain-des-Prés monastery to continue discussion from yesterday about individuals accused of counter-revolutionary statements concerning the Republic's victories in the Low Countries. Also on the Left Bank, further to the east, the Chalier committee meets in the former Mathurins monastery. Here, business started at 9.00 a.m. with the case of nuns from a small local hospital who have been denounced for not taking the oath of loyalty to the Republic and other offences. In the Marais, the Réunion committee has rejected a request by Cn. Barrois, drum-major in the 6th NG Legion for a *certificat de civisme* ('citizenship certificate'); he is angry as this could leave him politically exposed for conduct judged 'uncivic'. The Finistère Revolutionary Committee in the distant Faubourg Saint-Marcel has been following up a denunciation of a woman found to have smuggled fruit into the section at 3.00 a.m. the previous day.

In addition, a number of sections have this morning been actioning a CPS decree of 20 July which obliged sections to release all weapons confiscated from suspects, rebels, and malefactors that are in their possession. They will be placed into a central storehouse in the former Hôtel d'Elbeuf on the Place du Carrousel. The Tuileries section alone has come up with a list of over 30 rifles, 40-odd pistols, 20 sabres, five Swiss halberds, and much else. Are the sections being disarmed? Or maybe the idea is just to transfer the weapons to the NG battalions?

2.00 p.m.

Across the city

The Convention session is at a high dramatic pitch; but the vast bulk of the Parisian population is going about its normal business. There are disruptions in the city caused by worker assemblies protesting against the Wage Maximum, including outside the Maison Commune, but they are minor. The Convention decrees are still being printed, as are the posters which the bill-stickers will start placing around the centre of the city in a few hours' time. One wonders: how will Parisians receive news of the parliamentary coup once the news gets out more widely?

The answer depends to a considerable degree on the current state of Parisian public opinion regarding the Revolutionary Government, and Robespierre's role within it. Yesterday night, government spy Rousseville was reassuring Robespierre about Parisians' trust in the Convention, even as Robespierre's CPS colleagues were deferring taking action against him because of his great popularity. It is difficult to know what to believe.

A recent incident involving François-Vincent Le Gray and his friend Jean-Claude Saint-Omer, members of the Muséum sectional committee and staunch revolutionaries, illustrates the point. Following a conversation overheard a few weeks ago in the Tuileries gardens, the men were denounced for having deplored the shortage of decorations and lack of fuss that the CPS had permitted for the 14 July celebration of the storming of the Bastille. It showed a disrespect for the Rights of Man, the two had agreed, individual rights and the principle of a constitution. The Revolution, they went on, was in the wrong hands. Patriots were being sent to the scaffold, with the Revolutionary Tribunal placing patriots and aristocrats in the same cart. The whole court was rank with corruption. Barère and Saint-Just, who had been responsible for the exclusion of nobles from the city over the last few months, were both hypocritical ex-nobles themselves. The men cited (and this may have been the drink talking) pamphlets and brochures being produced against Revolutionary Government within the sections.

The incident occurred on the Convention's very doorstep and hit a nerve in the government, which came down firmly on both men. They were arrested forthwith and are destined for the Revolutionary Tribunal. The government has concluded that the incident shows seriously worrying signs of organized resistance to government among the popular classes. Robespierre has seized on it as evidence of the reality of the plots, conspiracies, and counter-revolution against which he has been inveighing for months. This level of anxiety has gained added traction from the fact that in late May a petition calling for the 1793 Constitution started in the Montagne section. It had attracted 2,000 signatures before the CPS forced its closure with a severe admonition regarding an idea they characterized as a vestige of radical Hébertism.

The government is worried that opinion is swinging in favour of the activation of the highly democratic 1793 Constitution, held in abeyance since the declaration on 10 October 1793 that the government would remain 'revolutionary till the peace'. This is not on the agenda of the key policy-makers at the heart of government: Robespierre, Saint-Just, Barère, Billaud, and others are prioritizing innovative social institutions to create the new Republic. They downplay the idea of individual rights enshrined within the constitution.

Anxiety at the heart of government is fuelled by the fact that it has no effective means of judging the state of Parisian opinion. The apparatus of repression that it has at its disposal—the atmosphere of terror, the prisons, the tumbrils, the guillotine, the police presence, the spies, the censors, the closed-down political clubs, and so on—may be giving government sufficient elbow room to enable them to quash the Republic's enemies. But the panoply of terror encourages superficial expressions of political conformity. This kind of dissembling gives Robespierre and Saint-Just nightmares: they are endlessly decrying 'intriguers in red bonnets', counter-revolutionaries who hide their true opinions under the outward signs of obedience and conformity.

The strengthening of the Committees has also choked off information and opinions coming up to the heart of government from the sections. The quality of intelligence from spy sources has deteriorated markedly since the suppression of the ministries in April. In addition, the venomous split that has emerged between the police services of the CGS and CPS means that messages are mixed and there is no unified picture of the state of opinion. Police informers often take the easy way out and simply tell their masters what they think they want to hear. The Le Gray story is full of holes, for example—the men were probably drunk and their boasts about sectional publications a figment of their overheated imaginations. But the police don't point this out to their betters. Time-serving thus exacerbates the problem and stimulates an atmosphere of fear and suspicion that breeds over reaction to criticism. Similarly, even though CPS attacks on popular clubs and free expression at sectional level in the spring have had a depressing effect on many sans-culottes, far from erasing dissent the attacks have helped to drive it underground. A few months ago, for example, police spies picked up a conversation about the guillotine between an apprentice printer and his friends, which took place on the Place de la Révolution.

> - If they guillotine people just for thinking [the apprentice asked], how many people will die?
> - Don't talk so loud [came a friend's reply]. They could hear us and take us in.

It would be easy to conclude from this *sotto voce* exchange that the forces of repression were crushing popular voices and creating blind conformism with central government. Yet were they? How many other Parisians were thinking like these young men, who while showing due caution about the expression of opinion, did not deny themselves the chance to speak their minds in spaces of freedom remaining in the city (even if on this occasion they were indeed overheard)?

It is easy to forget that nearly all the dominant figures in central government are new to policing—and new to Paris too. Most are provincials, whose exposure to the political culture of the French capital is recent and indeed in some cases quite superficial. This is important in that Paris has a long and highly distinctive tradition of dissent and contestation, quite opposed to the docility and conformity now expected of Parisians. 'The people of Paris are naturally *frondeur*,' proclaimed Louis-Sébastien Mercier in the last years of the Ancien Régime, evoking the free-wheelingly irreverent and subversive spirit in regard to authority that Parisians had learnt in the civil wars of the Fronde (1648–52). *Frondeur* is arguably still the default position of Parisian public opinion. 'They laugh at everything,' Mercier wrote of Parisians before 1789:

- They repulse cannon by vaudevilles, enchain royal power by epigrammatic sallies, and punish their monarch by their silence or absolve him by their applause.

It is simply impossible 'for government to tie the tongue of Parisians'. The people of the city, he warned, were generally 'gentle, well-mannered, easily led; but one should not take their lightness for weakness'. One might think that a full-scale riot could not happen in such a well-policed city. In fact, if such an event were to take place, Mercier wrote, it would soon get completely out of hand. The Parisian 'has sufficient confidence in himself not to fear despotic absolutism'.

'What people call a spirit of opposition,' Mercier claims, 'is innate in Parisians.' They see politics as a kind of spectacle in which they are critical observers. Conversely, the knowing reactions of theatre audiences show that they see spectacle as politics too. This *frondeur* attitude is also there in the 'typographical resistance' to be found in newspaper columns—as well as in the moral economy of the bread queue and the banter of the coffee-house. The tendency of government generally, but Robespierre in particular, to condemn all such reactions as 'counter-revolutionary' or 'aristocratic' (or even 'moderate') really does miss the point. The open expression of pro-monarchical views within the city has been virtually non-existent for some time. The evidence for enemy intervention or counter-revolutionary organization in the city is nugatory. Robespierre's over reaction to anything like criticism is actually counter productive. It generates false estimations—and indeed false news.

There are, it is true, some straws in the wind suggesting that all is not peace and light among Parisians. There has been widespread popular disappointment at the government's apparent unwillingness to countenance the country reaping the benefits of military success post-Fleurus. The Commune's repression of the spontaneous fraternal banquet movement celebrating the French victory seems just ridiculously over reactive. There are mutterings too about the ramping up of revolutionary justice just as conditions seem to be poised to make terror less necessary. In addition, the government's recent economic policy shifts seem to be worryingly inegalitarian: changes to the Price Maximum makes things easier for farmers and merchants rather than Parisian consumers, while the planned Wage Maximum seems to be a brutal attack on popular living standards.

Despite these areas of tension, the situation does not seem to suggest that government and Parisians are on a collision course. There is no seething mass of resentment building up and ready to explode. Indeed, there is a deep fund of goodwill towards the political state of affairs across Paris which the government seems determined to underestimate. This, after all, was spy Rousseville's point in his report last night: the people are 'full of confidence in the Convention'.

Revolutionary Government has carried the Parisian population along with it to a very considerable degree. Parisians seem especially enthusiastic about the war effort—witness the reception of Barère's *carmagnoles*—and patriotically willing to accept even the panoply of terror and the many of the hardships that result from national mobilization. The everyday, humdrum activities in which sectional authorities have been operating this morning are a reminder too of the continuing solidity of the pact between government and people of Paris on which Revolutionary Government was based: salt-petre collection highlights patriotic engagement, while the work of welfare committees demonstrate new levels of social solidarity that government has put in place. *Frondeur* attitudes and irritation over some policies don't suggest that Parisians are straining to burst the bonds imposed by Revolutionary Government under the authority of the Convention. But they do want a say, and lay claim to a right to an opinion, under Revolutionary Government just as under the 'despotic absolutism' evoked by Mercier.

If Parisians are generally supportive of Revolutionary Government, where does this leave Robespierre? How far have the whispering campaigns and the tyrant talk within the political elite reached down into the sections? Robespierre is implicitly included in praise but also in critical remarks aimed at the Revolutionary Government generally. People do notice that Robespierre rarely seems cheered by victories at the front: he is too worried about impending military despotism to relish battlefield success. Furthermore, there is no little disquiet about his celebrity status. The new phenomenon of celebrity has brought adulators to add to the many admirers of Robespierre's political mettle; but it has also multiplied denigrators. The emotional bonds on which celebrity is founded run against established notions about political rationality. Adulators follow the promptings of their emotions, it is held, not the exigencies of their minds. Robespierre's keenest supporters, says one journalist, cuttingly, are drawn from 'women and the weak-minded'.

Furthermore, there is a strengthening historical justification for distrust of celebrity, grounded in the experience of Revolutionary politics since 1789. The first celebrity politician of the Revolution was Mirabeau. His heroic role in the early days of the Revolution won him election to the Panthéon on his death in 1791. Yet the discovery of his treacherous secret dealings with the king in 1792 saw his stock plummet. Since then there has been a series of similar cases where the rising star of political celebrities is followed by crash-and-burn. Lafayette, the 'Hero of Two Worlds' deserted his command in 1792 to join the allies. Dumouriez, his successor as generalissimo, was lauded to the skies as a patriot general, before following Lafayette's example and deserting his post in 1793. These political exemplars have been deployed artfully against political opponents on the home front too. Thus the Revolutionary Government used the fame enjoyed by Danton and Hébert, critics of government policy, as an argument against them. These men had sought out celebrity, it was claimed, so as better to plot against the *res publica*.

'The Revolution,' Robespierre stated before the Convention during the Danton trial, 'lies in the people and not in the renown of individuals.' No individual, whatever their achievements for the Revolutionary cause, was above the rule of law and respect for republican institutions grounded in popular sovereignty. Republican institutions should always outrank individuals. One should instinctively distrust those political figures who achieve celebrity. The *Journal historique et politique* reported that Parisians were disgusted with themselves for credulously following Hébert and Danton. At least, the journal concluded a little wistfully, the episode 'had cured the people of its idolatry for individuals'.

The dangers of political celebrity have thus become a standard trope of public discourse to the extent that there is a real danger of Robespierre, the stern monitor of the celebrity of others, being hoist by his own petard. The halo of celebrity that he has enjoyed seems now, moreover, to be slipping. The stress on the sacrosanct character of republican institutions over any ephemeral individual fame has taken deep root in the Parisian political culture. In the spring, a police report mentioned how people in a group were praising Robespierre, but noted that one of the group then opined that

> despite the fact that Robespierre had rendered services to the Revolution, if he were to change, then the duty of a republican would be to forget everything he has done and only to see his crimes and to demand that the law strike him down.

Louis Martinet, Revolutionary Committee member in the Tuileries section was even more forthright: he went around telling his colleagues that what he called 'homomania' was making people lose sight of the *salus populi*, and roundly attacked Robespierre for 'viewing as a counter-revolutionary anyone who was not of his opinion'. How widespread are such views? Is Robespierre still as popular among Parisians as his colleagues in government have feared? Will Parisians rally to the cause of Robespierre-the-victim? The answer should be apparent in the next few hours. But in this first act of the anti-Robespierre drama, the Convention hall's public galleries suggests that Robespierre's popularity seems to have been overrated.

15.00/3.00 p.m.

National Guard Headquarters, Rue du Martroy (Maison-Commune)

- No one takes orders from anyone but me and the Commune.

The angry voice is that of Paris NG Commander, François Hanriot, and it is being raised at the NGHQ, the National Guard's central headquarters on the Rue du Martroy, a side street that skirts the southern side of the Maison Commune.

News about the early parts of the Convention's morning session has finally seeped into the eastern half of the city. Cn. Bazanéry, NG battalion commander of the Maison-Commune section (in which the city hall is situated), has been sent by a municipal official from his section to find out what is going on. He finds Hanriot in a rage and shouting out orders to all and sundry and also caballing with Paris's mayor, Jean-Baptiste Fleuriot-Lescot and National Agent Claude-François Payan.

Hanriot's spontaneous response to the news of the Convention's decree dismissing him is to take the path of armed resistance. He packs Bazanéry off to his section with orders to beat the *générale*, while his ADCs are already fussing around getting the command out more widely. This *générale* is the drum-beat signal convoking all serving national guardsmen to assemble at their sectional post. It also alerts the population as a whole that something important is up. In the past this has often prompted Civil Committees into calling an emergency meeting of their sectional General Assembly.

Hanriot is furious at being caught napping. This morning, he bumped into an old friend who was in the city for the day and when asked whether much was going on today Hanriot replied firmly in the negative. He really had not seen this coming. His anger at himself and fury at the world are further pricked by the arrival of Cn. Courvol, one of the Convention's bailiffs, to serve the men with copies of a Convention missive requiring the Mayor and National Agent to come to the bar of the assembly to show they are taking responsibility for public order within the city in the light of the change of NG command. Courvol asks the Mayor for a receipt for delivery of the message, but a fuming Hanriot seizes the pen from Fleuriot's hands, exclaiming to Courvol:

> – Oh, do fuck off. You can't expect a receipt at a moment like this. Go and tell those fucking scoundrels of yours that we are here deliberating over a purge of the Convention, and we will be along to see them in no time at all.

As Courvol seeks to retire, however, he is arrested and imprisoned. The same fate is reserved for another messenger from the Convention, CPS spy François Héron, who arrives at the NGHQ with a small delegation bearing the Convention's formal decree ordering Hanriot's dismissal. The commander launches a characteristically colourful volley of insults at them and orders their instant imprisonment.

The treatment of Courvol and Héron indicates that the Commune and National Guard have already taken the momentous decision to defy the Convention. Hanriot's vehemence has, moreover, swept up the assent of both Fleuriot and Payan while they were still taking in the news. The men had heard about today's events in the Convention halfway through an uneventful meeting of the Municipal Council within the adjacent Maison Commune. They rushed out and now find themselves turning their attention with all urgency from cemetery reform and drainage issues to the organization of armed resistance. All three Commune leaders cannot fail to realize the mortal risk this action entails. By consciously and impetuously rejecting the writ of the government, they are crossing a Rubicon into a terrain of formal illegality. They are implicitly invoking the people's inherent right to insurrection. This is one of the Rights of Man that the sansculotte movement has fought for since the early days of the Revolution. It is enshrined in the radical Declaration of the Rights of Man that prefaces the 1793 Constitution. Even though that constitution is in abeyance for the period of Revolutionary Government, the rights it itemizes are implicitly active.

The stakes in the crisis that looms are very high, causing stress levels to mount. Hanriot at least knows the ropes of rebellion (though the pressure seems to be getting to him, for his handwriting gets wild and shaky as he scribbles down his orders). But organizing a *journée* is unfamiliar territory for Fleuriot and Payan. The ease with which they have gone along with Hanriot may betray inexperience: after all, he is being charged with arrest not they, so it seems hasty for them to throw in their lot quite so swiftly. Both men are new to the task of leading a Parisian insurrection. Fleuriot was a long-term militant in the Muséum section, so at least has seen *journées* at first hand, albeit from the ranks. Payan has a measure of military experience and the kind of cool intrepidity useful in circumstances like these. But he is only 27 years old and has been in the city less than a year—indeed he arrived a year ago tomorrow: 28 July 1793. He has not witnessed the classic Parisian *journées*. Watering Can Day will give him quite a baptism.

A 31 May-style insurrection is now in the offing. The Commune will organize the people of Paris and mobilize the National Guard to conduct a purge of Robespierre's enemies within the Convention. But implementing this plan is made more challenging by the fact that the men in the Maison Commune are still rather in the dark about what happened in the Convention this afternoon, and do not yet know the identity of their opponents. Is the attack on Robespierre coming from the assembly's Left or the Right? They guess that after the Jacobin Club conflict last night, Billaud and Collot are probably involved. But who else? Moreover, Hanriot is regretting that the Commune is still on the back foot. The Convention's acts have completely taken them by surprise. There has evidently been quite a lot of talk about the possible eventuality of a 31 May-style *journée* recently. But it has remained at the level of talk. And indeed even today in the Convention the very man they are supporting will be denying point-blank a wish to organize such a move. The Commune leaders are thus unprepared for this sudden and unanticipated act on the Convention's part (not surprisingly, for the deputies are equally amazed at their own spectacular audacity). They now need to act fast to make up for lost ground.

Despite the air of fluster and concern, Fleuriot, Payan, and Hanriot can take comfort from the fact that, if today does indeed come down to an armed struggle, the odds are stacked heavily in their favour. In its own name, the Convention can call on absolutely no substantial local element of armed force from within the confines of the city. The CPS calls the shots as regards the republican armies, it is true: but these are on the frontiers, and none is less than a few days, ride from the city. Soldiers are simply out of the current equation, so long as the Commune acts fast. The guards protecting the

Convention amount merely to a few gendarmerie companies plus detachments of the NG sectional battalions amounting to a couple of hundred men. The battalions serve by rote, and answer to their Legion chief, and all ultimately do so to their Commander, namely, Hanriot.

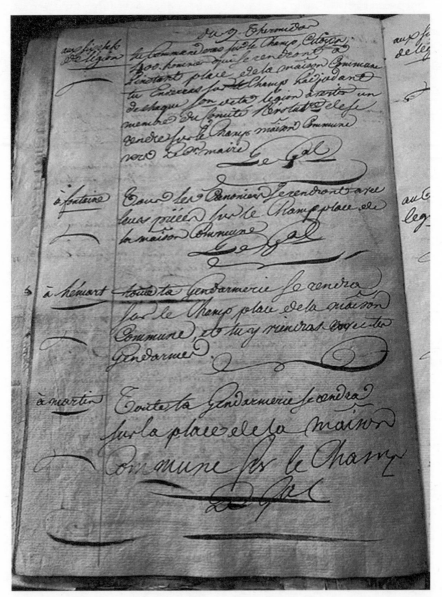

Figure 6. Paris National Guard Commander François Hanriot, order book, 9 Thermidor (AFII 47 pl. 368, pi. 38)

At midday today, forces from the Bonne-Nouvelle battalion, answerable to Second Legion Chief Julliot, replaced Panthéon section guardsmen under First Legion Chief Fauconnier. There are similar duty rotas and token detachments for the Temple prison, the Arsenal, the Treasury, and the law courts on the Ile de la Cité. These men are at the beck and call of the NG commander and the Commune, not the Convention.

The three Commune leaders know that in making their call for armed resistance, they have a strong hand. They also have history on their side. After all, it is the Commune which has generated popular action on all the great revolutionary days, through 31 May back to 10 August 1792 and to 14 July 1789. The men also realize that what ultimately will count, as on those other days of action, is numbers out on the street. The leaders of today's insurrection need above all else to get the people upstanding, and to do so swiftly. At the top of their immediate agenda is alerting the whole of Paris to the critical situation in which the Republic finds itself, getting sectional General Assemblies meeting, and mobilizing armed forces within the city for the cause. Military manpower will be essential if the arrested deputies are to be protected against the Convention's decrees; even more so if the Commune is to take the fight to the Convention.

Hanriot is leading on strategy and execution. His first general order is addressed to the six Legion Chiefs: each is to send 400 men instantly to the Place de la Maison Commune (thus 50 men from each section). They are also to order their sectional battalion commanders to come to the Maison Commune and receive orders. He sends out a summons too to Cn. Fontaine, the Parisian artillery commander (the gunners have a semi-autonomous command structure). A similar note is despatched to the commanders of the two mounted squadrons of the gendarmerie, Martin and Hémart. (Hanriot does not realize that the CPS has already nobbled the latter.) Finally, the NG in the outer ring of sections is primed to ensure that all gateways (or *barrières*) into and out of the city are closed. This is a classic move in all *journées*. It keeps Parisian *journées* Parisian.

Mobilizing Paris's armed forces as a first priority shows the seriousness of intent of the three men in the Maison Commune. But they are also aware that the active engagement of the city as a whole involves winning over the civilian authorities within the sections. The task is more difficult than it had been on 31 May 1793, moreover, as the Revolutionary Committees now report direct to the Committees of Government rather than the Commune. Civil Committees are less overtly line-managed from the Maison

Commune, however, and they are particularly crucial in that each Civil Committee President has the power to convoke an extraordinary sectional General Assembly in which all citizens may participate. This may be determinant in the scale of mobilization today.

Fleuriot has already given orders to those of the Municipal Council members who are leaving this morning's meeting to get things under way in their respective sections, and the *générale* is already being beaten in the adjacent sections of Homme-Armé and Droits-de-l'Homme. Only 22 of the 48 members of the Council have been present today, and a rump of them are continuing with that meeting. Other means of mobilization are therefore necessary. So Hanriot sends orders through the six Legion Chiefs to instruct the adjutant in each sectional battalion to alert the local President of the Revolutionary Committee as to what is going on, and in addition to summon them to come to the Maison Commune. To speed things up, Hanriot is barking out his orders rather than putting them in writing.

With Hanriot coordinating military aspects of their plans, Fleuriot and Payan also seek to legitimize their action not only by widening the call to action among civilians, but also by convoking the Commune's General Council. When this 144-strong body is in place the Commune will be plausibly able to claim to represent the people in insurrection. The Council meets only on the fifth and tenth day of every ten-day week, and the logistics of calling an emergency meeting are challenging. Messages to the sections have to be transcribed 48 times, and then transmitted to the most far-flung parts of the city. Hanriot orders drum-rolls within sections to get the message through.

It will take some time for the Council to foregather, so National Agent Payan probably thinks it is a good moment to slip away to dine. He lives a couple of hundred yards away, on the Rue des Arcis in the Lombards section. Maybe it is at this moment of lull too that Hanriot decides to release the hapless Courvol, to allow him to return to the Convention, with the words:

- Don't forget to tell Robespierre to stand firm; and say to all the good deputies not to worry; that we are going to hurry along to rid them of all the fucking traitors to the fatherland who sit amongst them.

Who does Hanriot imagine are the 'good' deputies and, equally important, who exactly are the 'fucking traitors'?

3.00 p.m.

Convention hall, Tuileries palace

C PS members are currently congratulating themselves on having established their control over the Convention. The tasks that they agreed last night in an air of general desperation have been successfully executed. The assembly has dismissed Hanriot as NG commander and his general staff with him, and instituted a more democratic, or at least less threatening, way of organizing the force. The deputies have also issued Barère's proclamation to the people of Paris urging them to rally around the Committees of Government.

Billaud, Collot, and Barère have profited more than they could have imagined from Tallien's unanticipated assault on Robespierre. By the end of their meeting last night, their fear of Robespierre's popularity had made them willing even to risk working with Saint-Just towards building a new consensus within the committees. Tallien's intervention dramatically put Robespierre in the firing line and has also revealed his lack of popular support. CPS leaders were also able to intervene in time just as Tallien looked like he was widening his attack to include a call for the rolling back of terror. Tallien the loose cannon has been effectively harnessed. The arrest of Revolutionary Tribunal President Dumas is an acceptable concession: he is one of Robespierre's staunchest supporters and had probably been licking his lips at the prospect of sentencing Tallien's lover, Theresa Cabarrus, to the guillotine. This apart, the institutions of Revolutionary Government have been otherwise unchallenged. Not just Robespierre will be under arrest, moreover, but also, as an unexpected bonus, his two principal allies in the Convention, Couthon and Saint-Just, and further acolytes in Le Bas and brother Augustin. It is all almost too good to be true.

Back in the President's chair now, Collot insists that Saint-Just should hand over the speech he was about to make. From Tallien's first interjection, Saint-Just has looked on the proceedings with dreamy impassivity, as though he was floating above the whole fracas. If the other arrested deputies are looking cowed and humbled, however, Robespierre is still breathing fire and continuing to stretch the patience of his erstwhile colleagues. When Collot addresses his fellow deputies:

> – Citizens! You have just saved the *patrie* . . . Your enemies were wanting another 31 May insurrection . . .
> Robespierre:
> – That's a lie!

Is it a lie though? Yesterday, Robespierre certainly came out strongly for a purge of government and a whole range of other measures. His speech in the Jacobins last night may have signalled his wish for the people of Paris to mobilize in his support, but he has done precisely nothing in the interim that could achieve this end or even to alert his confidants to the nature of his plans. Furthermore, the flustered response of Hanriot, Fleuriot, and Payan at the Maison Commune this afternoon underlines how far from their minds any sort of popular mobilization has been. The Maison Commune is currently improvising almost as furiously as the Convention.

On the face of it, then, Robespierre rather than Collot seems to be in the right, in that Robespierre has not formed plans for a *journée* today. Did he perhaps think that he could achieve his objectives by the sheer force of his words? Given the long history of antagonism between the non-Montagnard parts of the assembly and himself, it seems delusional for Robespierre to imagine he could ever get a non-Montagnard majority to support him on a lasting basis. The honeyed words for *hommes de bien* in yesterday's speech and his comments to landlord Duplay might provide him with enough support to ride out the current crisis. But it is not a long-term solution.

Collot, Billaud, and the others have seen Robespierre at work in the past. They realize he is no tribune of the people or street fighter, and, as Marat noted, pales at the sight of a drawn sabre. They know how he always seeks to position himself as adviser to the people rather than their leader. He merely seeks to point the way for the people to act. Robespierre believes that the people are constitutionally entitled to exercise oversight over the national representation. So if the people come to view the deputies as out of line, they have the inherent right to resist oppression.

Robespierre's particular mindset as regards popular oversight and intervention was very evident in his conduct preceding the 31 May and 2 June *journées*. In weeks of preparation from early in April, he and Couthon promoted the case for the expulsion of the Girondins, diffusing their arguments through the Jacobin club and the press, so as to reach militants in the Paris sections and also throughout the land. They also sought to hold back the movement from premature armed action, which risked backfiring. But then, on 26 May 1793, came a clarion call in the Jacobin Club for popular insurrection, which was also an exercise in self-effacement:

> – I invite the people to come into the Convention in insurrection against all the corrupt deputies... Loyal deputies are powerless without the people.

He was he said, with a characteristically martyrish nod, 'ready to die with republicans than to live with the victors'. He remained true to this approach, scrupulously refusing a role for himself on the organizing committee for the *journées* which were dominated by sans-culottes through to the days' aftermath.

Robespierre's conduct in the current crisis seems to conform very closely to his role in the earlier *journées*. Terror remains on the agenda, and purges within the political elite are essential if the social institutions that he glimpses on the horizon can transform the people in the ways of virtue. And it is the people who will need to act if, as seems to be the case, the Convention resists his path to these sunlit uplands. Deputies will need the people to pressurize them and if necessary to purge the recalcitrant, just as they did on 31 May and 2 June 1793.

Despite these forceful echoes of the earlier *journée,* developments have not yet reached maturity, and there is still some distance from the final paroxysm. For example, Robespierre and Couthon have not yet even reached the stage of publicly naming names. Indeed the former specifically refused the opportunity to do so several times in the last few days, at the Convention and the Jacobins. Parisians still need to be worked on in ways that bring to the surface the 'virtuous people' and consign to the depths the 'impure breed' within the popular classes which have so troubled Robespierre of late.

What Tallien has done today is to confound this careful strategy by forcing the issue when neither Robespierre nor indeed his supporters across the city is ready for it. Time has proved not to be on Robespierre's side. Tallien has taken the CPS and indeed the whole of the Convention by surprise.

Both the unexpectedness and the magnitude of today's events are such that the deputies do not yet seem to be quite mentally prepared for what they are doing. They had been so fearful about facing up to Robespierre. And now they need to screw up their courage again, to order the ushers to remove the accused from the benches and place them at the bar of the house. But even the ushers look nervous. Robespierre has so long been dominant within these walls, that they hesitate to carry out explicit orders against him. Couthon is carried towards the bar, but the others stay obstinately in place.

The President calls firmly for the most experienced of the ushers, Jacques-Auguste Rose, a man of Scottish extraction born in north America, to take the lead. Rose is a tough character with experience in the assemblies back to 1789. He played a courageous role on the *journée* of 10 August 1792, shepherding Louis XVI through a hostile crowd at the height of the action. Today he has already been active, working with the assembly's secretaries physically to block Robespierre's best efforts to gain access to the rostrum. When Rose now steps imposingly forward to invite the deputies to move towards the bar, the men initially show no inclination to do so. With the assembly dithering over its next move, deputy Lozeau pipes up to remind the deputies that Robespierre and his colleagues despatched the Girondins to the bar when they expelled them on 2 June 1793, so it seems only right to do the same to the five deputies now. To loud cries of 'To the bar!' the brow-beaten men are all finally forced to assemble at the bar of the house. Rose will hand the men over to CGS master spy Dossonville, who is present to conduct the next stage of the operation: he will take them to the offices of the CGS in the Hôtel de Brionne to await arrangements for them to be despatched to prison. The deputies seem finally to be getting a sense of purpose, and taking full cognizance of the startling fact: they are overthrowing Robespierre.

3.30 p.m.

Courtyard, Palais de Justice, Ile de la Cité

S ix tumbrils have entered the Conciergerie prison courtyard and are being readied to take those sentenced today to the guillotine. They are under the authority of public executioner Henri Sanson with his helpers (mostly his relatives: executioners from family dynasties, and the Sansons' involvement in the *métier* dates back to 1684). On his way here, Sanson has noticed large groupings of men and an air of unease abroad in the capital, particularly in the Faubourg Saint-Antoine, through which the convoy normally passes on its way to the Place du Trône. The executioner approaches Fouquier to share his anxieties, but the latter, who knows about the likely demonstrations against the Wage Maximum, hastily concludes that this is not a problem to worry about. He cuts his interlocutor short.

  - Do your business. The course of justice must not be obstructed.

Nor indeed, must one man's rendezvous with his dinner be postponed. Fouquier starts to make preparations to leave the Palais de Justice and head off for the Ile Saint-Louis, where a good meal and genial companions await him *chez* Cn. Vergne.

3.30 p.m.

Convention hall, Tuileries palace

J ust as the arrested deputies are finally moving under duress towards the bar of the house, Thuriot, in the President's chair, is informed that Mulot, Fifth NG Legion Chief, has arrived to take orders. Thuriot vacates the chair to talk to him in the small room behind the president's rostrum, passing on to him an arrest warrant for Hanriot.

Thuriot is aware that the six Legion Chiefs are crucial links in the NG chain of command, who will need to be on their toes today. They report to the NG commander, and the CPS will want to ensure that the Chiefs know that Hanriot has been dismissed from the post—and to get this message out swiftly to sectional battalions. Julliot, Second Legion Chief, who is commanding the duty force at the Convention today, has already been brought up to speed, as has Fourth Legion Chief Chardin. But neither acting Sixth Legion Chief Olivier nor First Legion Chief Fauconnier is currently to be found. There is a danger that they will implement Hanriot's orders without realizing that he has been relieved of his command. Fauconnier's absence is odd since he had been duty commander at the Convention till he was relieved by Julliot, and he was expected to stay close at hand. His absence is a concern, since on the rota system for NG command that the Convention just established Fauconnier is in line for the post as First Legion Chief. As he is not present, it seems the decision to appoint Hémart to the position is holding.

Third Legion Chief Mathis arrives and follows Mulot into Thuriot's cubby-hole. Mathis shows Thuriot Hanriot's summons, which he had just received, to send 400 men to the Maison Commune. 'This is just what we wanted to prevent,' mutters Thuriot, before sending the copy of Hanriot's

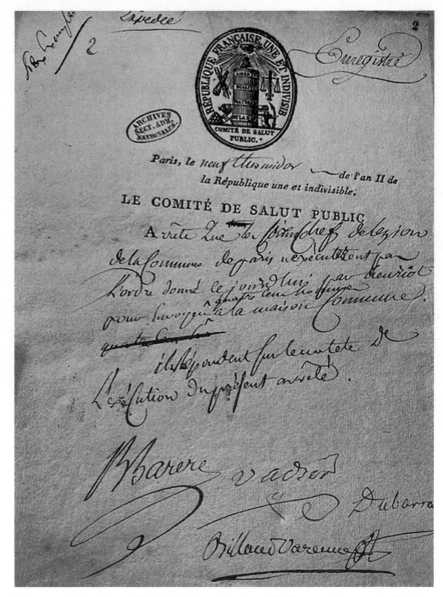

Figure 7. Committee of Public Safety to Legion Chiefs, around 3.30 p.m. (AFII 47 pl. 363, pi. 2)

order to the CPS for their urgent and immediate attention. Suddenly things are not going swimmingly for the Convention after all. It looks like Hanriot will not be going quietly, and armed resistance may be shaping up.

Meanwhile, at the suggestion of Collot, now back in the chair, the Convention has unanimously agreed that no one should leave the hall until all the arrest warrants have been signed. This will slow down the diffusion of the news across the city, no bad thing. The applause from the still-packed public galleries as well as from the deputies' benches is now long, loud, and prolonged, and it redoubles when one of the CGS secretaries enters the hall to inform the CGS members that they are expected at a meeting forthwith. They leave the hall as conquering heroes, to rapturous applause.

Hardly are they out of the room, when Thuriot is handed a decree from the CPS. The decree confirms that, in the light of Hanriot's illicit orders, he is officially removed from his command. The Legion Chiefs are prohibited from sending men to the Commune. The CPS has speedily grasped the paramount importance of stopping the formation of a supply chain of armed men to the Commune.

3.45 p.m.

Hanriot's ride: the eastern sections

P atience has never been Hanriot's strong suit. The pen-pushing punctiliousness of Courvol, the Convention's emissary, in asking for a chit acknowledging the delivery of his message, infuriated him, and he has been bawling out orders to his general staff and to anyone else in his presence to get things under way. The beating of the *générale* is leading guardsmen to muster at their sectional posts. The signal has also led to random groups of Parisians, curious as to what is going on, assembling on the Place de la Maison Commune to the front of the building, joining workers protesting against the Maximum.

At this precise moment, Hanriot would probably be best advised to stay in the NGHQ to await the arrival of the Legion Chiefs whom he has just summoned to the Maison Commune and to work through them to coordinate the NG call-up for the up-coming action. But Hanriot finds immobility challenging. He may suspect that some of the Chiefs favour the Convention. He may want also to verify how widely his orders are being obeyed. So after despatching his messages around the city, Hanriot decides it is his mission to go out and call the people to arms in person.

Leaping onto his horse and ordering three aides-de-camp to accompany him, Hanriot gallops eastwards along the Rue du Martroy to the back of the city hall in the direction of the Place de la Bastille and the Faubourg Saint-Antoine. His mounted group have only gone a hundred yards or so when they encounter, just by the site of the ancestral elm-tree outside the church of Saint-Gervais, Cn. Blanchetot, a member of the gendarmerie attached to the law courts on the Ile de la Cité. Hanriot rides up to him and, drawing his pistol and placing it against Blanchetot's chest, shouts in his foul-mouthed way:

- You fucking good-for-nothing! Get back to the law courts quickly and tell that rascal of a commander to assemble all his troops!

And he then gallops excitedly on, shouting, 'To arms, citizens!' ('*aux armes, citoyens!*') and ordering the *générale* to be beaten throughout the city.

Shaken by this encounter, Blanchetot rides post-haste to the law courts in the Palais de Justice, to report the incident to Cn. Degesne, his superior officer, so that he can alert the CPS to Hanriot's behaviour. It seems important that they should know just what Hanriot is up to.

3.45 p.m.

Across the city: sectional committee meetings

Currently it seems that only two of the six NG Legion chiefs have passed on Hanriot's mobilization orders to their sectional battalions. This means that they are being enacted by 16 of the 48 sections. Either through ignorance of events or pro-Hanriot sympathies, Sixth Legion Chief Cn. Olivier has sent out the Hanriot command. Confusion and ineptitude have reigned over Fauconnier's First Legion. Fauconnier was absent when the CPS earlier forbade the Legion chiefs from sending men to the Maison Commune, and when an emissary brought Hanriot's order to his home on the Ile Saint-Louis, assuming he might be there, his wife cavalierly assumed her husband's role and instructed the message to be sent out to the Legion's eight sections. Citizenness Fauconnier will have much to explain to her husband.

More broadly, however, Hanriot and his colleagues' precipitate action is spreading puzzlement and anxiety and also encountering resistance not only among NG commanders but also among the other sectional authorities. Those municipal councillors who have taken seriously Fleuriot's order at 2.00 p.m. to begin to mobilize have found it difficult to rouse sceptical sectional authorities. The Gravilliers Revolutionary Committee, for example, proved a stickler for legal forms: when Hanriot's ADC Ulrich brought them the Commander's message to send men to the Maison Commune and sound the *rappel*, they refused point-blank, pleading the need for written instruction before they would act. It is only at 4.00 p.m. when this duly arrives, that they agree to send 40 gendarmes to the city hall. But they refrain from sectional mobilization. They are suspicious of what Hanriot might be up to.

Similar reticence is evident elsewhere. On the Ile Saint-Louis, the Fraternité section's Revolutionary Committee indignantly refuses Hanriot's orders on the grounds that the Law on Revolutionary Government of 14 Frimaire forbids military officials from giving orders to civilian authorities. Over in the Marais, Lasné, the commander of the Droits-de-l'Homme battalion silences a drummer beating the *générale* to muster guardsmen, allegedly at the command of Hanriot on his ride. When he is shown a written order from Hanriot, he merely shrugs:

- I wash my hands of it.

On the Ile de la Cité, the Révolutionnaire section's Revolutionary Committee is more categorical. Informed by municipal official Alexandre Minier who has come hotfoot back from the Maison Commune where he has seen Hanriot, Fleuriot, and Payan mouthing off against the Convention and sending out their orders, they decide at once to go into permanent session and to declare unequivocally for the Convention, adding ominously:

- This raising of shields can only be the prelude to evil intent.

It is a similar story in the Left Bank Panthéon and Unité sections, where returning councillors seek to alert local authorities in ways that dispose them against the Commune, but get a chilly reception. The Commune's mobilization plans have not got off to the best of starts.

16.00/4.00 p.m.

Convention hall, Tuileries palace

Robespierre and his accomplices are waiting at the bar of the house, while the formal paperwork for their arrest is being prepared. Deputies are more than aware that their dinner break must be imminent, but Collot is using the moment to round off the session by spinning a narrative of the day that will comfort them in what they have done.

The Convention has thwarted a major conspiracy. A single event, Robespierre's speech, was going to be the trigger for insurrection and civil war. Collot's fellow deputies have today not only pre-empted a coup d'état. In addition they have carried out their own insurrection against incipient tyranny, an act that will pass into the annals of history. Had Saint-Just been allowed to speak, tomorrow would have been a day for mourning the Republic.

Robespierre's intervention on 8 Thermidor was designed to break up national unity and to demoralize the assembly. When he, Collot, had warned the Jacobins later that evening they had silenced him. No doubt, he states, this is an aberration on the part of a club that has always been respectful of the Convention. (He thereby proffers an olive branch to the Jacobins, by implying by implying that they were misled the previous evening.) He recounts what he and Billaud had to endure after being ejected from the Jacobin Club last night, with Couthon's threat of exclusion ringing in their ears. Back in the CPS offices, marble-faced Saint-Just was icily unsympathetic to the plight of his colleagues. The speech he was at that moment composing was full of lies, including accusations of conspiratorial complicity with Fouché. Those lies were based on mendacious reports from spies that Robespierre had been garnering over previous weeks. Saint-Just indicated that some CPS colleagues would be implicated in his report, but would not say more.

Saint-Just's deceitful conduct this morning beggars belief. On leaving the CPS committee room, he had promised to let the committees see his report before he presented it in the Convention. He had agreed that Fouché should be convened at a meeting to discuss the report so that he could explain his conduct. Yet with the committees in session awaiting his arrival, Saint-Just has come direct to the Convention to launch his attack. He had conspired with Couthon for the latter to provide a diversion in the CPS offices which would smooth the path for his speech. It seems too that he was planning to read the speech at the Jacobin Club this evening so as to continue to whip up feeling against the Committees of Government. One can only assume that the three men were planning to use the festival in honour of Bara and Viala tomorrow, on the decadal day of 10 Thermidor, to launch a terrible attack. A day of festivities would have turned into a day of mourning. Instead, Collot says, rallying to his argument, 10 Thermidor will be a day of triumph over tyranny. The committees will meet to consider the conspiracy that Robespierre and his accomplices have been hatching and then report back to the Convention.

This is a good point to leave this curious mélange of fact and fantasy, with cries of '*Vive la République!*' and '*Vive l'égalité!*' ringing round the hall. But Collot cannot resist the opportunity for some final petty digs against his opponents. They claim to respect the law but in fact have continually infringed it. Augustin Robespierre was ordered to go as deputy on mission to the front, but never went. Saint-Just has been recalled from the front on two occasions by Robespierre in defiance of the rest of the CPS so as to continue their plotting. As for Robespierre, he is nothing but a scheming hypocrite. He always speaks with reverence of Marat, whom Collot claims to have known well, yet at Marat's funeral, Robespierre managed to give an oration which failed to mention the man's name a single time. The people can see through such hypocrisy: they know that public virtues can be recognized by the virtues of private life . . .

The session is tailing off. It is getting on for 4.30 p.m. Barère is remembering that the Cardinal de Retz (whose memoirs of the civil wars of the Fronde in the seventeenth century form a kind of breviary of Parisian revolt that is well-known to many deputies) once sardonically remarked that Parisians resist any political action, however important, that disrupts the time that they set aside for dining. The deputies have pushed the claim to its limits, deferring their meal-break till now so as to deal with the urgent matters in hand. The inordinate length of the morning session, let alone the excitement it has engendered, has created healthy appetites. The deputies are hungry, but also intoxicated by their victory. They are starting to slip out.

Business is getting trivial. One deputy stands up to urge that arrangements should be speeded up to place Marat's ashes in the Pantheon, and to eject those of the traitor Mirabeau. The Montagnard Fayau reports that there is talk of arming the young people who will be taking part in the Bara and Viala festival tomorrow with rifles. In the circumstances, this is forbidden. And indeed, the whole festival will be postponed. But the deputies are hardly listening. The meeting is adjourned. There will be an evening session, it is belatedly agreed. Talk of arming and festivals can wait, at least for the moment. A memorable day in the Revolution's annals is drawing to a close. Dinner calls.

4.15 p.m.

Vergne's home, Ile Saint-Louis (Fraternité)

Vergne's dinner party is in full swing. The host, Coffinhal, Desbois-seaux, and an assortment of wives are helping Fouquier-Tinville unwind after the last nine days of ceaseless trials. He is proving hard to cheer up. After all, those days have seen him sending nearly 350 individuals to the guillotine. Morose, drink-sodden remarks recently overheard late at night by employees at the Café des Subsistances suggest he has been finding it hard to handle the pressure of his job. He has been telling the serving girl that the CPS is demanding he deliver 50 or more convictions a day. People think he is Robespierre's minion but he has endless conflicts with the man. The whole system is already creaking at the seams. 'How long can this go on?' he cries into his beer. He would prefer really to be a simple ploughman. But he is strapped to the mast, and if he tried to leave his post now he would be viewed as an aristocratic counter-revolutionary.

Vergne's home is on the western tip of the Ile Saint-Louis, in a tranquil spot relatively cut off from comings and goings from either Left Bank or Right. To get there, Fouquier chose not to cross onto the Right Bank where he has been told anti-Wage Maximum protesters are assembling, but instead took a route via the environs of Notre-Dame, crossing the Pont-au-Double onto the Left Bank and then crossing back onto the Ile Saint-Louis over the Pont de la Tournelle. This means that when, after a little while, the party catches the distant sound of drums rapping out the *générale*, they have little idea what this can be about. Vergne sends out one of his servants to discover what is going on. He returns to say that he has heard that it seems to be about workers on the Right Bank quais protesting against the Wage Maximum. He returns to the dinner-table.

4.15 p.m.

La Force prison

Hanriot's impetuous mounted cavalcade around the eastern sections has not been a rousing success. He is doubtless pleased to see the *générale* being beaten in a number of sections, but his strident calls for arming seem to be producing more anxiety among Parisians than militant adhesion. His appearance on the Boulevard du Temple on the edge of the Faubourg Saint-Antoine panicked proprietors of the many theatres there, who are considering cancelling this evening's performances which are due to start at 5.00 or 5.30 p.m. But at least his ride has brought one success, namely, the release of Payan from the clutches of the gendarmerie.

It seems likely that after setting off from the Maison Commune for a quick meal-break, Payan never reached his home in the Lombards section. CGS agents spotted him and had him arrested and escorted by gendarmes to the prison of La Force, in the Indivisibilité section in the Marais to the east of the Maison Commune. The cart conveying him was just unloading at the gates of the prison when by chance Hanriot and his troupe alighted on them. Hanriot ordered the gendarmes guarding Payan to release him, placing a pistol against their leader's throat:

– If you don't let him go I will blow your brains out!

The threat produced its effect. With Payan free, Hanriot arrested the gendarme escort. After recovering his equanimity in a nearby grocer's shop, the National Agent is now heading back with Hanriot to the Maison Commune.

4.15 p.m.

Conciergerie courtyard, Palais de Justice, Ile de la Cité

Today's accused are being processed for removal to the Place du Trône-Renversé for execution. Obliged to leave the courtroom at the moment that the jury retires, they remain outside for the rest of their own trial. Inside, when the jurors return, presiding judge Maire, Dumas's replacement, asks each of them in turn their verdict. He then proceeds to sentencing. The defendants milling around outside in the Conciergerie courtyard hear cheering from the courtroom, but do not know whether their own death is being announced. Only after the trial has drawn to a close do Conciergerie guards pass among the group and announce who is to be executed. It seems one person in each of the two trials has been acquitted. This means 44 individuals convicted today will be executed, plus the princesse de Monaco, left over from the day before. Fouquier believes that each tumbril should for humanity's sake only contain seven individuals. There are six carts waiting: the slight mis-match may be because he counted on a few more acquittals. Or it may simply be that since the recent CPS decree requisitioning Parisian horses and carriages for the war effort, transport has been in short supply.

The convicted enemies of the people must now be prepared for the scaffold. The Conciergerie guards take the men and women one by one into the small room known as the *salle de la toilette* (the 'dressing room' would be a translation in any other circumstance). The guards remove from them any effects and personal possessions that they have not been able covertly to slip to their fellow prisoners, remove their outer clothes down to their shirts, and then rip the shirts open and cut the hair of men and women back to the nape. Bare necks will offer the guillotine blade no resistance. Their hands are tied behind their backs, and they are pushed rudely out of a little door into the adjacent courtyard, the Cour de Mai, where Sanson and his men are ready to load them into the carts.

The convicted are a motley crew, as indeed such *fournées* always are, being for the most part composed of individuals who have no acquaintance with each other. There are fewer women than usual, but all social levels are represented. A large part of the evidence that Fouquier cited in his indictment in the Salle de la Liberté related to three men sent up from the Allier department where they had already been extensively investigated for economic offences. They shared the defendant benches with six noblemen, all with royalist and aristocratic links and sympathies. Mysteriously, Fouquier also accorded noble status to the Loison couple, entrepreneurs who ran the puppet-theatre on the Champs-Élysées. They had made scandalous comments against Marat, it appears. (A story that they had staged Charlotte Corday's assassination of Marat as marionette comedy was not brought up in evidence). A *valet de chambre* to the king's aunts (both now safely emigrated in Rome), two army officers, one of whom had escaped from prison, and a handful of individuals from the financial and administrative elite compose the contingent from the 'privileged classes' as they have been called since 1789. There are also two manufacturers, one who had worked at the national glass factory on the Rue de Reuilly and the other a tin-maker of indeterminate status. Then there is a school-teacher, a professor of astronomy who had spied for the German princes, and a few others making up numbers.

Over in the Salle de l'Égalité, it is the same kind of mix, though in differing proportions. Over half there are nobles, several from the highest court elite, while one, de Rouvière, had turned up at a deputy's house with concealed weapons and acted suspiciously. (Oddly, it is not stated that the deputy in question had been Maximilien Robespierre.) There is a handful of priests, while the old Third Estate is represented by a mixed group including a florist with Fayettist links, a hatter from Marseilles, a farmer from Dampierre who protested against the closure of churches, a cabinet-maker who had become rich through corrupt dealings in nationalized property and a bar-keeper who had tried to stop the recruitment of volunteers to fight in the Vendée. The enemies of the people come in many forms.

The equalizing force of the law is now bundling the convicted together. Some prisoners, however, still seek marks of distinction. The princesse de

Monaco has taken care to apply a little rouge for her final journey. She is determined not to give away her feelings to the jeering of crowds in the streets already craning their necks to see through the railings of the courtyard. She doesn't want her pallor to be thought to indicate fear.

Hardened executioner Sanson has seen it all before. The range of reactions to impending death runs from the sheerest terror to studied insouciance. Louis XV's last mistress, Mme du Barry, made a spectacular performance of shrieking and sobbing, while other individuals go laughing and joking to the scaffold as if they were off to a wedding feast. But even Sanson admits to feeling admiration for the way that stoical sang-froid has become the default conduct for these moments. Uncannily, unsettlingly, he finds that many of his charges struggling to master their feelings smile as he goes about his business. Despite Citizenness du Barry's example, this is especially true of women. Gently benign female smiles combine aristocratic sprezzatura with the practised sensibility learnt from reading Rousseau's *La Nouvelle Héloise* or viewing Madame Vigée-Lebrun's portraits. There is an 'emulation about dying well' to which many aspire. On the road to the guillotine, the smile has become a silent weapon of symbolic resistance.

4.15 p.m.

CPS Committee Room, Tuileries palace

W hile Collot's peroration is tying up the loose ends of the day in the Convention hall, the Committees of Government seated around the green table in the CPS committee room are busy at work in joint CPS–CGS session. CGS agents are being primed to make arrests of key individuals linked to Robespierre or known to have been in his entourage. The whole of the Duplay family must be brought in, as must Saint-Just's servant. Then there is Hanriot's groom; a couple of members of Popular Commissions; Rousseville, Robespierre's favourite spy; Nicolas and Renaudin from the bodyguard, and others. A quest starts up to locate Robespierre's sister, who has understandably taken fright at what is happening and sought refuge with a friend, reverting to her mother's maiden name, Carraut.

The arrest of Dumas in the Revolutionary Tribunal has been carried out effectively, but Hanriot is a harder nut to crack, ensconced as he is at the NGHQ next to the Maison Commune. Last night, the committees won over Jean Hémart, one of the gendarmerie commanders in the city, and they have chosen him for the task. They have handed him an order that specifies that he will go with a mounted squadron to the NGHQ, and make the arrest.

The committees also send out orders instructing the Revolutionary Committees of the Arcis and Indivisibilité sections to break up the crowds that they have heard are assembling in the environs of the Place de la Maison Commune. It is not sure whether these are Wage Maximum protesters or supporters of Robespierre. The Committee is getting the impression that news of today's arrest has not been welcomed with unanimous joy throughout Paris. The *générale* is being beaten in some sections, so a message goes out at once that sections should desist. Through intercepted orders, they are also getting a sense of what the Commune is up to. Decrees have been sent to the six Legion Chiefs to reverse Hanriot's order to expedite 400 men to the Place de la Maison Commune and his closure of the city gates. They are hoping that this raft of measures taken hastily will nip insurrection in the bud.

4.30 p.m.

Place de la Maison Commune
(or Place de Grève) (Arcis)

As Hanriot tracked back towards the Maison Commune, he will have perceived cannon being hauled towards the Place de la Maison Commune, where crowds are thickening. Although the CPS acted swiftly to prime the Legion Chiefs against Hanriot, and to win over the gendarmerie commanders to their cause, they have overlooked the parallel command structure enjoyed by the gunners. Fontaine, artillery commander for the city, has followed Hanriot's mobilization orders with alacrity. He has reached out to gunners in far more than the 16 sections of the First and Sixth Legions. Half a dozen sections are already on the Place and primed for action.

Hanriot is back on the Place, when he sees a troupe of gendarmes from the 29th Mounted Division ride up, led by Hémart. Hanriot has already sent out a call to Hémart without realizing where his loyalty lies. So he is astonished to see that he is wearing the insignia of Paris NG Commander that was Hanriot's as he reads out the arrest warrant.

Hanriot is thinking quickly as he listens to Hémart, and he calmly suggests that he accompany him into the NGHQ. Once there, out of sight of his gendarme troupe, he orders his men to seize Hémart, take his sword, remove his uniform, tie him up, and place him under armed guard.

Imprisoning the Convention's appointee as NG commander is quite a coup. But Hanriot feels he cannot afford to rest on his laurels, for the Hémart incident shows that the city's armed forces are probably going to be divided in their loyalties. Hanriot has been reflecting on his next step. His calls to the eastern sections of Paris have had little impact. He needs to try something else, in order to seize back the initiative. It suddenly comes to him like a bolt from the blue: he will lead a mounted rescue mission to seize the arrested deputies from under the noses of the Convention. Back on his horse, he harangues the crowd on the Place de la Maison Commune:

> – Citizens! Forty assassins want to kill Robespierre, . . . the virtuous and patriotic Robespierre, Couthon, Saint-Just, and Hanriot have had arrest warrants made out against them – the patriots are oppressed, the traitors triumph, they want me dead . . . those who ordered the arrests are knaves in the pay of Pitt and Cobourg. Let us set out and release our friends. Fear not, Hanriot is marching at your head. Let us spare blood, but the traitors must be arrested.

He summons his aides-de-camp to follow him and they gallop off at speed along the quais in the direction of the Louvre and Tuileries, followed by some 40 to 50 of Hémart's mounted gendarmes, who are mostly unaware of the trick Hanriot has played on their commander. Hanriot's rescue plan has the potential to swing the day dramatically in the Commune's favour.

4.30 p.m.

Mairie and Police Administration HQ, Ile de la Cité

I f the sections alerted to the news of Robespierre's arrest thus far seem rather lethargic in their reactions, there is one oasis of support for the Maison Commune which is hard at work in their cause: namely, the Police Administration located in the Mairie over on the Ile de la Cité. News of how Dumas was plucked from his presiding seat in the adjacent Revolutionary Tribunal earlier in the afternoon arrived a little while ago when most of the Administration's employees were taking their meal-break. Police clerks, duly fed, have returned to their desks to find that their bosses have made a bold beginning. The clerks are given urgent instructions to work in haste to copy and despatch to the warders of every one of the city's 100 gaols an order forbidding them from allowing entry or release to any individual without official police approval. It is important that this is done fast: the arrested deputies have not yet been expedited towards their respective prisons, so that the initiatives of the Convention may still be baulked. It seems as though all are readying themselves for a long night.

4.45 p.m.

Hanriot's raid: from the Maison Commune to the Tuileries palace

Hanriot's audacious raid to rescue Robespierre has a decent chance of success. He knows the habits of the deputies: they don't like to delay too long in the afternoon before adjourning to dine. A lightning strike may catch them unawares while Hémart, their choice as NG commander, languishes in the Maison Commune's cells. Yet as Hanriot's raiding party advances, the reception he receives from the sections through which he passes mirrors the mixture of incomprehension, apathy, and even hostility that marked his earlier cavalcade.

News leaking out of the Convention has already alerted some citizens to be wary of Hanriot. A stream of cries of '*Aux armes, citoyens!*' seems to fall on deaf but also forewarned ears. Near the Pont-Neuf, Hanriot's aide-de-camp Deschamps spots Cn. Savin, one of the CGS secretaries, and arrests him forthwith, pulling him along by his hair to deposit him with the Muséum section's Revolutionary Committee. Yet once Deschamps has rejoined his leader, the Committee addresses Savin:

- Arrested by Hanriot? The citizen is free to go!

As they approach the Tuileries palace, Hanriot's raiding party heads up from the quais towards the Rue Saint-Honoré, where they encounter a group of workers repairing the roadway. Hanriot calls them to arms, shouting, 'Your father is in danger.' The workmen down tools to give him a hearing and shout '*Vive la République!*' as Hanriot gallops off. They resume their labours as though nothing has happened.

Just south of the Palais-Royal, the Rue Saint-Honoré widens out into the
Place du Palais-Royal, only a few hundred yards away from the Tuileries
palace. Hanriot here spots the deputy Merlin de Thionville emerging from
the Rue de Saint-Thomas-du-Louvre where his lodgings are located. On 8
Thermidor, Merlin was out at Versailles supervising artillery practice with
fellow Montagnard deputy Léonard Bourdon and a member of the Commune with responsibility for armaments. He was thus probably absent for
Robespierre's speech. No matter: Hanriot assumes he is one of the enemy
and falls violently upon him, brandishing his pistol and ordering him to be
arrested and taken to the local NG cells. Hanriot cries out that patriot
deputies are being assassinated, but a voice from the crowd counters:

- Don't listen to him. He is a rascal who is tricking you. There is an arrest
warrant out for him. We must arrest him.

Members of Hanriot's mounted escort chase the man down but he seeks
refuge behind a wood-pile, and throws out logs as missiles to keep the
mounted soldiers at bay. Hanriot's dramatic exploit is in danger of turning
into farce.

Hanriot does manage to get Merlin to the NG guardroom of the Montagne section (where he is almost instantly released once Hanriot's back is
turned). Hanriot only extricates himself with some difficulty from a crowd
there that is becoming increasingly mutinous about his actions. Boulanger,
one of his ADCs, who rides up a little late with the intention of joining his
commander, is stopped by the crowd, who pull him off his horse and drag
him away.

As Hanriot and his men approach the CGS offices, where the arrested
deputies are being held, they are spotted by two deputies, Edme-
Bonaventure Courtois and Louis-Antoine Robin, who are sitting down to
dine. The two men represent the Aube, Danton's old department, so are
probably toasting Danton's memory as much as the overthrow of his
nemesis. They know a figure like Hanriot when they see him and are only
too well aware of what he might be up to. A crisis is clearly looming. They
pay up and while Courtois heads for the Palais-Royal to secure the support
of the Montagne NG battalion, Robin rushes towards the CGS offices in the
Hôtel de Brionne.

4.45 p.m.

CGS offices, Hôtel de Brionne (Tuileries)

Hanriot's raiding party has turned off the Rue Saint-Honoré down the narrow Rue de l'Échelle. It opens onto a small square in front of the elegant Hôtel de Brionne, which contains the CGS offices. His men dismount and enter the building, sabres in hand, and noisily scour the premises for the arrested deputies. They kick down a door to the room in which the CGS usually meets, and emerge gripping one of the committee—it must be André Amar—by the collar, calling him all the names under the sun and demanding that he tell them where Robespierre and the others are to be found. The hubbub brings troops out of the guardroom, led by brigadier Jeannolle. In the stand-off which ensues, Amar manages to escape, and scuttles out, passing deputy Robin on his way in.

Doubtless alerted by the racket being kicked up below, CGS member Ruhl has also just emerged. Leaping onto a table, he orders Jeannolle's loyal guardsmen to draw swords against the intruders. In the struggle, the raiding party seem to be getting the upper hand, until reinforcements, summoned by Courtois, arrive on horseback, led by Second Legion Chief Julliot. Many of Hanriot's little mounted force of 29th Division gendarmes, dismayed by the Merlin de Thionville incident, have lost their appetite for a fight and they promptly change sides. The fighting soon fizzles out, and with deputies Courtois and Robin cheering him on, Julliot sends out trooper Jeannolle to purchase rope to tie up the prisoners.

The CPS had been fretting about its inability to track down and arrest Hanriot. But Hanriot has fallen into their laps. This means that both the Commune and the Convention have their NG commanders in gaol. What are the implications, one wonders, for the wider conflict?

PART
IV

A Parisian *Journée*
(5.00 p.m. to Midnight)

At the end of their epic session, the deputies in the National Convention break off to dine, confident that their work is done. Robespierre and his allies have been identified, arrested, and await their fate. The crisis is over. Robespierre's bluff has been called. He is a paper tiger.

Even as the deputies make their way to their lodgings or to neighbouring restaurants, however, Paris's municipal government, the Commune, is declaring itself in insurrection over the arrest of Robespierre. It has been sending out commands while the Convention has been deliberating. It has begun assembling armed forces to bring their demands from the Maison Commune into the Convention hall. So far, anything out of the ordinary during Mulberry Day has been confined to the political elite. Not any longer. Parisians are being called on to mobilize for action by competing authorities, Convention and Commune, each claiming legitimacy. The date 9 Thermidor will prove to be a journée which engages the whole population of the city. After further rolls of the dice ordinary citizens will be obliged to make a fundamental choice regarding not only the fate of Robespierre but also the future character of the Revolution.

17.00/5.00 p.m.

Théâtre de la République, Palais-Royal environs (Montagne)

M ost theatre performances start at 5.00 or 5.30 and audiences are taking their places. Despite the scare that Hanriot caused theatre proprietors in his wild afternoon roving in the east of the city an hour or so ago, theatres are open.

This evening's offerings are a fair representation of the current repertoire. The Théâtre de l'Égalité will play Lemierre's patriotic, government-approved *Guillaume Tell*. At the other end of the stylistic spectrum, Astley's Amphitheatre over in the Faubourg du Temple, which specializes in circus-style entertainments, will be rehearsing a spectacular hippodrama. The classics are also on show: Quinault's *Armide*—libretto 1686, with Gluck's 1777 score—will be performed at the Opéra national. The persistent taste for light comedy is present too. The Théâtre du Vaudeville just across from the Palais Royal in the Rue de Chartres, where many deputies have their lodgings, has been cautioned by the government for frivolity, but it persists in the lighter vein, and three short plays are scheduled for this evening.

The Théâtre de la République near the Palais-Royal will play Legouvé's uplifting classical fable, *Epicharis et Néron, ou Conspiration pour la liberté*, first performed in early February. The play is an account of a plot to overthrow emperor Nero, a tyrant, of course. This has passed the censor, as it is easily presented as an attack on Bourbon absolutist 'tyranny'. But one wonders how many of the audience are abreast of the day's events. Will tonight's reactions show that they now equate emperor Nero with another, more contemporary 'tyrant'?

- *Tremble, tremble, Néron, ton empire est passé!*

5.00 p.m.

The streets of the city

The members of the Commune's 144-strong General Council are beginning to appear for the assembly convened by mayor Fleuriot-Lescot and National Agent Payan. Numbers are still not large. A couple of hours ago, the mayor sent colleagues who had attended the Municipal Council to rally support in their sections and then to return with all the fellow councillors for a full General Council. At the same time, Hanriot has also been trying to get NG Legion Chiefs to assemble troops outside the Maison Commune. That makes for a plethora of messages, oral and written, criss-crossing the city. Missives have not yet got through to many outer sections. The convocation is rendered more problematic by the fact that many would-be attendees are still at their workplace rather than at their home address. Telling them to drop everything and come to the Maison Commune is a tall order, even assuming they can be located.

The delegation from the nearby Indivisibilité section is already proceeding to the Maison Commune under the cheerful impression that the sections have been convoked

> for all to go en masse with them to the National Convention to congratulate it on the decrees of the afternoon session and for having arrested the tyrants who threaten our freedom.

Most councillors converging on the Maison Commune, however, will not yet have heard news of the arrests. Ignorance and uncertainty are widespread. A small but significant knot of around 20 were members of the Insurrectionary Commune of August 1792, while roughly half of the present Council served during the *journées* of 31 May and 2 June 1793. They are not so wet behind the ears as to be unaware that under government regulations, the General Council only meets on the fifth and tenth of every ten-day week. Thus calling a meeting like this is not only unusual, it could also be illegal. But then in revolutions, emergency situations arise where the *salus populi* can only be ensured by entering a zone of illegality. Such men know that, as councillor Jean-Jacques Chrétien puts it, the Commune is where 'in stormy times, duty calls any magistrate of the people'. Understandably, some councillors have chosen to lie low or claim illness.

5.00 p.m.

Police Administration HQ, Mairie, Ile de la Cité

The engraver Cn. Degouy, a member of the Panthéon section's Revolutionary Committee, has dropped into the Police HQ to see his Administrator friend, Claude Bigaud, a painter. He has heard that the Commune is calling for deputations from the sections to come to the Maison Commune, while NG commander Hanriot is also mobilizing. Surely, he states, these actions explicitly infringe the 14 Frimaire Law of Revolutionary Government? The reply comes back:

> – It's not now about a Revolutionary law. We are rising up to protect the interests of the people, which today is taking back its powers. If you and your committee are good patriots and good revolutionaries, you'll go back and get them to rise up too.

Bigaud rounds off the peroration by throwing his arms around Degouy's neck and giving him the kiss of fraternity.

The bulk of the membership of the Police Administration, like Bigaud, has come out determinedly in favour of the Commune against the Convention. Yet despite the red mist of Bigaud's enthusiasm, there are reservations and discordant voices. Prominent among the doubters is the Police Administration's longest-serving member, Étienne Michel. Renowned for his radical stance on most things (he has proclaimed the wish, for example, that the last lawyer on earth should be hanged with the guts of the last priest) he enters the Police HQ, to tell his colleagues the good news (in his view) about Robespierre's arrest, which he personally witnessed in the Convention hall. There he finds 8 to 10 of them, all wearing their tricolour sashes, sombrely announcing their collective decision to support the Commune.

No fraternal embrace for him. He angrily denounces their choice as illegal, but his colleagues strike back at him. He is

> – . . . a counter-revolutionary. He is betraying his municipal sash, he is a coward in letting the true representatives of the people be oppressed, and he is abandoning the Incorruptible.

He is roughly seized and after a sharp struggle thrown into the police cells, where he is joined shortly after by his colleague, the tailor Jean Benoit from the Halle-au-Blé section, who has also resisted the course of action. Another colleague, teacher Jean-Guillaume Guyot, is treated more leniently on arrival. The painter Jean-Léopold Faro, who is emerging as one of the most energetic of police administrators this evening, tells him that he is 'unsuited' to the upcoming activities of the night and orders him to go and see what is happening at the Maison Commune, with which the adminis-trators are seeking to establish liaison. The Commune has an ally and bastion on the Ile de la Cité. 'We are firm in our post,' Faro and fellow-administrator Jacques-Mathurin Le Lièvre write to inform the mayor. 'The Republic will triumph.'

5.30 p.m.

Place de la Maison Commune

The crowd that started forming on the Place de la Maison Commune from 2.00 p.m. has now swollen considerably. The speedy transmission to the six NG Legion Chiefs of the Convention's decree dismissing Hanriot and forbidding the Guard from following his orders has not prevented his orders from getting through to enough sections to produce a sizeable armed force alongside many curious or engaged civilians and protesters against the Wage Maximum. It has actually helped matters that the orders that Hanriot sent out have been garbled. He asked the Legion chiefs to send 400 men each to the Commune, 50 men per section that is. Yet some sections have taken the orders to mean that they themselves should contribute as near to 400 as they can manage. The beating of the *générale* in sections close to the Maison Commune has had a particularly impressive mobilizing effect, with sizeable contingents from Arcis, Lombards, and Réunion now present. Across the Seine, the Panthéon section is also busy mobilizing a force approaching 1,200 men.

Just arriving is a detachment of 200 men and two cannon from the Homme-Armé section, under the leadership of the President of its Revolutionary Committee, Claude Chalandon. That section was put on alert some time after 2.00 p.m. by the noise of the *générale* being beaten in the neighbouring Droits-de-l'Homme section. The painter Pierre-Alexandre Louvet, councillor for the section, had been present at the earlier Municipal Council. He heeded Hanriot and Fleuriot's call to go and mobilize the sections, shouting out through the streets, 'Virtue is oppressed! We need another 31 May!' His efforts to persuade Civil Committee president, Cn. Goujon, to take action failed by dint of him having no written orders to show him. Louvet was furious, and left with tears streaming down his face. But he has found a more willing ear in Chalandon, cobbler, businessman, and militant. Hearing that Hanriot at the Maison Commune was crying out for support, Chalandon went around the section between 3.00 and 4.00 p.m. with a drum, beating the *générale*. Under Louvet's guidance, he grouped together the men who answered the summons in the forecourt of the Hôtel de Soubise on the Rue des Francs-Bourgeois. The Homme-Armé artillery company is on active service outside Paris, but its cannon are still in place and Chalandon, as a former gunner himself, knows how to ready it for action. It takes some doing: the guns count as light cannon, but at 2840 kg each they need 8 strapping guardsmen in harness to pull them through the streets.

By the time Goujon arrived on the scene at around 4.00 p.m. to find out what was going on, there was still little clarity among the mobilized men about the nature of the apparent emergency. Some were saying that it was to do with the arrest of Robespierre, while others claimed it was in order to combat workers' disturbances caused by the 23 July Wage Maximum. (The Civil Committee had just received delivery of additional copies of that decree, which may have started the rumour.) A story is also circulating that workers have started attacking public buildings. Chalandon's energetic pro-Robespierre views are well-known in the section, and he has already arrested one colleague for claiming Robespierre is a counter-revolutionary. When his legal right to act is queried, he replies, 'We didn't need orders on 10 August 1792!' He has gathered that Hanriot wants half of the sectional Guard to come to the Maison Commune with both of the section's cannon. So at 5.00 p.m., he rolls the two cannons out of the Hôtel de Soubise, with lighted match in his hand. Challenged again over acting without written orders, he shouts out:

- When there aren't orders and no leader, we leave without a leader. It's me in command today. Let's go! Those who want to have only to follow me! And on my head be it!

5.30 p.m.

CGS and CPS offices, Tuileries palace complex

Second Legion Chief Julliot, the ranking officer in the Convention's duty guard for today, has despatched Livin, adjutant in the Bon-Conseil battalion, to inform the CPS that he has just captured Hanriot and put him under arrest. The contretemps at the Hôtel de Brionne leading to Hanriot's arrest attracted a large crowd of men and women but they seem highly supportive of the Convention. Julliot harangues them, urging them to return to their sections and to make preparations to defend the assembly.

The deputy Robin who was instrumental in Hanriot's capture still has his dander up, and frog-marches the general, his arms bound behind his back, to the CPS offices, where he finds Billaud-Varenne, Barère, and others. He explains what has happened and suggests immediate action against his prisoner. Billaud enquires what he has in mind, to which Robin replies:

> – If you don't have this traitor punished immediately, it is quite possible that by nightfall the villain and his allies will cut your throats in the assembly.

Barère seems strangely unperturbed by the drastic proposal. 'Do you want us to set up a military commission that can execute him by court-martial?' he idly asks. 'That,' Billaud, also oddly detached, chips in, 'would be highly energetic.' In the end, the men decide that Robin should lead Hanriot back to the CGS. They will make a decision on him after due consideration.

Robin can scarcely believe how lightly the CPS members are taking the situation. They are behaving as though they were Hanriot's accomplices, or at very least as though they are backing off from the use of deterrent force in self-defence. Surely this is a moment for the government to act with maximum energy against its enemies. If they do not, they may regret it.

5.30 p.m.

Place de la Maison Commune

The hot-headed Chalandon and his Homme-Armé detachment and cannons have now reached the Place de la Maison Commune. But his swashbuckling spirit is draining away. Along the route, his men have been yet again querying his lack of written orders for this drastic step, causing him to start harbouring doubts about the advisability of what he is doing. He finds the Place in a state of utter chaos and confusion. Leaving his men on the square, he enters the Maison Commune to seek orders and bumps into Pierre-François Vincent, a senior clerk in the NGHQ. Vincent has argued with Hanriot in the past and has a low estimation of his talents.

> - There's a storm breaking [he tells Chalandon]. The General is a real *jean-foutre*, a hopeless idiot, and you'd do well to go off to the National Treasury Building.

Chalandon takes the warning and seizes the mission with alacrity. Within a quarter of an hour of arriving at the Place, he and his troupe are heading for the Treasury to keep it safe, whether from mutinous workers or conspiratorial deputies, he is still not quite sure.

5.30 p.m.

Maison Commune Council Chamber

The impatience of Fleuriot and Payan at the tardiness of arrivals for the General Council meeting has been manifest. At 5.30 they adjudge that the 25 to 30 councillors present (out of a possible 144) form a quorum and so official business begins. The Council Chamber is located in the northern half of the long first-floor hall that extends the length of the western side of the building overlooking the Place. There is room for the public to gather on the southern half of this space, but there is also an outer passageway all around the chamber where the public can oversee events. There is not a big crowd.

The Fleuriot starts with a solemn declaration: it was here that the father-land was saved on 10 August 1792 and 31 May 1793, and it is here that the fatherland will be saved today. Having set today's events in the context of a series of popular insurrections, he reads out the decrees of the Convention relating to Payan, Hanriot, and Fleuriot himself, decrees, he explains, which the men have angrily rejected.

– The fatherland is in danger! It is we here who will save it!

Taking down from the wall a copy of the Declaration of the Rights of Man, Fleuriot intones:

– When government violates the rights of the people, insurrection is for the people the most sacred and indispensable of duties.

Fleuriot then calls on all present to stand and take an oath of loyalty to the Commune at this time of national emergency.

Payan and François-Louis Paris, a young writer who represents the Panthéon section (and who spent the morning in the Maison Commune solemnizing marriages), are delegated to write a proclamation to the people of Paris. It reads:

– CITIZENS! The fatherland is more in danger than it ever has been. Villains are dictating and oppressing the Convention. They are persecuting ROBE-SPIERRE, the man who established the principle of the Supreme Being and the consoling doctrine of the immortality of the soul; SAINT-JUST, this apostle of virtue who ended treason among the armies of the Rhine and of the North, and who along with LEBAS led the armies of the Republic to victory, along with COUTHON, this virtuous citizen whose only living parts, his head and body, burn with patriotism; and ROBESPIERRE the YOUNGER who presided over the victories of the Army of Italy. And who are their foes? AMAR, a nobleman who lives off 50,000 livres of rentes, and the viscount DUBARRAN along with others of their ilk: COLLOT d'HERBOIS, supporter of the infamous Danton, who as an actor stole the earnings of his troupe; BOURDON de l'OISE who endlessly berates the Commune; and BARÈRE, who has belonged to all factions in turn and who fixed the wages of workers at a level at which they die of hunger. These are the villains that the Commune's Council denounces to you. PEOPLE, RISE UP. We must not lose the fruits of 10 August and 31 May. We must hurl all these traitors into their tombs.

As a manifesto for an insurrection, this is very much a dog's dinner. The authors at least have the identity of those arrested correct, but clearly have little idea about the identity of the instigators of the attack on Robespierre. No Tallien? No Billaud? Amar is certainly involved in the day's actions thus far, but Dubarran not especially so. Bourdon de l'Oise is a perpetual thorn in the side of the Commune but has not had a leading role. There are several questionable notes too. Is Robespierre's support for the soul's immortality really a selling-point for Parisians? To hold Barère responsible for the 23 July Wage Maximum is simply wrong. It is a transparent attempt to win over protesting workers and to deflect attention away from the fact that it is the Commune not the CPS which has been strenuously enforcing the decree. How convincing will that appear? The Maximum protesters are amassing outside the Maison Commune, not the Convention, indicating whom they hold responsible. To get the people of Paris on its side, the Commune will have to try harder.

5.30 p.m.

CGS offices, Hôtel de Brionne

Crestfallen and humiliated, his hands tied behind his back, Hanriot enters the room in the CGS office, where the arrested deputies are being kept while preparations are under way to take them to different prisons across the capital. The deputies are eating. The CGS has pushed the boat out on the catering front, ordering in quite a feast for the prisoners, who remain, after all, representatives of the people. Soup is followed by a joint of roast mutton and boiled capon, with bread and two bottles of burgundy to wash it down. The guards suddenly notice that Hanriot is trying to establish secretive communication with the deputies by odd facial gesticulations. It is decided to separate them.

5.30 p.m.

Vergne's home, Ile Saint-Louis

T he Fouquier-Tinville dinner-party guests are hearing the drum-beat of
the *générale* coming louder, closer, and more insistent. Despite his post-
prandial state, Fouquier-Tinville is alert enough to realize that something
untoward is happening in the city. The news finally arrives: Robespierre,
Couthon, and Saint-Just have been arrested in the Convention. It is no longer
a question of worker's wage protests. It is . . . what? No one is quite sure.

Vergne and some of the other guests think it prudent to report to their
sectional headquarters: Vergne is secretary to the Fraternité section General
Assembly. Coffinhal dons his tricolour sash and heads for the Maison
Commune to find out what is going on there, taking with him fellow
guest, municipal councillor Desboisseaux. Fouquier heads for home and
workplace: the Revolutionary Tribunal at the Palais de Justice. En route,
rushing along the Quai des Ormes on the Right Bank before crossing back to
the Ile de la Cité he encounters another magistrate also aware of the situation
and hastening back to his post for what seems to be a major crisis ahead.

18.00/6.00 p.m.
Council chamber, Maison Commune

The Maison Commune has become a seething cauldron of insurrectionary activity. Fleuriot-Lescot's passionate opening speech has engendered an electrifying spirit of commitment around the room. The number of attendees is still not great, but it is growing. New arrivals are made to take an oath 'to save the fatherland, to exterminate all tyrants, and to enforce respect on and even to exterminate all those who would oppose the orders of the Commune'. But in the hectic and noisy throng, the oath is simplified and made to seem banal and unfocused: saving the fatherland and exterminating tyrants is the stuff of everyday life for patriots. Many are confused as to what exactly all this fuss is about.

The arrival in the Council of Jean-Jacques Lubin, one of Payan's two deputies as National Agent, imparts a new sense of urgency in the assembly hall. He was present in the Convention throughout the morning session and regales the assembled with the story of the arrests. Lubin has had radical moments in the recent past, but his appointment by the CPS in April 1794 has made him a firm supporter of Robespierre. (Perhaps being close to the centre of power is a means of protecting his family: for a younger brother has worked for Fargeon, Marie-Antoinette's favourite perfumer, and another brother Jean-Baptiste was only yesterday committed to the Revolutionary Tribunal. These are dangerous relatives to have at times like these.) Lubin readies himself for an energetic night.

It may well be Lubin who at this juncture states that precious time is being wasted with words when action is necessary. There is truth in this, for there is much to plan and organize. Earlier today, Robespierre categorically denied that he was instigating a 31 May-style *journée*; but under pressure of circumstances, his followers across the city are doing precisely that. The leaders of the Commune may not be clear about the names of their antagonists in the Convention; but they are well aware of the course of action upon which they have embarked. They have slipped effortlessly into a script for popular insurrection which, as their manifesto proclaims, goes back beyond 31 May 1793 to 10 August 1792. The script stipulates that city barriers are to be closed (as Hanriot has already ordered); representatives of each of the sections will be convoked to the Maison Commune; NG battalions will be primed for action; and General Assemblies will be called in each section 'to deliberate on the dangers to the fatherland' (a customary trope in such circumstances). The Parisian people rising in insurrection will lay claim to political legitimacy. In that spirit, they place under the safeguard of the people all those individuals whom the Convention has had arrested; and they also formally deny the legal status of the decrees of the 'so-called Convention' (as Fleuriot puts it), and command that their agents and emissaries are to be arrested on sight.

These messages need to go out swiftly, coordinating all means at the Commune's disposal. An order is given to go up to the Maison Commune belfry and ring the tocsin. The massive alarm cannon on the Pont-Neuf whose firing on 31 May signalled to Parisians that the fatherland was in danger should be brought into action. Payan also dictates an order for the Revolutionary Committee of the Cité section which includes the Temple of the Supreme Being (formerly Notre-Dame cathedral). The great Notre-Dame bell, the bourdon, has been used to signal major events, famous and infamous, in the city's history, from royal births and deaths through to the 1572 Saint Bartholomew's Massacre and beyond. Payan wants it rung today:

> – Patriots! On 31 May you assembled patriots by ringing the tocsin—and saved the fatherland. Today the fatherland is again in danger, and you will not hesitate in making the bourdon resound. It is the sure means of raising the people en masse and saving liberty.
>
> Greetings and fraternity!

Two delegates are also sent to the Jacobin Club, a crucial ally for the course of action being set in train. The Jacobin Club usually meets from around 7.00 p.m., but the Commune has every hope that, after last night's stirring session, members will be early into their seats. Contact needs to be established too with the Police Administration over at the Mairie. Closer at hand, two delegates are chosen to go out onto the Place and seek to raise awareness among the burgeoning crowds.

Commune clerk Blaise Lafosse has been in the building since 7.00 a.m. this morning. He and his colleagues managed a meal-break before the Council meeting but they are back now and, strapped to the oar, are furiously scribbling out orders and decrees for all the sections of Paris. They have been giving priority to messages ordering authorities in the 48 sections to convoke a General Assembly of all their citizens, and then to muster the presidents of the Revolutionary and Civil Committees in each section and the commander of each sectional battalion to come to the Maison Commune to swear an oath of loyalty. All hands are on deck in the mission to save the life of Maximilien Robespierre.

6.00 p.m.

Fouquier-Tinville's lodgings, Palais de Justice, Ile de la Cité

Fouquier enters his offices to find his employees bubbling over with the news. Shortly after 4.00 p.m., they heard that Dumesnil, the gendarmerie commander attached to the law courts, has been placed under arrest by the Commune. Half an hour later, news came through about the arrests of the deputies in the Convention. An hour or so of wild rumours of every description ensued. To crown it all, mayor Fleuriot-Lescot, who must have left National Agent Payan in charge at the Maison Commune, suddenly arrived in person to see Fouquier. Before he was appointed mayor in April 1794, Fleuriot served under Fouquier in the Revolutionary Tribunal. Their close friendship (they were like man and wife, claimed the wags) remains intact. But Fleuriot is on borrowed time and hastens back without managing to see Fouquier. He leaves a message requesting that his friend come at once to the Maison Commune. The Commune must be looking for signs of legitimation. Does Fleuriot's invitation to Fouquier suggest the municipality seeks to deploy the Revolutionary Tribunal to hand down capital sentences against Robespierre's enemies?

Fouquier is making some hasty mental calculations. He now sees that the arrest of Dumas which he witnessed in the Tribunal session earlier in the afternoon must be connected to Robespierre's arrest rather than to any other putative wrong-doing. There is no love lost between these men. Whatever Fouquier's feelings for Fleuriot, why should he throw in his lot with a hyper-ambitious colleague like Dumas who is impossibly difficult to work with? Or indeed with a politician like Robespierre who mistrusts him and wants him replaced? Quite apart from his personal hostility towards the two men, he is also moved by larger, personal considerations. The 47-year-old Public Prosecutor owes any success he has had in life to the Revolution. It has given him a second chance. His legal career was in a mess in 1789; now he is a national figure. In addition, he has always been a stickler for the law. He finds it easy to make up his mind. He despatches one of his secretaries to the CPS with the simple message: Fouquier is at his post; he awaits their orders.

6.15 p.m.

Place du Carrousel (Tuileries)

A set of carriages is being assembled outside the Hôtel de Brionne, where Robespierre and his arrested colleagues have been held. It is transport to take the arrested men to prison. They are expediting each arrested man to a different location. Augustin Robespierre will go to Saint-Lazare prison in the north, Le Bas to La Force in the Marais, while the others will be sent to distant locations south of the river. Couthon is designated the Port-Libre prison (the former Port-Royal convent on the southern edge of the city) and Saint-Just, the old Écossais monastery in the Faubourg Saint-Marcel. For Robespierre, they have selected the Luxembourg prison, a mile away to the south. Here, many elite figures from the Ancien Régime have been housed in the past, but it has also been the site of recent prison plots. Is the idea to tempt Robespierre into imprudent actions? Or to besmirch his reputation by placing him in a repair of aristocrats? It was also here that Danton, Desmoulins, and the rest were sent when they were placed under arrest four months earlier. So maybe the decision to send Danton's nemesis here too is a small act of revenge, served cold.

The arrested men step into their assigned carriage. Each will be accompanied by a CGS agent bearing the arrest warrant and a couple of gendarmes. As they leave the precincts of the Hôtel, groups of bystanders enjoying the spectacle choose to follow the carriages towards their destinations.

The prisoner despatch goes off smoothly. But the CPS remains alert to the possibility of the situation developing in unanticipated ways. They have prepared an order to go out to the Revolutionary Committee of each section: the committee members are to remain at their posts and to send the CPS hourly reports on what is happening within their jurisdictions. They need to keep watch on how Paris is going to react.

6.15 p.m.

Place du Trône-Renversé

With the mounted gendarme officer Cn. Debure leading the way, the tumbrils bearing today's convoy of prisoners have finally reached the place of execution. Debure has prudently chosen to avoid the usual route along the Rue du Faubourg Saint-Antoine because of the reported worker disturbances, preferring to take the quais. In the huge open scrubland of the execution site, the guillotine stands starkly bare against the evening sky. Despite the fall-off in attendance over the last weeks, there is a crowd, as this evening is the last day of the *décade*, and many workers (or at least those who have chosen not to demonstrate against the Wage Maximum) have received their wages and therefore have money to spend as well as a bit of end-of-week leisure time at their disposal.

Some prisoners may have received spiritual comfort from one of the small team of refractory priests who are accustomed to follow the procession clandestinely, seeking to catch the eye of the prisoners and offer them a discreet sign of absolution. Today is a Sunday, moreover, though they are a perennial presence. The priests have to be careful, since clerics who have refused an oath of allegiance to the Revolution are so closely linked with aristocratic counter-revolution that any open display of religious belief risks condemnation and possible imprisonment as a political suspect. In theory, the 1793 Constitution and the Cult of the Supreme Being envisage religious freedom. Yet nearly all Parisian churches are shut. Besides Notre-Dame's conversion into the Temple of the Supreme Being, many religious buildings are now government offices or arms manufactories. The Sainte-Chapelle is a flour-store, for example, the Oratory chapel is an arms dump and there are forges and a saltpetre magazine in the abbey-church of Saint-Germain-des-Prés.

On the raised platform where the guillotine is placed, public executioner Charles-Henri Sanson awaits today's batch of victims. He is elegantly dressed like an Ancien Régime *petit maître*. The story goes that when Marie-Antoinette accidentally stepped on his toe as she climbed onto the platform on her execution day, she blurted out 'Pardon, monsieur', as if the misfortune had been a trivial mishap in the Galerie des Glaces at Versailles. Sanson is, however, struggling to keep up appearances: he has complained bitterly to the CPS that he is losing money. He is not allowed a share of the effects of the executed, which now go to the state; and horse- and carriage-hire is increasingly expensive. Even so, he does his best. He is a professional. His father executed for the king and indeed then executed the king. Now he executes for the Committees of Government . . .

The stoicism of some of the prisoners is sorely tested as they approach the place of their execution. Sanson and his team act with practised efficiency, briskly taking the prisoners down from the carts, bundling the women in their arms, and assembling them all in line. Normally, to retain crowd interest, the most distinguished or heinous of the group will be executed last. Who will it be today? Already, Sanson's men are moving through the group, herding them up onto the platform. The guillotine is ready. The blade is raised high. Each victim is placed belly-down on a plank, head in the groove of the machine. The top half is closed around their necks. Hardly a moment has gone by when the blade falls and another head thuds into the basket. There are some cries of '*Vive la République!*' The headless corpse is swiftly removed and a new body thrust forward. The blade falls again, and again . . . The Sansons despatched the 22 Girondins deputies last October in 37 minutes precisely, and 15 Dantonists in 17 minutes. Today's performance with the 45 victims should take not much more than an hour.

6.30 p.m.

Council chamber, Maison Commune

Cn. Fauconnier, First Legion Chief, strides into the Commune's General Council meeting to inform it that he has been appointed commander of the Paris NG. He owes his post to the provisions of the Convention's decree instituting a rota system for command. He is Chief of the First Legion, so logically the first incumbent. However, his absence from the centre of things at an earlier key moment meant that the CPS placed initial responsibility in the hands of gendarmerie commander Hémart. But since then Hémart has been imprisoned by Hanriot who had been acting as though he was still legitimate NG Commander (until, that is, his own arrest in the Tuileries complex). But Fauconnier has entered the lions' den. He pays the price: he is placed under immediate arrest. His presumptuous appearance has been as naïve as Hémart's.

Following this short diversion, Payan is trying to impose order and objectives on the Commune's cause. He is sounding hoarse, however, from being kept up the previous night by the CPS and then having to endure arrest and the threat of imprisonment this afternoon. He takes the opportunity of a lull in proceedings to catch up with his lunch, as food and wine are thoughtfully supplied. As he eats, he is confronted by the Réunion sectional battalion commander, Jean Richard, who impatiently points out that he has received CPS instructions not to obey Hanriot; but not only is Hanriot in prison now but so too are both of his successors, Hémart and Fauconnier. Whom should he obey? Looking aimlessly around the room, Payan has a brainwave:

- Citizens! We have amongst us an army veteran, a true sans-culotte and a good citizen. I propose him as our provisional General Commander!

The proposal is put hastily to the vote and instantly confirmed. Hanriot's acting replacement is the wholly unsuspecting First Legion Adjutant Christophe-Philippe Giot.

Giot is absolutely amazed and indeed appalled. After a routine day of service, he had returned to his section at around 4.00 p.m. to attend to preparations for the Bara and Viala festival. The beating of the *générale* alerted him to the emergency in train. But not fully apprised of the Convention's decree against Hanriot, he sought out guidance from the elusive Fauconnier, his Legion Chief, and accompanied him here to the Maison-Commune.

The crowd now shout out to Richard:

- You don't need to worry any longer. There's your general!

Payan's first remark to the new appointment is, '*Mon brave*, what is your name?' He may have glimpsed him at the Jacobin Club. But one witness thinks Payan has picked 'the moustache man' because of the becomingly magnificent ferocity of Giot's facial hair. If he seems to look the part at least, a second glance makes Payan realize he may have chosen in haste: he swiftly appoints, as Giot's aide-de-camp his own brother Esprit, a career soldier who happens to be in Paris at the moment and in the room.

Giot may look the part, but he certainly does not feel up to what his metamorphosis demands of him. Making a tour of duty in the Place de la Maison Commune shortly afterwards, he is congratulated on his promotion by a friend. Turning a little pirouette, he self-mockingly exclaims:

- Me! Me! Fucking Commander of Potatoes more like!

Extraordinarily, Fauconnier's baulked mission is followed by the arrival in the Council chamber of yet another Legion Chief, in theory loyal to the Convention. This is Olivier, acting Sixth Legion Chief, who has also independently taken on the task of informing the Commune of the Convention's arrest order against Hanriot and his ADCs.

By now, Fleuriot and Payan are seeing the theatrical potential of their rejection of the Convention's legitimacy in stimulating enthusiasm in the hall. His voice dripping with irony, Fleuriot reads out the decree. Payan is more explicit: the document reveals, he states, the plot to destroy the patriots. 'We can pre-empt that by taking rigorous measures.' He goes on to express 'an infinite horror of the National Convention' in contrast with the Commune which is now 'the sole and unique representative of the people'. Grabbing the decree out of Olivier's hand, he tramples it under foot, berating its bearers as 'villains and good-for-nothings who abandon the cause of the people so as to serve the cause of brigands'. What the Convention is doing, he shouts, is tantamount to 'the abominable "Commission of Twelve"'. He is evoking the committee established by Girondins in April and May 1793 to enquire into the potential insurrectionary force of the Commune. The anger that the body stimulated among the popular movement contributed to the making of the 31 May *journée*.

Payan orders the arrest of Olivier and his retinue. Shortly afterwards he adds to the group the gendarmerie officer Degesne who dares to bring the Convention's order to the Commune to come to the bar of the house and is treated as a traitor for his pains. However, in the hubbub, Olivier is able to slip away and steal back with his followers to the Lombards section, where he issues an immediate command to all the sections in the Sixth Legion to refuse Hanriot's orders. This is a little late.

6.30 p.m.
Mairie and Police Administration
HQ, Ile de la Cité

The Police Administrators are aware that the municipality is doing its best to assemble an armed force of National Guardsmen on the Place de la Maison Commune. But they are concerned that their own HQ needs defending. There are crowds assembling at the Quai du Marché Neuf, just along from the Quai des Orfèvres and while they may be protesters against the Wage Maximum, the situation remains volatile. They also know that the Revolutionary Committee of the Révolutionnaire section in which their offices are situated has already declared its support for the Convention.

Police Administrator Ponce Tanchon, an engraver by trade, has skipped his duty service at the Temple prison this evening to remain in the thick of things. He is personally acquainted with Jean-Baptiste Van Heck, the commander of the NG battalion of the neighbouring Cité section. Tanchon sends a message to Van Heck formally requesting him to bring an armed force to the Mairie.

Van Heck was present in the Convention for the debate this morning and while others were cheering and shouting, he came away with grave reservations. He felt something was deeply wrong, and was shocked to see Robespierre being refused the right to speak in his defence, as is procedurally required, and is justified by the demands of natural justice. He finds it difficult simply to abandon the deep respect he has for Robespierre, so is still in two minds. Earlier this afternoon he received an appeal from Hanriot to take 50 of his men to the Place de la Maison Commune. Even though he will have witnessed the passing of the Convention decree ordering Hanriot's arrest, he responded positively to Hanriot's appeal. But then Tanchon's order makes him wonder whether he is getting too deep into something he cannot control.

After consulting with his senior officers, Van Heck determines to keep his artillery within the section on full alert, but to send a troop detachment to the Mairie under the orders of company commander Berger. When the latter asks what he should do once he is there, Van Heck replies, 'You will concert with Tanchon.' Berger and his men are just moving off when Van Heck, seemingly on impulse, decides to accompany them. The men enter the courtyard of the Mairie and a very satisfied-looking Tanchon comes out, takes Van Heck by the arm and leads him into the police offices. He is keen to get him onside.

6.30 p.m.

Talaru prison (Montagne) and the prison network

- Great arrest of Catiline Robespierre and his accomplices!

T he ears of prisoners in the Talaru gaol just north of the Palais-Royal suddenly prick up at the newsvendor's cry from the street outside. Prison guards rush to silence the cry, to stop alarm spreading among inmates.

- Go fuck yourselves! [the prisoners hear the vendor reply]. The poor people in there should know what is going on.

Across the prison network, a sense of numbing dread has been slowly spreading all day. At the Bénédictins-Anglais where many of the pro-Girondin '73' are housed, Louis-Sébastien Mercier and his fellow deputy, the Breton Honoré-Marie Fleury, began sensing in the early afternoon that something untoward was happening in the city. The gaolers seemed edgy too. They confined prisoners to their cells, made regular checks on inmates, and forbade contact with outsiders.

The news of Robespierre's arrest is a delight. But what comes next? Is it in fact going to be a triumph for the radicals who have been countenancing a prison massacre? Then again, the Collots, the Billauds, the Barères, the Vadiers of the world are just as enthusiastic for terror as Robespierre seems to be. And indeed in some quarters, aristocratic prisoners, as well as many of the '73' pro-Girondin deputies, have regarded Robespierre as their protector—their God even, in one claim. After Robespierre, what?

The very real fear within prison populations that a bout of bloodletting is in the offing is further stoked by the sound of the *générale* being beaten in many neighbourhoods from the late afternoon and early evening. From her cell in the Luxembourg, Sister of Charity Théotiste (comtesse de Valombray in an earlier life) glimpses horsemen charging in one direction then another, having clipped conversations whose content is difficult to pick up, but which seem marked by anger, fear, and other strong emotions. It is still far from clear what is going on. Whatever it is, prisoners are frightened for their lives.

6.45 p.m.

Rue Saint-Guillaume (Fontaine-de-Grenelle)

The moderate deputy, Francois-Jérome Riffard Saint-Martin, is having dinner in a restaurant on the Rue Saint-Guillaume in his Faubourg Saint-Germain neighbourhood. He is bathed in contentment at how the session in the Convention went. He thinks the day is all over, the mission complete once Robespierre and his allies were escorted out of the Convention hall. Many deputies, stomachs rumbling, left the session around that point to seek their dinners. They did not hear a decision being made towards the end of debates to hold a further, evening session starting at 7.00 p.m.

Riffard suddenly hears an emissary from the Maison Commune passing the open window, for it is a warm evening, yelling that the people should take up arms and rush to the Maison Commune

- . . . so as to defend Robespierre, the father of all of us, who has been arrested by those scoundrels in the Convention and faces death.

This is surprising news to the deputy. Very bad news in fact. Losing no time, he rushes out, crossing the river to find out from his colleagues in the Convention just what is going on.

19.00/7.00 p.m.

Place de la Maison Commune

The Commune has quite a fighting force at its disposal. With armed men still coming in, there are currently well over 3,000 National Guardsmen primed for action on the Place. A sizeable contingent of mounted gendarmerie has pledged allegiance, and a large amount of artillery is on show. The city's artillery commander, Adjutant-Major Fontaine, efficiently sent out his orders to all 48 artillery companies early in the afternoon. Besides benefiting from the artillery's semi-autonomous command structure, the notoriously active and enthusiastic gunners pride themselves on leaping at any chance to show their patriotism. Many brushed aside worries from the other sectional authorities in answering the call, in some cases not even bothering to inform them of their action. Even though Carnot's transfers of NG artillery to the front has reduced the number of companies in the city, the men leave their cannon behind. At present, there are between 20 and 30 pieces on the Place, making a powerful force at the Commune's disposal.

The sectional infantry companies first to appear this afternoon were those closest to the Maison Commune where action has been most apparent, but since 5.00 p.m. companies from far afield on the Left as well as the Right Bank have also been appearing. Although only two of the six Legion Chiefs have passed on Hanriot's order to sectional battalions, this still means that 16 out of 48 have received it. The 16 sections in question cover much of the populous workers' faubourgs of Saint-Antoine and Saint-Marcel. Overall, they represent over 40 per cent of Paris's population. As the number of battalion companies is directly related to sectional population, this means nearly half of the city's National Guard could potentially be raised in support of Robespierre. They pose a huge military threat to the Convention, whose defence forces look pathetically meagre in contrast.

7.00 p.m.

Convention hall, Tuileries palace

Deputy Riffard Saint-Martin has rushed pell-mell to the Convention to discover how the assembly is preparing for what seems to be brewing. Only 40 or 50 of his colleagues are present, with just a few ushers to hand. Everyone seems unaware of the dangers that confront them, and they are giving the impression of waking with difficulty from a deep post-prandial snooze.

Symptomatic of the complacency that is abroad in and around the Convention, duty commander at the Tuileries, Legion Chief Julliot has just turned away a large force of Guardsmen from the Maison-Commune sectional battalion who had arrived at the Tuileries intent, they said, on defending the deputies from the violence of the forces which they have witnessed assembling on the Place de la Maison Commune. Julliot informs them that all is well and they should simply return to their section, run patrols and await orders, which are currently being printed relating the afternoon's arrests. Julliot's ignorance of what is taking place a mile or so to the east is almost total. The deputies and their defenders do not realize just how weak their position is. Hanriot's arrest has not stopped the Commune from mobilizing the NG. There are the routine artillery and infantry units on duty outside the Convention hall, but their number, a few hundred men in total, is dwarfed by the forces amassing at the Maison Commune.

The deputies present have begun exchanging stories, news, and rumours about what is happening in this neighbourhood. They have discounted any threat from Robespierre. He looked utterly crushed by his experience in the Convention this afternoon, finished in fact. Some deputies are also reporting the inglorious end of Hanriot's quixotic raid on the CGS. But news of what is happening further afield in the city is harder to come by. Any danger seems likely to come from the popular classes, whipped up by the Commune and Jacobin Club.

There is no bureaucratic business or correspondence for evening sessions, so that, once brought to order, the assembly gets straight down to the issue at hand, as more deputies progressively filter in. Collot d'Herbois is absent: unknown to colleagues, he is fire-fighting in the CPS, as news has started to come in of growing resistance to the Convention across Paris.

In Collot's absence, Jean-Jacques Bréard, a Québecois who prides himself on being the only Canadian to have voted for the death of the king, is presiding. He summons Bourdon de l'Oise to address the deputies. The Commune this afternoon has picked out Bourdon as one of its prime targets and he heartily reciprocates their loathing:

> – Citizens! This morning the Convention took the security measures that circumstances required; all good citizens applauded them. However, a rumour is abroad that the Commune, in league with the Jacobin Club, is instigating an insurrection. (*Expressions of indignation*.) Such a resolution would be dangerous for any but the people of Paris; with them there is no cause for concern. I remind the Convention that in such cases it fraternizes with the people and by its presence calms popular effervescence. Even though I do not believe that such a measure is necessary, it is however useful to verify it. I therefore demand that the Commune should be immediately summoned to the bar of the house so as to receive the Convention's orders.

It is instantly agreed that both the Commune and the authorities of the Seine department should be convoked.

Supporting Bourdon's motion, Merlin de Thionville takes the opportunity at the rostrum to recount his afternoon experience, that is, his encounter with Hanriot and 40 of his men, the pistol placed against his chest, the threat of sabre blows to follow, his imprisonment in the Palais-Royal guardhouse, and his release at the hands of good patriots from the Montagne section. It seems clear to Merlin that a conspiracy has been hatched, and that freedom itself is in jeopardy. The cunning conspirator (Robespierre) who for six months has been hiding behind the mask of virtue so as to massacre citizens, may now, Merlin believes (incorrectly) be at the Commune.

Tallien (who does not know about the arrests of Hémart and Fauconnier) is just back from the Jacobin Club. He raises the temperature by giving credence to news dribbling in that suggests the Club is indeed coordinating resistance to the Convention with the Commune. The Commune, he concludes, is out of order. It must be purged.

Despite these notes of alarm, there is a lot of indecisive back-and-forth taking place, with confused deputies seemingly unwilling to accept the reality of the danger that they are facing. Thuriot announces that Hanriot's orders to Legion Chiefs to bring 400 men to the Place de la Maison Commune have been intercepted, while CGS member Amar speaks up to confirm Hanriot's imprisonment, and goes on to dismiss any real threat from the Parisian popular classes. The NG is now on full alert, he tells the deputies, with the people enthusiastically supporting them. 'In sum,' he smugly concludes, 'law and order reigns in Paris.' Other deputies follow him in seeking to damp down alarm. Poultier has a reassuring story to tell: when he stated his views on Robespierre to an angry supporter of the Commune in the street, the crowds around them shouted out, 'Long live the Convention! Down with Robespierre and the conspirators!' The Dantonist Legendre tells his fellow deputies they can unequivocally count on the people even if the Commune declares itself in insurrection. Thankfully, he says,

> – It is not easy to make the people rebel if they are well-instructed. The people will not idolize anyone in future.

Like the Convention, Legendre declares, the people is entirely Montagnard, and they will resist the influence of a single individual and stay firmly attached to principles. Lequinio has similarly soothing words. And when Rovère rises to say that he has seen a manifesto issued on behalf of the Commune by National Agent Payan, Merlin interrupts him to say that Payan has been arrested, which Barère confirms.

Merlin is not to know that Payan has also been released and is back leading developments in the Commune. The Convention's current complacency contrasts strikingly with the energy emanating from the Maison Commune.

7.00 p.m.

Maison Commune

Numbers of General Council members reporting for duty have gone up quite sharply; nearly one hundred are present, representing a good turnout. They even feel in a strong enough position to turn away Jean Guyot, the Police Administrator shunned by his colleagues at the Mairie, telling him to come back only when he is sporting his official tricolour municipal sash. With numbers also swelling nicely outside, the General Council makes a big decision. They will send an expedition to the Tuileries palace drawn from the forces on the Place de la Maison Commune and led by Louvet and Jean-Baptiste Coffinhal. Vice-president of the Revolutionary Tribunal, Coffinhal is blessed with a towering physique and a booming voice to which it is easy to defer. Their aim will be to free Robespierre, Couthon, Hanriot, and the others.

Coffinhal joins mayor Fleuriot in going down onto the Place to whip up enthusiasm among the crowds of guardsman and civilians for this key mission. Coffinhal harangues the crowd:

> – The fatherland is in danger, the best patriots have been imprisoned as well the Paris NG's General Staff. Members of the CPS and CGS have turned traitor. We must punish them. We must obey Hanriot and no other!

Fleuriot, in full municipal regalia, makes a beeline for the artillery companies of the famously radical Faubourg Saint-Antoine, and speaks to the gunners of the Popincourt section:

> – Would the men of 14 July, 10 August and 31 May lose from sight the fact that 9 Thermidor is necessary to save their country and the Republic? That it is

necessary that the people rise en masse? The people are being oppressed . . . What do you want: freedom or tyranny?

Fleuriot does not quite get the answer he expects. The men cry out 'Vive the Republic!' But then, 'Vive the Convention!' The Commune message has not fully got through.

There is similar uncertainty within the Commune hall. The municipal councillors hover around the entrance to the building, awaiting men from their section who are delegates from the Revolutionary and Civil Committees or else NG battalion commanders so that they can confront them straight away with taking the oath and adding their names to the list of the attendees. This is a way of cementing the support of all present. Yet in the haste to enrol support, little care is taken to ensure that the men know what they are signing up for. Many are new to a General Council meeting and assume that this is a routine signing-in procedure. With the ambient noise and excitement levels they don't all fully grasp what is going on. They don't all see their own presence as signifying hostility towards the Convention.

Worryingly for the Commune's cause, however, some do detect the intentions of the Commune leaders, and do their best to get away and run back to their sections with the news. Others are more circumspect. Surgeon-midwife Jean-Antoine-Gaspard Forestier is only too willing to accept a call to go out and deliver a couple of babies, for example, and then see what happens from outside. Around 7.00 p.m., moreover, it was noticed that the attendance list had gone missing. Does this mean that the full reality of what the Commune is embarking on has become clear to delegates? Is this a matter of cold feet? In any case, a new attendance list has been started. Jean-Nicolas Hardon who has just brought an NG group from the Finistère section in the Faubourg Saint-Marcel will be the first to sign the new attendance sheet (as he goes out and boasts to his men outside).

The Commune fears government spies are keeping the CPS and CGS informed of proceedings, but they are anxious too about a haemorrhaging of support from some sectional delegations. Consequently, they institute a *consigne* (or ban on exits), to stave off the possibility of dwindling numbers and to inhibit intelligence-gathering by the Convention's spies.

7.00 p.m.

Jacobin Club (Montagne)

People are milling about outside the Jacobin Club in anticipation of the evening's session. Anger and dismay have greeted the news of the arrests in the Convention. Rumour is rife: it is claimed that Le Bas was stabbed as he tried to defend himself in the Convention hall. The conspiracy that Robespierre warned against last night, and which has led to great anticipation about this evening's session, has shown its head.

Uncertainty about the day's events is causing disagreements, however, even among the women who have made a reputation for themselves by their pro-Robespierre presence in the public galleries. Most are incensed by what is happening. But some are not, including the former secretary of the Society for Revolutionary Women, Marie Dubreuil, who wants to drag the Commune back from the brink of civil war. It is reported that another regular Jacobin attender, Julie Couprye, has applauded Robespierre's arrest. She deserves to be assassinated, some fellow Jacobines state. In the mêlée outside the Club, someone—again, probably a woman—is heard saying, 'We have to march against the Convention and save Robespierre.' There is an immediate response:

- The people is not free. The public galleries in the Club are fomenting counter-revolution. The women there are a pile of *bougresses*. They are slaves to this man just as they were to Lafayette and Orléans.

The speaker is Jean-Baptiste Loys from the Bon-Conseil section. A radical with a record of terrorist activity in his native Arles as well as in Paris, he is no friend of Robespierre. Indeed, he was among the minority of the Club yesterday who tried to shout him and his supporters down with cries of

'Down with the slaves of Robespierre! Down with the tyrant!' He is just as opposed to Revolutionary Tribunal President Dumas (whom he once reported to the CGS for having said in his presence that all people of intelligence should be guillotined).

Loys now continues:

- All good citizens should support the Convention, which has just saved the country by the measures it has taken. For a long time there has been a move to mislead the people. The galleries in the Club are unwitting instruments of the despot. We don't want idols any more. Robespierre has been flattered too much in the past. He should be subject to the laws of the Convention like anyone else.

But there is muttering against Loys's forthright views and his attacks on 'idolaters'. Municipal official Joseph Fénaux, a cobbler from the Bondy section on his way into the meeting, intercepts Loys before he can go further and has him arrested and sent to the sectional authorities.

Yet why is Fénaux here? As municipal councillor he should be at the Commune. In fact, despite his bravado, Fénaux's ardour is cooling. For some time he has been wishing he had never been elected to the Commune or appointed juryman on the Revolutionary Tribunal, but he realizes it is too dangerous to resign. But tonight he will stay away from the Maison Commune.

Inside the Club, in the absence of serving Club President, CGS member, Élie Lacoste, who is understandably busy elsewhere, vice-chair Nicolas-Joseph Vivier is presiding. A judicial official, and a man of no distinction and little experience, Vivier is an uninspiring choice for Club President on such a day, when the Club's star speakers are absent on account of their arrests.

The first business of the session helps focus minds. It is a letter from the CGS demanding that the Club immediately send them the speech Robespierre had made the previous evening and which the Club had rapturously decreed should be printed. Vivier rejects the request: they have no document to hand over. Passions are ramped up when two Councillor envoys from the Commune, ex-priest Jacques-Claude Bernard and lawyer Edme-Marguerite Lauvin, enter to tell the assembled Jacobins that the Commune's General Council has declared a state of insurrection. The two men formally invite the Jacobins to enter into correspondence with the Insurrectionary Commune. To much applause, this proposal for collaboration is acclaimed, the Club declares itself in permanent session, and all present take an oath, swearing to die rather than to live under the Convention. Crime is seeking to overthrow virtue, a speaker proclaims, echoing Robespierre's last night speech. They will not disperse until the plans of the traitors are thwarted.

Some Jacobin deputies from the Convention, perhaps unaware that an evening session of the assembly is taking place, or else wishing to bring the Club back within the paths of political righteousness after the excesses of the previous evening, have come to show their faces at the Club. They have been receiving a chilly reception. Tallien chose to go back to the Convention straight away to tell deputies about the state of the Club. Vivier demands of another of the deputies, Jacques Brival, how he voted in the Convention earlier in the day. Brival can hardly deny that he voted against Robespierre, since as one of the assembly's secretaries, his signature is on some of the decrees. Boos fill the air. Brival is struck off the list of Jacobins forthwith, and forced to hand in his membership card. Prosper Sijas, the declared enemy of Pille, Carnot's high-ranking appointee in the Army bureaucracy, begins a long tirade against Carnot.

Brival's colleague Pierre-Jacques Chales also gets a rough ride. Though no Fouché, Chales is among those deputies accused of excesses while on mission in the departments. On his return, he made his defence in the Convention walking on crutches, following wounds sustained while fighting on the northern front in late 1793. He has been talking to a crowd in the courtyard outside the assembly room, explaining that Robespierre thought all the generals and all members of the government were traitors. He is overheard by fellow Jacobin, Jean-François Lagarde, who has been defending Robespierre and attacking Collot d'Herbois inside the Club. Lagarde has used a lull in the proceedings to go out and buy some tobacco. He contradicts Chales, and when the latter pulls rank and tries to correct him Lagarde insults him calling him a mere priest (Chales was a canon of Chartres cathedral before the Revolution). Chales vigorously rips Lagarde's Jacobin membership card from his lapel and threatens him with arrest, then angrily pulls aside his own clothing to show livid wounds incurred fighting for the Republic.

The two men take their quarrel inside to the Jacobin hall, but here sympathy for Chales is scarce, particularly when the deputy informs them that the vote against Robespierre in the Convention was unanimous. Jean-Charles Riqueur, one of the acting secretaries to the meeting—a man whose reputation for Robespierre 'idolatry' has led to him being called 'the

Robespierre of the Guillaume–Tell section'—yells out that Chales is 'a tartuffe and a scoundrel'.

Efforts within the Club meeting to identify Robespierre's enemies in the Convention have been hugely undercut by the news of the overwhelming scale of opposition to him in the Convention. The 31 May and 2 June 1793 *journées* led to the expulsion of 22 Girondin deputies. But hearing that Robespierre has not just 22 enemies but as many opponents as there are deputies has had a chastening effect on the assembled Jacobins.

Despite establishing links to the Commune, the Jacobins are dithering. The meeting is confused and lacklustre. Vivier in the chair seems incapable of whipping up passion, dynamism, or strategic thinking. Symptomatically, the meeting has second thoughts about expelling Brival. The proposal that not only Brival but all deputies who have voted against Robespierre should be excluded from the Club is not put in the end. Then they decide to reinstate Brival and send a messenger to him in the Convention returning his membership card. There is nothing like leadership coming from the Jacobins tonight: Cn. Portières is probably not the only member to walk out and publicly tear up his membership card in frustration at the meeting's equivocation.

7.15 p.m.

Luxembourg prison (Mutius-Scévole)

Jean Guyard, the concierge of the Luxembourg, is a *mouton* and a 'list-maker': that is, he is an informer who composes lists of alleged conspiratorial counter-revolutionaries in his gaol to be sent to the Revolutionary Tribunal—and then the guillotine. Mutinous mutterings against him by his charges have swollen as news of events in the city has filtered in, and as the beating of the *générale* has been heard throughout the Left Bank. Guyard has just received the order that concierges are not to permit any admissions or releases of prisoners without police approval. The order has been delivered by Police Administrator Wichterich and one of his colleagues. They are still present and with Guyard start to hear sounds of a crowd of noisy Parisians coming up the Rue Tournon directly in front of the prison entrance. This is how the 1792 September Massacres started . . .

The crowd, which Guyard reckons is between 2,000 and 3,000 strong, is accompanying a carriage bearing Maximilien Robespierre. Yelling their support for the Incorruptible? The mood is difficult to judge. As likely to be shouting insults, one might surmise. Filleul, the CGS agent in charge of the human cargo, presents the imprisonment order, as Guyard hears voices in the crowd demanding the opening of the prison gates. This is the last thing that Guyard wants: it could trigger a prison massacre. He is also aware of the Commune's order forbidding entrance to those they have not authorized, and he does not want to infringe—after all, the Commune pays his wages. He timidly suggests that the convoy should try another prison instead?

Police Administrator Wichterich, who is still present, has recognized the man in the carriage, and imperiously demands that the carriage be redirected to the Police Administration HQ in the Mairie on the Ile de la Cité. He personally will accompany it. The gendarmes who have been guarding Robespierre are arrested and taken along. As the carriage sets off with the crowd following, Guyard breathes a large sigh of relief. He has saved his own skin, and quite possibly the lives of his charges too.

7. 45 p.m.

Coffinhal's raid: Rue Saint-Honoré (Tuileries)

Coffinhal is leading an impressive army of several thousand armed men through the twilight towards the Tuileries palace on their rescue mission. Desboisseaux, Fouquier's dining companion this afternoon, and Councillor Louvet are his improvised lieutenants. As well as gendarmerie cavalrymen, the Amis-de-la-Patrie section is particularly well represented, with 400 infantrymen in the force, while there are artillery companies, pulling along between 15 and 20 cannon, from all over the city: from Bon-Conseil and Marchés in the central zone on the Right Bank, from Popincourt and Quinze-Vingts in the Faubourg Saint-Antoine and from Fontaine-de-Grenelle on the Left Bank. On the way, their path crossed at the Pont Notre-Dame with a crowd of 1,200 men coming from the Panthéon section to the Place de la Maison Commune in response to Hanriot's orders in the afternoon. These men tail along after Coffinhal. The Convention has no inkling of just what is coming its way.

7.45 p.m.

Police Administration HQ, Mairie, Ile de la Cité

P olice Administrator Wichterich is leading the carriage containing Maximilien Robespierre into the courtyard of the Police Administration's
offices in the Mairie. The accompanying crowds find it difficult to penetrate
the cramped entrances to the courtyard, and are left standing around along
the Quai des Orfèvres.

Robespierre, is not in a good state at all. Popular insults as well as
expressions of support must be ringing in his ears after his hour-long itinerary
across the city. He is not used to this level of immersion into the Parisian
popular classes. Wichterich's reassurances notwithstanding, the turbulence
and dramas of the day have got through to the deputy.

Three Police Administrators in their tricolour sashes rush out of their
offices. One opens the carriage door, to see Robespierre elbowing his
companions to get out first. He has a distracted look about him, and is
clutching a handkerchief to his mouth, as he leaps unsteadily to the ground,
then turns around to face towards the carriage, away from the welcome
party. He is pale and dejected.

The Administrators promptly place the accompanying gendarmes under
arrest, saying it will cost them dear for having had the temerity to lift a finger
against the father of the people. To Robespierre himself, they are all smiling
reassurance. One of the group takes his arm. Another places an arm around
his shoulders and holds him close as they walk him towards their office.

– Don't you worry. Aren't you with your friends?

But these faces are unfamiliar. Does Robespierre know who anyone is? Can
he trust these people?

7.45 p.m.

Across the city

There is still a widespread belief abroad that public disorder today is connected to protests against the 23 July Wage Maximum. In some cases, so it is. Over in the gunpowder factory at Grenelle, on city limits in the far south-west of the city, building workers have been protesting vigorously against the measure and demanding release from their contracts. In their dinner break, some went over to the Maison Commune and noted crowds gathering there to demonstrate against the Wage Maximum.

In Popincourt, towards the eastern periphery of the city, two explanations are currently being offered for the order to mobilize: it is either over the Wage Maximum or else it follows on from an incident in the Convention where, it is confidently asserted, some deputies have plotted to kill Robespierre. 'Villains have planned to murder patriots and make counter-revolution,' artillery Adjutant-Major Fontaine advises the Popincourt gunners.

It is a confusing situation. It is only around now in fact that authorities in some of the outer sections—Champs-Elysées and République in the north-west, Observatoire in the south, Faubourg-du-Nord in the north, Montreuil in the east—are receiving their first communication from the Commune. In many cases, the first written order is the command to close the city gates. This denotes some sort of emergency. But it is not clear what.

Once alerted to the existence of a crisis, these outer sections wait on events, but in the interim proceed with normal business. Getting on for a dozen sections are preoccupied by the distribution to charcutiers of pork received from the municipal provisioning department. A stray case of pork discovered in the Faubourg Saint-Martin has the Civil Committees of the Poissonnière and Faubourg-du-Nord sections much exercised. For the last hour, in fact, women have been rushing around the neighbourhood staking claims on the pork, the authorities report, and generally making nuisances of themselves. The turbulence is continuing even as, at around 7.30, news has come in of the arrests in the Convention. Evening newspapers are helping spread the news of the arrest, with vendors yelling the headlines at full volume. What is less evident is a sense of what exactly this means for the Revolution. Neither the Commune nor the Convention has yet managed to get across a plausible narrative that fully explains and legitimates their actions.

20.00/8.00 p.m.

Police Administration HQ, Ile de la Cité

Hardly is Robespierre out of his carriage than the Police Administrators are penning a message conveying news of his safe arrival in their midst to the Commune. One of their number, Jacques-Mathurin Le Lièvre, has been entrusted with conveying the missive. It states that Robespierre is already in agreement with them over the imperative need to imprison journalists. Newspapers must not become rallying point for false news put out by the Convention. This is certainly a familiar Robespierre theme, but one wonders whether the proposal is his. For what the note does not disclose is that in the new environment in which he finds himself, Robespierre seems entirely discombobulated.

It is highly unlikely that Robespierre has ever set foot in the Mairie. However much he may figure in the minds of the Police Administrators, they are probably all personally unknown to him, though he just might have glimpsed one or two of them in the Jacobin Club. For the last few years he has lived by and for high politics. His forays outside the golden triangle of Convention hall, CPS offices and Jacobin Club and beyond the protective cocoon that the Duplay womenfolk provide have been few; and they have been directed less into the heart of the city than out into the greener and more gently smiling public gardens and meadows to the west of the city. Generally speaking, individuals wanting to see Robespierre come to him, not vice versa. In the new world of municipal and sans-culotte politics in which he has been thrust, he is completely out of his element. Who are these new self-styled 'friends'?

The Police Administrators led by Tanchon and Faro are doing their best to calm him down and restore his spirits. They have hand-picked the commander of the Cité NG, Jean-Baptiste Van Heck, to take personal charge of his protection, and there is a NG troop from that section waiting below in the HQ courtyard. The choice seems shrewd, given Van Heck's reputed track record of patriotism and direct action, and the doubts he harbours about the legality of the Convention's silencing of Robespierre this morning.

Tanchon now proudly ushers Van Heck into the room where they have placed Robespierre, and beckons towards the deputy as he addresses Van Heck:

- Do you know who this is? Your proven patriotism and your known energy have led us to choose you to command the NG that will ensure his safety . . . My friend, we must unite, for the Convention wants to destroy liberty. A new Swamp has formed within it that spreads as many deadly vapours as its earlier incarnation. Do you see Robespierre here? We have saved him from the hands of those wanting his destruction. You are the man to guard him.

Van Heck's response to this invitation is surprisingly blunt.

- I know that an arrest warrant has been issued against him and he has yet to respond to the charges brought against him. I neither wish nor am I able to accept this post . . . Moreover, I have brought the armed forces to the Mairie in order to protect the interests of the public, not of an individual.

This impressive bow to impartiality and the rule of law over celebrity appals Robespierre:

- Great God! In whose hands were you going to place me? This man is nothing but an aristocrat and a counter-revolutionary!

Van Heck is hustled speedily out of the room, his ears ringing with accusations. Placed in custody, he is soon wangling his way out an hour or so later, while the Police Administrators redouble their soothing words to Robespierre, still reeling from his encounter with one of the 'impure breed' of people.

8.15 p.m.

Fouquier-Tinville's office, Palais de Justice, Ile de la Cité

G endarmerie officer Debure enters the offices of Public Prosecutor Fouquier-Tinville to report that the evening guillotinings have taken place in good order. He finds Fouquier deep in conversation with a couple of senior Tribunal colleagues. There is nothing else to be done but sit and wait. Fouquier must be wondering whether he has done the right thing by throwing in his lot with the CPS. Robespierre will be unforgiving if he prevails. But Debure offers some consolation at least: the executions took place in an atmosphere of great tranquillity. Maybe news of Robespierre's arrest has yet to reach the extremities of the Faubourg Saint-Antoine. Fouquier feels he is probably right to stick with the Convention. He will stay put at his place in the Palais de Justice. This is not a night for venturing abroad. Friend Fleuriot will have to fend for himself.

8.15 p.m.

Maison Commune

It has not taken long for police emissary Le Lièvre to reach the Maison Commune with news of Robespierre's arrival at the Mairie. He enters the Council chamber just as Fleuriot and Payan are castigating a messenger from the Convention who has ordered the General Council to come to the bar of the house. The Council will indeed go to the Convention, Payan threatens, 'but so will all the people in arms', and he goes on to rant wildly against Collot d'Herbois and the CPS. But then all stops for Le Lièvre to step up and make a dramatic announcement.

- Robespierre is free!

The applause is deafening. Even so, there is a certain bafflement about how this has happened. Has Robespierre been released by Coffinhal's expedition? Yet it seems Robespierre is currently at the Mairie. Then what is happening to the expeditionary force despatched to the Tuileries?

Such questions will have to wait. In the interim, Robespierre's position has to be secured. Orders are instantly given to despatch to the Mairie the provisional NG Commander, moustachioed Giot, to buttress its defences. Once in place, Giot tells his men, 'Citizens, Robespierre is here. You will be defending a man who has sought only to do well by the people.'

Yet Payan and Fleuriot have no intention of allowing Robespierre to remain in the Mairie for long. They realize that his iconic physical presence among the General Council will give a massive boost to the Commune's cause. Getting Robespierre on their side is also the best guarantee imaginable for Fleuriot and Payan's own physical security.

Plans are already afoot outside to bring Robespierre to the Maison
Commune. Le Lièvre has gone down to the Place and is energetically
amassing a troupe to lead to the Mairie so as to escort Robespierre back to
the Commune. He finds troops from the Sans-Culottes and Faubourg-du-
Nord sections willing to act and is in the process of complementing them
with men from his own Lombards section when the Lombards battalion
second-in-command, Quevreux, arrives with an order from Sixth Legion
Chief Olivier to return all the men to their section. Le Lièvre flies into a rage
when Quevreux tells him that he is merely following the Legion Chief's
orders:

– Today it is not Legion Chiefs who command, it is the people.

He then sweeps off with his improvised following in the direction of the
Mairie.

8.15 p.m.

Convention hall, Tuileries palace

T he mood in the Convention is changing. For all the endorsements of the fidelity and devotion of the Parisian people, the drip-drip of news, rumour, and anecdote coming in is suggesting that things are less rosy than deputies have been imagining. And they can surely hear, noises off, the swelling hum of people gathering on the Place du Carrousel just outside their windows. Some deputies may even be able to distinguish the squeaking of the wheels of cannon train being brought up en masse. Complacency is giving way to apprehension.

The Montagnard deputy Goupilleau de Montaigu has just returned to the Convention hall from CGS offices where he tells deputies he encountered crowds of citizens sporting the tricolour. One man there asked him who he was and when he replied that he was a Representative of the People, the man sneered, 'You are contemptible.' He gathers that the man involved was Dumas's deputy at the Revolutionary Tribunal, who is reported to have said that the Convention will receive some mighty blows this evening and that there is nothing more vile than a member of the Convention.

Danger is on the assembly's doorstep. A deputy cries out that the man that Goupilleau encountered is Louvet, whose arrest is decreed forthwith. (In fact, it was Coffinhal.) Since the municipal authorities have not responded to the deputies' call to come and account for themselves in the Convention hall, they must be held to be in contempt of the assembly. Mayor Fleuriot must be arrested at once. It is reported that he has simply torn up the Convention's orders.

Courvol, the usher temporarily arrested by the Commune in mid-afternoon, has made it back to the Convention now and he approaches the President's chair with bad news: the group that Goupilleau encountered has swollen in size and is endeavouring to free Hanriot from the CGS offices. They have trained their cannon on the hall, specifically at the President's chair. Commendably, Bréard keeps his cool, replying quietly to Courvol with no little sangfroid to keep the news from the deputies:

> – We mustn't trigger alarm. If we are to perish, I will be the first to go. Let us see what develops. Keep me constantly informed what is going on.

Despite this stoical attitude, the Convention is getting a sense of the perils that confront them.

CPS member Billaud-Varennes has rejoined the assembly, and starts speaking in a reassuring manner. The good news is that Payan is under arrest and the Mayor soon will be (untrue of course); and the rebellious Commune will be besieged by government forces within 20 minutes (similarly). Loud applause erupts at these unwitting untruths, but then there is an abrupt change of mood when Billaud continues more sombrely, and indeed more accurately:

> – The satellites of Hanriot have run through the streets sabre in hand . . . Sijas is currently in the Jacobin Club fomenting disquiet.

Worse follows:

> – There is a fact I cannot withhold from you. A company of gunners, misled by Hanriot, has sought to aim its cannons against the Convention (*Movement of indignation.*) The National Guard has opposed them. (*Loud applause.*) Vigorous measures are called for and we must be willing to die at our posts. (Yes, Yes! *All deputies cry*, we all will; *from the public galleries there is applause*). This is the time to stand and fight. The Committees of Government will present you with measures to save the *patrie.*

8.30 p.m.

Place du Carrousel

C n. Pellerin, artillery adjutant for the Popincourt section, has arrived at the Place du Carrousel to the east of the Tuileries palace to find a large group of cannon lining up inside the iron railings protecting the palace. When Coffinhal's force left the Place de la Maison Commune, Pellerin had remained behind. But he became worried by Coffinhal marching so aggressively on the Convention with a force bristling with pikes, rifles, mounted gendarmes, and artillery trains. So he decided that he could do his duty better alongside his comrades, and ran after them.

Initially, he is happily reassured to see that Coffinhal's cannon on the Place du Carrousel are pointing outwards, away from the palace itself. They may be preventing access to any relief force, but at least they are not directly threatening the deputies. Cannon also cover the Rue de l'Échelle to the north, thereby blocking any putative relief force coming from the Rue Saint-Honoré. However, he then discerns another group of cannon, including pieces from the Mutius-Scévole battalion, that have fanned out towards the vicinity of the CGS offices in the Hôtel de Brionne to the north edge of the Place, and are in fact disposed with guns facing inwards. They thus seem to be targeting both the Hôtel de Brionne and the adjacent Convention hall where the deputies are sitting. Moreover, the city's artillery Instructors Pionnier and Brizard (who outrank the sectional commanders) have ordered the men to load their guns with grapeshot, a devastatingly lethal weapon of crowd control. The gunners mean business.

Coffinhal and his comrades are currently ransacking the Hôtel de Brionne, in the hunt for the prisoners. They got past the Convention guard through knowing the password of the day (that the CPS has not had the forethought to change). Sabre in hand and yelling Robespierre's name, Coffinhal insulted the deputy Goupilleau *en passant*, but is by now concluding that Robespierre and his accomplices have already been despatched to their individual prisons. As CGS members have joined their colleagues in the Convention hall, the building is temporarily deserted. Coffinhal eventually stumbles across the room in which Hanriot is being kept. He and his men easily overpower the gendarme guard. The ropes binding Hanriot are cut, and one of those present, Jean-François Damour, a JP in the Arcis section, seizes the severed ropes and brandishes them aloft like a trophy.

Julliot, the commanding officer of today's Convention duty guard, has come galloping up. In the confusion he is taken prisoner too and he and his aides are in turn tied up. Hanriot leaps onto a table to proclaim that from now on the Paris Commune has to be obeyed. The victors then file out from the Hôtel de Brionne. One of the CGS secretaries hears Desboisseaux crowing on departure, 'That's good,' nodding towards Hanriot. 'We've still got this one.'

Mutius-Scévole gunners are standing by their charged cannon among the crowd, as Hanriot emerges from the Hôtel de Brionne side, accompanied by the newly released ADCs, and dozens of gendarmes. Artillery Instructor Pionnier gets the gunners to prime their cannon, ready to open fire on any pursuing force.

The applause that greets the emergence of the beplumed Hanriot in this confined space is loud enough to be heard from the courtyard entrance on the Place du Carrousel. The forces assembled there think that what they are hearing is the acclamation of the Convention and its public galleries for the liberation of the general. The cry goes up: *Vive la République*! Hanriot has been acquitted by Convention decree! Our brave general is acquitted!'

Yet Cosme Pionnier still has his guns trained on the Convention hall doorway.

8.30 p.m.

Convention hall, Tuileries palace

C ollot rushes in and in haste assumes his presiding role to exclaim:
   - Citizens, this is the moment to die at our posts. Armed scoundrels have invested the CGS and taken it.

The members recoil with horror at the imminent threat. Fréron cannot be the only deputy to see this moment a sublime echo of Roman senators confronted with the barbarians. (They know their Livy: they are thinking of the sack of Rome by the Gauls under Brennus in the fourth century BCE). Yet dying in their seats soon loses its appeal. They would rather go down fighting. Above the hubbub, the voice of Goupilleau is heard:

   - We must take the measures needed to save liberty! If we want to lay the conspirators low, we must be swifter than they.

The public galleries have entered into the spirit of the moment and many citizens rush out determinedly to general applause from those remaining.

   As Collot returns to CPS offices, Thuriot steps forward to preside in his place. It has now become clear, he states, that by 9.00 a.m. this morning a plot had been hatched to mobilize the NG against the Convention. If it is successful, there will be not a virtuous citizen still alive within 24 hours. But just as Thuriot is rallying the deputies, Goupilleau rushes in with more news:

   - Hanriot has escaped and is being led out in triumph!

A deputy stands to demand why the newly appointed NG commanders are not more active. Someone points out that local guard commander Julliot has just been taken prisoner by Coffinhal's forces, while Hémart and Fauconnier are languishing in Commune cells. Dauminval, a company captain from the local Tuileries section, confirms the lamentable state of the defences and Thuriot commandeers him to speed away to his battalion commander to secure arms and men. He does so forthwith, only for his battalion commander to refuse to act on the grounds that he requires a written rather than a verbal order. The Convention is defenceless.

8.45 p.m.

Place du Carrousel

- They have outlawed me, but with cannon we'll see about that!

T he angry Hanriot, cut free from his ropes, has emerged from the Hôtel de Brionne seemingly with vengeance in his heart. The immediate response he gets from the artillerymen from the Amis-de-la-Patrie section gives him pause:

- You may be an outlaw, but our cannon aren't!

This is not a good start. And Hanriot's perplexity is amplified when he sees some of the 29th Division Gendarmerie who accompanied him on his earlier raid a few hours ago, and then changed side and arrested him at the Hôtel de Brionne. Some of the men assure him that they are now back on his side, but others refuse allegiance. He angrily commands loaded cannon to be trained on the resisters. It is a stand-off. But Hanriot blinks first:

- The CGS has recognized my innocence. I am still your general! Not a drop of blood has been spilled. Liberty will triumph once more.

He is lying for the cause, as he struggles to grasp a situation which has evolved considerably since his arrest.

Hanriot is unaware that he has a virtually defenceless Convention at his mercy. It is in fact extremely difficult for him to size up the chaotic state of the forces in and around the Place du Carrousel, especially with crowds tumbling out of the public galleries and adding to the confusion. Night is falling (the sun set at 7.37 p.m.), and the cramped environs of the Hôtel de Brionne make the creeping darkness seem worse than it is. Bad light would throw any military action here into the lap of the gods. It could well cause indiscriminate bloodshed and even swing the day the Convention's way.

Nor is Hanriot's stated wish to avoid bloodshed an empty promise. The victories of 31 May and 2 June were achieved without deaths on either side—why not the 9 Thermidor too?

Hanriot has been under lock and key for more than three hours. He will have noted, from the outward-facing disposition of the cannon in the Carrousel, that his liberators are expecting resistance from Parisians loyal to the Convention. He has little idea of how things are going back at the Maison Commune or indeed across Paris. Coffinhal's forces came here to release Robespierre, but Robespierre is in prison elsewhere it seems. Issues have become complicated, and Hanriot struggles to grasp all the threads. He cannot be sure who is for and who is against him. And indeed it would seem that a great many of the men milling around are as confused as he as to their sympathies. It may be better all round if he were far away from the Place du Carrousel before his newly minted claim that he has been freed by Convention decree or CGS diktat is put to the test. An ill-considered act at this stage could ruin the whole strategy that Hanriot, together with Payan and Fleuriot, were developing in the middle of the afternoon.

Suddenly, impulsively, he cries out:

- *Vive la République*! My friends, follow me! To the Commune!

Hanriot's snap decision to return to the Place de la Maison Commune must puzzle men like trigger-happy artillery officer Pionnier, who was well primed for a bloody assault on the Convention. But this is not Hanriot's intention. As he leaves the courtyard, he passes the Amis-de-la-Patrie guardsmen, to whom he says in conciliatory tones, 'Friends, if you follow your magistrates, no blood will flow.' Drums beat the retreat, and the assembled forces start to evacuate the Carrousel, taking their cannon with them. Hanriot leads a large force down towards the quais, and is saluted warmly by the crowds on his passage. The other forces take the Rue Saint-Honoré route.

The wish to avoid bloodshed is commendable. It reflects how Hanriot is seeing today's insurrection in terms of the 31 May and 2 June mobilizations. But it is always possible too, that beneath Hanriot's bravura exterior beats a cowardly heart. Probably unique among the Republic's divisional generals, Hanriot has never seen a battlefield, let alone engaged in armed conflict. He has been badly shaken up by his experiences this afternoon. So the path of prudence seems very inviting: return to the Maison Commune, reflect, regroup, possibly reschedule—and get his courage back.

8.45 p.m.

Convention hall, Tuileries palace

I n the Convention, where deputies are as yet unaware of Hanriot's decision, bad news keeps coming. CGS member Élie Lacoste enters to announce that a number of the arrested deputies despatched to the prisons in the afternoon have been freed. Robespierre in particular has been refused entry to the Luxembourg prison and has been taken to the Commune where he is being welcomed and embraced by municipal officers who are brazenly flouting the Convention's decree. This is factually incorrect (for Robespierre is at the Mairie), but the rumour produces an immediate reaction:

 – I demand [Lacoste concludes] that these officials be outlawed.

There is universal assent, which is given added acuity by the announcement that Hanriot is still on the square outside the assembly hall, parading his cavalry and giving orders. It seems unlikely that these will be orders to retreat.

As one man, the assembly yells, 'Outlaw! Outlaw!'

Amar enters to give more information and to puff his own patriotic credentials. Hanriot has been instigating the sectional gunners against the Convention, but Amar went up to address them, calling on their sense of patriotism to support the assembly.

 – One of Hanriot's aides-de-camp threatened me with a sabre; but the gunners protected me. If we can enlighten the people, we can brook any danger.

Féraud rushes in out of breath to confirm that the gunners are not obeying Hanriot's orders. There seems as much confusion outside as inside the Convention hall.

Thuriot now seizes the initiative. From the presidential chair, he declares:

– All the conspirators are now outlawed. It is the duty of all republicans to kill
them. The Pantheon awaits the man who can bring us the head of Hanriot!

This savage decree hurried through at a moment of impending catastrophe is
big with consequence. A decree of outlawry is on a much more elevated and
forbidding level than an arrest warrant or a *mise en accusation*. Individuals
targeted as outlaws are formally assimilated to enemies of the people. When
captured, they are denied a right to trial. On simple identification, they can
be taken out and executed. This kind of treatment originated in the law of
19 March 1793, aimed at Vendée rebels captured with arms in their hands. It
has been refined by the Law of 23 Ventôse (13 March 1794) introduced by
Saint-Just, no less, which included in the outlaw category individuals fleeing
from justice. The high emotion of the moment has just made executing
alleged conspirators against the Convention easier. For the category includes
those fleeing justice or resisting imprisonment. Does that not include Maximilien Robespierre?

8.45 p.m.

CPS Committee Room, Tuileries palace

Around the CPS committee-room green table at the southern end of the Tuileries palace, members of the CPS are hard at work. When were they ever not? The deputies may relish their dinner, but CPS food-breaks are short so as not to interrupt business.

With two members of the CPS on mission outside Paris, and three now in gaol, the task of government has been assumed by the six remaining members. But the CGS offers willing hands. Le Bas is in prison and David on his sickbed, while Jagot has reported ill and Lavicomterie is lying surprisingly low. But the other CGS members are actively engaged in the day's operations. Some are based in their offices at the Hôtel de Brionne too, though only Amar and Ruhl appear to have been in the premises there when Hanriot made his 5.00 p.m. raid. Vadier, who has retreated from the limelight following his rumbustious attack on Robespierre in the Convention, is a more persistent presence at the green table. He and Voulland have their heads down and sleeves rolled up as they endeavour to manage the crisis.

When decisions are made, committee members do not dictate orders to their staff. Instead, they write them out by hand and pass them round the table for signature by whoever is close at hand, before banks of clerks make copies and seek further signatures. Frenetic moments come and go in tempo with the cycle of reports coming in. At times paperwork procedures are lax. To give certain decrees the impression of government unity and force, signatures are taken for granted. One or two have even gone out with bed-bound David listed among the signatories. Most of the police work is done by the CGS, but the CPS adds its weight for some, often random orders. The 9 Thermidor is not a day for punctilious policing of intra-governmental boundaries. All available hands are on deck.

There is quite a bit of back and forth between the committee room, CGS offices and, since 7.00 p.m. , the Convention hall, where deputies need to be kept informed and their morale boosted. With Collot spasmodically attending to his duties as assembly President, Barère and Billaud are continuing their customary role as committee work-horses. The CPS 'specialists' snatch time away from collective decision-making to manage their departments. Lindet, for example, is hard at work on food provisioning with customary dedication, finding time to give commands about payment for mule-hire on the Alpine front, provisioning for Paris with butcher's meat, the manufacture of espadrilles for the troops, and the use of Breton seaweed to make sodium for industry.

For a couple of hours now, however, it has been clear to the Committees of Government that the success of the day has been neither as complete nor indeed as certain as it looked when the Convention session broke up at 4.30 p.m. Their initial reaction was that once the arrested deputies had been packed off to their prisons, all that was needed was to ensure that the key Convention decrees were printed and posted up swiftly through the city. Some routine police work to bring in supporters and contacts of the arrested men would complete the task.

The government has proved to be naïve in many ways. First, it sent the NG detachment from the Maison-Commune section back to their quarters just as they were offering to defend the Convention against the impending threat from the Commune that they had seen brewing with their own eyes around the Commune building. Second, they expected Hanriot to give in gracefully when subject to arrest. It was also excessively hopeful of them, third, to expect the Commune to accept Robespierre's arrest without protest. The committees may have thought that the very completeness of their victory in the Convention hall (the vote for Robespierre and his colleagues' arrest was unanimous) would oblige the Commune's respect and obedience. They did not predict the rash impetuousness of Fleuriot, Payan, and Hanriot. To compound matters they are just sending over to the Mairie a new set of Police Administrators, expecting those in place to defer—in fact, they are about to be gaoled themselves.

As if all this was not bad enough, the Committees of Government have complacently failed to prioritize the printing and diffusion of the proclamation which Barère pushed through the assembly early on during the morning session. It is possible that Robespierre supporter Martial Herman at the Convention's print offices has deliberately slowed down its circulation as a means of giving the Commune more time to get its message across. Or it may simply not have been viewed as important once the arrests had taken place. The Hanriot raid, and the sudden realization after 7.00 p.m. that all was far from well across the city, have impelled the CPS to order the immediate diffusion of the document. Even so, it takes time for it to be delivered throughout the city to Civil Committees and to be posted on walls and trees. It is now almost 9.00 o'clock and only a handful of Civil Committees have actually received the document, let alone proclaimed it. The CPS has finally taken on the task just proposed by Amar in the Convention: they must 'enlighten the people' as to what is going on. The diffusion of information will be crucial. There is much to do.

The experience of the last hour or so has also starkly revealed to the Committees of Government that they lack a decent strategy for their own defence. They really have been caught napping. What they had imagined was a routine administrative matter has now become a major military dilemma on which the Republic's future depends, to say nothing of their own lives. Hanriot's impulsive raid on CGS offices to secure Robespierre's release, and then the sudden appearance of Coffinhal trailing thousands of angry National Guardsmen and most of Paris's artillery, have provided a rude wake-up call. CPS and CGS intelligence in the city has not provided alerts. Tonight's crisis has exposed the pathetic frailty of the forces surrounding the Tuileries in the face of an insurrectionary force. At least they have had the good sense to send out orders to Revolutionary Committees a couple of hours ago to stay at their posts and report to them hourly on their sections. But most of these missives have not reached their destination yet, let alone been acted on.

Seeing the error of their ways, the two committees now make desperate call-ups for NG reinforcement to the close-by Guillaume-Tell and Bonnet-Rouge sections, which they assume remain loyal. But this can only be a stop-gap measure. The Committee is working at full stretch and does not seem equipped to undertake by themselves the task that confronts them. They need reinforcement; but the source of that reinforcement is moot. From reports they have received about the state of the Place de la Maison Commune, it would appear that nearly all of the Paris NG supports the Commune. The Convention's confusion earlier in the day over who exactly was the new commander of the Paris armed forces—CPS nominee Hémart or the rota system candidate, Fauconnier—has been compounded by the fact that not just one but both men have been arrested and imprisoned. For several hours now, the Paris NG has no commander. Losing one commander may be accounted a misfortune. Losing two begins to look like carelessness. A pro tem solution would be to nominate Julliot, today's duty commander at the Convention, who has already done sterling service. But Julliot too has been imprisoned by Coffinhal's forces (though in fact he is currently wriggling free). Carnot within the CPS would be another possible choice: he has genuine military experience and is highly respected in military circles. Yet Robespierre and Saint-Just's antagonism towards him in the last few months have been such that he cannot be guaranteed an easy ride in the sections, which is where the government now needs support. And anyway, can the CPS do without his set of hands around the green table?

The gravity of the situation compels radical thinking. The government's fall from grace in a matter of hours has been vertiginous. They and the Convention are now fighting for their lives. Thinking outside the box has become a necessity forced by the exceptional circumstances of the moment. The question emerges: perhaps they should appoint a field commander from within the ranks of the Convention to rally loyal NG battalions, to defend the Convention hall and even to go out into the city and take the battle to the Commune?

This would be a very major decision, It would break entirely new political ground. Since the very beginnings of the Revolution, the municipality of Paris has had the legal monopoly of ensuring the security of the city. The NG commander has always reported to the Mayor, never to the national legislature or executive. There have been stormy debates in the past about the rights and wrongs of the national assembly seeking to recruit military muscle. They have always foundered on the long-lasting respect for the notion that the legislature should not have policing and military powers. In the immediate aftermath of the 31 May and 2 June *journées* in 1793, it was Robespierre who blocked any thought of revisiting the possibility of the Convention being allowed to requisition armed force in its own name. This partly explains why he gets so angry when he is accused of forming a personal bodyguard, as though he could not trust the NG, the proper emanation of popular sovereignty. Robespierre is no longer in the assembly of course, but even so, the notion of a deputy being made generalissimo of the Paris armed forces is still a breathtakingly audacious break with constitutional tradition. But frankly, in present circumstances, needs must.

If the Committees of Government are to take this decision, whom should they nominate for the role? Perhaps an outsider to government with a background of military competence would do the trick? Whom should they choose?

8.55 p.m.

Convention hall, Tuileries palace

V oulland and a number of his colleagues from the CGS and CPS are cowering in the little room behind the President's chair in the Convention hall. Fréron comes to join them.

Voulland to Fréron: how can we save the Convention?
Fréron: There is only one way to do this. The Convention must appoint deputies to command the armed forces of Paris.

Voulland, who has just torn himself away from the CPS green table where such an eventuality has been under consideration, is all ears. Fréron has a suggestion: his former colleague on mission in the Midi, Paul Barras.

Voulland at once emerges from the cubby-hole, takes the rostrum, and proclaims:

- Citizens, we need a chief for the National Guard. But this man must be one of you, selected from within your ranks. The two committees propose the name of Barras. He will have the courage to accept.

21.00/9.00 p.m.
Convention hall, Tuileries palace

To great cheers from the deputy benches, Barras is being acclaimed chief of Parisian armed forces. Paul Barras, or vicomte de Barras as he was before 1789, is a career soldier and marine officer from Provence. Elected by the Var department in 1792 after making an impact in local politics, he has proved a staunch Montagnard in the Convention. He can also boast a fine record of battlefield and siegecraft experience back to 1778, when he had seen action in India defending Pondichery against the English, but the deputies will have more in mind his striking success on mission alongside Fréron in the siege of Toulon in 1793. This is pertinent as he is now being given a role that, in essence, is that of deputy on mission for the city of Paris.

Barras accepts his role, but has a confession to make to his fellow deputies:

> – I am sensitive to the honour that the Convention has bestowed on me. I will not betray this confidence. However, as I don't know the geography of Paris, I request that I be given assistants.

This is a poor start. The former marine feels all at sea in Revolutionary Paris. Due to his extensive service on mission in the provinces, he has only lived here for a matter of months, and has been enclosed within the Rue Saint-Honoré bubble. One wonders whether the Committees realized Barras's reservations when it proposed his name. It has already had more than its fair share of trouble with commanders today.

The Convention willingly accords him his wish: it is agreed to provide him with adjuncts drawn from the ranks of the assembly, six deputies initially, then, following instant reflection on the scale of the task before them, twelve. To underline their role as deputies on mission, the men are to be kitted out in the approved uniform for these, designed by David in 1793 and comprising tricolour sash, plumes, cockade, sabre, and pistols.

Barras's adjuncts are a mixed bag, united in their hostility to Robespierre, but representing a range of political perspectives, very much like the cross-party coalition which expelled Robespierre this afternoon. Montagnards are there in force (Fréron, Léonard Bourdon, Rovère, Merlin de Thionville, Goupilleau de Fontenay), including some Dantonists too (Legendre, Bourdon de l'Oise), as well as deputies from the Plain and even the Right (Auguis, Bollet, Beaupré, Camboulas, Féraud). Prior career experience in the army is doubtless a factor in deputies' decision to offer their services (Auguis, Delmas, Rovère), but duty as a deputy on mission, notably with the armies, is also particularly in evidence, whether on the left or right. The moderate Féraud, for example, is from a merchant background in the Massif Central, yet showed great bravery as deputy on mission on the Pyrenean border, leading troops into battle from the front (and enduring spells in military hospitals as a result). Physical courage is probably the strongest common element for volunteering. Surprisingly, considering the reasons Barras gave for wanting help, less than half of the adjuncts are Parisians, though quite a few have lived in the city for a number of years. Has the Convention chosen wisely?

9.00 p.m.

Tuileries palace environs

The few NG companies remaining in the environs of the Convention appear troubled by what has just occurred. Artillery Instructor Cosme Pionnier's earlier orders to load the cannon of the Mutius-Scévole section with grapeshot in preparation for conflict has shocked the men. Corporal Levasseur has a reputation for radicalism, but even for him this was an excessive act. When Pionnier was distracted, Levasseur used his handkerchief to extinguish the match, and he now expresses his discontent to his comrades about the whole turn of events.

When the order came to evacuate the Carrousel, Levasseur and his troupe were still complaining. Artillery Adjutant-General Fontaine came over to tell them to ready themselves for their departure, to which Levasseur replied that he was more than ready to serve the public good. 'When the Commune gives the order to march,' Fontaine stated, 'we march.' Levasseur replied, 'It is the Convention that we rally round, and we only march on its orders.' An irritated Fontaine, whom bystanders judge to be drunk, goes off to try his luck with other artillery companies, leaving the Mutius-Scévole men muttering darkly about what seems to be going on and grumbling about the complicity of their officers in something which just didn't seem right.

The Mutius-Scévole gunners are not alone in their concerns. Elsewhere in the Place men from the Panthéon section who had followed the procession from Commune to Convention, are also having heated discussions. They have heard about the arrest orders against Hanriot just agreed within the Tuileries and the news that one of the Legion Chiefs is under arrest at the Commune has also got through to them. They decide to send an emissary to the CPS to ask for enlightenment and guidance. National Guardsmen are beginning to think that they need more reliable information about what is going on than what their leaders are providing.

9.00 p.m.

Place de la Maison Commune

There is an air of boredom, incomprehension, even anger abroad on the Place de la Maison Commune. Many National Guardsmen have been here kicking their heels for four or five hours now. They are being given little sense of what is going on. They arrive, their officers leave them to go up to report at the Maison Commune Council Chamber, and they don't return. The Council's embargo on exits—the *consigne*—prevents the officers from coming down to rejoin their men and to keep them updated. The men discover that their colleagues from other sectional battalions are equally in the dark. All listen out for news.

9.00 p.m.
Council chamber, Maison Commune

Joseph Bodson is the youngest of three brothers all of whom have become committed sectional militants in Révolutionnaire (formerly the Pont-Neuf) section on the Ile de la Cité. A painter and engraver by trade, Joseph, like his jeweller brother, Louis-Alexis, is a member of the sectional Revolutionary Committee. In fact, he is only just back in the saddle after a period in gaol as a suspected Hébert supporter. He was released ten days ago and he has arranged to meet in Paris this afternoon with friends from the nearby village of Villetaneuse to go out and celebrate with a few drinks and a few pipes.

Bodson's plans are however interrupted. When at around 3.00 p.m. he and his fellow members of the Revolutionary Committee heard that Fleuriot and Payan at the Commune were bad-mouthing the Convention, their first reaction was to think that this presaged ill. The section sent Bodson and others to observe the Commune (rather than to express support), and to find out what is going on.

In the frenetic Council chamber, Bodson and his friends have by now witnessed numerous delegations of guardsmen, gendarmes, and gunners taking the oath. They have observed the Commune theatrically ignoring CPS orders and Convention decrees, and arresting their message-bearers. They have seen Payan, Fleuriot, and others calling down the vengeance of the people on named members of the Convention (Collot seems a particular *bête noire*). Now, to his and his friends' astonishment, Bodson sees the arrival, out of the blue and to a rapturous reception, of the younger Robespierre, Augustin, who is led into the Council chamber by municipal councillor and Police Administrator, Joseph Lasnier.

Two hours earlier, Augustin's escort had taken him to the prison of Saint-Lazare. But such is the overcrowding problem, that the prison lacked facilities to keep him in solitary confinement as ordered, so he was shuttled on to the La Force prison, where the concierge proved more accommodating. News of this arrival reached the Maison Commune, a little over a quarter of a mile away, and in no time a force of 60 horsemen arrived, commanded by two municipal officers, Lasnier and Pierre-Jacques Legrand, who insisted that they take the prisoner into their own hands, saying that 'it was in the name of the people that they were demanding him'. They and supporting National Guardsman overpowered the protesting concierge, and the escort party dragged Augustin out into a carriage destined for the Maison Commune.

Dragged is in fact the word, for Augustin was reluctant to be lifted out of gaol by individuals he has never met, and who were making claims about the Commune's actions that he must have found difficult to take in. He had been sitting in his cell preparing for death. He has no illusions about what is in store for him: he expects to be guillotined with his brother tomorrow. Both men, he proudly believes, will die as free men, innocent of all crime.

Many in the Council chamber do not recognize Augustin when he is brought in, for he is not well known on Parisian streets. Some confuse him with his brother, to his advantage. The assembled crowd started to express noisy approbation. Called on to speak, Augustin invokes virtue and patriotism, as he thanks those present for freeing him. He is delighted, he says, to be among men who desire freedom and public safety. The most important and urgent task now for the Commune, he goes on, is 'to unite with his brother'. Maximilien will know what to do. As for himself, he is in two minds as to how to react. Despite his surroundings, he has an odd feeling that he should be defending the very Convention that has gaoled him this afternoon. He equates the CPS with the 'Commission of Twelve', the Girondin committee set up to identify conspirators within the popular movement and whose creation was one of the instigating factors of the 31 May *journée*. All the same, he insists, the National Convention must be respected and treated with consideration. Otherwise all will be lost. The Convention has been misled by a gang of conspirators but as a whole it remains committed to the task of saving the fatherland. It must not be destroyed.

It is not clear how this message of reconciliation is going down with the assembled. The pro-Convention sentiment does not chime well with the claim, voiced most pungently by Payan, that it is the Commune now that is 'the sole and unique representative of the people'. But Augustin gets back on track with his companions when he begins to vent his anger against members of the Committees of Government. These traitors have consistently misled him. They need to be confronted. The Commune must march on the Convention.

But already the spotlight is moving away from Augustin. It is around 9.30 now and news comes in that Coffinhal's expeditionary force has secured the release of Hanriot, whom it is bringing back to the Maison Commune. Levels of enthusiasm run high and are further stoked by the unheralded arrival of Cn. Lerebours, who holds a high-level position in the national welfare bureaucracy. He brandishes, then kisses, a briefcase: in it, he declares, are key elements of 'the web spun against the patriots of the 10 August and the 31 May'. Is this a moment when the government bureaucracy comes over to the Commune? Hopes are high.

Lerebours' crowd-pleasing gesture suffices to get him elected by the assembly to a new 'Enforcement Committee' (*Comité d'exécution*) which will take charge of the organization of insurrection, along the lines of earlier *journées* in which the Commune has assumed a vanguard role. Others who have played a part in the course of the evening are also elected: alongside Payan, there are the three key figures from the successful expedition to rescue Hanriot—Coffinhal and his lieutenants, Louvet and Desboisseaux. Three others—the painter Châtelet, one of the 'solid' jurymen on the Revolutionary Tribunal, plus the wallpaper industrialists Arthur and Grenard—are from the Piques, Robespierre's section. Police Administrator Pierre-Jacques Le Grand, who supervised the release of Augustin Robespierre, makes up the number. They are nine in all, the same number— surely this is deliberate?—as organized the 31 May *journée*.

The new Committee straight away decrees that it shall appoint 24 further councillors tasked to execute their orders across the city. In fact there are downright refusals to serve and it proves surprisingly difficult to winkle volunteers out of those individuals still sitting on the benches. They have to settle for only twelve adjuncts. This dilatory reaction is not a good sign.

By now, Joseph Bodson has seen more than enough. Bearing all this sensational news, Bodson extricates himself from the chamber and after bluffing his way past the *consigne* hurries back to his section to report the calamitous state of affairs. On his way out he may well pass the gaoler from La Force, being led in for severe admonition over Augustin Robespierre's treatment.

9.00 p.m.

Across the city

Despite the chaotic air evident in and around the Maison Commune, the Commune is still ahead of the game. It has recovered from the lead the Convention had at the start of the afternoon. The Commune's best efforts over the course of the late afternoon and early evening, plus word of mouth, the effect of the ringing of the tocsin, and the beating of the *générale* have all combined to considerable effect. An impressive military presence is assembled on the Place de la Maison Commune. Currently, it matches and may even exceed the 3,000 plus who were there at 7.00 p.m. Coffinhal's expedition funnelled off a thousand or more men from the Place, not all of whom have yet returned, but new arrivals have been taking their place. The force would have been even more substantial had four of the six NG Legion Chiefs not got wind of Hanriot's illegal continuation in authority, and refused to circulate his mobilization orders.

Even so, the Commune is finding the logistics of consolidating their position problematic. Just getting messengers together in numbers and on the hoof is proving a problem. Couriers often trail around a number of sections, slowing down transmission, especially now that it is dark. Within the Maison Commune, Fleuriot has had to order the Council clerks (including Blaise Lafosse) to stay at their desks without a break: they must deal with the mountains of paperwork involved in strategizing for insurrection. They will be bayoneted, they are told, if they try to leave. The Commune's problems are aggravated by the fact that the Commune does not have a print-shop to hand. For printing the Wage Maximum a few days earlier, they relied on the print works of Robespierre's bodyguard Charles-Léopold Nicolas, but these are located near Robespierre's house, which is hardly a safe location at the moment (and Nicolas has been arrested and is currently in the Pélagie gaol). In contrast, much of the Convention's printing tonight is being done on their doorstep in a workshop on the Place du Carrousel.

A couple of hours previously, the Commune's Police Administration, allegedly with Robespierre's backing, urged the arrest of key journalists so as to control the narrative of the day. They have plans to descend on newspaper offices at 5.00 a.m. tomorrow, to make arrests and place seals on presses. Tonight, around the Maison Commune, they have hauled in and imprisoned some news vendors for retailing news of the Convention's acts. Yet all this is too little, too late. While Lafosse and his friends are writing furiously to keep up, hordes of printed posters announcing the decree ordering Hanriot's arrest and also carrying Barère's proclamation are finally starting to go up in the central sections. In addition, this evening's papers are currently being diffused more widely, allowing the Convention's narrative to hit news venues and claim legitimacy. There is a danger this evening's that print will trump word of mouth and manuscript transmission, which is pretty much all the Commune can manage.

Many sectional authorities, unsure about what exactly is going on and what the issues are, seek guidance by reading aloud the evening papers' accounts of the Convention arrests. They also are becoming even more resolute about wanting to stick to the letter of the law. They demand to see signed and sealed orders, not simply airy oral commands, before they will lift a finger. Even when the letter protocols are properly met, problems remain. When summoned for the Commune oath, the Lombards' Civil Committee, for example, tells the courier that the order appears to be illegal under Article 2 of Section 2, and also Section 3, Article 16 of the Law of 14 Frimaire on Revolutionary Government. There are similarly motivated refusals in some other sections. All sectional officials have been instructed to carry with them a tiny printed version of the 14 Frimaire law, so it can be consulted at all times with minimum fuss. They have the rule of law in their pockets.

A good number of committees acknowledge their uncertainty and concern by simply forwarding the orders they receive from the Commune directly to the CGS for their urgent consideration, for they judge very easily that the Commune is straying over the line. This and the cavalier way that the Commune is treating legal forms is inhibiting mobilization. It is proving difficult to convince Parisians that the Commune has legitimacy on their side.

The rebels on 31 May gave the city the sense of the dangers to the fatherland in two ways, namely by the tolling of the great Notre-Dame bell and by the firing of the alarm cannon on the Pont-Neuf. Yet Payan's stirring letter of invitation to the Cité section to toll the ancient Notre-Dame bourdon has fallen on stony ground: the Civil Committee has rejected the invitation point-blank and confiscated the keys to the towers so as to avoid mishaps. The Révolutionnaire section, with help from a gendarmerie detachment headed by Cn. Dumesnil (who has freed himself from earlier arrest) also seems to be holding out against pro-Commune guardsmen seeking to fire the alarm cannon on the Pont-Neuf.

Despite high spirits and optimistic vibes in the Commune Council Chamber, the municipality is finding it tricky to impose its will even on sections on its doorstep. The Droits-de-l'Homme section, which abuts the building to the north, was one of the very first sections in Paris to beat the *générale* and start mobilizing men. Yet battalion commander Étienne Lasne was highly resistant to the Commune's action from the start, and Fifth Legion Chief Mulot has warned him off from dabbling in insurrectionary activity. Since then there has been a lively back-and-fro between the section and the Commune over the sending of men and cannon to the Place de la Maison Commune. The section's artillery men are fully mobilized and mustard-keen to lead out their cannon to join the side of the Commune, but the section's National Guardsmen and civilian authorities have been simply blocking the exit from their quarters. There has been a frustrating correspondence all evening between the Commune and Lasne. At the most recent refusal to acknowledge the Commune's orders and to insist on his obedience to the Convention, the municipality's emissary leaves Lasne muttering that if he does not recognize them soon, Lasne's head will roll.

9.15 p.m.

Convention hall, Tuileries Palace

Barras and his dozen adjuncts, that is, the deputies about to venture out into the city with the mission of propagating the Convention's message, are preparing themselves for the task. While they are out of the hall, commander Barras decides that an order should go out to all sectional NG battalion commanders, under the signature of himself and two of his most intrepid aides, Goupilleau de Fontenay and Féraud. It states that battalion commanders are to rally their men: half of them are to patrol the streets and ensure the defence of all public buildings, while the other half should come to defend the Convention, where duty commander Julliot, who has escaped his earlier captivity, is back in place and still running the show.

The adjuncts now enter the hall—to some surprise. The idea has been that they should wear the full official regalia of deputies sent out on mission in the departments or to the armies. But in May 1794 David also displayed for the Convention a set of uniforms of his devising for citizens and legislators. The adjuncts seem to have stumbled into the wardrobe and found the prototypes designed for deputies. Léonard Bourdon—and maybe others—take a fancy to this new classically inspired dress. The tights and calf-length boots are quite an item, though Bourdon eschews David's exotic feathered toque, preferring the more conventional plumed headgear of a deputy on mission. Fully booted and spurred, the men are going to make something of a performance of their mission, as ambulatory incarnations of popular sovereignty. Sabre in hand, they swear to save the *patrie* and then storm out of the hall to universal cheering. Outside, they take the horses of gendarmes who have been guarding the Convention hall. Some remaining mounted gendarmes will add force to their mission, leaving the rump still on guard.

There are still a few stragglers remaining from the Coffinhal expedition around and about the palace, and Barras summons some of the Fontaine-de-Grenelle guardsmen to accompany him on his rounds. As the men venture out into a city increasingly shrouded in darkness, the deputies find the environs of the Tuileries eerily empty. Many of today's NG duty guard for the Convention have taken the road to the Commune along with the rejoicing Hanriot and Coffinhal. The utter defencelessness of the assembly signals just how daunting Barras's task is.

9.30 p.m.

Maison Commune

The Commune's General Council has been working on the composition and remit of its new Enforcement Committee. Suddenly, enthusiasm in the Council is unbounded as another of the arrested deputies—this time Philippe Le Bas—is led into the assembly hall. He has been released almost by accident. On receiving a tongue-lashing from the Mayor for his ignoble treatment of Augustin Robespierre, the La Force gaoler confessed that he had left the prison's keys back within the prison. Three municipal officials, including Le Grand who had commandeered Augustin Robespierre's release, were despatched to collect them. To their surprise, they discovered that Le Bas was also being kept in the prison.

Le Grand's force arrived at the prison for this second time just as Le Bas's young wife, accompanied by her sister-in-law Henriette Duplay, arrived there in a coach, bearing a camp-bed, a mattress and a blanket that her husband had requested. Le Bas had been anticipating the possibility of being in gaol some little time while charges against him were formed. After Le Grand's men had fought off the attentions of government spy Dossonville, who had been escorting Le Bas, the two women accompanied the young deputy as, freed from his cell, he walked towards the Maison Commune. Le Bas is under no illusions as to what awaits him as a result of today's events. He is walking out of prison in artificial freedom, for his steps have taken him into a realm of formal illegality. He knows the likely consequences. His earlier pessimism about the situation has been confirmed. There will be no happy ending. He urges his wife to return home and to bring up their young baby not to hate those who are about to kill his father.

- Nurse him at your breast; inspire in him the love of his fatherland; tell him that his father died for that; adieu, Elizabeth, adieu!

And as he takes leave of her,

- Live for our dear son; inspire in him noble feelings; you are worthy of that! Adieu! Adieu!

9.45 p.m.

Quai de Gesvres (Arcis)

Joseph Lasnier, the municipal official from the Mutius-Scévole section who rescued Robespierre *jeune* and brought him into the Commune Council Chamber, has a new task in hand. He is leading a delegation of six men with orders to escort the elder Robespierre from the Mairie to the Maison Commune. The message states simply:

- The Enforcement Committee, authorized by the General Council of the Commune, has need of your advice. Come quickly.

The messenger is told to make clear to Robespierre that 'he no longer belongs simply to himself, and that he owes himself whole and entire to the *patrie*, to the people'. The Committee's names are listed and the presence of three individuals from his own Piques section (Arthur, Grenard, and Châtelet) will hopefully set his mind at rest that he will not be placing himself in the hands of complete strangers, as has been the case at the Mairie.

One wonders whether the plea in Lasnier's despatch will indeed succeed in winkling Robespierre out of his niche in the Mairie. The delegation from the Maison Commune that Le Lièvre led more than an hour ago failed to persuade him to budge. The force that provisional NG commander Giot took to the Mairie some time after has had no impact either and Giot has contented himself with simply deploying troops to defend the offices.

Robespierre can feel safe in the Mairie: eight NG cannon seal all entrances. Yet it is about more than armed defence: Robespierre is also aware that he is teetering on the edge of legality, and needs to compose his thoughts. He is unsure whether to believe Police Administrators (whom he does not know) when they speak of the strong position of the Commune.

Are they perhaps exaggerating? If he were to remain here and if the Convention prevailed, the deputies would probably still send him to the Revolutionary Tribunal. As things stand, he could frame his removal from the Luxembourg to the Mairie as a police abduction, and indeed it is certainly true that he had little to say about the episode. He may well fancy his chances of not being convicted (he might think differently about this option if he knew about the Convention's outlaw decree). The Revolutionary Tribunal is full of patriots. He knows: he helped put them there. But if he accepts the Commune's invitation to come to the Maison Commune, he will be irremediably breaking the law. He would then have banked everything on an essentially military solution: the Commune's violent crushing of the Convention's will.

As Lasnier's delegation passes along the Quai de Gesvres on the Right Bank, he encounters Hanriot leading mounted cavalrymen as well as NG forces in his triumphant withdrawal from the Place du Carrousel. A brief parley between the two men follows and Hanriot agrees to offer protection to the delegation as it proceeds towards the Mairie, and perhaps to add the commander's voice to the entreaties to Robespierre from the Maison Commune. It would be his first major act as reinstated NG Commander, replacing the incompetent Giot.

To command support across Paris, the Commune really wants Robespierre at its head. He doesn't need to get involved in organizing resistance: his iconic self embodies it. He is no longer his own person; as the General Council has put it, Robespierre 'belongs to the people'. Is that how Robespierre sees it?

22.00/10.00 p.m.

Police Administration HQ, Mairie, Ile de la Cité

Hanriot, Coffinhal and Lasnier are leading their men into the courtyard of the Mairie offices on the Ile de la Cité, where a big crowd has gathered.

> - Everything has been sorted out [they shout to the assembled]. Robespierre has been freed, Hanriot is free too and he is still our commander.

They don't want to complicate matters by raising suspicions about Hanriot's official outlaw status.

An over-energized Hanriot, freshly released from the Tuileries, and seemingly convinced that Giot had actively usurped his command, tears into him with furious contempt. Grabbing Giot's sword hilt as though to disarm him, he yells that he is a moderate who would hand everyone over to the enemy:

> - Get away, you scoundrel. Don't try to hide your unworthiness. The guillotine awaits you. Here (*indicating his military escort*) are your judges.

Giot retains his dignity enough to hand over to Hanriot his sword and swagger stick, and to bow to his command.

Hanriot then joins the others in going up to meet with Robespierre and the Police Administrators. Time passes, and then Lasnier alone comes down and rides off. More time passes. Then suddenly there is great excitement, and a large delegation emerges in a rush and mounts horses. Hanriot, calmer now, pauses only hastily to restore Giot to his command with the words:

> - You are all right here. Follow orders you receive and love your country!

And then Hanriot and the escort gallop excitedly off towards the Commune, shouting:

   - Citizens! Look out! We have a representative of the people with us!

To which the crowd reply:

   - *Vive* Hanriot! *Vive* our brave general!

10.00 p.m.

Maison Commune

The mood within the Council chamber has remained buoyant, following the arrival of Augustin Robespierre and Le Bas. Brother Maximilien is expected imminently, while Saint-Just and Couthon are also thought to be on the way. There is sufficient confidence in the strength of the Commune's position that a decision is taken to lift the *consigne*, the exit embargo which has been in place most of the evening. The fear had been that outgoing intelligence might compromise the Commune cause. Now the Council feels they will not weaken their position if they allow the embargo to be lifted. Individuals who have witnessed the stirring debates within the Maison Commune will be able to circulate within the city, amplifying mobilization efforts. In particular, the Enforcement Committee has primed its 12 adjuncts to go out into the city and chivvy along the General Assemblies which the General Council summoned earlier in the evening to strengthen the Commune's cause among the people of Paris.

It must be said that, despite the general allegresse, many citizens within the Council Chamber are only too pleased to get out. Some have been trying to leave for some time. Many are hungry, thirsty, and grateful for some fresh air. It is a warm night. Some of the leavers cut off straight away for their sections, but others, before deciding on their next move, go down to talk to friends and colleagues on the Place. A fair crowd go and share a drink at Belhomme's bar on the Rue du Mouton on the north-west corner of the Place, which is doing good business.

What they there discover is sensational. The news now beginning to sweep across the Place is that Hanriot has been declared an outlaw. And so, the story goes, have the members of the Commune. And the same is going to happen, rumour has it, to Robespierre and the other arrested deputies. This puts a new and frightening complexion on the evening.

Leavers also learn that some sections are pressurizing their armed forces on the Place and even, as far as contact has been possible, their colleagues within the Council chamber to return to their sections. Réunion battalion commander Jean Richard, who crossed swords with Payan earlier in the evening, is under sectional instruction to remove his 200 men, which he is doing by platoons so as avoid raising suspicion. The 1,200 men from the Panthéon section have also been ordered to return home and are currently in a face-off with pro-Commune troops who are trying to stop them crossing the Pont Notre-Dame without Hanriot's permission. What with the detachment of a good body of troops to protect the Mairie, and the dispersal of some of Coffinhal's forces, these defections are making the Place de la Maison Commune seem far less populated than earlier.

With rumours running rampant on the Place, the men still left are questioning their presence there. Men from the Amis-de-la-Patrie were a major component in Coffinhal's expeditionary force. Many were amazed to discover they had been sent to release Hanriot, and though they then returned to the Place de la Maison Commune after his release, they have been berating their battalion commander Thiéry about the legality of their actions. 'We all see now that this is not our place,' one of the men tells him. Thiéry counsels just following orders for the meanwhile, but he sends a message back to his section for advice on what he should do. If there is still great enthusiasm among the organizers of tonight's insurrectionary movement, worrying signs are appearing that the base is starting to crumble.

10.15 p.m.

Across the city

The Commune's emissaries are leaving the Maison Commune and are fanning out across the city to bolster the loyalty of the sectional General Assemblies whose convocation the Commune ordered earlier in the evening. A large majority of sections are holding or have convoked Assemblies. This is encouraging, since it means that they are following the Commune's orders. Only nine of the 48 sections, mostly located in central areas close to the Convention, refused the Commune's instruction outright and came out strongly in favour of the Convention.

Fleuriot, Payan, and Hanriot had realized from the outset that they were involved in a numbers game and that the Commune's claim to legitimacy would rest on a massive engagement by Parisians in their action. At first appearance, then, the fact that attendance at most assemblies is very much higher than it has been for some little time is a real plus point for the Commune's cause. The more the merrier. In fact, increased attendance in general assemblies is having the effect of changing their political complexion in ways the Commune leaders did not foresee. Over the last several months, Revolutionary Committees have controlled business closely in many sections, reducing the decision-making role of the assemblies. With assembly meetings in danger of becoming rubber-stamping exercises dominated by radical cliques with a power base within the Revolutionary Committee, attendance has slumped. The sometimes unpleasantly personal and threatening nature of disputes in meetings has also dissuaded many citizens from attendance. This evening, however, the frenetic hurly-burly out on the streets has stirred into action a huge part of the population. Parisians want to be involved. There suddenly seems a point in coming to a General Assembly.

Assemblies thus are more genuinely representative of Parisian opinion, rather than the views of dedicated radical local cliques, than they have been for a long time. Some of those cliques must be worried about this invasion of what they think of as moderates, but at the moment the more urgent issue is taking the right political decision to get their section through this crisis.

In the Bon-Conseil section, Jacques-Louis Ménétra is leading the Assembly back into the paths of pro-Convention righteousness. He was on NG duty earlier when he bumped into his friend Auguste Jemptel, who just a few weeks earlier had beaten him in elections to the Commune. Councillor Jemptel takes him for a drink in a nearby café to tell him how bitterly he is now regretting his success. He knows what the Commune is up to and has been powerless to stop the section's artillery from going to join the throng at the Maison Commune. Leaving gloomy Jemptel with his drink, Ménétra goes back into the sectional Assembly to declare:

> – Citizens, our cannon was taken to the Maison Commune at 5.00 p.m. Yet our civic devotion is for the Convention. Let us at instantly appoint commissaries to bring it back and to find out if our gunners (as must be the case) support the Convention.

Furious applause greets his words and part of the battalion goes off to the Maison Commune to bring the men back.

Decision-making elsewhere is not helped by the fact that contradictory information and conflicting pieces of information about what is happening are still flying about. Legendre's comment in the Convention this evening that 'it is not easy to make the people rebel if they are well-instructed' is all well and good. But at the moment no one is 'well-instructed'. The assembly has been incredibly laggardly in getting information out across the city. Sectional assemblies in particular are acutely aware that they lack hard information as regards what is going on in the city. For many, hedging the bets seems the best option. A substantial number of sections send delegates, and in some cases, simply observers, to both the Commune and the Convention. Indivisibilité and Poissonnière have sent observers to the Jacobin Club too. This is the kind of situation across the city that the Commune is hoping that its adjuncts will change, and win assemblies over to its cause.

The cover of darkness adds to the levels of nervous anxiety in many of the groups meeting to decide on a proper course of action, and makes it more difficult for them to gather hard information. This is particularly so in outlying sections where news is scarcer and where there is little by way of street lighting. People hear rather than see traces of the insurrection. It is obvious that this is a major crisis, but people fear taking a decisive course of action when friends and family might find themselves on the other side. In these circumstances, the side that can get its messages out most widely and inspire confidence in its pronouncements is going to be at a big advantage.

10.15 p.m.

Convention hall, Tuileries palace

B arère is rising to speak in the Convention. The retreat of Hanriot, Coffinhal, and the armed expedition towards the Commune has given the deputies breathing space. They have been lucky, very lucky indeed. They must now sit patiently and wait to see whether Barras and his men can have an effect on the people of Paris. In the meanwhile they listen to Barère.

Barère is perfect for a situation like this. He knows better than anyone how to manage the Convention. He specializes in spouting feel-good perorations, soothing worried brows, crystallizing situations, steadying the ship, celebrating successes, filling in time. He is currently telling the deputies that the events of the last few hours have indicated the existence of a long-nurtured conspiracy against the *res publica*.

> - All preparations for this counter-revolution were made, all dispositions readied . . . While you were passing salutary legislation, Hanriot was spreading the rumour in the streets of Paris that Robespierre had been assassinated. The most infamous stories were broadcast against you. Cartouches were distributed to gendarmes with orders to shoot the deputies . . .

His statements are informed by the rumours that have been flying around the sections closest to the Tuileries. But he is also being a little fanciful about alleged conspiratorial preparations.

He continues. Hanriot is continuing to act as though he still commands the NG. He has countermanded CGS arrest warrants against Boulanger and others of the aides-de-camp, arrested the Convention's envoys, summoned National Guardsmen to the Maison Commune and sounded the tocsin, as well as closing the city barrier-points. Before being arrested, he rode around the street shouting, 'They are assassinating the patriots! Arm against the

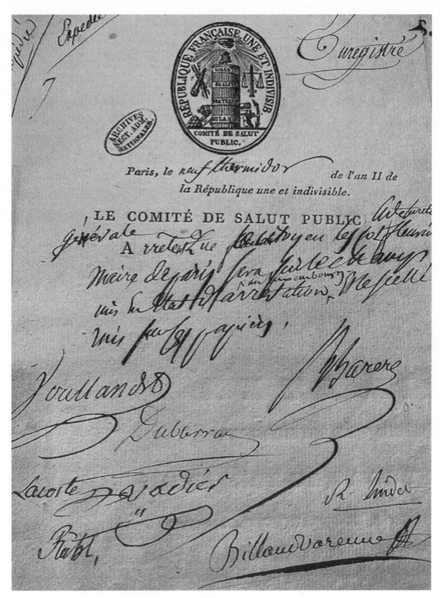

Figure 8. Committee of Public Safety, Arrest Warrant for Paris Mayor Fleuriot-Lescot, after 10.00 p.m. (AFII 47 pl. 363, pi. 10)

Convention!' The Commune has declared itself in open insurrection against the Convention and when summoned by a Convention envoy to come to the bar of the house, one of the municipal officers shouted, 'Yes, we'll go there—but with the people at our sides!'

> – As you can see, the most atrocious conspiracy, a military conspiracy, a conspiracy hatched with a latitude, an artfulness and a coldbloodedness that neither Catiline nor Pisistratus could rival!

Many sections have declared themselves supporters of the Convention, though some, Barère reports, are misguidedly holding out. The Convention's task is now to win them all back over to the side of right. With courage and virtue, the Convention will prevail. In the meantime (Barère is working up to this), the Convention must do the following:

> – Outlaw all those who take up arms against the assembly or give orders that seek to countermand the Convention! And outlaw too any individual who refuses to accept an arrest or detention warrant against them! . . . The fatherland is watching Paris and the Convention will know how to judge good citizens.

Voulland steps up to support Barère. The original outlawry decrees were against Hanriot and conspirators at the Commune. This proposal is a significant step up from the *mise en arrestation* and *mise en accusation* debates of this morning. The motion is thunderously applauded. It makes it crystal clear that Robespierre is targeted, for he has indeed refused to accept a detention warrant and has fled the Luxembourg prison. The Law of 23 Ventôse means that Robespierre's death is suddenly at the top of the agenda.

10.15 p.m.
Jacobin Club

Pierre Burguburu, an official in the Paris war manufactory, based in the Gardes-Françaises section, is not having the honeymoon he would have wished. Yesterday he was married and this evening he has brought his new wife to the Jacobin Club where he had heard that Robespierre would be unveiling a huge conspiracy. To his dismay, he had learnt not only that Robespierre has been attacked but also that arrest warrants are out for fellow Jacobins he admires who are alleged idolaters of Robespierre. The victims include his new brother-in-law, Prosper Sijas, no less, who has been using the Jacobin rostrum this evening to inveigh against Carnot and his acolyte Pille. Fearing that this crisis will cause a schism in the Club, Burguburu believes that the Commune should be the compass for the Paris sections and indeed for the Jacobins.

The Jacobins have played a pivotal role in so many Parisian *journées*. But tonight, they are hearing the news rather than making it. Under Vivier's uninspiring chairing, the Club is proving highly undynamic and waits on reports from outside. Burguburu admits to not understanding exactly what is going on, and he is not alone in this. There have already been a number of low-key delegations to the Commune to express solidarity and to clarify the situation. At one visit, the delegates rhetorically demanded where exactly 'the true representatives of the people were located', which allowed the mayor grandiloquently to respond that 'at this time tomorrow the factious will have been annihilated'.

Now, the Club is greeting a deputation sent by the municipality to provide an update on the accelerating pace of events. The delegates inform their brothers-in-arms that the CPS no longer exists, and that legitimate power now resides in the just-established Enforcement Committee drawn from the Commune's Council. The latter is henceforward to be called the 'General Council of 10 August'. The people is at its post, the delegates declare. The liberty bell—the tocsin at the Maison-Commune—is ringing.

It is true that the Maison Commune's tocsin is still working overtime, but as for the people being at their post? In fact, messages already coming into the Commune are presenting a less rosy picture. And in the Jacobins, the public galleries are not at their fullest either. Many Jacobin members have observed the *générale* and the tocsin in their different sections and are now bedecking themselves in their NG uniforms and reporting for duty at their sectional NG headquarters. Others are frightened and have run home.

The Club is being bypassed by events. Robespierre's whole strategy seems to have pivoted on the Jacobins being able to reach out and diffuse to the people of Paris the need for them to act in the interests of the nation. But the flaccidity of their actions tonight suggests that they are a broken reed.

To show willing at least, the remaining Jacobins appoint a delegation of around a dozen members to visit the Commune and to fraternize with them. Among the group are Robespierre's landlord Maurice Duplay and his bodyguard-friend Jean-Baptiste Didier, both of them fretting about what will become of Robespierre. Since abandoning him to his fate at the Convention early in the afternoon, Didier had been agonizing about what to do. At least now there is a mission. But there is no reason for thinking that this new move will produce anything but hot air, of which there has been no shortage on all sides this evening. The delegation sets out as a group—but how many arrive at their destination? Catching the mood of the streets, Didier decides it is in his interests to opt out altogether and go straight home, leaving his hero to his fate.

10.30 p.m.

Convention hall, Tuileries palace

CGS member Élie Lacoste is drawing deputies' attention to a new threat. There is an urgent need to ensure the loyalty of the young cadet solders serving in the École de Mars out on the Sablons plain near Neuilly. The danger of them being swayed to support the conspirators is amplified by the fact that Le Bas with fellow Montagnard, Jean-Pascal Peyssard was responsible for the camp. The École may only be composed of boys; but they could be sitting on an arsenal.

Somehow or other this afternoon, Le Bas has managed to get a message out to the director of the institution, the multi-scarred veteran Bertèche:

> A frightful plot has just broken out, I am among the loyal deputies that the conspirators have arrested. My suspicions about intentions for using the camp have been confirmed. It is up to you to oppose it marching under the banner of traitors. The people is watching. Stay loyal.

In fact, Le Bas is quite wrong in thinking that Robespierre's opponents plan to enlist the military might of the École, who were to have a starring role in the Festival for Bara and Viala planned for 10 Thermidor. In fact they are discounting it completely.

Billaud-Varennes intervenes in the debate to note that the École commander Bertèche has been under arrest for four hours (in fact for quite different reasons). But he accepts the reality of the threat the cadets might pose if they follow Le Bas's prompt. The assembly indefinitely postpones tomorrow's Bara and Viala festivities. On Tallien's suggestion, three deputies, Brival and Bentabole along with Peyssard, are instructed to ride out to the École and secure it.

While deputies have had to wait and see what impact Barras will have in defusing the political threat within Paris, there have been some encouraging straws in the wind. Jean Devèze, a member of the Commune's General Council, comes to the bar of the house to declare his complete opposition to the Commune and his undying support for the Convention. This is a major step for someone who in the past has been a convinced supporter of Robespierre and a radical sans-culotte in the République section who describes himself as 'a carpenter who has fun making heads roll'. Devèze is followed by a gunner from the Faubourg Saint-Antoine who announces, somewhat Delphically, that the Faubourg 'is on its feet, but not in a worrying way'. Not worrying for the Convention, one hopes. Then a delegate from the Unité section's Civil Committee also reports their rejection of advances from the Commune. These are good signs. It looks as though many, who less than 24 hours ago one would have thought were fully enfeoffed to Robespierre, are changing their minds.

10.30 p.m.

Maison Commune

The young schoolteacher, Jean-Philippe Charlemagne, from the Brutus section, has taken over chairing duties in the Council chamber. The appointment of the Enforcement Committee has removed much of the earlier buzz in the hall. The ending of the *consigne*, the blockade on individuals leaving the meeting, means that delegates can now go out into the city to spread the word of the Commune. Here, most of the time seems to be taken up with administering the oath to newcomers. At least there are newcomers—though not as many as might be hoped. Just as in the Convention, deputies are impatiently waiting on news of Barras's impact on the city, so the Commune is waiting to hear of the impact made across the city by the Enforcement Committee's twelve adjuncts despatched into the sections to win the support of Parisians.

In this rather reserved, low-key mood, a disappointed Lasnier is just declaring to the meeting that his mission to persuade Robespierre to come to the Maison-Commune has failed and that he has decided to remain in the Mairie. But suddenly, with Lasnier still in mid-sentence, the man himself enters the room, flanked by Hanriot and Coffinhal.

- Vive Robespierre!

It is not clear how Hanriot has managed to extract Robespierre from his niche in the Mairie; but extract him he has.

The crowd can now see that the great man is speaking and making gestures, but the excited hubbub is so noisy and intense that just what he is saying cannot be heard. Something about the need to support liberty, perhaps? It is probably apparent that Robespierre has been deeply shaken by the experience of the day. He seems much less willing than his brother to whip up the crowds.

As the meeting deliriously celebrates the new addition to their forces, Payan reaffirms the Commune's refusal to accept the Convention's legitimacy. Suddenly, however, a voice from the floor makes itself heard:

> – It is only scoundrels who think like that. Patriots should rally in support of the Convention.

It is François-Louis Juneau who is speaking. A second-hand clothes dealer, he is here as a marching member of the Amis-de-la-Patrie section who has come up to the Council chamber to see what is going on. His battalion colleagues down below share his lack of enthusiasm about supporting the Commune, indeed many are defecting back to the section.

The councillors react quickly and guardsmen and gendarmes leap on Juneau, beating him and ripping off his hat and coat (they just cost me 150 livres, thinks Juneau, true to his trade). Robespierre springs to life as he witnesses the struggle, shouting out, 'Knock him down! Knock him down!' Juneau is brought under control and despatched to the cells in the Mairie to await his fate.

Undeterred by this little incident, Hanriot and Coffinhal have gone on to milk the applause. Quite apart from Robespierre's arrival, the Commune has its NG commander back, Coffinhal exults. Coffinhal has rescued the now preening Hanriot from the clutches of 'villains, former police spies, enemies of the people and conspiring tyrants' (he means the CGS and the CPS). There is a call for all of the victims of the Convention's ire to be rescued and brought to the Maison Commune to join the three deputies present. Couthon and Saint-Just, as well as Dumas of the Revolutionary Tribunal, are now the priorities, while Hanriot's return is a reminder that his general staff should also be brought back into the fold.

It is perhaps revealing that Coffinhal's speech highlighted Hanriot's release rather than Robespierre's. Maybe the latter really was looking a broken man when he came in. He seems to have passed quickly out of the Council chamber limelight into the Salle de l'Égalité where Payan and Fleuriot are pressing ahead with action. Payan has drawn up a new proclamation for instant release. It contains a revised list of names of the alleged enemies of the people in the Convention:

- The Revolutionary Commune of 9 Thermidor, created by and for the people to save the fatherland and the National Convention from attacks by worthless conspirators decrees that Collot d'Herbois, Amar, Léonard Bourdon, Fréron, Tallien, Panis, Carnot, Dubois-Crancé, Vadier, Javogue, Dubarran, Fouchet, Granet, and Moise Bayle will be arrested so as to free the Convention from the oppression in which these men are holding it . . .

A civic crown will be awarded any citizen who makes the arrests.

It is a curious list of enemies. It does not inspire confidence that the Enforcement Committee either has a firm grasp of what has been happening in the Convention hall, or is even approaching its insurrectionary business in a methodical way. Only two members of the CPS are cited (and no Billaud or Barère even! Was the latter omission Robespierre's doing, one wonders?); four CGS members; and then a mixture of radicals and moderates involved in this morning's *coup de théâtre*. It looks like a ragbag, held together less by ideological considerations than by the personal animosities of those drawing up the list. Some of the putative enemies that Robespierre and Couthon have been attacking are there, but the fact that Fouché's name is mis-spelt suggests that Robespierre's engagement has been exiguous.

All the same, with Robespierre and Hanriot now back onside, the Commune's leaders are convinced that they have the wind in their sails. They roll up their sleeves for action, issuing an order to NG Commander Hanriot 'to direct the people against the conspirators who oppress the patriots and deliver the National Convention from the oppression of the counter-revolutionaries'. One notes in this echoes of Payan's proclamation. One also notes that the desire for the repression of the news media, highlighted by Robespierre from the Mairie earlier in the evening, has fallen off the bottom of the agenda for action.

Back in the saddle, Hanriot is eager to act. He informs Popincourt battalion gunner Cn. Pellerin that he should prepare to lead 600 men and ten cannon back to the Place du Carrousel. He then writes to the adjutants of the six Legion Chiefs (he seems to have given up on the Legion Chiefs themselves) ordering them each to keep 100 men in reserve and ready for action. An order also now goes out that the National Guardsmen defending the Convention should come to the side of the Commune. All individuals found making the Convention's proclamation should be arrested forthwith. Then finally a further order is formulated:

- The sections are ordered to save the fatherland, to ring the tocsin, to beat the *générale* across Paris and to merge forces at the Maison Commune where they will receive orders from General Hanriot, whom the sovereign people has just released from prison along with all the other patriot deputies.

A new *journée* is swinging into action. And Hanriot will have the chance to redeem himself following his humiliations earlier in the day.

10.45 p.m.

Guillaume-Tell section and across the city

Wig-maker Pierre-Louis Moessard is presiding in the Guillaume-Tell section's General Assembly which opened at 10.00. He is currently making amends for his actions earlier in the evening. Around 5.00 p.m., he witnessed Hanriot being arrested outside the CGS offices, and while others in the crowd yelled, 'He is a scoundrel! Place him under arrest', Moessard had gone to shake Hanriot's hand and say, 'Come on, Hanriot, don't be frightened. We'll support you.' Shortly after, Moessard was appalled to discover that Hanriot's arrest had been decreed by the Convention, so that his action has put him massively in the wrong. Now determined to brandish pro-Convention sympathies with all his might, he tells his assembled section to rally round the Convention:

– Individuals are wanting to seize supreme power at a moment when our armies are triumphant on all fronts.

With a transparent evocation of Robespierre, he concludes that it is always better 'to be attached to things rather than to individuals'. Fréry, one of the section's representatives on the Commune's General Council, hotfoot from the Maison Commune, has been trying to persuade the assembly to rally to the Commune. Yet the assembly is having none of it, and when someone shouts out that he should be arrested as an outlaw, Fréry disappears smartly. Resisting the temptation to burn the messages it has received from the Commune, the assembly also decides that these should be sent to the Committees of Government.

In the Faubourg Saint-Antoine, the Quinze-Vingts section is also currently gripped by sectional divisions. Early in the evening, the authorities here were so confused by conflicting orders they were receiving that they penned a letter to the Convention seeking guidance in the face of what they regarded as tricks and traps being created by the Commune. At this moment, pro-Commune militants in the Revolutionary Committee, led by Etienne Pellecat, a clerk in the municipal bureaucracy, are doing their best to sway local opinion towards the Commune. In answer to fresh-faced colleagues pressing him to support the Convention over the Commune, Pellecat replies:

> – You are still young in Revolution and you don't realize what a Commune is when it rings the tocsin and beats the *générale*. As our representatives (in the Convention) were not doing their duty, the Commune has the right to dismiss them and drive them out.

He finds support from François-Louis Fournerot, a hunchback dwarf with a glittering curriculum of radicalism that includes active participation on revolutionary *journée*s going back to 1789, as well as bureaucratic service culminating in a post on one of the Popular Commissions, where he has shown scant mercy to enemies of the Republic. Now he addresses his section:

> – Citizens, the Commune has been saved and now has the upper hand; Robespierre and Hanriot have escaped the scoundrels' clutches and tomorrow we will disarm the gendarmerie. The General Council has just appointed an Enforcement Committee.

Perhaps this kind of speech would have gone down well in most recent meetings of the General Assembly. The opposite is the case tonight, with Fournerot's fellow citizens showing scepticism about the legitimacy of the Commune's action. Pellecat and Fournerot's interventions in fact have the effect of actively antagonizing their listeners. The consensus is strengthened even more shortly afterwards, when the Quinze-Vingts battalion commander, François Bourbault, who earlier in the evening helped supervise today's guillotinings over on the Place du Trône-Renversé, returns from observing the Maison Commune to tell his fellow citizens that the Commune was now passing decrees that are frankly, he declares, 'liberticidal'. The Commune wants to kill the people's freedom. It seems that the twelve adjuncts that the Commune's Enforcement Committee has sent out to rally the people of Paris are going to have a tough job on their hands.

Before 11.00 p.m.

Paris prisons

- Shut up, Robespierre! Go and lie down!

The nervous tensions rampant across the prison system have spread to gaolers, and their guard-dogs. The gaoler at the Left Bank prison of Pélagie is having trouble stopping Robespierre, his favoured mastiff, from barking wildly. It is making it harder to hear the noises of the city.

As the evening has worn on, prisons closest to the centre of the city have registered the intensification of street action, as the air is rent with shouts, the clash of arms, the gallop of horses, the creaking of artillery trains and the tramp of National Guard companies. Many prisoners at the Luxembourg witnessed the imbroglio over Robespierre's non-admission to the gaol, and their narrow escape (so they feel) from massacre. Soeur Théotiste discovers more when a projectile hurled from outside on the street clatters onto the floor of her cell. Around the stone is a message:

- Robespierre has just been outlawed by the Convention. He and his satellites are closeted together in the Hôtel de Ville; but numerous battalions are surrounding the building.

She and her friends run to tell their fellow inmates. Can it all be true? Or is it merely wishful thinking?

The Luxembourg gaol is better-informed than most. Elsewhere ignorance is still rife, and dread at the possibility of a reprise of the September Massacres very much in the air. In the Port-Libre prison, gaoler Haly's response to the news of the arrests has been worryingly emotional: striking himself on the forehead, he groaned that Robespierre is the helmsman and if he died, the Republic will be lost. Will he take out his bad feelings on inmates? Over at La Force prison in the Marais, where Theresa Cabarrus is kept, inmates have improvised defensive preparations in the eventuality of a mob break-in: beds now barricade cell doors, and inmates have armed themselves with chairlegs and any knives that have escaped the official round-up of sharp objects. Their emotions have been wrung by news that Robespierre himself has been admitted to their prison (in fact it was Augustin not Maximilien), and then even more so when he was released and set off for the Maison Commune.

Similar acts of self-defence take place in other prisons. At the Plessis, children are pressed into service collecting ashes and cinders to throw into the eyes of their putative assailants. At the Bénédictins-Anglais, guards are making frequent visits to cells, and have been noisily loading their rifles. Mercier's colleague Fleury and other deputies overhear their gaolers talking among themselves in a way that suggests there will be a mass killing at midnight. 'No one,' they hear, 'must escape.' Fellow deputy Laurenceot takes in the news with weary resignation, and simply lies down on his bed with his face to the wall and goes to sleep. Fleury is beside himself with fear and shakes his colleague to wake him. Laurenceot remains resigned:

- If they start killing on the ground floor, tell me and I will kill myself by jumping out of the window.

Fleury's frenzied agitation is more typical of the prison mood than Laurenceot's calm. The prisons, and the whole city, are living on their nerves.

23.00/11.00 p.m.
Salle de l'Égalité, Maison Commune

The Commune's Enforcement Committee has got hold of copies of the Convention's proclamation that Barère drafted earlier today. They have taken this in their stride. Now, however, they receive copies of the Convention's outlaw decree. This has shaken them more than a little. It underlines the life-and-death struggle in which they are engaged.

The Committee determines to issue a counter-proclamation, an act of defiance that will rally their own supporters, bring over waverers and frighten those who have thrown in their lot with the Convention. The fact that it is the third such missive within an hour suggests real worries that their words are not having the impact they would wish and are failing to keep up with the speed of events.

> – The Revolutionary Commune in the name of safety of the people commands all citizens who compose it to recognize no other authority than itself, to arrest all those who abuse the title of Representative of the People and who make perfidious proclamations that outlaw its defenders; and declares that those who do not obey this supreme order will be treated as enemies of the people.

In a version targeted at the inhabitants of the village of Choisy, it adds:

> – The friends of liberty are on the march against the conspirators. The Commune is the rendezvous for all patriots. March with your cannon, your weapons and your republican wives and daughters.

The Commune has been more antagonistic than most towards the involvement of women in political and public life. Wanting 'wives and daughters' to join their forces seems decidedly desperate.

Payan gathers that the news about the outlaw decree has penetrated the Council Chamber and so he goes back in to bolster the meeting's defiance. He rejoices in the outlaw label:

> – Yes, we are *out-laws*, conspirators, counter-revolutionaries, royalists and *in-the-laws* of Liberty and Equality!

Yet Payan ruins the effect of his bold language by making a major gaffe. For he tells the assembled that they can assume that anyone who supports the Commune at this hour can expect to be included in the list of the Convention's outlaws—for the wording of the Convention decree does indeed target aiders and abettors. This is a formidable statement to the assembled which Payan clearly believes will redouble people's commitment. However, although there is some routine initial cheering, it does not take long for the implications of the message to sink in. If the Convention prevails, anyone present could be taken out and shot. The public galleries, already less populated after the lifting of the *consigne*, thin out swiftly and markedly. People want to save their own skin. The Commune's cause does not seem worth the wager.

It is not just the public who react in this way to the sudden threat to their lives. Councillor Charles Ballin, who has found it difficult to make head or tail of this evening's events, feels like he has been struck by a bolt from the blue by Payan's revelation. He rushes home to the Quinze-Vingts section to seek consolation from his wife, convinced his death is near. The signature of Cn. Fleury, the Commune clerk formerly known as Bourbon, stops appearing on Commune decrees at around this time. Fleury-Bourbon has cut and run. This is a worrying trend. Panic is setting in at the Maison Commune.

11.00 p.m.

Café des Subsistances, Palais de Justice, Ile de la Cité

D umesnil, the gendarmerie commander attached to the law courts, has managed to extricate himself from the Commune after being held under arrest for several hours. Rushing back to the law courts, he discovers Fouquier-Tinville not in his offices but in the *buvette*, aka the Café des Subsistances. Fouquier likes a drink. In circumstances such as these, he probably feels he needs a drink. From these improvised headquarters he has been receiving news, sending out employees to gauge the mood in the streets, and despatching the occasional message to the CPS assuring them of his continuing fidelity. Envoys from the Maison Commune have been finding their way to the *buvette*, seeking to shift his loyalty away from the Convention to the Commune. But Fouquier is having none of it, though he is far from clear about the pattern of the day: 'I do not know what is taking place nor what it means,' he tells his *buvette* hosts. Perhaps news has trickled back to him that the Commune has finally abandoned its efforts to win him over to their side: the story is that they have decided to start tomorrow by having Jean Hémart, the Convention's choice as Hanriot's putative successor, shot by firing squad, presumably on the Place de la Maison Commune. What exactly Fouquier will be doing tomorrow is still unclear; but the Commune evidently wishes to start off the *journée* of 10 Thermidor with a bang.

11.00 p.m.

Across the city

The Commune is banking heavily on the success of the adjuncts to the Enforcement Committee in speeding up the radicalization of the sections. One wonders whether they realize it, but it is a very tall order. The failure to secure 24 volunteers for the role suggests that even in the then ebullient atmosphere of the Council chamber it is a daunting task. In addition, they are setting out very late in the evening. Many sections have convoked General Assemblies all right, but they have not been adequately supplied with information by the Commune. The *consigne*—another blunder to lay at Payan and Fleuriot-Lescot's door—has kept militants within the walls of the Council chamber who could have returned to their section to plead the Commune's cause. In their absence, sectional Assemblies have been receiving more information and claims on their allegiance from the Convention. The delay caused by the *consigne* means that the adjuncts are often going into assemblies which have already made up their mind to support the Convention.

The twelve chosen adjuncts represent only nine fairly random sections among the city's 48. The levels of competence and commitment varies. Aubert, a wood-worker of little education and even less grasp of what is going on this evening, simply goes back to his section, Poissonnière, tells the authorities what the Commune is up to and throws himself on their mercy. Michée and Leleu seem to have simply slipped into the night rather than risk going back to their sections at all. Jault and Dhazard, knowing that their sections—Bonne-Nouvelle and Gardes-Françaises respectively—have opened general assemblies rather late in the evening and are coming out strongly pro-Convention, choose another target. Along with Mercier from

Finistère, they are set to visit the strategically important Arcis section, in which the Place de la Maison Commune is located. Cochois tried his luck at Bonne-Nouvelle, but his appeals cut no ice. The story was similar with Simon, ex-governor to the young 'Louis XVII' in the Temple, who found the Marat section too loyalist to shift. After his expression of pro-Commune sentiments, Simon and fellow councillors Warmé and Laurent were placed under arrest. Gibert and Barelle had little chance of prevailing in Faubourg-du-Nord either: by the time they reached it, the section had declared for the Convention and was recalling its NG troops from the Place de la Maison Commune.

Councillors Gencey and Delacour showed a bit more gumption in Finistère and Brutus respectively. The Faubourg Saint-Marcel barrel-maker Gencey even arrested members of the section's Revolutionary Committee for their pro-Convention views. But when he went into the General Assembly to justify his moves, and tried to make even more arrests, he was shouted down and ended the night in gaol. In the Brutus section, notary Pierre-Louis Delacour had been working since the early evening with a clique of Commune supporters on the Revolutionary Committee to shake the growing pro-Convention consensus within the section. They sought in particular to influence Charles Chardin, Fourth Legion Chief. Though Chardin was earlier obedient to the Convention and rejected Hanriot's command to send 400 men to the Place de la Maison Commune, he subsequently received a message that the Commune wanted to appoint him one of Hanriot's adjutants. Chardin wavers. A staunch member of the Cordeliers, who underwent trial by the Revolutionary Tribunal for his alleged Hébertist sympathies (he was acquitted), he can see many of his close sans-culotte allies now lining up with the Commune. Though he speaks in the assembly for the Convention, as he leaves shortly after 10.00 he states that he fully expects to be arrested by one side or the other. Even then Delacour continues to try to suborn him, whispering to one of Chardin's NG aides:

- If you love Chardin, if you are friendly with him, go and get him to abandon the Convention and the two of you get your troops to march to the Commune. We have Robespierre, Couthon, Saint-Just, Dumas and Le Bas and we no longer recognize the Convention.

Despite the honeyed words, the section's progressive move towards the Convention leaves Delacour out on a limb. He soon returned to the Maison

Commune with his tail between his legs. There the conclusion can only be, as news filters in, that the Enforcement Committee's use of adjuncts to galvanize Parisian opinion in favour of the Commune has proved a complete flop. They have comprehensively failed to halt the pro-Convention shift of the sections.

All this is certainly too much for Chardin. Despite his high rank in the NG, he now throws in his hand, and leaves his post to spend the night with a female friend and a bottle of wine. He will see how the dice have fallen in the morning.

11.00 p.m.

Convention hall, Tuileries palace

To loud acclaim, Barras and a number of his aides sweep back into the Convention. Barras presents his report on the state of the city:

- I have covered much of the city, accompanied by the gunners from the Fontaine-de-Grenelle section, and have found the people everywhere primed for freedom and crying '*Vive la République! Vive la Convention nationale!*' at our passage. Military orders have been given and a huge band of republicans surrounds the Convention to provide defence. I have just arrested a gendarme sent by the Commune to Bertèche out at the École de Mars.

Barras then leaves the hall accompanied by Fréron to report to the Committees of Government, leaving his aide Féraud to continue with the good news:

- I have visited the posts around this part of Paris. Wherever I have been I have found true republicans ready to die for the Convention. [*We would die too!, cry citizens in the public galleries.*] I have arrested a Commune emissary who was trying to get the National Guard surrounding the Convention to withdraw.

Pleased with their evening's work, and the striking success of the use of adjuncts, Barras and Fréron have meanwhile entered the CPS committee room to find Billaud-Varenne stretched out on a mattress. His exhaustion is understandable, and he is snorting snuff to give himself a bit of pep. He is characteristically unimpressed with what has been achieved so far. There is a rumour that Robespierre has said he will march on the deputies within two hours. Billaud states sharply:

- You need to march on the Commune and surround it. You are leaving time for Hanriot and Robespierre to come here and slit our throats.

Fréron leaves Barras to discuss the issue with Billaud and returns to the Convention hall, and further shapes the debate by reeling off the government's achievements. The plot that traitor Hanriot and Catiline Robespierre had devised using the École de Mars has been thwarted. Five brave gunners have gone to the Place de la Maison Commune to try to win back their colleagues to the cause of the people. As soon as people realize the real state of affairs, they come over to the Convention's side. The Pont-Neuf is finally in Convention hands and the deputies have 1,500 troops guarding it.

Fréron looks to the people of Paris to rise to the occasion:

- Time is crucial, and with Barras now concerting action with the Committees of Government, the rest of us are ready to march against the rebels.

As for the rest:

- We will summon the misguided allies of Robespierre in the Commune to hand over the traitors. If they refuse, we will reduce the Maison Commune to dust! [Yes! Yes! and much applause]

Tallien has assumed the President's chair, seemingly by acclamation for his actions today, and contributes to the air of urgency:

- I invite my colleagues to leave immediately so that the sun will not rise before the conspirators are flushed out from their lair and punished.

The Convention is passing hectically from a posture of defence to one of active aggression. While there is a need to defend the Convention militarily, the best form of defence will be attack.

- We must beat Robespierre to it. And we'll only sleep when the traitors have been annihilated.

Cries of 'To arms! To arms!' spring up. In the public galleries, this has an immediate impact, as men stream out in droves, leaving only women behind. But Tallien urges the mass of deputies present to stay at their posts while those of their colleagues, assigned the task under Barras's command, move against the enemy.

The Convention's cause is going well. Besides the delegations from loyal sections who have been heard, there are deputations lining up out of the assembly hall wishing to be admitted to the bar. Legendre, another of Barras's troupe, reports that he has been in Hanriot's own Sans-Culottes section in the Faubourg Saint-Marcel. Even there everyone is rallying to the cause of the Convention.

11.00 p.m.

Lombards section and across the city

In the Lombards section, newspaper vendor Jeanne Jouannes, *femme Deschamps*, is still yelling the news of Hanriot's arrest when she is assaulted by an individual who tears up her stock of the *Messager du Soir*. The individual, who is arrested by bystanders, proves to be Charles Joly, a worker in a wall paper factory. He has been at the Commune, where he witnessed news vendors being brought in and excoriated for peddling propaganda. He thought he was performing a public service in preventing government 'false news' from getting out.

The Commune has certainly lost the battle of news reporting this evening. Payan has failed to develop a strategy to combat the Convention's flow of information, and neither its agents nor the Police Administration have shown much energy in checking the diffusion of the Convention's printed narrative across the city. The Police Administrators have a plan to swoop on presses, editors, and journalists at 5.00 a.m. tomorrow. At the present rate of progress, that will be far too late.

Print is playing a major role tonight, and helping to turn the move by Paris's sections to support the Convention into a Gadarene rush. The confusion of the evening has been consistently driven on by the role of rumour and the absence of hard information regarding not just the political stakes at issue but even very basic facts about what had happened and what was going on. But now harder information, or at least the Convention's version of hard information, is coming through. The evening newspapers bear the headlines plus a good measure of detail on the first Convention session. Newspaper accounts are read aloud in sectional committees and assemblies. They stimulate individuals to attend their section's assembly.

Revealingly, most sections whose assembly meets after 10.00 p.m. declare immediately for the Convention. The more hard information there is, the less convincing the Commune's cause.

The shift in the ground-level mood in favour of the Convention is accelerated by two crucial printed documents which are coming into the hands of sectional committees and assemblies, namely, Barère's proclamation and the Convention's decree outlawing those who resist the Convention and the rule of law. The hold-up in the diffusion of Barère's proclamation in mid-afternoon, whether caused by inadvertence or else by the studied negligence of Robespierre's allies, Herman and Lanne, is at an end. The proclamation is being distributed not only in letter form but also as full-blown posters stuck up around the city. Copies of the proclamation are read aloud within General Assemblies, invariably provoking loud and enthusiastic cheers, and decisions are then made to proclaim the document *vive voce* in the main thoroughfares and crossroads of the section. The Jacobin Club is a predictable place of repulsion: 'we don't care a fuck about your proclamation,' Jacobin women shout as the Tuileries sectional officials pass the Club. This is an exception.

It is the outlaw decree that has been the real game-changer. The way that Payan's reading of the decree in the Council chamber frightened many of the assembled out of their seats and back to their homes is a telling comment on its impact. It is not just that it is a deterrent aimed to frighten people into obedience. It is also recognized as a key legal statement that places the Convention's opponents on the same level as the enemies of the people against whom Revolutionary Government has devoted its policies of terror over the last year.

11.30 p.m.

Révolutionnaire section

The Convention's proclamation reached the Révolutionnaire section on western side of the Ile de la Cité at around 10.30. Sectional authorities recognized its importance and appointed commissaries (including two of the Bodson brothers) to be responsible for its diffusion. Over the last hour or so, their torch-lit band has been reading it out at more than a dozen locations within their section, which includes the strategically important Pont-Neuf.

The Ile de la Cité is still split over tonight's actions. While the Révolutionnaire section is clearly pro-Convention, the Police Administration in the Mairie is still among the most gung-ho supporters of the Commune. An early reading of Barère's proclamation took place within hearing distance of the Mairie, situated on the boundary with the Cité section. A large gang from the Mairie led by Police Administrator Bigaud descended on the group and made several arrests, claiming that the proclamation is inauthentic. The Révolutionnaire authorities sent news of this to the Committees of Government, and appointed substitutes for the arrested men to carry on with the proclamations away from the boundary with the Cité. Shortly afterwards, as they tried to gain access to the courtyard of the Sainte-Chapelle (again close to the Cité boundary) they found their way blocked by a large group of National Guardsmen whom ex-commander Giot had led out from the Mairie. When they started reading the proclamation aloud, Commune Council member Jacques-Claude Bernard, armed to the teeth and wearing his tricolour sash, stepped forward from the troops to proclaim solemnly:

- I arrest you, in the name of the people assembled at the Maison Commune and the Enforcement Committee. Behind me are two hundred men ready to execute my orders if you resist.

Thereupon, one of the Révolutionnaire officials, unphased by the threat, seized Bernard by the throat and countered:

– And I arrest you in the name of the National Convention.

Giot's NG delegation back off and allow Bernard to be led away to the sectional cells, where he is unceremoniously stripped of his sash, pistol, cartridges, and bayonet.

The Convention has still not, however, secured the whole of the Ile de la Cité for its cause. The Pont-Neuf bridge allowing access from the Left Bank for those seeking to advance on the Tuileries to the north is both a strategically crucial hub for a city in insurrection, and a major bottleneck. Fréron has claimed in the Convention that control of the bridge is now in government hands, but this is far from clear on the ground, with remnants of a variety of battalions milling around. Just after the Bernard incident, in fact, Third Legion Chief Mathis, who has had a very energetic day keeping his sectional battalions true to the Convention cause, crossed the bridge to visit battalions located on the Left Bank. On the Ile de la Cité, he stumbled across gangs of men from the Marat and Sans-Culotte sections professing loyalty to the Commune. When the men realized Mathis was not pro-Commune, they turned on him with sabres and pikes, wounding him and his horse. He tried to run away along the Quai des Orfèvres, but a dozen shots were fired and he collapsed wounded. The guardsmen took him off, covered in blood, to the Police Administration cells in the Mairie.

11.30 p.m.

Place Saint-Sulpice (Mutius-Scévole)
and across the city

The shutters must be opening a crack on the corner of the Rue des Canettes, where diarist Guittard de Floriban resides. Loud drum rolls have woken the neighbourhood to the fact that on the adjacent Place Saint-Sulpice two mounted deputies are presiding over the public reading of the Convention's proclamation, with sectional authorities and uniformed gendarmes looking solemnly on.

The presence of the deputies produces considerable éclat as torchlight picks up the bright tricolour hue of their sashes, plumes, and cockades. Being present also allows the deputies to update a document that Barère drafted last night in very particular circumstances. It had to be studiedly vague on detail. Now specificity is the order of the day. The deputies can add the outlaw decree to their presentation. They improvise a little speech: the Commune is in a state of rebellion and must not be obeyed. Hanriot has been declared an outlaw. A handsome reward awaits him who strikes the traitor dead.

These impromptu ceremonial readings taking place across the city are having the effect of getting the Convention's narrative about the day into wide circulation. Imposingly staged, they stake a claim for legitimacy that is altogether more convincing than anything the Commune is producing. The Police Administration decides to send out agents to combat the readings: but they lack the manpower to have any effect. Many more Commune declarations end up in waste paper bins or are forwarded to the Committees of Government than are read out in public.

Barras's dozen adjuncts are planning to work through the night, covering the length and breadth of the city. Their presence is noted out to the west, in

Champs-Elysées and in the area of Neuilly; but also in Arsenal and Popincourt to the east. They are in Marat as well as Mutius-Scévole on the Left
Bank, Gravilliers as well as Faubourg-Montmartre on the Right. By dint of
being mounted, the deputies cover more ground, including the outer
sections, in a shorter time than the pedestrian messengers sent out by the
Commune. Overall, they produce a reassuring effect, buttressing the efforts
of the sectional authorities to produce calm and resolution in the population.
The city has been swept with waves of anxiety and fears for the worst. The
Convention's firm line seems to be appreciated. It brings reassurance as well
as clarity, and inspires commitment. In the Unité section, when the reader of
the Barère's proclamation for the Convention came to the section in which
Barère asked rhetorically, 'Do you want to lose in an instant the fruit of six
years of labour?', the assembled crowd yelled back in unison, 'No! No!'

The mounted deputies are also ensuring that sectional authorities have
received and are implementing the mobilization of their NG forces. On
setting out on their expedition just after 9.00 p.m., Barras had ordered NG
battalion commanders to call up their men, and while keeping half of them
patrolling the streets and ensuring the defence of all prisons and public
buildings in their section, to send the other half to the Place du Carrousel
to defend the Convention. The Convention's recent decision to direct the
massed NG forces against the Maison-Commune has added a new urgency
to the message. Paris is on the march.

Between 11.00 and Midnight
Place de la Maison Commune
and Place du Carrousel

The story of the night is becoming a Tale of Two Places: the Place de la Maison Commune, which is becoming progressively deserted, and the Place du Carrousel, which is filling up. These changes will determine the outcome of the *journée*.

The Carrousel is an open space extensive enough to contain very large numbers of people, as it has indeed done on several moments of agitation this evening. But its considerable capacity is currently being severely tested by the huge numbers of National Guardsmen who are filing into the square, often accompanied by their cannon, while bystanders and onlookers do their best to get out of the way. New arrivals report to Second Legion Chief Julliot, who is still acting as duty commander following his earlier adventures. He is certainly working overtime tonight, for as well as marshalling new detachments, he is also receiving a constant stream of information from the sections, despatched every hour through the night as the CPS requires.

Julliot finds he is running out of niches on the Carrousel for the new arrivals. They are already filling the approach streets to the Place—Rue de l'Échelle, Rue Saint-Nicaise, stretches of the Rue Saint-Honoré, and so on. He has put some battalions on the other side of the palace in the Tuileries garden, and some out in reserve on the Place de la Révolution. They are on the quais too and so as to avoid too much flowback towards the Pont-Neuf crossing-point, battalions are also being stationed to the east up the Quai du Louvre towards the Quai de l'École.

While the Place du Carrousel is full to overflowing, the Place de la Maison Commune is being progressively drained of numbers and vitality. The forces there started to receive calls to return to their sections from around 10.00 p.m. The Bon-Conseil group, whose withdrawal Jacques-Louis Ménétra had called for earlier, heeded sectional demands around then to withdraw. By now, the list of those battalions that remain is shorter than the list of those who have left. Captain Voyenne, a company commander from the Muséum NG, who has 60 men guarding the main stairway within the Maison Commune, has so far resisted pressure from his section to return. Outside, substantial forces from Lombards, Finistère, Quinze-Vingts, and Popincourt remain on the Place as well as quite a few stragglers from other units. The force from Mutius-Scévole is just in the process of slipping its men out of the Place, including Lasnier who an hour or so before had led the delegation to bring Robespierre from the Mairie to the Maison Commune. The hardened attitudes of the Enforcement Committee may have made him turn coat.

The Commune can't even count on the sections that abut the Maison Commune and the Place. The artillery of the Droits-de-l'Homme section has been retained in barracks much of the evening by battalion commander Lasne. The section as a whole declared for the Convention after 10.00, but a huge Commune force eventually pushed aside pro-Convention guardsman to allow the gunners to exit their premises and march to the Place de la Maison Commune. Once there, in the speediest of reversals, their commander led them off to the Place du Carrousel to support the Convention.

The Arcis section, which has the Place de la Maison Commune within its perimeter, took a little more time to come round. It was on the brink of declaring for the Convention when shortly after 10.00 the section's JP, Jean-François Damour, who had been out all day checking worker demonstrations against the infamous Wage Maximum (and had been drinking heavily), entered announcing that he was back from the expedition that had rescued Hanriot. He held proudly aloft the ropes with which Hanriot had been bound. But this failed to impress the Assembly as a whole, and he was roundly criticized for his support of the Commune (and Robespierre in particular). One man stated:

- Marat went before the Revolutionary Tribunal and he emerged innocent and without inciting an insurrection. If Robespierre is innocent, the people will be with him in order to ensure justice triumphs . . .

Damour thereupon started a fight with his legalistic interlocutor, waving around his badge of office. But it was to no avail. He was arrested and stripped of his insignia and arms.

At some time after 11.00, councillors within the Maison Commune note that there were two individuals, both from the Arcis section, reading the Convention's proclamation aloud to bystanders and guardsmen. This has been facilitated by a prior decision to light torches on the façade of the Maison Commune. The men were arrested and found to be Cns. Tugot and Dehureau, who had actually been in the Council chamber early in the evening and even signed the attendance sheet. They are 'scoundrels, royalists, counter-revolutionaries and rascals', they are told, and consigned to the cells. Examining a copy of the proclamation, the Committee noticed that David's name is listed as a signatory: they triumphantly proclaim it counterfeit. The Committee instructed three of its appointed adjuncts, Jault, Dhazard, and Mercier, to go at once into the Arcis section 'so as to enlighten it on the true interests of the people and the dangers to the *patrie*'. On arrival, the three men are arrested: the section is not for budging.

The Homme-Armé section, also in the Marais, has resisted the efforts of General Council member Jean-Étienne Forestier to support the Commune, as, he claimed, all other sections were doing, and has stayed solidly pro-Convention. Shortly after 10.00 a.m., 'citizens with a tricolour flame and a respectable escort' read out the Convention's proclamation. At the same time, the section's assembly decided not only to send a delegation with a message of support to the Convention but also to send 24 delegations of two men from their ranks to every one of the 47 other sections to share their allegiance with them. In their message they declare

> – that they do not wish to recognize any authority except the National Convention, that they will never deviate from this principle and that the inhabitants that compose the section will make of their bodies a rampart against the blows that could be directed against the National Convention.

Before midnight, two new Parisian-wide movements are taking place. First, a stream of delegations, all expressing their undying loyalty to the assembly, is being received at the bar of the Convention. Second, this inter-sectional messaging devised by the Homme-Armé section catches on and with astonishing speed snowballs into a major phenomenon. Before midnight, it is becoming evident that the fraternization process is having a significant impact in swaying the city as a whole towards wholehearted support for the Convention. Early imitators of the Homme-Armé's gesture are Guillaume-Tell, Bonne-Nouvelle and Droits-de-l'Homme, but the practice soon spreads far and wide. There are some initial waverers. The Fraternité section discovered it was a bad idea to visit the Jacobins, for example. But with very few exceptions the reception of the fraternal delegations is warm and enthusiastic.

These fraternal messages come in thick and fast into the General Assemblies, where they are read to whoops of enthusiastic cheering and clapping. The preponderance of support has the effect of deciding waverers and encouraging political conversions. Over the night an average section will receive over 20 sectional delegations, a considerable number bearing in mind movements by NG forces on the streets restrict mobility, especially beyond the Maison Commune.

The delegations diffuse the Convention narrative, backing up the proclamation. The quirky expression of the Homme-Armé section, about 'men making of their bodies a rampart' finds its way into numerous sectional motions and messages to the Convention. The delegations also find themselves being pumped for hard information in sections where this has been sadly lacking. Fraternization is proving the best way to make the people 'well-instructed' about the night's events, to use deputy Legendre's term.

The fraternization practice initiated by the Homme-Armé section is not new. It was used very powerfully in the late spring and summer of 1793 as a means of crushing pro-Girondin majorities in some sections. Nor, it is worth noting, is it legal. In fact, the Revolutionary Government has clamped down hard on this kind of inter-sectional political sociability, which is expressly forbidden by the Law of 14 Frimaire, which many sections are tonight using as their bible. It also seems to link up with the more ecumenical spirit shown by many sections in the 'fraternal banquets' movement in Messidor. Then Robespierre and Payan attacked it furiously. But no one is attacking the spirit of fraternization tonight. The Convention is certainly not complaining. For it is winning for the assembly the night's battle for public opinion.

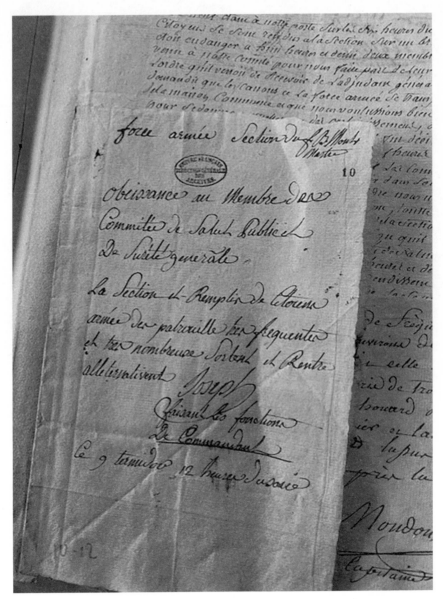

Figure 9. Joseph, Acting Commander, Faubourg-Montmartre National Guard battalion, to Acting Commanding Officer, Place du Carrousel, 12 midnight (AFII 47 pl. 364, pi. 10)

11.30 p.m.

Maison Commune

Nicolas-Paul Hugot and a fellow citizen from the village of Bercy, situated on the Seine just outside the south-east corner of Paris, have come to the Commune with a letter from their commune enquiring when the city gates on that side of the city will reopen. Villagers need to enter the city with their fruit and vegetable carts or just to get to their workplace early tomorrow morning.

Admission to the Maison Commune is less restricted than earlier in the evening and the men got easily into the Council Chamber where they were surprised to hear a decree of the Commune's Enforcement Committee ordering that Legion Chief Jean Hémart, who has been languishing in the cells since the late afternoon, should be publicly executed by firing squad at dawn. They show their papers to Fleuriot, who is presiding and he permits them access to the Enforcement Committee, meeting in the Salle de l'Égalité. There, Committee member Arthur comes out to greet them warmly:

- Ah here we are! The fatherland is saved yet again!

Arthur then takes hold of the letter and writes:

Bercy patriots! Come at once and in arms into the bosom of the Paris Commune so as to support the rights of freedom and the cause of the patriots oppressed by the conspirators! Vive the Republic!

Hugot is mystified, so Arthur continues:

- Don't you realize that Robespierre, Saint-Just, and the other patriot deputies have been arrested by a conspiratorial faction? Well, the people has released them and here they are in this committee.

Arthur opened the door more widely so that the men could look in at the committee at work, before urging the men to go off quickly.

The men are obliged to take the oath downstairs and when they seek clarification over whom they should obey, Councillor Lubin, Payan's deputy, is at hand to tell them categorically:

- The Commune. The Convention only exists in the form of a factious few. The people has taken the reins of government. The Convention issues its proclamations and we issue ours.

The men are then led into the adjacent NGHQ, where Hanriot greets them warmly and instructs his staff to give them unlimited powers. As they examine their new papers, Hanriot continues:

- If you get something from the Convention, take hold of it and show it to no one. And if you see deputies leading patrols making proclamations, seize them and their proclamations. Firmness, energy—and the cause of the people will triumph!

Before they have time to leave, a young man enters whom they are surprised to discover is Saint-Just. He has been released from the Écossais prison by the Commune forces, and now states with an ironic smile:

- It is I who am the supposed dominator of all France, the new Cromwell.

He is repeating Tallien's charge against him from first thing this morning. Then, less sardonically, he comments:

- All this is the last blow of the Foreign Plot. But the veil will soon be torn asunder—in fact it already has been!

One wonders whether he is also reflecting on his own role in the outlaw legislation, of which he is a current target. The Law of 23 Ventôse, which he drove through, states unequivocally that those resisting judicial process should be viewed as enemies of the people and outlawed. The day of 9 Thermidor Year II has sufficed to turn Saint-Just, Robespierre, Couthon, and their allies into enemies of the people.

The men from Bercy leave Saint-Just in a world of his own as they return home. The Place de la Maison Commune is semi-deserted, but as they move away from it they find the dark streets of the city surprisingly crowded and animated for this time of night. There are citizens on their way to General Assemblies; deputies and their gendarme escorts on their city-wide itineraries; numerous delegations of NG companies performing their intra-sectional patrols; others on their way back from the Place de la Maison Commune, or else marching towards the Place du Carrousel. There are still some protesters against the Wage Maximum about, exacerbating confusion. And then there are the many teams of fraternizing delegations buzzing around the sections. The city is mobilized for action—action for the Convention and the rule of law and against the Commune and other outlaws.

PART
V

Midnight, Around Midnight, After Midnight

Midnight

Salle de l'Égalité, Maison Commune

The Day of the Mulberry, 9 Thermidor, has given way to the 10th, the Day of the Watering Can. Robespierre is sitting in on the Commune's Enforcement Committee. He has only been at the Maison Commune for a little over an hour, having finally agreed to throw in his lot with the insurrection that Hanriot, Fleuriot, and Payan launched in mid-afternoon. In order to inveigle him out of the Police Administration offices, Hanriot will have fed Robespierre the story that the Commune's emissaries are trying to spread through the city: the Commune is being supported by dozens of sections; the Place de la Maison Commune is full of troops; and enthusiasm levels are high. The more time goes on in the Maison Commune, however, the more these seem exaggerated. The Commune's Enforcement Committee also seems wavering as regards its strategy.

What is Robespierre contributing to the discussions? The kind of strategizing and logistical work of hows and whens and whats taking place around him are certainly not his forte. Deputies know—and members of the Commune are learning—that he is no man of action or street-fighter. Marat's view that he shrank at the first sign of turbulence and went pale at the sight of an unsheathed sabre may well be close to the mark. A man who has never been called on to manage is unlikely to be able to manage an insurrection. In the past, he has been more remarked by his absence than his visibility on the great days of action like 10 August 1792, 31 May and 2 June 1793, as his enemies have always reminded him. He is certainly courageous, but in a negative way, characterized by moral strength and obdurate resistance rather than energetic action or physical exertion.

It is difficult not to imagine Robespierre's mind straying, as the Enforcement Committee endeavours to come to terms with the nitty-gritty of insurrectionary organization. Today has certainly been a learning experience for him, and one from which he can take comfort, albeit cold comfort. For it has indubitably proved to him that he has been right all along. There is a massive counter-revolutionary conspiracy to get rid of him and to lead the Republic onto uncharted counter-revolutionary terrain. All the proofs are not there yet, but it must link to the Foreign Plot being run from London and Westminster. And it clearly extends right to the heart of the Revolutionary Government of which he has formed part. The involvement of the maverick Tallien today was far less revealing than the fact that it was Robespierre's closest colleagues in government who joined the traitors in the hall in taking up cudgels against him. Ultimately, to Robespierre, his humiliation today has been his utter vindication and it confirms him in the correctness of his views on everything.

Robespierre must also surely reflect on how far he has come since last night. A good night's sleep was followed by busy morning preparations for a hard day in the Convention. He had realized the difficulties that would be involved in switching his allies from the Montagnards to the deputies of the Plain. It was a manoeuvre he was confident that he could negotiate as a means of surviving the Montagnard onslaught he anticipated. But then a bolt from the blue in the Convention occurred, to thwart his plans completely. Were he a military strategist, he might have borne in mind the adage that no plan survives contact with the enemy. But no one could have predicted that Tallien would have condensed his enmity towards Robespierre into a missile of such deadly force. What has utterly confounded him, moreover, even more than Tallien's *coup de théâtre*, is the hugely enthusiastic support that it instantly gained from the Convention, encouraged by the Committees of Government. Robespierre had not counted on that at all. He has long been concerned with the conspiracies he believes are being hatched throughout the political class. Conspiracies, arrests, perfidious journalists, and the Revolutionary Tribunal have been his *idée fixe* for months, as his CPS colleagues know all too well, to the detriment of his contribution to running the country. But he remained confident he could sail above it all, and manipulate factions in the assembly in ways that ensured his survival. What has stunned him is the Convention's newfound audacity, its intractable unanimity and its seemingly bottomless antipathy to his own person and thereby to the cause of the people which he incarnates.

Robespierre realizes that the Convention session on 8 Thermidor went badly wrong and that it represented a setback as well as something of a personal mortification. Even so, the unanimity and the sheer intensity of his fellow deputies' reaction to his presence today has been utterly crushing, especially for someone with such egg-shell *amour-propre*. His silencing was brutal. It was also, he is well aware, illegal, unparliamentary, and in contravention of his natural rights. The Convention used procedural irregularity so as to deny the people the benefits of the 'useful truths' that Robespierre's 8 Thermidor speech had offered.

This torturous session turned out to be only the beginning of Robespierre's trials and tribulations. First, there was his having to suffer the marked lack of enthusiasm for his cause from the public galleries in the Convention hall. Then being held under arrest as a common prisoner, before having his carriage followed through the streets by coarse crowds yelling his name. All that was bad enough. It was followed by worse: the wretched experience at the sinister Luxembourg prison; the transfer to the Mairie, with police administrators he had never met treating him like a long-lost brother; and then his being whisked away to the Maison Commune, and thereby not only entering the terrain of formal illegality but also becoming an insurrectionary leader, a prospect he does not cherish. All the more, in that the fine words about the buoyancy of the insurrection that Hanriot and others fed him have proved to be hollow: the Commune is not at all the shining popular beacon he was led to expect.

Robespierre's predicament was highlighted soon after his arrival at the Maison Commune when he was led into the Enforcement Committee. It was suggested that they might make a dedicated call to the Piques section. After all, this is where Robespierre lives, as do three of the Committee, painter Châtelet, and wallpaper magnates Arthur and Grenard. All are well-known in sectional circles there. A letter is drafted:

> Courage, patriots of the Piques section! Liberty triumphs. Already those whose firmness has rendered them formidable towards traitors are free. Everywhere the people shows its true character. The rendezvous is at the Commune. The brave Hanriot will execute the orders of its Enforcement Committee, that has been created to carry out the Commune's orders.

The letter is passed around the table for signatures. It comes to Robespierre. He picks up the pen. 'Ro . . . ' No: he does not sign. He cannot sign. To sign would mean that he was a full member of the Insurrectionary Commune. It would mean he had given up the formal status of a representative of the people, elected to the national assembly. It would make him an agent of insurrection rather than a wronged victim of counter-revolutionary mendacity. The letter goes out anyway, with his half-finished signature at the bottom. Will it have any impact?

The scale of his defeat in the Convention today has alienated him even more profoundly against the whole of the Convention. In his 8 Thermidor speech, he envisaged a purge of his (and the people's) enemies among the deputies. But the unanimity of the assembly in forcing his exclusion must be making him ponder whether it is not the legislature as a whole rather than a circumscribed set of deputies which is the problem. These musings are in line with similar ideas mooted within the Commune. Rather than follow the model of a purge on the lines of the 31 May/2 June *journées*, the approach adopted on the 10 August 1792 *journée* might be more appropriate. On that day the overthrow of Louis XVI was accompanied by the thorough discrediting of the Legislative Assembly, requiring a new legislature (the Convention) to be elected. The rhetoric of the Commune leaders, amplified within the Enforcement Committee, has become violent enough to suggest that they have begun thinking of themselves as a contra-Convention, whose legitimacy derives from incarnating popular sovereignty. They have even given themselves the title of 'Commune of 10 August' (though no one seems to be using it).

If Robespierre's views may be converging with the Commune's in regard to the night's objectives, he must have reservations about the timing of the action involved. Can the Enforcement Committee really be serious about initiating action when it is still the middle of the night? Around the table, adrenaline is pumping, but people are looking tired and in need of rest. Given the lateness of the hour, deferring full mobilization for tomorrow when minds and bodies will be fresher seems the sensible way forward. The Commune will have more time then to get its narrative across to the people of Paris.

By simply looking out of the window, moreover, Robespierre must be getting the impression that the people of Paris are currently a lot less committed to the Commune cause than the Enforcement Committee has been claiming. The Place de la Maison Commune has visibly leaked National Guardsmen, even in the short time since his arrival. The Commune is increasingly giving the impression of generals who are fast losing their foot-soldiers. Fewer sections across Paris are remaining in contact with the Enforcement Committee than seems healthy. The fact that the Enforcement Committee has instructed Hanriot to supply them with rifles, pistols, and ammunition does not seem a sign of self-confidence.

In addition, the more Robespierre hears about the Convention's new-found courage and resolution, the less he likes it. Indeed, rather than temporize now, there is a powerful counter-argument being mooted that if the Commune forces don't strike first, the Convention might do so, with deadly effect. Reports may be coming in by now that the Convention's NG forces have started to advance on the Maison Commune. The deputies are showing themselves in a new light, as a fighting force.

Looking around the Salle de l'Égalité, Robespierre must wonder if this handful of assorted individuals is really of the calibre required to win the day—let alone to imagine a new kind of future for the Republic. He is well aware that he is the most significant figure in the room, but though his iconic value is good for morale among the Commune's forces, he knows his own nullity in popular mobilization. His brother Augustin, Le Bas, and Saint-Just have commendable records as deputies on mission; but are any of them either really cut out for street-fighting? Saint-Just, moreover, has looked in a dazed state of shock from the moment Tallien challenged him at noon. Payan and Fleuriot seem competent enough, but have little spark or vision and their lack of clarity over strategy does not inspire confidence. The colleagues from the Piques section are solid in their way, but they are unusual sans-culottes, who would be happier running a wallpaper factory than organizing an insurrection. Newcomer Revolutionary Tribunal President Dumas, sprung from his prison some time after 11.00 is not a man of the streets either (indeed, he is much hated on the streets). Coffinhal and Hanriot are the most energetic members of the committee, but the two of them seem at odds: Coffinhal thinks Hanriot is drunk and incompetent. It may just be that the Commander is intoxicated with excitement, but his behaviour is certainly becoming more and more erratic. Earlier there was talk of no blood being spilled. Now, as well as threats of shooting at dawn, and an ever-accumulating mountain of swearing, Hanriot has added the prospect of hanging someone with the ropes with which Robespierre was earlier tied up.

Robespierre has to contemplate the real possibility of the victory of his enemies—and his enemies of course are the enemies of the people. The day's sombre experience has, moreover, confirmed his idea, which has been growing in his mind over the last several months, that sometimes the worst enemies of the people can be the people themselves. Generally, Robespierre prefers the people as a rhetorical abstraction rather than as concrete reality, let alone as a collection of individuals to whom he needs to appeal if he is to survive the day. He has not enjoyed his enforced immersion into the general population, so very different from the ring-fenced life he has recently enjoyed, shuttling between the Tuileries, the Jacobin Club, and his Duplay lodgings. The word *peuple* is forever in his mouth, but close physical encounters like today tarnish his cherished image of the people that has been nurtured by distance rather than propinquity. The popular classes rallying to the Convention are not his 'virtuous people' but more like the 'impure breed', to whose existence he has become increasingly attuned. And now he faces the real prospect of coming oblit-eration at their hands.

One wonders if, as he gazes around the decorations of this former 'Zodiac Room', his eye alights on Taurus, his own, cold and dry birth sign. But no, Robespierre finds such superstitious determinisms ridiculous. Much more in mind will be the thought that one way forward for him at this fateful moment is to enact the scenario that he has evoked so many times in his speeches in the last few years, and that has in fact already been in the minds of his brother and Philippe Le Bas this evening. That is, death by his own hand. Robespierre's evocation of his own death in recent years has not been just a rhetorical trope, a badge of insincerity, as his more virulent enemies claim. It is a thought that endlessly plays in his mind.

If Robespierre has to lose everything, taking his own life would surely be preferable to a guillotining in which he would be humiliatingly subjected to the vengeance (and worse, the mocking laughter) of his enemies. His suicide would not mean that all he had striven for was in vain: rather, it would open it up to posterity. Robespierre has less respect for the so-called lessons of ancient history than most of his fellow deputies. His vision is more firmly positioned towards the future. The Revolution and the advent of the Republic marked a genuine epochal change in the history of humanity. He still believes absolutely in the ideas he championed in the early days of the Revolution: social justice, democratic values, individual freedom, reli-gious toleration, humane institutions, the end of slavery, rights for women. Many of these have had to be shelved temporarily in time of civil and foreign war, but the fight in which the Republic is engaged is precisely about preserving the possibility of those gains for future generations. And if this battle in the larger campaign for justice were to fail, there would indeed be, after all, a case for dying a martyr's death. He would die, as he put it in the Convention two days ago as 'freedom's slave, the living martyr of the Republic, the victim even more than the enemy of crime'. The fame he would accrue would be so much more substantial than the fleeting and meretricious celebrity he has enjoyed in his life. His death would mean that Robespierre would live on as a name and an inspiration in the golden annals of posterity.

Around Midnight

Private lodgings, Quai de l'École (Muséum)

Marguerite Barrois was expecting 9 Thermidor to be a normal day. She arrived from her village in eastern France by coach a couple of days ago, looking for work, probably in domestic service. She hoped to draw on a network of emigrants from her village. A cousin who is a second-hand clothes dealer on the Quai de l'École on the riverbank close to the Louvre agreed to put her up. But new to the city, she lost her way today. Unable to find her cousin's residence, she accepted an offer of a bed from a shopkeeper in that vicinity. But in the course of the night she received a visit from her host's shop-boy, Charles Miquet, a lad from her region, who slept along the corridor. Perhaps it was to comfort her, as the National Guardsmen lining the quais in the early hours must have been kicking up a racket. There was nothing to fear, the boy whispered, there was no danger, and anyway the two of them could always return to their home and get married. He came twice that night into her bed and she really could not hold him back. By the end of the night she will be pregnant. Life will go on. And in nine months' time, Marguerite Barrois will have something by which to remember 9 Thermidor.

Convention hall, Tuileries palace

While leaving the environs of the Tuileries mightily defended, Barras has led a large column of National Guardsmen off towards the Maison Commune. He has Bourdon de l'Oise and two other adjuncts marching with him. They will follow the course of the river: Quai du Louvre, Quai de l'École, then the Quai de la Mégisserie and the Quai de Gesvres, leading into the Place de la Maison Commune from the south. They are well-equipped with cannon, including pieces from the artillery of the Droits-de-l'Homme section which caused so much trouble earlier in the evening protesting in favour of the Commune.

Barras has also decided to form a second column which will take a more northerly route to the Place. He has had the good sense to appoint to its command his adjunct Léonard Bourdon. Bourdon is an interesting and complex character, with a passion for pedagogy that has led him to open a patriotic school, the Jeunes Français, based in the Gravilliers section. But he also has a reputation for being a tough operator, and has already achieved a great deal this evening visiting sections to the east of the Tuileries to alert them to the crisis. In Réunion he galvanized the NG battalion commander Jean Richard to send 2,500 men and two cannon to bolster the Convention, and he did much the same in nearby Bon-Conseil and Halle-au-Blé. Bourdon also has the signal advantage, from Barras's point of view, of having invaluable hands-on knowledge of the terrain, as he lives in this part of north-eastern Paris, well away from the political bubble around the Rue Saint-Honoré that most deputies inhabit. For a number of years in fact he has lodged within the former priory of Saint-Martin-des-Champs, and has a strong popular following in the Gravilliers section within which the building is located.

Imposingly, even nattily dressed in David's prototype costume for legislators, Bourdon leads out from the Place du Carrousel what must be at first quite a small force. His intention is to take them eastwards along the Rue Saint-Honoré, and to pick up the Rue de la Verrerie, drawing additional recruits from sections along his path. He will then call a temporary halt at the junction between the Rue de la Verrerie and the Rue Saint-Martin, and branch northwards to visit the assembly of the Gravilliers section which meets in the ex-priory where he lives.

The two columns prepare to set out from the environs of the Tuileries around midnight. Within the Convention hall itself at this time, the session is becoming a victory parade before victory has been pronounced, indeed before the combatting forces have even been fully formed and battle joined. Little is being done but much is being said, to many cheers. Deputy after deputy keeps up a triumphalist rhetoric which is taking as read a good result emerging from the night.

The high morale of the deputies is boosted by the copious throng of citizens who are lining up at the bar of the house in order to declare their imperishable love for the Convention and their wish to consign to damnation the Commune and all its works. Sometimes it is a case of just two or three individuals, but there are often between eight and twelve delegates, while some sections bring over 20. They come from far and wide: the west (Champs-Elysées, République), the central sections through which Bourdon is going to be marching (Halle-au-Blé, Gardes-Françaises, Contrat-Social, Lombards, Réunion), the islands (Cité, Fraternité, etc), and the Left Bank (Unité, Marat, Fontaine-de-Grenelle). There are sections to the north and east of the Maison Commune too (Arsenal, Homme-Armé, Indivisibilité, Faubourg-du-Nord, etc). Only the far south-eastern and eastern sections of the Faubourgs Saint-Antoine and Saint-Marcel are not represented—yet.

The sectional delegations report invaluable intelligence about the state of the city to the deputies: demands they have received from the Commune, arrests, local reactions, patrols, signal actions of individuals, and so on. But they have also come to express their attachment to the Convention, the sole rallying-point of the Republic, for which they are willing to shed blood and 'make a rampart of their bodies' (one of the expressions of the night, copied endlessly from the Homme-Armé section's petition) so as to repel the plots hatched by the enemies of liberty. Such phrases are used repeatedly. Sectional delegate statements also chime with the sentiments expressed in Barère's proclamation. Why indeed should they wish to put at risk the gains the people have had from six years of Revolution? The echo effect produced in the language of the delegations makes them seem hackneyed, stereotyped, and often highly bombastic. But the strength of the feeling that they express seems more than sincere.

Place de la Maison Commune

The National Guardsmen defending the Maison Commune are becoming sullen and resentful. Many of them have been here for hours now, without provisions and, even more galling, without any real sense of what is going on. Many arrived here without taking on board that their presence at the Maison Commune was an anti-Convention act. Had not the mayor been charged with the maintenance of law and order in the city? Was there not a problem with protesters against the Wage Maximum? Guardsmen have been left to their own devices while their senior officers have been up in the Maison Commune Council chamber deliberating, but not being allowed out. The *consigne* has now ended, but such has been the riotous disorderliness of the Commune meeting that not all those leaving the meeting profess any certainty about what was decided. Or at least if they do know, they are not saying. Hanriot's release causes further confusion since it is widely thought that this has been on government instruction, a view which he encourages. What then to make of the Convention's outlaw decree aimed at Hanriot and then the Commune generally? The outlaw decree and the Convention's proclamation, which many on the Place will have heard being read aloud, provides more clarity. But it is a clarity that triggers anxiety and fear. Realization has grown that there really do seem to be two sides now. And that the price for choosing the wrong side will be very high.

Company commander Voyenne and his force from the Muséum section, stationed on the staircase of the Maison Commune, resisted efforts earlier on in the evening to make them return to the section. But when Voyenne hears the outlaw decree he realizes that its is only a matter of time before he leaves. After further contacts with his section, he will start to evacuate his men from around 1.30 a.m.

The National Guard is not an army: it is a citizen's militia. Although guardsmen respect discipline, they are not the chess-piece automata of Ancien Régime warfare. They take their role to defend the Republic and protect the public with great dedication. Their officers are keen to follow orders from on high, but the men know that they have elected the officers in the first place and that they are fellow citizens. They talk, they discuss, they argue.

Guardsmen from the Finistère battalion on the Place have been very active tonight. A group of them contributed to the release of Augustin Robespierre and then Le Bas from the La Force prison. But for hours now they have been talking eagerly among themselves and passing on their complaints to their senior officers. 'What are we doing here?' asks Cn. Ouy, a printer. The question is not rhetorical. A group of the force have in fact left their post earlier in disgust after one of their officers reported hearing the General Council applaud the idea of shooting a man arrested as a Convention spy, as well as a proposal to start massacring prisoners. But most remain, in a subdued and resentful mood. Some time after 1.00 a.m., they manage to persuade their commanding officer, captain Vian, to agree to take them home. But he feels he must inform the mayor first. In the Council chamber, he explains that the Lombard men and then also most of the gendarmes have been leaving. Fleuriot tries only weakly to prevail on him to stay: 'if the Finistère men do not wish to swear the oath to save the *patrie*, then the detachment may retire.'

The Lombards artillery company are similarly disenchanted with what is happening. They have been here on the Place since around 4.00 p.m. Two of the men shook hands and embraced Hanriot when he reappeared after his captivity, but their and their colleagues' mood changed once Hanriot's outlaw status became clear. A strong consensus has emerged that they should all leave and return to the section. They have seen streams of other detachments doing this. They have even put their cannon back on its train for withdrawal. Company captain Gigue, however, is hesitant about leaving: he wants to discover what is happening back in the section. He has been squabbling about this with Cosme Pionnier, who, as Instructor for the city's artillery force, outranks him. Pionnier is urging him to remain. But after havering for some time, Gigue bows to the majority feeling and orders the move. Pionnier is still unhappy and declares that the mayor should be informed. 'All right, do it yourself!' says Gigue as he marches off. Pionnier finally accepts the democratic decision and reluctantly joins the retiring troupe.

After the Finistère men left, a staff officer ran after them, catching up with them at the Port au Blé to the east of the Place de la Maison Commune. The men noted that he was trembling. No wonder: no regular NG detachments remain on the Place, just scattered groupings of Commune enthusiasts and sundry stragglers and bystanders. Company captain Le Grand explains to the officer, 'this detachment is made up wholly of working men; they need to eat'. They are going home. Another emissary from the Enforcement Committee tries to halt their progress, telling them that General Hanriot is offering them money for food and drink. But these working men are above such mercenary considerations, Le Grand retorts:

– The men recognize neither the Commune nor the general who is an outlaw. And they are not soldiers for hire.

Mairie, Ile de la Cité

Since walking out of his front door this morning at 8.00 a.m., Giot's whole day has been a story of being the wrong man in the wrong place. Selected on National Agent Payan's whim, following Hanriot's arrest, to command the Commune's armed forces he has shown an embarrassingly high level of incompetence throughout.

From some time after 9.00 p.m., Giot was nominal leader of the forces at the Police Administration within the Mairie protecting Robespierre. He is becoming increasingly depressed. He witnessed the stand-off incident between guardsmen around the Mairie involving municipal councillor Bernard. Later he saw Fourth Legion Chief Mathis, brought in dripping with blood to be put in the cells. He has endured Hanriot gratuitously tearing him off a strip. He now has to deal with a growing ground-swell of discontent from the men under his command, notably those from his own section, Marat, under the battalion's second-in-command Vincent Typhaine. They, like their colleagues on the Place de la Maison Commune, are becoming discontented with their position. Faced with commanders who are either absent, in prison, incompetent or else traitors, they have been thinking through their situation for themselves as a group. When after midnight Typhaine came to tell Giot that he was acceding to his men's wishes and withdrawing, Giot could only gloomily reply:

– You can do what you want. I haven't got a head for any of this. I don't know what it all means.

The Commander who doesn't understand what it all means stays in post, while the Marat men go back to their section to join anti-Commune forces under their commander Typhaine, who is already planning the denunciation he will make to the CGS of his brother-officer.

Temple prison

In the city's prisons, inmates are having the distinct feeling that they are ageing by 80 years in a single day. At the changing of the duty guard of Police Administrators at 9.30 p.m. at the Temple prison, they could already hear in the distance the ceaseless ringing of the Maison Commune tocsin. One of the three-man Police Administrator relief group failed to turn up: it is Ponce Tanchon in fact, who has been busy at the Mairie offering Robespierre support. Tessier from the Invalides section drew the short straw, and was obliged to sleep over another night. He was not at all sure what was taking place in the city, and a request to the mayor for information failed to elicit a response. With a force of over 200 guardsmen established in the prison, the Temple is unlikely to be targeted for a prison massacre. Their charges, the last two survivors of the royal family in Paris, are particularly valuable. They are blissfully unaware that both the Commune and the

Convention would be circulating stories that the other side was planning to seize the young 'Capet' ('Louis XVII').

The prison staff turned in at midnight but they were awoken around 3.00 a.m., by loud knocking at the outer gate. It was a force of around 300 men from the Temple NG battalion demanding to come in so as to offer reinforcement. They showed an order from Barras empowering them to do this. But the police administrators were loath to accept this: they only took orders direct from the Convention. It would not be till 6.00 a.m. when a fuming Barras arrived on the scene that they would open their gates to their defenders. By then any danger had long passed, and here and across the city prisoners will be able to breath a sigh of relief.

Maison Commune

In a lull in proceedings in the Council chamber, councillor Pierre-Louis Paris, who spent this morning performing marriage ceremonies in the building, and the early part of the afternoon drafting the Commune's first proclamation, is writing to the Revolutionary Committee in the Panthéon section, where he lives:

> – My brothers, I was pleased to see a delegation from the Panthéon section. I would have liked to say to it that there should always be someone here to keep the section *au courant*. The majority of the sections has come to support the measures we have taken today. Robespierre *jeune* and Le Bas are here and Couthon is free, as are the elder Robespierre and Hanriot. The different tasks I have had and the distance of the section from the Maison Commune have prevented me from coming to see you.
>
> Good day and good night
>
> 10 Thermidor, midnight and half an hour.

It must be shortly after this that Cn. Paris perks up, to witness and join the applause for Couthon who is being carried into the Council chamber by one of his duty gendarmes. Like the other arrested deputies, Couthon has shown reluctance to leave his prison: all those arrested today realize that resisting or circumventing lawful imprisonment identifies them as enemies of the people, under the provisions of the Law of 23 Ventôse. Couthon had been saying he entered the prison by Convention decree and needs another to get out. But eventually, he has ceded to the entreaties of his friends:

– Couthon, all patriots are proscribed, the whole people have risen. It would
be a betrayal of them not to come to the Maison Commune where we are.

In making this plea to their colleague, Robespierre and Saint-Just have
played the people card, and won. But it is to Couthon's loss, and indeed
their own. For despite the energy which Hanriot has been expending, the
message now coming through to the Enforcement Committee from the city
is that they are failing on all fronts. The people are rising all right: but not for
the Commune, and not for Robespierre. Hanriot's call for the tocsin to
sound across the sections has been almost totally ignored; bells have stayed
silent. The appeal to the forces around the Convention to come to the
Commune was intercepted before it arrived; the orders sent to Legion
adjutants have been ignored; their serial proclamations all seem to have
sunk without trace; their own Council chamber is emptying and the
mood in the room is getting flatter and flatter. Hanriot has been down on
the Place, talking to the fast-dwindling numbers of gunners and guardsmen,
trying to boost morale. This did not stop the troops haemorrhaging away
back to their sections.

Perhaps the Enforcement Committee is in denial, but it is clear enough
that the Convention has the upper hand. It is Barère's proclamation, not the
Commune's, which is being read throughout the city, even by the Arcis
militants, on the Maison Commune doorstep. The Convention is attracting
the allegiance of the Parisians, and the Committee has recently learnt that
the Convention is marching against them. Everything that the Commune is
hearing produces dismay and a sense of hopelessness. No wonder Arthur was
so pleased to see supporters from Bercy this evening. With Parisians so
resistant to the Commune's messages, perhaps the outlying villages can
bring additional resource. However, frankly, today is about Paris and all
will be settled within Paris, by Parisians.

Couthon's arrival at the Commune at this moment of the turning of the
tide is being observed by CPS spy Pierre-Honoré-Gabriel Dulac. Dulac has
had a busy day. His main preoccupation in recent weeks has been generating
prison plot lists to get the inmates of Parisian gaols to the guillotine in ever
larger numbers. Today, he has been following the action around the city and
reporting it back to his masters. At around midnight, he and fellow spy
Dossonville attempted to repeat the performance of the brave Arcis militants
by staging a public reading of the Convention's proclamation in the Place de
la Maison Commune, on the Commune's very doorstep. They were under

pressure, for Hanriot was lurking, so in order to save time Dossonville cut to the chase, shouting at the top of his voice:

> You are Frenchmen. The National Assembly calls you to come and defend it. The Convention has decreed that the man you are obeying is an outlaw. Those of you who defend the assembly will be rewarded; death awaits the conspirators and their accomplices. I order you in the name of the deputies to march to the Convention.

The two men then made themselves scarce so as to avoid arrest.

After being policed so strictly earlier in the evening, access to and from the building is altogether freer now the *consigne* has been lifted. Dulac was able to inveigle himself into the Maison Commune and then follow Couthon and his gendarme escort into the Council chamber where he found the two Robespierres and Le Bas present. With Couthon in tow, they proceeded back into the Salle de l'Égalité and Dulac followed, accompanying a group of gawpers who seemed able to enter without check.

Couthon embraced his comrades. One of the men in Couthon's entourage addresses Robespierre:

> – It is good to see you. You are not as rattled as you were when you stepped out of your carriage in the Mairie courtyard.

(Robespierre seems to have got some of his equanimity back here where there are people he knows and esteems.)

There is no time to lose, and Couthon at once addresses the Committee:

> – We must write straight away to the armies.

Robespierre does not slap the suggestion down, but enquires:

> – In whose name?

> Couthon: In the name of the Convention. Is that not where we are still? The rump are just a handful of plotters that our armed forces will scatter and give their just deserts.

Couthon is thus accepting that the Convention has no right to continued existence, and will have to be replaced (rather than merely purged). The proposal gives Robespierre pause. To call in the army is the exact opposite of what he has advocated in any political crisis, right back to 1789. He has always looked to the people of Paris as the main protagonist in defence of the Republic. Now, seemingly, the people of Paris cannot be counted on and armed support is needed. Robespierre goes over to his brother and whispers in his ear, then remarks:

– My view is that we should write in the name of the people.

Even as the people—or at any rate the people of Paris—are manifestly turning against him, for Robespierre everything is still about the people. It is a figleaf that he hopes will confer respectability on a summons for military aid.

Robespierre has not completely given up on the people in action, however, and he turns to Couthon's trusty gendarme:

– Brave gendarme, I have always valued and esteemed your bodily support. Do continue to be loyal to us. Go outside and do what you can to embitter the people against the plotters.

The gendarme and his companions state that they are under orders to remain, but they reassure him that the Police Administrators are well on top of things and there should be nothing to fear as regards security.

Couthon meanwhile has a pen in hand and has been writing:

– The traitors will perish! There are still humans in France and virtue will triumph!

Further conversation is halted, however, by noise of a scuffle coming from the Council chamber. On investigating, it proves to be the interception of two government spies, Longueville-Clémentières and Morel. An hour or so ago, the two men had audaciously wagered that they would go to the Commune, find Hanriot and shoot him. There is after all a price on his head. They got into the Council Chamber (again highlighting the abysmal security) but they are soon discovered. They are restrained and led into the meeting of the Enforcement Committee. Besides the nine members of the Committee there is maybe a score of other individuals present, including Robespierre and Le Bas. Sensing an opportunity. Morel reaches for his gun, but he is immediately seized and disarmed. Coffinhal takes over:

Why did you do that?
Morel: To use against enemies of the people.
Coffinhal: Here is another CGS agent come no doubt to spy on us. Get a firm hold on the bugger. We are going to have him shot. But let's search him first and get his papers.

The two men's pockets contain their identity papers, house-keys plus a couple of copies of the *Journal du Soir* announcing Robespierre's arrest, but not much else. Coffinhal sneers at their efforts at resistance:

– Come on, you won't need your papers. In two hours you'll be shot.

The two men had obviously been sent by the CGS with assassination in mind, Coffinhal concludes. Robespierre comments disdainfully:

– That doesn't surprise me: I would not have expected less from them.

It all conforms to Robespierre's analysis. The conspirators' use of assassination as a political weapon is fully in line with his ideas of the Foreign Plot. Le Bas angrily agrees that the men should be shot. But that can wait, for they must first be pumped for information. So they are sent down to the Maison Commune's cells, where they will be able to console themselves with gendarmerie ex-commander Hémart and a dozen or so others, all nervously awaiting the firing squad at dawn.

Gravilliers section

It is a little after midnight as two mounted deputies, Léonard Bourdon and Simon Camboulas, enter the grounds of the priory of Saint-Martin-des-Champs, where the Gravilliers section's General Assembly is taking place. Some 6,000 citizens from this, one of Paris's most populous and most working-class sections, are ready, waiting, and in arms. Camboulas, deputy for the Aveyron department, is a new face to the crowd, but Bourdon has been a well-known presence in the section long before being elected to the Convention.

The two deputies have left the bulk of their attack column back on the Rue de la Verrerie, but Bourdon has chosen to make a detour of a quarter of a mile because he knows he can count on his section for support. Straight away, he whips up the crowds:

– Citizens, the Maison Commune is the conspirators' den. We must march on it. Let not the sun shine on these tyrants!

He and his aides organize the men in a marching column, and they place a company of young lads from Bourdon's school for Jeunes Français in the van.

Is it a little rash to allow these adolescents to lead the force into battle? Bourdon may have heard that there was a bit of a scuffle at the Maison Commune around 1.00 a.m. when NG militants from the Arcis section, lined up on the Quai de Gesvres, were prompted by deputy Jean-Augustin Penières (who seems to have been in the vicinity by chance) to try to get to the Place de la Maison Commune from along the quais. They were however rebuffed, showing there were still pro-Commune forces to encounter. However, intelligence since then will have established that the Place de la Maison Commune is increasingly empty. Bourdon has a further, and very considerable asset too. He has been given the password that Hanriot devised this afternoon for the NG battalions following his orders. It came from Ulrich, one of Hanriot's aides-de-camp. Ulrich had accompanied Hanriot on his raid on the CGS this afternoon, but since then has seen the error of his ways. He passed the code onto his friend Jean-Paul Martin, from the Gravilliers section, who is also trying to retrieve his reputation following earlier support for the Commune in the section. Hanriot's password, Bourdon learns, is 'Justice', followed by 'Innocence'—very much the Commune's cause in a nutshell. The password that Barras has devised is similarly, if cryptically revealing: it is 'National Convention' and 'People'.

Across the city

What is happening across the city after midnight is even worse for the Commune than the Enforcement Committee fears: not only is armed force mobilized in large numbers and closing in on it, but out on the streets and right across the city, Parisians have accepted the narrative of the day on offer from the Convention.

In many sections of the city, between around 11.00 p.m. and 2.00 or 3.00 a.m. there have been final, despairing attempts by pro-Commune militants to persuade their fellow citizens that they have taken the wrong course. In rare cases, as with Gencey in Finistère and Delacour in Brutus, these came from adjuncts to the Enforcement Committee appointed after 9.00. A further cohort of councillors have taken it upon themselves to return to their sections to drum up pro-Commune support, joined sometimes by simple citizens who remain enthusiasts in the Commune cause, like the newly married Pierre Burguburu, who left the Jacobins at around 11.00 in order to try to influence debate in his own section of Gardes-Françaises.

Some of these emissaries still talk in terms of a purge of the Convention, but others are more emphatic, reflecting the change of thinking within the Enforcement Committee. The locksmith-councillor Jean-Nicolas Langlois shocks his fellow citizens in Mont-Blanc by claiming that 'it wasn't the Commune that was in insurrection but rather part of the National Convention was being counter-revolutionary by oppressing the patriots'. In Contrat-Social, the young maths professor Nicolas Le Pauvre, who played a big role in getting the section to send delegates to the Commune earlier in the evening, returned around midnight and, it was reported, spoke 'not with sangfroid but rather with a fieriness that was clearly counter-revolutionary (if not mad'). In Lepeletier, Bertrand Arnauld was equally emphatic when he arrived back in his section. The section should make haste, as they would not want to be on the losing side. He claimed there were already 39 to 40 sections loyal to the Commune and more than 6,000 men on the Place as well as 1,200 cavalrymen. The figure of 40 for pro-Commune sections (a complete fiction) was cited by others, and is being bandied around in the Jacobin Club too.

This rearguard action in the sections by pro-Commune forces has only delayed rather than reversed collective decisions to support the Convention. The lack of hard information for most of the evening allowed rumour and uncertainty to run riot, and encouraged holding back on firm decisions. The Droits-de-l'Homme section on the Commune's doorstep claimed to have received no fewer than seven different orders from seven different individuals or bodies between 4.00 and 8.00 p.m. before they received a single missive from the Convention. Things did not slow down thereafter. Close by, the Indivisibilité section concurred: 'All the different reports we received were mutually contradictory.'

Although the communications network of the Convention has been far from perfect, it has certainly proved far abler and more efficient than anything the Commune has been able to devise or improvise. The Committees of Government have everyday experience in contacting and coordinating across the sections, whereas the Commune lost much of that power after the Law of 14 Frimaire. This eastern side of the city has been more troubled with communication problems than the west, while the river is a factor too as regards Left Bank sections, for the surveillance of key bridges disrupts communication. It was no accident that the very last four sections to declare for the Convention were all on the Left Bank. At 1.00 a.m., when the assemblies of Panthéon and Bonnet-Rouge finally came out for the Convention, this left only Chalier and Observatoire still holding out.

The main cause for the tardiness of these sections in declaring for the Convention seems to have been distance from the Convention hall rather than any particular ideological commitment on their part. Torpidity in the traffic of information seems to have been critical. Explaining why the Revolutionary Committee of the Observatoire section was so hesitant over the night, NG, Jean-Baptiste Goulart, observed that

> the committee, borne down under the weight and number of reports all the more alarming than the others, believed that it perceived a kind of plot being woven against the people but it was unable to locate the thread nor the objective.

His fellow Committee member, cabinet-maker, Jean-Louis Lefebvre, who subsequently claimed only to have received the Convention's outlaw decree at 7.00 a.m., concurred: 'that night we found ourselves abandoned to ourselves and in a state of ignorance, as the reports we received were discordant'. It was like entering 'a labyrinth of uncertainty', commented Charles Ballin of the similarly peripheral section of Quinze-Vingts.

Uncertainty bred fear of the consequences. Lefebvre in the Observatoire spoke for others across the sections when he noted his predicament in making a choice:

> – I said to myself that I could not decide on the basis of what I have heard and that I had to remain calm and wait, and that orders would be sent us, and that the least rashness on my part could spark a civil war.

If the Commune prevailed, the situation could lead to the national government besieging Paris as they did at Lyon during the Federalist revolt of 1793. The Convention had wreaked terrible vengeance on the city, and Lefebvre feared that the same could happen to Paris. At the height of the Girondin-Montagnard struggles in 1793, the Girondin deputy Isnard had threatened such retribution on the city of Paris that in the future 'people will scan the banks of the Seine for traces of the city'. If the Commune won, Lefebvre now concluded, 'the wretched prediction of Isnard would be accomplished . . .' The future of Paris and the fate of the Revolution are coming to depend on the defeat of its municipality.

École de Mars encampment, Plaine des Sablons

Hyacinthe Langlois is on guard-duty on the perimeter of the École de Mars encampment. Although his fellow cadets are sleeping soundly in their tents, Langlois can hear the faint sounds of tocsin bells from churches and the drum-beats of the *générale* that indicate that something extraordinary for this time of night is taking place a mile or so away at the heart of Paris.

Suddenly, there is the sound of hooves, and deputies Peyssard, Brival, and Bentabole enter through the main gate. With drum and trumpet, the alarm is sounded and the youths form into battle-order to be addressed by the deputies. The deputies lay bare the conspiracy of Robespierre and the others. The boys' commander Bertèche is already under arrest in Paris. (This seems to have been done quietly despite Bertèche's professed support for the Convention.) Their École's administrator Le Bas, who shares oversight of the École with Peyssard, is also in custody. The cadets must arm and be ready to defend the Convention if necessary.

The cadets are very excited by this midnight adventure. They realize they will miss their starring role in the cancelled Bara and Viala ceremonies. But if the Convention prevails, they will be allowed to have their moment of glory. In the meanwhile, in between shouts of 'Long live the Convention!' and 'Down with Le Bas!', they wait to be summoned to action.

They don't realize it but in the last week or so, down to this evening's debates in the Convention, their institution has been ascribed violent intent by both political camps, pro- and anti-Robespierre. They are innocent of all charges. No one seems aware of it at this moment, but the camp stores are almost completely lacking in ammunition.

Guyot's wandering: from the Maison Commune to the Sans-Culottes section

This has not at all been the day that Jean-Guillaume Guyot expected. Checking into his post in the Police Administration at the end of the afternoon, he had not anticipated his colleagues' mobilization in support of the Commune, and was dismayed when they banished him from their midst and suggested he go to the Maison Commune. This he has done, in fact, and the more the evening has progressed the more he has found his sympathies shifting away from the Commune to the Convention. Such was the crush in the Council Chamber that he could hear more than he could see what was going on. He heard one of the Robespierre brothers—he was not sure which—regaling an enthusiastic crowd with tales of a faction that wished to enslave the people, murder patriots, and take the young Capet out of his prison. He witnessed the scornful treatment that Fleuriot has handed out to emissaries from the Convention who had brought the assembly's outlawry decree. Yes, he stated ironically, we are all outlaws, conspirators, counter-revolutionaries, and royalists. There was a handful of traitors, a further speaker stated—Guyot picked out the names of Collot-d'Herbois, Bourdon de l'Oise, Amar, Dubarran, and Ruhl—who used the Convention's names to hide their own plans to arrest patriots and proclaim 'liberticidal' decrees, snuffing out the people's freedom. It was they, he understood the speaker to be arguing, who needed to be purged and not the Convention itself (which some speakers eulogized). The debate gets wilder and wilder before Guyot chooses to slip away. When he is outside, he is amazed to see the Place de la Maison Commune, that was so full and effervescent on his arrival a matter of hours before, almost completely deserted.

His head in a whirl, Guyot realizes he is a marked man. As a member of the General Council, he has just been designated an outlaw. He concludes he has no alternative but to hand himself in to the authorities. But first, he must see his beloved wife, now pregnant with their fourth child. It is quite a trek to his home in the Sans-Culottes section in the Faubourg Saint-Marcel, and Guyot takes a circuitous route so as to avoid numerous police identity checks. He has to show his *carte de sûreté* to several patrols, protesting his ignorance of the night's events. Finally he gets home to his wife, before the two of them strike out to the sectional headquarters of the Maison-Commune section, where he will turn himself in, and hope for a miracle. If Guyot was amazed by how fast the Place de la Maison Commune had emptied while he was inside struggling to follow debates, now, in contrast despite this late hour, he observes the streets of the city are buzzing. All of Paris, he reflects, is armed, armed to defend the Republic . . .

Bourdon's expedition: from the Gravilliers section to the Place de la Maison Commune

Léonard Bourdon and his Gravilliers-based force have reached the Rue de la Verrerie. The intersection with the Rue Saint-Martin is their rendezvous with Bourdon's remaining force, but they also encounter here the Lombard section artillery on its way home from the Place de la Maison Commune. Bourdon asks for the commander, and in the absence of one accepts Cosme Pionnier, Artillery Instructor, as the ranking officer. The decision may be influenced by the fact that Pionnier hails from the Gravilliers section, and the two men probably know each other already. Do you want to fight for the tyrant? Bourdon asks the troops. The men shout back, no, they want to fight against the tyrant. No names are needed: everyone knows, Robespierre is the tyrant. Bourdon has got the men where he wants them. He instantly places the two Lombards cannon as the advance-guard of his force and they move on the Place de la Maison Commune. They keep the noise down so as to maintain a level of surprise as they enter the square, which is indeed effectively deserted. Men stealthily seal off all points of access to the Place, and then form a semi-circle around the front of the building in battle formation. Use of Hanriot's password helps: the few men guarding the main entrance come over to their side at once. On a signal, the forces in the square break the quiet with a huge 'Vive la Convention!' Leading an elite group of 50 riflemen, the two deputies, Bourdon and Camboulas, brush unchallenged past the guards at the main entrance to the Maison Commune. Pionnier has his artillery primed in case things go badly. They await the outcome.

And so it has come to pass that Cosme Pionnier, Paris artillery Instructor, reputed participant in the Lyon *mitraillades*, who a matter of hours previously, had primed his cannon on the Convention hall and the CGS offices on the Place du Carrousel, and who, minutes earlier had shown continued respect for the insurrectionary Commune, is now here, alert and commanding the Convention's artillery forces on the Place de la Maison Commune primed to overthrow the Commune, thus completing a day of many ironies and many changes of heart, a day which witnessed the fall of Robespierre.

After Midnight

At some time shortly after 2.00 a.m. on 10 Thermidor, the deputy Léonard Bourdon had led his expeditionary squad speedily yet stealthily up the main staircase of the Maison Commune. The huge numbers of his marching column stationed outside at the ready were being reinforced by Barras's main column entering the Place de la Maison Commune from along the quais. Mounted gendarmerie were present in the unlikely event of cavalry being needed, while Artillery Instructor Cosme Pionnier was expertly marshalling the cannon. In a night of several mobilizations, this was the most impressive show of force yet.

The conflict was all over bar the shouting. Even were the cadres of the Insurrectionary Commune in the building to offer resistance, they lacked an armed force to put up a fight. Not a shot was needed.

The early sounds of cannon being dragged onto the Place had triggered an initial round of *sauve-qui-peut* in the Council chamber. Seeing that the Convention's main forces were coming from the north-west direction, councillors and the very few remaining members of the public rushed to the other side, to exit on the Arcade Saint-Jean and the Rue du Martroy. As the boot-tramp of Bourdon and his men could be heard on the staircase, the meetings of both General Council and Enforcement Committee broke up in disorder and panic. If they could get beyond the Maison Commune environs and remove the tricolour sash that now marked them out, councillors might just manage to get away completely. Joining the ranks of those fleeing at the last moment were four of the nine-man Enforcement Committee: Grenard, Lerebours, Desboisseaux, and Coffinhal. Coffinhal's last gesture before taking flight was to hurl Hanriot out of a window into an inner courtyard in fury at his dismal, drunken performance as commander. Most individuals remaining knew that death was just around the corner.

In the Council chamber, councillor and man-midwife Jean-Antoine-Gaspard Forestier suddenly woke up to a nightmare. He had been napping following a long night in which he had been out and about delivering two babies. As Bourdon's forces were breaking open the doors to the chamber, Forestier made a run for it. He passed through the Secretariat offices (the clerk Blaise Lafosse had already managed to make his escape), then ran up a tiny staircase at the back of the building hoping to find a hiding place. But all doors were locked. He tried the latrines: but there was no room, for four trembling colleagues were already cowering in a cubicle. He continued his reckless, headlong, panicky search, hearing the Convention's guards find the latrine refugees behind him as he fled. Just as he was running out of hope, he bumped into a fleeing colleague with a better knowledge of the layout of the building. He led him up backstairs into the garret of the Maison Commune. There the men would spend the next several days holed up together, joined by other lucky escapees. Candle-stumps and stagnant water from an abandoned wooden clog would be their main diet.

CPS spy Dulac was in Bourdon's train as he and his men broke into the main Council chamber to find thirty-odd remainers. Dulac grabbed Charlemagne, who was in the chair, causing him to drop his bell in shock. Others stood around dumbfounded and despondent at their predicament. While arrests were being made, Bourdon, Dulac, and their men ascertained the location of the Enforcement Committee's meeting place.

Figure 10. Jean-Louis Prieur, Léonard Bourdon at the Maison Commune, 9–10 Thermidor

Some two hours later, Léonard Bourdon would recount to an enraptured Convention how he and Barras had led the people of Paris to a glorious victory over the conspiracy of Robespierre and the Commune. And he would commend to them the young gendarme at his side, Charles-André Merda, whom, he alleged, had fired a pistol-shot that pierced Robespierre's cheek on encountering the Enforcement Committee at the Maison Commune. The Convention had spent the 24 hours silencing Robespierre; a pistol shot had completed the task. Robespierre would not say another word. Had it been Merda's shot? The streets of Paris that night were full of the news that Robespierre had sought to end his own life, with no mention of a gendarme, heroic or otherwise.

It was a much-decimated and utterly demoralized Enforcement Committee that remained *in situ*. Robespierre was still alive, though in agonies caused by his face wound, but Le Bas had shot himself and lay dead on the floor. Fleuriot, Payan, and Dumas were present, the latter allegedly hiding under a table. Couthon was found at the bottom of a staircase with blood streaming from a headwound. Had he fallen, been pushed, or were he and his gendarme carrier merely seeking a way out? There was no Hanriot, though in fact he was lying dazed and undetected on a dung-heap in the internal courtyard where Coffinhal had hurled him. Saint-Just was present too, still stoical and passive. In contrast to those around him, his clothing remained neat, tidy and unbespattered by blood. Augustin Robespierre had climbed out of one of the upper floor overlooking the Place, and gaping onlookers were left wondering whether he was trying to escape or to commit suicide. He had removed his shoes and was carrying them in one hand. After a perilous few moments he lost his balance and fell headlong into the crowds below, landing on and severely injuring National Guardsman Claude Chabru, as well as causing himself serious fractures, cuts, and bruises.

Bourdon's forces set swiftly about making mass arrests of anyone they found in the sealed building and tying them together in twos ready for transfer to the CGS offices. Jacques-Louis Ménétra from Bon-Conseil was present outside and he shuddered to see mayor Fleuriot, with whom he had been drinking only a week before, roped together with the Municipal Councillor from his section, his friend, Antoine Jemptel. Ménétra had recently lost the election to the Commune to Jemptel by a mere handful of votes. There but for the grace of God . . .

Meanwhile, on the Ile de la Cité, the capture of the Mairie, the other Commune stronghold, was also taking place. Like the Place de la Maison Commune, the environs of the Mairie had suffered many NG abandonments, the Marat battalion most recently, and Giot, their commander, was showing no trace of leadership. By now, the majority of men remaining were better disposed towards the Convention than the Commune. They offer no resistance when, at some time after 2.00 a.m., Barras's adjunct Merlin de Thionville arrived with around 60 mounted gendarmes to reinforce guardsmen from the Révolutionnaire section. The force surrounded and seized the Mairie and the Police HQ, arresting the ten (out of 20) Police Administrators present, who were consigned to cells from which their own recent victims were removed. These included fellow Administrators Michel and Benoit and wounded Legion Chief Mathis. There were also four of the CPS-appointed replacements for the Police Administration who had arrived too early and were arrested.

Also shortly after 2.00 a.m., the Jacobin Club fell into government hands. It was the final centre of Commune-led resistance, though resistance is hardly an apposite description given its torpor throughout the night. Communication between the Club and the Commune had been increasingly insubstantial as the night went on. The exchange of delegations has been ongoing all night but produced no concrete actions. Deputy Louis Legendre took it upon himself to close the Club by force, and left the Convention hall with a small group of determined patriots. Their arrival at the Club broke up the session, though Vivier, who had presided all night, managed to slip away in the mêlée. Legendre evacuated the chamber and locked the doors, returning triumphantly to the Convention dangling the keys. The Convention applauded the action and outlawed Vivier. The feared Jacobins had been a pushover.

Strangely, on this night when the possibility of civil war had loomed ominously, extraordinarily little blood was spilled. Barras's adjunct deputies encountered nothing but enthusiastic crowds across the city, and easily mopped up isolated cases of resistance, much helped by the sections' fraternization, the movement of itinerant delegations linking sections in the Convention's cause together. Throughout the night, fighting between the sides had rarely got much further than fisticuffs. The physical assault on Third Legion Chief Mathis was about as bad as it got. In the afternoon, Hanriot and his expeditionary team had been imprisoned without physical harm, apart from some rope burns. Coffinhal's frontal attack on the Convention, with Pionnier's grapeshot at the ready, was averted once Hanriot decided to withdraw. The Commune had threatened its own prisoners with shootings at dawn; but dawn had not come. On the other side, too, Léonard Bourdon had just taken the Maison Commune with scarcely a shot being fired. The story was the same at the Mairie and the Jacobin Club.

Violence had been contained, at least for the moment, but the Convention was gearing up to mete out exemplary punishment on Robespierre, his colleagues and the Commune in a huge blood-letting. Of the blood that would flow over the next few days, a single death stood out: that of Maximilien Robespierre. Following Bourdon's attack, he had been laid out wounded and in shock in the Maison Commune. He was then transported to the offices of CPS and placed on a table where he was subjected to cruel taunts from bystanders—'Isn't he a fine king?', 'Sire, is Your Majesty suffering?'—before being stretchered over to the offices of the CGS. It was proposed to the Convention that his body might actually be brought into the Convention hall; but Thuriot spoke for all in stating that such an act would tarnish rather than enhance the day:

– The corpse of a tyrant carries with it only plague. The spot marked out for him is the Place de la Révolution!

The Place de la Révolution had seen the execution of the tyrant Louis XVI; it would be a fitting location for the death of tyrant Robespierre.

Soon joining Robespierre's suffering body in the government offices were Payan, along with Saint-Just and Dumas. Deputy Thibaudeau glimpsed Saint-Just, who retained his haughty air, while also contriving to look like a pickpocket caught in the act. The irony of the fact that he was on the receiving end of severe practices of revolutionary justice that they had helped create was not lost on him. Noticing a copy of the constitutional act pinned on the wall of the waiting area, he mused to one of his guards, 'This was my work . . . And the Revolutionary Government too . . .' The arrival of CGS member Élie Lacoste brought him down to earth. He ordered all the men to be sent to the Conciergerie to pass before the Revolutionary Tribunal.

Lacoste was concerned that Robespierre's wounded state made him in more pressing need of medical than legal examination. He was indeed in an appalling condition, his shirt soaked in blood, his breeches half-unbuttoned, and his silk stockings around his ankles. His horribly mutilated mouth produced only grunts, as he reached out for pen and paper, which were denied him. Not wanting his deteriorating condition to prevent a full public execution, Lacoste called in surgeons to inspect and clean the shattered jaw. They wrapped a bandage around his head to keep everything just about in place.

The Convention ended its mammoth 9 Thermidor session at 6.00 a.m., but a new session began only a few hours later, at 9.00 a.m., 10 Thermidor, or 28 July 1794. Waiting at the bar of the house was Public Prosecutor Fouquier-Tinville. Fouquier's wager the previous evening had paid off.

Sitting tight, staying loyal, keeping within the bounds of legality, and neglecting his old friend Fleuriot-Lescot in the latter's time of need, had allowed him to survive. He realized that his decadal rest-day was now out of the question: today would be exceptionally busy. But he was on hand with a quandary that only would have occurred to a stickler for the letter of the law: he would be unable to follow the identification procedures prescribed for outlaws, since this required the presence of two municipal officers, and in the current situation of the Commune's collective outlawry, these could not be found. The Convention graciously (if perplexedly) allowed him to proceed without observing the formality, with the instruction that executions had to take place by the end of the day.

– The soil of the Republic [stated Thuriot from the chair] must be purged of a monster who was already prepared to make himself king.

Le Bas's suicide had removed him from today's humiliations. (He had been buried overnight in the Saint-Paul cemetery in the Marais. His pet dog would whimper for three days on his tomb.) The other deputies—the two Robespierres, Couthon, Saint-Just—had been joined at the Palais de Justice by other captured principals, notably Payan and Dumas, plus the defenestrated Hanriot whose body had been latterly discovered coated in filth. He was in a pitiable state: either in his fall or along his route to the Hôtel de Brionne his eye had been gouged and hung out of its socket. He kept company with his aide-de-camp Lavalette, who had been sprung from the Pélagie prison around midnight with Dumas and had come to the Maison Commune. Jacobin president Vivier had escaped Legendre's clutches at the closure of the Club but was picked up from his home in the Muséum section. Mayor Fleuriot was also present. A disorderly transfer had presented him with an opportunity to make a run for it, but after a hue and cry near the Pont-Neuf he was recaptured.

In a way it was fitting, and very much in line with current Revolutionary Tribunal practice, that the *fournée* destined for the guillotine on 10 Thermidor included individuals quite unknown to each other. The Robespierre group were acquainted with Vivier through the Jacobins, but not with the dozen or so sectional militants who were destined for the same tumbrils. Robespierre's 'conspiracy' was full of strangers. Bonnet-Rouge Councillor Adrien-Nicolas Gobeau had tried to commit suicide with a pen-knife as Bourdon's men broke into the Maison-Commune and had been taken to the Hôtel-Dieu for treatment. Patched up, he was expedited to the Conciergerie along with Couthon. Augustin Robespierre, also badly wounded, was brought along later. Besides Gobeau, there was only one other General

Council member arrested at the Maison Commune, Christophe Cochefer. Poignantly, in his pocket was the little edition of the Law of 14 Frimaire on Revolutionary Government whose stipulations he had spent the night zealously infringing. The other men, who included a number of the Enforcement Committee's ill-starred adjuncts, had been arrested and handed over by loyal sectional authorities.

The identification procedures required by the Law of 23 Ventôse began late in the morning. For each of the 22 outlaws dealt with during the course of the day, a range of private individuals was called on, two per suspect, to make the requisite identification. Most were employees of the Tribunal or else persons living in the neighbourhood of the courts. Tribunal Vice-President Scellier was the presiding magistrate, with Maire and Deliège (who had sat alongside the condemned Dumas the previous day) as subaltern judges. Fouquier was present, but left the chamber when it was the turn of Fleuriot, formerly his bosom friend.

In the late afternoon, the 22 identified men passed through the *salle de toilette* and were bundled aboard three tumbrils that had been readied for them. At around 6.00 p.m., they set out for the Place de la Révolution for their encounter with public executioner Sanson and his team. Sanson had executed for Louis XVI, then had executed him. He had executed on Robespierre's behalf. Now he was about to dispatch him too.

A huge, enthusiastic crowd had gathered as the men made their way to the execution site, following the old route along the Rue Saint-Honoré. A later story had it that the tumbrils stopped outside the Duplay residence and women performed a little dance of joy around Robespierre's carriage. The cry of 'Fucking Maximum!' was heard—it was most likely hurled at Payan and Fleuriot rather than at Robespierre. Anyway, 9 Thermidor had been about a lot more than wages. Robespierre's cart made slow progress through the throng of people shouting insults, threats, sarcastic comments, and crude oaths. They arrived a little before 7.00 p.m. at the Place. Sanson set to work at once, starting with disabled Couthon and wounded Augustin Robespierre. A cheer greeted every falling head. Fleuriot was reserved till last: the *journée* had been on his mayoral watch after all. Before him went Maximilien Robespierre. One of Sanson's crew pulled the bandage from around his face and as he was thrust forward to the blade he emitted a blood-curdling animalistic shriek.

Resistance to Robespierre had been all about stopping a purge of the Convention or worse. The *journée* ended with the would-be purger spectacularly put to death. Moreover, the 22 executions on 28 July were followed by a further 71 on the 29th and 12 on the 30th. With a few latecomers, in total some 108 capital sentences were handed out under the outlaw decrees. Of this number, 87 were municipal councillors out of the 91 who had signed the attendance sheet. Most of those who fled Bourdon's attack, such as wallpaper manufacturer Grenart, had been picked up in the locality. Desboisseaux wandered from pillar to post in the south-east of the city in the company of Coffinhal before he returned to the Ile Saint-Louis to see his wife, and was arrested in a bar. Coffinhal, who would have been instantly recognizable at the city gates because of his height, pushed west and spent a couple of days, isolated and starving, among the faecal matter on the Ile des Cygnes to the west of the Champ de Mars before being captured. Few managed to get clean away: among those who did were secretary Bourbon-Fleury, state bureaucrat Lerebours, and Payan's elder brother Joseph. Payan even managed to collect a stack of silverware from his brother's lodgings before stealing out from the city.

A fair number of members of the Commune managed to avoid execution by other means. Three councillors threw themselves on the mercy of the Convention in their session of 9–10 Thermidor, while others pleaded their cause before their sectional authorities. In the eyes of the latter, a record of adherence to and especially service for the Convention's cause on the night was a mitigating factor. Pierre Lestage was only briefly in the Maison Commune and came back to the Montagne section to fight for the Convention: on leading a delegation to the Convention in the early hours he was even offered a fraternal accolade by the assembly's President. In Lepeletier, Pierre-Nicolas Vergne had not been at a General Council for more than a fortnight because of illness but rose from his sickbed to preside over the section's General Assembly, urging support for the Convention and fighting off resistance from Commune emissary Arnauld. Councillors who had rotated doing service at the Temple on the night could hardly be held responsible for the vagaries at the Maison Commune. Neither could Police Administrators Benoist and Michel, who had spent the whole night in the police cells at the Mairie. Then again, the Lombards section accepted Pierre-Henri Blandin's appeal that his severe bladder condition prevented him sitting still and paying attention throughout his evening at the Commune. The 68-year-old Pierre-Jean Renard had left the Commune meeting after a short while and spent most of the night wandering the streets utterly disconsolate until finally turning himself over to his section's authorities, who protected him. Perhaps the most striking examples of mercy were Cosme Pionnier whom Léonard Bourdon appointed in charge of the artillery on the Place de la Maison Commune, but who a matter of hours earlier had trained his guns on the CGS and the Convention; and Homme-Armé's Claude Chalandon. The latter had led his section's cannon to the Place de la Maison Commune in the afternoon, but by the end of the night joined with other members of his Revolutionary Committee in arresting supporters of the Commune.

In September, a batch of around 40 individuals from a dozen or so sections who had signed the Commune attendance sheet went before the Revolutionary Tribunal and were acquitted. The Tribunal thereby acknowledged that many of those who supported the Commune had been guilty only of having been misled. Arcis section's Tugot and Dehureau, for example, had signed the Maison Commune attendance sheet but then gone back to their sections and risked their lives by going out to the Place de la Maison Commune in the early hours of 10 Thermidor to read the Convention's proclamation.

Generally speaking, Parisians offered no resistance or hostility to the mass executions of their elected representatives in the immediate aftermath of the 9 Thermidor *journée*. Even Robespierre's final shriek did not stop the huge

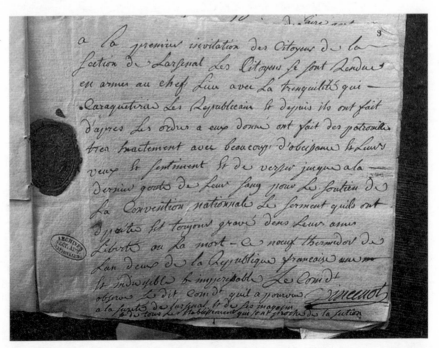

Figure 11. Vincenot, Commander, Arsenal National Guard battalion, to Acting Commanding Officer, Place du Carrousel, 9–10 Thermidor (AFII 47 pl. 367, pi. 3)

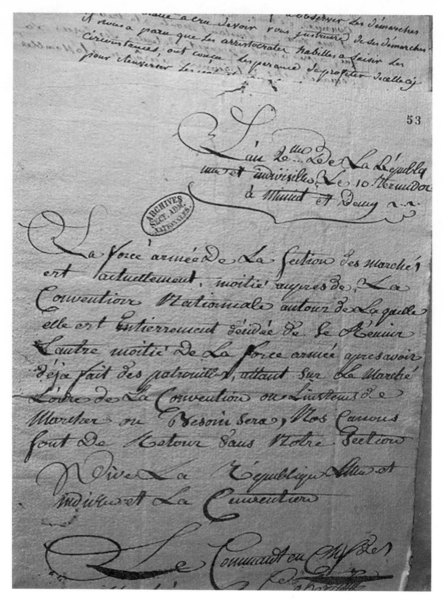

Figure 12. Goubert, Commander, Marchés National Guard Battalion, to Acting Commanding Officer, Place du Carrousel, 12.30 a.m., 9–10 Thermidor (AFII 47 pl. 367, pi. 53)

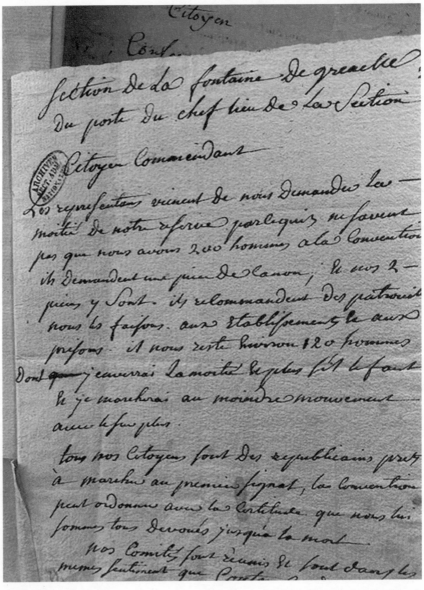

Figure 13. Contou, Commander, Fontaine-de-la-Grenelle National Guard battalion, to Acting Commanding Officer, Place du Carrousel, 9–10 Thermidor (AFII 47 pl. 365, pi. 2)

crowd who came to see his guillotining on 28 July from going home happy. Across the city, the mood was light-hearted and positive. All afternoon and evening on 10 Thermidor, the Muséum Revolutionary Committee noted,

> the most perfect tranquillity reigned in the section . . . At the moment when the tyrant Robespierre passed with his agents, conspirators and scoundrels on their way to expiate their crimes, there were cries of *Vive la République!* and *Vive la Convention!* They gave the signal for the joy of all patriots over the death of the traitors who were stealthily forging chains for them. They joyfully intended to keep their oath and rally around the Convention.

Towards the end of the night of 9–10 Thermidor, the Montagnard deputy François-Omer Granet had proposed the motion to a unanimously positive Convention that 'the Convention affirms their heartfelt view that the sections of Paris have never ceased to deserve well of the *patrie*'. The motion expressed the powerful feeling across the city that the *journée* of 9 Thermidor had been essentially a harmonious co-production between the Robespierre-purged Convention and the people of Paris. It was neatly encapsulated in the fact that the NG's required password exchange in the final, victorious stage of the *journée* of 9 Thermidor had been 'National Convention', with the rejoinder, 'The People'.

Louis-Sébastien Mercier was still in gaol, so had not himself witnessed the day and the ensuing rejoicings, though he certainly heard some of them. Looking back on the huge popular wave of celebration that swept through Paris at the execution of Robespierre, he was firm in his judgement on the *journée* and its meaning:

> 14 July 1789 and 9 Thermidor Year II: these are the two days of unanimity among French men and women about their revolution. On both days, the people made their appearance as one. The sovereignty they established was both striking and decisive . . . On 14 July, the French people said: I want freedom. On 9 Thermidor it said: I want justice.

The culling of the Commune on 28–30 July suggested that any justice was going to be pretty rough. It also remained to be seen how else the Convention would acknowledge in the longer term the people who had pulled its chestnuts out of the fire.

Afterword

9 Thermidor From Afar

> Writing the history of the Revolution will be an almost impossible task for up to a half-century afterwards. This is because its agents are even more mobile than their emotions and they often escape even the most attentive eye that follows them; and one sees that the principles that governed the day before differ from those of the day after.

Writing in 1798, Louis-Sébastien Mercier confessed to being an observer of the Revolution rather than its historian, a role that his own mortality prevented. His 'up close' approach to the Revolution was essential, he argued, to get any sort of grip on its fast-moving and unpredictable course. But only future historians could loosen the focus on the historical lens—'the optic', in his vocabulary—to get the wide-angle perspective needed to understand the meaning of such a complex phenomenon.

Mercier's challenge thrown down to historians writing 'from afar' rather than 'up close' is all the greater when we are at not just 50, but at well over 200 years remove from 9 Thermidor Year II, or 27 July 1794. The importance of the day has always been acknowledged. From the very outset, it was viewed as one of the great symbolic and pivotal moments of the French Revolution, a status it shared with 14 July 1789 and 10 August 1792. All three were accorded an annual national festival in their honour: for the rest of the 1790s, July 14 marked the advent of liberty, 10 August the birth of equality and 9 Thermidor the triumph over tyranny. All three were *journées* on which decisive direct action on the streets of Paris secured the Revolution and its gains. Each was often described as a revolution in its own right. They became the three landmarks around which historians ever since have constructed their narratives of the 1790s.

If the importance of 9 Thermidor was clear enough, however, its full meaning was less immediately evident than was the case with the other two landmark days. In 1789, the Estates General had already established a national assembly and the principle of a constitutional monarchy weeks before 14 July. Then again, because of the military crisis that beset the regime over the spring and summer of 1792, the king was being politically bypassed months before his overthrow on 10 August. In contrast, as I have shown, 9 Thermidor came as a surprise, a shock even, and this delayed the understanding of the full impact. Initially it was far from certain what the overthrow of Robespierre, and those adjudged to have supported his resistance to the Convention, entailed for the regime and the direction of policy. Unlike the other great symbolic *journées*, 9 Thermidor was a day that had to wait for its meaning to be established. This process took place over what came to be called the Thermidorian period, which lasted from Robespierre's fall through to the opening of the new Directorial regime in November 1795. In this time, the political atmosphere altered in ways that powerfully influenced the way people thought about what had gone before.

The two leading impressions arising from the *journée* as I have portrayed it were, first, that it was a day of action to remove a man and not a regime; and second, that it was a joint victory for the elected deputies and for Parisians. Barère, always the man with the *mot juste*, highlighted as key factors in the overthrow of Robespierre 'the tyrant' 'the power of the people, the energy of the Convention and the patriotism of the sections of Paris'. The theme of partnership and mutual trust—neatly incarnated in the 'Convention'-'People' NG password for the night of 9 Thermidor—was endlessly and rhapsodically evoked in the dozens and dozens of delegations presenting their congratulations to the assembly throughout the sessions of 10, 11, 12 Thermidor and beyond. It was also echoed in speeches and pamphlets by deputies.

This view held the field for only a short period, however. Within a year, the story would be completely transformed, and the day's meaning viewed very differently. On 8 Thermidor Year III (26 July 1795) in fact, the Dantonist deputy Edme-Bonaventure Courtois, whom the Convention had commissioned to report on the 9 Thermidor *journée*, presented his findings to his colleagues. Strikingly, his *Rapport sur les événements du 9 thermidor an II* widened the attack so that it targeted not just a tyrant but also a tyranny, a form of government deadly to liberty run by a group of would-be 'usurpers of supreme power' allegedly under Robespierre's leadership. In addition, it completely rejected the co-production model evident a year earlier. For Courtois, there was only one hero on the day, and that was the Convention, which had overthrown the tyrant and his fellow conspirators. The people of Paris had been under the dominance of the Commune, so implicitly the defeat of the Commune was a defeat for Parisians and popular politics.

Courtois's report was a straw in the wind. Endorsing what had become current thinking in the interim, it helped set in place a template for understanding 9 Thermidor that lasted well beyond the 1790s. The Revolutionary Government of Year II was hereafter conceived of as 'the Terror'—a regime-defining usage (definite article, capital T) that post-dated 9 Thermidor. Whereas the Revolutionary Government had deployed intimidatory violence and terror alongside other policies including war mobilization and social reform, now 'Terror' was essentialized, causing other features of the policies of Revolutionary Government to fade in significance. Robespierre was viewed as the ambitious tyrant-in-the-making who was conspiring to seize dictatorial powers on 9 Thermidor, aided and abetted by 'terrorists' and 'Robespierrists' (terms whose usage also now sky-rocketed). On 9 Thermidor, the Convention stopped Robespierre and 'the Terror' in their tracks.

In this book, I have deliberately set out to research the pivotal day of 9 Thermidor without having recourse to the analytical vocabulary and inter-pretative schema that were developed in the Thermidorian period after Robespierre's fall, before being endorsed by Courtois and carried forward by generations of historians. To take a single example: I have avoided the term 'the Terror' as an unhelpful anachronism. Researching and writing about 9 Thermidor in the 'up close' manner advocated by Mercier allows us to explore and analyse the event in terms that were contemporaneous with the event.

In this Afterword, I will first present a brief overview of the changes in the political atmosphere in Paris in the Thermidorian period, to give a sense of the way in which the co-production interpretation of the *journée* was erased and its meaning extended beyond the removal of a tyrant, Robespierre, to incorporate the removal of a system of tyranny, the Terror. I will go on to lay out the interpretation of the day that has emerged from the approach I have adopted and the research that has underpinned it. Most of my argument is implicit in the account I have provided; but bringing it to the surface and making explicit the key lines of the argument will allow readers to set findings in the context of the broader study of the Revolution, and also to consider what has been gained for a historian writing 'from afar' by observing 9 Thermidor 'up close'.

Against the people

The erasure of the notion of 9 Thermidor as co-production between the people of Paris and the Convention in the months following the event was a consequence of the collapse of the relationship of the two protagonists in the Thermidorian period. It was closely tied up with moves to broaden the attack on Robespierre so as to incorporate other elements and other personnel within Revolutionary Government in Year II.

In the immediate aftermath of the day, the artisans of the fall of Robespierre in the Convention on 9 Thermidor, most notably Barère, Billaud-Varenne and Collot d'Herbois, basked in their own reflected glory. But they were very soon on the defensive, as they discovered that many of their parliamentary allies on the night wanted to rid the regime not simply of Robespierre but also of policies of terror which he and they had been promoting. Some wanted to be shot of the whole régime too. The three CPS leaders had wanted Revolutionary Government to function more efficiently with their difficult colleague removed, rather than to have their wings clipped in any way. They had thought the policies of Revolutionary Government, terror included, would simply continue under less-divided management. Other deputies, however, scented a chance to make much bigger changes. The events of 9 Thermidor had not yet stopped 'the Terror' in its tracks—far from it. The work was still to be done, but the opportunity to effect for more substantial change was on the agenda.

Chief among early opportunists was Tallien, whose conduct on the day had won him great political capital. 'Rising on the ruins of Robespierre', as Thibaudeau noted, he became one of the defining figures of the Thermidorian period, vehemently attacking the pre-Thermidor 'system of Terror', calling for a relaxation of policies of repression he regarded as quintessentially 'Robespierrist', and campaigning for the freedom of the press and the release of unjustly gaoled political prisoners. This put a heavy strain on his relations with Billaud-Varenne, Collot d'Herbois, and Barère, whose position was further weakened by the intervention in debates of the Dantonist deputy Laurent Lecointre. Despite his huffing and puffing about his homicidal hatred of Robespierre, Lecointre had played no part in the 9 Thermidor events. But from autumn 1794, he re-entered the fray with the accusation that it was not only Robespierre but also his other colleagues in the Revolutionary Government who were responsible for 'the Terror'. Initially, this approach was widely mocked and Lecointre's sanity questioned: it seemed ridiculous to see as Robespierre's accomplices CPS members like Billaud-Varenne, Collot d'Herbois and Barère when these were the men who had led his overthrow.

Undaunted, Lecointre battled on, however, and his arguments started to be better received as the public mood changed. The trial in autumn 1794 of Jean-Baptiste Carrier, who had committed atrocities as deputy on mission in Nantes, produced public revulsion for what had occurred under the Revolutionary Government's watch. Greater press freedom allowed the wide diffusion of such accounts. A wave of prison memoirs depicting the gaols of the Terror as gothic sites of heartless cruelty made a particular impact. The revocation of the Law of 22 Prairial endorsed whole-hearted rejection of practices of revolutionary justice—it would later be followed by the outright abolition of the Revolutionary Tribunal. By the spring of 1795, public prosecutor Fouquier-Tinville had gone to the scaffold, while Collot, Billaud, and Barère, along with CGS stalwart Vadier, were arraigned for past offences under what was now universally regarded as 'the Terror'. They would be sentenced to deportation.

By then, the Convention itself had changed in significant ways. In December 1794 it had been agreed that the '73' gaoled Girondin supporters (Mercier included) should be readmitted to the assembly. In March 1795, it was the turn of the survivors of the 1793 Girondin purge. A symptomatic returnee was Maximin Isnard whose anti-Parisian comments had so enraged the sans-culottes in May 1793. The overthrow of Robespierre had been engineered by Montagnards, but these shrank to a small rump of around 70 deputies. A strong majority for the Right emerged in the Convention, and it strongly favoured a decisive move away from policies and institutions of terror. Besides changes to the CPS to reduce its authority, and the abolition of the Revolutionary Tribunal, the Jacobin Club was closed down and the social and economic policies of terror were removed. The troublesome 23 July (5 Thermidor) Wage Maximum had been withdrawn as early as 30–31 July (12–13 Thermidor), and this was followed in December 1794 by the abolition of the General Maximum, the shining symbol of the Montagnard-sans-culotte pact of Year II.

Mercier had remarked that the *journée* of 9 Thermidor was characterized by a wish for justice. In the event, what emerged less resembled justice than vengeance, from Day One onwards. Formal politics in the assembly and in the prints were increasingly complemented by street violence from retaliatory Right-wing gangs of youths—the *jeunesse dorée* or *muscadins*, marshalled by 'turncoat terrorists', Tallien and Fréron. These violently harassed the 'men of Year II', by which they meant essentially anyone who had been in a position of power under 'the Terror'. This extra-parliamentary pressure was even more intense in the provinces, moreover, where 'White Terror' was pitted against 'Red'.

The Convention was already on a path to 'depopularize' the Revolution, as one journalist put it. Deputies made the people of Paris the particular butt of their quest for vengeance. Parisians might have helped bring Robespierre down; but they had, after all, given him power in the first place, and had to be punished in a way that prevented such a thing ever happening again. The brutal purge of the Commune in the days after 9 Thermidor was followed not by the municipality's reform and the replacement of purged councillors, but by its outright abolition. The municipal council and the post of mayor were simply removed. Municipal services hitherto superintended by the Commune were placed under the authority of the central government. A purged Police Administration was appointed by and reported to the Convention under advice from the CGS. Sectional police commissaries were henceforth appointed rather than elected. The National Guard command stayed a rotational office, in line with the 9 Thermidor anti-Hanriot decree, while 'men of Year II' were expelled from National Guard battalions. The 48 sectional Revolutionary Committees were reduced into twelve Arrondissement Committees, again reporting direct to government. The electoral system at the heart of municipal government across France since 1789 now had a Parisian bypass.

If the Thermidorian Convention of Year III was no longer the Convention of Year II days, neither were the Parisian people of Year III the people of Year II. The popular unity of the night of 9–10 Thermidor soon started to crumble. The slackening of terror and the granting of greater press freedom allowed for a wider diversity of views to emerge, with the release of prisoners stoking a spirit for revenge at local as well as national level. In addition, the stabilization of the military situation post-Fleurus, and then the marked improvement in France's international fortunes, seemed to reduce the regime's need to placate the popular movement.

For much of Year II, Parisian public opinion had been dominated by the radical views of the sans-culotte movement. This had been in decline for several months before 9 Thermidor, and the *journée* released a wave of critical energy that had been pent up for some time. The ensuing months saw a rebalancing of Parisian opinion. The egalitarian aspirations implicit in the Revolutionary Government's Year II social and economic policies were subjected to withering attack. The Thermidorian elite favoured social differentiation and fostered inequality. As a result, Parisian public opinion became hopelessly fractured and a widening gulf opened between haves and have-nots.

These tensions were put into tragic relief by the exceptionally harsh winter of 1794–5. The Seine was frozen over for more than a month, crippling provisioning and etching 'Nonante-cinq' ('ninety-five') on popular memory for decades. With the abolition of the Maximum, the return to the free market, together with runaway inflation and the depreciation of the assignat, made conditions for urban consumers exceptionally challenging. Moreover, the Convention's attack on Parisian self-governance meant that there were no welfare policies worth their salt to cushion the hit, and neither a Commune nor a Jacobin Club nor a strong Montagnard deputation in the Convention to champion, channel, or cheerlead popular demands. Bread queues lengthened as hunger ravaged the masses in a way that had been forgotten, while the regime seemed indifferent to suffering. By early 1795, nostalgic evocations of the name of Robespierre began to be heard on Paris streets.

– Under Robespierre [it was reported as being said], blood flowed and there was no bread-shortage; today blood flows no longer and we lack bread. Blood must flow if we are to have bread . . .

Remaining sectional militants also began speaking warmly of the highly democratic but never-implemented 1793 Constitution.

The burgeoning social crisis came to a head in two despairing popular outbursts: the *journées* of 12 Germinal and then 1–4 Prairial Year III (1 April and 20–3 May 1795). Mass demonstrations targeted the Convention, with 'Bread and the Constitution of 1793' as their slogan. On 1 Prairial, crowds besieging the Convention (once again on the 31 May/2 June 1793 model) got out of hand, and struck down and decapitated deputy Féraud, one of Barras's doughtiest adjuncts on the night of 9 Thermidor. The assembly's widespread revulsion against this unprecedented act led to further anti-

Parisian repression, with over 2,000 arrests and a score of executions. Deputies also acted with striking harshness towards six Montagnard deputies held to have supported the social aims of the Prairial rebels following Féraud's murder. The men were sent before a Military Commission set up to sentence rioters and after a collective attempt at suicide they were executed on 17 June 1795.

The Prairial *journées* set the context for the view of the Parisian people conveyed in Courtois's 9 Thermidor report. It also cleared the ground for the creation of the new constitution, which completed the 'depopularization' of power. The violence of the Prairial episode led to the Convention rejecting the idea of an eventual implementation of the democratic 1793 constitution championed by the rebels. Instead, the Constitution of Year III (1795), which instituted the regime of the Directory from November 1795, was a liberal rather than a radical charter. Symptomatically, the universal male suffrage guaranteed by the 1793 constitution was replaced by a property franchise.

It had taken some time, but 9 Thermidor had set in train a process by which the people were disenfranchised and Parisian radicals silenced. The idea that the people of Paris had played a key role in the fall of Robespierre appeared in these circumstances unacceptable, unpalatable, and indeed implausible. The move to the Right transformed the meaning of the *journée*, at the people's expense. In a double paradox, the leading Montagnards who had organized the fall of Robespierre within the Convention and the people of Paris who led the overthrow on the city's streets were both viewed as the enablers of a figure subject to ever-increasing vilification.

Initial attacks on Robespierre in the Convention following the *journée* freely disparaged him by comparing him to tyrants of Antiquity (Pisistratus, Catiline, Julius Caesar, Nero) or more modern vintage (Cromwell). Picking up stray comments heard in debates, and following the chance discovery in searches of the Commune offices of a seal with a fleur-de-lys design, Barère added another comparator: Robespierre had aspired to be king. The idea was a somewhat desperate ploy to appeal to the wide population that they believed better versed in recent history than in lessons from Antiquity.

In a month or two, a new perspective opened up, with critics of Robespierre shifting the framework for their accusations from history ancient and modern to natural history. Focusing on Robespierre's alleged physical appearance, journalists and pamphleteers compared him to a vampire, a monster, a sphynx, a chameleon, a wolf, and especially a tiger, an animal notorious for its irrational appetite for blood. Barras's adjunct Merlin de Thionville authored a much-copied, very widely circulated *Portrait de Robespierre*, which highlighted Robespierre's feline, tigrish appearance, which cartoons and caricatures soon copied. The tiger image would run and run, underlying and seeming to justify Robespierre's reputation as a *buveur de sang* ('blood-drinker'). It received reinforcement from a pamphlet subgenre aimed at flushing Robespierre's supporters out of public life and based on the zoomorphic idea of cutting off the tyrant's tail (*la queue de Robespierre*). Comparing Robespierre to a historical tyrant suggested a tragically human dimension to his wish to dominate. In contrast, making him a monstrous, bestial, demonic specimen put him beyond the reach of humanity or rationality.

The Black Legend of Robespierre's political monstrosity was to prove amazingly resilient and long-lasting. It still surfaces in histories and biographies in our own day. From the time of the Thermidorian debates onwards, moreover, Robespierre's Black Legend was associated with a similar and no less defamatory denigration of the Parisian popular movement. It was not only Robespierre who was a *buveur de sang*, whose judgement had been fatally impaired by inward passions; this was also the stock phrase that came to be reserved for any of the popular classes who had engaged in politics in Year II. It was their passionately inflamed support for Robespierre that had made his popularity and his monstrous power possible: Robespierre's nemesis on the night of 9 Thermidor were transmuted into his cheerleaders. Only as a democratic movement emerged from the 1830s did the *buveur de sang* image and the Black Legend that yoked together Robespierre and the people of Paris begin to be challenged.

Conspiring against Robespierre: a myth?

From the day itself onwards, 9 Thermidor was swamped in talk of conspiracy. Robespierre felt he was the victim of conspiracies, while his opponents justified their action against him by the threat of the conspiracy which he had hatched to seize power. The view from 'up close' challenges these narratives at every level. It is very moot whether there was substance to any of these alleged 'conspiracies'. By the time of Thermidor, Robespierre was certainly attracting a great deal of hostility from within the political elite. Many deputies will doubtless have ardently wished for his removal and death. But imagining is not the same as doing, and the evidence of serious organized plotting against him is exiguous and largely discountable.

The most substantial 'conspiratorial' grouping within the assembly, around Laurent Lecointre and Bourdon de l'Oise, certainly talked big (and even bigger after the event). But they did nothing concrete, and their brand of opposition did not eventuate in anything that resembled logistical planning. Fouché is sometimes seen as part of the group, and his own memoirs paint him as a leading conspirator in the run-up to the day. Yet the little evidence we have suggests that he did nothing more than engage in anti-Robespierre propagandizing among his colleagues. Tallien was part of the Lecointre group, it is true. But the evidence suggests that he acted as a loner, looking for support less to his Lecointre cronies than to new-found allies on the Right, that he recruited a matter of hours before the action of the day.

Lecointre talked of a group of fellow conspirators numbering 40 or 50 deputies. That this number was so small—the total strength of the assembly was 749—highlights how equivocal many deputies were towards Robespierre. Genuine hatred in many cases was tempered by fear: the brutal fates meted out to the Girondins and Dantonists encouraged hiding heads below the parapet. In addition, however, there were some deputies from the Plain and even on the Right who felt that the removal of Robespierre would mark a shift to the Left that could make matters even worse for them. Robespierre encouraged this thinking by offering ostentatious defence of the gaoled '73', the moderate pro-Girondin deputies.

For the most part, then, deputies just rubbed along with the status quo, however disagreeable they found it. It was only when Robespierre's speech on 8 Thermidor suggested that he was wanting an immediate and scattershot intensification of Terror that they became anxious for their lives. Tallien played perfectly to this anxiety in his midnight calls on 8–9 Thermidor: Robespierre was spinning out of control, he contended, and no colleague to Left or Right was safe. The number of deputies that Tallien recruited was probably quite small: most deputies were as amazed at what was happening in the Convention on 9 Thermidor as a thunderstruck Thibaudeau.

In the blame game over 'the Terror', that Tallien and especially Lecointre initiated after 9 Thermidor, Robespierre's former CPS and CGS colleagues sought to exculpate themselves from responsibility for 'the Terror' by stressing Robespierre's monstrous authority, and also by claiming proportionate credit for conspiring against him. But here too there was gross exaggeration. There was much dissatisfaction and even hatred for

Robespierre around the CPS green table in the months before Thermidor, and a good deal of underhand dealing and Robespierre-baiting, by Carnot and Vadier in particular. That is hardly surprising, as he had become a quite impossible colleague. However if, like the Lecointre group, some members of the Committees probably talked among themselves about Robespierre's removal, they did little or nothing concrete about it. Not only did they not conspire, they went out of their way actively to dissuade others outside the committee (notably the Lecointre group) from attempting a premature move against Robespierre. Their reticence was partly due to their fear that Robespierre was simply too powerful and that his popularity would make him impossible to dislodge, at least for the moment. Some may also have cherished the vague hope, expressed by Robert Lindet, that if one gave Robespierre enough rope he might hang himself.

In addition, it is difficult to resist the feeling that Robespierre's colleagues retained a sense of loyalty to a unified Revolutionary Government and baulked at the idea of divisions which would harm the war effort. When during the negotiations of 4–5 Thermidor (22–3 July), Billaud sought to win over Robespierre by saying, 'We have come so far together . . .', he was not simply making sycophantic small talk. It was true. The long-term domestic goals of all the men around the CPS green table had not been so very different. The core members had been on the same side on all the major issues throughout the Revolution. All accepted the need to continue the use of terror, and many prioritized the workings of social institutions over the return to the 1793 constitution. This was as true for Collot, Billaud, and Barère as for Robespierre and Saint-Just. Much of what separated the two sides came down to issues of personality rather than ideological differences. There was divergence over how some of the institutions might work, with Robespierre's peers notably anxious about the role that Robespierre seemed to be giving himself in the Cult of Supreme Being. But they had only latterly fallen out seriously. The fact that they were open to working with him until nearly midday on 9 Thermidor suggests that he was far from the monstrous dictator of reputation whose image they later portrayed. Nor were they the inspired dragon-slayers of their later imaginings.

In the Thermidorian atmosphere in which negotiating with Robespierre was equated with supping with the Devil, CPS members downplayed these earlier commonalities and occluded their willingness to cooperate with Robespierre. Things look different when seen from 'up close'. The negotiations with Robespierre and Saint-Just seem to have been a genuine effort to find common ground and to heal divisions. Yet even as their patched-up truce was unravelling, Robespierre's colleagues still nurtured lingering hope that he might be brought back onside. Despite his highly provocative conduct since 5 Thermidor (23 July), they determined in advance not to attack him on 9 Thermidor but rather to remove Hanriot from the command of the National Guard, thus depriving Robespierre, they calculated, of his ability to do harm. Tellingly, the Proclamation that Barère drew up that night made no mention of Robespierre at all. In addition, the men basically agreed to hold off any further action until Saint-Just returned for discussions before the Convention met next morning. It was only when he missed the rendezvous that they gave up on Robespierre and Saint-Just altogether.

If there was a conspiracy to topple Robespierre, it began at or around midnight with Tallien's late night visits to deputies of the Right and Centre. Tallien did not, it should be stressed, extend those calls to the Committees of Government. Even at this late hour, there was no unified plot to overthrow Robespierre. The reactions in the Convention hall at midday show that Tallien not only took Robespierre by surprise—he took the government by surprise too.

The CPS's success on the day owed a great deal to the way that Billaud, Collot, and Barère exploited the flying start that Tallien had given them, pivoting around and improvising in a way that unified the Convention completely. They did this not simply against Robespierre but also—in a way that no one had in any way anticipated—so as to implicate his two allies, Saint-Just and Couthon, and his brother and Le Bas. What occurred on 9 Thermidor was a masterclass in extemporization by the CPS.

The improvisational aspect of the Convention and the CPS's role in the fall of Robespierre was also evident later in the day, in the way the government overcame the dangerous military thrust of the Commune at 9.00 p.m. that evening. The assembly was struggling with the real prospect of losing the day altogether, with the Commune's forces led by Hanriot and Coffin-hal baying at the door, and with artilleryman Cosme Pionnier training his loaded cannon on the assembly. It was at that moment that the Convention took the momentous step of appointing as commander of the city's armed forces one of their own, Barras. Crucial in the outcome of the day, this decree merged legislative, executive, and military power to create a kind of legislator on horseback. The Paris National Guard had reported to a commander appointed by the Commune since 1789. Since 1790, legislation placed all responsibility for law and order in the hands of municipalities.

The Convention's decree was thus not only a vital step in ensuring the day's success. It was also a signal break with the past—and one that was entirely unplanned, arising as it did from the heat of the moment and the tightness of the spot in which the Convention found itself.

From this act of inspired unplanned improvisation, moreover, a political tradition was born. In the final *journées* of the Thermidorian period, Parisian protests would be put down in the same way, by the Convention appointing one of their own to act as generalissimo. For the Prairial disturbances, the post fell to Delmas, one of Barras's adjuncts on 9 Thermidor. The same line of defence was offered in October when the assembly faced a final act of Parisian resistance to the new constitution in the *journée* of Vendémiaire (5 October 1795). Deputies fell back on using Barras, whose success was immensely assisted by his use of his young protégé, Napoleon Bonaparte, a legislator on horseback in the making, if ever there was one.

Robespierre conspirator?

We have suggested that the idea of planned conspiratorial machinations against Robespierre in advance of 9 Thermidor was largely a myth, fabricated in the post-Thermidorian atmosphere of accusation and justification. Can the same be said of Robespierre's 'conspiracy', on which his fall was predicated? From that very afternoon, all the talk was of his conspiracy. Yet it is far from easy to identify what Robespierre's aims and intentions were on 9 Thermidor. Not only did he keep his cards close to his chest, he was silenced in the Convention, and made few utterances through the day. From midnight, his facial injury prohibited speech, and he was not granted his wish for pen and paper.

The question of Robespierre's intentions is often muddied by claims that his behaviour at the end of his life manifested some form of either mental or physical sickness. This scenario is implausible, however, when seen from 'up close'. He was certainly under stress, but frankly in government circles in the first *décade* of Thermidor, who wasn't? When ill earlier in the year, his health was widely reported and indeed commented on by himself. There was none of that leading up to 9 Thermidor. He missed Convention and CPS meetings but was an assiduous regular at the Jacobin Club. It has also been argued that the language of martyrdom and victimhood evident in his 8 Thermidor speech suggests some kind of mental crisis. But such language was neither exceptional nor symptomatic. If anything, it comprised Robespierre's signature trope. He had used it literally dozens of times in this way before. It should not be taken literally as a serious death wish or as a planned objective but rather a token of his stoical willingness to die for the cause.

On the basis of that speech, moreover, it is difficult to argue that he was aiming to initiate a move away from terror, and overall, Robespierre outlined objectives that were fully in line with his earlier positions. They revolved around extensive purges—purges of the CGS, CPS, and Cambon's Finance Committee, cleansing the government bureaucracy, especially the CGS's spies, and the removal of at least some of his opponents within the Convention. In association with those purges, his speech categorically defended the key institutions and practices of terror—Committees of Government, Revolutionary Tribunal, CPS Police Bureau, repression of the press, no quarter to the English on the battlefield, deferral of the 1793 constitution, and so on.

It is true that Robespierre's speeches in the last months of his life had allowed his audience a tantalizing glimpse of a better world in the future beyond the need for terror and characterized by still-to-be-defined social institutions. Still, there seems little doubt that he recognized that there would be a need for violence to get there: in sum, an intensification rather than a relaxation of terror. He certainly envisaged greater clemency and beneficence being extended towards patriots; but in his Manichean vision, this had to be matched by a merciless campaign against all counter-revolutionaries, wherever they were to be found. Given the range of targets that the 8 Thermidor speech indicated, the number of potential victims would be far higher than the 'five or six' promised by Couthon. As the historian Alphonse Aulard remarked, his listeners on 8 Thermidor thought he sounded less like a man determined to die for the cause than a man who wanted to kill. And a man who wanted to kill quite profusely, it seemed.

The personal attacks that Robespierre launched, with manifestly mortiferous intent, on 8 Thermidor were not targeted at colleagues for wanting to continue the Terror. He wanted that too, maybe more than some of them. They were directed at individuals who in his view were corrupt. Terror had to be continued so as to root out corruption. His 8 Thermidor speech which made this very clear, was in a way a reversion to type. His lifelong mission was as critic of power and as whistleblower against any move towards corruption at the heart of government. Viewed from 'up close', it appears that this remained his goal right through to his death, even though he had personally shared in power for a year.

If we accept that Robespierre's objective was to purge every part of Revolutionary Government, how was he to achieve this? It is conceivable that he thought that simply the force of his words on 9 Thermidor could do the trick. Yet given his reception on 8 Thermidor, this seems implausible. It is also difficult to imagine that he could form a durable strategic alliance with the moderate *hommes de bien* whose favour he planned to curry on 9 Thermidor as a means of keeping his Montagnard enemies at bay. It might have given him some breathing space in the short term, but he must have been aware that most of the Right and the Centre hated him intensely, while his inclusion in his list of targeted enemies of centrist deputies like Cambon and Dubois-Crancé on 8 Thermidor hardly inspired them with confidence in any new-found moderation on his part.

The likely scenario that Robespierre envisaged was the exertion of popular pressure on the assembly on the lines of the *journées* of 31 May and 2 June 1793. When Billaud accused him of planning such a coup for 9 Thermidor, he responded with a vehement denial. But this is most likely explained, as I have suggested, by the fact that he had not in fact been planning the move for that day, but for a later date. As we have seen, no evidence exists of conspiratorial machinations with others to bring his plans to fruition on 9 Thermidor. We lack evidence that those subsequently viewed as his alleged fellow conspirators and who would probably have played starring parts in any such coup—the Payan brothers, Dumas, Herman, Hanriot, and others—were engaged in preparations of any sort. Moreover, Saint-Just's undelivered speech on the day, for example, suggests that even his closest political ally was moving out of his immediate ambit and mindset. And after his Jacobin Club apotheosis on 8 Thermidor, Robespierre did not go on to engage in nocturnal networking. He went home, reassured his landlord, and slept the night away.

Furthermore, Robespierre's sheer discombobulation on 9 Thermidor, and the muddle that Hanriot, Payan, and Fleuriot-Lescot made of insurrection similarly suggests an absence of any kind of planning or prior coordination by him or his main supporters. The surprise, consternation, and puzzlement that their actions caused among the sections and in the Jacobin Club confirmed that neither Robespierre nor his supporters had conducted logistical work among the people of Paris in preparation for some sort of coup on 9 Thermidor. The 'conspirators' were improvising throughout the day.

Everything points towards Robespierre looking for a popular intervention to purge the Convention at a later date. We have suggested that his behaviour in the weeks leading up to 9 Thermidor strongly indicate that he saw the *journées* of 31 May and 2 June 1793 as providing the script to follow in order to achieve his objective. This was not only because those *journées* had been successful, but also because they conformed to the notion that Robespierre had of his relationship with the people. The people, for Robespierre, were the fundamental source of sovereignty, the alpha and omega of legitimate power. His very last known words in the Maison Commune in the early hours of 10 Thermidor associated his own destiny with theirs. Even though the people delegated power to elected representatives, Robespierre maintained that it retained powers of oversight and surveillance in regard to the national assembly. If the people lost confidence in its representatives, then it could and should resist oppression, as was constitutionally its right.

Robespierre regarded his role not as a potential popular leader—he was anything but a street activist—but rather as a patriot who could use his oratory to recount 'useful truths' (to cite the 8 Thermidor speech) about the state of politics to the people. It was his way of speaking truth to power—the legitimate power of the people. His task was thus to hold back the unleashing of popular force until the moment when the people had grasped its role as historical actor and was ready to move. Timing was vital for success. A few days before 9 Thermidor he warned that the moment was not yet right. This echoed exactly his conduct in April and early May 1793. The people still needed time, patience, and Robespierre's application. The date 9 Thermidor thus would not mark the dénouement of a deep-laid plot. Rather, it was a step in a process whose end was still a little way off. He had only got partway through the script. The day was a complete surprise for him, one that took him off guard when he still had his eye on a further horizon.

Had Robespierre's timing worked, had a popular purge of Revolutionary Government been carried out in the near future, what then? We should discount Barère's claim, in the immediate aftermath of 9 Thermidor, that Robespierre was grooming himself for kingship. Robespierre also vehemently rejected the idea that he wanted to be a dictator too. 'If I were dictator,' Robespierre claimed on 8 Thermidor, as he sought to contradict his enemies, 'they would be grovelling at my feet.' He was intensely irritated by accusations about his ambitions, which had followed him around since the autumn of 1792. He seems to have held that no would-be dictator would step back from action and encourage the people to be the key protagonist when the fate of the Revolution was in the balance. His sincere dedication to the cause of the people proofed him against any claim to dictatorship—at least in his own eyes. Others saw it rather differently, as he realized. He placed blame for the accusations on English propaganda, whose targeting of his person seemed to form part of that Foreign Plot of whose existence he was so convinced. Carnot's throwing the 'ridiculous dictators' taunt in his and Saint-Just's faces around the green table will have merely confirmed him in his anxiety about the tentacles of the Foreign Plot reaching inside and corrupting the government of which he formed part.

It is not difficult to see how Robespierre's colleagues in government feared his ambitions. His obsessive talk over his last months of 'arrests, newspapers and the Revolutionary Tribunal' and his erratic behaviour caused them increasingly to doubt his judgement too. They worried about the power he, Couthon, and Saint-Just were building up through the Police Bureau—a quite misguided assessment of a lacklustre body. Had the purges of his enemies in government, legislature, and bureaucracy that he called for on 8 Thermidor been effected, however, he would achieve a level of authority, probably from within a revamped CPS, a Convention purged of his enemies and the news media curtly brought to heel, that no individual had enjoyed since 1789. Nor did he seem to be viewing this level of power in the mode of a temporary stewardship in the style of Cincinnatus, a name he seems never to have used. Once he had achieved that personal authority there seemed to be no exit strategy. This seemed to his colleagues to represent a scenario for marking out with purges the road to some form of personal power, that they were happy to call tyranny.

The Commune and the people

The Paris Commune had served as the leading edge of Parisian popular action since the July crisis of 1789, through the overthrow of the monarchy in 1792 and beyond. The night of 9 Thermidor ended this role within the Revolution once and for all. When push came to shove, the people of Paris refused to follow the Commune's marching orders. The huge counter-mobilization that the Convention was able to muster late in the evening highlighted popular acclaim for national over municipal authority. It involved all 48 sections, and numbers involved dwarfed the strength of forces that had gathered outside the Maison Commune earlier in the evening. The achievement was all the greater for being carried out at night under cover of darkness. The level of enthusiasm shown the next day for the guillotining of Robespierre underlined the very widespread popularity of his overthrow.

This historic demotion of the Commune in Parisian political life owed much to the Convention's superior strategic sense. In addition, one should also note the woeful performance of the Commune on the day. The Commune's leadership of the insurrection was highly deficient. Recovering from a slow start, the Commune had built up a powerful force by early evening, with contingents representing nearly half of the city's population. But incompetent leadership ruined its chances. NG Commander Hanriot was wildly erratic, got himself needlessly arrested for over-impetuousness, and missed a chance of seizing the Convention when it was at his mercy. Mayor Fleuriot and National Agent Payan, both new to insurrectionary command, were well out of their depth. Their poor tactical decisions and organizational blunders are too numerous to list. Major gaffes included agreeing to Coffinhal's larger expeditionary force later in the evening (whose only result was the release of the ineffectual Hanriot), the fast-and-loose policy of the *consigne*, and their ill-considered reaction to the outlaw decree.

The Commune really never worked out what its strategy was. Were they going to start the insurrection on the spot or on the morrow? Would they purge the Convention of ringleaders on the model of the 31 May/2 June *journées*—or remove it completely from power, in the style of 10 August 1792? What level of violence was anticipated: was the aim a bloodless coup to take power, or a bloodbath initiated by shootings at dawn? The answers to these questions are as unclear to historians as they appear to have been to participants in the *journée*. With this level of confusion in its ranks, it is little wonder that the Commune found it impossible to identify a mere 24 councillors to go out into the city at midnight and get its message across. The performance of the twelve adjuncts they did manage to raise was pitiful when compared with Barras's twelve deputy adjuncts.

In retrospect, probably the most egregious of the serial blunders the Commune committed on the night of 9 Thermidor was its decision to convoke sectional general assemblies. Those assemblies had become rather uninspired talking-shops in recent months. Yet once summoned by tocsin and *générale*, they were instantly transformed into an open forum on which sectional opinion could express itself. The Commune paid the price for unleashing the Parisian people's voice which had lain semi-dormant, as that voice expressed itself overwhelmingly in favour of the Convention.

In the aftermath of the *journée*, radicals claimed that the sectional assemblies had been invaded by 'moderate' opinion. Doubtless there is an element of truth in this, though one should note that 'moderate' was a term used indiscriminately by sans-culotte militants to designate those who did not share their views. But this overlooks the fact that many newcomers and returnees to assemblies were from the Left as well as the Right. Sectional purges over the previous months had targeted heterodox opinion on both ends of the political spectrum. Assemblies contained radicals as well as moderates, and indeed, at every stage of the night we find individuals with impeccable sans-culotte credentials making strong and principled contributions to the Convention's cause—from Cité section's Van Heck (whom Robespierre called an aristocrat counter-revolutionary to his face), to Révolutionnaire's Bodson brothers, to Réunion's Étienne Michel, to Montagne section's Jean-Baptiste Loys, and to many more besides. The coalition in the Convention which toppled Robespierre had been a cross-party grouping led by Montagnards. In much the same way, the popular contribution to his fall came from individuals from across the full political spectrum.

Public opinion redivivus

The 9 Thermidor *journée* demonstrated that public opinion was not as dead and buried under Revolutionary Government as is sometimes claimed. The Committees of Government had silenced monarchist and counter-revolutionary forces in the city and muted Right-wing views, but it proved quite unable to erase all debate within the public sphere. Analysis from 'up close' reveals that, despite the government crackdown on sans-culotte institutions, Parisians made free use of the weapons of the weak developed prior to 1789, that were available to them. They were still obdurately resilient under measures limiting freedom of expression, and remained true to their *frondeur* inheritance that Mercier had celebrated. Much public debate and dissent had gone underground—but it was still there, if one knew how and where to look for it—in queues, bars, gatherings in public places, and also, for those who could decipher the codes, in newspapers, pamphlets, and theatres, prime locations for Parisian *frondeur* wit and fighting spirit. Furthermore, some spaces of freedom still existed, where opinions could be openly expressed. Outside the home, most prominent among these were the companies and guardrooms of the National Guard. It was this civilian militia who formed the vanguard of popular support for the Convention and opposition to Robespierre and the Commune on the night of 9 Thermidor.

National Guardsmen had become far more representative of Parisian opinion than sectional institutions, whose autonomy had weakened under government pressure. Perhaps, however, historians have taken sans-culotte claims to 'represent' the people of Paris too literally. In fact, despite its semi-hegemonic status in parts of 1793, 'sans-culotte opinion' was never more than a subset within the broader spectrum of Parisian opinion. Politically active sans-culottes never formed a majority in the city. In addition, the policy over the previous year, encouraged by government, of conducting political purges of sectional authorities and political clubs and associations meant that they had been increasingly groomed into conformity with government views and thereby lost much of their ability to reflect grass-roots opinion.

As the city-wide political mobilization of 9 Thermidor suggests, Parisians might have tired of Robespierre but they had not tired of political life. Parisians remained, in the words of a pamphlet describing the *journée*, 'the generous and intrepid athletes of liberty' who were only too keen to flex their muscles in the Republic's defence. The tendency among many historians to see the night as one in which Parisians revealed political indifference is quite wrong. By turning out in such large numbers to support a national assembly voted by universal male suffrage over against a municipal government increasingly out of touch with the people it was supposed to represent, they sent an immensely powerful political message. Furthermore, although we should not underestimate the impact of Barras and his adjuncts across the city in ensuring the success of the Convention, we should not lose from sight the cross-sectional fraternization movement which rose up spontaneously on the night, out of the revivified sectional Assemblies, and made the popular and Convention victory so complete. The movement proved crucial in bringing the sections up to speed on what was happening in the city and in aligning them with the cause of the Convention.

There were many emotions on display throughout the fast-moving hours of the *journée* of 9 Thermidor, with strong feelings heightened by the lack of hard information forthcoming in the context of an extremely tense situation. Unplanned and unexpected, the day was riven with gossip and rumours that further generated anxiety and fear. Fear of the attack on individuals many regarded as model patriots. Fear of a popular day of action that could get out of hand and end up with street killings and prison massacres. Fear that judicial terror would be ramped up. Fear that civil war might result. Fear that Paris could have meted out on it the exterminatory violence with which Isnard had threatened in May 1793 and which the Revolutionary Government had imposed on Federalist Lyon. Fear, especially as the night wore on, that one might end up on the losing side of the battle and be subject to harsh punishment.

Undoubtedly, the fear that counted for most on the streets of the city was the fear that counter-revolution was lurking out there somewhere, threatening the gains of Revolution since 1789. Barère, moreover, had brilliantly made this anxiety into a massive mobilizing agent for the Convention. 'Citizens,' his proclamation, read and read aloud across the city all night, had demanded, 'do you wish to lose in a single day six years of revolution, of sacrifices and of courage? Do you wish to go back beneath the yoke that you broke?'

The words played into the strong popular attachment in Paris to the Convention for safeguarding the gains of the Revolution. Writing to Robespierre and the CPS on the eve of 9 Thermidor, the spy Rousseville had not been wrong: 'the people retains confidence in the Convention'. Areas of discord still existed, but people could remember what Paris was like before 1789. The Revolution had delivered improvements in many aspects of their everyday lives: the abolition of feudalism and the old status order and the advent of personal and economic freedoms, democratic practices, representative government and all the rest. At sectional level, alongside the political manoeuvrings, new administrative forms—civil committees, justices of the peace, beneficence committees—delivered significant local service. Revolutionary gains might be much attenuated under Revolutionary Government, and Parisians felt they had every right to criticize. But they also accepted that the government was defending the Revolution and defending France against allied forces threatening a return to the Ancien Régime. This was a war that had to be won, and Revolutionary Government was winning it. At this moment, Parisians were still willing to cut Revolutionary Government some slack.

LE TRIOMPHE

DES PARISIENS,

Dans les Journées des 9 et 10 Thermidor,
avec l'abrégé de la Lettre trouvée dans
la paillasse de la soi-disant mere de
Dieu, adressée à Robespierre.

V IVE la République une indivisible et impérissable! vive la représentation Nationale, si digne de notre amour et de notre reconnoissance! vive le peuple Français, qui ne peut rien souffrir d'impur dans son sein! vivent les Parisiens, ces généreux et intrépides atheletes de la liberté, qui n'ont point

A

Figure 14. 'Triomphe des Parisiens' saluting 'the generous and intrepid athletes of liberty' (British Library, French Revolution Pamphlets)

The people's choice: institutions over personalities

If Parisians on 9 Thermidor acted out their pre-existing confidence in the Convention, they also by the same token demonstrated opposition towards the person of Robespierre. This owed something to the CPS's improvisational skills. By presenting Robespierre as a hypocritical conspirator against the Revolution, the CPS consciously played to a trope that had significant purchase in popular political culture: from Mirabeau, through Lafayette and Dumouriez, to Hébert and Danton, the idea had played that it was sometimes the most apparently patriotic of political figures who were in fact most suspect. Ironically, this critique of political hero-worship formed a lesson in republican pedagogy that Robespierre had done more than most to popularize. His whistle-blowing against political celebrities from early on in the Revolution, combined with his role in explaining the alleged treachery of Dantonists and Hébertists in spring 1794, stressed the need to be vigilant against patriots who hid their evil intent and corruption beneath protestations of patriotism. This narrative was easily fashioned so as to fit Robespierre himself like a glove, and to make the charge of conspiracy only too plausible. A very firmly held theme within the comments that sectional delegations made to the Convention on the night was the priority that needed to be shown to republican institutions rather than over persons. The same discourse studded discussions and debates all night. 'Homomania' was unacceptable in the Republic, and so Robespierre's very celebrity made his own conspiracy only too credible.

Although it necessarily took coded forms, moreover, expressions of hostility and resistance to Robespierre had been circulating in the public sphere before Thermidor. 'Tyrant-talk' was in the air. His distancing himself from government was puzzling and open to interpretations that did not flatter him. Even some of his most fervent admirers, like Herman and Lanne, found it difficult to understand what game he was playing. There was, moreover, residual distrust of the new phenomenon of political celebrity: 'idolatry', it was widely believed, was the terrain of 'women and the weak-minded'. It is also the case that Robespierre himself showed only partial understanding of the emergent rules of celebrity. Celebrities did not go sulking in their tent for six weeks without losing much of their aura. Life, and public opinion, moved on. By 9 Thermidor they had moved beyond Robespierre. Parisians were being risk-averse in refusing to follow a single individual who would lead them who knew where, and in putting their trust in republican institutions. To rely on celebrity was a perilous way forward, as indeed Robespierre had always told them. In a way, Robespierre's fall was both self-inflicted and his greatest contribution to democracy.

The events of 9 Thermidor showed popular acceptance of the Convention's view that the defence of the Republic depended on the fall of Robespierre. Action on the night was not therefore an attack on the system of government in place—or 'the Terror', as it was subsequently called. Of course there were many on the Right—in the Convention as on the city streets—who rejoiced in attacking the system as a whole (though some feared that what might follow Robespierre could be even worse). But the common denominator, the rationale for armed mobilization and the red thread through the ups-and-downs of the night was to defend the Republic by rescuing rather than replacing the threatened Convention.

The 9 Thermidor *journée* did not mark the climax of a build-up of popular resentment against 'Terror' (to utilize a term that was not yet current). There was certainly hostility towards some policies of Revolutionary Government. The Wage Maximum was one source of discord, although it was the Commune rather than the Convention, and Payan and Fleuriot rather than Robespierre, who were held to be responsible for it. The government's dwindling commitment to egalitarianism in social policy also had a damaging impact, while there was a growing swell of public discomfort over some of the things going on at the Revolutionary Tribunal. Curiously, perhaps the most telling symptom of discord was the manifest overreaction by Robespierre, Barère, the Jacobins, and the Commune over the fraternal banquet movement triggered by victory at Fleurus. The movement originated and spread spontaneously and quite independently of the structures of central or local government. This independence of mind on the part of Parisians seemed massively threatening to the men in power. It was a reminder of the limits of the government's ability to control Parisian opinion. Parisians didn't need prompts from government to be fraternally patriotic over victories at the front—any more than they needed permission to set in train the fraternization movement across the sections on 9 Thermidor.

Parisians mobilized on 9 Thermidor to defend the Convention and the Republic against a conspiracy, even though, as I have suggested, there was a strong imaginary element in Robespierre's 'conspiracy'. There was little or no logistical planning in advance of the day, by either Robespierre or his opponents. The day was not pre-planned. It just happened. After the event it seemed that it had to have happened—but that was a combined result of

20/20 hindsight and the quickly shaping ideological agenda across the Thermidorian period that I have delineated. What transpired on 9 Thermidor was not a move to overthrow a system of government but to defend it against alleged conspirators. It would only be the passage of time that rewrote the script in such a way that the day was held to have been an attack on one man and the system of government that he managed.

The system of government did not recover from the impact of 9 Thermidor. In that sense the *journée* deserves to retain its pivotal place in histories of the Revolution. But ultimately, the 'Terror' was only overthrown by the Thermidorian regime which coined the term. In crushing what they named the Terror, the Thermidorians also destroyed much of the democratic promise and the progressive social and economic policies that have also characterized the period of Revolutionary Government before 9 Thermidor. The ultimate irony was that the person who, in the early part of his career, expressed belief in those values most luminously—and in a way that can speak to us still—was Maximilien Robespierre, the great loser of 9 Thermidor.

NOTES

ABBREVIATIONS

AAG   Archives administratives de la Guerre
ADP   Archives départementales de Paris
AHRF   *Annales historiques de la Révolution française*
AP   *Archives parlementaires de 1787 à 1860, recueil complet des débats législatifs et politiques des Chambres françaises.* Multiple editors, 102 volumes at present, Paris, 1867-present (Volume 93 unless otherwise stated).
APP   Archives de la préfecture de police, Paris
Atlas   *Atlas de la Révolution française, 11: Paris,* Émile Ducoudray, R. Monnier, & D. Roche, eds. Paris: ÉHESS, 2000.
BHVP   Bibliothèque historique de la ville de Paris
BNF   Bibliothèque nationale de France
B&R   *Histoire parlementaire de la Révolution française,* P. J. B. Buchez & P. C Roux, eds. 40 vols. Paris: Paulin, 1834–8.
Caron   *Paris pendant la terreur. Rapports des agents secrets du ministre de l'Intérieur, publiés pour la Société d'histoire contemporaine,* P. Caron, ed. 7 vols. Paris: Picard, 1914.
Courtois I   E. B. Courtois, *Rapport fait au nom de la commission chargée de l'examen des papiers trouvés chez Robespierre et ses complices.* Paris, Imprimerie nationale des lois, 1795.
Courtois II E. B. Courtois, *Rapport sur les événements du 9 thermidor, précédé d'une préface en réponse aux détracteurs de cette mémorable journée.* Paris, Imprimerie nationale, 1795.
CPS   *Recueil des actes du Comité de salut public avec la correspondance officielle des représentants en mission et le registre du Conseil exécutif provisoire,* A. Aulard ed. 28 vols. Paris: Imprimerie nationale, 1889–1951 (Volume xv unless otherwise stated).
d.   dossier
DHRF   *Dictionnaire historique de la Révolution française,* A. Soboul, ed. Paris: Presses universitaires de France, 1989.
FHS   French Historical Studies
Hamel   E. Hamel, *Histoire de Robespierre: d'après des papiers de famille, les sources originales et des documents entièrement inédits.* 3 vols. Paris, A. Lacroix, Verboeckhoven, & Cie, 1865.
Jacobins   *La Société des Jacobins. Recueil des documents pour l'histoire du Club des Jacobins de Paris,* A. Aulard, ed., 6 vols. Paris: Jouaust, Noblet, and Quantin, 1889–97. (Volume vi unless otherwise stated).
NG   National Guard
NP   L. S. Mercier, *Le nouveau Paris,* ed. J.-C. Bonnet. Paris, Mercure de France, 1984.

OCR	Maximilien Robespierre, *Œuvres complètes*, E. Hamel, ed. 11 vols. Paris: Société des Etudes Robespierristes, 1910–67.
Papiers	*Papier inédits trouvés chez Robespierre, Saint-Just, Payan, etc supprimés ou omis par Courtois*. 3 vols. Paris, Baudouin frères, 1828.
pi.	Document number *pièce*
pl.	plaque (bound set of documents)
pr.	present-day
S&M	A. Soboul & R. Monnier, *Répertoire du personnel sectionnaire parisien en l'an II*. Paris, Publications de la Sorbonne, 1985.
SCD	P. Sainte-Claire Deville, *La Commune de l'an II: vie et mort d'une assemblée révolutionnaire*. Paris, Plon, 1946.
TP	L. S. Mercier, *Le Tableau de Paris*. 2 vols. ed. J.-C. Bonnet. Paris, Mercure de France, 1994.

To reduce space, I have not indicated location for manuscripts at the Archives nationales. All manuscript call marks are thus from the Archives nationales unless otherwise stated.

INTRODUCTION: THE FALL OF ROBESPIERRE UP CLOSE (PP. 1–7)

p. 1   **'From up close, things are different':** Chapter 248, 'Tout est optique' in *NP*, p. 881 (written from the vantage-point of 1798). For biographical information on Mercier, see the excellent editorial material in Jean-Claude Bonnet's editions of his *Tableau de Paris* (1780–8) and *Le Nouveau Paris* (1799) (both 1994). See also Béclard (1903).

p. 1   **Time seemed to speed up in 1789:** Boissy d'Anglas's speech in the Convention on 23 June 1795 is cited in Perovic (2015), p. 180. This sense of time accelerating in the late eighteenth century is explored by Koselleck (1985) and Hunt (2008). For discussion on this point, I also thank Jonathan Sachs (and see Sachs [2019]).

p. 1   **not giving an exact time:** For an example, see the testimony of Cn. Gouin, Fraternité NG battalion second-in-command, in his report at AFII 47 pl. 365, pi. 8.

p. 2   **'can one write such a history':** *NP*, p. 881. Mercier's words in the last part of the quotation are 'Car tel événement a été produit d'une manière si inattendue [qu']il semble avoir été créé et non engendré . . .'.

p. 2   **French Revolutionary Calendar:** See Shaw (2011) and Perovic (2015).

p. 4   **'popular movement':** Classic works on the popular movement and the sans-culottes: Soboul (1958), Cobb (1987), Rudé (1959), and more recently Burstin (2005, 2013) and Sonenscher (2008).

p. 4   **democratic space:** Woloch (1994).

p. 4   **'Federalist Revolt':** See Hanson (2003); and for how this led into the period of Revolutionary Government, see Biard & Linton (2020).

p. 4   **Committee of Public Safety:** The best introduction remains the classic Palmer (1941).

p. 5   **Maximilien Robespierre:** For key studies of Robespierre, see Note on Sources, p. 533.

p. 6 **'Paris is so big':** *NP*, p. 644.

p. 6 **no chance for the environs:** Some villages on the edge of the city as it then was (and which now fall within Paris's circumscription) did hear of what was taking place during the day (notably Bercy, Montmartre, and Belleville). But they remained external to the action. For the swiftness of the conclusion, see Baczko (1989).

p. 6 **archival documentation:** The sources for the study are briefly passed under review in Jones (2014); and below, p. 533, Note on Sources.

p. 7 **'A fact that seems minor':** Barras commanded armed forces within the city from the night of 9 Thermidor. There is an example of the order in W 501 d. 3. See also below, p. 7.

p. 7 **a report on the day:** This was E. B. Courtois, *Rapport fait au nom de la commission chargée de l'examen des papiers trouvés chez Robespierre et ses complices* (Paris, 1795).

p. 7 **'at once terrible and singular':** *NP*, p. 446.

p. 7 **Changing our customary focus:** On this approach, through micro-history and *jeu d'échelles* (changing scales, changing focus), see esp. Revel (1996) and Ghobrial (2019).

PRELUDE: AROUND MIDNIGHT (PP. 11–24)

p. 11 **Pierre-Henri Rousseville rents a room:** Although most residences in Paris by 1794 had numbers, these were based on an arbitrary system which is impossible to decipher. We do know, however, that Robespierre's dwelling at 366 corresponds to pr. 398 Rue Saint-Honoré, while Rousseville's was about a quarter of a mile along the road to the east, at pr. 297. Both locations are in the pr. Ie., as is the Place de la Révolution, pr. Place de la Concorde. For the residence's location and the tumbrils, see Hillairet (1997), ii, p. 439, and a reference to the lodging at ADP A20 (arrestations). There are brief biographies of Rousseville in Caron (1914), i, pp. XLII–XLVI; and Calvet (1941), pp. 62–5. Written in the late 1790s, the anonymous hatchet-job, *Aperçus sur la conduite en politique de Rousseville, inspecteur général de la police*, contains useful biographical information. (Copy in ADP, 1AZ74). The Caron volumes contain Rousseville's reports to the Minister of the Interior in 1793–4. For his work outside Paris, see Cobb (1975), esp. pp. 98–138. Most of the reports on which Cobb drew are located at F7 4781–4 and F7 3688. The report discussed may be found at F7 4781 d. Auteuil & Passy. See too his personal dossier in F7 4775/2. Here he denies working individually for Robespierre; but his letters to the CPS were directed through their Police Bureau of which Robespierre was a member. The Bureau's archives contain summaries of Rousseville's reports: see esp. F7 3822. See also below, pp. 122–3.

p. 13 **denouncing Dossonville:** F7 4680 d. Dossonville (though note that the contents of the file have become dispersed throughout the box). See too files at F7 6318B and F7 4774/75 d. Pigasse or Pigace. D'Hauterive (1928) is a serviceable biography. Dossonville's name comes up frequently throughout the alphabetical police files, F7 4557–4775 (as do those of Rousseville and Héron). For an outline of his powers in a letter from the CGS to the Bonne-Nouvelle section, dated 18 Pluviôse II, see F7 4680, which also contains the Amis-de-la-Patrie denunciation.

p. 14 **the Police Bureau:** Ording (1930), the standard source. See too below, pp. 122–4. For Couthon and Saint-Just, see below, pp. 49–50 and 85–6.

p. 14 **Rousseville is a true patriot:** Using the Index and the supplementary indices to CPS (while noting that Aulard sometimes gets Rousseville's name wrong), one observes a high incidence of acts relating to Rousseville which are either in Robespierre's handwriting or signed by him, and in many cases only by him.

p. 14 **a quiet warning whistle:** Caron (1914), i, p. 3.

p. 14 **reporting on counter-revolutionary wrongdoings:** This passage draws on F7 4781–4; F7 4775/2 d. Rousseville; and Cobb (1975), pp. 98–138. The Law of 27 Germinal II (16 April 1794), introduced by Robespierre's ally Saint-Just, banned aristocrats from Paris.

p. 15 **'seeing what a tyrant looked like':** AP 91, pp. 32–3.

p. 15 **taking British prisoners of war:** For the broader context of the law, which was not generally applied, see Jones & Macdonald (2018).

p. 15 **'full of confidence in the Convention':** F7 4781: 'l'esprit public de Paris: le peuple est plein de confiance en la Convention'.

p. 15 **chalk signs:** See the letter sent to the Commune, 29 Messidor: BHVP, ms. 741, pi. 157. Thanks to Simon Macdonald for this reference. According to the *Almanach national*, over 20 deputies resided on the Rue Traversière. The street was subsumed within the Avenue de l'Opéra (pr. Ie. & IIe.) in the nineteenth century. The other incidents were noted within the Convention from early Thermidor: see AP, pp. 368–70 (2 Thermidor), 450–3 (5 Thermidor) and 514–15 (7 Thermidor). The news was also carried in the *Moniteur* and other newspapers. For bread queues, see below, pp. 104–5 and for the 'fraternal banquets', pp. 112–3.

p. 16 **Alexandre Vernet:** Vernet's dossier is located in police files at APP A70 (Arsenal). The street, renamed in 1817, is pr. Rue de La Reynie (Ie. & IVe.) The Place du Trône-Renversé is pr. Place de la Nation (XIe. & XIIe.).

p. 16 **'sans-culotte':** Cf. Wrigley (2002), pp. 183–227. For the history of the term, Sonenscher (2008), pp. 57–63. For Robespierre's vestimentary correctness, see Thompson (1968 edn), pp. 273–4; and Ribeiro (1988), p. 70. Deputies conspicuously wearing sans-culotte attire included Chabot, Granet, and Thibaudeau: Baudot (1893), p. 108.

p. 16 **men of his social type:** See the still classic Soboul (1958); and Burstin (2005b). For the representation of the luxury trades among sans-culotte militants, see S&M, pp. 11–12 & 15.

p. 17 **faubourgs of Saint-Antoine and Saint-Marcel:** The Faubourg Saint-Marcel (covering roughly the outer parts of the pr. Ve. and XIIIe.) has been well served by Burstin in two major works (1983, 2005b). For the Faubourg Saint-Antoine (roughly XIe. and XIIe.), see Monnier (1981).

p. 17 **the location for the guillotine:** From the guillotine's invention in 1792 through to May 1793, executions took place on the Place du Carrousel in front of the Tuileries palace. The guillotine relocated when the Convention moved into the Salle des Spectacles of the palace. There was a brief experiment with the Place de la Bastille, 9–13 June 1793.

p. 17 **austere morality play:** Arasse (1989) gives details of the critique aimed at the Place de la Révolution: esp. pp. 107–11. For the performance aspect, see too Friedland (2012), esp. pp. 239ff. For pre-1789 capital punishment, see the famous description in Foucault (1975), pp. 3–5.

p. 17 **accounted for many more:** Godfrey (1951), p. 137. Cf. Jones (1988), p. 121. From its inception on 6 April 1793 through to 10 June 1794, the guillotine executed 1231 individuals; and between 10 June and 9 Thermidor, 1376.

p. 17 **people from humble backgrounds:** See W 433 d. 972 for the listing including professions. Newspapers give name lists but not always professions.

p. 18 **'the year for patriots':** Cf. F7 4708 d. Florian ('year for patriots'); [Sanson], *Journal de Charles-Henri Sanson* (2007), p. 249 ('No children'). Probably apocryphal, these memoirs are sufficiently well-informed to be useable. For the Carmelites, see Bernet (2008).

p. 18 **Rue de Birague:** Rue de Birague, pr. IVe.

p. 18 **'making my dream come true':** Bourquin (1987), p. 217 (the letter was dated 7 Thermidor). This well-researched dual biography of Cabarrus and Tallien lamentably has virtually no footnotes. On Tallien, see too Harder in Andress (2013). The La Force prison was situated on the pr. Rue Pavée (IVe.).

p. 19 **Federalist Revolt:** See above, p. 4.

p. 19 **he met Theresa Cabarrus:** For Tallien in Bordeaux, see Forrest (1975), pp. 229–37.

p. 19 **recommended behaviour for a deputy on mission:** Mathiez (1925), which draws on *Mémoire du Citoyen Héron au peuple français* (no date), a rare copy of which may be found in F7 4403 d. Héron.

p. 19 **now believed to be in Paris:** See Jullien's reports in Courtois I, docs. LXXIII & CVII (a–m), pp. 244–5, 333–64. OCR, iii contains many of the same letters. For Rousseville, see F7 4782 d. Chatenay.

p. 20 **Servais-Beaudoin Boulanger:** See esp. Cobb (1987), pp. 65–6 and passim; and Calvet (1941), pp. 57–8. Robespierre had publicly defended him against accusations of radicalism and corruption. For Hanriot, see below, pp. 31 & 159–62.

p. 20 **admissions register:** Cf. Bourquin (1987), p. 211. French measurements equate to around five foot three inches in fact. This depiction may be compared with Laneuville's flattering portrait reconstruction of her in gaol (1796), for which see Freund (2014), esp. 127–59.

p. 20 **the use of a mirror:** Bourquin (1987), p. 214. This striking story may be apocryphal.

p. 21 **revolted by these shocking incidents:** OCR, ix, p. 93 (a passage worth reading). For evidence of Robespierre's personal revulsion, see McPhee (2012), p. 130.

p. 21 **'Tallien is one of those individuals':** AP, p. 549; & OCR, x, p. 496. For a fuller discussion of the law, see below, pp. 166–8.

p. 21 **frighteningly formidable:** For Bourdon de l'Oise, see Lecointre, *Les crimes* (1795), pp. 90n., 97n. For the encounter, see AP, pp. 546–8 & OCR, x, pp. 493–5. For the assassination rumour, see F7 4587 d. Baroy. On Tallien, see *Papiers* I, pp. 115–17 and, for the expulsion, *Moniteur*, 1 Messidor, p. 2. There is no mention of this in Jacobins. The Rue de la Perle is in the pr. IIIe.

p. 21 **a watch on Tallien's moves:** Courtois I, doc. XVIII, pp. 130, 132–3, 135. As with the Rousseville reports, these are addressed to the whole CPS but with the expectation that Robespierre would read them. They found their way into Robespierre's private papers.

p. 22 **'the tyrant will be brought low':** Bourquin (1987), p. 229 ('be prudent'); plus the memoirs of the banker Laffitte: Laffitte (1932), p. 42 ('by the end of the week').

p. 22 **Legracieux's lodgings:** W 79 d. Legracieux. See too his police files at F7 4774/13 (dossier marked Le Granois) and F7 4558 d. Gracieux. For his place in the Bureaux des lois, see listing in AFII 23B. The Rue Denfert was a southern prolongation of the Rue de la Harpe (Ve.), and has been built over by the pr. Boulevard Saint-Michel.

p. 22 **Virtue personified:** W 79. There are fuller extracts in SCD, pp. 195–6. Saint-Paul-les-Trois-Châteaux is in the pr. department of the Drôme. See below for Fleuriot and Payan, pp. 131–3.

p. 22 **the famous Paris Jacobin Club:** Scholarship on the Jacobins has tended to focus on the national network of clubs or on Jacobin discourse, and the Paris Club has been short-changed save as the locus of speeches (notably by Robespierre). The study most focused on the Club itself is Walter (1946). See too Brinton (1930); Kennedy (3 volumes, 1982, 1988, 1999); and Higonnet (1998). The fundamental printed primary source is Jacobins. The Club was situated on the pr. Marché Saint-Honoré (Ie.). For Robespierre's speech, see AP, pp. 530–6 (includes the speeches against); and OCR, x, pp. 542–87. See the discussion of them below at pp. 38–40.

p. 23 **keeps a diary:** [Guittard de Floriban], *Journal* (1974). The section on 9 Thermidor is at pp. 433–6. Daily information on sunrise etc is carried in many newspapers and in the *Almanach national*. The Rue des Canettes is in the pr. VIe. I have also consulted the meteorological records of the Paris Observatory.

p. 24 **27 July will see no rain:** Archives of the Observatoire, AF 1–14. This is worth stressing in light of a myth of a violent storm at the end of the day.

PART I: ELEMENTS OF CONSPIRACY
(MIDNIGHT TO 5.00 A.M.)

00.00/Midnight, 9–10 Thermidor (pp. 27–42)

p. 27 **'I expect nothing from the Montagne':** B&R, 34, p. 3. The quotation allegedly originated from the Duplay family. Testimony on Robespierre's bedtime by Duplay *fils* in police interrogation, 3 ventôse III: W 79 d. Duplay.

p. 27 **Robespierre has repeated his Convention speech:** For Legracieux, see above, p. 22. For the Jacobin Club speech, see, Jacobins, pp. 246–81, and below, pp. 44–5. The lateness of the hour is endorsed in comments by Robespierre's CPS colleague Billaud-Varenne, *Réponse de J. N. Billaud-Varenne* (1795b), p. 36 (in Club till nearly midnight). For the Club generally, see note above, p. 23 and note, 'the famous Jacobin Club'; for affiliates, see Boutier, Boutry, & Bonin (1992), esp. p. 15.

p. 28 **theoretical strength of the Convention:** Brunel (1989), p. 11 for this estimate. Many deputies were not regular attenders.

p. 28 **He respects anniversaries:** For his early commemorations of 14 July, see Scurr (2006), p. 212. He spent 14 July 1794 rather differently: in the Jacobin Club, proposing the expulsion of Fouché. See OCR, x, pp. 526–9. The king's speech on 5 May 1789 opened Estates General business, making 6 May the first full day of resistance.

p. 28 **a mastiff called Brount:** For Brount and the walks, see Hamel (1865), iii, pp. 295–6.

p. 29 **the 'populomaniac deputy':** OCR, viii, p. 91 (2 January 1792); and for royalist attacks: ibid., vi, p. 507; vii, p. 339 (to much laughter).

p. 29 *'je suis peuple'*: OCR, viii, p. 89. The phrase is difficult to translate: perhaps 'I am of the people' or 'I embody the people'.

p. 29 **'Flight to Varennes'**: For this episode, see Tackett (2003). For the ensuing Champs de Mars massacre, see Andress (2000).

p. 30 **lodgings that provided greater protection:** There are a number of accounts of how Robespierre ended up at the Duplays. See e.g. Hamel (1865), iii, pp. 284–5. The Rue Saintonge (pr. IIIe.) is nearly two miles from the Manège within the Tuileries complex, then the assembly's meeting place.

p. 30 **the advent of the Legislative Assembly:** Robespierre in fact proposed the so-called self-denying ordinance which prohibited deputies in the Constituent Assembly from sitting in the Legislative Assembly. The Assembly lasted from October 1791 to September 1792, at which moment it was replaced by the National Convention. All Robespierre's journalism is available in OCR, vols. iv and v. For the period generally, see Leuwers (2014), ch. 15, pp. 215ff.; and for the 10 August *journée*, see Reinhard (1969).

p. 30 **Girondins or Brissotins:** For the Girondins/Brissotins, see Sydenham (1961); Kates (1985); Soboul ed. (1980); and Tackett (2015).

p. 30 **September Massacres:** For the September Massacres, see below, p. 76.

p. 30 **Maximin Isnard:** AP 65, p. 302.

p. 31 **80,000 guardsmen:** Slavin (1986).

p. 31 **just how far France has come:** AP, pp. 510–15.

p. 31 **the city lost even its identity:** Edmonds (1990) and Biard (2013).

p. 32 **'a new 31 May':** AP, pp. 510–11.

p. 32 **a foreign-financed conspiracy:** For the Foreign Plot, Mathiez (1918) remains a good place to start. See also Hampson (1976).

p. 32 **he has pestered CPS colleagues:** See *Réponse des membres des anciens comités* (1795), pp. 101–2.

p. 33 **'impure breed':** OCR, x, pp. 476–7.

p. 33 **he did not actively seek:** OCR, x, p. 65 (11 August 1793). In the same speech (p. 75) he also reported his shock at colleagues. Cf. for similar, his speech on 13 Messidor, in OCR, x, p. 515.

p. 33 **Robespierre couldn't boil an egg:** Michelet accepted this quotation, which is however contested by the hagiographical Ernest Hamel: Hamel (1865), iii, p. 84. The comment of Robespierre's friend Rosalie Jullien in early 1793 speaks in the same sense: "il est propre à être chef de parti comme à prendre la lune avec les dents'. [Jullien] (2016), p. 23. See too Barère's comment, below, p. 52.

pp. 33–4 **his expert knowledge:** McPhee (2012) is good on Robespierre's administrative inexperience. For expert knowledge on international affairs, see the amusing anecdote cited in OCR, vi, p. 231 (11 February 1790); on military affairs, see Simon Duplay's comment in his interrogation, W 79; and for pay-cheques, see C 2443/2. It seems Simon Duplay drew Robespierre's salary for him for most of Year II. See too Garmy (1962–3: two parts); and Baudot (1893), p. 264.

p. 34 **a neophyte's enthusiasm:** For his management ideas, see the 'Organisation du comité' in his hand at AFII 23A.

p. 34 **'pales at the sight of a drawn sabre':** Cited in Gauchet (2018), p. 88n.

p. 34 **'the very purest of principles':** F7 4599 d. Billaud-Varenne. The copious contents of this box are a mess, so no clearer indication of location is possible.

p. 35 **'idolaters':** For women, see Fleischman (1908); McPhee (2012), pp. 137–40; Sepinwall (2010); and Shusterman (2014). For the cult of celebrity, see Lilti (2014), and below, pp. 118–9.

p. 35 **he can weave a spell:** See below, p. 197, for the magic spell. Robespierre's major policy speeches included interventions in 1793 on 17 November (27 Brumaire) on the state of the Republic; on 5 December 1793 (15 Frimaire); on 25 December (5 Nivôse) on the principles of Revolutionary Government; and in 1794 on 5 February (17 Pluviôse) on the principles of political morality. The 'republic of virtue' tag derived esp. from the latter. See also the speech of 7 May (18 Floréal) setting up worship of the Supreme Being.

p. 35 **grasp of detail:** For the 14 Frimaire law, see AP 80, pp. 624–35. The text was also published as a brochure for handy use: see below, p. 343. For Barère's jingoistic so-called *carmagnoles* announcing victories, see below, p. 108. Barère notably introduced the law of 22 Floréal/11 May on public welfare and also sponsored the creation of the École de Mars.

p. 35 **'Virtue without which terror is destructive':** OCR, x, p. 357. For the history of usage of the word 'terror' prior to 1793–4, see Schechter (2018), plus the broader perspective in Edelstein (2009); and Biard & Linton (2020), esp. pp. 31–49.

p. 36 **Jean-Jacques Rousseau:** See esp. Manin (1988), pp. 872–87.

p. 36 **his signature trope:** For the sentimental narrative, see Reddy (2001) and Andress (2011). It would be a sizeable task to list all the times that Robespierre evoked his own death or the mortal danger in which he found himself. A sampler from 1791 onwards includes: OCR, vii, p. 590; vii, p. 310, 523; p. 375; viii, p. 157, ix, p. 150, p. 523; x, p. 514. For an early example of the martyr trope, see the Dupaty brochure at OCR, iii, p. 166 (though his authorship of this piece has been challenged).

p. 36 **not at all a natural orator:** See discussion in Jordan (1985), esp. pp. 64–79; and Leuwers (2014), pp. 152–3. For stage fright, see Étienne Dumont, cited in Jacob (1938), p. 88.

p. 37 **Roberts-pierre:** See below, p. 212. For Damiens, see Van Kley (1984).

p. 37 **Catherine Théot:** For the Théot case, see Eude (1969). See Zobkiw's excellent unpublished PhD thesis (2015): for previous lack of laughter, pp. 211–13, and in general p. 5.

p. 37 **'Let me speak or else kill me':** OCR, ix, p. 174 ('let me speak'); ibid., p. 48 ('freedom's defender'). For the stare see ibid., p. 73. For a Medusan reference, Jacobins, p. 344. See too his interventions over the Law of 22 Prairial targeted at Bourdon de l'Oise and Tallien, discussed above, p. 21. Examples of playing to the gallery are too numerous to list.

p. 37 **associating them with his putative victimhood:** For this tactic, see Zobkiw (2015), p. 85.

p. 38 **Robespierre presented his remarks:** The speech may be consulted in full in AP, pp. 530–2; OCR, x, 542–76 gives a fuller version. The manuscript of the speech, with

Robespierre's amendments and crossings-out has recently passed into the Archives nationales and may be consulted at Collection Robespierre 683 AP 1 d. 12. See Geffroy (2013). It is a very difficult speech to summarize. The excellent account by Leuwers (2014), pp. 356–61, is the first to take full account of the manuscript version. The six-week absence is cited at p. 565.

p. 38 **to unveil plots and to denounce conspiracies:** OCR, x, p. 546 ('unburdening his heart'); p. 543 ('useful truths'); pp. 546–8 ('system of terror'); p. 548 (sleeping away); ibid., p. 531 ('grovelling at my feet').

p. 39 **corrupt and aristocratic hands:** Ibid., p. 546 (to initiate accusations); pp. 557, 560–1 (Festival of the Supreme Being, 'émigrés and crooks'); pp. 558–9, 563–5, 570–1 (accusations against committees).

p. 39 **Robespierre generally eschews naming names:** Ibid., p. 568 ('academic lightness'); pp. 572–3 ('military despotism'); p. 562 (Vadier and Théot: see also attacks on Amar and Jagot in a deleted part of the speech at p. 552n.); pp. 552n., 568, 572–3 (celebration of successes, military despotism); p. 570 (artillery units); p. 567 (Catiline). For Robespierre resenting laughter provoked by victories, see Zobkiw (2015), passim.

p. 39 **the taking of British prisoners of war:** Ibid., pp. 547, 548 (Revolutionary Tribunal); p. 568 (prisoners of war). For the latter issue, see above, p. 145.

p. 39 **'freedom's slave':** Ibid., p. 554 ('dictator'); p. 556 ('freedom's slave'); p. 576 (governed criminally).

p. 40 **a word indicating conspiracy:** Robespierre crammed in 15 *conspirations*, 16 *conspirateurs*, 18 *conjurés*, 1 *conjuration*, 5 *complots*, 5 *trames*, and 40 *factions* making 100 conspiracy words in 120 minutes. My count includes a handful of usages in possibly erased sections.

p. 40 **a man who wants to kill:** I have been unable to locate this brilliant aphorism in Alphonse Aulard's published oeuvre. It may be found in his lecture notes at the Houghton Library, Harvard University, Aulard Collection, Cours 1899–1900.

p. 40 **precise list of demands:** They are mostly summed up on p. 546.

p. 40 *hommes de bien:* See p. 575.

p. 40 **a quandary:** The following account of reactions in the Convention is drawn from AP, pp. 532–5; and OCR, x, pp. 583–6.

p. 40 **deep-dyed enemies of Robespierre:** For Lecointre and Bourdon, see below, pp. 61–2.

p. 41 **'time to tell the whole truth':** Ibid., p. 533. For the Cambon-Robespierre conflict, see Hincker (1994).

p. 41 **deputy Joseph Fouché:** Ibid., p. 554. For Fouché, see below, pp. 59–61.

p. 42 **Louis-Stanislas Fréron:** For Fréron, see below, pp. 57–8. Other speakers on these lines were Bentabole, Charlier, and Thirion.

p. 42 **Jean-Baptiste Mailhe:** Baudot (1893), p. 123.

01.00/1.00 a.m. (pp. 43–55)

p. 43 **the CPS meeting room in the Tuileries palace:** For the CPS Offices, see Lenôtre (1895), pp. 117ff. Lenôtre gleans much from the account of a CPS clerk, Jean-Gabriel-Philippe Morice, who was auditory witness to a dispute: de Broc (1892), pp. 453–98. For the Tuileries, see below, p. 176. The best guide to the events of the night in the

CPS are the accounts of various CPS and CGS members after the event, particularly when in Year III, Barère, Billaud-Varenne, Collot d'Herbois, and Vadier were under attack for their leading role in the Terror. Although the passage of time and the underlying rationale of self-justification make these crucial sources subject to caution, they provide much more useable detail than most existing secondary works indicate. Laurent Lecointre, the deputy who led the attacks, also provided several accounts of the night. Saint-Just's undelivered speech for 9 Thermidor also offers insights.

p. 43 **earfuls of confidential government business:** *Réponse des membres des anciens comités* (1795), p. 109. The meeting was about the Law of 22 Prairial.

p. 43 **attacks on the government:** Although there are a few Robespierre signatures to CPS decrees after 11 Messidor, it is likely that his policy of personal absence dated from this time. See Leuwers (2014), p. 345.

p. 44 **joint CPS/CGS meetings:** My account of the high-level negotiations of 4–5 Thermidor suggests that they produced a broad measure of agreement, with concessions on both sides. This negotiation has perhaps been underplayed by historians because the course of events on and after 9 Thermidor made it politically inexpedient (even harmful) for Robespierre's opponents on the *journée* to hint that they came close to an agreement with him a few days earlier. The best analysis is still Mathiez's chapter in his *Girondins et Montagnards* (1930). See also the important account of the 5 Thermidor meeting by CGS member Ruhl in F7 4775/5 d. Ruhl. The report is reproduced by Cobb (1955): see esp. p. 111. Ruhl claimed that Robespierre was specific in his attacks on individuals, but confirms that agreement was reached by the end of the meeting.

p. 44 **'We are your friends':** The quotation comes from Saint-Just's account of the meeting in his undelivered 9 Thermidor speech: AP, p. 561.

p. 45 **the idea of a purge of the Convention:** Although other accounts do not include this latter point, it was specifically referred to by Barère in his 7 Thermidor speech.

p. 45 **Popular Commissions:** For a recent evaluation of the Popular Commissions, see Jourdan (2016). The decision on the Commissions was taken at the 4 Thermidor meeting, the tribunals decree on 5 Thermidor. The latter was very short on detail, suggesting it was provisional or possibly even something of a sop. See CPS, p. 375.

p. 45 **Saint-Just agreed to Carnot's proposal:** Herlaut (1951). His data is considered and updated in Cobb (1987), pp. 610–13 which suggests little malice on Carnot's part. For the order, see CPS, p. 375. The sections involved were Chalier, Champs-Élysées, Gravilliers, and Montreuil.

p. 46 **'hands are laden with wealth':** Jacobins, p. 238.

p. 46 **'five or six turbulent creatures':** Ibid., p. 239 for Couthon; for Robespierre, OCR, x, p. 539. The editors, noting the absence of this extract in volume vi of Aulard's Jacobins, suggest that the statement indicates Robespierre's readiness to act.

p. 46 **the NG gunners being evacuated from Paris:** Jacobins, p. 236. The full title of Pille's commission was *de l'organisation et du movement des armées de terre*. Sijas had made earlier attacks on 28 Messidor and 3 Thermidor: Jacobins, pp. 223, 236. Pille gave his side of the story in *Réponse de L. A. Pille* (1794). See too Brown (1995), pp. 136–8.

p. 47 **a ruse to make him look ridiculous:** For the Magendie case, see Jacobins, pp. 240, 243. Some context is provided in his police file at F7 4774/28 d. Magenthies (sic), and in W 135 and W 153. No mention is made of Robespierre's intervention on Magendie in either OCR or Aulard: but see mention of it in the *Journal de Perlet*, 9 Thermidor (printed and diffused before the Convention session on that day).

p. 47 **Both glared furiously at Gouly:** Gouly, *A ses collègues* [1794], p. 4. Gouly claimed that the omission of the episode in minutes or newspapers was due to the hold Robespierre had over the press.

p. 47 **'notorious for his patriotism':** AP, p. 504. Barère later unconvincingly claimed he was saying this with irony. Barère, *Observations sur le rapport du 12 ventôse* (1795), pp. 8–9. See too AP, pp. 510–15 (speech) and pp. 504–5 (delegation).

p. 48 **an intricate complex of corridors and rooms:** Besides the account of Morice (de Broc, 1892), we get some glimpses of the room in various deputy memoirs. On all organizational matters, see Matta-Duvigneau (2013) and for the other committees and their work, id. (2012). For personnel, see Gainot (1990) and Palmer (1941). For CPS office expansion, see esp. AFII 23B: the box also includes detailed information on the size and salaries of CPS staff. See Year II's *Almanach national*, p. 105 for an indicative (but slightly out of date) listing of committee locations.

p. 48 **'God forbid':** OCR, x, p. 203.

p. 49 **formal plenary meetings:** For a personal account of procedures from CPS member Prieur de la Côte d'Or, see Bouchard (1946).

p. 49 **military engineer Lazare Carnot:** For Carnot, see H. Carnot (1907) and Reinhard (1950–2); for Prieur, Bouchard (1946); and for Lindet, Montier (1899).

p. 49 **Saint-Just:** Saint-Just has attracted three very different biographies: Gross (1976), Vinot (1985), and Hampson (1991). For Couthon generally, see Soboul (1983); Bouscayrol (2002); Couthon's police file at F7 4656 (including information on the baths); and W 501 (Fouquier-Tinville on Couthon's evening absences).

p. 50 **Barère, Billaud-Varennes and Collot d'Herbois:** For Barère, see Gershoy (1962); and for Collot, Biard (1995). There is no modern scholarly biography of Billaud, though see his memoirs (1893 edition). The huge file relating to his trial in 1795 in W 499 is also worth consulting, as is his police file at F7 4599. See also Billaud-Varenne (1992) and Klemperer (2018).

p. 50 **professional backgrounds:** A few had a smidgeon of nobility: Saint-Just was the son of an ennobled military officer; Prieur's father had held an ennobling financial post; and Barère's mother was noble.

p. 50 **pressure of work:** Matta-Duvigneau (2013), p. 257. See too [Billaud], *Réponse de J.N. Billaud* (1795), p. 57 (claiming he personally signed up to 300 a day). See Lenôtre (1895), p. 120 (beds). For the Carnot anecdotes, see [Carnot], *Opinion* (1795), pp. 3–4 (trust) and Faure, *Sur le procès*, p. 4n. (restaurateur).

p. 51 **young Philippe Le Bas:** For Le Bas and Augustin Robespierre, see Cousin (2010).

p. 51 **with unconcealed contempt:** Over Amar's report on the Compagnie des Indes scandal in Ventôse, see OCR, x, pp. 379–85; and over Vadier's reporting of the Catherine Théot case, see above, pp. 37–9. For the CGS generally, see the articles by Michel Eude in the *AHRF* (1933–8). The notes which Eude collected for his planned, but never completed *thèse d'état* are located in the Library of the Institut de la

Révolution française in the Sorbonne. I consulted them with the kind permission of Pierre Serna. See too Cadio (2012).

p. 51 **complex patterns in regard to policy, procedures, and personalities:** CGS members Amar, Voulland, and Grégoire Jagot were also involved in the selection of suspects in the prison plots in ways that irked Robespierre.

p. 51 **Cult of the Supreme Being:** For the cult, see Smyth (2016). There a cross-over between the two groups: Protestant Ruhl became an atheist and broke the vial of sacred chrism in Reims with which generations of kings of France had been crowned.

p. 51 **Tonight's joint session of the CPS and CGS:** CPS presence during this night session: Barère, Collot, Billaud, Carnot, Prieur de la Côte d'Or, Lindet. CGS presence: Lacoste, Dubarran, Vadier, Amar, Louis du Bas-Rhin, Bayle, Vadier, and Voulland. See also Montier (1899), p. 249 (for Lindet's testimony on Saint-Just). There are a number of accounts of episodes during the Jacobin session but no overall description. Jacobins, pp. 282–9 has a helpful compilation of key accounts (notably by Billaud, Courtois, the deputy Toulongeon, and Buchez & Roux).

p. 52 **provincial Jacobin Legracieux:** See above, p. 22.

p. 52 **'you have calumnies against us in your pockets':** *Réponse des membres des anciens comités* (1795), p. 106. In this chapter, quotations from this meeting come, unless otherwise stated, from this account (esp. pp. 103–9). Also useful is [Billaud-Varenne]. *Réponse de J. N. Billaud* (1795), reprinted in Jacobins, pp. 282–7. The text of Saint-Just's 9 Thermidor speech refers to Billaud and the others' anxiety about the following day. For the presence of Javogues, Dubarran, and Bentabole in the Club, see Thibaudeau (2007), p. 112. The radical Loys also later described himself as attacking Robespierre: see F7 4774/26 d. Loys (statement at 3 Brumaire III).

p. 52 **'You couldn't even run a farmyard':** Cf. above, p. 33 and note, 'boil an egg'.

p. 52 **credit in Jacobin circles:** Partly this credit was a vestige of the support he attracted over the Ladmiral assassination attempt on his life. See above, p. 15.

p. 53 **'the enemies of the fatherland':** *Réponse*, in Jacobins, p. 282. Note Robespierre's characteristic equation of his own with the Republic's enemies.

p. 53 **'dominators at the Jacobins!':** Leuwers (2014), p. 361, drawing on *Conservateur décadaire*, 20 Fructidor.

p. 53 **'If you drink hemlock':** Traditions noted by B&R, 34, and cited in Jacobins, p. 287. In the Convention debate on David's conduct on 13 Thermidor, David stated that Robespierre found physical contact repellent and that no embrace took place. AP 94, pp. 22–3.

p. 54 **'I too was under the assassin's knife!':** F7 4764 d. Lanne. Lanne was present at the session.

p. 54 **'We'll cut their cackle!':** AP, p. 557. This part of the evening draws on Collot's peroration in the Convention in the evening session of 9–10 Thermidor. See below, p. 52.

p. 54 **'No usurpation goes unpunished':** *Réponse des membres des anciens comités*, p. 106.

p. 55 **plotting with radical deputy Joseph Fouché:** AP, p. 557.

p. 55 **There is no coming storm:** Ibid. Reading between the lines of his speech next day, finally composed in anger, one gets a strong sense of Saint-Just's effort to placate the meeting.

p. 55 **a letter to a group of fellow patriots:** Mathiez (1927c), pp. 175–9. One letter is dated 8 Thermidor, while a second is dated 9 Thermidor and written either late on the night of 8 Thermidor or else early the next morning.

02.00/2.00 a.m. (pp. 56–68)

p. 56 **Laurent Lecointre is writing an urgent message:** Lecointre, *Robespierre peint par lui-même* (1794), p. 5. As noted earlier, I am drawing heavily for the actions in and around the CPS this evening on the post-Thermidor pamphlets of Laurent Lecointre (which often repeat themselves) and replies by those members of the CPS he attacked.

p. 57 **refused access to the committee:** Lecointre, *Robespierre peint par lui-même*, pp. 4–6. For Fleuriot-Lescot and Payan, see below, pp. 131–4.

p. 57 **'either Robespierre or I will be dead':** Duval-Jouve (1879), p. 188n. For Cambon's intervention against Robespierre, see above, p. 41. See Saumade (1939) for his wealth.

p. 58 **deputies sent out on mission:** Biard (2002) provides an excellent overview of the phenomenon. Fréron's father, Élie-Catherine, was a literary critic and renowned anti-philosophe.

p. 58 **Napoleone Buonaparte:** Gueniffey (2015), pp. 137–45. For Toulon, see Crook (1992).

p. 58 **to usher themselves out:** Fréron cited in Jacob (1938), pp. 157–60 (a very partial and possibly untrustworthy account of course that does, however, capture Robespierre's habitual hauteur).

p. 58 **Couthon managed a spell in Lyon:** Couthon served in the expedition to Lyon, August-October 1793. He was due to undertake another mission in early July 1794 but this fell through presumably because of his progressive paralysis. Biard (2002), p. 484.

p. 58 **his younger brother Augustin:** Cousin (2010) and (for details of his missions) Biard (2002), p. 576. For correspondence between Augustin and Maximilien, see Courtois I, docs. XLII and LXXXIX, pp. 177–9, 293–4, and OCR, iii.

p. 59 **Marc-Antoine Jullien:** For the correspondence between the two, see above, p. 20.

p. 59 **Joseph Fouché:** Tulard (1997) is probably the best recent biography.

p. 59 **he cordially detests him:** Charlotte Robespierre (1835), pp. 106–10.

p. 59 **dechristianization:** See Vovelle (1991), pp. 126–9; and Cobb (1987), ch. 6, pp. 442–79.

p. 60 **Robespierre castigated him in person:** According to Robespierre's sister Charlotte: Robespierre (1835), p. 108.

p. 60 **radical sans-culottes from Lyon:** The so-called 'friends of Chalier' included men like Renaudin, Gravier, Fillion, and Achard who inveigled themselves into Robespierre's good graces and fed his hatred of Fouché. The Fouché–Robespierre spat can be followed in Jacobins.

p. 60 **Robespierre's 'tablets of death':** Fouché uses the phrase in his *Mémoires* (1946), p. 45; and see above, pp. 41–2. In the debates following Robespierre's speech on

8 Thermidor, his name was suggested as someone likely to be on Robespierre's list. OCR, x, p. 583.

p. 60 **the imminent overthrow of Robespierre:** AFII 47, pi. 1–8. The letters were seized by deputy on mission, Bo. They only reached Paris after 9 Thermidor.

p. 60 **Joseph Lebon:** It is unclear how much Robespierre supported Lebon. The latter was recalled from his mission on 10 Thermidor, suggesting Robespierre may have been an obstacle to this happening earlier. CPS, p. 484.

p. 61 **Robespierre detests them all:** For Léonard Bourdon, see Sydenham (1999), pp. 150–66. Biard (2002) makes a good case for the role of rumour and calumny behind many of the charges against deputies on mission. But then at this moment it was rumour that counted. For the missions of the deputies cited, see ibid., pp. 474, 496, 533, 579, 588; and generally, chs. 4 and 5. The best account of a deputy on mission at work focuses on Javogues: Lucas (1975).

p. 61 **frightened out of their wits:** The idea of the 'politician's terror' forms a key argument in Linton (2013).

p. 61 **Robespierre had been misled:** AP, pp. 505–6. See Robespierre's private notes on Dubois-Crancé in Courtois I, doc. LI, pp. 189–90.

p. 61 **'I despise you as much as I hate you':** Lecointre, *Robespierre peint par lui-même*, pp. 3n., 16 ('overthrow one tyrant'); ibid., p. 3 (Amar & Bayle). He claimed that he had as many as 50 supporters in the assembly: id., *Les crimes des sept membres du comité de salut public et de sûreté générale* (1795), p. 72. See too Baudot (1893), p. 5; and OCR, x, p. 560.

p. 62 **he spoke to Robert Lindet:** This was seemingly on 24–25 July. Lecointre, *Robespierre peint par lui-même*, pp. 3–4. He also had approached Carnot earlier and got a similar response. Reinhard (1950–2), p. 471.

p. 62 **disgruntled ex-supporters of Danton:** This is the Courtois who edited Robespierre's papers and wrote the official report on 9 Thermidor for the Convention. Lecointre had, it appears, already prepared a text or manifesto for the coup, entitled *Robespierre opposé à lui-même* that Guffroy would publish. Guffroy, deputy for Arras like Robespierre, also published a newspaper *Rougyff* (an anagram of his name). Robespierre's notes on Delmas and others are published in Courtois I, doc. LI, pp. 190–2.

p. 62 **Dantonist Bourdon de l'Oise:** Bourdon consulted the lawyer Berryer: [Berryer] (1839), esp. 228–9.

p. 62 **an open secret:** See above, pp. 40–1 and note. Letter of Scellier to Robespierre, cited in Lecointre, *Les crimes des sept membres*, pp. 181–2n.

p. 62 **Lecointre's craven behaviour:** OCR, p. 532. Lecointre's later statement about his conduct, which was that his attack was to be on the whole of the CPS and not just Robespierre, seems deeply unconvincing. Lecointre, *Les crimes des sept membres*, p. 73.

p. 63 **a big batch of paperwork:** *Opinion de Carnot* (1795), p. 4.

p. 63 **sent out a messenger:** For the summons to Lecointre's brother, see CPS, pp. 461–2. This states a time of 1.00 a.m., but Lecointre later recorded it as being at 4.00 a.m. For the Hémart summons, ibid., p. 462; and Birembault (1959), p. 305.

p. 65 **deputies' lodgings are very concentrated:** Jones (2020), esp. pp. 264–5. Tallien's interlocutors were based as follows: Boissy on the Rue du Bouloi (Ie.), Durand on the

Rue neuve de l'Égalite (part of pr. Rue d'Aboukir, IIe.) and Palasne on the Rue Saint-Honoré (Ie.). See the account of these discussions in Durand-Maillane (1825), p. 199. For Tallien at the theatre, see F7 4710 d. Fourcade. Payan was also supposed to be there.

p. 66 **the '73':** According to some estimates, 75 deputies were actually imprisoned. But the label 'the "73"' generally stuck.

p. 66 **thence no doubt to the guillotine:** See esp. OCR, x, pp. 133–6, 376–9.

p. 66 **expressing their gratitude:** Robespierre's correspondence contains nearly a dozen such letters, plus a collective letter by 31 deputies, dated 3 Messidor: OCR, iii, pp. 299 and passim. Cf. Hamel (1865), iii, pp. 157–8.

p. 66 **Robespierre appeared to have been distancing himself:** OCR, x, p. 550. Inter-estingly Ruhl records the impression that Robespierre was changing his attitude towards the 73. Cobb (1955), p. 112.

p. 66 **'You are on the list! Me too!':** Fouché (1946), p. 46. Fouché's self-aggrandizing memoirs overplay his role in the making of the *journée*. We have no evidence except his own later say-so that he was bolstering Tallien's efforts during the night. See the purported listing of 47 deputies cited in Walter (1974), pp. 91–2.

p. 67 **he does not seem to be sick:** When he was ill in February and March, there was huge public concern. See e.g. W 112 d. 1 and Courtois I, docs V–VIII, pp. 104–6. There is no indication that anyone ascribed his absences before 9 Thermidor to illness. I differ on this point from McPhee (2012).

p. 67 **all respected men:** See above, p. 57.

p. 67 **the so-called *amalgame*:** These military reforms are discussed in Bertaud (1979), pp. 96–9 & 158–60.

p. 67 **No one stepped forward:** See above, p. 61.

03.00/3.00 a.m. (pp. 69–83)

p. 69 **denizens of the dark hours:** The famous author and night-walker Restif de la Bretonne held that night-walking was less common at this time.

p. 69 **Jules Messidor:** Most of the *état civil* for Paris was destroyed in the Commune fires of 1871. The few reconstituted vestiges that remain are located in the Archives de Paris, where they are consultable on microfilm. The time of 3.00 a.m. is stated in both cases cited here. Also born on this day was the more appropriately named Pierre François Thermidor Lefebvre. Other demographic examples are from the same source.

p. 69 **24,000 births:** This and other demographic data from *Atlas*, pp. 94–5. Figures given in newspapers provide, for Messidor, the figure of 74 deaths and 65 births, close to these averages.

p. 70 **ceremonial around births, marriages, and deaths:** BNF NAF 2690 ('lugubrious'); ADP VD★7 724 (tricolour); *Journal historique et politique*, 23 Nivôse/12 January 1794 (tunic). It would be interesting to know how widely these were observed.

p. 70 **25 marriages:** The *Messager du soir* gives 22 marriages and nine divorces on the day.

p. 70 **'the couple is joined in marriage':** ADP D3U1 30. The proceedings began in the Guillaume-Tell section on the Right Bank where the husband has relocated. For another divorce case active on this day see ADP D3U1 42 (Poissonnière) It seems that 75 per cent of French divorces in Revolutionary and Napoleonic periods were lodged by women: Phillips (1980), p. 96.

p. 70 **huge baskets:** de Bohm (2001), p. 79; Bijaoui (1996), p. 160. See APP AA220 (quicklime being brought through the Quinze-Vingts section to the cemetery).

p. 72 **princesse de Monaco:** Blanc (1984), pp. 92–3. For her arrest, see APP AA148; and for her trial W 434 d.972. For the pregnancy declaration, Berthiaud (2014) updates existing literature on the subject, but there is still useful anecdotal material in Billard (1911).

p. 72 **Robespierre appointee:** OCR, iii, p. 168 (May 1793), letter to Fouquier Tinville. Thiéry did not serve on the Monaco panel.

p. 72 **little time for medical certainties:** Berthiaud (2014), pp. 10–11, n. 51.

p. 72 **'I am not pregnant':** W 431, pi. 968. Also Blanc (1984), pp. 92–3. My thanks to Stephanie Brown for conversations about this fascinating case.

p. 74 **'of you I thought':** Cited in Guillois (1890), p. 312 (my translation).

p. 75 **Bénédictins-Anglais prison:** The prison is in the pr. Ve. For Mercier, I am drawing on the letters to his wife cited in full in the Introduction to *NP*, pp. XXXV–CLVI. For his claim to sound sleep on this night, see *NP*, p. 198. On the Bénédictins-Anglais generally, see de La Laurencie (1905). There is a very rich literature on Parisian prisons under the Terror. There was a particular outpouring in Year III/1794–5, when prison writing almost became a new literary genre. See Brown (2018), pp. 132–3. Care is required in using these accounts, some of which sensationalize. A pioneer in the field was P. E. Coittant, who composed four volumes of different accounts in 1795, which were largely crowd-sourced from victims. See [Coittant], *Almanach des prisons*; [id.] *Tableau des prisons de Paris*; [id.] *Second Tableau des prisons*; and [id.], *Troisième Tableau des prisons*. Other compilations include Nougaret (1797); Riouffe (1795); and Proussain-ville [= Pierre Roussell] (1815). Besides these, I have drawn especially on Delahante (1881); La Chabeaussière (1795); and Soeur Théotiste [Christine de Saint-Vincent comtesse Valombray] (1875); as well as more recent editions of prison accounts including Billecocq (1981); de Bohm (2001); Lacroix de Lavalette (1992); and Maussion (1975). Bijaoui (1996) provides a serviceable overview. For Sade at the Madelonn-ettes, see F7 4436 d. 3, pi. 61.

p. 75 **a visit:** Documentation on this in Courtois I, docs. XXXIII (a–e), pp. 146–54; and F7 4435 d. 6). For the slop-bucket, see Blanqui (1794), pp. 72–3. For corroboration about conditions here in F7 4659 d. Dabray. See also *TP*, i, p. 35 (Rue Saint-Jacques).

p. 75 **the organ from the chapel:** See AFII 22A.

pp. 75–6 **roughly seized him:** F7 4774/42 d. Mercier provides details on the arrest. See too the record of the arrest in BB 30 (dossier on arrested Girondin supporters).

p. 76 **September Massacres:** The standard works on the September massacres are Caron (1935) and Bluche (1986). This nightmarish idea of a massacre within the prisons gained further traction after 9 Thermidor, but there is evidence that suggests that there was a kind of panic about such holes being dug within the prisons at this time. See F7 4768 d. Lannay (Police Administrator Teurlot inspecting such a pit in the Abbaye prison on 9 Thermidor); Audouin (1795), p. 36 (opening up of *fossées d'aisance*); F7 4594 d. Berryeter (municipal purchase of land for huge burial pits).

p. 76 **'the perpetrators of the massacres':** *NP*, pp. 785–8.

p. 76 **'a zero in the Convention':** Roland (1905), i, p. 189; *NP*, i, p. XVI (citing Fleury).

p. 76 **the wedding of Camille Desmoulins:** Leuwers (2018), pp. 173–4. Danton was also present among a starry guest-list. Cf. *NP*, p. LVII.

p. 77 **the petition of the '73':** The clash in debate can be followed in OCR, ix, pp. 580–1.

p. 77 **Robespierre's hostages:** See above, p. 75. Mercier was one of 31 signatories to a prisoners' letter of 3 Messidor, and noticeably stressed the principle of justice rather than gratitude: OCR, iii, p. 299. For the visit to the Madelonnettes, see *NP*, p. 198. Cf. F7 4336 d. 6; and Courtois I, docs. XXXIII (a–e), pp. 146–54.

p. 77 **'government by fools':** *NP*, p. 36; and F7 4774/42 d. Mercier: see the letter from Germinal III ('mistaken multitude', 'government by fools', etc); and *NP*, passim.

p. 77 **one hundred prisons:** For the prison network, *Atlas*, pp. 70, 112–13.

p. 78 **Jacques Belhomme:** On the Belhomme institution, see esp. Lenormand (2002). Following a scandal in January 1794, it closed down, but had resumed functioning by Thermidor.

p. 78 **stained by the blood of their victims:** *NP*, pp. 26–7. See also Coittant, *Tableau des prisons*, p. 54.

p. 78 **the princesse de Lamballe:** *NP*, pp. 98–9. The veracity of this account is contested. Brutality is however unquestioned.

p. 78 **a few hundred wild men:** *NP*, p. 88 (Mercier claimed 300 individuals were involved).

p. 79 **'Let us exercise terror':** 'Soyons terribles, pour dispenser le peuple de l'être': AP 60, p. 63.

p. 79 **'Septembrization':** Blanqui (1794), p. 27.

p. 79 **Prisoners feel hated:** Caron (1914), v, p. 332 (resentment at prisoner food); Audouin (1795), p. 23 (cannibalism).

p. 79 **new lists of prison plotters:** F7 4594 d. Pierre-Guillaume Benoist. The figures here are derived from Wallon (1880–2), iv and v. The personal dossiers of particular *moutons* from F7 4557 to 4775/53 are instructive: see under the names Armand, Beausire, Benoit, Leymarie, Manini, Rohan, etc.

p. 79 **the notorious Law of 22 Prairial:** See below, pp. 166–8.

pp. 79–80 **'to purge the prisons at a stroke':** F7 4436 pl. 1, pi. 10. In the margin Robespierre has written 'approuvé'. Note that Aulard's transcription does not mention Robespierre at all: CPS, p. 518.

p. 80 **'one of us':** *Papiers*, i, pp. 279–80. The private conversation was recorded by Herman's colleague Lanne: F7 4764.

p. 80 **the prison population:** *Atlas*, p. 70. Names and numbers of prisoners were carried in the *Moniteur* and all major newspapers. The deterioration of prison conditions is a commonplace in prison accounts cited at note for p. 74.

p. 80 **a wearying trek:** See, for example, de Bohm (2001), pp. 62–3; and Riouffe (1795), p. 25. The centralization law was passed on 16 April/27 Germinal, but in fact some tribunals continued to function, notably at Orange, Arras, and Cambrai.

p. 81 **the little necessities of his life:** See *NP*, 'Lettres de prison', passim; and esp. *NP*, pp. CLIII ('I will live') and XC ('I am crying').

p. 81 **'enigmatic and ambiguous wording':** F7 4436; Courtois I, doc. XXXIII (d), p. 152.

p. 81 **sharp and cutting objects:** The change of regime was worse in some places than others. For toothpicks, see Coittant, *Tableau*, p. 175; and nappy-pins, Audouin (1795), p. 21. See Nougaret (1797), ii, pp. 329, 336 (pets); Proussainville (1815), p. 313 and Coittant, *Tableau*, p. 96 (Wichterich). See also Coittant, *Troisième Tableau*, p. 30 (meals) and Périer de Féral (1955), p. 188 (beards, etc).

p. 82 **'our sole point of contact with humanity':** de Bohm (2001), p. 134.

p. 82 **newspaper hawkers:** Nougaret (1797), iii, p. 3.

p. 82 **threatened with potshots:** Foignet, *Encore une victime* (no date), p. 25.

p. 82 **Guyard, the new gaoler:** Bitaubé (1826), p. 13. For more on warders, see Nougaret (1797), iii, p. 200 & de Bohm (2001), p. 106 ('une véritable ménagerie'); [Duras], *Journal* (1889), p. 150; Coittant, *Troisième Tableau*, p. 36; F7 4597 d. Bertranon ('guillotine meat/fodder' or *gibier de guillotine*); F7 4738 d. Haly (sexual favours).

p. 83 **Ferrières-Sauveboeuf:** Beugnot (1866), pp. 211–13; Coittant, *Troisième Tableau*, p. 73. See too Blanc (1987), pp. 19–21. After Thermidor, Ferrières went before the Revolutionary Tribunal but was acquitted: W 494.

p. 83 **nervous twitches:** Coittant, *Tableau*, p. 73.

p. 83 **the new norm:** Beugnot (1866), p. 226; Rouy, *Assassinats commis* (no date), passim (for around 6 Thermidor); [Duras] *Journal*, p. 115; Périer de Féral (1955), pp. 150–7. For the Oiseaux convent, see Coittant, *Tableau*, p. 5ff.

p. 83 **the Talaru prison:** Coittant, *Troisième Tableau*, p. 65.

04.00/4.00 a.m. (pp. 84–99)

p. 84 **Saint-Just is working by candlelight:** It is possible to piece together the events in the CPS after the initial row between Collot and Saint-Just using the content of Saint-Just's undelivered speech for the next day. I am drawing on the transcription in AP, pp. 558–62. I am assuming that his thinking was influenced by the recent hours: indeed he explicitly stated this in his opening remarks ('quelqu'un cette nuit a flétri mon coeur'): AP, p. 558. This is generally taken to be Collot.

p. 84 **conciliatory truce meetings:** See above, pp. 44–6. AP, p. 559 (a brief and partial account of the 4–5 Thermidor meetings and the Magendie issue).

p. 85 **a new idea in Europe:** 'Le bonheur est une idée neuve en Europe' (1793), one of Saint-Just's most famous aphorisms.

p. 85 **At the CPS's request:** Gross (1976), p. 331 (Couthon's suggestion).

p. 85 **'community of affections':** I am quoting fairly accurately Saint-Just's comment on *la communauté des affections*. See Gross (1976), p. 544. The idea of an 'emotional community' is developed in the work of Barbara Rosenwein (2006).

p. 85 **'Saint-Juste':** This is especially noticeable in his signatures on CPS decrees, notably relating to police matters in F7 4436. Saint-Just's ideas for reform are found in a number of unconnected passages, known as the 'Fragments républicains'. See the Fragments publication in 1831, in *Oeuvres* (1908), ii, pp. 492–530.

p. 85 **'you are a great man':** OCR, iii, pp. 87–8. For some unsavoury background, see F7 4701 d. d'Evry.

p. 86 **fresh-minted aphorisms:** Walzer (1974) discusses the speeches at pp. 61–9 and 70–4.

p. 86 **neck scars:** Duval (1844), p. 191 (also citing Camille Desmoulins).

p. 86 **Théroigne de Méricourt:** According to Courtois II, pp. 131–2, a mad missive awaits Saint-Just at his home. See too Roudinesco (2010), pp. 201–5.

p. 86–7 **talking of him as a tyrant:** AP, pp. 559, 561. For the tyrant claim, see Jones & Macdonald (2018). See too below, pp. 200–1.

p. 87 **related to conspiracy:** See above, p. 40, and note, 'related to conspiracy' for Robespierre. Factionalism is denounced throughout Saint-Just's speech, which begins, 'Je ne suis d'aucune faction.' But I count only one *conjuré*, and around half a dozen *faction* or *factieux*. Dispersal is much more powerfully evoked than plotting.

p. 87 **he cannot simply overlook:** AP, pp. 559–62.

p. 88 **Saint-Just and Carnot:** See Reinhard's admirable biography of Carnot (1950–2) as well as Gross (1976); Bertaud (1990); and H. Carnot (1907).

p. 88 **'He would give his own head':** Levasseur (1829–31), i, p. 324.

p. 89 **'an armed missionary':** OCR, ii, p. 81.

p. 89 **The conflict between Carnot and Saint-Just:** Accounts of this series of incidents is fragmentary and ex post facto, which makes it difficult to sketch their exact chronology and content. The main accounts of disputes come from CPS members post-9 Thermidor, notably: Réponse, p. 106 ('dictateurs ridicules') and p. 108 (Prairial); *Discours de C.A. Prieur de la Côte-d'Or, 3 Germinal III* (no date, III?), p. 4; and for Carnot, H. Carnot (1907), i, pp. 536–7. See too Baudot (1893), p. 206; Reinhard (1950–2), ii, pp. 463–4; and the testimony of Deschamps in F7 4333, pi. 56.

p. 90 **a private fiefdom:** Robespierre would go direct to the Police Bureau, dropping in on the main committee room to give a few signatures at the day's end: see *Réponse des membres des anciens comités*, p. 61.

p. 90 **Soirée du Camp:** The newspaper's early output is remarkably innocuous.

p. 90 **Robespierre's conduct has always been irreproachable:** AP, p. 559; but then again on p. 562, where Saint-Just considered Robespierre's 8 Thermidor speech: 'il ne s'est plaint non plus des comités', a manifest falsehood. There are no hints about dictatorship in the speech, and Saint-Just is somewhat condescending towards his ally.

p. 91 **at least six signatories:** AP, p. 562.

p. 91 **prelude to a bloody purge:** Bathetically, the speech concludes of those he has denounced: 'je désire qu'ils se justifient et que nous devenions plus sages'. AP, p. 562.

p. 91 **jours de gloire:** Cf. 'Ils ne sont point passés, les jours de gloire': AP, p. 558.

p. 92 **Billaud's conception:** Billaud-Varenne (1992) and Klemperer (2018) highlight overlaps in their thinking. See too Gauchet (2018), p. 189.

p. 92 **'social institutions':** For Saint-Just, see *Oeuvres* (1908), pp. 492–508.

p. 93 **'we are on the edge of a volcano':** For Billaud's phrase, see Saint-Just's undelivered speech, AP, p. 599. For the Vesuvius report, see e.g. *Courrier républicain*, 1 Thermidor.

p. 93 **more credibility:** Robespierre's use of death tropes is extensive: see above, p. 36, and note, 'his signature trope'.

p. 93 **except for men he doesn't like:** *Réponse de Billaud-Varenne* (1795), p. 26.

p. 94 **waiting for defeats:** Ibid., p. 24.

p. 94 **loyally stuck by Robespierre:** See his speech on 24 Prairial, AP 91, pp. 549–51. Most recently he also backed him up over the fraternal banquets issue. See below, pp. 112–3.

p. 94 **Robespierre's demand for heads seems insatiable:** Lyons (1975b), p. 140 (citing Vilate).

p. 95 **'digging his own grave':** Lindet cited in Walter (1974), p. 95n.

p. 95 **to expel Danton:** On the arrest and its aftermath, see esp. Hampson (1991), pp. 155–74.

p. 95 **a charge-sheet against Danton:** OCR, xi, pp. 429–49 (Robespierre's memorandum which formed the basis for the charge-sheet against Danton). No fuss was made of the fact that Robert Lindet did in fact refuse to sign the arrest warrant.

p. 96 **defenceless submission:** See above, p. 31.

p. 96 **a few infant steps:** For these moves, see esp. *Réponse des anciens membres des comités*, p. 107. See also above, p. 63.

p. 98 **talk of Fouché being there:** Most accounts do not mention Fouché and his presence may have been left vague.

p. 98 **to the representatives of the nation:** As noted near the start of his speech: AP, p. 558.

p. 98 **the *gens de bien*:** Pro-Jacobin sentiments at AP, p. 561. He invokes the 'gens de bien' at the start of his speech. A footnote suggests he may have been thinking 'meilleurs gens de bien': p. 558.

PART II: SETTING FOR A DRAMA: 5.00 A.M. TO MIDDAY (PP. 101–87)

05.00/5.00 a.m. (pp. 103–13)

p. 103 **'where Morpheus never sprinkles his poppy-dust':** *TP*, i, p. 877. Mercier's *TP* and *NP* are essential sources for times of the Parisian day: see esp. *TP*, pp. 873ff., 'Les heures du jour'. Delattre (2004) is also helpful. Les Halles was not the only major marketplace within the city by the late eighteenth century: see *Atlas*, p. 46. The Farmers-General wall had been built as a customs barrier. Mainly constructed in wood in fact, it was 15 feet high and 15 miles long. For food specialities, see Abad (2002), esp. pp. 660–6.

p. 103 **a strict embargo on noise:** Mercier waking, *TP*, i, p. 876. Clamart is in the pr. XIIe. See also Delattre (2004), pp. 216–17 ('whip in hand').

p. 104 **municipal street-cleaners:** Ibid., pp. 240–1; and for animals in the city, see Serna (2017), esp 32–5. For the cats, see *TP*, i, p. 914, and more generally, ibid., pp. 240–1.

p. 104 **coffee-houses, bars, and taverns:** Mercier, *TP*, i, p. 878 & ii, p. 206. See too Roche (1985). For labour-markets, see Delattre (2004), pp. 255–6. The Pont-au-Change (pr. Ie. & IVe.) joins the Right Bank to the Ile de la Cité.

p. 104 **queue:** APP AA (Montblanc), for early starts. Mayor Fleuriot-Lescot tried to ban queues, but to no avail. Pierre Caron (1914) contains extensive Ministry of the Interior spy reports on queues from late 1793 through to spring 1794. For the period after the abolition of the ministries in April 1794, there are less copious CPS and CGS spy reports (e.g. see above, for Rousseville, pp. 11–16). There is much in the F7 series, however, while many newspapers pick up street conversation and rumours.

p. 105 **an *émeute*:** For the vocabulary range, see Nicolas (2002), pp. 19–25.

p. 105 **'Queue' is a freshly coined word:** Discussion of the word in the newspaper, *Courrier de l'égalité*, 4 Prairial II. It is echoed in the *Courrier républicain*, 2–4 Prairial and in the *Nouvelles politiques, nationales et étrangères*, 7 Prairial.

p. 105 **The 1793 Constitution:** A decree of 10 October 1793, introduced by Saint-Just, ruled that the government would be 'revolutionary until the peace'. The 1793 Constitution had been agreed but was not implemented.

p. 105 **an implicit contract:** This is one of the central points of Albert Soboul's classic thesis (1958). For 'measly merchandise', see OCR, ix, pp. 275–6.

p. 105 **Jacques Roux:** For Roux and the *enragés*, besides Soboul, see Rose (1968).

p. 105 **the Price Maximum:** Besides older work by Mathiez (1927d) and Calvet (1933), see a number of recent essays by Dominique Margairaz, notably (1991), (1993: with Philippe Minard), (1994), and (2008).

p. 106 **effective action against the aristocracy of wealth:** Calvet (1933) for the commissioners; and Cobb (1987) for *armées révolutionnaires*.

p. 106 **Robert Lindet:** Montier (1899) refers to and quotes from untraced memoirs by Lindet. See also below, p. 49.

p. 106 **confiscating hoarded goods:** APP AA240 (Temple), 7–8 Thermidor. For a similar case in the Droits-de-l'Homme section, see APP AA136, 9 Thermidor.

p. 107 **'the locks of liberty':** AP 74, p. 535. & ibid., 72, pp. 678. On war industry, see Alder (1997), esp. pp. 253–91 (which updates the still valuable Richard [1922]), and Le Roux (2011), esp. ch. 4, pp. 167–213.

p. 107 **the foremost centre for military manufacture:** Besides Alder, Le Roux, and Richard, see Gillispie (2004), p. 424; and for the geography of war manufacture, *Atlas*, p. 73. For street uncleanliness generally, see Mercier, *NP*, p. 645 and Saddy (1977). It is a constant leitmotiv in spy reports in Caron (1914), passim. There was also universal condemnation of worsening street lighting.

p. 108 **'We'd have to be real buggers':** Caron (1914), iii, p. 279. Courtille was at the edge of the city in the area now covered by Belleville (pr. XIX. & XXe.).

p. 108 **Barère's *carmagnoles*:** *Carmagnole* speeches should be distinguished from the *carmagnole* jacket worn by sans-culottes.

p. 108 **popular thirst for military victories is unquenchable:** See Barère's comments to this effect in *Observations de Barère* (25 ventôse III), pp. 8–10. For this occasion, AP, p. 536. For the *carmagnoles*, see Gershoy (1962), pp. 217–21.

p. 108 **to encourage trade and not to kill it:** AP 86, p. 80 (4 March/14 Ventôse).

p. 109 **economic offenders:** Calvet (1933), p. 36; and Greer (1935) who shows less than one per cent of indictments were for economic offences. See also Jones (1988), p. 120.

p. 109 **Workers have still felt the pinch:** For these disturbances and their context, see Soboul (1958), pp. 932–51 and Eude (1936). See too, for the print-workers, Cohen (2011), pp. 143–9.

p. 109 **imprisons strikers:** Ording (1930), pp. 78–9.

p. 110 **the assignat:** On the assignat, see Spang (2015). For the assignat's cash value over time, see Jones (1988), p. 237. For the bonfire, see *Moniteur*, 10 Thermidor (issued on 9th). The Capucines convent was located on the Rue Saint-Honoré.

p. 110 **the assignat presses:** Robespierre's ally Martial Herman had all striking print workers thrown into gaol, where they were still languishing. Ording (1930), p. 79; F7 4708 d. veuve Fontenas; and SCD, pp. 176–7. For an attempted burglary in 1793 aimed at stealing huge piles of assignats, see Cohen (2011), p. 100.

p. 110 **'if everyone shared the same dearth':** Caron (1914), v, p. 29. See too ibid., iii, p. 82; v, p. 4; v, p. 21 (black market) and v, p. 158 (restaurants).

p. 111 **a transformation of consumer behaviour:** See the classic work of Daniel Roche (1987); and Jones & Spang (1999).

p. 111 **Robespierre's first act:** OCR, x, pp. 9–10. For food riots, see Rudé (1959), pp. 115–19.

p. 111 **Anger drives protest:** For the culture of the queue, see esp. Caron (1914), passim; Alder (1997), p. 272 ('pretty speeches'); and Caron, iv, p. 317 ('fucking Republic').

p. 111 **the best way to bring back abundance:** F7 4594 d. Beryetter. The comment was made by a militant from the Unité section.

p. 112 **'fraternal banquets':** For an important overview, see Aberdam (2013). He corrects Soboul (1958), pp. 980–5. Payan's long attack on the banquets as an aristocratic plot in a speech in the Maison Commune on 28 Messidor was extensively quoted in newspapers: see e.g. *Messager du soir*, 30 Messidor. For Robespierre, see OCR, x, pp. 533–5. Cf. Soboul (1958), pp. 983n. and 984. For examples of the crackdown at local level, see APP AA49 (Amis-de-la-Patrie) and AA70 (Arsenal).

p. 112 **'a first draft of the image':** *Correspondance politique de Paris*, 22 Messidor. For the 'impure breed', see above, p. 33.

p. 112 **Wage Maximum:** The actual document is rather rare: I consulted a copy at F12 1544/30. See too BNF NAF 2663 (Lepeletier section papers). Discussion with the Commune was started by Carnot and Prieur de la Côte d'Or, the CPS's two military experts. It was noted that such a measure would cause major wage reductions which would need to be handled carefully. DXLII/11 d. Commune de Paris.

p. 113 **salary of National Agent Payan:** Payan's salary was increased from 4,000 to 5,000 livres: AFII 65. See AFII 23A for the CPS.

p. 113 **'they will work':** F7* 2482 (Faubourg-Montmartre), entry for 9 Thermidor.

06.00/6.00 a.m. (pp. 114–25)

p. 114 **the home of Maurice Duplay:** The account of Robespierre's home life draws especially on the descriptions of Elizabeth Le Bas, née Duplay, the daughter of Maurice, in Stéfane-Pol (1900). For the room, see ibid., pp. 149–50. See too Charlotte Robespierre (1835), esp. pp. 84–5; Hamel (1865), i, pp. 518–21 & iii, pp. 281–99; and Lenôtre (1895), pp. 15–64 (this contains illustrations and descriptions of the house and courtyard). Robespierre's preference for the old calendar is suggested by his description of his time absent from the CPS as six weeks rather than four *décades*: OCR, x, p. 565.

p. 115 **Timber for these constructions:** F1c 84 d. 'Fêtes messidor et thermidor'. There is an account item for 7,515 livres for 'Duplay menuisier' for expenses incurred, with indications that his men were working through till the night of 9–10 Thermidor on the Bara and Viala festival.

p. 115 **Antoine Auzat:** F7 4583 d. Auzat. See too Auzat, *Pétition* (1795).

p. 115 **Philippe Le Bas:** For Le Bas, see Cousin (2010). The blue eyes are mentioned in Langlois (1836), p. 17, describing an encounter in the École de Mars. The Rue de l'Arcade is in the pr. VIIIe.

p. 115 **Maurice Duplay's nephew, Simon:** Members of the Duplays have a police file in F7 4694. The file on Simon is a long one. See too the interrogations of family members in W 79 d. Duplay. Simon denied being Robespierre's secretary. However, the files noting collection of deputies' pay-cheques show 'Duplay fils' picking up Robespierre's salary monthly between Pluviôse and Prairial. I have assumed Jacques-Maurice Duplay was too young for this task and that it must have been Simon. C 2443/2. See too Garmy (1962–3). Simon entered the CPS bureaucracy at the end of Floréal: AFII 24 pl. 192.

p. 116 **a cosy family life:** Although it appears some deputies came socially *chez* Duplay, this fell away in the last months. Saint-Just and Le Bas were still regular attenders.

p. 116 **harmonious domestic milieu:** For Robespierre's childhood, for which there are highly conflicting accounts, see McPhee (2012), pp. 1–12; and Leuwers (2014), pp. 17–32. For 'Bon-Ami', see Stéfane-Pol (1901), pp. xxii, 120, 131, etc.

p. 116 **leisure moments:** Choisy, where Mme Duplay came from, was a favoured haunt. See the dossiers on Robespierre's contacts there in W 79.

p. 116 **elder brother to Augustin:** Biographical treatments in Luzzatto (2010) for Augustin, and Cousin (2010) for Augustin and Le Bas.

p. 117 **'All lungs, no brain':** Courtois (1887), p. 940.

p. 117 **plans for a military offensive:** Barrier (2019) provides an excellent recent discussion of the episode.

p. 117 **'They love me so':** Charlotte Robespierre (1835), p. 87.

p. 118 **'not a drop of blood':** OCR, ii, p. 293. Ricord lived at Rue neuve Saint-Eustache (pr. Rue Aboukir, IIe.). Augustin had moved there from the Rue Saint-Florentin (pr. Ie.)

p. 118 **the somewhat severe Eléonore:** Hamel claims that she and Robespierre were affianced, on the basis of Le Bas family testimony: Hamel, iii, p. 293. It was said at Choisy the two lived 'en concubinage': F7 4769 d. Lauveaux. For Danton ('balls'), see Riouffe (1795), p. 75. I have noted that this obscene comment is not present in all copies of Riouffe. I consulted a version at the Houghton Library, Harvard University (which had belonged to Arthur Young). See too Mantel (2000), a striking analysis.

p. 118 **Robespierre has become a celebrity:** For Robespierre, women and celebrity, see Fleischmann (1909) and Shusterman (2014). For a marriage proposal, see OCR, iii, p. 292. Lilti (2014) is fundamental to the study of celebrity in this period. He does not attach the description to Robespierre, but my sense is that his analytical framework matches Robespierre well.

p. 118 **'bombastically repeat your name':** OCR, ii, p. 262.

p. 118 **engravings and table-top busts:** Mentions of this are found in descriptions of visits to the Duplays by fellow deputies La Révellière-Lépeaux, Fréron, and Barbaroux. See

Leuwers (2014), pp. 245–7. For the trade in reproductions of images of deputies, see Freund (2014). For the letters, see de Baecque (1994), pp. 166–8.

p. 118 **letters from provincial patriots:** On naming, see F7 4774 13 d. Le Gentil (Le Gentil case); F7 4775/48 d. Vincent and Courtois I, doc. XIV, p. 111 (Deschamps, godfather); ibid., pp. 111–12; F7 4336 pl. 6 (sons named Maximilien); F7 4774/40 d. Mauvage (daughter Maximilienne); OCR, iii, p. 292 (marriage proposal); and for pets, see below p. 371.

p. 119 **'Tiger covered with the purest blood of France':** Courtois I, doc. LX, p. 224. See also the discussion by Bell & Mintzker (2018), pp. 124–8.

p. 119 **suspicious incidents:** For the Renault incident, see AP 91, pp. 32–3. Rouvière who was a further suspected assassin was guillotined on 9 Thermidor: F7 4775/3 d. Rouvière and W 433. For another example of suspicious pestering, see F7 4775/8 d. veuve Ruvet. There was an incident involving Saint-Just too: see CPS, xii, p. 399; xiii, pp. 311–12, 339, 388; and also one for Collot in [Saladin], *Rapport au nom de la Commission des 21* (III), p. 8.

p. 119 **'fear written in his face':** F7 4755 d. Lacombe. For his earlier illness, see above, p. 67. W 501 for the Fouquier quotation.

p. 120 **a line of defence:** Edme-Bonaventure Courtois, the editor of Robespierre's papers, cited as members of Robespierre's 'escorte', Nicolas, Garnier Delaunay, Didier, Girard, and Châtelet: Courtois I, LIX, p. 223. Of the three involved in the Renault affair, for Didier, see F7 4676 and W 501. Robespierre's sister Charlotte claimed that Didier served as her brother's secretary: F7 4774/94 (interrogation 13 Thermidor). One account had Didier sleeping in the same bed as Robespierre: F7 4676 d. Didier. See too Didier's interrogations in W 500 and W 501. For the Choisy connection, see above, p. 116. For Châtelet, see Higonnet (2011), esp. pp. 251–4. And for Boulanger, see esp. Cobb (1987), pp. 65–6; Calvet (1941), pp. 57–8. His army record is at AAG 8YD201.

p. 120 **Other members of the bodyguard group:** For François-Pierre Garnier Delaunay, see F7 4716 d. Garnier Delaunay; for Charles-Léopold Renaudin, see F7 4774/90 d. Renaudin; and for Pierre-François Girard, see his interrogation at W 501. See also S&M, pp. 83, 87, 123; and Calvet (1941), pp. 65, 75.

p. 121 **economic benefit:** For the case of Nicolas, see S&M, p. 83; Calvet (1941), p. 74. See too F7 4774/57, W 434, and T 1684. For glimpses of his career as a publisher under the Terror, see F7 4774/80 d. Potier; AFII 66; and OCR, x, pp. 465, n. 1 and 587, n. 4. See too W 500 (Girard's interrogation); OCR, iii, p. 262 (7 Ventôse II); and below, pp. 342–3.

p. 121 **'I would blow your brains out':** Stéfane-Pol (1900), p. 136. See too above, p. 115.

p. 122 *Messager du soir:* The newspaper is cited at OCR, p. 576, n 3. For misreporting, see below, pp. 145–6, 212–14.

p. 122 **CPS Police Bureau:** The best coverage of the work of the bureau is still provided by Ording, 1930. See also Walter (1989), pp. 581–91. What remains of the archive is retrievable from F7 3821–2 and F7 4437. For Simon Duplay's role, ibid., p. 42. See also above, the discussion of CPS spy Rousseville: pp. 11–15. Ording, pp. 47, 101, suggests the Bureau dealt with around 4,000 individual items for 474 cases. Secretary

Lejeune was doubtless exaggerating when he stated there were 20,000 cases: Bégis (1896), p. 18.

p. 123 **office staff:** AFII 23B pl. 191; see also Ording (1930), pp. 36–9.

p. 123 **working with the CGS:** Ording (1930), esp. chs. V, VI, pp. 87ff.

p. 123 **a gendarme at the entrance:** CPS, xiv, pp. 519–20.

p. 123 **closes down sectional committees:** In fact, there were accusations of peculation and corruption levelled against the individuals, but Robespierre adjudged these less important than the personal insults. Robespierre's attempts to purge a number of sectional committees (and the CGS response) can be followed in AFII 57. See too Soboul (1958), pp. 966–74.

p. 124 **the scale of his involvement:** In a noted passage in the speech (OCR, x. p. 565), he spoke of his 'momentary' involvement and 'short period of management' extending to some 30 cases of a 'weakly organized body'. This is clearly incorrect. Cf. Lejeune's testimony in Bégis (1896), p. 15.

p. 124 **Catherine Théot:** See above, p. 37.

p. 124 **marginalia:** See esp. Walter (1989), pp. 581–91.

p. 125 **Robespierre had seen off Louvet:** See Louvet (1792), and the exchanges in OCR, IX, pp. 63–7 (29 October) and 77–101 (15 November 1792). There were many other back-to-the-wall moments in Robespierre's career.

07.00/7.00 a.m. (pp. 126–39)

p. 126 **Blaise Lafosse:** F7 4758 d. Lafosse. See too W 79 (listing of municipal officers arrested after 10 Thermidor).

p. 126 **Today's agenda:** The record of municipal governance for this period vanished in the Commune fires of 1871. But following Payan's arrest, his briefcase was found to contain reports on the subjects listed, presumably for today's consideration. See AFII 48 d. 369.

p. 126 **Jean-Baptiste Avril:** F7 4583 d. Avril. See too W 79 d. Avril and F7 4430. F7 4332 pl. 2, pi. 19 shows that the festival was discussed.

p. 127 **sectional framework:** Mellié (1898) retains its value for details of sectional organization. See too *Atlas* (2000), pp. 14–15 and 132 (with following map, which includes name changes).

p. 128 **Paris Commune:** For an overview of the municipality see 'Commune de Paris/Département de Paris' by Emilie Ducoudray in *DHRF*, pp. 265–71. For the Commune's formation in 1789, see Godechot (1965). For the period under the Convention, see SCD, passim; Braesch (1911); and Eude (1933 to 1936). On the General Council's composition, SCD, pp. 98–102 and pp. 361–79. On Bernard, ibid., p. 100; and F7 4595 d. J. P. Bernard.

p. 128 **even relatively humble social positions:** SCD, pp. 361–79, passim; F7 4774/89 d. Renard; and F7 4582 d. Aubert. The ages of over 90 per cent are known. The breakdown is as follows: 20s, 7 per cent; 30s, 33 per cent; 40s, 35 per cent; 50s, 18 per cent; 60s, 60s, 6 per cent.

p. 129 **Writers and professionals:** SCD, pp. 361–78 for an overview of occupations, with added details from individual police files. For Paris, see above, p. 70 and for painters, see esp. Dowd (1948) on David, and his police file at F7 4663. For Châtelet, see above, p. 120 and Calvet (1933), p. 75. See too W 80 d. Cietty and F7 4702 d. Faro.

p. 129 **Jean-Jacques Arthur:** Arthur was the son of an English watchmaker who arrived in Paris in 1750 and from the 1770s worked in partnership with Grenard in the wallpaper business. Arthur *fils* took a growing interest in the trade and from c. 1791 was in partnership with François Robert as the former partnership broke down. See Velut (2005), passim, and F7 4581 d. Arthur. Grenard appears to have retired in 1789. The Rue Louis-le-Grand is in the pr. IIe.

p. 129 **Jean-Guillaume Barelle:** F7 4586 d. Barelle. He later explained his absence with reference to this being his pay-day.

p. 129 **the former Hôtel de Ville:** For municipal government prior to 1789, Chagniot (1988), pp. 93–151; Williams (1979) and Milliot (2011). The Place de la Maison Commune is now the Place de l'Hôtel de Ville (IVe.). For the relationship with the river, see Backouche (2000), esp. pp. 112–21.

p. 130 **have never made more noise:** *NP*, p. 916. *Bulletin républicain* reported on 25 Floréal that the cathedral had been so renamed (since 1793 it had been Temple de la Raison).

p. 130 **alarm cannon:** The cannon was fired during the 31 May 1793 *journée* and also for the festivities of the Supreme Being festival in June. All statues of rulers had been pulled down and most melted down for cannon.

p. 131 **democratic principles:** For a general account, see esp. the classic outline in part 3 of Soboul (1958), pp. 681ff. Cf. SCD, pp. 146ff.; and Eude (1934a and b).

p. 131 **existing councillors:** SCD, pp. 98–117.

p. 131 **Mayor Jean-Baptiste Fleuriot-Lescot:** SCD, pp. 160–1; and 'Lescot-Fleuriot', in *DHRF*, p. 669. For some reason, this reversion of name order was quite frequent. For the father comment, see F7 4774/9 d. Leclerc (Muséum).

p. 131 **Claude-François Payan:** F7 4774/65 d. Payan. See also W 79 (dossier relating to the Drôme department); his private papers at T 528; and the letters and other documentation in *Papiers inédits*, ii, pp. 347–405. For 'Robespierrization' of the Commune, see Eude (1935a).

p. 132 **'take care, spare the innocent':** *Papiers*, ii, p. 371.

p. 133 **more like Robespierre:** The term 'Robespierriste' did not achieve currency until after 9 Thermidor. These men were Robespierristes *avant la lettre*. For Payan's communication, see F7 4437 pl. 6, pi. 49, copied in Courtois I, doc. LVI, pp. 212–17.

p. 133 **proven patriots:** Of the group as a whole, see SCD, pp. 153–4; Courtois I, doc. XXIX, pp. 139–42. The originals may be seen at F7 4335, pl. 5. The only historian to have given this important document much attention is Hardman (2000), though we differ in interpretation.

p. 134 **'marching towards a dictatorship':** F7 4436 d. 1, pi. 21. See too ibid., pi. 17 (esp. testimony of Lamaignère); SCD, p. 112 (Lubin's brother). For Charlemagne, see F7 4639 d. Charlemagne. Bourbon was named on Robespierre's list of patriots: Courtois I, doc. XXIX, p. 140. See too DXLII 11 d. 'Commune de Paris'.

p. 134 **a visit to the theatre:** F7 4710 d. Fourcade. Fourcade claimed he saw Payan at the theatre that night.

p. 135 **the construction of audience seating:** F1c 84 d. 'Fêtes messidor et thermidor'. See above, p. 115, and note, 'timber'.

p. 135 **Bara and Viala-related performances:** David's painting was never finished. See too Guillaume (1891), iv, p. 850 (poems); APP AA60, 7 Thermidor (engravings).

p. 135 **management of the event:** On 8 Thermidor, the starting time was changed from 3.00 p.m. to 9.00 a.m.: Guillaume (1891), iv, p. 856. Fleuriot's order in AFII 48 d. 374 is often reproduced in sectional minutes for 8 Thermidor. Examples of preparations on 8 Thermidor include AFII 47 pl. 364 (Brutus: with Gossec contribution); and F7 4432 pl. 7, pi. 32 (Cité).

p. 136 **President of the Convention:** As President, he would have had the same leading role as Robespierre had done at the Festival of the Supreme Being.

p. 136 **pageant-master David:** David's police dossier at F7 4663 contains a letter of apology to his children's teacher that he would be unable to attend the 10 Thermidor festival, plus the prescription for his emetic. For Barère warning David, see Kuscinski (1916), p. 180.

p. 137 **system of pork rationing:** The system is set out in BNF NAF 2703 (Mutius-Scévole). It crops up as an item in many sectional accounts in AFII 47 and F7 4332. La Salpêtrière hospital is located in the XIIIe.

p. 137 **Sectional officials and committees:** For sections and sectional life, see esp. Soboul (1958), pp. 581ff. See also 'Comités civils', *DHRF*, pp. 256–7. For an in-depth sectional survey, see Slavin (1984), pp. 214–43. For Moulin, see F7 4774/54 d. Moulin. See also Adrien Binon who claimed to be unemployed as a ladies' tailor as he had had all his former aristocratic lady clients guillotined! F7 4601 d. Binon.

p. 138 **Jacques-Louis Ménétra:** Roche (1986): see esp. pp. 124–5 (Dauphin); 127, 180, 194 (Sanson); 181–6 (Rousseau); 192–4 (Condé). It is generally accepted that Ménétra's boasting is excessive. There is a supplement to this Ménétra document at BHVP ms. 768. It covers the Revolutionary period more closely.

p. 138 **a solid citizen:** Roche (1986), pp. 217–38 for the Revolutionary period.

p. 138 **Beneficence Committees:** In-depth study of the Droits-de-l'Homme beneficence committee in Slavin (1984), pp. 278–311. For the philanthropic aspects of section life, see too Woloch (1986); and Weiner (2002).

p. 138 **what the Revolution has achieved:** Although Ménétra's account stresses the bad side of the Terror, he welcomed 1789 and 'the almost supernatural effect [it had which] invigorated us all' (p. 217).

p. 139 **Revolutionary Committee:** See 'Comités de surveillance', *DHRF*, p. 258 for an overview. See too Slavin (1984), pp. 244–77.

p. 139 **Bonnet-Rouge section:** See F7 4774/75 d. Pigeau (a major dossier on sectional corruption). Petty corruption is such a leitmotiv in prison memoirs that it is unlikely to be sheer invention. Long-existent local power struggles constitute a strong theme in the work of Cobb (1970).

p. 139 **careful not to refuse any posts:** Roche (1986), p. 225 (this was the phrase that Ménétra used). For internal rivalries, see pp. 225–9. The theme of fear is explored for national politicians in Linton (2013). See too the example of Mailhe above, p. 42.

08.00/8.00 a.m. (pp. 140–9)

p. 140　**École de Mars:** For the École, see the institution archive at AFII 199; and Langlois (1836). Chuquet (1899) draws heavily on the latter source but is not always reliable. For the École's involvement in 9 Thermidor, Guillaume (1891), iv, pp. 857–9, is excellent. See Robespierre's reports on education in July 1793 based on a report by the assassinated deputy, Lepeletier de Saint-Fargeau: OCR, x, pp. 10–41. See too Palmer (1985), pp. 137–42.

p. 140　**children join in the fun:** *NP*, pp. 545–9.

p. 140　**Louis-Florentin Bertèche:** Often wrongly written la Breteche or Bretache. See Chuquet (1899), pp. 34–7 and 41–2; F7 4596 d. Bertèche. See Guillaume (1891), iv, p. 859 for his vulnerable position.

p. 141　**colourful *opéra-comique* mélange:** For the uniform, see Langlois (1836), pp. 12–13 and Chuquet (1899), pp. 76–8. For the haircuts, see Langlois (1836), pp. 6–7.

p. 141　**refuge for aristocrats:** F7 4783 (report by Rousseville, dated 2 Thermidor). See also the later petition to the CGS from the Neuilly 'citoyennes' who were among the 114 individuals arrested from the village on 16 Messidor: F7 4774/57. They make an appearance in de Bohm (2001), pp. 115–24 (their stay in the Saint-Lazare prison).

p. 141　**'nostalgia':** Dodman (2018). For the insalubrity, see Langlois (1836), pp. 22–3. For discipline and other features, see interviews with staff in Fructidor in F7 4774/72 d. Peyssard.

p. 141　**up since dawn:** See Chuquet (1899), p. 90; Langlois (1836), pp. 18–19. On the daily schedule, see too AFII 199; CPS, pp. 80–1.

p. 141　**a place of honour:** Guillaume (1891), iv, p. 854.

p. 142　**a thin, pale man:** Langlois (1836), pp. 16–17. (Chuquet [1899] is sceptical about the identification.)

p. 142　**Joseph Souberbielle:** For Souberbielle, Chuquet (1899), p. 86.

p. 142　**siege cannon:** Jacobins, pp. 239–40. Le Bas defended the École against these charges.

p. 143　**this morning's newspapers:** For print-shop locations, *Atlas* (2000), p. 80. For the press more generally, see esp. Popkin (1990); Gough (1988); and Darnton & Roche (1989). For the period of the Terror, cf. Bertaud (1994). For the *cris de Paris*, see Milliot (1995), esp. pp. 181–91 and Mercier, *TP*, i, pp. 1050–1.

p. 143　**freedom of the press:** Numbers of titles from Bertaud (2000), p. 302. In September 1789, the overall number of news vendors was set at 300, but this was not observed. See Gough (1988), pp. 51, 203–4, 224–5. Popkin, in Darnton & Roche (1989), p. 147, suggests that the popular *Journal du Soir* alone had 200 vendors.

p. 144　**extended the parameters of democratic debate:** See esp. Popkin (1990) on the press contribution to Revolutionary political culture. For the print industry, see Hesse (1989), p. 92. The pre-1789 daily was the *Journal de Paris*, established in 1777. For democratic space, see Woloch in Baker (1994). For songs, see Jones (1988), p. 261 and Mason (1996). Year II was to prove the zenith of song production across the decade. *Atlas* (2000) lists 38 theatres: pp. 81, 115–16. Exact estimations are made difficult as theatres changed identities, went dark, or moved locations in random ways. Newspaper listings suggest more than a dozen were open for 9 Thermidor. For the theatre generally, see esp. Tissier (1992, 2002); d'Estrée (1913); Maslan (2005); and Hemmings (1994).

p. 144 **by departments far from the capital:** Brissot was elected by the Eure-et-Loir, for example, Carra by the Saône-et-Loire and Fauchet by Calvados. Generally, see Popkin (1990); and Kennedy (1988), p. 322.

p. 144 **Journalists who have seen the scaffold:** See esp. Gough (1988), pp. 103–4 and Bertaud (2000). Mercier was editor of the popular *Annales patriotiques et littéraires* from 1789.

p. 145 **Jacobin line:** It is worth noting that only journalists approved by the Jacobin Club were currently allowed access to the journalists' gallery in the Convention hall.

p. 145 **'the least reporting error':** *Correspondance politique de Paris et des départements,* 8 Prairial II. The next day's issue gave a verbatim account of Robespierre's speech and said they would do the same for Barère's when it was available. This kind of caution is ubiquitous in newspapers consulted. See too the case of 8–9 Thermidor, above, p. 122. Subsidizing the press began in earnest under Roland's Girondin ministry in 1793. Which titles received subsidies changed over time. By Thermidor, editors had to be in the good books of the Jacobin Club.

p. 145 **tried his hand at journalism:** He repeated the exercise with his title, *Lettres à ses commettants,* from late 1792. For contents of both journals, see OCR, iv and v.

p. 145 **'for times of tranquillity':** This phrasing was used in reports in the *Feuille de Paris* and some other journals. The wording in the *Moniteur* was less categorical, though it did call for the arrest of 'faithless journalists' as 'the worst enemies of freedom'. OCR, ix, pp. 370–1 and n. 14. See too Courtois I, doc. XLIII, p. 180 (notebook).

pp. 145–6 **'brûler n'est pas répondre':** For this famous exchange, see OCR, x, p. 309.

p. 146 **'How can it be permitted':** Cited by Bertaud (1994), p. 301. It dates from December 1793.

p. 146 **'it is a most constant fact':** OCR, x, p. 503. For the clash in the Jacobin Club, see OCR, x, pp. 310–11; and for context, Leuwers (2018), pp. 302–3.

p. 146 **did not satisfy Robespierre:** OCR, x, p. 502.

p. 146 **'to mislead public opinion':** Ibid., pp. 502–3.

p. 146 **Foreign Plot:** As his ally Couthon puts it, 'Pitt has a cabinet in Paris just as he has in London', *Réimpression de l'ancien Moniteur,* xxi, p. 66.

p. 147 **A decree of the Convention on 2 August 1793:** Darlow (2012), pp. 152–4; and d'Estrée (1913), pp. 6–7.

p. 147 **'Newspapers are like theatres':** Gough (1988), p. 109.

p. 147 **the most popular play of the Revolutionary decade:** Tissier (2002), p. 488. For the popularity of particular plays, see ibid., pp. 488–9 (based on the whole decade).

p. 148 **two theatre censors:** Darlow (2012), p. 173.

p. 148 **traveller John Moore:** Hemmings (1994), p. 123.

p. 148 **a form of free speech:** Maslan (2005), pp. 23–4; for close attention by spies, see Caron (1914), esp. iii, p. 80; v, pp. 31, 130, 380, etc.

p. 148 **the play was withdrawn:** Courtois I, doc. LVI, p. 212 and F7 4435 d. 4, pi. 53. See too d'Estrée (1913), pp. 133–6, 214–6, 393.

p. 149 **the *Pamela* case:** Neuchâteau was a member of the Legislative Assembly but refused election to the Convention. For the *Pamela* incident, see Poirson ed. (2007). For Robespierre's intemperate attacks on actresses, see OCR, x, p. 101.

p. 149 **'arrests, newspapers and the Revolutionary Tribunal':** *Réponse des membres des anciens comités*, p. 104.

09.00/9.00 a.m. (pp. 150–163)

p. 150 **'Virtue is the order of the day!':** APP AA95 (Montagne). For prostitution generally, see Plumauzille (2016: the order is reproduced at pp. 247–8) and Conner (1995).

p. 150 **women playing a role in public life:** From a strong literature on the subject, see esp. Levy, Applewhite, & Johnson (1979); Godineau (1988); Landes (1988); and Jarvis (2019).

p. 151 **police commissary:** The key source for the commissaires is the unpublished thesis of Vincent Denis (2017). My thanks to him for allowing me to consult it. For the National Guard, see below, pp. 155–7; for JPs, Andrews (1971); and for Civil and Revolutionary Committees, see above, pp. 137–9.

p. 151 **This morning's business:** APP AA136 (Droits-de-l'Homme); AA254 (Fraternité). For similar smuggling offences, see AA163 (Lombards) and AA173 (Montreuil).

p. 151 **Other morning business:** For these issues, see APP AA153 (Gardes-Françaises); AA159 (Invalides); AA77 (Bonne-Nouvelle), AA228 (République).

p. 152 **a stronger NG presence:** AFII 47 d. 367, pi. 14 (Montagne); AFII 48 d. 374, pi. 10; and BNF Fonds français 8607 (Homme-Armé).

p. 152 **policing of suspects:** Boulant (1990) and Matharan (1986) provide overviews. See too 'Suspects', *DHRF*, pp. 1004–8 (by Matharan) and SCD, passim. Michel's police dossier is at F7 4774/45 d. Michel. The figure of 100 prisons includes 48 sectional police cells.

p. 153 **Martin Wichterich:** See above, p. 81. For his quotation, see SCD, p. 157. Note that some of the appointed police administrators were already municipal councillors, negating the need for a further election.

p. 153 **the night shift:** APP AA201 (Panthéon), AA140 (Maison-Commune).

p. 153 **a major cache of jewellery:** F7 3774/67 d. Perinat.

p. 154 **Alexandre Vernet:** APP AB3 26. See above, pp. 16–18.

p. 155 **Giot boasts a very fine moustache:** There are excellent accounts of Giot and his day in his police files: F7 4725 d. Giot and W 79 d. Giot. For the use of a sans-culotte-style moustache by aristocrats, see F7 4627 d. Bunou.

p. 155 **The National Guard:** The Paris National Guard has been sadly neglected by historians, partly at least because extant archives are very thin. The best description from the point of view of this section is Monnier (1989). See too the chapters devoted to the Revolutionary period in Dupuy (2010) and Bianchi & Dupuy (2006).

p. 156 **Floriban:** See above, pp. 23–4.

p. 156 **A hierarchical structure:** See the *Almanach national* for Year II, pp. 416–20.

p. 156 **Cosme Pionnier:** F7 4774/76 d. Pionnier (plus F7 4774/72 under 'Piaunier'). For the Lyon revolt and for the *armée révolutionnaire*, see above, pp. 59 and 106.

p. 157 **principle of election:** Monnier (1989), pp. 149–50.

p. 157 **Rue Hautefeuille:** Pr. VIe. For the weather, see Archives de l'Observatoire, AF1/ 14.1. See above, p. 24.

p. 158 **Louis-Charles:** It is very difficult to construct the former dauphin's life with any degree of accuracy. Reactionary narratives from the late 1790s depicted a scheme of sadistic cruelty on the part of the Simons and the other gaolers. However, there is little hard evidence to prove that these are anything more than counter-revolutionary fabulations. He probably suffered more from severe neglect rather than overt cruelty. The illness which killed him in mid-1795 was probably not evident in mid-1794. For Marie-Thérèse's waking hour, see AP 94, p. 68 (speech by Barras, 27 Thermidor).

p. 158 **Antoine Simon:** Beauchesne (1852), ii, p. 493 for the truss. See too the unusual reference in the letter-diary of Catherine-Innocente de Rougé, duchesse d'Elbeuf, F7 4775/1 (5 July 1793 entry) for Simon's herniotomy skills. For the incest claims, see Hunt (1991).

p. 158 **François Le Lièvre:** F7 4774/4 d. Le Lièvre.

p. 159 **three members of the Commune's General Council:** F7 4775/26 d. Tessier; F7 4775/21 d. Soulié. See also important materials on him in F7 4774/90 d. Renaudin.

p. 159 **a daily NG force:** F7 4391 (240 men). F7 4779 has a collection of orders which gives normal duty guard strengths as follows: Temple prison, 200 men & gunners; Convention, 240 men; Arsenal, 50; Place de la Maison Commune 120; Palais de Justice, 40. The major prisons also had NG detachments on hand along with some gendarmes.

p. 159 **François Hanriot:** F7 4738 d. Hanriot. There is no decent biography and he suffered so much at the hands of post-Thermidorian biographers that it is difficult to grasp the man. See, however, Moreau (2010).

p. 160 **His cheery daily bulletins:** Moreau (2010) is packed with quotations from Hanriot's bulletins on which I draw here. For other orders, see AFII 47 pl. 368, pi. 33; and Moreau (2010), p. 40 ('darning socks').

p. 160 **colourful braided uniforms:** AFII 47 pl. 368, pi. 30–9. See too Caron (1914): i, p. 72 (spies spot Hanriot's ADCs in the Opera); and iv, p. 225 (Hanriot's horse-riding).

p. 160 **Jean Hémart:** See above p. 63. Birembault (1959) provides an overview of Hémart (see esp. p. 315). For the gendarmerie forces within Paris, see Chambon (1793).

p. 162 **an old acquaintance:** AFII 47 pl. 368, pi. 38. Ibid. for his efforts to discover which section has been complaining.

p. 162 **'citizen washer-women':** Ibid., pi. 37.

p. 162 **'Everyone does his guard-duty':** TP, p. 144. A meeting of the Military Council of the Bon-Conseil battalion suggests that here were 44 replacements in total for the section's battalion. Sorbonne Library, ms. 117 fol. 16. We lack other evidence.

p. 162 **'a little republic in each section':** Jacobins, p. 129 (15 May/26 Floréal).

p. 163 **reproduce neighbourhood friendships and solidarities:** See Burstin (2005b), p. 480n.

10.00/10.00 a.m. (pp. 164–75)

p. 164 **Fouquier-Tinville:** For Fouquier, no adequate biography exists. See however Dunoyer (1913), which contains long verbatim quotations from Fouquier's trial; Labracherie (1961); and T 28 (his estate).

p. 164 **Fouquier met Cn. Vergne:** Unless indicated, details of the Vergne dinner come from Fouquier's trial documentation, W 500 and W 501. The memoranda which he wrote for his own defence have been published in Fleischmann (1911). For Coffinhal, see his papers at T 1611 (mainly pre 1789) and his police file in F7 4650. Note that Courtois's canonical account mixes this Vergne up with a completely different Vergne from Lepeletier section: Courtois II, p. 131. For Desboisseaux, another denizen of the Ile Saint-Louis, see F7 4671 d. Desboisseaux.

p. 164 **assault by a NG patrol:** F7 4710 d. Fouquier-Tinville; F7 4662, d. Daubenton; F7 4774/13 d. Legrand; W 116; and APP AB353. The incident took place in the Montagne section. The men seem to have been drunk and the police were trying to deal with hordes of prostitutes from the Palais-Royal at the same time.

p. 165 **the main courtroom:** For the Revolutionary Tribunal, see Boulant (2018) which updates Lenôtre (1908), which though strong on archival material is not infrequently misleading on historiography and interpretation. Ibid., p. 125 for Dumas's colouring. Godfrey (1951) provides an overview of the Tribunal's workings. See too Wallon (1880–2) and Fairfax-Cholmeley (forthcoming).

p. 165 **humiliated and angry:** See above, p. 54.

p. 165 **a dark celebrity in Paris:** Lenôtre (1908), pp. 275–6. There were other denunci-ations of Dumas too, notably by Loys (F7 4774/26 d. Loys) and F7 4768 d. Lauchet (a high-level CGS secretary).

p. 165 **enemies from his native Jura department:** W 79 d. Dumas; F7 4687; F7 4768 d. Lauchet; and scattered material in W 500, W 501. See too his estate at T 715. See Dumas's highly motivated counter-attacks on CGS personnel in the Jacobins on 6 Thermidor. Jacobins, pp. 232–3.

p. 165 **no love lost:** For Fouquier's antipathy to Dumas, whom he claimed to have regarded as his 'mortal enemy', see Fleischmann (1911), p. 241 and passim. *NP*, p. 587, for physical differences.

p. 165 **cosies up to Robespierre:** Lenôtre (1908), pp. 272–3.

p. 166 **irascible characters:** These characterizations emerge strongly in the witness state-ments at Fouquier's trial: W 500, W 501. For the clerk story (Legris), see Wallon (1880–2), v, p. 59.

p. 166 **Dumas's offices:** Lenôtre (1908), pp. 120–1 (map of law courts), p. 2 (mattress).

p. 166 **Café des Subsistances:** W 500, 501. For the bar-staff's role, see the statements by café proprietor Morisan, his wife, and daughter. The trial documentation for 9 Thermidor is located at W 433 d. 975.

p. 166 **Félix is new to the job:** F7 4704 d. Félix; SCD, pp. 150–2.

p. 167 **good patriotic citizens:** Godfrey (1951), pp. 42–52, for judges and jurors. Today's jurors are listed in the trial record (W 433).

p. 167 **'solid' jurors:** See above, p. 137. The phrase '"solid" jurors' comes from juror Trinchard, cited in Wallon (1880–2), iv, p. 113. Desboisseaux, Fouquier's fellow

guest on the Ile Saint-Louis was also a 'solid' juror. The continuity in jury membership shown in the trials of the Hébertists, Dantonists, the motley grouping of their
followings, and the trial of Madame Elisabeth, King Louis XVI's sister, flatly rules out
the possibility of lot-drawing.

p. 167 **'a tribunal of blood'**: 'Tribunal de sang' was a phrase used by Robespierre to
recognize a perspective on the court with which he disagreed. See OCR, x, p. 558.
It is a section heading in Campardon (1862), i, p. 328. For numbers executed see the
classic Greer (1935), summarized in Jones (1988), pp. 120–1.

p. 167 **Law of 22 Prairial:** For 22 Prairial law, see AP 92, pp. 482–7. For the Couthon
quote, see AP 91, p. 546.

p. 168 **to centralize revolutionary justice:** However, there were exceptions, notably
tribunals established at Orange and Arras.

p. 168 **Martial Herman**: For Herman, see F7 4743 d. Herman, F7 4764 d. Lanne, and
W 501 (dossiers on Herman and Lanne). For the CPS Police Bureau, see above,
pp. 122–5. For his role regarding prisoners, see Jourdan (2018), pp. 265–8.

p. 168 **escape plots:** F7 4598 d. Biancourt.

p. 168 **engendering plot denunciation:** The historiography of the prison plots is murky.
One gets a sense of the games in play from the legal depositions at F7 4437. There is
helpful, if dated, coverage in Wallon (1880–2), v, pp. 53–177. See more recently
Jourdan (2018), pp. 271–7.

p. 169 **the man thought to be missing:** Wallon (1880–2), v, p. 171.

p. 169 **lack of adequate documentation:** This is a recurrent theme in depositions in
Fouquier's trial, W 500, W 501. See too F7 4335 d. 6.

p. 169 **personal reasons:** See above, p. 165.

p. 169 **Fouquier sometimes winces:** A number of references to this in W 500 and W 501.

pp. 169–70 **their guilt had already been established:** See the explicit comment to this
effect by juror Trinchard in W 500. *Fournées* were more numerous after 22 Prairial,
especially with the prison plots.

p. 170 **'good sans-culottes':** B&R, 35, p. 102. See too Roberts (2000), pp. 61–2 (sketching).

p. 171 **Antoine Thibaudeau:** See above, p. 157. Thibaudeau's memoirs were published in
1825, and again in 1827. However, he subsequently revised them extensively and
François Pascal published a revised version in 2007. Thibaudeau offers a very full
account of the day and one generally adjudged fair and accurate.

p. 172 **Mercier counselled:** *TP*, p. 1075.

p. 172 **Pont-Neuf:** Ibid., pp. 932 (oranges), 1256 (shoe-cleaners).

p. 172 **find a way:** Thibaudeau (2007), pp. 111–12.

p. 172 **Robespierre disgusts him:** Ibid., pp. 77–86 (for family disputes); and pp. 67–70,
111–13 (thoughts going into the day).

p. 173 **Locksmith Jean-Baptiste Didier:** See above, p. 120.

p. 173 **if he is needed:** I am drawing especially on two interrogations of Didier in W 501.
See also W 79 d. 'Notes et renseignements relatifs à différens prévenus'; and F7 4676
d. Didier.

p. 174 **as he and Didier leave the house:** B&R, 34, p. 3. It is sometimes claimed that Saint-Just visited Robespierre after leaving the CPS offices in the early hours. There is no evidence to this effect. The two men may have arrived at the same time.

11.00/11.00 a.m. (pp. 176–87)

p. 176 **the old Tuileries palace:** For the palace, see Boulant (2016), Carmona (2004), and Sainte-Fare & Jacquin (1989). These update Lenôtre (1895), pp. 67–138. See also above, p. 48.

p. 177 **planted with potatoes:** The Commune decided on this use for the gardens following the popular demonstrations of 4–5 September 1793. See Spary (2014), p. 167.

p. 177 **pilfering as usual:** Loss of wallets recorded for the day: APP AA250 (Tuileries), AA127 (Mont-Blanc), and F7 4764 d. Lanoy.

p. 178 **A very large majority of the 749 deputies:** See Jones (2020) for an analysis of deputies' addresses.

p. 178 **private lodgings:** Ibid.; and for the neighbourhood more generally see cf. Roche (2000), pp. 120–41 (esp. map III.3 on p. 131 for the hotel park); Coquéry (2011); and Spang (2000) (shopping and eating).

p. 178 **gambling and prostitution:** Plumauzille (2016), esp. pp. 94–114. This shows continuity with the Ancien Régime picture described in Benabou (1987). See F7 4335 d. 1 (case of Virolle, who treated Conventionnels for venereal infection).

p. 178 **large-scale removal of the aristocracy:** Roche (2001), p. 147. For Armonville, see Laurent (1924).

p. 180 **order of the day:** The meeting regulations are contained in the 'Règlement de la Convention nationale', passed 28 September 1792. See AP 52, 205–9.

p. 180 **meetings are averaging:** The estimate of 400 comes from Brunel (1989), p. 81. Details of missions in Biard (2002) suggests that around 60 deputies were on mission on this day in the departments or with the armies. Special leave was also needed for long-term permission to be absent. Records suggest less than six such absences at this time: C 312–13. The number did not include Chales who was present, but had been granted a period of spa convalescence on 1 Thermidor: F7 4637 d. Chales. Besides David, CGS member Jagot also claimed to be sick on this day. AP 94, pp. 29–30.

p. 180 **Duplay is there:** Thibaudeau (2007), pp. 112–13.

p. 180 **checked at the door:** Observance of rules of admission was policed by a special deputy-staffed committee of inspectors of the hall. See Cohen (2011), esp. pp. 98–9.

p. 180 **in larger numbers than usual:** See the untitled (and largely unknown) account of the day by Convention usher Jacques-August Rose (often written Roze) in the Merlin de Thionville papers in the BNF NAF 244. He states that more deputies than normal were present from 10.00 a.m. onwards. C 2458 shows extensive purchase of vinegar for cleaning purposes.

p. 181 **swallowed an emetic:** David's police dossier at AN F7 4663 contains the emetic prescription and other related materials. See too above, p. 136 (alleged tip-off by Barère).

p. 181 **expulsion from the Club:** This was certainly being said, but it isn't clear whether these were Couthon's words, from the fragmentary record of the meeting that we have.

p. 181 **Cambon:** See above, p. 57.

p. 181 **Robespierre ejecting his rivals:** Thibaudeau (2007), pp. 111–12; id. (1827), p. 88.

p. 181 **covertly coordinating their plans:** Durand-Maillanne (1834), p. 199.

p. 182 **in the Convention hall:** See references at p. 176 for the layout of the room. Lenôtre's account is particularly useful for drawing on contemporary descriptions.

p. 182 **bellows-lunged Danton complained:** Boulant (2016), p. 150.

p. 182 **Paris Jacobin Club delegation:** See above, p. 47.

p. 182 **six secretaries:** The current secretaries were elected at the meeting on 1 Thermidor. AP, p. 323.

p. 183 **'The lictors bring to Brutus the bodies of his sons':** The painting is currently in the Louvre.

p. 184 **routine items:** Besides the account in the AP, pp. 541–50, I have drawn on the originals at C 314. The order of the small business of the day is set out in C 311. It contains no mention of Saint-Just but major policy speeches were generally given priority on the nod. See Simonin (2008), pp. 285–8.

p. 184 **200 letters:** De Baecque (1994), pp. 165–6 for the statistics.

p. 185 **a certain nervousness:** Thibaudeau (2007), 112–13.

p. 185 **a report on the government:** See above, p. 45.

p. 186 **the joint meeting of the CPS and the CGS:** I draw here particularly on the account by CGS member Ruhl, at F7 4775/5. See Cobb (1955) for a transcription and brief commentary.

p. 186 **not Saint-Just:** Fouché's presence seems uncertain, despite evidence that he was convoked for the meeting. As well as above, p. 98, and note, 'talk of Fouché', see *Réponse des ancien membres des comités*, p. 8.

p. 187 **'the most evil of men':** Ibid., p. 108.

p. 187 **'Injustice has closed my heart':** For Barère's account on 13 Fructidor of the episode in the Convention, see AP 96, p. 121.

PART III: A PARLIAMENTARY COUP: MIDDAY TO 5.00 P.M. (PP. 189–266)

12.00/12 noon (pp. 191–9)

p. 191 **'This has got to end!':** For the account of the two Convention sessions on 9 Thermidor, I am following the reconstructed record in the AP, pp. 541–58. For political reasons, the official account was only agreed much later, in Year IV (late 1795). The AP draws on this but also other current accounts, notably in the minutes of the sessions and in early newspaper reporting. See too the relevant section in OCR, x, pp. 588–613. Like Françoise Brunel (1989), I also draw on the very early account by Charles Duval (III). There are some frankly insoluble differences between the different accounts, particularly regarding the order of some of the speeches. In addition, some deputy memoirs are also useful for the sessions, notably Thibaudeau's. For Tallien's exclamation, see Thibaudeau (2007), p. 113.

p. 191 **His controlled anger:** For Saint-Just's demeanour, see Duval (Year III), p. 3. His undelivered speech may be consulted at AP, pp. 558–62.

p. 192 **'Come into the hall':** Anecdote from Courtois II, p. 39n.

p. 192 **not privy to Tallien's intentions:** I differ from most historians in not seeing the action of this session as the unfolding of a single plot. There is no evidence of prior collaboration, and it is much more likely that Tallien's plans were unknown to the CPS and may not have got far either within the Lecointre group (few of whom joined in the day's course of events).

p. 192 **an electric shock:** Thibaudeau (1827), i, p. 82. The phrase comes from the earlier version of the memoirs.

p. 193 **Robespierre's faithful and ruthless henchman:** See above, p. 86.

p. 193 **the Tarpeian rock:** The speech seems ambiguous as to who would in fact be hurled from the Tarpeian rock.

p. 193 **Cunning or coincidence?:** It is impossible to know if there was indeed collusion between Robespierre, Saint-Just, and Couthon on the day's procedures. It is not implausible, but there is no evidence either way. It is worth bearing in mind how generally disorganized the three were throughout the day. But the way events transpired convinced many deputies of the reality of a conspiracy of the three.

p. 193 **a very low opinion of Tallien:** See Billaud's put-down of Tallien in the debates on the 22 Prairial law: AP 91, p. 549. For Collot and Tallien, see [Tallien], *Collot mitraillé par Tallien* (1795).

p. 194 **'with a dagger':** AP, p. 551. See too above, p. 24. For the dagger, Ruault (1976), pp. 359–60.

p. 194 **Cabarrus supplied the dagger:** See Bourquin (1987), pp. 236–7. There is no evidence that Tallien visited Cabarrus in gaol, while getting hold of a dagger and then sending it out from the La Force prison seems an implausible scenario. The memoirs of Ruault (1976) on this point seem suspect.

p. 195 **in their sights:** See above, p. 165.

p. 195 **antagonism to the Law of 22 Prairial:** See above, pp. 21–2.

p. 195 **rules of procedure:** See 'Règlement de la Convention nationale' (28 September 1792): AP 52, pp. 205–9. Key stipulations: quoracy at 200 (206); order of the day starting at midday (206), speeches normally at the rostrum (207), alternation between proposers and opposers (207), no personalia (207).

p. 195 **focus his attacks:** This was Espert (Arège), according to Courtois II, p. 39. For Billaud's speech, see AP, pp. 551–3. (It is not placed in the order in which it appears to have been given.)

p. 196 **patriotic sans-culottes:** This was the Revolutionary Committee of the Indivisibilité section. See Soboul (1958), pp. 973–4. Robespierre also handled political disputes with sectional authorities in Finistère, Unité, and Marat: ibid., pp. 968–70, 971, and 977–8. There are materials relating to these cases in AFII 57.

p. 197 **today's secretaries:** None of the published accounts gives the names of the secretaries. According to AP, p. 323, they were Bar, Levasseur de la Meurthe, and Portiez. The decrees listed in C 312 show Bar playing a major part, assisted particularly by Dumont and Legendre, who had both completed a round of service in late Messidor.

Other signatories of the decrees include Brival, a replacement secretary in late Messidor, and Thuriot, who presided alongside Collot on the day. For Robespierre's hostility towards deputies like Dumont, see above, p. 60. See too F7 4687 d. Dumont. Although his signature was not present, Portiez was also a designated secretary, and the Portiez de l'Oise collection in the Archives de l'Assemblée nationale collection shows Legendre as signatory to Barère's proclamation poster.

p. 197 **the spell is broken:** Duval (III), p. 7.

p. 197 **Jean-François Delmas:** Courtois I, doc. LI, p. 190.

p. 197 **Dumas is added:** Other names on the decree, besides these, are Daubigné and Prosper Sijas, though Hanriot's ADCs and adjutants were cited generically.

p. 197 **two speeches:** See above, p. 181. Thibaudeau (1827), p. 88.

p. 198 **the threat posed by Paris's NG:** He makes passing reference to Robespierre's 8 Thermidor speech at AP, p. 556.

p. 199 **the gendarmerie commander Jean Hémart:** See above, p. 63. There is no sign in C 311–12 of the Hémart decree mentioned in several of the accounts. This reflects a moment in the session that seems to have been very confused.

p. 199 **a few minor changes:** There are handwritten amendments on the text in C 311. For the final text, see AP, p. 543.

13.00/1.00 p.m. (pp. 200–14)

p. 200 **during the king's trial:** Walzer (1974) for the key speeches in debate. See also, on the trial, Jordan (1985) and Soboul (1973).

p. 200 **Greek city states and the Roman republican era:** This truism is frequently cited, though in-depth studies which explore it systematically are surprisingly rare. See Parker (1937) and Bouineau (1986). I have benefited from conversations with Dr Ariane Fichtle on this point.

p. 200 **Cincinnatus:** Two bouts of dictatorship were ascribed to Cincinnatus ($c.519–c.430$), in 448 and 439 BCE. For the idea of 'being Cincinnatus', see Linton (2013), pp. 185–200 (chapter 5: 'Being Cincinnatus: the Jacobins in power').

p. 201 **'sole centre of impulsion of government':** For the 14 Frimaire law, see AP 80, pp. 629–35.

p. 201 **'the people exercises dictatorship over itself':** Barère's words came from his speech on 5 April 1793: see AP 61, p. 343. See OCR, x, p. 357 ('despotism of virtue').

p. 201 **'a guide, a chief, and not a master':** Marat's speech, 3 June 1793, in Jacobins: Jacobins, v, p. 226. See too Gottschalk (1967).

p. 201 **'ridiculous dictators':** See above, p. 89.

p. 201 **aspirants to dictatorial power:** The conspiracy of Lucius Sergius Catilina (63 BC) is best known through Cicero's famous denunciations. Caesar's role as regards the Roman Republic, and Cromwell's in the English civil wars and the Protectorate were well known in France. See the discussions of dictatorship by Parent and Leuwers, in Biard & Ducange (2019); and by Leuwers, in Cottret & Grillard (2017).

p. 202 **calling him Pisistratus:** See Jones & Macdonald (2018); and above, pp. 86–7.

p. 202 **assassination-envy:** Cf. OCR, ix, p. 623 (claiming 'the honour of the dagger' alongside Marat); and ibid., x, pp. 649–53 (placing his own assassination attempt on the same level as Collot's).

p. 202 **'a despotism of opinion':** AP 53, p. 174, Deuxième Annexe (speech by Louvet); Aulard, *Jacobins*, v, p. 346.

p. 203 **many provincial affiliates:** Boutier & Boutry (1986); Biard & Linton (2020), p. 172.

p. 203 **'exclusive celebrity':** *Réponse de J. N. Billaud*, p. 93; Collot, *Réflexions rapides*, p. 8.

p. 203 **almost accidentally:** Although there is evidence of the operations of an organized claque behind Tallien, there was no discussion of such a silencing tactic in the CPS/CGS meeting as far as we can tell.

p. 203 **a new NG command structure:** AP, pp. 542–3.

p. 204 **were he dictator:** OCR, x, p. 554. See above, p. 38.

p. 204 **'If my eyes were pistols':** BNF NAF 244 (Rose testimony in the Merlin de Thionville papers).

p. 204 **the Catherine Théot case:** See above, pp. 37–9. Robespierre alluded to the affair in his speech the previous day: OCR, x, p. 562.

p. 206 **'Set me free':** The Dumont exchange does not appear in AP or Duval; it is recorded in the 10 Thermidor edition of the *Journal des hommes libres*. It seems plausible.

p. 206 **'The virtue that you invoke':** This exchange noted by Baudot (1893), p. 206 (including the 'men of virtue' phrase in Robespierre's remark). Baudot was not present in fact.

p. 207 **Robespierre paces wildly around:** Duval (III), pp. 18–19 has a good description of this scene.

p. 208 **'So it is Danton you are avenging':** B&R, 34, p. 32 for this exchange, which the AP does not include. Levasseur (1829–31), iii, p. 147 claims the speakers were Tallien and Legendre. But Levasseur was not present on the day.

p. 208 **'The voice of a man':** For this anecdote, see Nougaret (1797), ii, p. 285.

p. 209 **Jean-Baptiste Didier:** This passage of time in Didier's day is based on his answers to interrogations in W 501.

p. 210 **Jean-Baptiste Van Heck:** It seems his real name was Gratin, though most documents refer to him as Van Heck (or Gratin Van Heck). See S&M, p. 408. His police file (F7 4775/39 d. Van Heck) includes an impressive self-penned CV.

p. 210 **storm-clouds forming over the patriots:** Wording here draws on his statements in his section later in the evening.

p. 210 **its own procedural rules:** For the rules, see above, p. 195, and note, 'rules of procedure'.

p. 211 **Van Heck has qualms:** There were others critical of Convention procedures: see e.g. F7 4667 d. Delepine d'Andilly; and F7 4682 d. veuve Dubois.

p. 212 **Lanne, his political ally:** F7 4764 d. Lanne. The first conversation allegedly took place this morning.

p. 212 **'Roberspierre':** See above, p. 37; and Leuwers (2014), p. 182. The charge was repeated down to 1793: see McPhee (2012), p. 144. For more recent usage, 'Roberspierre' in *Trois décades*, 17 Frimaire issue. Other Jacobins received typographically disrespected too (e.g. 'Barrère', 'Couton', 'Javoc' (Javogues) and 'Jambon' (aka

Jean-Bon) Saint-André). The deliberate nature of the misprint is highlighted by the speed with which most newspapers at once and almost uniformly went back to using the deformed name after 9 Thermidor.

p. 213 **pen-portrait of the Incorruptible:** *Feuille de la République*, 5 Thermidor II. For the play, see Tissier (2002), p. 436. Several months later, Dumaniant also authored a more explicitly anti-Robespierre play with a 'tyrannical' narrative: *La Journée du 9 au 10 thermidor ou la Mort du tyran* (Paris, III). See Tissier (2002), p. 441.

p. 213 **'an enemy of the tyranny of Cromwell':** *Moniteur*, 9 Thermidor; *Feuille de la République*, 29 Messidor II. Olivier Lutaud devoted a book to editions of the text (1973), but states that the version published in the Revolution was in 1793 and related to Louis XVI. This evidence complicates the story (assuming this is a new edition and not the 1793 one).

p. 214 **weapons of the weak:** I am drawing in this section on the notions of 'weapons of the weak' and 'private transcripts' developed in the work of James C. Scott (2000, 2004). The examples cited are as follows: *Trois décades*, 21 Pluviôse II (a paper known for crypto-royalist sympathies, closed down in late spring. See Popkin [1979]); *Abréviateur universel, ou Journal sommaire des opinions, productions et nouvelles publiques*, 3 Thermidor II; ibid., 9 Thermidor II.

14.00/2.00 p.m. (pp. 215–32)

p. 215 **clerk Blaise Lafosse:** See above, p. 126.

p. 215 **councillor Daujon:** F7 4662 d. Daujon. Cf. SCD, pp. 106–7.

p. 215 **22 are present:** The attendance list may be seen at F7 4430, fol. 15. The Police Administration was not represented.

p. 215 **cemetery reform:** See above, p. 126.

p. 216 **she cannot be tried today:** Mme de Maillé benefited from the *journée*, was never tried and she gave evidence at Fouquier's trial. See her deposition in W 501.

p. 216 **ex-financier Puy de Vérine:** Wallon (1880–2), v, p. 169; Lenôtre (1908), p. 278, and W 501.

p. 216 **princesse de Monaco:** See above, p. 72.

p. 217 **Maire assumes the presiding role:** As noted by the court record in W 434. There is inconsistent testimony about the hour at which this occurred. In his deposition at the Fouquier trial, court official Wolff placed the event around midday, which does not match up with the timing of events in the Convention. Wolff and others also question whether Fouquier remained as much in the dark as he claimed. W 501, deposition Wolff. My sense is that Fouquier's testimony seems generally sound. SCD (p. 199) maintains Dumas's arrest was voted in the Convention around 12.45, which confirms this kind of time.

p. 217 **'I am lost!':** Lenôtre (1908), p. 281. See also SCD, p. 199.

p. 218 **to remain at their posts:** AFII 47 pl. 364, pi. 30; F7* 2472 (Revolutionary Committee, Tuileries section, minutes).

p. 218 **a state of shock:** SCD, p. 200, n. 1. See AN F7 4775/43 d. Véret (for the 2.00 p.m. time).

p. 218 **'a decisive speech for liberty':** F7 4743 d. Herman (statement by Lanne).

p. 219 **'worthy of being one of us':** *Papiers* I, pp. 279–80. See above, p. 80.

p. 220 **becomes unanimous:** B&R, 34, p. 34 for this detail.

p. 221 **differentiating between the two:** Biard (2015) esp. pp. 84–8 for clarity in this murky area. Thanks also to Mette Harder for guidance on the point.

p. 221 **Marat was acquitted:** Gottschalk (1967), pp. 157–62.

p. 221 **informal escort group:** See above, p. 120.

p. 222 **the motion for an arrest warrant:** Refraining from a *mise en accusation* can be interpreted in many ways.

p. 222 **tugging at his coat-tails:** Louis Blanc (1861), xi, p. 230 and Hamel (1865), iii, p. 760. Both stories were seemingly sourced from the Le Bas family.

p. 222 **Élie Lacoste wades in:** Lacoste was elected President of the Club for the first fortnight of Thermidor and served in this role on 3 Thermidor. I have been unable to find wording similar to this in accounts of recent debates in which Augustin intervened.

p. 223 **friends on the deputy benches:** Despite his close latter-day association with Robespierre, Couthon started close to the Girondins and has many friends and admirers from earlier days in the Convention.

p. 223 **triumvirate:** This was in 60–53 BCE. There was a 'Second Triumvirate' following Caesar's death, involving Octavian (later emperor Augustus), Mark Antony, and Lepidus, between 43 and 33 BCE. The common thread was that they marked the aftermath of the Republic and the advent of empire.

p. 224 **standard policing issues:** For arms collection, see F7★ 2472; and F7★ 2480 (Lepeletier). For other sectional committee work cited see F7★ 2783 (salpetre collection, Lombards); F7★ 2507 (Unité); F7★ 2511 (Chalier); F7 4587 d. Barrois (Réunion); F7★ 2519 (Finistère). The Chalier meeting place was close to the pr. Musée de Cluny, Ve.

p. 226 **posters:** For posters, F7 4432 pl. 3, pi. 15 suggests these were going up from around 5.00 p.m.

p. 226 **François-Vincent Le Gray and his friend Jean-Claude Saint-Omer:** The two men's police files—at F7 4774/14 and F7 4775/11 d. Saint-Omer—contain nearly all the relevant evidence, much of which is reproduced in 'L'Affaire Le Gray' in Mathiez (1930).

p. 227 **exclusion of nobles:** Saint-Just's 27 Germinal law had obliged all nobles to leave the city. See above, p. 14.

p. 227 **worrying signs of organized resistance:** It was mentioned in Barère's 7 Thermidor speech and Robespierre's 8 Thermidor speech. Saint-Just is planning to mention it today too. See above, pp. 90–1. For the Montagne petition, see Soboul (1958), pp. 979–80.

p. 227 **'intriguers in red bonnets':** Saint-Just (1831), p. 46.

p. 228 **tell their masters:** This is the vigorously argued theory of Richard Cobb (1970), part I. It is exaggerated, as Cobb's own heavy use of such reports confirms.

p. 228 **'They could hear us and take us in':** Caron (1914), v, p. 13.

p. 228 **provincials:** The two Robespierres, Saint-Just, and Carnot hailed from Artois-Picardy, Couthon from the Auvergne, Barère from the Pyrenees, Billaud from La Rochelle, Lindet from Normandy, etc, etc. Collot and Mercier were relatively rare breeds among prominent Conventionnels in being Paris born and bred.

p. 228 **'They laugh at everything':** For these views, see esp. three discussions in *TP:*, i, pp. 75–6 (*'Caractère politique des vrais Parisiens'*); i, pp. 1273–6 (*'Emeutes'*) and ii, pp. 419–28 (*'Gouvernement'*). See also *TP*, ii, p. 215 ('tie the tongue').

p. 229 **'a spirit of opposition':** *NP*, p. 506.

p. 230 **Rousseville's point:** See above, p. 16.

p. 230 **'women and the weak-minded':** *Chronique de Paris*, 5 November 1792 according to Leuwers, in Cottret & Galland (2017), p. 140.

p. 231 **'not in the renown of individuals':** OCR, x, p. 418.

p. 231 **'cured the people of its idolatry':** *Journal historique et politique*, 15 Germinal/4 April 1794.

p. 231 **'the law strike him down':** Caron (1914), vi, p. 221.

p. 232 **'homomania':** F7 4774/37 d. Martinet.

15.00/3.00 p.m. (pp. 233–50)

p. 233 **'No one takes orders from anyone but me':** Bazanéry in AFII 47 pl. 367, pi. 38. For Hanriot's rage, see also the statement made at 4.00 p.m. by municipal officer Alexandre Minier in the Révolutionnaire section: F7 4432 pl. 9, pi. 30.

p. 233 **caught napping:** See the testimony of Jean Masset from Villetaneuse (close to Hanriot's native village of Nanterre), at F7 4774/38.

p. 234 **'expect a receipt at a moment like this':** Courtois II, doc. XXXV, p. 199.

p. 234 **colourful volley of insults:** F7 4743 d. Héron; SCD, pp. 203–4; AFII 47 pl. 366, pi. 29 (not 368, as SCD states).

p. 234 **meeting of the Municipal Council:** Report of Maison Commune concierge Michel Bochard on timings: Courtois II, doc. XXXVI, p. 200. The meeting did continue: see F7 4578 d. Lafosse (which states 4.30 closure) and Lasnier in F7 4432 pl. 9, pi. 1.

p. 235 **his handwriting gets wild and shaky:** The signed orders can be viewed at AFII 47 pl. 368. Cf. SCD, p. 203 & n.

p. 235 **eventuality of a 31 May-style *journée*:** See above, p. 32.

p. 237 **duty rotas and token detachments:** F7 4779.

p. 237 **commanders of the two mounted squadrons:** See above, p. 63. The orders are grouped together in AFII 47 pl. 368, pi. 30–9.

p. 238 **continuing with that meeting:** Municipal clerk Lafosse indicates it lasted till 4.30 at least. F7 4758 d. Lafosse.

p. 238 **to release the hapless Courvol:** Courtois II, doc. XXXV, p. 199. Courvol states this occurred two and a half hours after his arrest but this does not square with Hanriot's movements in the afternoon. For Payan's address, see T 528 d. Payan.

p. 240 **hand over the speech:** This is the speech cited in full in AP, pp. 558–62.

p. 240 **by the sheer force of his words:** This is the argument in Gauchet (2018), see esp. p. 229: the 9 Thermidor speech as 'un 31 mai par la seule puissance de la parole'. But Gaucher does not consider the time factor and the wider appeal discussed here.

p. 240 **pales at the sight of a drawn sabre:** See above, p. 34.

p. 241 **'I invite the people':** OCR, ix, pp. 526–7.

p. 242 **Couthon is carried towards the bar:** Report on the session in the *Messager du soir.*

p. 242 **Jacques-Auguste Rose:** See above, p. 180, and note, 'in larger numbers'.

p. 243 **Six tumbrils:** There are contradictions in the evidence about the timing of the despatch of the prisoners. Wallon prefers an earlier timing in order to accommodate an exploit of Hanriot for which there is no confirmation: Wallon (1880–2), v, pp. 438–9. The tumbrils left normally between 5.00 and 6.00 p.m. An eyewitness who saw the tumbrils leave claimed it was at around 6.30: see Courtois II, doc. VI, pp. 91–2 (Foureau, Mutius-Scévole section). But this would probably cut it too fine for the convoy's commander to be back in the Palais de Justice by 8.00 p.m. See below, p. 316. One possible consideration is that Fouquier's trial finished earlier than the other one taking place—and indeed testimony suggests that this went on until 4.30 or even later. There would thus have been a considerable gap between Fouquier leaving which he himself placed between 2.00 and 3.00 (though it was probably later) and the departure of the tumbrils. [Scellier], *Précis de la vie* (no date)—from a judge at the other trial (4.30) and W 501, Girard deposition, from a juror (5.30).

p. 243 **Henri Sanson:** See the depositions of the Sanson clan at W 501.

p. 243 **'Do your business':** W 501: Depositions of Wolff, Simonet, and Comtat. Cf. Lenôtre (1908), pp. 281–2.

p. 244 **Mulot, Fifth NG Legion Chief:** Mulot was alerted to the situation at his home on the Rue du Plâtre (Réunion). See his deposition AFII 47 pl. 367, pi. 42. The complicated manoeuvres involving the Legion Chiefs are covered in SCD, pp. 204–12.

p. 246 **the decree confirms:** Aulard, CPS, p. 457.

p. 247 **assembling on the Place de la Maison Commune:** The sections in question include Arcis and Lombards (in which Payan may have played a role) and Homme-Armé: AFII 47, pl. 366.

p. 248 **'Get back to the law courts':** Blanchetot's report is doc. XXVIII in Courtois II, pp. 128–9.

p. 248 **alert the CPS:** Ibid. The document states that the Degesne letter was written at 4.00 p.m.

p. 249 **difficult to rouse sceptical sectional authorities:** It seems less than half a dozen councillors sought to mobilize their sectional authorities in favour of the Commune in mid afternoon. Positive examples include Talbot in the Temple section, Louvet in Homme-Armé (see below, pp. 274–5), Vaucanu at Maison-Commune, and Delacour in Brutus. Other councillors, who may have left the meeting before the news from the Convention arrived, were pro-Commune in sectional fora later in the evening. See too AFII 47 pl. 365, pi. 4 (Fraternité); and the Gosset deposition in W 501 for a similar argument in Marat section. It seems that on learning of his promotion to Commander, Fauconnier set off to visit numerous sectional battalions, leaving the Convention highly exposed. For the Mme Fauconnier intervention, see F7 4774/11 d. Lefebvre.

p. 250 **Droits-de-l'Homme battalion:** AFII 47 pl. 366, pi. 42. This was around 3.30 p.m. or after.

p. 250 **to declare unequivocally for the Convention:** F7 4432 pl. 9, pi. 30.

p. 250 **Panthéon and Unité sections:** In the Unité section, the Councillor was Pacquotte and his report led to sectional authorities coming out at once in support of the Convention. See SCD, p. 274; Soboul (1958), pp. 970–1; and F7* 2507 (Unité Revolutionary Committee).

16.00/4.00 p.m. (pp. 251–66)

p. 251 **a narrative of the day:** Here as earlier I am following the account in AP for all Convention business.

p. 252 **Marat's funeral:** See above for Robespierre's rivalry with Marat, p. 202.

p. 252 **getting on for 4.30 p.m.:** Duval (III), places the end of the session at 5.30 p.m., and other sources at around 5.00 p.m. However, I follow SCD in believing that a much earlier time is indicated. SCD, p. 205, n. 3.

p. 252 **Cardinal de Retz:** See Barère (1842), ii, p. 225. Cf. Jones (1981).

p. 253 **intoxicated by their victory:** The phrase used by Thibaudeau (1827), i, p. 83.

p. 254 **employees at the Café des Subsistances:** Numerous witnesses in the Fouquier trial represented him being a keen attender at the *buvette*, and complaining about the number of victims he seemed required to produce: W 501, depositions Wolff, Tavernier, Laucher, etc. The wife of the *buvette*'s proprietor records Fouquier drinking beer. (His family originated close to the Belgian border). For conflicts with Robespierre, besides W 501, see Eude (1985).

p. 254 **cut off from comings and goings:** Storm damage in the early 1790s to the bridge connecting the Ile de la Cité to the Ile Saint-Louis meant that there was no direct link between the islands. In his depositions before his trial, Fouquier made a point of stating that he had passed the Cloître Notre-Dame on his journey to *chez* Vergne: W 501, suggesting he followed the route outlined here.

p. 255 **proprietors of the many theatres:** SCD, p. 215n., citing a 13 Thermidor police report, F7 4432 pl. 1, pi. 48.

p. 255 **'I will blow your brains out!':** There is little documentation on Payan's arrest. See the discussion of this incident in SCD, 216n., which lists witnesses who refer to the incident. They often give different times. Gendarmerie commander Dumesnil claimed that Hanriot was arresting gendarmes around the prisons from 11.00 a.m., but there is no corroborating evidence and it is more likely he is referring to the arrest and imprisonment of Payan's gendarme escort. It seems to be this incident which is referred to in Aulard, CPS, p. 460, point 15.

p. 256 **requisitioning Parisian horses and carriages:** For discussion of the optimum number of individuals per tumbril, see W 501 (Fouquier's testimony). The timing I have ascribed to these events is a calculation based on very vague and conflicting accounts. See the standard works on the Revolutionary Tribunal: esp. Lenôtre (1908) and Boulant (2018).

p. 257 **a motley crew:** W 433. The list of the accused can also be seen in Fleischmann (1911), pp. 27ff. Greer's research suggests that overall around 10 per cent of those executed were women. See Jones (1988), p. 120.

p. 257 **the Loison couple:** See their police files at F7 4774/26 d. Loison. The puppet story may be a Thermidorian invention.

p. 257 **de Rouvière:** See Rouvière's file at F7 4775/3 d. Rouvière.

p. 258 **to apply a little rouge:** Coittant, *Troisième Tableau*, p. 157.

p. 258 **feeling admiration:** [Sanson], *La Révolution française vue par son bourreau*, p. 188. For Mme du Barry in contrast, see ibid., pp. 106–9.

p. 258 **'emulation about dying well':** Jullian (1815), p. 174, and more broadly Jones (2014), pp. 147–9.

p. 259 **arrests of key individuals:** For Rousseville's arrest (with others), see AFII* 255. Most arrests, as this, were organized by the CGS. CPS orders are noted in Aulard, CPS, pp. 457–61.

p. 259 **Carraut:** F7 4592 d. femme Béguin; F7 4594 d. Charlotte Robespierre.

p. 261 **primed for action:** AFII 47 pl. 364, pi. 47 (Lombards); AFII 47 366, pi. 20 (Arcis). The latter followed written orders received from a Hanriot ADC at 14.30.

p. 261 **led by Hémart:** This incident is recorded by Hémart in his own words in Birembault (1959): see esp. p. 317. The account was not known to SCD. The passage refers to a decree from the Convention making him NG commander of which no trace survives (p. 317). AFII 47 pl. 368, pi. 29 includes the order to place him in the Rue de Bouloi prison, which did not in fact transpire.

p. 262 **'Forty assassins want to kill Robespierre':** The speech as given is a composite of testimonies, notably the Civil Committee of the Marat section, AFII 47 pl. 365, pi. 39; and Cn. Basset from Lombards, F7 4332 pl. 6, pi. 27–9. See too SCD, p. 216 & n. 2.

p. 263 **forbidding them from allowing entry:** For a copy of the order, see F7 4333, pi. 11. See also the accounts by HQ employees Minier, F7 4774/46 d. Minier; and Bisson, F7 4332 pl. 7, pi. 4 (Réunion section). Bisson contains the point about the publishing houses. Cf. SCD, pp. 237–41.

p. 264 **Cn. Savin:** Savin statement in F7 4432 pl. 5, pi. 1–16.

p. 264 **'Your father is in danger':** Recorded in the Mutius-Scévole section: F7 4432 pl. 9, pi. 1.

p. 265 **turning into farce:** F7 4775/89 d. Renard. The following episodes are covered in an excellent account from the Montagne section, AFII 47 pl. 367, pi. 11.

p. 265 **Boulanger:** For the Boulanger incident, see F7 4794 d. Benoit Perlin (ADC to Boulanger); AFII 47 pl. 367 (Montagne sectional committees); also Merlin in AP, pp. 587–8. Cf. Viton testimony in Courtois II, doc. XXXI(4), pp. 186–7. See SCD, pp. 217–18.

p. 265 **sitting down to dine:** For restaurants, see Jones (2020), pp. 82–4; and Spang (2000).

p. 265 **A crisis is clearly looming:** Courtois is his own source in Courtois II, pp. 65–6n.

p. 266 **Amar manages to escape:** Ibid., 66n. Although no name was given, the identification with Amar is very strong.

p. 266 **Leaping onto a table:** Jeannolle's account is valuable on this whole episode: F7 4432 pl. 2, pi. 24. See too AFII 47 pl. 365 (Bon-Conseil: account by Livin) and F7 4406 (rope details); plus the Benoit account above (he was one of the gendarmes who changed sides). A certain Tremblay, a wigmaker by trade and corporal in the Gardes-Françaises NG, who happened to be there on an errand, had a major role in defending Ruhl as he was assaulted by Hanriot: Courtois II, doc. XLII, pp. 217–18.

PART IV: A PARISIAN *JOURNÉE* (5.00 P.M. TO MIDNIGHT)
(PP. 269–394)

17.00/5.00 p.m. (pp. 269–81)

p. 269 **theatres are open:** See above, p. 147. There is a full listing on the back page of the day's *Moniteur*, and in several other newspapers.

p. 269 **Astley's Amphitheatre:** Astley is conventionally seen as the originator of the modern circus; he had decamped back to England at this point, leaving the business in the hands of Franconi. See the Franconi police file at F7 4712. For the Hanriot scare over closure, see above p. 255.

p. 269 *Epicharis et Néron:* Tiesset, in Poirson (2008). The theatre was located in the pr. Ie.

p. 269 *'Tremble, tremble, Néron':* Tissier (2002), p. 45n. does make this suggestion in fact, as, more fully, does Tiesset, in Poirson (2008).

p. 270 **many outer sections:** In many more distant sections, news only got through from around 7.00 p.m. See e.g. Sans-Culottes section in the Faubourg Saint-Marcel (F7 4585 d. Ballin); the Faubourg-du-Nord section (F7 4586 d. Barelle); and below, p. 416. For the fewness of councillors at around 5.00 p.m. see F7 4735 d. Guilbert.

p. 270 **'all to go en masse':** W 80 d. Indivisibilité.

p. 271 **Jean-Jacques Chrétien:** F7 4648 d. Chrétien.

p. 271 **to lie low:** Besides the case of David (see above, p. 136), see F7 4750 d. Joigny (for Godefroy) and F7 4775/43 d. Vergne. In the case of Mouret (Guillaume-Tell), his wife's illness had kept him away from meetings for three weeks: F7 4774/54 d. Mouret.

p. 272 **the kiss of fraternity:** F7 4432 pl. 10, pi. 24 (Finistère). See too F7* 2521. For the 14 Frimaire law, see above, pp. 166–8.

p. 272 **among the doubters:** For Michel, see F7 4774/46 d. Michel; F7 4774/45 d. Minier; and F7 4432 pl. 7, pi. 4. For Benoit, see F7 4594 d. Benoit. For Michel's activity prior to his arrest, see F7 4735 d. Guilbert. For the arrest, see F7 4333, pi. 59–60, and Michel, *Pétition* (no date). See too SCD, pp. 239–41. The lawyer quotation is an adaptation of the wish of the materialist thinker Jean Meslier (1664–1729) that the great of the earth should be strangled with the guts of the last priest. For the Guyot case, see F7 4757 d. Guyot, plus the printed memoir by him at F7 4432 pl. 1, pi. 88. Minier, noted above, and Verdet (Bonne-Nouvelle) were among the first to be tasked with attending the Commune to report on its activities. See Verdet's interrogation at W 80. For Faro, see Courtois II, doc. XI, p. 101.

p. 274 **mobilizing effect:** The *générale* was beaten early in Arcis, Lombards, and Homme-Armé sections. See AFII 47 pl. 364, pi. 22 and ibid., pl. 366, pi. 24 (Arcis); ibid., pl. 366, pi. 20 and ibid., pl. 364, pi. 46 (Lombards). For Droits-de-l'Homme, see above, p. 238. For the numbers of troops, see ibid: pl. 366, pi. 18 (Arcis); and pl. 367, pi. 18 (Réunion). See also ibid., pl. 365, pi. 5 (Fraternité: 100 men after 5.30); and pl. 367, pi. 5 (Amis-de-la-Patrie: 400 men after 6.30). For Panthéon, see below, p. 310.

p. 274 **Claude Chalandon:** F7 4637 d. Chalandon, and for this episode also AFII 47 pl. 366, pi. 1–7. There is a very full set of testimonies dated 15 Thermidor at pi. 6. The Rue des Francs-Bourgeois is in pr. IIIe.

p. 274 **Pierre-Alexandre Louvet:** F7 4774/26 d. Louvet; and AP 95, p. 385 ('31 May'). Cf. S&M, p. 350. Cf. F7 4430 for attendance at the earlier meeting.

p. 275 **It takes some doing:** SCD, p. 211n. Sainte-Claire Deville notes that although the actual cannon themselves weighed only 290 kg each, the harness and train weighed 1,050 kg and the ammunition train a further 1,050 kg. Horses were at a premium because of recent requisitioning.

p. 275 **additional copies:** Mentioned in Louvet's account at AFII 47 pl. 366, pi. 6.

p. 276 **to inform the CPS:** AFII 47 pl. 365, pi. 33.

p. 276 **The deputy Robin:** Courtois II, p. 66n., for this episode.

p. 277 **'a storm breaking':** This may have been Jean-Baptiste Vincent who was municipal councillor. However, the hostility with which the Vincent in question spoke of his relations with Hanriot suggests it was administrator Pierre-Louis Vincent. See AFII 47 pl. 366, pi. 6; and the latter's police file F7 4775/48 d. Vincent. I have translated as 'storm breaking' Vincent's expression, 'coup de chien'. At the Treasury, Chalandon's men joined forces with men from the Arcis section: AFII 47 pl. 364, pI. 22.

p. 278 **General Council meeting:** The main account of the Council meeting is provided by the minutes of the Commune secretaries, filed in AFII 47 pl. 368, pi. 28. They were reproduced in the *Journal de Perlet*, 24 Thermidor II and a shortened version is given in B&R, 34, pp. 46–57. No guidance is given for the timing of different decrees and actions. The document gives a 6.00 start, but 5.30 is noted by Minier, in his careful and believable account, who also remarks an initial attendance of 25–30: F7 4432 pl. 9, pi. 30. SCD, p. 222 is in agreement. See also Courtois II, p. 47n.

p. 278 **outer passageway:** See the description in SCD, p. 4. There is an engraving of the same space in 1790 by Prieur, which may be seen at BNF document numérique, IFN-8411026.

p. 278 **'for the people':** *Journal de Perlet*, 24 Thermidor, p. 85. For the decrees signed Herman and Lanne, see F7 4433 pl.1.

p. 278 **oath of loyalty:** *Journal de Perlet*, 24 Thermidor, p. 85. Lombard gunner Pierre Pay claimed to see his superior officer take this oath at around 5.00 p.m.: F7 4432 pl. 6, pi. 29. But it would have been after the 5.30 opening of the session.

p. 279 **solemnizing marriages:** On Paris, see S&M, p. 498. See also above, p. 70 (marriages).

p. 279 **'We must hurl all these traitors':** AFII 47 pl. 368, pi. 28.

p. 279 **Bourdon de l'Oise:** Intriguingly, a later hit-list of conspirators listed Collot, Barère and Amar but then named Léonard Bourdon rather than Bourdon de l'Oise. SCD, p. 225n.

p. 280 **a feast for the prisoners:** F7 4406B for the full meal. For the signs, see the account by Chevrillon in Courtois II, p. 66n.

p. 281 **The news finally arrives:** Fouquier's account in Fleischmann (1911) and W 501 suggests a time before 6.00 which allowed Fouquier to get back to the Palais de Justice just after the visit by Fleuriot-Lescot.

p. 281 **secretary to the Fraternité section:** F7 4432 pl. 7, pi. 51. See above, p. 164, and note, 'Fouquier met Cn Vergne' for Courtois's misidentification of Vergne. Coffinhal is not listed in SCD as a councillor. He was however appointed on 9 Prairial, but seemingly not for his own section. See BNF NAF 2663. There was a tendency for CPS appointments not to respect councillors' sectional base.

18.00/6.00 p.m. (pp. 282–97)

p. 282 **take an oath:** This is a formulation of the oath recorded by the Bon-Conseil delegation: AFII 47 pl. 365, pi. 30. For more abbreviated wordings, see e.g. AFII 47 pl. 365, pi. 4 (Fraternité); F7 4332 pl. 7, pi. 7 (Indivisibilité): ibid., pl. 10, pi. 3 (Finistère); and ibid. pl. 9, pi. 15 (Marat). See too below, pp. 303, 306.

p. 282 **Jean-Jacques Lubin:** For Lubin, see above, p. 134; and Soboul (1958), esp. p. 869. Lubin's perfumer brother went on to found one of the great perfumery houses: see https://www.lubin.eu/en/history.

p. 282 **precious time is being wasted with words:** The minutes do not make clear who made this remark at this moment; but Lubin had just been speaking.

p. 283 **'so-called Convention':** B&R, 34, pp. 46–8.

p. 283 **'ringing the tocsin':** AFII 47, pl. 365, pi. 27. It is unclear whether the alarm cannon was fired in fact. As a key channel of communication from Left Bank to Right, the Pont-Neuf became a site of contestation. See below, p. 384.

p. 283 **The Jacobin Club usually meets:** SCD states that the delegates were at the Jacobin Club at 7.00 p.m. and suggests 6.30 p.m. as the moment the delegates were chosen. SCD, p. 226n.

p. 284 **strapped to the oar:** SCD, p. 224n.; and AFII 47 pl. 367, pi. 27 (Cité). SCD thinks this happens around 6.30, though Maison Commune official Bochard (Courtois II, doc. XXXVI, p. 200) states it was at 7.00 p.m. For Lafosse, see F7 4758 d. Lafosse, and above, p. 126.

p. 285 **Dumesnil:** Courtois II, doc. XXXI (2), pp. 182–4. Dumesnil's evidence in W 500 provides additional information.

p. 285 **like man and wife:** According to former clerk of the Revolutionary Tribunal, Fabricius, in his deposition, 'Nottes sur Gribeauval', W 500.

p. 286 **a national figure:** For Fouquier's pre-Revolutionary career, see Lenôtre (1908), pp. 33–66.

p. 287 **bearing the arrest warrant:** Courtois II, doc. XIX (3), p. 113. The bailiff used for Robespierre was Filleul, and the gendarmes were Chanlaire and Lemoine.

p. 288 **preferring to take the quais:** Testimony of Foureau in Courtois II, doc. XVI (1), p. 92.

p. 288 **churches are shut:** Réau (1994), pp. 382–91. For priests offering absolution, see Sabatié (1912), p. 260.

p. 289 **'Pardon, monsieur':** *NP*, p. 443.

p. 289 **effects of the executed:** Wallon (1880–2), iii, p. 365.

p. 289 **37 minutes precisely:** Bronne (1971), pp. 45–6 (Abbé Jehin de Theux recorded timings).

p. 290 **placed under immediate arrest:** SCD, pp. 206–8. For the rota system, see above, pp. 159, 198.

p. 290 **to catch up with his lunch:** See F7 4637 d. Chaguignée and F7 4636 d. Chevassu for Payan's behaviour. See too the report of Mauvage, Faubourg-du-Nord section: F7 4432 pl. 5, pi. 49.

p. 290 **'our provisional General Commander':** The episode is recounted in F7 4774/92 d. Richard, who puts it at around 7.00. I draw also on Giot's own account 'Détail des évenements arrivés dans la journée du 9 Thermidor . . . au citoyen Giost' [sic], in W 79 d. Giot. Note that SCD is ambiguous about the timing of Giot's promotion: on p. 245, he seems to place it at after 8.00 p.m.; but his account at p. 248 places it between 6 and 7. The latter concurs with the Mauvage account in F7 4432 (see previous note), and seems more plausible.

p. 291 **Giot's facial hair:** See above, p. 155. It is not certain that Giot accompanied Fauconnier. But why else would he be in the Commune? This supports the case for his appointment between 6 and 7 rather than between 8 and 9.

p. 291 **his own brother Esprit:** Many secondary accounts state that this was Joseph Payan. But Guillaume (1891), iv, p. 876, presents compelling evidence that Joseph remained in the Education Commission buildings for most of the day, and that it was a younger brother on military leave in the capital who was chosen.

p. 291 **'Commander of Potatoes':** W 79 account.

p. 291 **Olivier:** See esp. Olivier's own account of the episode at AFII 47 pl. 364, pi. 46. See too the Degesne account in Courtois II, doc. XIX (9), pp. 119–20, which puts this interview at around 6.30. The testimony of Maviez, second-in-command of the Bondy NG is confirmatory: AFII 47 pl. 367, pi. 31.

p. 293 **declared its support:** Notably as a result of their municipal councillor Minier reporting in mid-afternoon what had been going on at the Maison Commune: F7 4432 pl. 9, pi. 30.

p. 293 **Jean-Baptiste Van Heck:** For Van Heck, see above, p. 210.

p. 294 **leads him into the police offices:** This episode is well covered in F7 4432 pl. 365, notably in reports from the Civil Committee (pi. 32), the General Assembly (pi. 33), and NG commander Berger (pi. 35). The denunciation of Van Heck by Leblanc at pi. 34 is also of interest. See too the account by Van Heck himself (AFII 47 pl. 365, pi. 29), and his police file at F7 4775/9. Van Heck was a very involved radical: see S&M, p. 408 and the references there. Soboul is correct in arguing that Van Heck's later account airbrushes his more qualified views earlier in the day: Soboul (1958), p. 1016n.

p. 295 **'Great arrest of Catiline Robespierre':** Coittant, *Troisième Tableau* (1797), pp. 80–1.

p. 295 **something untoward:** de La Laurencie (1905), pp. 27–8.

p. 295 **their God even:** Remarks from prison of the celebrated entrepreneur Palloy in a letter to his wife: ADP 4AZ 15. See also above, p. 77.

p. 295 **Sister of Charity Théotiste:** Théotiste (1875), p. 160.

p. 297 **Riffard Saint-Martin:** Riffard Saint-Martin (2013), pp. 104–6.

19.00/7.00 p.m. (pp. 298–313)

p. 298 **a fighting force at its disposal:** The map of sectional involvement in *Atlas* (1989), p. 66 is instructive. While the north-west quadrant of the city west of the rue Poissonnière showed no artillery commitment to the Commune, all other areas were involved, notably the Left Bank (e.g. Mutius-Scévole, Bonnet-Rouge, Invalides), the islands (Fraternité), the central and eastern inner sections (e.g. Muséum,

Lombards, Arcis, Homme-Armé, Marchés) and the eastern faubourgs (e.g. Quinze-Vingts, Popincourt). It is very difficult to follow the actions of the gendarmerie in the evening, as many of them changed sides at least once and after the event looked to cover their tracks. Dumesnil's account in Courtois II, doc. XXXI, pp. 182–4 does not square at all with evidence of gendarme collaboration with the Commune in F7 4437 (deposition by Haurie) or F7 3822 (report of the Paris Department, 11 Thermidor).

p. 298 **the number of companies in the city:** Soboul (1958), pp. 1003, 1005, slightly corrects SCD, p. 213 on the number of cannon. But both men fail to note that the artillery companies did not always (perhaps ever) take their cannon with them. See the Chalandon example in the Homme-Armé, cited below. Thus in terms of guns, there was a full complement, rather than the number that SCD claims were on the Place. But not all companies would have brought both their company's cannon. Three companies were, moreover, engaged in duty service at the Convention, the Temple prison, and the Arsenal.

p. 298 **companies from far afield:** Besides the above, men from Finistère in the Faubourg Saint-Marcel and from Left-Bank sections Marat and Observatoire were present by around 7.00 p.m.

p. 298 **over 40 per cent of Paris's population:** This demographic point is not mentioned in historical accounts of the day yet it is highly significant. Disregarding the disappointing number of actual sections mobilized, the population figures are impressively high. For population statistics, see Soboul (1958), pp. 1093–4 and pp. 435–8.

p. 299 **how the assembly is preparing:** For the evening session I again draw freely from AP, pp. 583–95, corrected by Duval (1794), pp. 25–47. For the 40 to 50 members, see Riffard Saint-Martin (2013), p. 106.

p. 299 **a large force of Guardsmen:** AFII 47 pl. 365, pi. 19: report by Bouchefontaine who met the troops on their way back to their section. The section actually contains the Maison Commune building, and extends to the east.

p. 300 **the Commune and the authorities of the Seine department:** Duval (1795), p. 27. Cf. Courtois II, pp. 68–9.

p. 301 **Payan has been arrested:** This may be merely a rumour or else refer to the Payan arrest earlier, noted above, p. 255.

p. 302 **Numbers of General Council members:** Attendance at its maximum involved 91 councillors (listed in B&R, 34, pp. 43–4). For the Guyot case, see 'Mémoire du Citoyen Guyot, membre de la Commune et administrateur de police', in F7 4332 pl. 2, pi. 88.

p. 302 **to free Robespierre:** Courtois II, pp. 55–6.

p. 302 **'We must obey Hanriot':** AFII 47 pl. 366, pi. 37.

p. 303 **'Vive the Convention!':** Ibid., pi. 38.

p. 303 **councillors hover around the entrance:** Playing this role were, for example, Eude and Delacour for Droits-de-l'Homme (AFII 47 pl. 367, pi. 44); Cochefer for Réunion (F7 4735 d. Guilbert); and Hardon or Ardon for Finistère (F7 4332 pl. 10, pi. 4, containing testimony by Vian). For one among many cases of individuals not grasping the anti-Convention thrust of the meeting: see F7 4774/79 d. Ponsard (Finistère). For speedy exits, see too the case of e.g. Minier (Arcis) F7 4774/46 d. Minier.

p. 303 **Jean-Antoine-Gaspard Forestier:** F7 4609 d. Forestier.

p. 303 **a new attendance list has been started:** F7 4432 pl. 10, pi. 4 (especially testimony from Le Grand and Menuit). The attendance sheet, showing Hardon's name at the top, may be found at W 80.

p. 303 *consigne*: F7 4332 pl. 5, pi. 43 and F7 4774/40 (both Mauvage); and F7 4631 d. Cazenave.

p. 304 **milling about outside the Jacobin Club:** The minutes of the evening session (now lost) were seen by Courtois, who gives some extracts. These and other fragments are assembled in Jacobins, pp. 290–4. An account of the early part of the evening was given in the *Conservateur décadaire*, 20 Fructidor II. Some individual accounts also supply detail: e.g. Courtois II, p. 60 (Le Bas rumour).

p. 304 **She deserves to be assassinated:** See Godineau (1988), pp. 193–6 (citing F7 4683).

p. 304 **'We have to march':** Besides Godineau, see F7 4627 d. femme Butikère (for Couprye); F7 4669 d. Dembreville; and F7 4683 d. Dubreuil.

p. 304 **Jean-Baptiste Loys:** The Loys episode can be reconstructed from F7 4774/26 d. Loys; F7 4704 d. Faineaux; and AFII 47 pl. 367, pi. 13 (Montagne: testimony of Delassaux).

p. 305 **Nicolas-Joseph Vivier:** F7 4775/29 d. Vivier.

p. 306 **Crime is seeking to overthrow virtue:** Courtois II, p. 60. See above, p. 22 (Legracieux report).

p. 306 **Tallien chose:** Besides his speech in the Convention, see F7 4774 d. Le Gentil (testimony of Des Fosses) for evidence of Tallien's presence in the Jacobins.

p. 306 **Jacques Brival:** The copies of the outlaw decrees against the two Robespierres I consulted in the Newberry Library, Chicago, bear Brival's signatures.

p. 306 **Prosper Sijas:** See above, p. 46. For Sijas, speaking, see reports in Duval (III), p. 29; and AFII 47 pl. 366, pi. 39.

p. 306 **to show livid wounds:** F7 4758 d. Lagarde. Note especially the long and highly partial letter from Lagarde's father defending his son's conduct.

p. 306 **the vote against Robespierre:** See the testimony in F7 4631 d. Calvet (a man accused of having shaken his fist at Robespierre in the past). For Riqueur, see F7 4774/93 d. Riqueur.

p. 307 **the Jacobins are dithering:** Testimony by Philippe Durand in F7 4774/93 d. Riqueur suggested a time of around 8.00 p.m. for the discussion on deputy exclusion.

p. 307 **excluded from the Club:** F7 4631 d. Calvet.

p. 307 **they decide to reinstate Brival:** AP, p. 589. See SCD, pp. 234–4 for commentary on key timings.

p. 307 **Cn. Portières:** W 500 (testimony in Fouquier-Tinville's trial).

p. 308 **Parisians coming up the Rue Tournon:** For the prison plots and the September Massacres of 1792, see above, p. 76. I am drawing particularly on Guyard's own account, written from gaol after the night, to secure his release. Although we can discount some details as self-serving (such as his claim not to have recognized Robespierre), the account is largely credible. See too the file on him in W 79 (not W 80, as SCD states); and the report of one of the accompanying gendarmes in Courtois, doc. XIX, pp. 113–14. Cf. SCD, pp. 242–3.

p. 308 **the Commune pays his wages:** A point brought up by several gaolers and functionaries on the night: e.g. APP AA95 (Montagne).

p. 310 **between 15 and 20 cannon:** A member of the Tuileries section Civil Committee claimed 15–20 cannon were on the Place du Carrousel at 9.00 p.m.: AFII 47 pl. 364, pi. 33. Carlier, Mutius-Scévole gunner, talked of eleven in the part of the force close to the Convention hall (W 80 d. Mutius-Scévole). See also SCD, pp. 232–3.

p. 310 **crowd of 1,200 men:** Report of Bigot, second-in-command of the Panthéon NG, AFII 47 pl. 366, pi. 24 (not pl. 36 as SCD states).

p. 311 **these faces are unfamiliar:** I am following SCD in using the account of this episode which appeared in the accompanying texts to the published version of Serieys' play, *La Mort de Robespierre*. It seems to have been based on eyewitness accounts (SCD, p. 243n). See too the report of gendarmes Chanlaire and Lemoine in Courtois II, doc. XIX (3), pp. 113–14; and below, p. 411.

p. 312 **protests against the 23 July Wage Maximum:** For other presumptions about the Wage Maximum, see e.g. F7 4432 pl. 7, pi. 32 (Cité); AFII 47 pl. 366, pi. 50 (Marchés); and above, pp. 274–5 (for Homme-Armé).

p. 312 **to demonstrate against the Wage Maximum:** This in reports from the artillery company of the Maison-Commune section who were billetted at the factory: AFII 47 pl. 365, pi. 21. The protest was the subject of rumours in the Unité section later in the day: AFII 47 pl. 364, pi. 13.

p. 312 **'to murder patriots':** AFII 47 pl. 366, pi. 38 (report by Pellerin). See too for Popincourt AFII 47 pl. 366, pi. 29.

p. 312 **some sort of emergency:** The order from Hanriot in the early afternoon reached only a handful of sections by 6.00 p.m. Around half the sections had received the orders by 7.30. Poissonnière and Bondy received it between 9 and 10, and Montreuil not till 10.30. Even so, this was overall a faster transmission than for any other order (information culled esp. from AFII 47 and F7 4432).

p. 312 **a stray case of pork:** For Poissonnière, see AFII 47 pl. 367 and F7 4332 pl. 4. See also AFII 47 pl. 364 (Piques); pl. 365 (Contrat-Social); pl. 366 (Lepeletier); pl. 367 (Bondy); plus F7 4332 pl. 3 (Montagne); pl. 5 (Faubourg-du-Nord); pl. 6 (Gravilliers); and pl. 7 (Réunion).

20.00/8.00 p.m. (pp. 314–34)

p. 314 **the imperative need to imprison journalists:** Courtois II, doc. XIII, p. 102. See above, pp. 145–6. For Le Lièvre, see his and his brother's police files at F7 4774/14. See too above, p. 158.

p. 314 **in the Jacobin Club:** Of the dozen members of the Administration acting on the night, only Faro and Le Lièvre appear to have been members of the Club. See Jacobins, Index.

p. 315 **waiting below in the HQ courtyard:** There are three key, largely concordant accounts of this episode: AFII 47 pl. 365, pi. 29; F7 4432 pl. 7, pi. 33; and F7 4775/39 d. Van Heck. The Robespierre quotation below is from the first of the accounts. See too denunciations of Van Heck by Leblanc and Berger in F7 4332 pl. 7, d. 38 (Cité). Van Heck's achievements also included stopping the king's aunts from leaving Paris without permission in April 1791 and stopping the looting of the treasury after 10 August 1792. See above also, p. 210.

p. 316 **Debure enters the offices:** Notably Tribunal Vice-President Scellier and his own deputy Grébeauval. See W 501 (testimony of Debure).

p. 317 **to come to the bar of the house:** For this episode, see AFII 47 pl. 365, pi. 30 (an excellent account from the Bon-Conseil section, 15 Thermidor).

p. 317 **'Robespierre is free':** F7 4774/81 d. Poupart.

p. 318 **He then sweeps off:** F7 4432 pl. 6, pi. 24; AFII 47 pl. 364, pi. 48. Cf. SCD, pp. 245–6.

p. 319 **torn up the Convention's orders:** This last incident is recorded in Duval (1795), pp. 28–9.

p. 319 **Courvol:** See above, p. 234.

p. 320 **'Let us see what develops':** Courtois records this anecdote: Courtois II, pp. 68–9n.

p. 320 **Payan is under arrest:** Duval's account says Payan was arrested four hours previously. This presumably relates to the incident at around 4.00 p.m. See above, p. 255.

p. 321 **Cn. Pellerin:** AFII 47 pl. 366, pi. 38 for the account by Pellerin, Popincourt's artillery adjutant. It is excellent for this entire episode. SCD plausibly reckons (p. 233) that the force arrived at the Place du Carrousel at around 8.15.

p. 322 **insulted the deputy Goupilleau:** See esp. SCD, pp. 233–5, for this episode (drawing especially on the Pellerin account). See too the very full statements of gunners from the Mutius-Scévole section in W 80 d. Mutius-Scévole. For the force near the Hôtel de Brionne, see SCD, p. 234. On Pionnier, see above, p. 156.

p. 322 **The ropes binding Hanriot:** W 79, 'Dossier 13'. See also W 80, Damour file and F7 4660 d. Damour. Chaise (Fontaine-de-Grenelle) was later accused of cutting the restraining ropes: F7 4637 d. Chaise.

p. 322 **Julliot:** Livin report in AFII 47 pl. 365, pi. 33 (Bon-Conseil section); ibid., pl. 364, pi. 5 (Lambert, Brutus section).

p. 322 **'We've still got this one':** The testimony of the CGS secretary Rolland, W 434 d. 975. See too Jeannolle's statement in F7 4432 pl. 2, pi. 24.

p. 323 **Roman senators:** AP, p. 590; cf. Courtois, p. 69. The reference is to Livy's Roman History, book 5, 41. Thanks to Ariane Fichtl on this point.

p. 323 **Thuriot steps forward:** There was a delegation from the authorities of the Department of Paris at this time. They kept largely aloof from the night's events. AP, p. 590.

p. 324 **Dauminval:** See Dauminval's illuminating account at AFII 47 pl. 364, pi. 41.

p. 325 **'The CGS has recognized my innocence':** Besides the Pellerin source quoted, see too the testimony of Thiéry, NG commander of the Amis-de-la-Patrie section: AFII 47, pl. 367, pi. 5. For the standoff with artillery, see Courtois II, p. 132, and for the gendarmerie, AP 94, p. 103. It was reported that, as for the Pionnier incident, someone extinguished the match for the cannon.

p. 326 **'no blood will flow':** F7 4695 d. Dupré.

p. 326 **get his courage back:** I follow SCD, who argues that the much-repeated story that Hanriot was ordered back by the Commune is false. However, I am less certain than he about Hanriot's courage. SCD, p. 236, n. 3. Tales of his drunkenness were common after the event, partly as a result of comments by Coffinhal when in prison.

p. 328 **the Law of 23 Ventôse:** AP 96, p. 491. See above, pp. 80–3 for use of the legislation in prison plots. For the *mise en accusation*, see the discussion above, pp. 82–3.

p. 329 **the task of government:** Jean-Bon Saint-André and Prieur de la Marne were absent on mission. There is no record of the CPS/CGS meetings. CPS, pp. 457–68 provides a list of most decrees, which may also be consulted in AFII 47, pl. 363. Aulard failed to note some CPS decrees, and there is no full record of CGS decrees, many of which have, however, left traces in the archives. For David, see above, p. 136; for Jagot, see AP 94, p. 30 and for Lavicomterie, ibid., pp. 29–30 (the two latter both on 13 Thermidor).

p. 329 **when Hanriot made his 5.00 p.m. raid:** The number of signatures in Aulard provides a rough guide to activity. Of CPS members, Billaud leads with 15 signatures (no documents in his hand), followed by Lindet with 13, mostly on food supply issues. Then there are for Collot 9 (5 in his handwriting), Barère 8 (5), Carnot 7 (4) and Prieur 6. Vadier and Voulland's signatures are each found on 11 decrees, Dubarran on 8 (4) and Lacoste 7 (1). Lavicomterie signed none (and see the altercation about his fitful presence, cited in the previous note).

p. 330 **hard at work on food provisioning:** CPS, pp. 463–7.

p. 330 **a new set of Police Administrators:** Ibid., pp. 458–9. See also below, p. 422.

p. 331 **Martial Herman:** For Herman, see above, p. 168. This accusation was held against him: see his interrogation on 24 Thermidor in F7 4743 d. Herman.

p. 331 **only a handful of Civil Committees:** Sectional reports in F7 4332 and AFII 47 show the proclamation reaching most sections between 9.30 and shortly after 10.00.

p. 331 **a stop-gap measure:** CPS, p. 460.

p. 332 **currently wriggling free:** See above, p. 322. For Julliot's escape, see AFII 47 pl. 365, pi. 33.

p. 332 **ensuring the security of the city:** See SCD, pp. 353–4. More generally on the issue of the legislature's executive power, see Simonin (2008), esp. pp. 303–7.

p. 332 **forming a personal bodyguard:** See Jones & Macdonald (2018).

p. 334 **'only one way to do this':** Courtois II, p. 70n.

21.00/9.00 p.m. (pp. 335–50)

p. 335 **Barras:** The memoirs of Barras (1895–6) are important but notoriously mendacious and on most aspects of 9 Thermidor may be discounted (as also noted by SCD, pp. 324–6). For the bubble, see above, p. 178.

p. 335 **'I request that I be given assistants':** AP, p. 591.

p. 335 **Rue Saint-Honoré bubble:** The addresses we have for him are Rue Saint-Honoré and nearby Rue Traversière.

p. 336 **a mixed bag:** For potted biographies see Kuscinski (1916), with information on deputies on mission from Biard (2002).

p. 336 **moderate Féraud:** See *Moniteur*, 76, p. 688.

p. 337 **this was an excessive act:** A former member of the Paris *armée révolutionnaire*, Pionnier participated in the sectional popular society. He is included in the S&M dictionary of militants, p. 316. See too above, p. 156. The following account draws particularly on witness statements of gunners from the Mutius-Scévole section in W 80. Pionnier and other officers disputed the story, but the balance of evidence rests with the men. See also Courtois II, doc. XLIII, pp. 218–9, where Levasseur is identified as Vasseur.

p. 337 **to send an emissary to the CPS:** Bigot, Panthéon NG second-in-command statement: AFII 47 pl. 366, pi. 24.

p. 339 **The section sent Bodson:** See F7 4432 pl. 9, pi. 30 for this episode. See also Bodson's police file at F7 4604. Bodson stated that he left the Commune when Robespierre arrived which he says was around 9.45. This seems not to square with other evidence. For timings at this moment in the evening, SCD remains a good guide: esp. pp. 260–1.

p. 340 **the escort party:** One slipped away and reported the incident to the CGS. See testimony of Le Grand in F7 4432 pl. 10, pi. 4; and of René-Francois Camus, municipal officer from Guillaume-Tell, in W 79 d. 'Complicité de Robespierre'. See too F7 4632 d. Camus and F7 4702 d. Jacques Fabre. Two men held Augustin under the arms according to B&R, 34, pp. 87–9. For his beliefs, see his remarks to his captors at the end of the night, in Courtois II, doc. XXXVIII, pp. 203–6.

p. 340 **not well known:** For non-recognition, see the testimonies of Goupy, AFII 47 pl. 365, pi. 56 (Faubourg-du-Nord) and AFII 47 pl. 366, pi. 7 (Sans-Culottes Revolutionary Committee).

p. 340 **'to unite with his brother':** According to F7 4637 d. Chaguignée.

p. 340 **two minds as to how to react:** There are numerous testimonies about Augustin's interventions, including the references in the previous note; AFII 47 pl. 368, pi. 28; and AFII 47 pl. 365, pi. 57. They are vague and confusing for the most part, but do allow a reconstruction of his thinking on the lines indicated, bearing in mind his later remarks (see p. 519, note 'a pistol shot').

p. 340 **treated with consideration:** AFII 47 pl. 365, pi. 57 (Civil Committee, Faubourg-du-Nord). See W 79 d. 'Complicité de Robespierre' (testimony of Fréry and Camus, Guillaume-Tell section). See too F7 4632 d. Camus.

p. 340 **'the sole and unique representative':** Report by Olivier (Lombards), AFII 47 pl. 364, pi. 46.

p. 341 **march on the Convention:** See the report of Popincourt emissaries Courtois and François: AFII 47 pl. 366, pi. 37.

p. 341 **Hopes are high:** F7 4432 pl. 5, pi. 49 (Faubourg-du-Nord); and Commune minutes at AFII 47 pl. 368, pi. 28. There was subsequent discussion of Lerebours in the Convention: AP, p. 635, where it was suggested that he only used the briefcase as he had no entry card for the Commune. Lerebours proved the only chief of a government executive commission to join the Commune.

p. 341 **nine in all:** The decree is at Courtois II, doc. XVII, p. 110. The 1793 Commission des Neuf was better known as the Commission de l'Évêché (after its meeting place).

p. 341 **only twelve adjuncts:** See the testimony on this point of Poissonnière councillor Renard, at F7 4774/89 d. Renard. For a refusal to serve, see F7 4636 d. Cazenave. The list is given in Courtois II, doc. XVIII (2), p. 111.

p. 341 **hurries back to his section:** F7 4432 pl. 5, pi. 43 (Faubourg-du-Nord); AFII 47 p. 366, pi. 37 (sectional Revolutionary Committee report: Robespierre attacking Convention).

p. 342 **will be bayoneted:** F7 4669 d. Duval.

p. 343 **newspaper offices:** See above, p. 143. Report of Bisson, secretary in the Police Administration: F7 4432 pl. 7, pi. 4. For arrests of news vendors, see Courtois II, p. 149.

p. 343 **similarly motivated refusals:** AFII 47 pl. 364, pi. 43 (Lombards). It was a similar story elsewhere, notably in Cité: AFII 47 pl. 365, pi. 4. Cf. Fraternité: F7 4432 pl. 4, pi. 32 (initial refusal to act on an order from the military rather than civilian authorities). For the law, see AP 80, pp. 629–35. Section 2, article 2 highlights the role of the CPS and CGS in the organization of government; section 3, article 16 forbids functionaries and constituted bodies from exceeding their specific powers (article 16 extends this to convoking meetings and the like). AP 80, pp. 631, 633.

p. 343 **straying over the line:** There are simply too many examples to list. A copy of the small 14 Frimaire handbook may be consulted at F7 4764 d. Langlois.

p. 344 **in two ways:** AFII 47, pl. 365, pi. 27 (Notre-Dame); see the account of the gendarmerie attached to the law courts: testimony in AP 94, p. 77 (15 Thermidor: cannon).

p. 344 **battalion commander Étienne Lasne:** For Lasne's account, see AFII 47 pl. 367, pi. 42. The dossier includes other witness testimony. See too F7 4592 d. Becq; and, for Mulot, see above, p. 244.

p. 345 **still running the show:** SCD (p. 257) suggests the message went out twice in the course of the night. There seems no evidence that this was the case. For Julliot, see above, p. 332.

p. 346 **the rump still on guard:** The point about uniform does not appear to have been noticed by historians of the night. Léonard Bourdon's adoption of David's proposed uniform for legislators can be shown by comparing David's designs with Prieur's depiction of the capture of the Maison Commune (see below, p. 430). In the Prieur, the boots are very striking, but David's toque is missing. For the uniform generally, see Guillaume Nicoud, 'David habille la Révolution', *Histoire par l'image*, consulted 07 April 2020. http://www.histoire-image.org/fr/etudes/david-habille-revolution. For the gendarmerie, see the memo supplied by the 14 Juillet squadron of the gendarmerie, in AP 94, p. 102 (13 Thermidor); and AFII 224, doc. 1932.

p. 346 **today's NG duty guard:** This is strongly implied in the account by Tuileries militant Dauminval: AFII 47 pl. 364, pi. 41.

p. 347 **kept in the prison:** The Legrand account cited above is very confused. Cf SCD, p. 261 & n.

p. 347 **His earlier pessimism:** See above, p. 121.

p. 348 **'Adieu! Adieu!':** Stéfane-Pol (1900), pp. 137–8. Le Bas had earlier been taken to his home, presumably to have seals placed on his property, by CGS agent Dossonville according to the latter's testimony: F7 6318B.

p. 349 **'Come quickly!':** B&R, 34, p. 52.

p. 349 **eight NG cannon:** According to a report from the Révolutionnaire section reported in the Convention on 10 Thermidor: AP, p. 605.

p. 350 **he helped put them there:** See above, pp. 153–5.

p. 350 **Lasnier's delegation:** Lasnier's account, F7 4432 pl. 9, pi. 1.

22.00/10.00 p.m. (pp. 351–72)

p. 351 **'Hanriot is free too':** For this episode, see F7 4432 pl. 9, pi. 30 (report of Révolutionnaire Revolutionary Committee). Some details too from Marat NG personnel: AFII 47 pl. 365, pi. 41–4.

p. 354 **Jean Richard:** AFII 47 pl. 367, pi. 18; F7 4774/92 d. Richard. See above, p. 290 for the Payan incident.

p. 354 **less populated than earlier:** For the Panthéon battalion, see AFII 47 pl. 366, pi. 24 (report of Bigot, battalion second-in-command). Troops (with some artillery) guarding the Mairie at this time came from Marat, Lombards, Sans-Culottes, Arcis, and Faubourg-du-Nord sections. Men from Arcis and Droits-de-l'Homme were at the Treasury building.

p. 354 **Men from the Amis-de-la-Patrie:** Thiéry's file at F7 4775/28 contains over 20 anonymous declarations from Amis-de-la-Patrie guardsmen about this stage of the night.

p. 355 **A large majority of sections:** Over the course of the evening, some 33 of the remaining 39 sections would hold assemblies. SCD, p. 278n.

p. 355 **in central areas:** The central sections were Tuileries, Lombards, Muséum, and (on the Ile de la Cité) Révolutionnaire, plus on the Left Bank Fontaine-de-Grenelle. To the east, there were Réunion and Arsenal and to the west, République. SCD, p. 272n. Soboul (1958), p. 1013, notes that the Champs-Élysées only met much later and was antagonistic to the Commune.

p. 355 **changing their political complexion:** Although Soboul (1958) is less convinced (p. 1021), SCD argues strongly on these lines (pp. 272–3).

p. 356 **the paths of pro-Convention righteousness:** BHVP ms. 678: continuation of the journal of Jacques-Louis Ménétra.

p. 356 **'not easy to make the people rebel':** See above, p. 301.

p. 356 **sections send delegates:** For Indivisibilité, see AFII 47 pl. 365 pi. 38; and for Poissonnière, see F7 4432 pl. 4, pi. 30. See also for the latter section AFII 47 pl. 367, pi. 52–3; F7 4639 d. Chandellier; F7 4774/10 d. Lecomte; and F7 4774/80 d. Potier.

p. 356 **observers to the Jacobin Club:** Thibaudeau (1827), pp. 82–4 is esp. good on this aspect.

p. 358 **Barère is rising to speak:** AP, pp. 591–2.

p. 358 **informed by the rumours:** This is SCD's view (p. 254).

p. 360 **'neither Catiline nor Pisistratus':** For both classical references, see p. 39.

p. 361 **Pierre Burguburu:** Two excellent files on Burguburu in W 79 and F7 4627.

p. 361 **fellow Jacobins:** As well as Sijas, Burguburu cited Renaudin, Nicolas, and Chatelain among others either arrested or due for arrest.

p. 361 **'the factious will have been annihilated':** AFII 47 pl. 366, pi. 4 (testimony of Martellière).

p. 362 **'General Council of 10 August':** The delegate may have been confused between the Enforcement Committee of nine and the twelve appointed adjuncts. (Or it may have been the original nine with the two Robespierres and Le Bas added. The 10 August title was not widely used.) Those who had been on the Insurrectionary Commune in 1792 were given honorary membership of the Commune for this night, though there were few takers.

p. 362 **Didier had been agonizing:** There is detail on Didier's day in his interrogation in W 500. He claims to have left the Jacobins for his home after 10.00 p.m. Despite this act, he stayed loyal to Robespierrist principles in future years: S&M, p. 62. We have nothing about Duplay.

p. 363 **'Stay loyal':** Courtois II, p. 68.

p. 363 **Bertèche has been under arrest:** See above, p. 141. Indeed he seems to have already been placed under arrest for a counterfeiting offence earlier in the day: see his account in F7 4596. He claims to have resisted the calls of the rebels at 9.00 p.m.: F7 3822.

p. 364 **Jean Devèze:** F7 4765 d. Devèze. For these events, see AP, p. 591.

p. 365 **the man himself enters the room:** For the mid-sentence break, see SCD, p. 263n.

p. 365 **the need to support liberty:** F7 4432 pl. 10, pi. 4: testimony of Hardon (Finistère). For the liberty quotation, see F7 4431 d. Camus.

p. 366 **His battalion colleagues:** See above for the battalion's sympathies, p. 354. The incident is recorded in Courtois II, doc. XXXIV (2), pp. 196–7. Robespierre's phrase was '*assommez-le!*'. The document includes Juneau's claim for his lost property noted here, with costings.

p. 366 **'villains, former police spies':** AFII 47 pl. 366, pi. 37.

p. 367 **'to free the Convention':** F7 4333 pl. 1, pi. 18.

p. 367 **no Billaud or Barère:** Mathiez supposed that Barère's absence was Robespierre's doing: Mathiez, 'Robespierre à la Commune le 9 thermidor', in id. (1925), p. 223n.

p. 367 **roll up their sleeves:** Examples of the following decrees can be seen at AFII 47 pl. 368, pi. 1–16; F7 4333 pl. 1; and Courtois II, docs. XXI–XXVII, pp. 123–8.

p. 367 **come to the side of the Commune:** AFII 47 pl. 368, pi. 14 (Hanriot order); AFII 47 pl. 366, pi. 38 (Pellerin); AFII 47, pl. 368, pi. 12 (order to section); ibid., pi. 11 (pistols); AP, p. 592 (Convention capture of Hanriot order). See generally too SCD, pp. 283–5.

p. 369 **Pierre-Louis Moessard:** See the very full account in F7 4432 pl. 4, pi. 16–18; and for Moessard himself, F7 4774/47 d. Moessard. He would be investigated for his pro-Hanriot stance after the day. For Fréry, see also F7 4632 d. Camus.

p. 370 **penned a letter:** AFII 47 pl. 365, pi. 25. The letter was sent at 7.15. The sense of trickery was shared by officials in the Faubourg-du-Nord who had sent their artillery to the Commune under the impression they were being used for public order purposes. See AFII 47 pl. 365, pi. 55–7; and F7 4432 pl. 5, passim; plus F7 4637 d. Chaguignée and F7 4774/40 d. Mauvage. See too, for a similar case, AFII 47 pl. 366, pi. 47–8 (Marchés).

p. 370 **'still young in Revolution':** F7 4774/66 d. Pellecat. See too AFII 47 pl. 364, pi. 23–4 (Quinze-Vingts section: testimonies of Bourbault and his second-in-command Trouville). See too F7 4710 d. Fournerot. Fournerot was 4 feet six inches tall. See too SCD, pp. 270–1.

p. 371   **'Shut up, Robespierre!':** Coittant, *Almanach des prisons*, p. 157.

p. 371   **Can it all be true?:** Théotiste (1875), p. 160. This was rumour: at this time government troops were not at the Maison Commune.

p. 371   **take out his bad feelings:** F7 4738 d. Haly.

p. 372   **children are pressed into service:** Beugnot (1866). p. 228; Fleischmann (1908), p. 395, citing Beaulieu.

p. 372   **Laurenceot remains resigned:** de La Laurencie (1905), p. 29.

23.00/11.00 p.m. (pp. 373–94)

p. 373   **'enemies of the people':** F7 4333 pl. 1, pi. 23.

p. 374   ***'in-the-laws* of Liberty and Equality':** F7 4432 pl. 2, pi. 88 (memoir by Guyot: see below, pp. 417–8).

p. 374   **Fleury-Bourbon has cut and run:** F7 4585 d. Ballin. See SCD, pp. 280–1. For the decrees, see F7 4433, pl. 1.

p. 375   **improvised headquarters:** Fouquier's trial accounts, in W 500 and W 501. Cf. Lenôtre (1908), p. 288.

p. 375   **'what it means':** Dunoyer (1913), p. 290 (testimony of femme Morisan, *buvetière*, in W 500).

p. 376   **Aubert:** See above, p. 128 and F7 4582 d. Aubert.

p. 377   **little chance of prevailing in Faubourg-du-Nord:** F7 4437 (Gibert), F7 4586 (Barelle) and AFII 47 pl. 365, pi. 35 (Faubourg-du-Nord). See also F7 4650 d. Cochois, and AFII 47 pl. 364, pi. 42 (Cochois). For Simon, see above, p. 158 and AFII 47 pl. 365, pi. 39–42 and F7 4432 pl. 9, pi. 15 (Marat section). In Invalides, Michée did not support the pro-Commune Roussel and Vitry: F7 4432 pl. 8, pi. 34–5.

p. 377   **Gencey:** AFII 47 pl. 365, pi. 12.

p. 377   **to influence Charles Chardin:** F7 4432 pl. 4, pi. 6 (testimony of Lambert). See too the testimony of battalion second-in-command, Stainville, and the minutes of the Civil Committee.

p. 378   **his tail between his legs:** Besides these sources, see also B&R, 34, p. 47 for the Commune order.

p. 379   **'slit our throats':** Courtois II, p. 72n.

p. 380   **The Pont-Neuf:** See below, pp. 383–4.

p. 381   **'false news' from getting out:** W 80 d. Joly. See above, p. 000, for the Police Administration.

p. 382   **declare immediately for the Convention:** According to SCD (p. 274 & n.), ten such assemblies joined the nine sections who refused assemblies altogether because of fidelity to the Convention.

p. 382   **Herman and Lanne:** See above, pp. 168, 212.

p. 382   **full-blown posters:** For the poster format see Assemblée Nationale; Collection Portiez de l'Oise. (These were kindly brought to my attention by Laurent Cuvelier). Sections receiving the proclamation before 10.00 include Contrat-Social, Marchés, Bondy, Temple, Poissonnière, Arsenal, and Maison-Commune. The latter section contains the Maison Commune. In sections in which documentation provides timings after 10.00 p.m. (roughly half of the 48) nearly all readings were done between 10 and 11.30, though in some locations they took place after midnight.

p. 382　**'we don't care a fuck':** AFII 47 pl. 364, pi. 33 (Tuileries section).

p. 383　**Bodson brothers:** See above, p. 339.

p. 383　**gung-ho supporters of the Commune:** CPS, pp. 459–60. See too F7 4774/8 d. Le Camus.

p. 384　**unceremoniously stripped of his sash:** For this episode, see F7 4432 pl. 9 and AFII 47 pl. 365, as well as BNF NAF F7★ 2712. See too the dossiers of the Bodson brothers in F7 4604.

p. 384　**in government hands:** See above, p. 380.

p. 384　**to visit battalions:** The Third Legion's eight sectional battalions were located on the Right Bank (Tuileries, Champs-Elysées), the Ile de la Cité (Révolutionnaire) and the Left Bank (Fontaine-de-Grenelle, Bonnet-Rouge, Unité, Mutius-Scévole, and Invalides).

p. 384　**to the Police Administration cells:** AFII 47 pl. 364, pi. 1 & 14–17 (Unité). These materials include Mathis's account of the incident.

p. 385　**Rue des Canettes:** See above, p. 24. Floriban's house on the end of the Rue des Canettes overlooked the square.

p. 385　**The presence of the deputies:** F7 4432 pl. 9, pi. 1. See also Sorbonne Library (Paris), ms. 117 (fragment only). The identity of the two deputies is unknown.

p. 385　**wastepaper bins:** Many sections strove to maintain an archive of the night's communications, but the amount retained was very small overall.

p. 386　**'the fruit of six years of labour':** AFII 47 pl. 365, pi. 14; F7★ 2507.

p. 386　**a new urgency to the message:** See above, p. 345. It is possible, however, that the decree was sent out in two lots. Certainly the arrival times in some sections was very late (2.00 a.m. in Indivisibilité, 2.30 in Bonne-Nouvelle, 3.00 in Sans-Culottes, 5.00 in Arsenal).

p. 388　**The Bon-Conseil group:** See above, p. 356; and AFII 47 pl. 365, pi. 30.

p. 388　**made him turn coat:** F7 4432 d. 9, pi. 1 and AFII 47 pl. 366 pi. 14. For Lasnier's expedition, see above, pp. 349–51.

p. 388　**stripped of his insignia:** W 79, 'Dossiers Canonniers des Droits-de-l'Homme'; ibid., 'Dossier 13' (relating to Arcis) as well as AFII 47 pl. 366, pi. 20; F7 4660 d. Damour. See also accounts of the incident at F7 4774/49 d. Monoyer. Around the same time, the assembly agreed to recall its NG detachment from the Place de la Maison Commune.

p. 389　**the three men are arrested:** For Tugot and Dehureau, see W 80 d. Arcis. For Homme-Armé, AFII 47 pl. 366, pi. 4; and F7 4609 d. Forestier; B&R, 34, p. 55. For the 3 men, see below, p. 428. There is uncertainty over the time of these arrests.

p. 389　**Jean-Étienne Forestier:** See esp. F7 4609 d. Forestier; plus F7 4737 d. Guyard and AFII 47 pl. 366, pi. 20. The delegates were recorded in the Popincourt assembly at 10.45 p.m.: AFII 47 pl. 366, pi. 33. See too APP AA266 Popincourt; and Courtois II, p. 167, which records the wording of the Homme-Armé text.

p. 389 **Early imitators:** See AFII 47 pl. 367, pi. 43 (Droits-de-l'Homme). These names are very often listed among the first delegations to be received in individual sections. BNF Fonds française 8607 contains the minutes of the Homme-Armé section and its exceptional efforts at outreach. See too W 79.

p. 390 **to visit the Jacobins:** For the Fraternité section and the Jacobins, see F7 4432 pl. 7, pi. 44.

p. 390 **forbidden by the Law of 14 Frimaire:** See above, pp. 166–8. For the condemnation of the 'fraternal banquets', see above, pp. 112–13.

p. 390 **fraternization practice:** See Soboul (1958), pp. 31–5. SCD notes 33 out of 39 sections in which a General Assembly was held practised this form of inter-sectional fraternity.

p. 392 **Nicolas-Paul Hugot:** AFII 47 pl. 368, pi. 17. See also SCD pp. 285–7 and, with the Commune decree, Courtois II, doc. XXX, pp. 164–6.

p. 393 **'The new Cromwell':** See above, p. 194.

p. 393 **The Law of 23 Ventôse:** See above, p. 80.

p. 394 **protesters against the Wage Maximum:** See arrests noted in F7★ 2472 (Montagne).

MIDNIGHT, AROUND MIDNIGHT, AFTER MIDNIGHT

(A) Midnight

p. 397 **Marat's view:** See above, p. 34.

p. 398 **no plan survives contact with the enemy:** This phrase is usually attributed to nineteenth-century Prussian field marshal von Moltke. More recently it has been reformulated by boxer Mike Tyson as 'everyone has a plan until they get punched in the mouth'.

p. 398 **his *idée fixe* for months:** See above, p. 149.

p. 399 **'useful truths':** See above, p. 38.

p. 399 **a wronged victim:** Scholars will realize I am taking sides in a classic dispute. Many hold that this letter was Robespierre's last act and that a blot next to his semi-signature is the blood spilled as he was shot by the Convention's forces. I am largely following the arguments of Albert Mathiez, who pointed out the fallacies as well as the improbabilities of that claim. The letter did go out and was received in the Piques section before the hour of Robespierre's death. The overall interpretation here, however, is ultimately my own. The document is located in the Musée Carnavalet.

p. 401 **much hated on the streets:** See above p. 165 for his unpopularity. He had been released from Pélagie prison with Robespierre's ally Nicolas: F7 4677 d. Digeon; and F7 4662 d. Dauphinot.

p. 401 **hanging someone with the ropes:** F7 4432 pl. 7, pi. 2. For his excessive behaviour at this time, see also F7 4775/48 d. Vincent. The threat was odd in that Robespierre does not seem to have been tied up in the afternoon. In gaol, post Thermidor, Fouquier heard Coffinhal berating Hanriot for being drunk on the day: W 501.

(B) Around Midnight

p. 403 **expecting 9 Thermidor to be a normal day:** APP AA188 Muséum (déclaration de grossesse, 20 Pluviôse III). I was put on to the case by Cobb (1971), p. 225 & id. (1972), p. 142.

p. 403 **two other adjuncts:** Reference to the other deputies serving with Barras at F7 4774/ 92 d. Richard.

p. 403 **artillery of the Droits-de-l'Homme section:** See above, pp. 344 and 388.

p. 404 **Léonard Bourdon:** There is no evidence about Barras's decision-making. Bourdon's energy that night already and his knowledge of the terrain must have been key factors in Barras's mind in choosing him for this mission. See the biography of Bourdon by Sydenham (1999), pp. 236–41.

p. 404 **to bolster the Convention:** For Réunion, see F7 4774/92 d. Richard. (This is the same Richard that was involved in an incident with Payan earlier in the evening: see p. 290.) For Bon-Conseil, F7* 2490; and for Halle-au-Blé, AFII 47 pl. 364, pi. 50.

p. 404 **the copious throng of citizens:** Acts relating to these visits are mainly contained in C 314. They are also listed in AP, esp. pp. 565–73.

p. 405 **not represented:** There are no reports for Chalier in AFII 47 or F7 4432; the only official documentation we have is the Revolutionary Committee account in F7* 2511.

p. 405 **the gains the people have had:** This trope appears in nearly a dozen statements in the course of the night and is much repeated on later days.

p. 405 **hackneyed, stereotyped, and often highly bombastic:** This is Baczko's view in his influential work on post-Thermidor (1989). I argue against this in Jones (2014).

p. 406 **Voyenne:** F7 4775/49 d. Voyenne and W 80.

p. 406 **the Finistère battalion:** See the very full dossier on the Finistère group in F7 4432 pl. 10, pi. 4. For the La Force incident, see above, p. 347.

p. 406 **massacring prisoners:** Ibid., esp. testimonies of Ouy, Brehy, and Thibaux.

p. 406 **'the detachment may retire':** Ibid., testimony of Vian.

p. 407 **'All right, do it yourself!':** F7 4432 pl. 6, pi. 24–9.

p. 407 **'not soldiers for hire':** 'Ils n'étaient pas soldats d'argent': ibid., testimony Legrand (Finistère). See also testimonies by Manant, Bontemps, Vian, Prin, also in F7 4432 pl. 10.

p. 407 **the wrong man in the wrong place:** What follows draws on Giot's police files at W 79 d. Marat; and F7 4725 d. Giot. See too AFII 47 pl. 365, pi. 41 (Damour testimony); pi. 44 (Typhaine testimony); and F7 4432 pl. 9, pi. 16.

p. 408 **ageing by eighty years:** Vilate, *Causes secrètes* (III), p. 212 (on the La Force prison). For general background on the Temple see F7 4391. See the police files on administrators involved: F7 4775/26 d. Tessier; F7 4775/31 d. Tombe; F7 4775/21 d. Soulié; and F7 4774/90 d. Renaudin (for Soulié). See also F7 4432 pl. 6, pi. 39–41; and AFII 47 pl. 367, pi. 23–4.

p. 408 **Tessier from the Invalides:** For Tessier, see above, p. 159.

p. 409 **planning to seize the young 'Capet':** See below, p. 418.

p. 409 **writing to the Revolutionary Committee:** F7 4432 pl. 10, pi. 37.

p. 410 **'all patriots are proscribed':** See Courtois II, doc. XXXV (1), p. 198, for the circumstances of his release.

p. 410 **failing on all fronts:** For the sole effort at mobilization, in the Maison-Commune section, see AFII 47 pl. 365, pi. 18–20 and F7 4774/97 d. Roger. For the interception of the letter, see above, p. 379.

p. 410 **CPS spy Pierre-Honoré-Gabriel Dulac:** Dulac's account in Courtois II, doc. XXXIX, pp. 207–12 is an overwritten version of his printed memoir, to be found in F7 4432 pl. 2, pi. 90. I also draw on the account by the two gendarmes who were Couthon's escort, Javois and Muron. See ibid., pl. 2, pi. 13.

p. 411 **'in the Mairie courtyard':** It is unclear who is speaking. My guess is that it is a police administrator who was present earlier in the evening when Robespierre entered the Mairie. (See above, p. 311.) It may well have been police administrator Legrand, who was a member of the Enforcement Committee.

p. 412 **'embitter the people against the plotters':** This wording is from the Dulac account. The Javois and Muron account has, 'Gendarmes, go down at once to the Place and put the people in the right frame of mind and impassion them', plus the reply noted here.

p. 412 **Longueville-Clémentières and Morel:** Compare Morel at F7 4774/72 and Clémentières at W 79 d. Clémentières-Longueville. The two men's accounts differ in some particulars.

p. 413 **firing squad at dawn:** The threat of execution by firing squad the next morning does seem to have been current. See also e.g. Courtois II, doc. XIX (9), pp. 120–1.

p. 413 **Léonard Bourdon and Simon Camboulas:** I am drawing on the account of this incident in 'Récit de ce qui s'est passé dans la Maison Commune de Paris la nuit du 9 au 10 thermidor', from *Messager du soir*, 18 Thermidor issue, and then in the Convention on 16 Thermidor: AP 94, pp. 95ff. The accounts state that it was at 11.00 but this seems too early in view of the attack on the Maison Commune at 2.00 or 2.30 a.m. But the sectional report at AFII 47 pl. 366, pi. 27 also states the same time. Although Bourdon lived here, Camboulas resided on the Rue Saint-Honoré. Six thousand men represents a big force; but Gravilliers was one of the largest sections with around 25,000 inhabitants. Some of the force may have come from other sections.

p. 414 **a scuffle at the Maison Commune:** For this incident, see F7 4774/66 d. Penières and F7 4774/81 d. Poupart. The latter suggests that the move led to the occupation of the area around the NG HQ, but this is substantiated by no other source.

p. 414 **the password:** F7 4774/37 d. Martin; F7 4775/36 d. Ulrich; and W 80 d. Gravilliers. Pierre-Louis Vincent, a Commune functionary, claimed to have passed this to Ulrich and done his best to keep the password in use all day: F7 4775/48. See also above, pp. 321–2; and Ulrich's statement in Courtois II, doc. XXXVI, pp. 126–7. There was a good deal of password confusion all night: see e.g. F7 4748 d. Janson.

p. 414 **'National Convention' and 'People':** AFII 47 pl. 365, pi. 44 (testimony of Typhaine).

p. 414 **Gencey in Finistère:** Despite the energy of their interventions, neither Delacour at Brutus nor Gencey was successful in his efforts. For Burguburu, see above, p. 361. See also F7 4677 d. De l'Épine for a similar case in Gravilliers.

p. 415 **'oppressing the patriots':** Testimony of Bougon in F7 4764 d. Langlois. See too F7 4432 pl. 7, pi. 2. For Le Pauvre, see W 79 d. 'Complicité de Robespierre', and for Arnauld's behaviour, see Tachereau's account: F7 4775/25 (39 or 40 sections, 6,000 guardsmen, 1,200 cavalry).

p. 415 **pro-Commune sections:** Ibid. See also AFII 47 pl. 366, pi. 25–6. The 40 figure is cited also by Perrot in Maison-Commune: F7 4774/69. In Marat at 11.00 p.m., the figure was 20, in Invalides, 30: AFII 47 pl. 365, pi. 39 (Marat) and F7 4432 pl. 8, pi. 35. For the Jacobin Club claim, see e.g. F7 4774/92 d. Roch.

p. 415 **'mutually contradictory':** F7 4432 pl. 7, pi. 2 & pi. 6; AF II 47 pl. 367, pi. 42.

p. 416 **traffic of information:** F7 4730 d. Goulart; F7 4774/11 f. Lefebvre; F7 4585 d. Ballin.

p. 416 **'spark a civil war':** Lefebvre F7 4774/11 d. Lefevbre. See too the sectional reports in AFII 47 pl. 366. Cf. Vincenot, Arsenal NG second-in-command, AFII 47 pl. 367, pi. 2 for another Lyon reference; and F7★ 2510 (Invalides: civil war).

p. 416 **'people will scan the banks of the Seine':** See above, p. 31.

p. 417 **Langlois is on guard–duty:** For Langlois, see above, p. 140. His account of this day (Langlois [1836], pp. 26–33) is poor, and contains a number of errors of fact. There are a few minor details in Peyssard's police file: F7 4774/72.

p. 417 **Bertèche is already under arrest:** F7 4596 d. Bertèche. See above, p. 363.

p. 417 **lacking in ammunition:** Peyssard in the 11 Thermidor session: AP, pp. 584, 593.

p. 417 **not at all been the day:** See his printed account of his life and 9 Thermidor in F7 4332 pl. 2, pi. 88: 'Mémoire du Citoyen Guyot, membre de la Commune et administrateur de police'. See too F7 4737 d. Guyot.

p. 418 **from the Place de la Maison Commune:** See above, p. 407. See also the participant accounts for this episode in F7 4432 pl. 6, pi. 29.

p. 419–20 **they want to fight against the tyrant:** Ibid., esp. testimonies of Laroche and Lieyvus; and AFII 47 pl. 364, pi. 47 (account by Philippe and Dubois).

(C) After Midnight

p. 419 **the most impressive show of force:** See above, p. 302 (around 7.00 p.m.) and p. 342 (around 9.00 p.m.).

p. 420 **death was just around the corner:** This account draws particularly on Forestier's police file at F7 4609, as well as Dulac's account in Courtois II, doc. XXXIX, pp. 207–14. For earlier in the evening, see above, p. 303.

p. 420 **clerk Blaise Lafosse:** Lafosse was picked up on his way back to the Contrat Social section: see F7 4578; W 79; and W 80.

p. 420 **Candle–stumps and stagnant water:** Councillor Beauvallet was another escapee here: see F7 4432 pl. 5, pi. 34 (Bondy); and Courtois. They came out after the guillotinings of 10–12 Thermidor and survived.

p. 421 **Dulac grabbed Charlemagne:** According to Dulac's account in W 79 'Notes et renseignements relatifs à différents prévenus', as well as his report in Courtois II, doc. XXXIX, pp. 213–14.

p. 421 **a pistol-shot that pierced Robespierre's cheek**: AP, p. 594. This is not the place to enter into a debate over the circumstances of Robespierre's shooting which have divided historians for more than two centuries. The most recent contribution is Biard (2015). A number of supporters of the Merda hypothesis claim support from the blood to be found by Robespierre's semi-signature on his alleged final letter. However, as pointed out above (p. 399), there is sufficient evidence to discount the idea that this was in fact written at this time. It is worth noting that Augustin Robespierre confessed that his falling from a window of the Maison Commune had been a suicide attempt. Sainte-Claire Deville, whose acquaintance with primary materials for the *journée* is sans-pareil, also dismisses Merda's account unconditionally (p. 299 & n).

p. 422 **demoralized Enforcement Committee:** See for the carnage, Dulac's account in Courtois II, doc. XXXIX, pp. 213–14. Most historians state that Couthon had been pushed down the stairs, but the plausible eyewitness account by Arcis gunner Laroche suggests he had been taken to the place in efforts to flee: Cobb (1952). For Saint-Just's state of dress, *Faits recueillis aux derniers instants de Robespierre et de sa faction du 9 au 10 thermidor* (no date = 1794). For the younger Robespierre, see the reports in Courtois II, doc. XVIIII, pp. 203–6. The guardsman's name is given in *Journal de Perlet*, 18 Thermidor. SCD (p. 298) places the fall just as Bourdon was entering the building though other accounts differ on this.

p. 422 **Ménétra had recently lost the election:** BHVP, ms. 678, and above, p. 138.

p. 423 **seized the Mairie and the Police HQ:** This account draws from esp. AFII 47 pl. 365, pi. 53, 54 and F7 4332 pl. 9, pi. 30 (Révolutionnaire); AFII 47 pl. 367, pi. 47 (report by 5th Legion Chief Mulot); and the report given to the Convention on 12 Thermidor by the 31st mounted gendarmerie division: AP, pp. 653–5. For CPS decrees on the Police Administration, see CPS, ix, pp. 458–9; and F7 4774/8 d. Lecamus.

p. 423 **the Jacobin Club:** The main account of the Jacobin closure is Legendre's report to the Convention: AP, p. 594 and then the Jacobin Club on 11 Thermidor: Jacobins, pp. 297–8.

p. 423 **physical assault on Third Legion Chief Mathis:** Mathis wrote to the Convention from his sick-bed and received the deputies' commendation: AFII 47 pl. 364, pi. 4 and AP 94, p. 13.

p. 424 **cruel taunts from bystanders:** *Faits recueillis* (1794), pp. 3–4. Besides the testimony from this source, see also Courtois II, doc. XLI, pp. 215–17, notably on the transfers of Robespierre and Saint-Just.

p. 424 **'The corpse of a tyrant':** AP, p. 593.

p. 424 **contriving to look like a pickpocket:** As stated by deputy Thibaudeau (2007), p. 119. For the men's condition at this time, see esp. *Faits recueillis*.

p. 424 **Robespierre's wounded state:** See the surgeons' report on his wound at Courtois II, doc. XXXVII, pp. 202–3.

p. 425 **'The soil of the Republic':** For the 10 Thermidor session, see AP, pp. 597–618; and Duval (1795), p. 47ff.

p. 425 **His pet dog would whimper:** Le Bas's death was recorded in ADP Etat civil. See too ADP AA70 Arsenal; and for the dog, Stefan-Pol (1900), p. 146. Lavalette had been arrested early in the afternoon on 9 Thermidor by the Gardes-Françaises Revolutionary Committee and sent to Pélagie. See F7 4769 d. Lavalette; F7 4774/11 d. Lefaure and F7 4774/67 d. Percin (where part of Lavalette's police dossier has been misfiled). For the Pélagie incident, see F7 4662 d. Dauphinot. For Vivier, F7 4775/49 d. Vivier; and AFII 47 pl. 364, pi. 8. For Fleuriot's escape attempt, see F7 4432 pl. 7, pi. 6.

p. 425 **Robespierre's 'conspiracy' was full of strangers:** For Couthon, see Courtois II, doc. XXXV, p. 198; and AFII pl. 363, pi. 51, 52. For Gobeau, see F7 4727 d. Gobeau and, for his earlier strident support for the Commune in his section, F7 4432 pl. 8, pi.

30. See also F7 4650 d. Cochefer. For the CPS orders, AFII 47 pl. 363, pi. 51–2. Most councillors arrested at the Maison-Commune were still in process at this time.

p. 426 **ill-starred adjuncts:** These included Dhazard (see AFII 47 pl. 363, pi. 46); Gencey (F7 4432 pl. 10, pi. 3); Simon, along with Warmé and Laurent (F7 4432 pl. 9, pi. 14, 16 and CPS, ix, p. 483). Also in the execution convoy were Bernard (see above, p. 383); Jean-Étienne Forestier (F7 4609 d. Forestier: note that this was not Jean-Antoine-Gaspard Forestier, mentioned above, p. 420); Jean-Marie Quenet (Maison-Commune: a Police Administrator arrested at the Mairie); Bougon (see F7 4764 d. Langlois) and Guérin (both from Mont-Blanc).

p. 426 **identification procedures:** Full listings in W 434 d. 975. For subsequent days see ibid., dossiers 976–8.

p. 426 **formerly his bosom friend:** As noted by several witnesses in Fouquier's later trial: W 501.

p. 426 **they set out for the Place de la Révolution:** *Journal de Perlet*, 12 Thermidor, states three tumbrils were used for the 22 men. For the dance of joy, see Michelet (1979), ii, pp. 895–6. For Robespierre's shriek, ibid., p. 895. For the order of execution, there are good accounts in *Feuille de la République*, 12 Thermidor and *Journal de Perlet*, 18 Thermidor.

p. 426 **'Fucking Maximum!':** Rudé (1959), p. 140.

p. 426 **stopping a purge of the Convention:** Harder's analysis (2013) is a reminder that the purge of five deputies was less than the Girondins and the '73' in June–October 1793. For statistics on the executed, I use SCD's figures (pp. 340–1). He notes that non-councillors executed were four deputies, six municipal functionaries and eleven others. SCD is excellent on the repression generally: see ch. 5, pp. 315–47. For Grenart, see W 79 liasse 26; AFII 47 pl. 365, pi. 20. For Desboisseaux, see W 434 d. 975 and for Coffinhal, Courtois II, doc. XXX, p. 178. For both men, SCD, pp. 338–41.

p. 427 **Few managed to get clean away:** Fleury appears to have gone for ever; for Lerebours, see Hamel, iii (1865), p. 787n.; and for Payan, SCD, p. 302 and (for the silverware) F7 4437 (police report, 14 Thermidor).

p. 427 **Three councillors threw themselves on the mercy:** The three who attended the Convention were Devèze (République), Chrétien, and Renouard (both Amis-de-la-Patrie). See above, p. 364. For other examples of fugitives' fates, see Jean-Jacques Beaurieux who served in the Police Administration on the night but left early to hand himself in at the Plessis prison under the misguided impression that a friend was still gaoler: Foignet (no date), p. 29. The Quinze-Vingts Revolutionary Committee transferred him to the CGS regardless and he was executed on 11 Thermidor. F7 4432 pl. 1, pi. 21. For other examples, see F7 4774/63 d. Parizot (Gravilliers); F7 4775/31 d. Tonnelier, and see too AFII 47 pl. 364, pi. 12 (Faubourg-Montmartre); F7 4582 d. Aubert plus F7 4432 pl. 4, pi. 31, 32 (Poissonnière).

p. 427 **service for the Convention's cause:** F7 4774/20 d. Lestage, plus AFII 47 pl. 367, pi. 11 and 13 and F7 4432 pl. 3, pi. 31, and for the encounter in the Convention, AP p. 574; F7 4775/43 d. Vergne and AFII 47 pl. 366, pi. 25. Temple service involved Lorinet (Panthéon), Seguy (Montagne), Soulié (Gardes-Françaises), Tessier (Invalides), and Tombe (Amis-de-la-Patrie); and for Benoit and Michel, see above, pp. 272–3. Similarly, Félix served as Revolutionary Tribunal judge and steered clear of the night's events. See above, p. 166. See too F7 4602 d. Blandin and F7 4432 pl. 6, pi. 24; F7 4774/89 d. Renard; and for Guyot, see above, p. 417; For similar cases, see SCD, p. 371 (Legry) and F7 4774/54 d. Mouret. There are numerous similar examples.

p. 428 **Claude Chalandon:** See above, p. 277; F7 4637 d. Chalandon; and AFII 47 pl. 366, pi. 1. However, as the anti-Terror movement grew, both Pionnier and Chalandon did suffer imprisonment.

p. 428 **a batch of around 40 individuals:** The case dossier is W 444. Hardon was also among the acquitted: for his actions, see above, p. 303 The Droits-de-l'Homme artillery, however, which had ended the night under Barras, remained in gaol until well into 1795.

p. 431 **'the most perfect tranquillity reigned':** AFII 47 pl. 367, pi. 47. For Granet, see AP, p. 611. See Jones (2015), pp. 22ff. ('Thermidor as co-production').

p. 431 **the NG's required password:** AFII 47 pl. 365, pi. 44.

p. 431 **firm in his judgement on the *journée*:** NP, p. 699.

AFTERWORD (PP. 432–456)

p. 432 **'Writing the history of the Revolution':** NP, p. 882.

p. 433 **to wait for its meaning to be established:** Cf. Baczko (1989), which places emphasis on the quest for an end to Terror.

p. 433 **a joint victory for the elected deputies and for Parisians:** Barère's speech of 11 Thermidor: AP, p. 634.

p. 433 **delegations presenting their congratulations:** Brunel (1989), pp. 120–4; and Baczko (1989), p. 40. Baczko is severe on these statements; Jones (2015) provides a more sympathetic reading (pp. 23–6).

p. 433 *Rapport sur les événements du 9 thermidor an II*: Courtois II (p. 28 for the quotation).

p. 434 **conceived of as 'the Terror':** On the 'invention' of 'the Terror' in the Thermidorian period, see esp. Martin (2018).

p. 435 **Against the people:** For this theme within Thermidorian history, see esp. Mason (2015–17), esp. the contributions of Mason and Jones. See also Baczko (1989), Luzzatto (2001), and Woronoff (2004).

p. 435 **'Rising on the ruins of Robespierre':** For the Talliens at this phase of their lives, see Bourquin (1987), pp. 254–67; Harder (2013), pp. 98–103 (quotation from Thibaudeau on p. 101); and Adams (2014).

p. 435 **Dantonist deputy Laurent Lecointre:** This maverick figure deserves a biography. See Jones (2015), for this stage of his career, and p. 17 for the insanity claim.

p. 436 **the gaols of the Terror as gothic sites:** Brown (2018), pp. 132–3; Baczko (2008). See too above, p. 472, and note, 'Bénédictins-Anglais prison'.

p. 436 **Fouquier-Tinville:** After a long trial, Fouquier was guillotined on 7 May 1795.

p. 436 **Maximin Isnard:** See above, p. 30.

p. 437 *jeunesse dorée*: Gendron (1979). For reaction in the provinces, see Vovelle (1997), Sutherland (2009), and Cobb (1970), pp. 131–50.

p. 437 **'depopularize' the Revolution:** See Monnier in Vovelle (1997): the phrase was Audouin's. Tonnesson speaks of 'de-sansculottization' (1959), pp. 111–16—but the phenomenon was wider than that. For administrative changes, see SCD, pp. 348–52; Tulard (1989), pp. 357–405; and Tonnesson (1959), pp. 46–51.

p. 437 **post of mayor:** In 1795, mayors were established in the twelve new arrondissements. With the exception of the period of the Commune if 1871, there was no a mayor for the whole of Paris until 1977.

p. 438 **'Nonante-cinq':** See Lyons (1975a), chapter 1, 'Nonante-Cinq': esp. pp. 15–16; Tonnesson (1959); and Cobb (1970), p. 160ff.

p. 438 **'there was no bread-shortage':** Tonnesson (1959), p. 240. By the same token there was also nostalgia for the monarchy in some quarters.

p. 438 **the *journées*:** Tonnesson (1959), pp. 253–323.

p. 438–9 **anti-Parisian repression:** Besides Tonnesson, see esp. Brunel & Goujon (1992); and S&M, 'Introduction', p. 19. These pages are excellent on the direction of popular radicalism after 1794.

p. 439 **Constitution of Year III (1795):** For the debates on and the context of the new constitution, see Conac & Machelon (1999); and Vovelle (1997). For the Directory generally, Lyons (1975a) is an excellent introduction.

p. 439 **Robespierre had aspired to be king:** Vadier later described the claim as a cynical move to win popular support: see Baczko (1989), p. 16 & n. In my view, based on manuscript sources, Baczko appears to exaggerate the importance of the monarchy rumour at this time.

p. 439 **Robespierre's alleged physical appearance:** See Jones (2012), pp. 1–26 & 34–5; and Baczko, '"Comment est fait un tyran . . ."', in id. (2008). Passages from the *Portrait de Robespierre*, including the tiger comparison, were published in a very large number of newspapers within a week of 9 Thermidor. For the *queue de Robespierre* literature, see esp. Brown (2010); Biard in Vovelle (1997); and de Baecque (2001), pp. 161–5. J. J. Dussault's widely circulated *Véritable portrait de Catilina Robespierre* (Year III) took the monstrous comparisons to extreme lengths.

p. 440 **political monstrosity:** For the Black Legend generally, and the emergence of a Counter- ('Golden') Legend, see Belissa & Bosc (2013) and Jones (2012).

p. 440 **a democratic movement emerged:** See Luzzatto (1991) and Belissa & Bosc (2013), pp. 138–56 and passim. A pivotal figure in the reevaluation of Robespierre from the left was Albert Laponneraye, for whom see Hazareesinghe, in Deleplace (2009). He was linked to Robespierre's sister Charlotte: see C. Robespierre (1835); and Labracherie & Pioro (1961: 2).

p. 442 **actively to dissuade others:** See above, p. 61.

p. 442 **Robespierre enough rope:** See above, p. 442.

p. 442 **'We have come so far':** See above, p. 44.

p. 443 **legislator on horseback:** Cf. Bell (2020); Gueniffey (2015, 2018).

p. 443 **responsibility for law and order:** SCD, pp. 353–5; and Simonin (2008), esp. pp. 303–7. For the Vendémiaire rising, see Rudé (1959), pp. 160–77.

p. 445 **'five or six' promised by Couthon:** See above, p. 46.

p. 445 **a man who wanted to kill:** See above, note to p. 40.

p. 447 **His very last known words:** See above, p. 412.

p. 447 **oversight and surveillance:** See Bosc (2019). This appeared too late to shape my argument.

p. 448 **'arrests, newspapers and the Revolutionary Tribunal':** See above, p. 149.

p. 448 **Cincinnatus:** See above, p. 200.

p. 450 *frondeur* **inheritance:** For these weapons of the weak, see esp. above, pp. 228–9.

p. 451 **'the generous and intrepid athletes of liberty':** See the pamphlet, *Triomphe des Parisiens*, (1794). See p. 453.

p. 452 **spy Rousseville:** See above, p. 15.

p. 454 **'women and the weak-minded':** See above, p. 230.

LIST OF CHARACTERS

★ = guillotined for actions on or concerning 9 Thermidor

THE COMMITTEES OF GOVERNMENT

CPS

Barère, Bertrand

Billaud-Varenne, Jacques-Nicolas

Carnot, Lazare

Collot d'Herbois, Jean-Marie

★Couthon, Georges

Lindet, Robert

Prieur de la Côte d'Or, Claude-Antoine

★Robespierre, Maximilien

★Saint-Just, Louis-Antoine

[André-Jean Bon Saint-André and Pierre-Louis Prieur de la Marne were absent from Paris before and during Thermidor.]

CGS

Amar, André

Dubarran, Joseph-Nicolas Barbeau

Bayle, Moyse

David, Jacques-Louis

Jagot, Grégoire

Lacoste, Élie

Lavicomterie, Louis-Charles

Le Bas, Philippe (suicide 9-10 Thermidor)

Louis du Bas-Rhin, Jean-Antoine

Ruhl, Philippe

Vadier, Marc-Guillaume-Alexis

Voulland, Jean-Henri

CONVENTION

Barras Adjuncts

Barras, Paul: Commander of Paris Armed Forces

Auguis, Pierre-Jean-Baptiste

Bollet, Philippe-Albert

Bourdon, Léonard

Bourdon de l'Oise, François-Louis

Camboulas, Simon

Delmas, Jean-François-Bertrand

Plet de Beauprey, Pierre-François

Féraud, Jean-Bertrand

Fréron, Louis-Stanislas

Goupilleau de Fontenay, Jean-François

Legendre, Louis

Merlin de Thionville, Antoine-Christophe

Rovère, Stanislas-Joseph

Other

Baudot, Marc-Antoine: Montagnard, memoir-writer

Bentabole, Pierre-Louis: Montagnard

Boissy-d'Anglas, François-Antoine: Moderate

Bréard, Jean-Jacques: Montagnard

Brival, Jacques: Montagnard, Convention secretary

Cambon, Joseph: Chair, Finance Committee

Carrier, Jean-Baptiste: radical deputy on mission in Vendée

Chales, Pierre-Jacques-Michel: Montagnard

Courtois, Edme-Bonaventure: Dantonist

Danton, Georges: Montagnard, executed with Dantonists, 5 April 1794

Desmoulins, Camille: Montagnard, executed with Danton, 5 April 1794

Dubois-Crancé, Edmond-Louis-Alexis: military reformer, moderate

Dumont, André: radical deputy on mission, Convention secretary

Durand-Maillane, Pierre-Toussaint: Moderate

Duval, Charles: Montagnard, author of an account of Convention, 9 Thermidor

Fouché, Joseph: radical deputy on mission, Robespierre enemy

Goupilleau de Montaigu, Philippe-Charles-Aimé: Montagnard

Isnard, Maximin: Girondin notorious for anti-Paris views; in hiding

Javogues, Claude: Montagnard, radical deputy on mission

Le Bon, Joseph: Montagnard, radical deputy on mission, friend of Robespierre

Lecointre, Laurent: Dantonist, enemy of Robespierre

Palasne-Champeaux, Julien-François: Moderate

Peyssard, Jean-Pascal: co-director (with Le Bas) of the École de Mars

Riffard Saint-Martin, François-Jérôme: Moderate

Robin, Louis-Antoine: Dantonist

Tallien, Jean-Lambert: radical deputy on mission, enemy of Robespierre

Thibaudeau, Antoine: moderate Montagnard

Thuriot, Jacques-Alexis: Montagnard

GOVERNMENT ADMINISTRATION

*Herman, Martial: chair of Commission of Civil Administration, Tribunals and Prisons, Robespierre supporter

Lerebours: chair of Poor Relief Commission, member of Commune Enforcement Committee

*Lanne, Emmanuel-Joseph: adjunct to Herman at Commission of Civil Administration, Tribunals and Prisons, Robespierre supporter

Lejeune, Augustin: secretary to CPS Police Bureau

Payan, Joseph: member Education Commission; brother of Claude-François

Pille, Louis-Antoine: chair of Military Commission, client of Carnot

*Sijas, Prosper: sometime adjunct to Pille at Military Commission, Robespierre supporter

COMMUNE

Management

*Fleuriot-Lescot, Jean-Baptiste-Edmond: Mayor

*Payan, Claude-François: National Agent

*Lubin, Jean-Jacques: deputy to National Agent Payan

*Moenne, Jacques: deputy to National Agent Payan

*Charlemagne, Jean-Philippe-Victor: Chair, Municipal Council

Lafosse, Blaise: clerk

Vincent, Pierre-François: Commune official, military commission

Enforcement Committee

*Arthur, Jean-Jacques (Piques)	*Legrand, Pierre-Jacques (Cité)
*Châtelet, Claude-Louis (Piques)	Lerebours (government bureaucracy)
*Coffinhal, Pierre-André (Fraternité)	*Louvet, Pierre-Alexandre (Homme-Armé)
*Desboisseaux, Charles (Fraternité)	*Payan, Claude-François (National Agent)
*Grenard, René (Piques)	

Municipal Councillors

*Arnauld, Bertrand (Lepeletier)

Aubert, Jean-Baptiste (Poissonnière)

Avril, Jean-Baptiste (République)

*Bernard, Jacques-Claude (Montreuil)

*Delacour, Pierre-Nicolas (Brutus)

Devèze, Jean (République)

*Dhazard, Jean-Baptiste-Mathieu (Gardes-Françaises)

Fénaux, Joseph (Bondy)

Forestier, Jean-Antoine-Gaspard (Gardes-Françaises)

*Frery, Antoine (Guillaume-Tell)

*Gencey, Antoine (Finistère)

*Jemptel, Antoine (Bon-Conseil)

*Lasnier, Jacques (Mutius-Scévole)

*Le Lièvre, Jacques-Mathurin (Lombards)

Martinet, Louis (Tuileries)

*Paris, Pierre-Louis (Panthéon)

Renard, Pierre-Jean (Poissonière)

*Simon, Antoine (Marat)

Soulié, Joseph (Gardes-Françaises)

Tessier, Louis-Pierre (Invalides):

*Warmé, Jacques-Louis-Frédéric (Marat)

SECTIONAL PERSONNEL AND SANS-CULOTTES

Bodson, Joseph (Révolutionnaire)

Burguburu, Pierre (Gardes-Françaises)

Chalandon, Claude (Homme-Armé)

Dehureau, Jean (Arcis)

Le Gentil, 'Robespierre', formerly Charles-François (Montmartre)

Lefebvre, Jean-Louis (Observatoire)

Le Gray, François-Vincent (Muséum)

Loys, Jean-Baptiste (Montagne)

Moessard, Pierre-Louis (Guillaume-Tell)

Saint-Omer, Jean-Claude (Muséum)

Ménétra, Jacques-Louis (Bon-Conseil)

Tugot, Louis (Arcis)

Vernet, Alexandre (Lombards)

POLICE AND SPIES

Benoist, Jean (Halle-au-Blé)

Dossonville, Jean-Baptiste: CGS spy

Dulac, Pierre-Honoré-Gabriel: CGS Spy

*Faro, Jean-Léonard (Poissonnière): Police Administrator

Guérin, Claude: CPS spy

Guyot, Jean-Guillaume (Sans-Culottes): Police Administrator

Héron, François: CPS spy

Jullien, Marc-Antoine: personal spy for Robespierre in provinces

*Le Lièvre, Jacques-Mathurin (Lombards): Police Administrator

Longueville-Clémentiéres, Thomas: CGS spy

Michel, Étienne (Réunion): Police Administrator

Morel: CGS spy

Rousseville, Pierre-Henri: CPS spy

*Tanchon, Ponce (Cité): Police Administrator

*Teurlot, Claude-François (Montreuil): Police Administrator

*Wichterich, Martin (Popincourt): Police Administrator

REVOLUTIONARY TRIBUNAL

*Dumas, René-François: President

*Coffinhal, Pierre-André: Vice-President

*Fouquier-Tinville, Antoine-Quentin: Public Prosecutor

Maire, Antoine-Marie (Arcis): judge

Deliège, Gabriel: judge

Félix, Jean-Baptiste-Henri-Antoine (Sans-Culotte): judge

Sanson, Charles-Henri: public executioner

PARIS PRISONS

Benoist: gaoler, Carmes prison

Cabarrus, Theresa: prisoner, La Force prison

Ferrières-Sauveboeuf, Louis-François: prison informer

Guyard, Jean: Luxembourg concierge

Haly: gaoler, Port-Libre prison

Le Lièvre, François: gaoler, Temple prison

Monaco, princesse de: prisoner

Mercier, Louis-Sébastien: deputy, one of '73', prisoner

Théotiste, Soeur (Sister): prisoner, Luxembourg prison

FORCES OF ORDER (INCLUDING NATIONAL GUARD)

Commanding Officers

*Hanriot, François: NG Commander

Chardin, Charles (Brutus): NG 5th Legion Chief

Debure: gendarme

Degesne: gendarme attached to law courts

Dumesnil: law courts gendarme commander

Fauconnier: NG 1st Legion Chief

Fontaine (Mutius-Scévole): artillery commander

Giot, Christophe-Philippe (Marat): Adjutant, 1st Legion, appointed NG commander, 9 Thermidor

Hémart, Jean: commander, mounted gendarmerie

Julliot: NG 2nd Legion Chief

Lasne, Étienne (Droits-de-l'Homme): NG battalion commander

Levasseur (or Vasseur): Mutius–Scévole gunner

Martin: Gendarmerie chief

Mathis: NG 3rd Legion Chief

Mulot: NG 5th Legion Chief

Olivier: NG 6th Legion Chief

Pellerin (Popincourt): gunner

Pionnier, Cosme (Gravilliers): artillery Instructor

Richard, Jean (Réunion): battalion commander

Typhaine, Vincent (Marat): battalion second-in-command

Ulrich, Joseph-Guillaume (Gravilliers): Hanriot ADC

Van Heck, Jean-Baptiste (Cité): battalion commander

Voyenne, Claude-François (Muséum): company commander

ROBESPIERRE CIRCLE

*Boulanger, Servais-Beaudouin: Hanriot ADC

*Châtelet, Charles-Louis (Piques): Revolutionary Tribunal juror; Robespierre bodyguard

*Deschamps, Hanriot ADC, Robespierre bodyguard

Didier, Jean-Baptiste (République): Revolutionary Tribunal juror; Robespierre bodyguard

Dufresse, Simon: ADC to Hanriot

Duplay, Maurice: Robespierre's landlord, Jacobin, Revolutionary Tribunal member

Duplay, Eléonore: daughter of Maurice, affective relations with Robespierre

Duplay, Elisabeth: daughter of Maurice, wife of Philippe Le Bas

Duplay, Jacques-Maurice: young son of Maurice

Duplay, Sophie: daughter of Maurice, wife of Antoine Auzat

Duplay, Simon ('Jambe-de-Bois'): disabled war veteran, nephew of Maurice Duplay, close friend to Robespierre

*Garnier-Delaunay, François-Pierre (Piques): Robespierre bodyguard

Girard, Pierre-François (Piques): Robespierre bodyguard

*Lavalette, Louis-Jean-Baptiste ADC to Hanriot, Robespierre bodyguard

Le Bas, Henriette: sister to Philippe Le Bas

*Nicolas, Charles-Léopold (Piques): printer and Robespierre bodyguard

*Renaudin, Léopold (Gardes-Françaises: Revolutionary Tribunal juror, Robespierre bodyguard

Souberbielle, Joseph: Robespierre's physician

OTHER

Bertèche, Louis-Florentin: commander, École de Mars

Legracieux, Stanislas: provincial Jacobin and Robespierre supporter

Guittard de Floriban, Célestin: Parisian rentier and diarist

Langlois, Hyacinthe: student, École de Mars

Courvol: Convention usher

Rose (or Roze), Jacques-Augustin: Convention usher

Théot, Catherine: visionary and prophetess, alleged supporter of Robespierre

NOTE ON SOURCES

For fuller details of printed works cited, see the Bibliography.

I. PRIMARY SOURCES
Robespierre
Robespierre's works have been collected in the scholarly edition, *Oeuvres complètes*, multiple editors, 11 vols. (Paris, 1910–2007). After his death the Convention established a commission chaired by deputy Edme-Bonaventure Courtois to examine his papers. It is generally accepted that this was done in an extremely partial and politically motivated way. However, Courtois's *Rapport fait au nom de la Commission chargée de l'examen des papiers trouvés chez Robespierre et ses complices* (Paris, III) remains invaluable. A fuller set of papers was published under the Restoration as *Papiers inédits trouvés chez Robespierre, Saint-Just, Payan, etc, et supprimés ou omis par Courtois*, 3 vols. (Paris, 1828). What these collections do not contain, however, are CPS papers penned by Robespierre located in CPS archives. Alphonse Aulard, *Recueil des actes du Comité de salut public*, 26 vols. (Paris, 1889–1923: vol. 15 covers 9 Thermidor) provides guidance on Robespierre's authorship and signature on CPS decrees, though not other memoranda; and it should be noted that Aulard's ascriptions are not 100 per cent accurate, nor is the list of decrees fully comprehensive. Finally, the Archives nationales in 2011 purchased the papers of Robespierre that passed into the hands of the Duplay and Le Bas families. These have been classified as 683AP/1 (Papiers Robespierre). See too the relevant documents in AP 35AP/1 (Papiers Le Bas). See Geffroy (2013) for a description.

Government and Politics
The *Archives parlementaires de 1787 à 1860*, multiple editors and 102 volumes thus far (Paris, 1867-present, 2012) are a crucial aid to research. Volumes of the series covering the years 1789–93 are available online at the Stanford French Revolution Digital Archive: https://sulphilologic.stanford.edu. Volume 93 of the series covers 2 Messidor to 12 Thermidor and volume 94 from 13 to 25 Thermidor. Both were edited by Françoise Brunel, who also commends the account of the Thermidor debates of the account by Charles Duval, *Projet de procès-verbal des séances des 9, 10 et 11 thermidor* (Paris, 1795). The newspaper of record, the *Moniteur* contains minutes of meetings of the Convention's sessions. In is available digitally through the BNF's Gallica, but one may also consult the *Réimpression de l'ancien Moniteur (1789–99)*, 32 vols. (1858–70: vol. 21 covers the period of the *journée*). Other newspapers are worth consulting for variants in reportage. The *Moniteur* also contains minutes and/or accounts of meetings in the Paris Commune and the Jacobin Club. The Commune reports are especially valuable as a huge amount of the municipal archive was destroyed in the 1871 Commune fires. For the Jacobin Club, see too Alphonse Aulard, *La Société des Jacobins: Recueil de documents pour l'histoire du Club des Jacobins de Paris*, 6 vols. (Paris 1889–97). Volume 6 covers Thermidor. The debates in the Convention in 1795 over responsibility for the Terror are not yet covered in the *Archives parlementaires*. Newspapers are useful for these, while many of the

major speeches of the protagonists were published separately as pamphlets. On the debates attacking former CPS and CGS members, see especially Laurent LeCointre, *Les crimes de sept membres des anciens comités de salut public et de Sûreté générale* (Paris, Year III) and Saladin, *Rapport au nom de la Commission des Vingt-Un* (Paris, Year III).

Memoirs and Other Primary Printed Materials

Alfred Fierro, *Bibliographie des mémoires sur la Révolution écrits ou traduits en français* (Paris, 1988) provides a very full list of memoirs from the Revolutionary period and is strong on deputies and on individuals held in Parisian prisons. For the actual day in the Convention, Thibaudeau's memoirs (1827, 2007) are especially useful. P. J. B. Buchez and P. C. Roux, *Histoire parlementaire de la Révolution française*, 40 vols. (Paris, 1834–8) is a potpourri of reprinted materials, but complemented by some oral and eye-witness testimony. Most relevant are volumes 33 (up to 9 Thermidor), 34 (mainly 9 Thermidor), and 35 (the aftermath and some papers of Le Bas and Saint-Just).

Sectional Reports on 8–10 Thermidor

Reports started coming into the CPS from sectional authorities directly after the events of 9–10 Thermidor. The demand from Barras, the acting commander of Parisian armed forces on 14 Thermidor (see above p. 7) was effective in generating well over 150 reports, mostly within the next few days. Most of these were seen by the Courtois Commission and also by the Saladin Committee of the Vingt-et-Un in Year III. Some reports have gone missing, but most are in two locations: AFII 47 and F7 4432. The standard range for each section contains reports from the Civil Committee, the Revolutionary Committee, and the Commander and in some cases the second-in-command from the sectional NG battalion of each section. There is a good deal of other relevant material too. All of the 48 sections except Chalier are represented in these two sources. Most sectional authorities kept minutes of meetings, but the destruction of Parisian archives in the Commune fires of 1871 saw most disappear. Some (particularly relating to Revolutionary Committees) remain with F7 or F7★ call-marks. This includes two notable subseries of papers, F7★ 2471–2522 and BNF NAF, 2638–2720. Lengthy extracts from these latter reports are given in Walter (1989), pp. 171–287. These plus some other outliers are included in the list of locations for sectional papers listed here:

1 Tuileries: F7 4332/3; AFII 47/364; F7★ 2472

2 Champs-Elysées: F7 4332/3; AFII 47/365; F7 4777; F7★ 2474

3 République: AFII 47/365

4 Montagne: F7 4332/3; AFII 47/367; BNF NAF 2675

5 Piques: AFII 47/364; F7 4778; F7 4778; F7★ 2475; W 501

6 Lepeletier: AFII 47/366; F7★ 2479

7 Mont-Blanc: F7 4332/3; AFII 47/367; BNF NAF 2651

8 Muséum: F7 4332/8; AFII 47/367

9 Gardes-Françaises: AFII 47/367

10 Halle-au-Blé: AFII 47/364; F7★ 2484

11 Contrat-Social: AFII 47/365; W 79

12 Guillaume-Tell: F7 4332/4; AFII 47/364

13 Brutus: F7 4432/4; AFII 47/364

14 Bonne-Nouvelle: AFII 47/364

15 Amis-de-la-Patrie: AFII 47/367; F7* 2490

16 Bon-Conseil: AFII 47/365

17 Marchés: F7 4432/5; AFII 47/366

18 Lombards: F7 4432/6; AFII 47/364; F7* 2485

19 Arcis: AFII 47/364; AFII 47/366

20 Faubourg-Montmartre: AFII 47/364; F7* 2482–3

21 Poissonnière: F7 4432/4; AFII 47/367

22 Bondy: F7 4432/5; AFII 47/364; AFII 47/367

23 Temple: F7 4432/6; AFII 47/367; F7* 2487

24 Popincourt: AFII 47/366; W 79; APP AA266

25 Montreuil: AFII 47/367

26 Quinze-Vingts: AFII 47/364

27 Gravilliers: F7 4432/6; AFII 47/366; F7* 2486

28 Faubourg-du-Nord: F7 4432/5; AFII 47/365: F7 4637 d. Chaguignée

29 Réunion: F7 4432/4; AFII 47/367; F7* 2494

30 Homme-Armé: AFII 47/366; F7* 2496l; W 79

31 Droits-de-l'Homme: AFII 47/367; F7* 2497; W 79

32 Maison-Commune: AFII 47/365

33 Indivisibilité: F7 4432/7; AFII 47/365; W 79

34 Arsenal: AFII 47/367

35 Fraternité: F7 4432/7; AFII 47/365

36 Cité: F7 4432/7; AFII 47/367

37 Révolutionnaire: F7 4432/9; AFII 47/365; BNF NAF 2712

38 Invalides: F7 4432/8; AFII 47/366; F7* 2510

39 Fontaine-de-Grenelle: AFII 47/365

40 Unité: AFII 47/364; F7* 2507; F7 4779; APP AA266

41 Marat: AFII 47/365; F7* 2512

42 Bonnet-Rouge: F7 4432/8; AFII 47/365

43 Mutius-Scévole: F7 4432/9; AFII 47/366

44 Chalier: F7* 2511

45 Panthéon-Français: F7 4432/10; AFII 47/366; F7* 2521; W 79

46 Observatoire: AFII 47/366; F7* 2516

47 Sans-Culottes: AFII 47/366

48 Finistère: F7 4432/10; AFII 47/365; F7* 2519

Individual Police Files

Within the F7 'Police générale' series at the Archives nationales is the so-called 'alphabetical series' covering call-marks F7 4577 to 4775/93. These 350 boxes, containing tens of thousands of individual files, hold great riches, many of them untapped. To locate dossiers relating to participants in 9 Thermidor, Albert Soboul and Raymonde Monnier's invaluably erudite *Répertoire du personnel sectionnaire parisien en l'an II* (Paris, 1985: in essence a biographical dictionary of sans-culottes) is a superb finding aid.

Main other Archives

Within the AN, the following were particularly useful: T (papers of individuals executed by the state) and W (Revolutionary Tribunal). Important boxes dealing with the repressive follow-up to the *journée* are to be found in W 79 and W 80. The Archives de Paris (ADP) are good for births, marriages, and deaths, Justice of the Peace archives, and other papers. The Archives de la Préfecture de la Police (APP) contain police commissary archives and some prison records. The Bibliothèque Nationale de France (BNF) has some important manuscripts, as does the Bibliothèque historique de la ville de Paris (BHVP).

II. SECONDARY SOURCES

A. Robespierre

Biographies of Robespierre are innumerable. Recent works of high quality include (in French) Leuwers (2014), Martin (2016), and Gauchet (2018). Belissa and Bosc (2013) provide a kind of 'Robespierre for and against'. Hamel (1865) is still useful for being very well-informed; its hagiographical approach to its subject makes it unreliable in many areas. In English, Jordan (1985), Scurr (2006), and McPhee (2012) stand out, but of older biographies, J.M. Thompson (several editions) and Hampson (1974) are still well worth consulting.

B. 9 Thermidor

The best and best-informed study is the brief volume by Brunel (1989). Both Walter (1974) and Bienvenu (1968) are lacking in analysis but strong for the inclusion of much primary material. For the Commune, Paul Saint-Claire Deville, *La Commune de l'an II. Vie et mort d'une assemblée révolutionnaire* (Paris, 1946), is a superbly detailed account, which draws on many of the sectional and police archives consulted for this volume, though its focus is on the Commune rather than the sections or the Convention. The sections are well covered, at least down to midnight 9–10 Thermidor in Albert Soboul's great thesis (1958). Burstin (2005b) covers in detail the sections of the Faubourg Saint-Marcel for the night. The francophone crowd-sourced website '9-Thermidor' (http://9-thermidor.com) is still in progress. It contains very useful summaries of many aspects of the day.

C. Revolutionary Government and Terror

The literature is too huge to recapitulate. The recent Biard and Linton (2020) is a useful overview, and introduces most of the key debates. For these see too Baker (1994), Edelstein (2009), Linton (2013), Martin (2018), Schechter (2018), Steinberg (2019), Tackett (2015), and Wahnich (2003).

BIBLIOGRAPHY AND PRINTED SOURCES

NEWSPAPERS

Abréviateur universel, ou Journal sommaire des opinions, productions et nouvelles publiques
Annales de la République française
Bulletin républicain, ou Papier-nouvelles de tous les pays et de tous les jours
Conservateur décadaire
Correspondance politique de Paris et des départements
Correspondance politique, ou Tableau de l'Europe
Courrier de l'égalité
Courrier républicain
Feuille du salut public (from Germinal, *Feuille de la République*)
Journal de Perlet
Journal historique et politique
Messager du soir
Moniteur, ou Gazette nationale
Nouvelles politiques, nationales et étrangères
Le Patriote républicain, ou Journal des sans-culottes: bulletin du soir
Le Républicain, ou Journal des Hommes libres de tous les pays
Soirée du camp
Vieux Cordelier

PRIMARY

Note: Works published in France after late 1793 usually bore the date of publication according to the French Revolutionary Calendar. These are wherever possible converted into the regular calendar.

Almanach national. 1793, Year II.
Aperçus sur la conduite en politique de Rousseville, inspecteur général de la police. No place, no date.
Audouin, X. (1795): *L'intérieur des maisons d'arrêt.* Paris, Pougin.
Aulard, F.-A. (1889): *La Société des Jacobins: recueil de documents pour l'histoire du club des Jacobins de Paris.* Paris, Jouaust.
Aulard, F.-A. (1889–1964): *Recueil des actes du Comité de salut public: avec la correspondance officielle des représentants en mission et le registre du Conseil exécutif provisoire.* Paris, Imprimerie.
Auzat, A. (1795): *Pétition à la Convention nationale.* Paris, Imprimerie Delafolie.
Barère, B. (1795): *Observations de Barère, sur le rapport fait le 12 ventôse, par Saladin à la Convention nationale* (25 Ventôse, III). Paris, Imprimerie républicaine.
Barère, B. (1842): *Mémoires*, ed. H. Carnot & D. d'Angers 4 vols. Paris, J. Labitte.
Barras, P. (1895–6): *Mémoires de Barras, membre du Directoire.* 4 vols. Paris, Hachette.

Baudot, M.-A. (1893): *Notes historiques sur la Convention nationale, le Directoire, l'Empire et l'exil des votants*. Paris, Imprimerie D. Jouaust.

Berryer, P.-N. (1839): *Souvenirs de M. Berryer, doyen des avocats de Paris de 1774 à 1838*. 2 vols. Paris, Ambroise Dupont.

Beugnot, J.-C. (1866): *Mémoires du Comte Beugnot l'ancien ministre*. Paris, E. Dentu.

Billaud-Varenne, J. N. (1794): *Réponse de J. N. Billaud, représentant du peuple, à Laurent Lecointre, représentant du peuple*. Paris, Imprimerie de R. Vatar.

Billaud-Varenne, J. N. (1795a): *Billaud-Varenne jugé par lui-même ou Réponse à la Réponse de Billaud-Varenne*. Paris, Hachete.

Billaud-Varenne, J. N. (1795b): *Réponse de J. N. Billaud, représentant du peuple, aux inculpations qui lui sont personnelles* (Ventôse III). Paris, Imprimerie nationale.

Billaud-Varenne, J. N. (1893): *Curiosités révolutionnaires. Mémoires inédits et correspondance de Billaud-Varenne et Collot d'Herbois*. Paris, Librairie de la Nouvelle Revue.

Billaud-Varenne, J. N. (1992): *Principes régénérateurs du système social*, ed. F. Brunel. Paris, Publications de la Sorbonne.

Billecocq, J. B. (1981): *En prison sous la Terreur. Souvenirs de J. B. Billecocq (1765–1829) suivis de quatre autres textes inédits*, ed. N. Felkay & H. Favier. Paris, Société des Études Robespierristes.

Bitaubé, P.-J. (1826): *Joseph, précédé d'une notice historique sur la vie et les oeuvres de l'auteur et d'un relation de sa captivité au Luxembourg par Mme Bitaubé*. Paris, Deschamps.

Blanqui, L. A. (1794): *L'Agonie de dix mois ou les souffrances des 73 députés pendant leur incarcération*. Paris, F. Porte.

Bohm, S. de (2001): *Prisonnière sous la Terreur. Mémoires d'une captive en 1793*, ed. J.-C. Martin. Paris, Cosmopole.

Carnot, H. (1907): *Mémoires de Lazare Carnot (1753–1823). Nouvelle édition des mémoires de Carnot par son fils*. 2 vols. Paris, Hachette.

Carnot, L. (1795): *Opinion de Carnot, représentant du peuple, sur l'accusation contre Billaud-Varenne, Collot d'Herbois, Barère et Vadier par la Commission des vingt et un*. Paris, Imprimerie nationale.

Caron, P. ed. (1914): *Paris sous la Terreur. Rapports des agents secrets du ministre de l'Intérieur, publiés pour la Société d'histoire contemporaine*. 7 vols. Paris, Picard.

Chambon (1793): *Rapport sur l'état actuel de Paris*. Paris. Convention nationale.

Chamfort, S.-R.-N. D. (1802): *Chamfortiana, ou recueil choisi d'anecdotes piquantes et de traits d'esprit de Chamfort . . . Notice sur sa vie et ses ouvrages*. Paris, Delance et Lesueur.

Coittant, P. E. (1794): *Almanach des prisons, ou anecdotes sur le régime intérieur de la Conciergerie, du Luxembourg, etc*. Paris, Michel.

Coittant, P. E. (1795a): *Tableau des prisons de Paris*. Paris, Michel.

Coittant, P. E. (1795b): *Second Tableau des prisons sous le règne de Robespierre*. Paris, Michel.

Coittant, P. E. (1797): *Troisième Tableau des prisons sous le règne de Robespierre*. Paris, Michel.

Collot d'Herbois, J. M. (1795): *Défense de J. M. Collot*. Paris, Imprimerie nationale.

Collot d'Herbois, J. M. (1795): *Discours fait à la Convention nationale, par J.-M. Collot, . . . prononcé le 4 germinal an III . . . à l'ouverture des débats sur le rapport de la commission des vingt-un dans l'affaire des représentants Billaud, Collot, Barère et Vadier*. Paris, Imprimerie nationale.

Collot d'Herbois, J. M. (1795): *Collot représentant du peuple, à ses collègues: réflexions rapides sur l'imprimé publié par Lecointre contre sept membres des anciens Comités de salut public et de sûreté générale*. Paris, Imprimerie de Guerin.

Courtois, E. B. (1795): *Rapport fait au nom de la commission chargée de l'examen des papiers trouvés chez Robespierre et ses complices . . . dans la séance du 16 Nivôse, an IIIe de la République Française, etc.* Paris, L'Imprimerie nationale des lois.

Courtois, E. B. (1795): *Rapport sur les événements du 9 thermidor, précédé d'une préface en réponse aux détracteurs de cette mémorable journée.* Paris, Imprimerie nationale.

[Courtois, E. B.] (1887): 'Notes et souvenirs de Courtois de l'Aube', *La Révolution française*, pp. 806–20, 922–42, 998–1020.

David, J.-L. (1794): *Rapport sur la fête héroïque pour les honneurs du Panthéon à décerner aux jeunes Bara & Viala.* Paris, Imprimerie nationale.

Dulaure, J. A. (1825–6): *Esquisses historiques des principaux événemens de la Révolution française, depuis la convocation des États-Généraux jusqu'au rétablissement de la maison de Bourbon.* 6 vols. Paris, Delongchamps.

Dumaniant & Le Brun, P. (1794): *La Nuit du 9 au 10 thermidor, ou La chute du tyran, comédie en deux actes et en vers.* Théâtre de la Cité, 4 septembre.

Durand-Maillane, P.-T. (1825): *Histoire de la Convention nationale.* Paris, Baudouin Frères.

[Duras, L. H. C. P.] (1889): *Journal des prisons de mon père, de ma mère et des miennes, par la duchesse de Duras, née Noailles.* Paris, E. Plon, Nourrit et cie.

Dussault, J. J. (1794): *Véritable portrait de Catilina Robespierre, tiré d'après nature.* Paris, chez le citoyen Hannaud.

Duval, C. (1794): *Projet de procès-verbal des séances des 9, 10 et 11 thermidor.* Imprimerie nationale.

Duval, G.-L.-J. (1844): *Souvenirs thermidoriens.* Paris, Magen.

Faits recueillis aux derniers instants de Robespierre et de sa faction, du 9 au 10 thermidor (1794). Paris, Impr. de Paix.

[Faure, P.-J.-D.-G.] (1795): *P. J. D. G. Faure, député de la Seine-Inférieure, à la Convention nationale sur le procès des quatre députés prévenus par acte d'accusation rédigé par la commission des vingt-un.* Paris, Imprimerie nationale.

Foignet, E.-J.-J. (no date): *Encore une victime, ou mémoires d'un prisonnier de la maison d'arrêt dite des Anglaises Rue de l'Ourcine.* Paris, Maret.

Fouché, J. (1946): *Les mémoires de Fouché*, ed. L. Madelin. Paris, Flammarion.

Gouly, B. (1794): *À ses collègues.* Paris, Imprimerie du Guffroy.

Guillaume, J. (1891–1907): *Procès-verbaux du Comité d'instruction publique de la Convention Nationale.* 8 vols. Paris, Imprimerie nationale.

[Guittard de Floriban, N. C.] (1974): *Journal de Célestin Guittard de Floriban, bourgeois de Paris sous la Révolution*, ed. R. Aubert. Paris, Éditions France-Empire.

Héron, L.-J.-S. (no date, 1794?): *Mémoire du citoyen Héron, au peuple français et à ses représentants* (no place, no publisher).

Jullian, P. L. P. D. (1815): *Souvenirs de ma vie depuis 1774 jusqu'en 1814.* Paris, Boissange et Masson.

[Jullien, R.] (2016): *'Les affaires d'état sont mes affaires de coeur': Lettres de Rosalie Jullien, une femme dans la Révolution, 1775–1810*, ed. A. Duprat. Paris, Belin.

La Chabeaussière (1795): *Les huit mois d'un détenu aux Madelonnettes.* Paris, Imprimerie de Pain.

Lacroix de Lavalette, M.-J. D. (1992): *Une Parisienne sous la Terreur: Marie-Angélique Bergeron (1756–1804) d'après les archives.* Paris, Téqui.

Laffitte, J. (1932): *Mémoires de Laffitte: 1767–1844*, ed. P. Duchon. Paris, Firmin-Didot.

Langlois, E.-H. (1836): *Souvenirs de l'École de Mars.* Rouen, F. Baudry.

Lecointre, L. (1794): *Robespierre peint par lui-même, et condamné par ses propres principes, ou, Dénonciation des crimes de Maximilien-Marie-Isidore Robespierre.* Paris, Imprimerie de Rougyff.

Lecointre, L. (1795): *Les crimes de sept membres des anciens comités de salut public et de Sûreté générale, ou dénonciation formelle à la Convention nationale, contre Billaud-Varenne, Barère, Collot-d'Herbois, Vadier, Vouland, Amar et David*. Paris, Maret.

Legouvé, G.-M. (1794): *Épicharis et Neron, ou Conspiration pour la Liberté: Tragédie en cinq actes et en vers*. Paris, Maradan.

Levasseur, R. (1829–31): *Mémoires de R. Levasseur*. 4 vols. Paris, Rapilly.

Lombard de Langres, V. (1819): *Les Souvenirs, ou Recueil de faits particuliers et d'anecdotes secrètes, pour servir à l'histoire de la Révolution*. Paris, Gide fils.

Louvet de Couvray, J. B. (1792): *Accusation contre Maximilien Robespierre*. Paris, Imprimerie nationale.

Maussion, A. (1975): *Rescapés de Thermidor*. Paris, Nouvelles Éditions latines.

Ménétra, J. L. (1982): *Journal de ma vie*, ed. D. Roche. Paris, Montalba.

Mercier, L.-S. (1994): *Le nouveau Paris*, ed. J.-C. Bonnet. Paris, Mercure de France.

Mercier, L.-S. (1994): *Le Tableau de Paris*. 2 vols., ed. J.-C. Bonnet. Paris, Mercure de France.

Merda, C. A. (as J. J. B.) (1825): *Précis historique des événements qui se sont passés dans la soirée du neuf thermidor, adressé au Ministre de la guerre, le 30 fructidor an X*. Paris, Baudouin frères.

Merlin de Thionville, A.-C. (1794): *Capet et Robespierre*. Paris, Rue de la Loi.

Merlin de Thionville, A.-C. (1794): *Portrait de Robespierre*. Paris, Rue de la Loi.

Michel, É. (1794): *Pétition à la Convention nationale*. Paris, Imprimerie de Gueffier.

Noms et domiciles des individus convaincus ou prévenus d'avoir pris part à la conjuration de Robespierre. (1794): Paris, Imprimerie nationale.

Nougaret, P. J. B. (1797): *Histoire des prisons de Paris et des départements*. 4 vols. Paris, Chez l'Éditeur.

Pille, L.-A. (1794): *Réponse de L.-A. Pille, commissaire de l'organisation et du mouvement des armées de terre*. Paris.

Prieur, C. A. (1795): *Discours de C.A. Prieur de la Côte d'Or*. Paris, Imprimerie nationale.

Proussainville (1815): *Histoire secrète du Tribunal Révolutionnaire*. 2 vols. Paris, Lerouge.

Réponse des membres de l'ancien Comité de salut public dénoncés aux pièces communiquées par la Commission des Vingt et un. Paris, Imprimerie nationale.

Riffard de Saint-Martin, F.-J. (2013): *Journal de François-Jérôme Riffard Saint-Martin, 1744–1814*, ed. J. O. Boudon. Paris, Éditions SPM.

Riouffe, H. (1795): *Mémoires d'un détenu pour servir à l'histoire de la tyrannie de Robespierre*. Paris, De Boffe.

Robespierre, C. (1835): *Mémoires de Charlotte Robespierre sur ses deux frères; précédés d'une introduction par Laponneraye, et suivis de pièces justificatives*. Paris, Dépôt central.

Robespierre, M. (1910–67): *Œuvres complètes*. Paris: Société des Études Robespierristes.

Roland, M. J. (1905): *Mémoires de Madame Roland*, ed. C. Perroud. Paris, Plon.

Rouy l'ainé (no date): *Assassinats commis sur 81 prisonniers de la prison dite St Lazare, le 7, 8 et 9 thermidor par le Tribunal Révolutionnaire*. Paris, Imprimerie de Guffroy.

Ruault, N. (1976): *Gazette d'un parisien sous la revolution: lettres à son frère 1783–1796*. Paris, Librairie Academique Perrin.

Saint-Just, L. A. (1908): *Œuvres complètes de Saint-Just*. 2 vols. ed. C. Vellay. Paris, Eugène Fasquelle.

Saladin, J. B. M. (1795): *Rapport de la commission des vingt-un*. Paris, Rondonneau.

[Sanson, C.-H.] (2007): *La Révolution française vue par son bourreau: Journal de Charles-Henri Sanson*, ed. M. Le Bailly. Paris, Cherche-Midi.

Serieys, A. (1801): *La mort de Robespierre: tragédie en trois actes et en vers.* Paris, Monroy.

Tallien, J. L. (1795): *Collot mitraillé par Tallien. Eclaircissemens véridiques de Tallien, représentant du peuple envoyé en mission à Bordeaux en réponse aux Eclaircissemens nécessaires de Collot, ancien membre du Comité de salut public.* Paris.

Taschereau, P. A. (1795): *A Maximilien Robespierre aux enfers.* Paris, les marchands de nouveautés.

[Théotiste, Soeur, or Valombray, C. de S.-V.] (1875): *Les mémoires d'une soeur de charité,* ed. E. Gagne. Paris, Didier et cie.

Thibaudeau, A.-C. (1827): *Mémoires sur la Convention et le Directoire.* 2 vols. 2nd edn. Paris, Ponthieu.

Thibaudeau, A.-C. (2007): *Mémoires sur la Convention et le Directoire,* ed. F. Pascal. Paris, SPM.

Welvert, E. (1891): *La saisie des papiers du conventionnel Courtois (1816): testament de Marie-Antoinette, papiers de Robespierre, lettres du comte de Provence.* Paris, Bourloton.

SECONDARY

Abad, R. (2002): *Le grand marché. L'approvisionnement alimentaire de Paris sous l'Ancien Régime.* Paris, Fayard.

Aberdam, S. (2013): 'L'heure des repas de rue (juillet 1794)', in P. Bourdin, ed., *Les nuits de la Révolution française.* Clermont-Ferrand, Presses Universitaires Blaise Pascal, pp. 237–50.

Adams, C. (2014): '"Venus of the Capitol": Madame Tallien and the Politics of Beauty under the Directory', *FHS,* 37, pp. 599–629.

Alpaugh, M. (2014): *Non-Violence and the French Revolution: Political Demonstrations in Paris, 1787–1795.* Cambridge, Cambridge University Press.

Alder, K. (1997): *Engineering the Revolution: Arms and Enlightenment in France, 1763–1815.* Chicago, IL, University of Chicago Press.

Andress, D. (2000): *Massacre at the Champ de Mars: Popular Dissent and Political Culture in the French Revolution.* Woodbridge, The Boydell Press.

Andress, D. (2005): *The Terror: The Merciless War for Freedom in Revolutionary France.* New York, Farrar, Straus, & Giroux.

Andress, D. (2011): 'Living the Revolutionary Melodrama: Robespierre's Sensibility and the Construction of Political Commitment in the French Revolution', *Représentations,* 114, pp. 103–28.

Andress, D. ed. (2013): *Experiencing the French Revolution.* Oxford, Voltaire Foundation.

Andrews, R. M. (1969): 'Political Elites and Social Conflicts in the Sections of Revolutionary Paris, 1792-an III', DPhil dissertation, Oxford.

Andrews, R. M. (1971): 'The Justices of the Peace of Revolutionary Paris, September 1792–November 1794 (Frimaire Year III)', *Past and Present,* 52, pp. 56–105.

Arasse, D. (1989): *The Guillotine and the Terror.* London, Allen Lane.

Backouche, I. (2000): *La trace du fleuve: La Seine et Paris (1750–1850).* Paris, ÉEHESS.

Baczko, B. (1989): *Ending the Terror: The French Revolution after Robespierre,* tr. M. Petheram Cambridge, Cambridge University Press.

Baczko, B. (2008): *Politiques de la Révolution française.* Paris, Gallimard.

Baecque, A. de (1994): 'The Trajectory of a Wound: From Corruption to Regeneration. The Brave Locksmith Geffroy, Herald of the Great Terror', in K. M. Baker, ed., *The Terror.* Oxford, Pergamon, pp. 157–76.

Baker, K. M. ed. (1994): *The Terror*, Oxford, Pergamon.

Beauchesne, A. H. D. B. de (1852): *Louis XVII: sa vie, son agonie, sa mort*. 2 vols. Paris, Plon.

Béclard, L. (1903): *Sébastien Mercier: sa vie, son oeuvre, son temps, d'après des documents inedits*. Paris, Champion.

Bégis, A. (1896): *Curiosités révolutionnaires. Saint-Just et les bureaux de la police générale au Comité de salut public en 1794*. Paris, Amis des livres.

Belissa, M. & Bosc, Y. (2013): *Robespierre: La fabrication d'un mythe*. Paris, Ellipses.

Bell, D. A. (2020): *Men on Horseback: Charisma and Power in the Age of Revolutions*. New York, Farrar, Straus, & Giroux.

Bell, D. A. & Mintzker, Y. eds. (2018): *Rethinking the Age of Revolutions: France and the Birth of the Modern World*. New York, Oxford University Press.

Benabou, E.-M. (1987): *La Prostitution et la police des moeurs au XVIIIe siècle*. Paris, Librairie Académique Perrin.

Bernet, J. (2008): 'Terreur et religion en l'an II: l'affaire des Carmélites de Compiégne', in M. Biard, ed., *Les politiques de la Terreur, 1793–1794*. Rennes, Presses universitaires de Rennes, Société des études robespierristes.

Bertaud, J.-P. (1979): *La Révolution armée: les soldats-citoyens et la Révolution française*. Paris, Éditions Robert Laffont.

Bertaud, J.-P. (1990): 'Carnot et le 9 thermidor', in J. P. Charmay, ed., *Lazare Carnot ou le savant-citoyen*. Paris, Presses de l'Université de Paris-Sorbonne, pp. 74–82.

Bertaud, J.-P. (1994): 'An Open File: The Press under the Terror', in K. M. Baker, ed., *The French Revolution and the Creation of Modern Political Culture, Vol. IV*. Oxford, Pergamon, pp. 297–308.

Bertaud, J.-P. (2000): *La presse et le pouvoir de Louis XIII à Napoléon Ier*. Paris, Le Grand Livre du Mois.

Berthiaud, E. (2014): 'Les femmes enceintes devant la justice révolutionnaire à Paris (1793–1810): l'état des enjeux et des représentations de la grossesse', in L. Faggion & C. Regina, *La culture judiciaire: Discours, représentations et usages de la justice du Moyen Age à nos jours*. Dijon, Éditions universitaires de Dijon, pp. 1–16.

Bianchi, S. & Dupuy, R. eds. (2006): *La Garde nationale entre nation et peuple en armes. Mythes et réalités, 1789–1871*. Rennes, Presses Universitaires de Rennes.

Biard, M. (1995): *Collot d'Herbois: Légendes noires et Révolution*. Lyon, Presses Universitaires de Lyon.

Biard, M. (1997): 'Après la tête, la queue! La rhétorique anti-jacobine en fructidor an II— vendémiaire an III', in M. Vovelle, ed., *Le tournant de l'an III: Réaction et Terreur blanche dans la France révolutionnaire*. Paris, Éditions du CTHS.

Biard, M. (2002): *Missionnaires de la République. Les représentants du peuple en mission (1793–1795)*. Paris, Éditions du CTHS.

Biard, M. ed. (2008): *Les politiques de la Terreur, 1793–1794*. Rennes, Presses universitaires de Rennes, Société des études robespierristes.

Biard, M. (2013): *1793, le siège de Lyon entre mythes et réalités*. Clermont-Ferrand, Lemme.

Biard, M. (2015): *La liberté ou la mort. Mourir en député, 1792–1795*. Paris, Tallandier.

Biard, M. & Ducange, J.-N. (2019): *L'Exception politique en révolution: pensées et pratiques (1789–1917)*. Mont-Saint-Aignan: Presses universitaires de Rouen et du Havre.

Biard, M. & Leuwers, H. eds. (2014): *Visages de la Terreur: l'exception politique de l'an II*. Paris, Armand Colin.

Biard, M. & Linton, M. (2020): *Terreur! La Révolution française face à ses demons*. Paris, Armand Colin.

Bienvenu, R. (1968): *The Ninth of Thermidor: The Fall of Robespierre*. New York, Oxford University Press.

Bijaoui, R. (1996): *Prisonniers et prisons de la Terreur*. Paris, Imago.

Billard, M. (1911): *Les Femmes enceintes devant le Tribunal Révolutionnaire*. Paris, Perrin.

Birembault, A. (1959): 'Hesmart et son rôle au 9 thermidor', *AHRF*, 31, pp. 306–27.

Blanc, L. (1861): *Histoire de la Révolution française, t. xi*. Paris, Pagnerre, Furne et Cie.

Blanc, O. (1984): *La dernière letter. Prisons et condamnés de la Révolution*. Paris, Robert Laffont.

Blanc, O. (1989): *Les Hommes de Londres: histoire secrète de la Terreur*. Paris, A. Michel.

Blanc, O. (1992): *La Corruption sous la Terreur: 1792–1794*. Paris, R. Laffont.

Blanc, O. (1995): *Les Espions de la Révolution et de l'Empire*. Paris, Perrin.

Bluche, F. (1986): *Septembre 1792: logiques d'un massacre*. Paris, Éditions Robert Laffont.

Bosc, Y. (2019): *Le Peuple souverain et la démocratie: Politique de Robespierre*. Paris, Editions critiques.

Bouchard, G. (1946): *Un Organisateur de la victoire, Prieur de la Côte-d'Or, membre du Comité de salut public*. Paris, Clavreuil.

Bouineau, J. (1986): *Les Toges du pouvoir ou la révolution de droit antique (1789–1799)*. Toulouse, Eché.

Boulant, A. (1990): 'Le suspect parisien en l'an II', *AHRF*, no. 280, pp. 187–97.

Boulant, A. (2016): *Les Tuileries: château des rois, palais des révolutions*. Paris, Tallandier.

Boulant, A. (2018): *Le tribunal révolutionnaire: punir les ennemis du peuple*. Paris, Perrin.

Bouloiseau, M. (1983): *The Jacobin Republic 1792–1794*. Cambridge, Cambridge University Press.

Bourquin, M.-H. (1987): *Monsieur et Madame Tallien*. Paris, Perrin.

Bouscayrol, R. (2002): *Georges Couthon: ange ou démon*. Clermont-Ferrand, Société des amis des universités de Clermont-Ferrand.

Boutier, J. & Boutry, P. (1986): 'Les Sociétés populaires: un chantier ouvert', *AHRF*, 266, pp. 393–5.

Boutier, J., Boutry, P., & Bonin, S. (1992): *Atlas de la Révolution française. Vol. 6: Les Sociétés politiques*. Paris, Éditions ÉHESS.

Braesch, F. (1911): *La Commune du 10 août 1792. Étude sur l'histoire de Paris, du 20 juin au 2 décembre 1792*. Paris, Hachette.

Brinton, C. C. (1930): *The Jacobins: An Essay in the New History*. New York, Macmillan.

Broc, M. H. de (1892): 'Un Témoin de la Révolution française à Paris: Jean-Gabriel-Philippe Morice', *Revue des questions historiques*, 8, pp. 453–98.

Brionne, C. (1971): 'Le journal inédit d'un témoin de la Terreur'. *Revue Générale: Perspectives européennes des sciences humaines*, 1, pp. 29–55.

Brown, H. G. (1995): *War, Revolution, and the Bureaucratic State: Politics and Army Administration in France, 1791–1799*. Oxford, Oxford University Press.

Brown, H. G. (2008): *Ending the French Revolution: Violence, Justice and Repression from the Terror to Napoleon*. Charlottesville, VA, University of Virginia Press.

Brown, H. G. (2010): 'Robespierre's Tail: The Possibilities of Justice after the Terror', *Canadian Journal of History*, 45, pp. 503–35.

Brown, H. G. (2018): *Mass Violence and the Self. From the French Wars of Religion to the Paris Commune*. Ithaca, NY, Cornell University Press.

Brunel, F. (1989): *Thermidor: la chute de Robespierre*. Bruxelles, Complexe.

Brunel, F. & Goujon, S. (1992): *Les Martyrs de Prairial: textes et documents inédits*. Genève, Georg.

Burstin, H. (1983): *Le Faubourg Saint-Marcel à l'époque révolutionnaire: structure économique et composition sociale*. Paris, Société des études robespierristes.

Burstin, H. (2005): *L'Invention du sans-culotte. Regard sur le Paris révolutionnaire*. Paris, Odile Jacob.

Burstin, H. (2005): *Une Révolution à l'oeuvre: le faubourg Saint-Marcel, 1789–1794*. Seyssel, Champ Vallon.

Burstin, H. (2013): *Révolutionnaires. Pour une anthropologie politique de la Révolution française*. Paris, Vendémiaire.

Cadio, É. (2012): 'Le Comité de sûreté générale (1792–1795)', *La Révolution française* 3. https://doi.org/10.4000/lrf.676.

Calvet, H. (1933): *L'Accaparement à Paris sous la Terreur. Essai sur l'application de la loi du 26 juillet 1793*. Paris, Imprimerie nationale.

Calvet, H. (1941): *Un instrument de la Terreur à Paris. Le Comité de salut public ou de surveillance du département de Paris, 8 juin 1793—messidor an II*. Paris, Librairie Nizet et Bastard.

Campardon, E. (1862): *Histoire du Tribunal révolutionnaire de Paris, d'après les document originaux conservés aux Archives de l'Empire*. 2 vols. Paris, Librairie de Poulet-Malassis.

Carbonnières, P. D. (2006): *Prieur: les tableaux historiques de la révolution: catalogue raisonné des dessins originaux*. Paris, Paris Musées Éditions.

Carbonnières, P. de (2009): 'Le sans-culotte Prieur', *AHRF*, 358, pp. 3–17.

Carmona, M. (2004): *Le Louvre et les Tuileries. Huit siècles d'histoire*. Paris, Éditions de la Martinière.

Caron, P. (1910): 'Les publications officieuses du ministère de l'Intérieur en 1793 et 1794', *Revue d'histoire moderne et contemporaine*, 14, no. 1, pp. 5–43.

Caron, P. (1935): *Les Massacres de septembre*. Paris, Maison du Livre Français.

Chagniot, J. (1985): *Paris et l'armée au XVIIIe siécle: étude politique et sociale*. Paris, Economica.

Chagniot, J. (1988): *Paris au XVIIIe siècle*. Paris, BHVP.

Charnay, J. P. ed. (1990): *Lazare Carnot, ou, Le savant citoyen: actes du colloque tenu en Sorbonne les 25, 26, 27, 28 et 29 janvier 1988*. Paris, Presses de l'université de Paris-Sorbonne.

Chuquet, A. (1899): *L'École de Mars, 1794*. E. Plon, Nourrit & Cie.

Cobb, R. (1955): 'Le témoignage de Rühl sur les divisions au sein des Comités à la veille du 9 thermidor', *AHRF*, 27, no. 139, pp. 110–14.

Cobb, R. (1961, 1963): *Les armées révolutionnaires: instrument de la Terreur dans les départements*. 2 vols. Paris, Mouton.

Cobb, R. (1965): *Terreur et subsistances, 1793–1795*. Paris, Librairie Clavreuil.

Cobb, R. (1970): *The Police and the People. French Popular Protest, 1789–1820*. Oxford, Oxford University Press.

Cobb, R. (1975): *Paris and its Provinces, 1792–1802*. Oxford: Oxford University Press.

Cobb, R. (1981): 'Thermidor or the Retreat from Fantasy', in H. Lloyd-Jones, V. Pearl, & B. Worden, eds., *History and Imagination. Essays in Honour of H. R. Trevor-Roper*, London, Duckworth, pp. 272–5.

Cobb, R. (1987): *The People's Armies: The Armées Révolutionnaires: Instrument of the Terror in the Departments April 1793 to Floréal Year II*, tr. M. Elliott. New Haven, CT: Yale University Press.

Cohen, A. (2011): *Le Comité des Inspecteurs de la salle. Une institution originale au service de la Convention nationale (1792–1795)*. Paris, L'Harmattan.

Conac, G. & Machelon, J. P. (1999): *La Constitution de l'an III: Boissy d'Anglas et la naissance du libéralisme constitutionnel*. Paris, Presses universitaires de France.

Conner, S. (1995): 'Public Virtue and Public Women: Prostitution in Revolutionary Paris, 1793–4', *Eighteenth-Century Studies*, 28, pp. 221–40.

Coquéry, N. (2011): *Tenir boutique à Paris au XVIIIe siècle: luxe et demi-luxe*. Paris, Éditions du Comité des travaux historiques et scientifiques.

Cottret, M. & Galland, C. eds. (2017): *Peurs, rumeurs et calomnies*. Paris: Éditions Kimé.

Cousin, A. (2010): *Philippe Lebas et Augustin Robespierre. Deux météores dans la Révolution française*. Paris, Bérénice.

Couty, M. (1988): *La vie aux Tuileries pendant la Révolution, 1789–1799*. Paris, Tallandier.

Crook, M. (1992): *Toulon in War and Revolution: From the Ancien Régime to the Restoration, 1750–1820*. Manchester, Manchester University Press.

Daline, V. (1964): 'Marc-Antoine Jullien après le 9 thermidor', *AHRF*, 176, pp. 159–73.

Darlow, M. (2012): *Staging the French Revolution: Cultural Politics and the Paris Opera, 1789–1794*. Oxford, Oxford University Press.

Darnton, R. & Roche, D. eds. (1989): *Revolution in Print: The Press in France, 1775–1800*. Berkeley, CA, University of California Press.

Dauban, C.-A. (1869): *Paris en 1794 et en 1795: histoire de la rue, du club, de la famine, composée d'après des documents inédits, particulièrement les rapports de police et les registres du Comité de salut public*. Paris, Plon.

Delahante, A. (1881): *Une Famille de finance au XVIIIe siècle*. 2 vols. Paris, Hetzel.

Delattre, S. (2004): *Les Douze heures noires. La nuit à Paris au XIXᵉ siècle*. Paris, Albin Michel.

Denis, V. (2017): 'Policiers de Paris. Les commissaires de police en Révolution, 1789–99', University of Paris.

Dodman, T. (2018): *What Nostalgia Was: War, Empire, and the Time of Deadly Emotion*. Chicago, IL, University of Chicago Press.

Dowd, D. L. (1948): *Pageant-master of the Republic: Jacques-Louis David and the French Revolution*. Lincoln, NE, University of Nebraska.

Ducoudray, E., Monnier, R., & Roche, D. eds. (2000): *Atlas de la Révolution française. 13. Paris*. Paris, Éditions EHESS.

Dunoyer, A. (1913): *Fouquier-Tinville, accusateur public du Tribunal Révolutionnaire, 1746–1795*. Paris, Perrin.

Dupuy, R. (2010): *La Garde nationale 1789–1872*. Paris, Gallimard.

Duval-Jouve, J. (1879): *Montpellier pendant la Révolution*. 2 vols. Montpellier, Coulet.

Edelstein, D. (2009): *The Terror of Natural Right: Republicanism, the Cult of Nature, and the French Revolution*. Chicago, IL, University of Chicago Press.

Edelstein, D. (2018): *On the Spirit of Rights*. Chicago, IL, University of Chicago Press.

Edmonds, B. (1990): *Jacobinism and the Revolt of Lyon, 1789–93*. Oxford, Clarendon.

Ehrard, J. (1996): *Images de Robespierre. Actes du colloque international de Naples (1993)*. Naples, Biblioteca europea.

d'Estrée, P. (1913): *Le théâtre sous la Terreur (Théâtre de la peur), 1793–1794*. Paris, Émile-Paul frères.

Eude, M. (1933): 'La Commune robespierriste', *AHRF*, 59, pp. 412–25.

Eude, M. (1934): 'La Commune robespierriste (suite)', *AHRF*, 64, pp. 323–47.

Eude, M. (1934): 'La Commune robespierriste: Chapitre II (suite)', *AHRF*, 66, pp. 528–56.

Eude, M. (1935): 'La Commune robespierriste: L'arrestation de Pache et la nomination de l'agent national Claude Payan', *AHRF*, 68, pp. 132–61.

Eude, M. (1935): 'La Politique économique et sociale de la Commune Robespierriste', *AHRF*, 72, pp. 495–518.

Eude, M. (1936): 'La Politique sociale de la Commune Robespierriste le neuf thermidor', *AHRF*, 76, pp. 289–316.

Eude, M. (1969): 'Points de vue sur l'affaire Catherine Théot', *AHRF*, 198, pp. 606–29.

Eude, M. (1983): 'La loi de Prairial'. *AHRF*, 254, pp. 544–59.

Eude, M. (1985): 'Le Comité de Sûreté Générale en 1793–1794', *AHRF*, 261, pp. 295–306.

Fairfax-Cholmeley, A. (forthcoming): 'Resisting the Terror: Suspects, Victims and Revolutionary Justice in France, 1793–4'.

Fleischmann, H. (1908): *Les Prisons de la Révolution, d'après les mémoires du temps et les lettres des guillotinés*. Paris, Publications modernes.

Fleischman, H. (1909): *Robespierre et les femmes*. Paris, A. Michel.

Fleischmann, H. (1911): *Réquisitoires de Fouquier-Tinville*. Paris, Charpentier & Fasquelle.

Fontaine, J.-P. (2013): 'Chardin, l'agent bibliophile de Beckford: le "Fou de Fonthill"', *Histoire de la bibliophile*, viewed 22 January 2020, http://histoire-bibliophilie.blogspot.com/2013/07/chardin-lagent-bibliophile-de-beckford.html.

Forrest, A. (1975): *Society and Politics in Revolutionary Bordeaux*. Oxford, Oxford University Press.

Foucault, M. (1975): *Surveiller et punir: Naissance de la prison*. Paris, Éditions Gallimard.

Freund, A. (2014): *Portraiture and Politics in Revolutionary France*. University Park, PA, Penn State University Press.

Friedland, P. (2012): *Seeing Justice Done: The Age of Spectacular Punishment in France*. Oxford, Oxford University Press.

Furet, F. (1981): *Interpreting the French Revolution*. Cambridge, Cambridge University Press.

Furet, F. & Ozouf, M. (1988): *A Critical Dictionary of the French Revolution*, tr. A. Goldhammer. Cambridge, MA, Harvard University Press.

Gainot, B. (1990): *Dictionnaire des membres du Comité de salut public*. Paris, Tallandier.

Garmy, R. (1962–3): 'Robespierre et l'indemnité parlementaire (I)', *AHRF*, 169 (1962), pp. 257–87; and (II), *AHRF*, 171, pp. 25–43.

Gauchet, M. (2018): *Robespierre: L'homme qui nous divise le plus*. Paris, Gallimard.

Geffroy, A. (2013): 'Les manuscrits de Robespierre', *AHRF*, 371, pp. 39–54.

Gendron, F. (1979): *Le jeunesse dorée: épisodes de la Révolution française*. Quebec, Presses de l'Université du Québec.

Gershoy, L. (1962): *Bertrand Barère, a Reluctant Terrorist*. Princeton, NJ, Princeton University Press.

Ghobrial, J. P. ed. (2019): 'Global History and Micro-History', *Past and Present Supplement*. Oxford, Oxford University Press.

Gillispie, C. C. (2004): *Science and Polity in France: The Revolutionary and Napoleonic Years*. Princeton, NJ, Princeton University Press.

Godechot, J. (1965): *La prise de la Bastille: 14 juillet 1789*. Paris, Gallimard.

Godfrey, J. L. (1951): *Revolutionary Justice: A Study of the Organization, Personnel, and Procedure of the Paris Tribunal, 1793–1795*. Chapel Hill, NC, University of North Carolina Press.

Godineau, D. (1988): *Citoyennes tricoteuses: Les femmes du peuple à Paris pendant la révolution française*. Paris, Perrin.

Gottschalk, L. R. (1967): *Jean Paul Marat: A Study in Radicalism*. New edn, first published 1927. Chicago, IL, University of Chicago Press.

Gough, H. (1988): *The Newspaper Press in the French Revolution*. London, Routledge.

Gough, H. (1998): *The Terror in the French Revolution*. New York, St. Martin's Press.

Grasilier, L. (1913): *Un secrétaire de Robespierre. Simon Duplay (1774–1827) et son Mémoire sur les sociétés secretes et les conspirations sous la Restauration*. Nevers, L. Cloix.

Greer, D. (1935): *The Incidence of the Terror during the French Revolution: A Statistical Interpretation*. Cambridge, MA, Harvard University Press.

Gross, J.-P. (1976): *Saint-Just: sa politique et ses missions*. Paris, Bibliothèque nationale.

Gueniffey, P. (2000): *La politique de la Terreur. Essai sur la violence révolutionnaire (1789–1794)*. Paris, Fayard.

Gueniffey, P. (2015): *Bonaparte (1769–1802)*. London, Harvard University Press.

Gueniffey, P. (2018): *Le dix-huit Brumaire: l'épilogue de la Révolution française, 9–10 novembre 1799*. Paris, Gallimard.

Guillois, A. (1890): *Pendant la Terreur: le poète Roucher, 1745–1794*. Paris, C. Lévy.

Hamel, E. (1865): *Histoire de Robespierre: d'après des papiers de famille, les sources originales et des documents entièrement inédits*. Paris, A. Lacroix, Verboeckhoven & cie.

Hamel, E. (1897): *Thermidor: d'après les sources originales et les documents authentiques*. Paris, Flammarion.

Hampson, N. (1974): *The Life and Opinions of Maximilien Robespierre*. London, Gerald Duckworth and Company.

Hampson, N. (1976): 'François Chabot and his Plot', *Transactions of the Royal Historical Society*, 26, pp. 1–14.

Hampson, N. (1991): *Saint-Just*. Oxford, Blackwell.

Hanson, P. R. (2003): *The Jacobin Republic Under Fire: The Federalist Revolt in the French Revolution*. University Park, PA, Pennsylvania State University Press.

Harder, M. (2013): 'Reacting to Revolution: The Political Career(s) of J.-L. Tallien', in D. Andress, ed., *Experiencing the French Revolution*. Oxford, Voltaire Foundation.

Hardman, J. (2000): *Robespierre*. London, Longman.

Hauterive, E. d' (1928): *Figaro-policier: un agent secret sous la Terreur*. Paris, Perrin.

Haydon, C. & Doyle, W. eds. (1999): *Robespierre*. Cambridge, Cambridge University Press.

Hazareesingh, S. (2009): 'Une profonde haine de la tyrannie: Albert Laponneraye et les paradoxes de la mémoire républicaine', in M. Deleplace, ed., *Les discours de la haine: Récits et figures de la passion dans la Cité*, Villeneuve-d'Ascq, Presses universitaires du Septentrion.

Hemmings, F. W. J. (1994): *Theatre and State in France, 1760–1905*. Cambridge, Cambridge University Press.

Herlaut, A. P. (1951): 'Carnot et les compagnies de canonniers des sections de Paris au 9 thermidor', *AHRF*, 23, pp. 9–16.

Hesse, C. (1989): 'Economic Upheavals in Publishing', in R. Darnton & D. Roche, eds., *Revolution in Print: The Press in France, 1775–1800*. Berkeley, Los Angeles, CA, University of California Press.

Higonnet, P. L. R. (1998): *Goodness Beyond Virtue: Jacobins during the French Revolution*. Cambridge, MA, Harvard University Press.

Higonnet, P. L. R. (2011): *La Gloire et l'échafaud: vie et destin de l'architecte de Marie-Antoinette*. Paris, Vendémiaire.

Hillairet, J. (1997 edn): *Dictionnaire historique des rues de Paris*. Paris, Éditions de Minuit.

Hincker, F. (1994): 'L'affrontement Cambon-Robespierre le huit thermidor', in J. P. Jessenne, G. Deregnaucourt, J.-P. Hirsch, & H. Leuwers, eds., *Robespierre. De la Nation artésienne à la République et aux Nations*. Lille, Publications de l'Institut de recherches historiques du Septentrion.

Hunt, L. A. ed. (1991): *Eroticism and the Body Politic*. Baltimore, MD, Johns Hopkins Press.

Hunt, L. A. (2008): *Measuring Time, Making History*. Budapest, Central Europe University Press.

Jacob, L. (1938): *Robespierre vu par ses contemporains*. Paris, A. Colin.

Jacquin, E. (2000): *Les Tuileries, du Louvre à la Concorde*. Paris, Editions du Patrimoine, Centres des Monuments Nationaux.

Jarvis, K. (2019): *Politics in the Marketplace: Work, Gender, and Citizenship in Revolutionary France*. New York, Oxford University Press.

Jones, C. (1988): *The Longman Companion to the French Revolution*. London, Longman.

Jones, C. (2002): *The Great Nation: France from Louis XV to Napoleon*. London, Penguin.

Jones, C. (2004): *Paris: Biography of a City*. London, Penguin.

Jones, C. (2012): Presidential Lecture. 'French Crossings III: The Smile of the Tiger', *Transactions of the Royal Historical Society*, 22, pp. 3–35.

Jones, C. (2014): 'The Overthrow of Maximilien Robespierre and the "Indifference" of the People', *The American Historical Review*, 119, no. 3, pp. 689–713.

Jones, C. (2014): *The Smile Revolution in Eighteenth-Century Paris*. Oxford, Oxford University Press.

Jones, C. (2015): '9 Thermidor, Cinderella of French Revolutionary *Journées*', *French Historical Studies*, 38, pp. 9–31.

Jones, C. (2020): 'La vie parisienne des Conventionnels en 1793', in P. Bastien & S. Macdonald, eds., *Paris et ses peoples*. Paris, Presses de la Sorbonne, pp. 75–88.

Jones, C. & Macdonald, S. (2018): 'Robespierre, the Duke of York, and Pisistratus during the French Revolutionary Terror', *The Historical Journal*, 61, pp. 643–72.

Jones, C. & Spang, R. (1999): 'Sans-culottes, *sans café, sans tabac*: Shifting Realms of Necessity and Luxury in Eighteenth-Century France', in M. Berg & H. Clifford eds. *Consumers and Luxury: Consumer Culture in Europe, 1650–1850*. Manchester: Manchester University Press.

Jordan, D. P. (1979): *The King's Trial: The French Revolution vs. Louis XVI*. Berkeley, CA, University of California Press.

Jordan, D. P. (1985): *The Revolutionary Career of Maximilien Robespierre*. Chicago, IL, University of Chicago Press.

Jourdan, A. (2016): 'Les journées de prairial an II: le tournant de la Révolution?', *La Révolution française*, https://journals.openedition.org/lrf/1591, 10.

Jourdan, A. (2018): *Nouvelle Histoire de la Révolution*. Paris, Flammarion.

Kates, G. (1985): *The Cercle Social, the Girondins, and the French Revolution*. Princeton, NJ, Princeton University Press.

Kennedy, M. L. (1982, 1988, 1999): *The Jacobin Clubs in the French Revolution*. 3 vols. Princeton, NJ, Princeton University Press; New York, Berghahn Books.

Klemperer, D. (2018): 'The Political Thought of Jacques-Nicolas Billaud-Varenne', MPhil thesis, University of Cambridge.

Koselleck, R. (1985): *Futures Past: On the Semantics of Historical Time*. Cambridge, MA., MIT Press.

Kuscinski, A. (1916): *Dictionnaire des Conventionnels*. Paris, Société de l'Histoire de la Révolution Française.

Labracherie, P. (1961): *Fouquier-Tinville, accusateur public*. Paris, A. Fayard.

Labracherie, P. & Pioro, G. (1961): 'Charlotte Robespierre et ses amis', *AHRF*, 166, pp. 469–92.

Lacombe, P. (1886): *Les noms des rues de Paris sous la Révolution*. Nantes, Imprimerie Vincent Forest et Emile Grimaud.

Lacroix, C. (1872): *Bertèche (Louis-Florentin), colonel, chevalier de la Légion d'honneur*. Lille, Imprimerie. de C. Robbe.

La Laurencie, J. de (1905): *Une Maison de détention sous la Terreur. L'hôtel des Bénédictins anglais.* Paris, Schola.

Landes, J. B. (1988): *Women and the Public Sphere in the Age of the French Revolution.* Ithaca, NY, Cornell University Press.

Laurent, G. (1924): 'Jean-Baptiste Armonville, ouvrier conventionnel', *AHRF,* 1, pp. 217–315.

Lemay, E. H. ed. (2007): *Dictionnaire des législateurs, 1791–1792.* Ferney-Voltaire, Centre international d'étude du XVIIIe siècle.

Lemay, E. H. & Favre-Lejeune, C. eds. (1991): *Dictionnaire des Constituants: 1789–1791.* 2 vols. Paris, Universitas.

Lenormand, F. (2002): *La Pension Belhomme: une prison de luxe sous la Terreur.* Paris, Fayard.

Lenôtre, G. (1895): *Paris révolutionnaire.* Paris, Firmin-Didot et Cie.

Lenôtre, G. (1908): *Le Tribunal révolutionnaire (1793–5).* Paris, Perrin.

Le Roux, T. (2011): *Le laboratoire des pollutions industrielles, Paris, 1770–1830.* Paris, A. Michel.

Lestapis, A. de (1956): *L'Envers d'un conspirateur: le baron de Batz.* Dax, Imprimerie de P. Pradeu.

Lestapis, A. de (1959): 'Admiral [Admirat] et l'attentat manqué (4 prairial an II)', *AHRF,* 157, pp. 209–26.

Leuwers, H. (2014): *Robespierre.* Paris, Fayard.

Leuwers, H. (2018): *Camille et Lucile Desmoulins.* Paris, Fayard.

Levy, D. G., Applewhite, H. B., & Johnson, M. D. (1979): *Women in Revolutionary Paris, 1789–95.* Chicago. IL, University of Illinois Press.

Lévy-Schneider, L. (1900): 'Les démêlés dans le Comité de salut public avant le 9 thermidor', *La Révolution française,* 7, pp. 97–112.

Lilti, A. (2005): *The World of the Salons: Sociability and Worldliness in Eighteenth-Century Paris.* Oxford, Oxford University Press.

Lilti, A. (2014): *Figures publiques: l'invention de la célébrité, 1750–1850.* Paris, Fayard.

Linton, M. (2013): *Choosing Terror: Virtue, Friendship, and Authenticity in the French Revolution.* Oxford, Oxford University Press.

Lucas, C. (1975): *The Structure of the Terror. The Example of Javogues and the Loire.* Oxford, Oxford University Press.

Lutaud, O. (1973): *Des Révolutions d'Angleterre à la Révolution française: Le tyrannicide & Killing No Murder (Cromwell,* Athalie, *Bonaparte).* La Haye, Nijhoff.

Luzzatto, S. (1991): *Mémoire de la Terreur: vieux montagnards et jeunes républicains au XIXe siècle.* Lyon, Presses Universitaires de Lyon.

Luzzatto, S. (2001): *L'Automne de la Révolution: luttes et cultures politiques dans la France thermidorienne.* Paris, Champion.

Luzzatto, S. (2010): *Bonbon Robespierre: la terreur à visage humain,* tr. trans. S. Carpentari-Messina. Paris, Arléa.

Lyons, M. (1975a): *France under the Directory.* Cambridge, Cambridge University Press.

Lyons, M. (1975b): 'The 9 Thermidor: Motives and Effects', *European History Quarterly,* 5, pp. 123–46.

Manin, B. (1988): 'Rousseau', in F. Furet & M. Ozouf, eds., *Dictionnaire critique de la Révolution française.* Paris, Flammarion.

Mansell, P. (2005): *Louis XVIII.* London, John Murray.

Mantel, H. (2000): 'What a man is this, with his crowd of women round him', *London Review of Book,* 22/7, 30 March.

Margairaz, D. (1991): 'Le Maximum: une grande illusion libérale, ou de la vanité des politiques économiques', in *État, finances et économie pendant la Révolution française*. Paris, Librairie de Imprimerie nationale, pp. 399–428.

Margairaz, D. (1993): 'Les institutions de la République jacobine ou la révolution utopique', in *Révolution et République: l'exception française*. Paris, Kimé, pp. 237–51.

Margairaz, D. (1994): 'Le maximum, politique économique ou politique sociale?' in J. P. Jessenne, G. Deregnaucourt, J.-P. Hirsch, & H. Leuwers, eds., *Robespierre. De la Nation artésienne à la République et aux Nations*. Villeneuve-d'Ascq, IRHIS, pp. 263–78.

Margairaz, D. & Minard, P. (2008): 'Marché des subsistances et économie morale: ce que "taxer" veut dire', *AHRF*, 352, pp. 53–99.

Martin, J.-C. (2016): *Robespierre: la fabrication d'un monstre*. Paris, Perrin.

Martin, J.-C. (2018): *Les échos de la Terreur: vérités d'un mensonge d'Etat, 1794–2001*. Paris, Belin.

Martin, J.-C. (2019): *Nouvelle histoire de la Révolution française*. Paris, Perrin.

Maslan, S. (2005): *Revolutionary Acts: Theater, Democracy, and the French Revolution*. Baltimore, MD, Johns Hopkins University Press.

Mason, L. (1996): *Singing the French Revolution: Popular Culture and Politics, 1787–1799*. Ithaca, NY, Cornell University Press.

Mason, L. (2008): 'Après la conjuration: le Directoire, la presse, et l'affaire des Égaux', *AHRF*, 354, pp. 77–103.

Mason, L. ed. (2015–17): 'Forum: Thermidor and the French Revolution', *FHS*, 38 (2015), no. 1 & *FHS*, 39 (2017), no. 3.

Matharan, J.-L. (1986): 'Les arrestations de suspects en 1793 et en l'an II', *AHRF*, no. 263, January–March, pp. 74–83.

Mathiez, A. (1917): 'La politique de Robespierre et le 9 thermidor expliqués par Buonarroti', in *Études Robespierristes: La Corruption parlementaire sous la Terreur*. Paris, A. Colin.

Mathiez, A. (1918): *La Conspiration de l'étranger*. Paris, A. Colin.

Mathiez, A. (1925): *Autour de Robespierre*. Paris, Payot.

Mathiez, A. (1927): *La Corruption parlementaire sous la Terreur*. 2nd edn. Paris, Armand Colin.

Mathiez, A. (1927): 'Les Séances des 4 et 5 Thermidor an II aux deux Comités de salut public et de Sûreté générale', *AHRF*, 21, pp. 193–222.

Mathiez, A. (1927): 'Trois lettres inédites de Voulland sur la crise de Thermidor', *AHRF*, 19, pp. 67–77.

Mathiez, A. (1925): 'La vie de Héron racontée par lui-même', *AHRF*, 11, pp. 480–3.

Mathiez, A. (1927): *La vie chère et le mouvement social sous la Terreur*. Paris, Payot.

Mathiez, A. (1930): *Girondins et Montagnards*. Paris, Firmin Didot.

Matta-Duvigneau, R. (2012): 'Le Comité de salut publique (6 Avril 1793–4 Brumaire An IV)', *La Révolution française: Cahiers de l'Institut d'Histoire de la Révolution Française*, 3.

Matta-Duvigneau, R. (2013): *Gouverner, administrer révolutionnairement: le comité de salut public (6 avril 1793–4 brumaire an IV)*. Paris, L'Harmattan.

McPhee, P. (2012): *Robespierre: A Revolutionary Life*. New Haven, CT, Yale University Press.

McPhee, P. ed. (2013): *A Companion to the French Revolution*. Chichester, Wiley-Blackwell.

Mellié, E. (1898): *Les sections de Paris pendant la Révolution française (21 mai 1790–19 vendémiaire an IV): organisation, fonctionnement*. Paris, Société de l'histoire de la Révolution française.

Milliot, V. (1995): *Les Cris de Paris ou le peuple travesti. Les représentations des petits métiers parisiens (XVIe–XVIIIe siècles)*. Paris, Éditions de la Sorbonne.

Milliot, V. (2011): *Un policier des Lumières: Suivi de Mémoires de J.C.P. Lenoir, ancien lieutenant general de police de Paris écrits en pays étrangers dans les années 1790 et suivantes*. Seyssel, Champ Vallon.

Monnier, R. (1981): *Le Faubourg Saint-Antoine (1789–1815)*. Paris, Société des Études Robespierristes.

Monnier, R. (1989): 'La garde citoyenne: eléments de démocratie parisienne', in M. Vovelle, ed., *Paris et la Révolution*. Paris, Publications de la Sorbonne, pp. 147–59.

Monnier, R. (1994): *L'Espace public démocratique. Essai sur l'opinion politique à Paris de la Révolution au Directoire*. Paris, Éditions Kimé.

Montier, A. (1899): *Robert Lindet, député à l'assemblée législative et à la Convention, membre du Comité de salut publique, ministre des finances*. Paris, Ancienne librairie Germer Ballière.

Moreau, J. (2010): *Enfant de Nanterre: François Hanriot, général-citoyen*. Nanterre, Société d'histoire de Nanterre.

Nicolas, J. (2002): *La rébellion française: mouvements populaires et conscience sociale (1661–1789)*. Paris, Seuil.

Ording, A. (1930): *Le Bureau de police du comité de salut public. Étude sur la Terreur*. Oslo, Jacob Dybwad.

Palmer, R. R. (1941): *Twelve Who Ruled: The Year of Terror in the French Revolution*. Princeton, NJ, Princeton University Press.

Palmer, R. R. (1985): *The Improvement of Humanity: Education and the French Revolution*. Princeton, NJ, Princeton University Press.

Palou, J. (1958): 'Documents inédits sur le 9 thermidor', *AHRF*, 153, pp. 44–50.

Parker, H. T. (1937): *The Cult of Antiquity and the French Revolutionaries*. Chicago, IL, University of Chicago Press.

Périer de Féral, G. (1955): *La Maison d'arrêt des Oiseaux d'après les souvenirs de captivité du Président Dompierre d'Hornoy*. Paris, Imprimerie de Daupeley-Gouverneur.

Perovic, S. (2015): *The Calendar in Revolutionary France: Perceptions of Time in Literature, Culture, Politics*. Cambridge, Cambridge University Press.

Phillips, R. (1980): *Family Breakdown in Late Eighteenth-century France: Divorces in Rouen, 1792–1803*. Oxford, Clarendon Press.

Plumauzille, C. (2016): *Prostitution et Révolution: les femmes publiques dans la cité républicaine (1789–1804)*. Paris, Champ Vallon.

Poirson, M. ed. (2007): *'Paméla, ou La Vertu récompensée'*. Oxford, Voltaire Foundation & Liverpool University Press.

Poirson, M. (2008): *Le théâtre sous la Révolution: politique du répertoire, 1789–99*. Paris, Desjonquières.

Popkin, J. D. (1979): 'The Royalist Press in the Reign of Terror', *The Journal of Modern History*, 51, pp. 685–700.

Popkin, J. D. (1990): *Revolutionary News: The Press in France, 1789–1799*. Durham, NC, Duke University Press.

Réau, L. (1994): *Histoire du vandalisme. Les monuments détruits de l'art français*. Paris, Laffont.

Reddy, W. M. (2001): *The Navigation of Feeling: A Framework for the History of Emotions*. Cambridge, Cambridge University Press.

Reinhard, M. (1950, 1952): *Le grand Carnot*. 2 vols. Paris, Hachette.

Reinhard, M. (1969): *La Chute de la royauté: le 10 août 1792*. Paris, Gallimard.

Reinhard, M. (1971): *Nouvelle histoire de Paris, 1789–1799*. Paris, Hachette.

Revel, J. (1996): *Jeux d'échelles: la micro-analyse à l'expérience*. Paris, Gallimard.

Ribeiro, A. (1988): *Fashion in the French Revolution*. London, Batsford.

Richard, C. (1922): *Le Comité de salut public et les fabrications de guerre sous la Terreur*. Paris, F. Rieder.

Roberts, W. (2000): *Jacques-Louis David and Jean-Louis Prieur, Revolutionary Artists. The Public, the Populace, and Images of French Revolution.* Albany, NY, State University of New York Press.

Roche, D. (1984): 'Le Cabaret parisien et les manières de vivre du peuple', in M. Garden & Y. Lequin, eds., *Habiter la ville XVe–XXe siècles.* Lyon, Presse universitaires de Lyon, pp. 233–51.

Roche, D. (1985): 'Le cabaret parisien et le manière de vivre du peuple', in M. Garden, & Y. Lequin, eds., *Habiter la ville, XVe–XXe siècles.* Lyon, Presses universitaires de Lyon, pp. 233–51.

Roche, D. (1986): *Journal of My Life by Jacques-Louis Ménétra.* ed. D. Roche. New York, Columbia University Press.

Roche, D. (1987): *The People of Paris: An Essay in Popular Culture in the 18th Century.* Berkeley, CA, University of California Press.

Roche, D. (2000): *La Ville promise: mobilité et accueil à Paris (fin XVIIe—début XIXe siècle).* Paris, Fayard.

Roche, D. (2001): *Almanach parisien en faveur des étrangers et des personnes curieuses.* Saint-Etienne, Publications de l'université de Saint-Etienne.

Rose, R. B. (1968): *The Enragés: Socialists of the French Revolution?* Sydney, Sydney University Press for Australian Humanities Research Council.

Rose, R. B. (1978): *Gracchus Babeuf: The First Revolutionary Communist.* Stanford, CA, Stanford University Press.

Rosenwein, B. (2006): *Emotional Communities in the Early Middle Ages.* Ithaca, NY, Cornell University Press.

Rudé, G. (1959): *The Crowd in the French Revolution.* Oxford, Oxford University Press.

Rudé, G. & Soboul, A. (1954): 'Le Maximum des salaires parisiens et le 9 thermidor', *AHRF,* 26, pp. 1–22.

Sabatié, A. C. (1914): *Le Tribunal révolutionnaire de Paris.* Paris, Lethielleux.

Sachs, J. (2019): *The Poetics of Decline in British Romanticism.* Cambridge, Cambridge University Press.

Saddy, P. (1977): 'Le cycle des immondices', *Dix-huitième siècle,* 9, pp. 203–14.

Sainte-Claire Deville, P. (1946): *La Commune de l'an II: vie et mort d'une assemblée révolutionnaire.* Paris, Plon.

Sainte-Fare Garnot, P.-N. (1988): *Le Château des Tuileries.* Paris, Herscher.

Saumade, G. (1939): 'Cambon et sa famille acquéreurs de biens nationaux (1791 et 1793)', *AHRF,* 93 & 94, pp. 228–44 & 313–38.

Schechter, R. (2018): *A Genealogy of Terror in Eighteenth-Century France.* Chicago, IL, University of Chicago Press.

Scott, J. C. (2004): *Weapons of the Weak: Everyday Forms of Peasant Resistance.* New Haven, CT, Yale University Press.

Scott, J. C. (2009): *Domination and the Arts of Resistance: Hidden Transcripts.* New Haven, CT, Yale University Press.

Scurr, R. (2006): *Fatal Purity: Robespierre and the French Revolution.* New York, Metropolitan Books.

Sepinwall, A. G. (2010): 'Robespierre, Old Regime Feminist? Gender, the Late Eighteenth Century, and the French Revolution Revisited', *Journal of Modern History,* 82, pp. 1–29.

Serna, P. (1997): *Antonelle: aristocrate révolutionnaire, 1747–1817.* Paris, Éditions du Félin.

Serna, P. (2005): *La République des girouettes: Une anomalie politique: la France de l'extrême centre (1789–1815 . . . et au-delà).* Paris, Champ Vallon.

Serna, P. (2017): *Comme des bêtes: histoire politique de l'animal en Révolution (1750–1840)*. Paris, Fayard.

Shaw, M. (2011): *Time and the French Revolution: The Republican Calendar, 1789–Year XIV*. Woodbridge, Boydell.

Shusterman, N. C. (2014): 'All of His Power Lies in the Distaff: Robespierre, Women and the French Revolution', *Past & Present*, 223, pp. 129–60.

Simonin, A. (2008): *Le déshonneur dans la République. Une histoire de l'indignité, 1791–1958*. Paris, Grasset.

Slavin, M. (1984): *The French Revolution in Miniature. Section Droits-de-L'Homme, 1789–1795*. Princeton, NJ, Princeton University Press.

Slavin, M. (1986): *The Making of an Insurrection: Parisian Sections and the Gironde*. Cambridge, MA, Harvard University Press.

Slavin, M. (1994): *The Hébertistes to the Guillotine: Anatomy of a 'Conspiracy' in Revolutionary France*. Baton Rouge, LA; London, Louisiana State University Press.

Smyth, J. (2016): *Robespierre and the Cult of the Supreme Being: The Search for a Republican Morality*. Manchester, Manchester University Press.

Soboul, A. (1958): *Les Sans-culottes parisiens en l'an II: Mouvement populaire et gouvernement révolutionnaire (2 juin 1793–9 thermidor an II)*. Paris, Librairie Clavreuil.

Soboul, A. (1973): *Le Procès de Louis XVI*. Paris, Julliard.

Soboul, A. ed. (1980): *Girondins et Montagnards: actes du colloque, Sorbonne, 14 décembre 1975*. Paris, Société des études Robespierristes.

Soboul, A. (1983): 'Georges Couthon', *AHRF*, 55, pp. 510–43.

Soboul, A. & Monnier, R. (1985): *Répertoire du personnel sectionnaire parisien en l'an II*. Paris, Publications de la Sorbonne.

Sonenscher, M. (2008): *Sans-culottes: An Eighteenth-Century Emblem in the French Revolution*. Princeton, NJ, Princeton University Press.

Spang, R. (2000): *The Invention of the Restaurant. Paris and Modern Gastronomic Culture*. Cambridge, MA, Harvard University Press.

Spang, R. (2015): *Stuff and Money in the Time of the French Revolution*. Cambridge, MA, Harvard University Press.

Spary, E. C. (2014): *Feeding France: New Sciences of Food, 1760–1815*. Cambridge, Cambridge University Press.

Stéfane-Pol (1900): *Autour de Robespierre: le conventionnel Le Bas d'après des documents inédits et les mémoires de sa veuve*. Paris, Ernest Flammarion.

Steinberg, R. (2019): *The Afterlives of the Terror: Facing the Legacies of Mass Violence in Postrevolutionary France*. Ithaca, NY, Cornell University Press.

Sutherland, D. M. G. (2009): *Murder in Aubagne. Lynching, Law, and Justice during the French Revolution*. Cambridge, Cambridge University Press.

Sydenham, M. J. (1961): *The Girondins*. London, Athlone Press.

Sydenham, M. J. (1999): *Léonard Bourdon: The Career of a Revolutionary (1754–1807)*. Waterloo, Wilfred Laurier Press.

Tackett, T. (2003): *When the King Took Flight*. Cambridge, MA, Harvard University Press.

Tackett, T. (2015): *The Coming of the Terror in the French Revolution*. Cambridge, MA, Harvard University Press.

Thompson, J. M. (1968 edn): *Robespierre*. New York, H. Fertig.

Tiesset, L. (2008): 'Une réécriture de la tragédie du complot: Gabriel Legouvé, *Épicharis et Néron*', in M. Poirson, ed., *Le Théâtre sous la Révolution. Politique du répertoire*. Paris, Desjonquères, pp. 381–93.

Tissier, A. (1992, 2002): *Les spectacles à Paris pendant le Révolution. Répertoire analytique, chronologique et bibliographique (de la proclamation de la République à la fin de la Convention nationale)*. Paris & Geneva, Droz.

Tonnesson, K. D. (1959): *La défaite des sans-culottes. Mouvement populaire et réaction bourgeoise en l'an III*. Paris, Clavreuil.

Tulard, J. (1989): *Nouvelle histoire de Paris: la Révolution*. Paris, Hachette.

Tulard, J. (1997): *Fouché*. Paris, Fayard.

Van Kley, D. K. (1984): *The Damiens Affair and the Unraveling of the Ancien Régime, 1750–1770*. Princeton, NJ, Princeton University Press.

Velut, C. (2005): *Décors de papier: production, commerce et usages des papiers peints à Paris, 1750–1820*. Paris, Éditions du patrimoine.

Vetter, C., Marin, M., & Gon, E. (2015): *Dictionnaire Robespierre: lexicométrie et usages langagiers: outils pour une histoire du lexique de l'Incorruptible*. Tome 1. Trieste EUT, Edizioni Università di Trieste.

Vinot, B. (1985): *Saint-Just*. Paris, Fayard.

Vovelle, M. (1991): *The Revolution Against the Church: From Reason to the Supreme Being*. Cambridge, Polity Press.

Vovelle, M. ed. (1997): *Le tournant de l'an III: Réaction et Terreur blanche dans la France révolutionnaire*. Paris, Éditions du CTHS.

Wahnich, S. (2003): *La Liberté ou la mort—Essai sur la Terreur et le terrorisme*. La Fabrique, Paris.

Wallon, H. (1880–2): *Histoire du tribunal révolutionnaire de Paris*. 6 vols. Paris, Hachette.

Wallon, H. (1886): *La Révolution du 31 mai et le fédéralisme en 1793*. 2 vols. Paris, Hachette.

Walter, G. (1946): *Histoire des Jacobins*. Paris, A. Somogy.

Walter, G. (1974): *La Conjuration du Neuf Thermidor*. Paris, Gallimard.

Walter, G. (1989): *Maximilien de Robespierre*. Paris, Gallimard.

Walton, C. (2009): *Policing Public Opinion in the French Revolution: The Culture of Calumny and the Problem of Free Speech*. Oxford, Oxford University Press.

Walzer, M. ed. (1974): *Regicide and Revolution: Speeches at the Trial of Louis XVI*. Cambridge, Cambridge University Press.

Weiner, D. B. (2002): *The Citizen-Patient in Revolutionary and Imperial Paris*. Baltimore, MD, Johns Hopkins University Press.

Williams, A. (1979): *The Police of Paris 1718–1789*. Baton Rouge, LA, Louisiana State University Press.

Woloch, I. (1986): 'From Charity to Welfare in Revolutionary Paris', *Journal of Modern History*, 58, pp. 779–812.

Woloch, I. (1994): *The New Regime: Transformations of the French Civic Order, 1789–1820s*. New York, W. W. Norton.

Woloch, I. (1994): 'The Contraction and Expansion of Democratic Space during the Period of the Terror', in K. M. Baker, ed., *The French Revolution and the Creation of Modern Political Culture, vol. 4, The Terror*. Oxford, Pergamon.

Woronoff, D. (2004): *La République bourgeoise: de Thermidor à Brumaire, 1794–1799*. Paris, Éditions du Seuil.

Wrigley, R. (2002): *The Politics of Appearance: Representations of Dress in Revolutionary France*. Oxford, Berg.

Zobkiw, J. C. (2015): 'Political Strategies of Laughter in the National Convention, 1792–4', PhD thesis, University of Hull.

INDEX

Allen, William, *A Political Treatise* 213
Allier department 257
Alsace 11
amalgame 67
Amar, André 42, 51, 61, 66, 75, 77,
    149, 266, 279, 301, 327, 329, 331,
    367, 418
  relations with Robespierre 51
Angers 166
Anseaume, Louis, *Les deux chasseurs et la
    laitière* 147
Ardèche 65
Ardennes 69
aristocracy 14–21, 37, 39, 48, 57, 61,
    78–9, 82–3, 106, 110–12, 125, 127,
    133, 141, 144, 146, 148, 155, 157,
    170, 176, 178, 198–9, 215, 226,
    257–8, 287–8, 295, 315, 408, 450
Arles 304
armée révolutionnaire, Paris 106, 109, 120,
    156
Armonville, Jean-Baptiste 178
Arnault, Bertrand 415, 427
Arras 60, 116–18
Arsenal 15, 159, 237
Arthur, Jean-Jacques 129, 341, 349,
    392–3, 399, 410
assignat (currency) 110, 438
Aube department 62, 265
Aubert, Jean-Baptiste 376
Auguis, Pierre-Jean-Baptiste 336
Aulard, Alphonse 445
Austria 13, 29–30, 90, 198
  Vienna 89, 117
Auteuil 14
Auvergne 114
Auzat, Antoine 115
Aveyron department 220, 413
Avril, Jean-Baptiste 126, 215

Ballin, Charles 374, 416

Bar, Jean-Etienne 197, 210
Bara, Joseph 24, 135, 141
Bara and Viala festival 70, 75, 126, 129,
    135, 141–3, 152, 157, 162, 164,
    215, 252–3, 291, 363, 417
Barelle, Jean-Guillaume 129, 377
Barère, Bertrand 52, 92, 107, 149, 181,
    185, 201, 295, 301, 367, 436, 442
  carmagnoles 108, 230
  École de Mars 140
  exclusion of nobles from Paris 226–7
  never been on mission 58
  relations with Robespierre 14, 39, 56,
    94, 112, 145, 195, 203, 239, 433,
    435–6, 439, 447
  role in CPS 31–2, 35, 40, 45, 47–8, 50,
    97, 197–9, 218, 227, 276, 279, 330,
    343, 358, 360, 373, 382–3, 385–6,
    405, 410, 443, 452
  use of military victories 88, 455
Barras, Paul 7, 60, 334–6, 345–6, 358,
    364–5, 379–80, 385–6, 403–4, 409,
    414, 419, 422–3, 438, 440, 443–4,
    449, 451
  deputy on mission 58, 62, 334
Barrois, Cn. 224
Barrois, Marguerite 403
Barry, Jeanne Bécu, comtesse du 258
Bastille, the 2, 25, 62, 130, 155
Baudot, Marc-Antoine 61
Bayle, Moise 51, 61, 367
Bazanéry, Cn. 233
Belhomme, Jacques 78
Benoist, gaoler 79
Benoit, Jean 272, 423, 427
Bentabole, Pierre-Louis 52, 363, 417
Bercy 129, 392–3, 410
Berger, NG company commander 294
Bernard, Jacques-Claude 305, 383–4, 408
Bernard, Jean-Pierre 128

Bertèche, Louis-Florentin 140–1, 363, 379, 417
Bicêtre 15, 77–9
Bigaud, Claude 129, 272, 383
Billaud-Varenne, Jacques-Nicolas 34, 43, 45, 48, 51–4, 84, 87–8, 91, 94, 99, 107, 181, 191, 193, 195–6, 203, 223, 235, 251, 276, 295, 320, 363, 367, 380
    relations with Robespierre 39, 41, 44, 86–7, 92–3, 165, 196–7, 202–3, 239–40, 279, 379, 435–6, 442–3, 446
    role in CPS 35, 50, 92–3, 133, 227, 330
Blanchetot, Cn. 247–8
Blandin, Pierre-Henri 427
Blanqui, Denis 79
Bodson, Joseph 339, 341, 383, 450
Bodson, Louis-Alexis 339, 383, 450
Boissy d'Anglas, François-Antoine 1, 65–6
Bollet, Philippe-Albert 336
Bon Saint-André, André-Jean 49–50, 87
Bordeaux 19–20, 30, 59
Bosphorus, the 83
Bouches-du-Rhône 60
Boulanger, Servais-Beaudoin 20, 120, 197, 265, 358
Bourbault, François 370
Bourbon monarchy 130, 157, 269
Bourdon, Léonard 61, 265, 336, 345, 367, 404–5, 413–14, 418–23, 425, 427
Bourdon de l'Oise, François-Louis 133, 279, 300, 336, 403
    plot against Robespierre 62, 94, 96, 101, 121, 181, 418, 441
    relations with Robespierre 23, 41, 221
Bréard, Jean-Jacques 300, 320
Brennus 323
bridges 415
    Pont-au-Change 104, 135
    Pont-au-Double 254
    Pont de la Tournelle 254
    Pont National 172
    Pont-Neuf 130, 156, 172, 264, 283, 344, 380, 383–4, 387, 425
    Pont Notre-Dame 310, 354
    Pont Saint-Michel 171
Brissot, Jacques-Pierre 30–1, 77, 144

Britain 30, 39, 89, 198, 335, 398
    British prisoners of war 15, 94, 145, 184
    press 38, 146
    Royal Navy 58, 111
    see also Foreign Plot
Brittany 61, 65
Brival, Jacques 197, 306–7, 363, 417
Brizard, artillery instructor 321
Brussels 132
Brutus, Lucius Junius 147, 166, 183
Brutus, Marcus Junius 183, 194
Buonaparte, Napoleone, see Napoleon
Burguburu, Pierre 361, 414–15
Burgundy 61

Cabarrus, Theresa 19–20, 22, 24, 59, 65, 189, 194, 239, 372
Caesar, Julius 183, 194, 197, 201–2, 223, 439
Café des Subsistances 166, 254, 375
Calendar, French Revolutionary 2–3, 24, 142, 164
Calendar, Gregorian 24, 114
Cambon, Joseph 38, 40–1, 57, 67, 88, 181, 445–6
Camboulas, Simon 336, 413, 419
Cambrai 60
Camillus 183
Capucines convent 110
Carnot, Lazare 39–40, 43–6, 49–50, 57, 87–92, 123, 142, 186–7, 201, 298, 306, 332, 361, 367, 442, 448
Carra, Jean-Louis 37, 144
Carrier, Jean-Baptiste 59–60, 436
Catiline 39, 201–2, 295, 360, 380, 439
Chabru, Claude 422
Chalandon, Claude 274–5, 277, 428
Chales, Pierre-Jacques 306–7
Chardin, Charles, Legion Chief 244, 377–8
Charente-Inférieure 220
Charlemagne, Jean-Philippe-Victor 134, 365, 420
Chartres cathedral 306
Châtelet, Claude-Louis 120, 170, 341, 349, 399
Chaumette, Pierre Gaspard 150
Chénier, André 74

Chénier, Marie-Joseph
   Caius Gracchus 148
   Timoléon 148
Choisy 120, 373
Chrétien, Jean-Jacques 271
churches
   Oratory 288
   Saint-Eustache 127
   Saint-Germain-des-Prés 289
   Sainte-Chapelle 288
Cicero 201
Cietty, Laurent 129
Cincinnatus 183, 200–1, 448
Cobourg, Frédérique Josias, prince
   de 262
Cochefer, Christophe 425–6
Cochois, Jean-Baptiste 377
Coffinhal, Pierre-André 164, 254, 281,
   302, 310, 317, 319, 321–3, 326,
   331–2, 341–2, 346, 351, 354, 358,
   365–6, 401, 412–13, 420, 422–3,
   427, 443, 449
coffins 70
Collot d'Herbois, Jean-Marie 45, 48, 51–4,
   57, 59, 60, 84, 87–8, 91–2, 94, 99,
   165, 181, 191, 235, 251–2, 259, 279,
   295, 300, 306, 317, 330, 339, 367,
   418, 442
   assassination attempt on his life 15, 184
   deportation 436
   President of the Convention 136,
      185–6, 192–3, 206–7, 210, 240,
      246, 323
   relations with Robespierre 39, 43–4,
      54–5, 93, 196, 203, 239–40,
      435–6, 443
   role in CPS 50, 93, 106, 133, 149, 162,
      195, 218
Commission du Muséum, *see under*
   popular commissions
Commission of Civil Administration,
   Prisons and Tribunals 123, 168,
   212, 218
Committee of General Security 13–15,
   31, 37–42, 44–6, 51–2, 54–6,
   60–2, 66, 75, 77, 79, 84–7, 92, 94,
   96–7, 113, 115, 120, 124, 129, 133,
   151, 165, 169, 187, 192, 195–6,
   201, 217, 222, 242, 246, 255, 259,

264, 280, 287, 299, 301–3, 305,
   308, 322–3, 325–7, 329, 331, 334,
   343, 358, 363, 366–7, 398,
   408, 412–14, 424, 428, 436–7,
   441, 445
   bureaucracy 38–40, 133, 165
   offices 48, 119, 148, 242, 265–6, 276,
      280, 319–21, 329–31, 369, 419,
      422, 424
   police force 14–15, 228, 329
   rivalry with the Police Bureau 123
   Robespierre distrusts the 14, 37,
      51, 123
Committee of Public Safety 13, 31,
   38–41, 46, 57–62, 79–81, 85–8, 90,
   92–6, 99, 106–8, 111–13, 124, 135,
   139–41, 147–9, 151, 153, 159,
   162–3, 167, 192–3, 195–6, 198–9,
   201, 204, 211–12, 215–16, 218,
   221, 226–8, 234–5, 237, 239, 241,
   244, 246, 248–9, 254, 261, 266,
   279, 286–7, 289–90, 300, 302–3,
   316–17, 320–2, 331–2, 334, 337,
   339–40, 361, 366, 375, 387, 398,
   410, 423, 435–6, 441–5, 448,
   452, 454
Bureau of Administrative Surveillance
   and General Police 14, 22, 49, 51,
   86, 90, 94, 109, 115, 122–4, 206,
   445, 448
   bureaucracy 50, 132, 229–30
   code of confidentiality 89, 98
   Committee Room 43, 48–9, 51, 63,
      151, 252, 259, 329, 379
   decrees 14, 50, 93–4, 200, 225, 246, 256
   dysfunctionality 39, 87, 91, 181, 198
   friction with CGS 13, 51, 55, 96, 228
   joint CPS/CGS meetings 44–5, 51,
      55–7, 84, 186, 191, 193, 203, 259
   offices 49, 56, 115, 122–3, 134, 177,
      181, 186, 251–2, 276, 314, 323
   personnel 4–5, 11, 13, 15, 20, 32,
      34–5, 48–51, 123, 131, 133, 282,
      367, 423
   Robespierre
      avoids the 28, 41–4, 54, 66, 89, 117,
         122, 212
      elected to the 28, 31, 33–4

Commune, Paris 6, 22, 57, 59, 70, 81, 96,
    109–10, 112–13, 123, 128–35, 139,
    148, 150–3, 158, 163, 174, 199, 203,
    215, 219, 229, 234–5, 237, 246, 260,
    262, 266–7, 271–3, 278–9, 282–5,
    290, 292, 298–301, 303–5, 307–8,
    313–14, 319–20, 322, 324, 326–7,
    330, 332, 337, 339–44, 346, 349–50,
    352–3, 355–6, 358, 360–2, 364–7,
    369–70, 374–86, 388, 392–4,
    399–401, 404–10, 412, 414–17,
    419, 421–3, 425, 427–8, 431, 434,
    437–9, 443, 448, 450–1, 455
  early history (to 1792) 30, 130
  Enforcement Committee 341, 347, 349,
    353, 362, 365, 367, 370, 373, 376,
    378, 383, 388, 392, 397, 399–400,
    407, 410, 412, 414–15, 420–2, 426
  General Council 128–31, 134, 138,
    158–9, 238, 270–1, 278–9, 282, 284,
    290, 302–3, 305, 317, 338–40, 344,
    347, 349, 353–4, 362, 364–6, 369–70,
    376, 406, 418, 420, 425, 427
  Municipal Bureau 131
  Municipal Council 126, 131, 215, 234,
    238, 249, 270, 274, 303, 305, 408,
    422, 427, 437
  purge of the 437
  relations with sections 113, 158, 237–8,
    250, 272, 274, 312, 331, 343–4,
    354–6, 361, 364, 366, 388–9, 397,
    405, 415
  role in journées 130, 237, 270, 341
Conception monastery 120, 173
Constituent Assembly, National 2, 23,
    29–30, 32, 34, 36–7, 67, 120,
    132, 145
Constitution (1793) 105, 156, 227, 234,
    288, 438–9, 442, 445
Constitution of Year III (1795) 439, 444
Convention, National 3–7, 13, 15–16,
    19, 21–3, 25, 27–8, 30–4, 38–39–
    43, 45–51, 53, 56–9, 61–2, 66–7,
    76–7, 79, 82, 84–7, 90, 93–9, 101,
    105, 108, 110–13, 115–18, 121–2,
    124–5, 128, 133–4, 139–42, 144–5,
    147, 151, 156, 158–9, 165, 167,
    170–4, 176–82, 184–7, 191–206,
    209–13, 215–16, 218–20, 222–4,

    226–7, 230–40, 244, 246–7, 250–3,
    259, 261–4, 266–7, 270, 272, 274–6,
    278–9, 281–3, 285, 290–3, 297,
    299–301, 303–7, 310, 312–17,
    319–32, 334–7, 339–46, 350, 355–6,
    358, 360, 362, 364, 366–7, 369–71,
    373–86, 388–90, 393–4, 398–402,
    404–6, 409–11, 413–28, 431, 433–9,
    441, 443–5, 447–52, 454–5
  Convention hall 15, 31–2, 42, 49, 53–4,
    121, 135, 171, 177–8, 180, 182–5,
    187, 189, 191–4, 200–1, 209–11,
    218, 220, 232, 239, 244, 246, 251–2,
    259, 267, 272, 297, 299, 304, 314,
    319–23, 327, 330, 332, 334–5, 345,
    358, 363, 367, 379–80, 399, 403–4,
    419, 423–4, 443
  Education Committee 147, 171
  Finance Committee 40–1, 57, 67,
    88, 445
  Manège 27, 416
  moderate deputies 4, 28, 32, 42, 57,
    67–8, 90, 133, 144, 159–60, 206,
    210, 297, 336, 351, 356, 367,
    441, 450
  public galleries 108, 118, 151, 180,
    182–3, 195, 202, 209–12, 218, 220,
    232, 246, 320, 322–3, 325, 374,
    379–80, 399
Corday, Charlotte 257
Cordeliers club 83, 377
Corneille, Pierre 116
Couprye, Julie 304
Courtois, Edme-Bonaventure 62, 265–6,
    433–4
  Rapport fait au nom de la Commission
    chargée de l'examen des papiers trouvés
    chez Robespierre et ses complices
    459, 533
  Rapport sur les événements du 9 thermidor
    an II 433–4, 439
Courvol, Cn. 234, 238, 247, 319–20
Couthon, Georges 82, 87, 149, 191, 218,
    242, 279, 302, 353, 377, 410, 412
  arrested 281, 287, 409, 426
  deputy on mission 58
  disability 54, 58, 186–7, 223
  earlier life and career 49
  guillotined 425

head-wound 422
  relations with Robespierre 14, 21, 41,
    44, 47, 54, 67, 89, 96, 167, 223,
    239, 241, 367, 393, 443
  role in CPS 14, 46, 48–9, 51–2, 59, 61,
    66, 79, 89–90, 122, 167, 181,
    186–7, 193, 195–6, 251–2, 262,
    411, 445, 448
Couturier, Jean-Pierre 197
Crassus 223
Cromwell, Oliver 194, 197, 201–2, 213,
    393, 439
Cult of the Supreme Being 36, 39, 45, 51,
    59, 61, 94, 177, 205, 288, 442

Damiens, Robert, regicide 37
Damour, Jean-François 322, 388
Dampierre 257
Danton, Georges 20, 32–4, 37, 53, 62, 79,
    95–6, 118, 182, 196, 204, 208, 213,
    221, 231, 265, 279, 287, 454
Dantonists 62, 80, 86, 92, 94, 139, 144,
    146, 181, 197, 204, 208, 213, 289,
    301, 336, 433, 435, 441, 454
Daujon, François, sculptor 215
Dauminval, NG company captain 324
dauphin, see Louis-Charles
David, Jacques-Louis 51, 53, 96, 129,
    135–6, 141, 181–3, 329, 336, 345,
    389, 404
Debure, Cn. 288, 316
Degesne, Cn. 248, 292
Degouy, Cn., engraver 272
Dehureau, Jean 389, 428
Delacour, Pierre-Nicolas 377, 414
Deliège, Gabriel 166, 426
Delmas, Jean-François-Bertrand 62, 197,
    336, 444
Demosthenes 183
Desboisseaux, Charles-Huant 164, 254,
    281, 310, 322, 341, 420, 427
Deschamps, Robespierre's bodyguard 264
Desmoulins, Camille 32, 76, 86, 95–6,
    117, 144–6, 204, 287
Devèze, Jean 364
Dhazard, Jean-Baptiste-Mathieu 376, 389
Didier, Jean-Baptiste 120, 167, 173–4,
    176, 209, 362
Directory, the 433, 439

divorce 70
Dossonville, Jean-Baptiste 13–14, 38,
    242, 347, 410–11
Drôme, department 132
Dubarran, Joseph-Nicolas Barbeau 52,
    279, 367, 418
Dubois-Crancé, Edmond-Louis-Alexis
    56, 61, 67–8, 186, 367, 446
Dubreuil, Marie 304
Ducy, Cn. 106
Dulac, Pierre-Honoré-Gabriel 410–11,
    420
Dumaniant, Antoine-Jean, Hypocrite en
    révolution 213
Dumas, René-François 46, 53–4, 132,
    165–6, 168–70, 195–6, 219, 256,
    305, 319, 446
  arrest 197, 216–18, 239, 259, 263, 285,
    366, 377, 401, 422, 423–6
Dumesnil, gendarmerie commander 285,
    344, 375
Dumont, André 60, 197, 206–7, 210
Dumouriez, Charles-François du Périer,
    called 29, 231, 454
Duplay, Eléonore 118–19, 174
Duplay, Madame 117–18, 120, 174
Duplay, Maurice (Robespierre's
    landlord) 20, 27–30, 40, 51, 114–
    15, 121, 135, 142, 167, 175, 180,
    196, 206, 240, 362, 446
Duplay, Simon 115, 122
Duplays, the 58, 62, 114–17, 119–21,
    173–4, 221, 259, 314, 402, 426
Durand-Maillane, Pierre-Toussaint 65,
    67, 181, 193, 206
Duras, Louise-Charlotte, duchesse de 82
Duval, Charles 197, 222

École de Mars 14, 140–3, 363, 379–80,
    416
Elisabeth, Louis XVI's sister 157
émigrés 17, 19, 57, 106–7, 126–7, 165, 169,
    217, 257
English Channel 88
enragés 105
Estates General 28–9, 116, 130, 257, 433
Europe, war against 3, 5, 30, 108,
    112, 115
Ezekiel 204–5

Fargeon, Marie-Antoinette's
        perfumer 282
Faro, Jean-Léonard 129, 148, 153, 314
Fauchet, Claude 144
Fauconnier, Legion Chief 157, 237, 244,
        249, 290–1, 300, 323, 332
Fayau, Joseph-Pierre-Marie 253
Federalist Revolt 4, 19, 49, 58–9, 61, 93,
        156, 416, 452
Félix, Jean-Baptiste-Henri-Antoine 166
Fénaux, Joseph 305
Féraud, Jean-Bertrand 327, 336, 345, 379,
        438–9
Ferrière-Sauvebœuf, Louis-François 83
Feuillants, the 29
Filleul 308
Flanders 88
Fleuriot-Lescot, Jean-Baptiste 22, 84, 98,
        131, 134, 136, 152, 157, 159, 215,
        233–5, 238, 240, 249–50, 270, 274,
        278, 282–3, 285, 291–2, 302–3,
        316, 326, 330, 339, 342, 355, 366,
        376, 392, 397, 401, 406, 417, 422,
        425, 446, 449, 455
    arrest 319
    before 1794 132, 285
    execution 426
    relations with Robespierre 57, 97, 174,
        203, 219, 317
Fleurus, battle of 5, 31, 67, 85, 88,
        112–13, 115, 229, 455
Fleury (formerly known as Bourbon) 134,
        374, 427
Fleury, Honoré-Marie 295, 372
Fontaine, NG artillery commander 156,
        237, 261, 298, 312, 337
Fontenay-aux-Roses 20
food riots 111
Foreign Plot 14–15, 22, 28, 32, 38, 46–7,
        59, 86, 146, 149, 393, 398,
        413, 448
Forestier, Jean-Antoine-Gaspard 303,
        389, 420
Fouché, Joseph 41, 55, 59–60, 66–7, 93,
        98, 101, 186, 213, 251–2, 306,
        367, 441
Fouquier-Tinville, Antoine-Quentin 72,
        164, 167, 169–70, 243, 254, 256–7,
        286, 310, 316, 375, 424–6, 436

relations with Dumas 165–6, 217, 285
relations with Robespierre 119, 124,
        132, 204
Fournerot, François-Louis 370
'fraternal banquets' 15, 112–13, 133, 229,
        390, 455
Fréron, Louis-Stanislas 42, 57–8, 60, 62,
        67, 222–3, 323, 334–6, 367,
        379–80, 384, 437
Fréry, Antoine 369
Fronde, the 228, 252

Garnier de l'Aube, Antoine-Marie-Charles
        62, 208
Garnier Delaunay, François-Pierre 120,
        167
Gencey, Antoine 377, 414
Germany 21
    Cologne 81, 153
Gibert, Jean-Louis 377
Gigue, captain 407
Giot, Christophe-Philippe, provisional
        NG commander 155–7, 159, 171,
        291, 317, 349–51, 383–4, 407–8,
        423
Girard, Pierre-François 120–1
Girondins (or Brissotins) 29–30, 32, 37,
        50, 65, 76–7, 86, 125, 144–5, 151,
        174, 202, 221, 289, 292, 295, 340,
        390, 416, 436, 441
    expelled from the Convention 4, 31,
        56, 66, 75, 92, 145, 156,
        241–2, 307
Gluck, Christoph Willibald von 269
Gobeau, Adrien-Nicolas 425
Gorsas, Antoine-Joseph 144
Gossec, François-Joseph 136
Gouges, Olympe de 151
Goujon, Cn. 274–5
Goulard, Jean-Baptiste 416
Gouly, Benoît 47
Goupilleau de Montaigu,
        Philippe-Charles-Aimé 192,
        319–20, 322–3, 336, 345
Granet, François-Omer 367, 431
Grenard, René 129, 341, 349, 399,
        420, 427
Gros-Caillou military hospital 159
Guérin, Ambroise 69

Guérin, Claude 22, 123
Guérin, Jules Messidor 69
Guffroy 62
guillotine 17–18, 21, 23–4, 38, 46, 54, 59,
    66, 70, 74, 76, 79, 82–3, 89, 111,
    132, 134, 139, 144–5, 149, 151,
    153, 156–7, 164, 166–8, 216, 219,
    221, 227–8, 239, 243, 256–8,
    288–9, 305, 308, 316, 340, 351,
    370, 402, 410, 425, 431, 449
  number of victims 23–4, 31, 59, 70, 79,
    82, 243, 254, 289, 410
  Place de la Révolution 11, 17–18
  Place du Trône-Renversé 16, 70, 370
Guittard de Floriban, Célestin 23–4, 156,
    385
gunpowder production 107
Guyard, Jean 82, 308–9
Guyot, Jean-Guillaume 273, 302, 417–18

Haly, gaoler 82, 371
Hanriot, François 277–8, 283, 290, 292–
    3, 298, 300, 302, 323, 328, 341,
    346, 354–5, 366, 368, 370, 375,
    377, 380, 393, 400–1, 408–9, 411–
    12, 419
  arrest 186–7, 194–5, 197–9, 218, 244,
    261–2, 266, 276, 280, 291, 293,
    299, 301, 326, 330, 337, 343, 369,
    381, 423, 449
  defenestrated 420, 422, 425
  dismissed from his post 234, 239, 244,
    246, 274, 437, 443
  imprisonment, escape from 322, 325,
    388, 449
  mobilizing the city 31, 56, 236, 247–50,
    255, 259–62, 264–5, 269–70, 272,
    275, 299, 301, 310, 320, 326–7,
    329, 342, 350, 352, 358, 397, 399,
    410, 414, 443, 446
  National Guard Commander 63, 84,
    96, 120, 151–2, 155, 157, 159–60,
    162, 235–8, 240, 367
  outlaw status 351, 353, 360, 385, 406–7
  plot against him 162, 196, 203, 220,
    233–4
  prior to 1793 31, 159–60
  raid on the CGS 264, 266, 299, 325,
    329, 331, 414

  reinstated 350
  relations with Robespierre 56–7, 174,
    203, 264, 331, 351, 365, 367, 379
Hardon, Jean-Nicolas 303
Hébert, Jacques-René 32, 53, 134, 144,
    196, 231, 454
Hébertists 32, 36, 92, 108, 139, 141, 146,
    153, 160, 197, 227, 339, 377, 454
Hémart, Jean, Gendarmerie
    commander 63, 96, 160, 162, 199,
    237, 244, 259, 261–2, 264, 290,
    300, 323, 331, 375, 392, 413
Hénault, Charles-Adrien 70
Henri IV, king of France, 130, 172
Hérault de Séchelles, Marie-Jean 48
Herman, Martial 79–80, 123, 132–3,
    168–9, 208, 212, 218–19, 330, 382,
    446, 454
Héron, François 19, 234
Hôtel-Dieu 103, 106, 126, 425
hôtels particuliers
  Hôtel de Brionne 48, 242, 265–6, 276,
    280, 287, 321–2, 325, 329, 424–5
  Hôtel d'Elbeuf 225
  Hôtel de Longueville 109
  Hôtel de Soubise 275
  Hôtel de Taranne 179
  Maison Penthièvre 218
Hua, Marie-Thérèse 69
Hugot, Nicolas-Paul 392

Île-de-France (Mauritius) 47
Île de la Cité 107, 128, 130–1, 152, 165,
    171, 173, 210, 224, 237, 247, 263,
    273, 281, 309, 339, 351, 383–4,
    422
Île des Cygnes 126, 427
Île Saint-Louis 128, 151, 164, 243,
    249–50, 254, 281, 427
Isnard, Maximin 30, 416, 436, 452

Jacobins, the 22, 27, 29, 46, 48, 52–3, 98,
    115, 120, 134, 142, 145–7, 178,
    223, 304, 306–7, 361–2, 382,
    423, 455
Jacobin Club 11, 21, 23, 27–30, 34,
    41–7, 49–50, 52–4, 60–1, 67, 83,
    90, 94, 112, 116–20, 122, 125, 134,
    136, 142, 145, 151, 163, 165, 171,

Jacobins, the (*cont.*)
    174–5, 178, 181–2, 194–6, 202–3,
    211, 213, 222–3, 235, 241, 251–2,
    283, 291, 300, 304–7, 314, 320,
    356, 361–2, 382, 390, 402, 414–15,
    423, 425, 436, 438, 444, 446
  public galleries 27, 35, 37, 212,
    304–5, 362
Jagot, Grégoire 66, 329
Jardin Marbeuf 116, 121
Jault, Pierre-Simon-Joseph 376, 389
Javogues, Claude 52–3, 60, 367
Jeannolle, brigadier 266
Jemappes, battle of 141
Jemptel, Antoine 138, 356, 422
Joly, Charles 381
Jouannes, Jeanne 381
journées 1–2, 4, 6, 147, 194, 235, 237,
    241, 361, 368, 370, 375, 387, 426,
    431–4, 437–9, 444, 450–1, 455–6
  14 July 1789 1–2, 28, 226, 302, 432–3
  5–6 October 1789 155
  10 August 1792 3, 30, 144, 155, 176,
    242, 275, 278–9, 283, 302, 341,
    397, 400, 432–3, 448–9
  31 May and 2 June 1793
    (anti–Girondins) 4, 31–2, 56, 95,
    130, 155–6, 160, 181, 210, 235,
    237, 240–2, 270, 274, 278–9,
    282–3, 292, 302, 307, 326,
    332, 340–1, 344, 397, 400,
    446–7, 449
Jullien, Marc-Antoine 20, 59
Julliot, Legion Chief 237, 244, 266, 276,
    299, 322–3, 332, 345, 387
Juneau, François-Louis 366
Jura, department 165

La Balue, Magon de 46
Lacombe, Claire 119, 151
Lacoste, Élie 52, 222–3, 305, 327, 363, 424
Ladmiral, Henri 15, 54, 94, 118
Lafayette, Marie-Joseph Paul-Yves Roch-
    Gilbert Motier, marquis de 29,
    155, 304, 454
La Flèche, François 113
Lafosse, Blaise 126, 130, 132, 134, 215,
    284, 342–3, 420
Lagarde, Jean-François 306

Lamballe, Marie-Thérèse-Louise,
    princesse de 78
Langlois, Hyacinthe 140–2, 416
Langlois, Jean-Nicolas 414
Lanne, Emmanuel-Joseph 168, 212, 218,
    382, 454
Lasne, Étienne 250, 344, 388
Lasnier, Joseph 339–40, 349–51, 365, 388
Laurenceot, Jacques-Henri 372
Laurent, Denis-Étienne 377
Laurent, Marie-Antoinette 69
Lauvin, Edme-Marguerite 305
Lavalette, Louis-Jean-Baptiste 425
Lavergne, Pierre-Nicolas 427
Lavicomterie, Louis-Stanislas 56, 329
Le Bas, Elisabeth (*née* Duplay) 115, 121,
    347–8
Le Bas, Henriette 115, 347
Le Bas, Philippe 116, 304, 348, 353, 363,
    402, 406, 409, 411–13, 417, 443
  arrest 223, 239, 287, 329, 347, 377
  deputy on mission 88, 115, 279, 401
  relations with the Duplay family 51,
    115, 121, 142, 196, 347
  relations with Robespierre 51, 96, 115,
    142, 196, 222
  suicide 422, 425
Lebon, Joseph 60
Lecointre, Laurent 40, 56–7, 61–3, 94, 96,
    101, 435–6, 441–2
Lefebvre, Jean-Louis 416
Legendre, Louis 62, 95, 197, 204, 210,
    301, 336, 356, 380, 390, 423, 425
Le Gentil, Charles-François 118
legislation
  Law of 7 Prairial 145
  Law of 14 Frimaire 92, 131, 201, 250,
    272, 343, 390, 415, 425
  Law of 22 Prairial 51, 61, 79–80, 89, 94,
    166–8, 195–6, 204, 221, 346
  Law on Suspects 139, 152, 163
  Law of 23 Ventôse 168, 328, 360, 393,
    409, 426
  'Laws of Ventôse' 45
Legislative Assembly 30
Legouvé, Gabriel-Marie Jean-Baptiste,
    Epicharis et Néron 269
Legracieux, Stanislas 22–4, 27–8, 52
Legrand, Pierre-Jacques 340–1, 347, 407

Le Gray, François-Vincent 226–8
Lejeune, Augustin 123
Leleu, Charles-Nicolas 376
Le Lièvre, François 158
Le Lièvre, Jacques-Mathurin 148, 158, 273, 314, 317–18, 349
Lemière, Antoine-Marin, *Guillaume-Tell* 269
Le Nôtre, André 176–7
Léon, Pauline 151
Le Pauvre, Nicolas 415
Lepeletier de Saint-Fargeau, Louis-Michel 147, 166, 183
Lequinio, Joseph 301
Lerebours, Cn. 341, 420, 427
Lestage, Pierre 427
Levasseur, gunner 337
levée en masse 93, 106, 108
Lhermina 39
Lindet, Robert 49–50, 57, 62, 87, 95, 106, 112, 330, 442
Livin, adjutant 276
Livy 323
Loizon 257
Longueville-Clémentières, Thomas, 412–13
Louchet, Louis 220–1
Louis XIV, king of France 176
Louis XV, king of France 37, 258
Louis XVI, king of France 2–3, 28–30, 78, 86, 92, 130, 144, 150, 153, 157–8, 169, 200, 231, 289, 300, 424, 426, 433
 'Flight to Varennes' 29
Louis XVIII, comte de Provence, brother of Louis XVI 78
Louis-Charles (Louis XVII) 158–9, 377, 409, 418
Louis du Bas-Rhin, Jean-Antoine 51
Louis-le-Grand, college 116
Louvet, Pierre-Alexandre 274–5, 302, 310, 319, 341
Louvet de Couvray, Jean-Baptiste 125
Louvre, the 176, 181, 262, 403
Low Countries, the 5, 13, 32, 224
 Netherlands, the 88
Loys, Jean-Baptiste 304–5, 450
Lozeau, Paul-Augustin 220–1, 242
Lubin, Jean-Baptiste 282
Lubin, Jean-Jacques 134, 282, 393

Luxembourg gardens 107
Lycurgus 183
Lyon 4, 31, 49, 58–61, 67, 82, 93, 134, 156, 186, 416, 419, 452

Mably, Gabriel Bonnot de 200
Machard, Louise 76, 81
Magendie, Jean-François 46–7
Mailhe, Jean-Baptiste 42
Maillé, Madame 216
Maire, Antoine-Marie 166, 217, 256, 426
Mairie 131, 152, 224, 263, 283, 293–4, 302, 309, 311, 314–15, 317–18, 327, 330, 349–51, 354, 365–7, 383–4, 388, 399, 408, 411, 422–3, 427
Maison Commune (Hôtel de Ville) 104, 126, 129–31, 157, 159, 199, 226, 233–5, 237–8, 240, 244, 247, 249–50, 255, 259, 261, 263–4, 270, 272–5, 277–9, 281–5, 297–9, 301–2, 305, 312, 317–18, 326, 340–3, 347, 349–50, 355–6, 358, 362, 366, 368–72, 374–5, 377, 380, 383, 386, 388–90, 392, 397, 399, 401, 403, 405–6, 408–11, 413–14, 417, 419–21, 423, 425, 427–8, 447, 449
 Council Chamber 278, 282, 290–1, 317, 338–41, 344, 349, 353–4, 365–6, 374, 376, 382, 389, 392, 405–6, 409–12, 417, 420–1
 Zodiac Room (Salle de l'Égalité) 215, 366, 373, 392, 397, 401–2, 411
Mallarmé, François-René 38, 57
Marat, Jean-Paul 34, 58, 147, 166, 183, 201–2, 221, 240, 252–3, 257, 388, 397
Marie-Antoinette, queen of France 48, 78, 120, 149, 157–8, 289
Marie-Thérèse, daughter of Louis XVI 158–9
marriage 70
Marseilles 4, 31, 257
Martin, Jean-Paul 237, 414
Martinet, Louis 231–2
Massif Central 336
Mathis, Legion Chief 244, 384, 408, 422–3

Maximum
  Price Maximum 105–6, 108–9,
    111–13, 116, 151, 229
  Wage Maximum 112–13, 120, 152–3,
    215, 224, 226, 229, 243, 247, 254,
    259, 274–5, 279, 281, 288, 312,
    342, 388, 394, 405, 426, 436,
    438, 455
Mayet, Madame 216
Ménétra, Jacques-Louis 138–9, 356, 388,
    422
Merchants' Provost, the 130
Mercier, Louis-Sébastien 1–2, 6–7, 76–7,
    103–4, 130, 162, 172, 228–30, 432,
    434, 437, 450
  imprisonment 75, 79, 81, 144, 154,
    295, 372, 431, 436
  Tableau de Paris 77
Mercier, Marc-Martial-André 377, 389
Merda, Charles-André 422
Méricourt, Théroigne de 86, 151
Merlin de Thionville,
    Antoine-Christophe 265–6,
    300–1, 336, 423, 440
Michée, Jean-Baptiste 376
Michel, Étienne 153, 272–3, 422, 427, 450
Minier, Alexandre 250
Miquet, Charles 403
Mirabeau, Honoré Gabriel Riqueti, comte
    de 29, 230, 253, 454
mitraillades 59, 156, 419
Moenne, Jacques 134
Moessard, Pierre-Louis 369
Monaco, Marie-Thérèse Françoise de
    Choiseul, princesse de 72–4,
    76–7, 83, 217, 256–8
Montagnards, the 4–5, 27–8, 30–1, 40,
    42, 50, 52, 57–8, 60–1, 65, 76–7,
    105, 113, 121, 142, 171, 174,
    180–1, 192, 197, 202, 206, 222, 253,
    265, 301, 319, 335–6, 363, 398, 416,
    431, 436, 438–9, 446, 450
Montesquieu, Charles de Secondat, baron
    de La Brède et de 200
Montpellier 41, 57
Moore, John 148
Morel, CGS spy 412–13
moustaches 155
Moutard, Marguerite 70

moutons 80, 82–3, 308
Mulot, Legion Chief 244, 344
muscadins 437

Nanterre 159
Nantes 60, 436
Napoleon Bonaparte 1, 58, 89, 117, 444
National Guard, Paris 19–20, 29, 31, 56,
    96–7, 105, 120, 138, 144, 152, 164,
    174, 196, 198–9, 203, 220, 225,
    233, 235, 237, 249, 259, 261,
    265–6, 270, 274, 277, 283, 293,
    298, 299, 301–3, 315, 320, 323,
    330, 332, 334–5, 338, 340, 344–6,
    350, 358, 362, 367, 377–9, 383–4,
    386–8, 390, 394, 400, 403–7, 409,
    414, 422, 431, 433, 451
  artillery and gunners 39, 45–7, 156,
    237, 261, 274–5, 277, 298, 302,
    310, 312, 319–22, 325–7, 331, 337,
    339, 344, 349, 356, 364, 367, 371,
    379–80, 387–8, 403–4, 407, 410,
    418–19, 428, 443
  organ of public opinion 159, 162, 451
  organization 151, 155–7, 159–60,
    162–3, 239, 244, 290, 437, 443
  see also under Hanriot
Nero 269, 439
Neufchâteau, François de 148–9
Neuilly 14–15, 140–1, 363, 386
newspapers 67, 143–7, 149, 160, 178, 203,
    212, 214, 229, 241, 313–14, 343,
    367, 381, 445, 448, 451
  Abréviateur universel 213
  Bulletin des lois 145
  Correspondance politique de Paris et des
    départements 145
  Le Défenseur de la Constitution (ed.
    Robespierre) 145
  Feuille de la République 213
  Journal de la Montagne 120, 146
  Journal des hommes libres 146
  Journal du soir 413
  Journal historique et politique 231
  Messager du soir 122, 381
  Moniteur, Le 146, 159, 213, 533
  Soirée du Camp 90
  Trois décades 212
  Vieux Cordelier, Le 145

Nicolas, Charles-Léopold 120–1, 167, 259, 342–3
Nieuport, siege of 108, 182
Nièvre 59–60
nobility 19, 38, 107, 128–9, 147, 178, 257, 279
  laws against the 14, 227
Normandy 140
Notre-Dame cathedral (Temple of the Supreme Being) 103, 130, 157, 254, 283, 288, 344

Olivier, Legion Chief 244, 249, 291–2, 318
Orléans, Philippe, duke of 29, 304
Ouy, Cn. 406

Pache, Jean-Nicolas 134
Palais de Justice 72, 243, 248, 281, 316, 425
Palais-Royal (Maison-Égalité) 65, 110, 143, 164, 178, 265, 269, 295, 300
Palasne-Champeaux, Julien-François 65
Panis, Étienne-Jean 41, 62, 367
Paris 1, 4–5, 6, 14–15, 21, 24–5, 30–2, 39, 56, 58–9, 65, 69–71, 75–6, 95, 101, 107–8, 111–12, 126, 130, 133, 142–3, 178, 228, 235, 237, 300–1, 326, 330–2, 335–6, 340, 350, 392, 416–17
  counter-revolutionary trials centralized in 80, 168
  industry, heavy 107
  manufacturing 107
  Panthéon, the 24, 135, 157, 231, 253, 310, 328
  population size 15, 69, 298
  Robespierre's poor acquaintance with 314
  mentioned 16, 19–20, 29, 60, 63, 89, 114–18, 120, 129, 132, 140–1, 146, 186, 291, 329, 360, 364, 368, 408, 432
Paris, locations within
  abbey of Saint-Germain-des-Prés 107
  Belleville 11, 103
  Bois de Boulogne 140
  Champ de Mars 30, 107, 121, 427
  Champs-Élysées 17, 20, 116, 257, 386
  Clamart 103
  Courtille 108
  Faubourg du Temple 269
  Faubourg Saint-Antoine 17–18, 243, 247, 255, 298, 302, 310, 316, 364, 369, 405
  Faubourg Saint-Germain 107, 127, 172, 178, 297
  Faubourg Saint-Honoré 172
  Faubourg Saint-Marcel 17, 77, 156, 160, 224, 287, 298, 303, 377, 380, 405, 418
  Faubourg Saint-Martin 312
  Grenelle 103, 107, 312
  Halles, Les 16, 103–4, 106, 118
  Latin Quarter 172
  Marais, the 18, 20–1, 28, 30, 69, 77, 131, 157, 224, 250, 255, 287, 372, 389, 425
  Montmartre 103, 118
  Montmorency 103
  Montreuil 103
  Montrouge 76, 103
  Picpus convent cemetery 70–1
  Port au Blé 407
  Saint-Eustache 120
  Saint-Martin-des-Champs, priory 404, 413
  Saint-Roch 153
  Vincennes 151
Paris, Pierre-Louis 70, 129, 278, 409
Parisians, the 1–7, 14–18, 25, 31, 36, 66, 76–8, 84, 95, 97, 101, 103–4, 107–8, 110, 112, 118, 120–2, 130–1, 133, 135, 148, 156, 159, 162, 165, 175, 179, 185, 203, 209, 214, 220, 226–7, 231–2, 237, 239, 241, 247, 255, 259, 279, 287, 311, 319, 326, 353, 355–6, 358, 362, 365, 386, 389–90, 411–12, 421, 428, 431, 433–5, 437–8, 444, 446–7, 454–5
  character 228–9, 252, 450–1
  diet 177
  insurrections 235, 237–8, 251, 260, 267, 278–9, 282–3, 292, 300–1, 305, 331, 341–2, 354, 357, 360, 367, 384, 397, 399, 401, 415, 419–20, 446, 449

Parisians, the (*cont.*)
    popular mobilization 5–6, 21, 230, 235,
        238, 240, 249, 267, 274–5, 283, 297,
        299–303, 305, 308, 310, 312, 317,
        323, 341–4, 353–4, 370, 378–80,
        386, 394, 400–1, 410, 414–15,
        417–18, 419–20, 448–52, 454–5
    see also under Hanriot
    public opinion fractured 438
    role in Robespierre's fall
        contested 439–40, 451
    Thermidorian repression of 439
Parlement of Paris 152, 166
Pas-de-Calais 60, 80, 115
Passy 14
Payan, Claude-François 22, 57, 84, 97,
        109–10, 112–13, 123, 131–4, 147,
        150–1, 153, 159, 174, 215, 233–5,
        238, 240, 250, 255, 270, 278,
        282–3, 285, 290–2, 301, 317, 326,
        330, 339–41, 344, 354–5, 366–7,
        374, 376, 381, 393, 397, 401, 407,
        422, 424–6, 446, 449, 455
    arrest 301, 320
    relations with Robespierre 22, 97, 123,
        132–3, 149–50, 174, 203, 219,
        317, 390
Payan, Esprit 291
Payan, Joseph-François 132, 147–8, 427,
        446
Pellecat, Etienne 370
Pellerin, Cn. 321, 367
Penières, Jean-Augustin 414
Pétion, Jérôme 77
Peyssard, Jean-Pascal 142, 363, 417
Piedmont 89, 117
Pille, Louis-Antoine 46–7, 306, 361
Pionnier, Cosme 156, 321–2, 326, 337,
        407, 418–20, 423, 427–8, 443
Pisistratus 39, 87, 202, 360, 439
Pitt, William 14–15, 119, 262
Plain, the 28, 40, 65–6, 98, 101, 174, 182,
        336, 398, 441
Plato 183
Plet de Beauprey, Pierre-François 336
Plutarch 202
Poitiers 172
Police Bureau, *see* Committee of Public
        Safety, Bureau of Administrative

Surveillance and General Police
    under Committee of Public Safety
Pompey 223
Popular Commissions 45, 123, 168–9,
        259, 370
Portières, Cn. 307
Poultier, François-Martin 301
pregnancy 72
press freedom 144–6, 149, 435–7
priests 14, 59, 69, 105, 128, 257, 288
Prieur, Jean-Louis 170
Prieur de Côte d'Or, Claude-Antoine
        49–50, 87, 107, 112
Prieur de la Marne, Pierre-Louis 49, 87
prison population 45, 77, 80–1, 152, 168,
        295, 410
    acts of self-defence 372
prisons, Paris 81–3, 111, 145, 152, 178,
        227, 263, 280, 371, 386, 408
    Abbaye 78, 154, 196
    Bénédictins-Anglais 2, 75, 77, 154,
        295, 372
    Carmes 78–9
    Conciergerie 17, 72, 77–8, 83, 167,
        170–1, 243, 256, 424–5
    Couvent des Oiseaux 78, 83
    Écossais monastery 287, 393
    La Force 19–20, 75, 78, 83, 154, 255,
        287, 340–1, 347, 372, 406
    Luxembourg 77, 79, 81–2, 168, 287,
        295–6, 308, 327, 350, 360, 371, 399
    Madelonnettes 75, 77
    Pélagie 343, 371, 425
    Pension Belhomme 78
    Plessis 372
    Port-Libre 77, 81–2, 287, 371
    Saint-Lazare 79, 287, 339–40
    Salpêtrière, La 77–8, 137
    Talaru 78, 83, 295
    Temple 157, 159, 237, 293, 408–9, 427
prostitution 150–1, 178
Provence 65, 335
purges, political 27–8, 31–2, 40, 44–7,
        54–6, 60, 66–7, 87, 91, 94, 131,
        153, 163, 165, 197–8, 234–5, 301,
        415, 418, 425–6, 431, 436–7, 445,
        447, 450–1
    see also *journées* of 31 May and 2 June
        1793; *and under* Robespierre

Puy de Vérine, ex-financier 216
Pyrenees, the 31, 336

queue de Robespierre, la 440
queues 104–5, 110–11, 124, 137, 160,
    163, 212, 229, 438, 450
Quevreux 318
Quinault, Philippe, *Armide* 269

Racine, Jean 116
Raffet, Nicolas 159
Ramel, Dominique-Vincent 38, 57
Renard, Pierre-Jean 129, 427
Renaudin, Léopold 120, 167, 259
Renault, Cécile 15, 118–20, 202
Retz, Jean-François-Paul de Gondi,
    cardinal de 252
Revolutionary Tribunal 16–21, 32, 37–9,
    45–6, 50, 53, 66, 69–70, 72, 74,
    78–80, 82–3, 87, 89, 95, 109, 114,
    120, 124, 132, 142, 145, 149,
    164–71, 173, 195, 204, 208, 212–3,
    215–16, 219, 221, 226–7, 259, 263,
    281–2, 285, 302, 305, 308, 319,
    341, 350, 377, 388, 398, 401,
    424–6, 428, 445, 448, 455
  abolition of the 436
  juries 114, 120, 132, 142, 164, 167–70,
    173, 221, 256, 305, 341
  medical panel 72
Rhine, the 31
Richard, Jean 290–1, 354, 404
Richardson, Samuel, *Pamela* 148
Riffard Saint-Martin, François-Jérôme
    297, 299
Rights of Man and the Citizen,
    Declaration of the 3–4, 105, 143,
    148, 166, 234, 278
Riqueur, Jean-Charles 306–7
Robespierre, Augustin-Bon-Joseph 58,
    60, 89, 116–18, 174, 176, 209,
    221–3, 239, 252, 279, 287, 339–41,
    347, 349, 353, 366, 372, 401–2, 406,
    409, 411–12, 422, 425–6, 443
Robespierre, Charlotte 59, 116–8,
    121, 259
Robespierre, Maximilien-Marie-Isidore
  366 Rue Saint-Honoré 11, 23, 27–8,
    30, 114, 117, 122, 173

accused of dictatorship/tyranny 22, 25,
    28, 38–9, 42, 48, 61, 89–90, 125,
    133–4, 197, 200–2, 204, 208, 210,
    213, 222, 251, 305, 418–19, 424,
    432–4, 439, 447–8
against praising military victories 88,
    94, 112, 230
in Arras 29–30, 59, 80, 90, 114,
    116, 208
arrest warrant against him 222, 251,
    287, 315
Black Legend 440
bodyguards 120–1, 146, 167, 173, 202,
    209, 259, 332, 342, 362
Brount [his dog] 28, 116
celebrity status 118–19, 203, 211–12,
    221, 226, 230–1, 239, 315, 403,
    440, 442, 454
eschews naming names 39, 241
fears of conspiracies 14–15, 22, 25,
    28, 32, 38, 40, 46–7, 51, 53, 59,
    85, 87, 91, 93–4, 119, 122, 125,
    146, 149, 205, 227, 304, 398,
    440, 448
form of dress 16, 174
ideas of the French Revolution 16, 36,
    92, 124, 402, 448, 456
impracticality 33
journalism 30
and money 34, 41
nostalgia for 438
personality 116, 142, 145, 197, 397–8
pessimism 33
pistol wound 422–4
provincial lawyer 33, 80, 90
purifying government 33, 41, 61, 67,
    96, 175, 240–1, 400, 445–8
reputation 22, 25, 27–9, 47, 93, 199,
    202, 212, 287, 440, 442
Rue Saintonge 30
self-exile from government 41, 43–4,
    79, 211–12, 454
sexual identity 118
speeches 34–7, 44, 114, 136, 173, 203,
    213, 402, 445
  at the Convention 22, 27, 38–42, 51,
    53, 61–2, 67, 86–7, 98, 108, 121–2,
    124, 171, 174, 182, 203, 205, 218,
    399–400, 441, 444–5, 447

Robespierre, Maximilien-Marie-Isidore
  (*cont.*)
    at the Jacobin Club 27, 43, 94–5,
      98, 181, 203, 205, 240, 305–6,
      399–400, 446
    oratory 28, 34, 36–8, 197, 240–1, 447
    threats to his life 15, 121, 184, 202
Robin, Louis-Antoine 265–6, 276
Roland, Manon (*née* Phlipon) 76, 151
Roque, Antoinette 151
Rose, Jacques-Auguste 242
Roucher, Jean-Antoine 74
Rousseau, Jean-Jacques 36, 116, 138, 151,
  160, 200
  Julie, ou La Nouvelle Héloïse 258
Rousseville, Pierre-Henri 11–16, 18, 20,
  24, 108, 112, 123, 141, 226, 230,
  259, 452
Rouvière, de 257
Roux, Jacques 105, 144
Rovère, Stanislas-Joseph 60, 62, 181,
  301, 336
Ruhl, Philippe 51, 187, 193, 266, 329, 418

Sade, Donatien-Alphonse-François,
  marquis de 75
Saint Bartholomew's Massacre 283
Saint-Just, Louis-Antoine 151, 202, 259, 353
  arrest 223, 262, 281, 287, 366, 377, 393,
    410, 422, 424–5
  as deputy on mission 49, 88, 115, 122,
    279, 401
  earlier life and career 88
  relations with Robespierre 21, 43–4, 86,
    93, 95–6, 101, 174, 194–5, 201, 446
  role in CPS 14, 45–6, 48–52, 54–5, 57,
    61, 63, 80, 84–5, 87–93, 97–9, 121,
    123–4, 168, 174, 181, 185–7, 189,
    191–3, 196, 200, 226–7, 239–40,
    251–2, 328, 332, 442–3, 448
Saint-Omer, Jean-Claude 226–7
Saint-Paul-Trois-Châteaux 22
Sans-Culottes 4–6, 16–17, 24, 30–2, 45,
  50, 60, 75, 77, 81, 105–6, 109,
  111–14, 116, 118, 120, 129, 133–4,
  139, 153, 155, 158, 160, 162–3,
  170, 173, 177, 196, 210, 234, 241,
  290, 314, 364, 377, 401, 436, 450–1
  breeches 4, 16

Sanson, Charles-Henri 243, 257–8,
  289, 426
Sarthe, the 60
Saudraye, Madame 117
Savin, Cn. 264
Scellier, Gabriel-Toussaint 426
sectional organization
  Beneficence Committees 138, 452
  Civil Committees 137–9, 151, 156,
    233, 237–8, 275, 284, 303, 312,
    331, 343–4, 364, 452
  justices of the peace 70, 138, 151, 452
  Revolutionary Committees 139,
    151–3, 157, 218, 231, 237–8,
    249–50, 259, 264, 272, 274, 283–4,
    287, 293, 303, 331, 339, 355, 370,
    377, 409, 415, 428, 431, 437
sections, Paris 4, 6–7, 39, 45, 56, 106–7,
  109, 113, 123, 127–8, 131, 135–7,
  162–3, 174, 177, 196, 199, 224,
  227, 230, 233, 237–8, 247, 249,
  260–1, 264, 274, 283–4, 298, 332,
  343, 354–8, 360–1, 365, 376,
  380–3, 385, 390, 400, 410, 422,
  425–6, 431, 433, 449–51, 454
  Amis-de-la-Patrie (15) 13, 128, 310,
    325–6, 354, 366
  Arcis (19) 259, 274, 322, 377, 388–9,
    410, 413–4, 428
  Arsenal (34) 154, 386, 405
  Bon-Conseil (16) 138, 276, 304, 310,
    356, 388, 404, 422
  Bondy (22) 305
  Bonne-Nouvelle (14) 13, 152, 177,
    237, 376–7, 389
  Bonnet-Rouge (42) 128, 139, 331,
    415, 425
  Brutus (13) 128, 136, 365, 377, 414
  Chalier (44) 128, 156, 224, 416
  Champs-Élysées (2) 143, 312, 405
  Cité (36) 156, 210, 283, 293–4, 315,
    344, 383, 405, 450
  Contrat-Social (11) 126–7, 138,
    405, 415
  Droits-de-l'Homme (31) 128, 151,
    238, 250, 274, 344, 388–9,
    403, 415
  Faubourg-du-Nord (28) 129, 312, 318,
    377, 405

Faubourg-Montmartre (20) 113, 386
Faubourg-Poissonnière (21) 129, 312, 356, 376
Finistère (48) 156, 224–5, 303, 377, 388, 406–7, 414
Fontaine-de-Grenelle (39) 69, 178, 310, 346, 379, 405
Fraternité (35) 128, 156, 164, 250, 281, 389, 405
Gardes-Françaises 151, 159, 178, 361, 376, 405, 414
Gravilliers (27) 128, 137, 156, 386, 404, 413–14, 418–19
Guillaume-Tell (12) 128, 178, 307, 331, 369–70, 389
Halle-aux-Blé (10) 120, 178, 273, 404–5
Homme-Armé (30) 69, 128, 238, 274–5, 277, 389–90, 405, 427–8
Indivisibilité (33) 128, 204, 255, 259, 270, 356, 405, 415
Invalides (38) 128, 152, 159, 408
Lepeletier (6) 128, 178, 415, 427
Lombards (18) 16, 154, 158, 178, 238, 255, 274, 292, 318, 343, 388, 405–7, 418–19, 427
Maison-Commune (32) 233, 299, 330, 417
Marat (41) 128, 143, 155–8, 171, 178, 377, 384, 386, 405, 408, 422–3
Marchés (17) 310
Montagne (4) 128, 159, 178, 227, 265, 300, 427, 450
Mont-Blanc (7) 414–15
Montreuil (25) 312
Muséum (8) 132, 153, 178, 226, 235, 264, 388, 406, 425, 431
Mutius-Scévole (43) 128, 156, 321–2, 337, 349, 386, 388
Observatoire (46) 156, 312, 415–16
Panthéon-Français (45) 128, 137, 177, 237, 250, 272, 274, 278, 310, 337, 354, 409, 416
Piques (5) 120, 128, 132, 178, 341, 349, 399, 401
Popincourt (24) 302, 310, 312, 321, 367, 386, 388
Quinze-Vingts (26) 310, 369–70, 374, 388, 416

République (3) 312, 364, 405
Réunion (29) 128, 153, 224, 274, 290, 354, 404–5, 450
Révolutionnaire (37) 128, 250, 293, 339, 341, 344, 383–4, 422
Sans-Culottes (47) 128, 156, 160, 318, 380, 384, 417–8
Temple (23) 128, 409
Tuileries (1) 128, 151, 178, 218, 225, 231, 324, 382
Unité (40) 128, 165, 178, 224, 250, 364, 386, 405
Seine department 300
Seine, river 31, 50, 129, 152, 171, 274, 392, 416, 438
Seine-et-Oise department 76
Sellier, Madame 23
September Massacres (1792) 21, 30, 76–9, 154, 308, 371
Seven Years War 155
Sexby, Edward, *Killing No Murder* 213
Sijas, Prosper 46, 306, 320, 361
Sillery, comte de 77
Simon, Antoine 158, 377
singing culture 144
Soisy, Françoise-Nicole 70
Solon 183
Somme, the 60
Souberbielle, Joseph 142
Soulié, Joseph 159
Spain 19
squares and places, Paris
  Place de la Bastille 247
  Place de la Maison Commune (Place de Grève) 104, 129, 237, 247, 259–62, 274, 277, 291, 293, 298–9, 301–2, 310, 318, 321, 326, 331, 338, 342, 344, 353–4, 375, 377, 380, 387–8, 393–4, 397, 400, 403–4, 406–8, 410, 413–14, 418–20, 422, 428
  Place de la Révolution (Place de la Concorde) 11, 17–18, 71, 228, 387, 424, 426
  Place des Vosges 18
  Place du Carrousel (Place de la Réunion) 109, 176, 225, 287, 319, 321–2, 325–6, 337, 343, 350, 367, 386–8, 394, 404, 419

squares and places, Paris (*cont.*)
  Place du Palais-Royal 265
  Place du Panthéon 157
  Place du Trône-Renversé 16–17, 70,
    243, 256, 370
  Place Saint-Sulpice 24, 385
  Place Vendôme 218
streets, boulevards, and quais, Paris
  Boulevard du Temple 147, 255
  Quai de l'École 387, 403
  Quai de Gesvres 350, 403, 413–14
  Quai de la Mégisserie 403
  Quai des Orfèvres 152, 293, 311, 384
  Quai des Ormes 281
  Quai du Louvre 387, 403
  Quai du Marché Neuf 293
  Rue Croix-des-Petits-Champs 55
  Rue de l'Arcade 115
  Rue de Birague 18, 154
  Rue de Chartres 269
  Rue de Conti 69
  Rue de l'Échelle 266, 321, 387
  Rue d'Enfer 103
  Rue de la Perle 21
  Rue de la Tour 106
  Rue de la Verrerie 404, 413, 418
  Rue de Reuilly 257
  Rue de Richelieu 78
  Rue de Saint-Thomas-du-Louvre 265
  Rue de Seine 165
  Rue de Sèvres 78
  Rue des Arcis 238
  Rue des Canettes 24, 385
  Rue des Francs-Bourgeois 275
  Rue des Lavandières 153
  Rue du Faubourg Saint-Antoine 288
  Rue du Jour 126
  Rue du Martroy 233, 247, 420
  Rue du Mouton 353
  Rue Hautefeuille 157, 171
  Rue Louis-le-Grand 129
  Rue Poissonnière 103
  Rue Saint-Antoine 20
  Rue Saint-Denis 103, 179
  Rue Saint-Florentin 117
  Rue Saint-Guillaume 297
  Rue Saint-Honoré 11, 14, 17, 23, 65,
    120, 178, 264–6, 321, 326, 335,
    387, 404, 426

Rue Saint-Jacques 2, 70, 75–6, 103
Rue Saint-Martin 103, 404, 418
Rue Saint-Nicaise 387
Rue Tournon 308
Rue Traversière 15
Rue Troussevache 16
strikes 109–10
Sylla 223

Tallien, Jean-Lambert 65, 178, 191, 193,
    209–10, 223, 240, 279, 300–1, 306,
    363, 367, 380, 393, 398, 401,
    435, 437
  deputy on mission 62
  plot against Robespierre 66, 68, 101,
    181, 183, 192, 194–5, 197–8,
    201–2, 205–6, 220–2, 239, 241,
    441, 443
  relations with Robespierre 20–1, 60, 67
  and Theresa Cabarrus 19–20, 22, 24,
    59, 65, 189, 194, 239, 372
Tanchon, Ponce 293–4, 314–15, 408
terror 2, 5, 13, 18, 25, 32, 35–6, 40, 50, 61,
    79, 88, 92, 95, 106, 124–5, 148,
    227, 229–30, 239, 241, 295, 382,
    434–7, 441–2, 445, 452
  'Terror, the' 434–7, 441, 454, 456
Tessier, Pierre-Louis 159, 408
Teurlot, Claude-François 153–4
theatres, Paris 65, 134–5, 144–5, 147–9,
    163, 214, 229, 255, 257, 269, 451
  Opéra Comique 160
  Opéra national 269
  Théâtre de la Cité-Variétés 213
Théot, Catherine 37, 39, 47, 124, 133,
    204–5
Théotiste, Sister of Charity (comtesse de
    Valombray) 295, 371
Thermidorian period 434–5, 438, 440,
    444, 456
Thibaudeau, Antoine 171–2, 176–7,
    180–2, 185, 192, 194, 197, 424,
    435, 441
Thiéry, battalion commander 354
Thiéry, physician 72
Thirion, Didier 60, 62
Thouin, Marguerite 151
Thuriot, Jacques-Alexis 207–8, 210, 222,
    244, 246, 301, 323–4, 328, 424–5

Toulon 4, 31, 58, 335
Treasury, the 159, 237, 277
Trinchard, François 170
'triumvirate' 52, 223
Tugot, Louis 389, 428
Tuileries gardens 22, 43, 135, 176, 209, 226, 387
Tuileries palace (Palais-National) 11, 29, 43, 47–8, 55, 63, 65, 84, 109–10, 118, 123, 128, 171, 176–8, 209, 218, 262, 264–5, 276, 290, 299, 302, 310, 317, 319, 321, 323, 329, 331, 337, 346, 351, 358, 384, 402–4
Typhaine, Vincent 408

Ulrich, Joseph-Guillaume 249, 414
Uzès 55

Vadier, Marc-Guillaume-Alexis 37, 39–40, 51, 60, 62, 124, 133, 204–5, 212–13, 223, 295, 329, 367, 436, 442
Valerius Publicola 183
Valmy, battle of 115
Van Heck, Jean-Baptiste 210–11, 293–4, 315, 450
Var department 335
Varennes 29
Vendée, insurrection 4, 31, 59–60, 62, 72, 80, 158, 166, 257, 328

Verdun, fall of 21
Vergne, Cn. 164, 243, 253, 281
Vernet, Alexandre 16–18, 24, 77, 154
Versailles 14, 19–20, 29, 61, 120, 138, 176, 265, 289
Viala, Agricol-Joseph 24, 135, 142
Vian, captain 406
Viard, Jean-Baptiste-Guillaume 70
Vienne department 171
Vigée-Lebrun, Elisabeth 258
Villetaneuse 339
Vincent, Pierre-François 277
Vivier, Nicolas-Joseph 52–3, 305–7, 361, 423, 425
Voltaire 116
Voulland, Jean-Henri 51, 55, 75, 77, 92, 329, 334, 360
Voyenne, Claude-François 388, 406

Warmé, Jacques-Louis-Frédéric 377
Wichterich, Martin, police administrator 81, 308–9, 311
women in public life 150, 373
  'citizen washer-women' 161–2
  Society of Revolutionary Republican Women 151, 304

York, Frederick Augustus, duke of 39